The Relative Mountains of Earth:

The Ribus

Daniel Patrick Quinn

2024

with major contributions from
Oscar Argudo, Petter Bjørstad, Alan Dawson, Jonathan de Ferranti, Deividas Valaitis and Rob Woodall

additional research, writings and photographs from
Sean Caulfield, Andy M Dean, Eric Gilbertson, Alastair Govan, Anne Gray, David Jamieson, Jude Newton-Stock, Martin Richardson, James Stone, Mark Trengrove and Nikolaus Żuliński

A Pedantic Press publication
PPB005

First published in Great Britain in 2024 by Pedantic Press

pedantic.org.uk

ISBN 978-1-9163662-3-7

Some rights reserved. The data tables in this work are licensed under the Creative Commons Attribution-NoDerivs Licence CC-BY-ND. This licence allows for copying and redistribution as long as the data is reproduced unchanged and in whole, with credit to the original author.

All text and photographs by those attributed. Text and photographs without attribution are by Daniel Patrick Quinn.

Copyright in all text rests with the writers. Copyright in all images rests with the photographers. Rights for these are reserved but permission for use may be obtained for some purposes.

Peak distribution maps reproduced courtesy of Adam Schneider via the GPS Visualizer website, with background images from Esri ArcGIS. Maps also created with QGIS using the Here Satellite layer.

Front cover: Gunung Merapi and Gunung Merbabu as seen from Gunung Lawu in Java, Indonesia at dusk, 2009

Back cover: Pointe Percée, France by Alastair Govan, 2023

Contents

The Concept	1
The List	5

North and Central America

NA10 Alaska – Yukon Ranges	7
NA11 North America Arctic Islands	21
NA12 Pacific Ranges	31
NA13 Inter-mountain West	46
NA14 Rocky Mountains	59
NA15 North America Plains	67
NA16 Appalachian Mountains	69
NA17 Central Mexican Ranges	70
NA18 Central America Ranges	75
NA19 Caribbean Area	79

South America

SA20 Coastal South America	83
SA21 Andes North	87
SA22 Andes South	99
SA23 Guiana Highlands	110
SA24 Brazilian Highlands	113
SA25 South-east South America	115

Europe

EU30 Scandinavia – European Arctic	117
EU31 North-west Europe	122
EU32 Iberian Peninsula	124
EU33 Alps	128
EU34 Italian Peninsula and Islands	137
EU35 Eastern Europe Ranges	140
EU36 Balkan Peninsula	141
EU37 Ural Mountains	147
EU38 Caucasus Mountains	148

Asia West

AS40 Anatolia	151
AS41 Levant Ranges	155
AS42 Zagros Mountains	156
AS43 Iranian Plateau	160
AS44 Arabian Peninsula	165
AS45 Central Asia Ranges	168
AS46 Tien Shan	179
AS47 Tibet and Central China	183
AS48 Himalaya	196
AS49 Indian Subcontinent	206

Asia East

AS50 Central Siberia	209
AS51 Eastern Siberia	211
AS52 Baikal Area Ranges	218
AS53 Mongolia Ranges	220
AS54 East China	223
AS55 Korea – Amur Area	231
AS56 Japanese Archipelago	233
AS57 Southeast Asia	238
AS58 Malay Archipelago	246
AS59 Philippines	258

Africa

AF60 Atlas Mountains	261
AF61 Sahara Desert Ranges	263
AF62 West Africa Mountains	265
AF63 Ethiopian Highlands	267
AF64 East Africa Mountains	270
AF65 Southern Africa	275
AF66 Mid-Atlantic Islands	278
AF67 Indian Ocean Islands	280

Oceania

OC70 New Guinea	281
OC71 Lesser Australian Ranges	286
OC72 Great Dividing Range	287
OC73 New Zealand	288
OC75 Melanesia	291
OC76 Polynesia	293

Antarctica

AN80 West Antarctica Ranges	296
AN81 Transantarctic Mountains	298
AN82 East Antarctica Ranges	300

Articles

Relative mountains of the ocean	294
The relative importance of prominence	301
The research process	305
Accuracy of digital elevation models for the Pyrenees	309
Restless Earth	312
The Seven Summits	314
The Volcanic Seven Summits	317
Relative mountains of the Moon	320

Indexes

Top 50 Ribus by prominence	321
Top 50 Ribus by elevation	323
Top 50 islands	325
Sub-Ribus	327
Index of countries and territories	333
Ribu density	337
Author and contributors	339
Glossary	341

Acknowledgements	342
References	343

The concept

A Ribu is a mountain with one thousand metres of topographic prominence. This book lists all of them. They are the 7150 most prominent peaks on our planet.

Topographic prominence – also known as drop, or relative height – is an objective way of identifying separate, individual mountains. A point on a Himalayan ridge over 6000 metres above sea level may be very impressive, but if it is near another peak 6500 metres high then the 6000-metre peak becomes less important in the landscape, and the views from it are likely to be limited by its higher neighbour. Contrast this example with a 1200-metre peak in Australia with no higher neighbouring peak for hundreds of kilometres. If the view at the top is not obstructed by vegetation then it is likely to offer an incredible panorama over the lower lands, stretching further than the eye can see in all directions.

To take a specific example, the south summit of Mount Everest is 8749 metres high and is arguably the second-highest peak in the world, yet it has a prominence of only eleven metres, and that is why it is not included in the list of 8000-metre peaks. Those who pass over this summit tend to have their eyes firmly fixed on Everest itself. The south summit is merely part of Everest and does not qualify as a separate mountain either objectively or subjectively. Owing to its lack of prominence, it is barely regarded as a distinct entity.

All lists of hills or mountains group them together in a particular category, whether that be region, country, elevation, prominence or a combination of several factors. The use of prominence has taken time to become established but has proved to be a robust and consistent principle for producing lists of peaks. It eliminates subjective judgements based on appearances, routes, personal experiences, favouritism and emotional associations.

The project

The concept for the Ribus owes much to previous summit lists including Corbetts, Marilyns and Ultras, which are looked at in more detail later. The Ribus project began life in Java in Indonesia in 2009, when I met Andy Dean on a hike up Gunung Lawu (3265m). The image on the front cover of this book is from that very hike. We got together again a few weeks later on Gunung Salak (2211m) in West Java and decided to create a list and website detailing the many mountains and volcanoes of the Indonesian archipelago, along with information about how to climb them. I suggested the thousand-metre prominence definition required for inclusion in the list, and Andy immediately responded with the name Ribu for these peaks, which comes from the Indonesian and Malay word for thousand. The Gunung Bagging website was launched a few weeks later with an afternoon event at the Eastern Promise bar in Kemang, South Jakarta.

> 'Hiking Gunung Rinjani a few months after arriving in Indonesia, I was frustrated by the lack of a good write-up of the routes and options. It was all about selling tour packages. I wanted impartial hike planning advice and GPS tracks. I saved my tracks and was thinking about a website or blog on climbing Indonesia's mountains. The next hike was a Java Lava hiking group trip to Gunung Lawu. Chatting with Dan early on the ascent, he introduced the idea of a list of prominent mountains and soon afterwards the concept of the Ribu and gunungbagging.com were born.' Andy M Dean

A decade later, discussions on an online forum led to an international research team forming with the aim of identifying all of the summits across the globe with one thousand metres of prominence. They were to be known as Ribus or P1000s, where P stands for prominence. The question of what definition to use for any list of summits depends on the scope of the project. A list of Ribus in England or the Netherlands would have no entries at all. A global list of peaks with 100 metres of prominence would have over 1.6 million entries. A figure of 1000 metres seemed to make good sense in Indonesia back in 2009, as any higher prominence led to some great peaks being left out of the list, and anything lower meant including a large number of obscure summits of little mountaineering interest. It was a good fit for the region and 1000 is a nice round number. It was much later discovered that a list of 7150 peaks worldwide can just about fit in a single printed volume.

A good starting point for the project was the list of Ultras, which are peaks with 1500 metres of topographic prominence, also known as P1500s. There are currently believed to be 1566 of them. This list was compiled in 2004-2006 and was already available, via the Peaklist.org website. One of the research team, Oscar Argudo, designed a web application that allowed editors to analyse individual peaks in conjunction with various data sources and to amend a central database. The Ribus project has taken around five years to reach a point where the list is considered to be good enough for publication. There will inevitably be many changes to the list still to come, as data sources are refined, new technology emerges, more appropriate local names are discovered and the mountains themselves change over time due to natural processes. There is more on this topic later in the book.

The mountains

Plenty of mountains are technically illegal to climb, for many different reasons including local religious or superstitious beliefs, hostile landowners, volcanic activity or political rules and administrative regulations. The list of Ribus is not influenced in any way by local access issues, because religions, nations, rulers and landowners tend to come and go more frequently than the mountains themselves. Inclusion on the list is solely determined by a single criterion, that the mountain has been found to have at least 1000 metres of topographic prominence.

The main purpose of the Ribus project has been to create a catalogue not a challenge. No-one is ever going to climb all the Ribus. Even climbing the 1566 Ultras would be an immense undertaking that may well be impossible over the course of a single lifetime. Even before putting one foot in front of the other on the mountains you would need more disposable income and free time than most people could ever dream of having. It would be as much a financial and logistical challenge as a physical one, regardless of ethical considerations. Yet the list of Ribus is more accessible to more people than the Ultras. For example, British residents would have to travel to France or Norway to climb their closest Ultra, whereas there are three Ribus in Great Britain and one over in Ireland. There is also one Sub-Ribu, the brilliant Sgurr Alasdair (992m) on the Scottish island of Skye.

Sub-Ribus are peaks that just miss out on the main list by ten metres or less, with a prominence of from 990 to 999.9 metres. A list of them is included towards the back of the book, because some of them may turn out to be Ribus when improved data becomes available. This publication will certainly not be the end of the story.

Ground zero

The Earth is not a perfect sphere. It bulges at the equator. This explains why Volcán Chimborazo in Ecuador is the mountain summit farthest from the centre of the Earth (6384.4 kilometres away) rather than Mount Everest (6382.3 kilometres away), though Everest is over 2500 metres higher (above sea level) than Chimborazo. Everest is located at 28 degrees north of the equator, which is over 3000 kilometres from the equatorial bulge. As a result of the bulge, Everest is not in the top ten summits farthest from the centre of the Earth.

The sea is not perfectly flat. Sea level varies according to regional differences in gravity. Many national or regional topographic maps use a locally-derived sea level. Mean Sea Level (MSL) is usually based on hourly readings over a nineteen-year period and constitutes zero elevation locally. Vertical datums differ from one another, meaning that zero elevation in Australia is different from zero elevation in Sweden. The World Geodetic System 1984 (WGS84) is a global standard in cartography and satellite navigation yet it does not align perfectly with Mean Sea Level. One great advantage of using topographic prominence is that most Ribus are not affected by any change in sea level. Only the highest points of islands and continents have a key col of zero, which is sea level.

To date there is no perfect model which accounts for the complexity of the Earth's shape, regional differences, the spinning of the planet and a constantly varying actual sea level. It is thought that if the planet stopped spinning then its oceans would split into two separate polar seas, leaving the equator completely dry. This would have massive implications for the list of Ribus but would have even bigger implications for life on Earth.

Data sources

Establishing the prominence of a mountain requires four crucial pieces of information: the location and elevation of its summit and the location and elevation of its key col. This is the specific point that separates a peak from its nearest higher neighbour. If the peak is the highest point of an island then the key col is sea level. Creating a list of peaks based on this data also requires establishing a name for the peak, which is a less precise process.

The dataset for the Ribus has been compiled from a wide range of sources with varying levels of accuracy. Different sources often provide different information, and it has been the task of editors on the Ribus project to scrutinise all of the accessible sources and use their best judgement. Some parts of the world have been so well surveyed and mapped that accurate elevation and prominence figures can be given to within tens of centimetres. Other regions are not so nearly well surveyed.

Data sources have included traditional topographic paper maps, online digital map layers such as OpenTopoMap and the Google Maps terrain layer, personal GPS readings from hikers and numerous online sources of mountain information such as the Peakbagger.com website. However, the single most important factor in making the project feasible has been the availability of global digital elevation models (DEMs), which are elevation datasets representing terrain that can be visualized and analysed. These DEMs have made it feasible to compile lists of peaks worldwide with a reasonable degree of accuracy. The results produced are not usually as accurate as those from ground surveys or satellite GPS based surveys, but the completeness and consistency of coverage has made these models an invaluable resource.

Locating the key col for every peak with a high degree of accuracy would have been an immense challenge if it had not been for the work of three pioneering individuals: Edward Earl, Jonathan de Ferranti and Andrew Kirmse. In the early 2000s, Edward Earl created a computer program called WinProm which was used to calculate prominence values based on raw terrain data. It was a remarkable achievement. Jonathan de Ferranti created a DEM terrain dataset that was the ideal companion to use in conjunction with the WinProm program, and Andrew Kirmse used these to produce his global datasets.

Kirmse was previously engineering director and terrain database specialist for Google Earth and Google Maps. He released two datasets – in 2017 and 2023 – covering the entire planet and including all peaks down to a prominence of 100 feet. This was another huge achievement. The 2017 dataset was used as the starting point for the Ribus project in 2019, along with an earlier provisional list provided by Edward Earl. Team members carried out manual research into all individual peaks, and this was later cross-checked with the 2023 dataset. More details on the research process are given later.

Tragically, Edward Earl died in 2015 during a hiking trip to Mount Isto, which is coincidentally the first mountain listed in this book.

Mount Everest, the most prominent peak on Earth (Oscar Argudo)

The list

The Ribus database and website at WorldRibus.org include extensive data for every peak. The most important information is included in the data tables that form the main body of this book. Peaks are organised into regions, grouped together geographically based on a modified version of the pioneering Peakbagger Mountain Range Classification System (PEMRACS). This system divides the entire land surface of the Earth into ranges and sub-ranges. The seven continents form the seven Level 1 regions. The Level 2 regions organise peaks into major mountain ranges, islands and areas. Aerial maps show the distribution of Ribus in each Level 2 region. Many of these regions are very large. For example, there are only ten Level 2 ranges in the whole of North America and only nine in Europe, leading to very large lists. The tables in the book use smaller Level 3 regions to make the mass of data more meaningful and accessible. For example, there is one table for each of seven Level 3 regions in the Rocky Mountains. Within each table, the summits are listed in order of prominence, though in some tables the peaks on islands are grouped together for clarity.

The data in each table is displayed in six key fields for each entry: Id, Height, Name, Drop, Country and Location, with an Island column added where this is helpful.

Id – Every peak has a unique, fixed identification number. The numbering system starts at 30001 to avoid any conflict with the well-established Database of British and Irish Hills (DOBIH). The four Ribus in the British Isles use the same Id numbers as already exist in the DOBIH and on websites such as hill-bagging.co.uk. Id numbers are arbitrary but follow a pattern. Ribus in North America begin with Id 30001, in South America with 40001, in Europe 50001, in Asia 60001, in Africa 70001, in Oceania 80001 and in Antarctica 90001.

Height – Also known as elevation, this is the height above sea level of a mountain summit. Figures are rounded to the nearest metre.

Name – Where possible, names are taken from the most appropriate map. Some famous mountains have several names in multiple languages. To keep things simple, there are only one or two names shown for most peaks, with a forward slash separating different names. The aim is to give the name or names most relevant for the purposes of this book, with the most popular or well-used name first, though this is not always straightforward to ascertain. For some peaks, the name given refers to a mountain range, e.g. Khrebet Arga-Tas in region AS513 in Siberia (*Khrebet* means *range*). In such cases, the location specifies the highest point of the range. In other cases a single dash separates a range name and peak name, such as Mount Lyell – Ernest Peak.

Many of the peaks in the more sparsely populated areas of the world have no name on any readily available map. Local names may exist for some of these peaks but it is not currently feasible to discover what these may be. In some cases there will be names in different local languages on different sides of the same mountain.

Ascertaining which ought to be the main name applied to a Ribu is a monumental task in itself. Numerous rivers and lakes are named on current digital mapping, and so the names of some peaks have been derived from these landscape features, using some common local words for mountain or summit to help formulate the name of the Ribu.

Derived names are indicated by an asterisk after the peak name, e.g. Gora Kantakan * in region AS512. If more applicable names come to light for any peaks, their names will be updated on the Ribus website and in any future publications.

Island – In some tables, an Island column is added to clarify the location of the peaks. If there is no Island column, the name of an island or peninsula may be included in the Name field, if neither are obvious from the region heading. In such cases a comma is used to separate peak name from island name, e.g. Mount Iraya, Batan Island in region AS590.

Drop – Also known as prominence and relative height, this is the key figure that defines Ribu status and is a measure of the independence of a summit. It refers to the height of a mountain or hill's summit relative to its key col. The drop figure may be as low as 1000 and as high as the elevation of the mountain. The highest peak of any island will have identical height and prominence figures. For example, Ben Nevis in Scotland is 1345 metres above sea level at its highest point and also has a drop of 1345 metres. This is the highest point on the island of Great Britain and so the key col is zero, which is sea level. Similarly, Pico del Teide on the Spanish island of Tenerife has height and drop equal to 3718 metres. This is listed in region AF660 which is part of the African Level 1 region. Like Indonesia, Spain has its highest point in a different continent to most of the country.

For all peaks other than island high-points, the key col is the lowest point on the highest ridge or slope connecting the peak to a higher mountain. In some cases the key col will be many hundreds of kilometres from the summit. For example, the key col for Elbrus, the highest peak in Europe, is in Pakistan. The prominence of Elbrus is less than its height because Europe is not an island. There is one Ribu, Ale Bagu in Ethiopia, with a drop that is greater than its elevation. This is an extremely rare case of a key col being below sea level.

Country – The Natural Earth dataset has been used to determine which country each summit is located in, with some minor amendments to reflect recent political changes. Many Ribus are on or close to international borders and some regions and territories are disputed. In such cases two or three countries are listed. In the list of Ribus the country of a peak is of secondary importance to topographic region, but if a hiker wishes to choose to focus on one country then that is entirely up to them. For Ribus in the USA, the state code is also given, to assist those who may wish to focus on specific states.

Location – Summit co-ordinates for latitude and longitude are provided for each entry, using decimal degrees to four decimal places. These figures give the location of a summit to the nearest eleven metres at the equator or better, with a greater degree of precision for peaks located further from the equator. The locations are given using the standard international convention of latitude followed by longitude. This is different to some national systems which use X, Y coordinates, such as the Ordnance Survey two-letter grid system used in Britain.

North and Central America

NA10 Alaska – Yukon Ranges

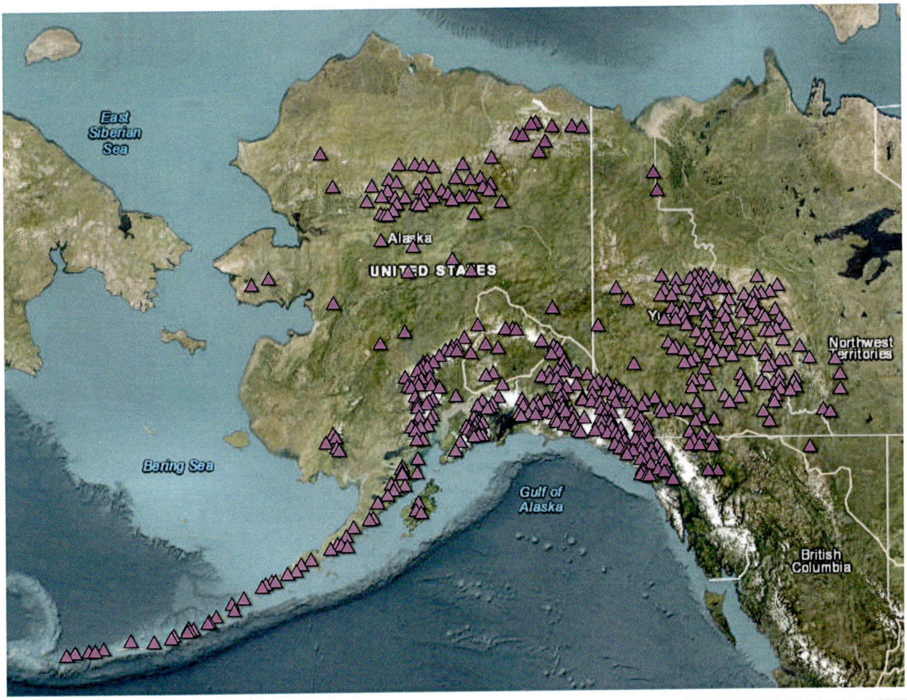

Mount Cairnes, NA105 (Rob Woodall)

NA100 Brooks Range

Id	Height	Name	Drop	Country	Location
30016	2736	Mount Isto	2416	USA-AK	69.2025, -143.8017
30042	2523	Mount Igikpak	1857	USA-AK	67.4126, -154.9650
30097	2240	Verdant Peak *	1422	USA-AK	68.2792, -153.5550
30121	1884	Poss Mountain	1359	USA-AK	67.4408, -149.7192
30124	2220	Kurupa Mountain *	1340	USA-AK	68.2583, -154.7183
30135	2248	Echooka Peak	1312	USA-AK	69.0167, -146.3767
30147	2452	Accomplishment Peak	1285	USA-AK	68.4433, -148.0942
30161	2713	Mount Chamberlin	1257	USA-AK	69.2775, -144.9108
30163	2206	Killik Peak	1250	USA-AK	67.8033, -154.8617
30165	2205	Mount Greenough	1248	USA-AK	69.1625, -141.6658
30177	1799	Bluecloud Mountain	1226	USA-AK	67.4062, -150.4245
30189	2298	Thibedeau Mountain	1212	USA-AK	68.2842, -150.0975
30207	1791	Ipnek Peak *	1184	USA-AK	67.3383, -150.9517
30209	1347	Narvak Peak *	1180	USA-AK	66.9450, -155.7442
30211	2140	Geroe Peak *	1175	USA-AK	67.6908, -148.6925
30217	2298	Mount Chandalar *	1170	USA-AK	68.8217, -144.3508
30221	1904	Tunukuchiak Peak *	1166	USA-AK	67.7108, -156.6450
30223	1886	Sillyasheen Mountain	1163	USA-AK	67.7692, -152.7133
30237	1998	Iniakuk Peak	1151	USA-AK	67.4750, -152.9042
30251	2140	Iriklaklik Peak	1140	USA-AK	68.2367, -152.9192
30253	1716	Thazzik Mountain	1137	USA-AK	67.2767, -147.4258
30258	1976	Thru Creek Mountain *	1134	USA-AK	67.8998, -148.8457
30279	2145	Sann Benchmark	1117	USA-AK	68.9892, -145.8992
30281	1443	Mount Hal Waugh	1116	USA-AK	67.1908, -153.2275
30285	2192	Oyukak Mountain	1115	USA-AK	67.5699, -155.5017
30288	1395	Reed River Mountain *	1112	USA-AK	67.0836, -155.1376
30308	2273	Mount Doonerak	1092	USA-AK	67.9042, -150.6267
30318	2061	Inualurak Mountain	1085	USA-AK	68.2092, -152.2108
30325	1407	Fritts Mountain	1081	USA-AK	66.9239, -155.5051
30335	1888	Chandalar Peak *	1071	USA-AK	67.7273, -148.1507
30364	1350	Tobuk Mountain *	1053	USA-AK	67.2439, -153.4489
30373	2050	Old Woman Peak *	1046	USA-AK	68.5544, -144.7200
30378	1584	Cummings Creek Mountain *	1044	USA-AK	67.3000, -152.9617
30380	1651	Rock Creek Mountain *	1043	USA-AK	67.4063, -152.2499
30381	1433	Mount Angayukaqsraq	1041	USA-AK	67.7083, -159.4042
30382	1946	Pingaluk Peak *	1039	USA-AK	67.6375, -153.2158
30383	1710	California Creek Mountain *	1039	USA-AK	67.4158, -149.4250
30385	1942	Mount Weyahok *	1038	USA-AK	67.8817, -155.3708
30393	2360	Plateau Peak	1037	USA-AK	69.2675, -145.3078

Id	Height	Name	Drop	Country	Location
30402	1682	Agnes Creek Mountain *	1031	USA-AK	67.5175, -151.1817
30408	1660	Inyuilak Peak *	1031	USA-AK	67.2464, -154.8806
30423	2182	Arrigetch Peaks – Xanadu	1023	USA-AK	67.4005, -154.2295
30424	1530	Black Mountain	1023	USA-AK	68.5598, -160.3281
30431	1986	Shulakpachak Peak	1021	USA-AK	67.4317, -155.9350
30448	1741	Sirr Mountain	1012	USA-AK	67.5725, -151.6475
30457	2185	Egaksrak Mountain *	1007	USA-AK	69.1858, -142.4192
30465	1691	McNett Peak *	1005	USA-AK	67.5742, -148.2992
30468	1189	Ambler Mountain *	1003	USA-AK	67.3092, -157.0033
30469	1975	Mount Mathews *	1003	USA-AK	67.8700, -149.5945

NA101 Alaska Inter-mountain Ranges

Id	Height	Name	Drop	Country	Location
30107	1994	Mount Harper	1384	USA-AK	64.2367, -143.8433
30118	1600	Chikuminuk Peak *	1357	USA-AK	60.1159, -159.3241
30129	1437	Mount Osborn	1331	USA-AK	64.9925, -165.3292
30157	1682	Mount Tozi	1267	USA-AK	65.6875, -150.9500
30166	1517	Wolf Mountain	1247	USA-AK	65.3133, -154.0733
30181	1532	Mount Waskey	1221	USA-AK	59.7623, -159.2249
30208	1801	Moore Creek Mountain *	1182	USA-AK	66.9725, -149.3492
30242	1873	Pine Peak	1147	Canada	63.6955, -140.6046
30266	1245	Zane Peak *	1127	USA-AK	66.2400, -156.0075
30270	1374	Von Frank Mountain	1122	USA-AK	63.5400, -154.3342
30282	1414	Sawtooth Mountain	1116	USA-AK	65.3649, -149.5771
30310	1291	Indian Mountain	1090	USA-AK	66.0692, -153.6875
30322	1844	Wolf Lake Peak *	1082	Canada	61.9040, -140.0281
30346	1501	Gold Lake Mountain *	1062	USA-AK	60.2367, -159.5358
30369	1228	Kalasik Mountain *	1048	USA-AK	64.4533, -159.4150
30398	1291	Cloudy Mountain	1033	USA-AK	63.1892, -156.0783
30410	1420	Mount Oratia	1029	USA-AK	59.9292, -160.0142
30439	1137	Mount Bendeleben	1019	USA-AK	65.1742, -164.0942
30449	1100	Amakuk Mountain *	1012	USA-AK	59.6517, -159.0898

NA102 Alaska Range

Id	Height	Name	Drop	Country	Location
30001	6190	Denali / Mount McKinley	6164	USA-AK	63.0691, -151.0062
30005	4216	Mount Hayes	3500	USA-AK	63.6200, -146.7175
30012	3479	Mount Torbert	2642	USA-AK	61.4092, -152.4125
30022	3141	Mount Kimball	2247	USA-AK	63.2392, -144.6408
30023	5304	Mount Foraker	2229	USA-AK	62.9608, -151.3992
30028	2996	Mount Hesperus	2117	USA-AK	61.8041, -154.1467

Id	Height	Name	Drop	Country	Location
30039	2739	Kichatna Spire	1886	USA-AK	62.4233, -152.7225
30056	3557	Mount Russell	1687	USA-AK	62.7983, -151.8842
30065	3761	Mount Deborah	1592	USA-AK	63.6378, -147.2382
30066	2541	Tlikaklia Peak *	1588	USA-AK	61.1125, -153.4683
30069	2587	Snowcap North *	1580	USA-AK	61.4950, -153.6225
30081	2441	Merrill River Mountain *	1488	USA-AK	61.2225, -153.4342
30095	4442	Mount Hunter	1432	USA-AK	62.9500, -151.0908
30140	1984	Distin Peak	1296	USA-AK	62.0892, -152.5425
30168	2307	Dillinger Peak *	1245	USA-AK	62.4760, -153.0164
30185	2016	Soule Mountain *	1216	USA-AK	63.1642, -148.5958
30187	2067	Hartman Mountain *	1214	USA-AK	61.8442, -153.4058
30188	2128	Indian Pass Peak *	1214	USA-AK	62.8475, -143.9625
30195	3968	Mount Moffit	1203	USA-AK	63.5683, -146.3975
30199	2669	Mount Dall	1196	USA-AK	62.5792, -152.2942
30222	2048	Bartell Peak *	1164	USA-AK	63.0076, -143.5394
30233	2926	Jezebel	1155	USA-AK	61.7800, -153.9250
30241	2131	Trimokish Peak *	1147	USA-AK	62.1178, -154.3469
30243	1887	Kenibuna Mountain *	1146	USA-AK	61.2129, -152.8636
30260	2063	Terra Cotta Peak *	1131	USA-AK	61.9732, -153.4967
30298	1737	Mount Trimble *	1101	USA-AK	61.7658, -151.8867
30304	2103	Big Salmon Mountain *	1097	USA-AK	62.5917, -153.0183
30309	2271	Dry Tok Mountain *	1090	USA-AK	63.0942, -143.7617
30312	1340	Mount Susitna	1088	USA-AK	61.4733, -150.7367
30320	1957	Spring Creek Ridge *	1082	USA-AK	61.8692, -152.4466
30323	2088	Pingston Peak *	1082	USA-AK	62.6393, -152.7119
30359	1771	Post River Peak *	1054	USA-AK	62.2976, -153.4467
30376	2691	Scott Peak	1045	USA-AK	63.3442, -150.1258
30391	2057	Harpoon Mountain *	1037	USA-AK	61.3266, -152.6769
30395	1880	Watana Mountain *	1035	USA-AK	63.0164, -147.7081
30397	2058	Teocalli Peak *	1034	USA-AK	62.0553, -153.2339
30422	1433	K'esugi Mountain	1024	USA-AK	62.8667, -149.6800
30436	3150	The Moose's Tooth	1020	USA-AK	62.9692, -150.6133
30453	1868	Tatina Peak *	1009	USA-AK	62.3619, -153.3075
30458	4029	Mount Silverthrone	1007	USA-AK	63.1158, -150.6750
30460	1905	Mount Hines *	1007	USA-AK	63.7550, -149.1275

NA103 Aleutian Ranges

Id	Height	Name	Drop	Country	Location
30010	3108	Redoubt Volcano	2780	USA-AK	60.4852, -152.7440
30014	2507	Mount Veniaminof	2493	USA-AK	56.2192, -159.2975
30015	2499	Pavlof Volcano	2484	USA-AK	55.4174, -161.8934
30017	3053	Iliamna Volcano	2412	USA-AK	60.0320, -153.0917

Id	Height	Name	Drop	Country	Location
30024	2334	Mount Griggs / Knife Peak	2218	USA-AK	58.3533, -155.0933
30031	2103	Mount Chiginagak	2023	USA-AK	57.1335, -156.9910
30035	2873	Mount Neacola	1928	USA-AK	60.7983, -153.3958
30041	2139	Mount Douglas	1866	USA-AK	58.8592, -153.5350
30051	1769	Frosty Peak	1751	USA-AK	55.0673, -162.8351
30080	1896	Mount Kupreanof	1489	USA-AK	56.0125, -159.7908
30084	1890	Tlikakila Mountain *	1473	USA-AK	60.4562, -153.6762
30094	2078	Double Peak	1432	USA-AK	60.7292, -152.5867
30110	1474	Mount Peulik	1375	USA-AK	57.7506, -156.3698
30119	2165	Mount Mageik	1356	USA-AK	58.1946, -155.2543
30152	1463	Mount Katolinat East	1280	USA-AK	58.4639, -155.4339
30179	1354	Mount Dana	1225	USA-AK	55.6417, -161.2150
30186	2057	Mount Currant *	1214	USA-AK	60.3442, -153.6642
30229	1646	Pile Mountain *	1159	USA-AK	60.0125, -153.5167
30239	1346	Aniakchak Peak	1148	USA-AK	56.8625, -158.1300
30250	1497	Mount Dutton	1141	USA-AK	55.1867, -162.2742
30257	1675	Strike Mountain *	1134	USA-AK	58.7933, -154.5908
30262	1176	Yellow Bluff Mountain *	1130	USA-AK	56.5142, -158.6067
30275	1603	Portage Mountain *	1119	USA-AK	60.4390, -153.8658
30296	1127	Virgin Peak	1102	USA-AK	56.1233, -158.5142
30316	1946	Black Peak	1085	USA-AK	60.8534, -152.4238
30337	2299	Mount Denison	1067	USA-AK	58.4175, -154.4508
30348	1600	Mount Kialagvik	1059	USA-AK	57.2020, -156.7461
30384	1483	Kamishak Ridge *	1039	USA-AK	58.9150, -154.6383
30418	1373	Chignik Peak *	1027	USA-AK	56.1775, -158.9858
30440	1311	Paint Peak *	1018	USA-AK	59.0825, -154.6342
30450	1424	Pirate Lake Peak *	1011	USA-AK	59.0117, -154.6886
30452	1676	Becharof Wilderness Peak *	1010	USA-AK	58.0208, -155.6700
30461	1859	Chokotonk Mountain *	1006	USA-AK	60.4358, -153.2942

Aleutian Islands

Id	Height	Name	Island	Drop	Country	Location
30009	2869	Shishaldin Volcano	Unimak	2869	USA-AK	54.7555, -163.9705
30037	1991	Pogromni Volcano	Unimak	1887	USA-AK	54.5708, -164.6925
30018	2471	Isanotski Volcano	Unimak	1771	USA-AK	54.7680, -163.7293
30464	1112	Eickelberg Peak	Unimak	1005	USA-AK	54.6765, -164.4811
30027	2149	Mount Vsevidof	Umnak	2149	USA-AK	53.1250, -168.6950
30212	1984	Mount Recheshnoi	Umnak	1175	USA-AK	53.1535, -168.5385
30213	1253	Tulik Volcano	Umnak	1174	USA-AK	53.3733, -168.0567
30044	1811	Makushin Volcano	Unalaska	1811	USA-AK	53.8858, -166.9442
30403	1141	Udamak Mountain *	Unalaska	1031	USA-AK	53.6475, -166.6892
30046	1806	Tanaga Volcano	Tanaga	1806	USA-AK	51.8833, -178.1433

Id	Height	Name		Drop	Country	Location
30052	1740	Great Sitkin Volcano	Great Sitkin	1740	USA-AK	52.0758, -176.1117
30053	1730	Mount Cleveland	Chuginadak	1730	USA-AK	52.8225, -169.9467
30274	1170	Mount Corwin *	Chuginadak	1120	USA-AK	52.8383, -169.7583
30062	1610	Mount Carlisle	Carlisle	1610	USA-AK	52.8917, -170.0583
30070	1573	Mount Gareloi	Gareloi	1573	USA-AK	51.7879, -178.7943
30076	1533	Korovin Volcano	Atka	1533	USA-AK	52.3817, -174.1650
30137	1307	Kanaga Volcano	Kanaga	1307	USA-AK	51.9242, -177.1650
30143	1296	Akutan Peak	Akutan	1296	USA-AK	54.1333, -165.9858
30153	1280	Herbert Volcano	Herbert	1280	USA-AK	52.7417, -170.1150
30176	1227	Augustine Volcano	Augustine	1227	USA-AK	59.3625, -153.4325
30183	1221	Anvil Peak	Semisopochnoi	1221	USA-AK	51.9858, 179.6017
30184	1220	Kiska Volcano	Kiska	1220	USA-AK	52.1025, 177.6033
30201	1196	Mount Moffett	Adak	1196	USA-AK	51.9367, -176.7417
30214	1174	Little Sitkin Volcano	Little Sitkin	1174	USA-AK	51.9532, 178.5369
30224	1163	Segula Peak	Segula	1163	USA-AK	52.0150, 178.1367
30249	1142	Chagulak Peak *	Chagulak	1142	USA-AK	52.5717, -171.1383
30339	1067	Amukta Peak *	Amukta	1067	USA-AK	52.4975, -171.2550
30361	1054	Pyre Peak	Seguam	1054	USA-AK	52.3158, -172.5100

NA104 South-Central Alaska

Id	Height	Name	Drop	Country	Location
30004	4996	Mount Blackburn	3534	USA-AK	61.7317, -143.4375
30007	4016	Mount Marcus Baker	3285	USA-AK	61.4375, -147.7525
30019	4949	Mount Sanford	2342	USA-AK	62.2133, -144.1300
30021	3411	Mount Tom White	2330	USA-AK	60.6525, -143.6975
30030	3661	Mount Drum	2052	USA-AK	62.1158, -144.6400
30038	2464	Mount Chosin Few	1887	USA-AK	60.8300, -145.1333
30040	2441	Copper River Peak *	1878	USA-AK	61.1608, -144.8133
30043	2015	Truuli Peak	1832	USA-AK	59.9125, -150.4342
30047	2592	Hanagita Peak	1800	USA-AK	61.0675, -143.7083
30048	2697	Sovereign Mountain	1790	USA-AK	62.1308, -148.6042
30050	1991	Isthmus Peak	1771	USA-AK	60.5771, -148.8913
30054	4317	Mount Wrangell	1701	USA-AK	62.0058, -144.0183
30059	3205	Mount Steller	1645	USA-AK	60.5200, -143.0925
30063	2440	Bashful Peak	1608	USA-AK	61.3075, -148.8699
30064	2550	Mentasta Mountains – Tetlin Peak	1600	USA-AK	62.6217, -143.1083
30068	3261	Mount Miller	1585	USA-AK	60.4608, -142.3008
30074	2108	Copper River Mountain *	1545	USA-AK	61.3292, -144.9600
30079	1740	Mount Ascension	1489	USA-AK	60.2583, -149.4992
30085	1864	Excelsior Peak *	1464	USA-AK	60.1717, -148.8542
30086	4091	Mount Jarvis	1458	USA-AK	62.0233, -143.6200
30090	2286	Mount Tasnuna *	1441	USA-AK	61.1250, -145.3000

30099	1622	Pestle Peak	1409	USA-AK	60.4767, -149.5233
30104	2926	Mount Leeper	1396	USA-AK	60.2858, -142.1033
30108	1768	Iceworm Peak	1379	USA-AK	59.6088, -150.7946
30109	1699	Bench Peak	1376	USA-AK	60.6492, -149.1342
30112	1922	Sheep Mountain	1371	USA-AK	60.3356, -149.2651
30120	4220	Regal Mountain	1351	USA-AK	61.7442, -142.8675
30126	2890	Mount Allen	1338	USA-AK	62.2442, -142.2350
30133	3048	Mount Gannett	1320	USA-AK	61.2425, -148.1967
30138	1786	Mount Godwin	1298	USA-AK	60.1596, -149.1622
30151	2489	Goodlata Peak	1280	USA-AK	61.0533, -143.1350
30159	2190	Mount Taylor	1261	Canada	61.9567, -140.6633
30162	2295	Summit Lake Ridge *	1256	USA-AK	61.2975, -144.3650
30167	2613	Nutzotin Mountains	1246	USA-AK	62.1358, -141.4540
30180	1506	Fiddlehead Mountain	1223	USA-AK	60.7550, -149.3075
30182	2763	Steller Ridge *	1221	USA-AK	60.5783, -143.6175
30191	1606	Cooper Mountain	1210	USA-AK	60.3775, -149.8417
30196	2274	Mount Stairway *	1203	USA-AK	61.0426, -148.5598
30200	1646	El Tercero	1196	USA-AK	60.5858, -149.3608
30216	2037	Klu Peak *	1171	USA-AK	61.2217, -143.2875
30218	2064	Falls Creek Mountain *	1169	USA-AK	61.3583, -144.2275
30225	1860	Trident Peak	1162	USA-AK	60.3975, -149.0750
30238	1606	Madson Mountain	1149	USA-AK	60.4550, -149.4333
30248	1548	Frenchy Peak	1142	USA-AK	60.7450, -149.5400
30252	1984	Crystalline Hills	1140	USA-AK	61.4307, -143.3827
30263	2214	Mount Nabesna *	1130	USA-AK	62.3758, -143.0958
30268	2192	Mount Benet	1125	USA-AK	61.1583, -146.0158
30276	1794	Mount Denson	1118	USA-AK	60.9017, -146.3633
30303	1134	Olsen Bay Mountain *	1098	USA-AK	60.7934, -146.1506
30306	2213	Boyden Hills	1094	USA-AK	62.4758, -142.9375
30313	1992	Mineral Cairn	1086	USA-AK	62.8692, -143.3692
30332	1935	Twelvemile Mountain *	1072	USA-AK	60.9050, -143.8508
30341	1884	Hearth Mountain	1064	USA-AK	60.2308, -149.1892
30343	2318	Mount Muir	1063	USA-AK	61.1076, -148.3813
30347	2344	Kiagna Peak *	1060	USA-AK	60.9258, -143.0367
30356	1316	Russian Mountain	1056	USA-AK	60.4492, -150.0408
30358	2173	Mount Tom	1054	USA-AK	62.2792, -143.1917
30362	2356	Golconda Mountain *	1053	USA-AK	61.0942, -143.5350
30365	1963	Gunsight Mountain	1052	USA-AK	61.8442, -147.4675
30366	2283	Chugach Peak *	1052	USA-AK	60.8748, -145.6248
30374	2211	Worthington Ridge *	1046	USA-AK	61.2056, -145.8684
30401	2142	Canyon Mountain	1032	Canada	61.8167, -140.9396
30406	2128	Organ Mountain	1031	USA-AK	61.1325, -149.2425

Id	Height	Name	Drop	Country	Location
30409	2852	Tanada Peak	1029	USA-AK	62.3025, -143.5058
30414	2722	Yahtse Peak *	1029	USA-AK	60.2517, -141.9267
30428	2120	Fireweed Mountain	1023	USA-AK	61.4663, -143.1474
30434	1581	Phoenix Peak	1021	USA-AK	60.1222, -149.5385
30435	2385	Nowhere Mountain *	1020	USA-AK	62.2192, -148.1250
30443	1410	Kenai Peak *	1017	USA-AK	60.4390, -149.7776
30446	2452	Klutina Peak *	1014	USA-AK	61.3409, -146.0858
30451	3240	Frederika Peak *	1010	USA-AK	61.8280, -142.2455
30467	1675	Mount Resurrection *	1004	USA-AK	60.2945, -149.5923
30473	2103	Mount Bremner *	1000	USA-AK	60.9442, -144.3008
30115	1362	Koniag Peak, Kodiak Island	1362	USA-AK	57.3546, -153.3247
30273	1327	Browns Lagoon Peak, Kodiak Island *	1120	USA-AK	57.4508, -153.6250
30445	1159	Helmet Mountain, Kodiak Island	1015	USA-AK	57.7322, -153.4200

NA105 Saint Elias Mountains

Id	Height	Name	Drop	Country	Location
30002	5956	Mount Logan	5250	Canada	60.5671, -140.4056
30003	4671	Mount Fairweather	3976	Canada, USA-AK	58.9064, -137.5265
30006	5489	Mount Saint Elias	3449	Canada, USA-AK	60.2931, -140.9307
30008	5245	Mount Lucania	3052	Canada	61.0217, -140.4658
30011	4812	Mount Vancouver	2769	Canada	60.3589, -139.6982
30013	4557	Mount Hubbard	2497	Canada, USA-AK	60.3193, -139.0723
30020	4194	Mount Cook	2335	Canada, USA-AK	60.1819, -139.9810
30025	3879	Mount Crillon	2209	USA-AK	58.6625, -137.1717
30029	5040	Mount Bona	2103	USA-AK	61.3850, -141.7508
30032	2722	Alsek Peak	2002	Canada	60.0325, -137.5917
30033	2805	Mount Cairnes	1974	Canada	60.8683, -138.2767
30034	2721	Buckwell Peak	1961	Canada	59.4187, -136.7655
30036	2550	Detour Peak	1908	Canada	59.8423, -137.5854
30045	4095	Mount Natazhat	1810	USA-AK	61.5217, -141.1025
30049	2512	Mount Martha Black	1779	Canada	60.6714, -137.6222
30055	3155	Mount Seattle	1700	USA-AK	60.0682, -139.1888
30057	2588	Mount Archibald	1667	Canada	60.7844, -137.8740
30060	2596	Granite Range Peak *	1622	USA-AK	60.9283, -142.5233
30061	3353	Mount Foresta	1617	USA-AK	60.1908, -139.4325
30067	2706	Basement Peak	1588	Canada	59.3551, -137.1617
30071	4520	Mount Bear	1566	USA-AK	61.2842, -141.1425
30073	2329	Dalton Peak	1551	Canada	60.4767, -137.1733
30075	4289	Mount Augusta	1536	Canada, USA-AK	60.3080, -140.4585
30087	2098	Battle Peak	1451	Canada	59.5746, -138.1914
30092	1774	Chunekukleik Mountain	1439	USA-AK	59.2922, -135.9529
30093	2326	Super Cub Mountain *	1436	Canada	59.9633, -138.0133

30096	2830	Mount Aylesworth	1423	Canada, USA-AK	59.9244, -138.7994
30098	1680	Mount Case	1415	USA-AK	58.8179, -135.9701
30116	4507	Mount Walsh	1360	Canada	61.0036, -140.0171
30117	1399	Mount Hendrickson	1359	USA-AK	59.8190, -139.4722
30123	1549	Mount Merriam	1342	USA-AK	58.9008, -136.4367
30128	3928	Mount Queen Mary	1332	Canada	60.6285, -139.7247
30136	2181	Gribbles Peak *	1307	Canada	60.2788, -137.1647
30146	2708	Ross Green Mountain *	1285	USA-AK	60.8083, -142.3758
30150	2287	Samuel Peak	1281	Canada	59.6299, -136.8508
30158	3715	Mount King George	1265	Canada	60.5315, -139.7841
30170	3709	Mount Salisbury	1242	USA-AK	58.8508, -137.3717
30175	1737	Mount Reaburn	1228	USA-AK	59.4325, -138.6400
30178	2293	Lynx Creek Mountain *	1226	Canada	61.6088, -140.0786
30197	4841	Mount Wood	1203	Canada	61.2327, -140.5122
30205	2015	Noisy Peak	1189	Canada	59.5639, -137.6763
30215	2707	Mount Hay	1173	Canada, USA-AK	59.2444, -137.6087
30228	3634	Lituya Mountain	1160	USA-AK	58.8055, -137.4367
30231	3530	Mount Upton	1157	Canada	60.8059, -140.1639
30232	3609	Logan Glacier Peak *	1156	Canada	60.6000, -140.0492
30264	2491	Mount Barnard	1130	Canada, USA-AK	59.1013, -136.9693
30280	2570	Mount Tweedsmuir *	1117	Canada	60.0525, -138.8442
30283	2286	Mount Tlingit Ankawoo	1116	USA-AK	59.1591, -135.8860
30291	1728	Mount Draper	1110	USA-AK	59.8062, -139.0799
30324	2514	Thompson Ridge	1081	USA-AK	60.6667, -142.4525
30327	2225	Arch Creek Mountain *	1079	Canada	61.4867, -139.5550
30340	2960	Jefferies Peak *	1064	USA-AK	60.7100, -141.6450
30353	2004	Four Winds Mountain	1056	USA-AK	59.4929, -136.1480
30355	5173	King Peak	1056	Canada	60.5833, -140.6549
30388	2018	Sockeye Mountain *	1038	Canada	60.4332, -137.7072
30390	1732	Battle Glacier Mountain *	1038	USA-AK	59.6436, -138.5767
30392	3110	Mount Bertha	1037	USA-AK	58.6866, -137.0271
30407	1677	Beartrack Mountain *	1031	USA-AK	58.7914, -135.8125
30412	2105	Mount Beaton	1029	Canada	60.0118, -137.0399
30413	1705	Mount Pinta	1029	USA-AK	59.6817, -139.1619
30416	4377	McArthur Peak	1027	Canada	60.6067, -140.2142
30417	4410	University Peak	1027	USA-AK	61.3272, -141.7862
30419	2043	Kusawak Peak	1026	Canada	59.7042, -136.4781
30444	3709	Donjek Peak *	1016	Canada	60.8856, -139.6527
30447	1604	Chilkat Peak *	1013	USA-AK	58.5514, -135.3626
30455	1370	Echo Creek Mountain *	1008	USA-AK	58.7406, -137.6402
30471	3000	Mount Hoge	1002	Canada	61.2400, -139.3990
30472	1600	Yakutat Peak *	1002	USA-AK	59.5939, -138.5128

Mount Cairnes, NA105

Rob Woodall, August 2023

Yukon Ribus tend to be remote, but Dave Hart is Alaskan and had identified a line of four Ultras close to the paved Alaska Highway. Some of them seemed feasible for a day hike during our Alaska to Calgary road trip. Mount Cairnes had a single undated log on the Peakbagger website, with no information. Someone on YouTube called Foresty Forest had provided useful footage and a GPS track but had turned back before reaching the summit.

An hour in, we parked the e-bikes and undertook the first of seven unfriendly creek crossings, well outside my softie European comfort zone but seemingly quite normal for Alaskan Dave, who always managed to find a spot that somehow worked, tossing back his hiking poles for me to use. Ahead lay a long graceful ridge topped with snow and ice. An initial scree slope led to excellent hiking, with occasional easy scrambling, and in time we arrived at the east top, where Foresty had turned back. We had more equipment and carried on, crossing the top edge of the glacier. This was initially mellow, then steep, with a huge drop-off and no margin for error. Further on, a climb on loose, unstable rock led to a tottering arete, its components attached by gravity only but heavy enough to safely put a sling around. I led this section and the summit was easily attained after a short crampon climb, although a nearby rocky top might become higher in time.

The descent hit the buffers when we discovered that we couldn't cross the Bryson Creek. The weather was unusually warm and the increased melt water had turned it into an ugly mass of raging water which even Dave wouldn't consider crossing. We had to make an unplanned, unequipped and unprovisioned bivouac. Dave found a foil bivvy bag deep in his pack. I got up once an hour and walked around to generate body heat. On one occasion I tripped over some driftwood and bruised my quadriceps muscle on a sharp rock. Next morning I could barely walk but the torrent was crossable again, and we made it back to the camper van. I knew the injury from a previous trip, to Japan in 2012. I had kept on climbing and it had taken over a month to heal. Here I was grounded as there was nothing I could reasonably climb. The next day Dave soloed the nearby Mount Archibald, which took him thirteen hours, while I stayed in the van with ice-pack and painkillers.

Afterwards we called at Logan Lodge. The owner knew the next peak south, Mount Martha Black, as a serious three-day outing. He knew nothing of the fourth one, Dalton Peak. The weather window was closing so we headed south. In the nearby settlement of Smithers I found a physiotherapist and engaged in some retail therapy while Dave enjoyed rainy ascents of Kispiox and Cronin, which I had climbed on a previous trip. As part of my rehab plan I took my brand new hiking poles up Mount Harvey, a 900-metre ascent that was mostly on a path.

Other planned peaks in northern British Columbia weren't feasible due to poor weather and poorly leg, so we continued to the Rockies. There we failed on Mount Hector as it was too icy. It was then Dave's turn to take time out, after tweaking a tendon, so I made a two-day solo ascent of Mount Joffre, my rehabilitation apparently on track. We then parted, with Dave continuing to Montana for Mount Cleveland, which was to be his final Ultra in the 48 contiguous states. I spent a fortnight in British Columbia enjoying its excellent supply of reasonably feasible Ribus before visiting New Hampshire for Mount Washington, which became my own final Ultra in the 48 states.

NA106 Yukon Inter-mountain Ranges

Id	Height	Name	Drop	Country	Location
30077	2214	Grey Hunter Peak	1520	Canada	63.1356, -135.6367
30088	2295	Kluane Lake Mountain *	1447	Canada	61.5847, -138.7780
30089	2403	Fox Mountain	1443	Canada	61.9242, -133.3664
30100	2107	Mount Minto	1406	Canada	59.9410, -133.9005
30101	2350	Swanson Creek Mountain *	1405	Canada	61.2458, -138.2500
30102	2157	Mount Armstrong	1403	Canada	63.1940, -133.2561
30105	2088	Mount Patterson	1393	Canada	64.0651, -134.5849
30106	2150	Sifton Peak	1390	Canada	61.0108, -136.2406
30113	2174	Gray Creek Mountain *	1369	Canada	61.1801, -133.6190
30122	2142	Mount Snowdon	1349	Canada	59.7164, -132.4919
30125	2189	Glenlyon Peak / Mount Hodder	1339	Canada	62.5315, -134.4854
30127	2350	Mount Frank Rae	1337	Canada	64.4706, -138.5550
30130	2058	Mount Hinton	1331	Canada	63.8689, -135.1294
30132	2084	Joe Mountain	1324	Canada	60.9364, -134.7056
30141	2170	Nuntaea Peak *	1296	Canada	61.6155, -139.0386
30144	1679	Richardson Mountains Peak *	1290	Canada	67.5512, -136.3396
30148	2142	Mount Connolly	1282	Canada	62.5338, -132.3516
30154	1715	White Mountains Peak *	1279	Canada	67.9934, -136.5856
30155	2089	Mount Byng	1278	Canada	60.9131, -134.3397
30156	1994	Stewart Plateau Peak *	1277	Canada	63.3919, -132.8583
30173	2109	Tay Mountain	1239	Canada	62.5564, -134.0356
30174	2330	Pelly Peak *	1234	Canada	61.3651, -130.5023
30190	1907	Kalzas Mountain	1210	Canada	62.9431, -135.2928
30198	2054	Pilot Mountain	1201	Canada	61.0264, -135.5369
30206	1923	Sunday Peak	1188	Canada	59.7469, -134.1037
30210	2037	Hess Mountains Peak *	1179	Canada	63.1353, -132.5930
30219	1969	Mount Keish	1168	Canada	59.9662, -132.5529
30227	2011	Mount Cameron	1161	Canada	64.0726, -135.0136
30246	2087	D'Abaddie Ridge *	1146	Canada	61.6881, -133.9743
30247	2219	Mount Bark	1144	Canada	61.0910, -137.5071
30256	1839	Mount Haldane	1135	Canada	63.8606, -135.8439
30261	1980	Crystal Peak	1131	Canada	62.9072, -134.5071
30265	2091	Mount Barham	1128	Canada	59.7497, -133.3825
30267	2305	Gladstone Creek Mountain *	1126	Canada	61.3900, -138.4300
30284	2061	Mount Mye	1116	Canada	62.3120, -133.1010
30286	1844	Mount Edwards	1114	Canada	63.7230, -134.2639
30290	1953	Toshingermann Mountain *	1110	Canada	61.7868, -139.3743
30295	2130	Mount Creeden	1103	Canada	61.2668, -137.2552
30297	1972	Nahlin Mountain	1101	Canada	58.8574, -132.0879

Id	Height	Name	Drop	Country	Location
30305	1908	Clarke Peak	1095	Canada	63.0378, -135.0823
30307	2240	Lapie Mountain *	1094	Canada	61.7839, -132.7133
30314	1877	Swede Johnson Peak	1086	Canada	61.6617, -139.4683
30315	2026	Apex Mountain	1086	Canada	62.4689, -138.0665
30330	2001	Fork Range Peak *	1076	Canada	62.7917, -132.7164
30333	2106	Mount Patterson	1072	Canada	61.9383, -133.8956
30336	1894	Streak Mountain	1071	Canada	60.5767, -133.6555
30350	1997	Thirtymile Range	1059	Canada	60.6348, -132.3644
30351	2010	Red Granite Mountain	1059	Canada	61.3443, -136.5997
30363	1840	Mount Roop	1053	Canada	63.8739, -134.3964
30370	1923	McQuesten Mountain *	1047	Canada	64.2229, -135.3820
30371	1703	Inklin Peak *	1047	Canada	58.8592, -132.7792
30379	2197	Ogilvie Mountains Peak	1044	Canada	64.8145, -139.3349
30387	1997	Mount Grant	1038	Canada	60.7368, -133.3455
30389	1947	Mount Bryde West	1038	Canada	60.1050, -133.2475
30396	1814	Jubilee Mountain	1035	Canada	60.1967, -134.1192
30400	2253	St Cyr Peak *	1033	Canada	61.1940, -131.2064
30404	1787	Pleasant Creek Mountain *	1031	Canada	63.4760, -133.5896
30429	1986	Twopete Mountain	1022	Canada	62.6836, -133.7111
30433	2138	Worm Lake Mountain *	1021	Canada	64.5794, -136.1514
30442	2173	Ragged Peak	1018	Canada	61.4044, -131.5757
30459	2114	Quill Mountain *	1007	Canada	61.6170, -139.2411
30466	1978	Stony Creek Peak *	1004	Canada	60.9049, -136.0492

NA107 Mackenzie Mountains

Id	Height	Name	Drop	Country	Location
30026	2952	Keele Peak	2154	Canada	63.4313, -130.3242
30058	2773	Mount Nirvana	1661	Canada	61.8751, -127.6805
30072	2755	Mount MacDonald	1564	Canada	64.7250, -132.7781
30078	2703	Sheepbed Peak	1490	Canada	62.5486, -127.2842
30082	2316	Mount Hamilton Gault	1485	Canada	61.6889, -126.5156
30083	2504	Pass Mountain	1482	Canada	64.5140, -133.6254
30091	2674	Backbone Peak	1440	Canada	64.1932, -130.3335
30103	2575	Mount Shannon	1402	Canada	61.8891, -128.8981
30111	2350	Mount Caribou Cry *	1374	Canada	64.0489, -129.1774
30114	2545	Sayunei Peak *	1366	Canada	64.3333, -129.5028
30131	2405	Stelfox Peak *	1326	Canada	63.5580, -127.9119
30134	2273	Mount Joy	1315	Canada	63.7556, -132.8939
30139	2565	Snake River Mountain *	1297	Canada	65.0065, -133.4122
30142	2550	Itsi Range Peak *	1296	Canada	62.9067, -130.2967
30145	1536	Nizone Peak *	1289	Canada	61.5913, -123.3516
30149	2350	Little Wind Mountain *	1282	Canada	64.7797, -135.1225

30160	2357	Hyland Mountain *	1260	Canada	61.7644, -128.6359
30164	2504	Bear Pass Creek Peak *	1249	Canada	61.5961, -127.5908
30169	2170	Mount Murray	1243	Canada	60.8925, -128.8189
30171	2514	Horn Peak	1242	Canada	63.5771, -131.1084
30172	2371	Stone Knife Peak *	1241	Canada	64.5186, -129.5203
30192	2605	Stone Knife Mountain *	1209	Canada	64.6003, -130.1947
30193	2230	Bastard Plume *	1205	Canada	64.8861, -133.6619
30194	2368	Tigonankweine Peak	1204	Canada	64.1225, -127.9447
30202	2309	Natla Mountain *	1193	Canada	63.4650, -128.3531
30203	2173	Mount Selous	1192	Canada	62.9772, -132.5128
30204	2265	Niddery Mountain *	1190	Canada	63.1909, -131.1789
30220	2440	Branching Mountain *	1168	Canada	64.8111, -132.1950
30226	2305	Ekwi Mountain *	1161	Canada	63.8974, -128.6304
30230	2490	Broken Skull Peak *	1159	Canada	62.9311, -128.6703
30234	2514	Tagish Peak	1154	Canada	64.7478, -133.9111
30235	2230	Hart River Mountain *	1152	Canada	64.7277, -135.9076
30236	2154	West Coal Peak *	1152	Canada	61.1678, -128.0947
30240	2340	Cranswick Mountain *	1148	Canada	65.0731, -132.3381
30244	2364	Shattered Range Peak *	1146	Canada	64.6128, -128.9264
30245	2520	Twitya Mountain *	1146	Canada	63.8200, -129.7028
30254	2195	Arctic Red Ridge *	1137	Canada	64.7580, -131.2570
30255	2539	Plume Peak	1135	Canada	64.4272, -131.2505
30259	2223	Mount Emerald *	1133	Canada	63.4056, -131.3597
30269	1894	Thunder Mountain *	1123	Canada	60.5344, -128.4125
30271	2321	Sheep Lick Peak *	1122	Canada	64.6739, -128.3605
30272	2275	Mount Wilson	1121	Canada	62.8893, -129.7057
30277	1985	Tlogotsho Range Peak *	1118	Canada	60.9272, -124.5381
30278	2125	Surveys Range Peak *	1118	Canada	63.6456, -131.9547
30287	2525	Ravens Throat Ridge *	1113	Canada	63.1954, -127.4184
30289	2492	Black Wolf Peak *	1110	Canada	62.5364, -127.6503
30292	2325	Rapitan Peak *	1107	Canada	65.1461, -133.7162
30293	2197	Nadaleen Mountain	1105	Canada	64.2539, -133.0422
30294	2411	Dome Mountain *	1105	Canada	61.5723, -126.9504
30299	2015	Mount Pinguicula *	1101	Canada	64.6817, -133.5272
30300	2336	Mount Haywire *	1100	Canada	62.4217, -128.1956
30301	2759	Mount Sir James MacBrien	1099	Canada	62.1236, -127.6800
30302	2107	Mount Sheldon	1098	Canada	62.7258, -131.0861
30311	1678	Liard Range Peak *	1090	Canada	60.8633, -124.0492
30317	1950	Royal Mountain	1085	Canada	65.0220, -135.0387
30319	2062	Mount Ortell	1084	Canada	63.9822, -132.8219
30321	2389	Moose Horn Mountain *	1082	Canada	63.6814, -127.2444
30326	2377	Icefield Peak *	1080	Canada	62.7338, -128.6330

30328	2105	Mount Fortin *	1078	Canada	61.9130, -130.2339
30329	2067	Traffic Mountain	1078	Canada	62.1162, -130.4396
30331	2516	Middlecoff Mountain *	1076	Canada	64.0531, -130.2219
30334	1985	Knorr Mountain *	1072	Canada	65.0650, -134.0632
30338	2505	Mount Shale *	1067	Canada	64.3583, -129.7322
30342	2183	Stenbraten Ridge *	1064	Canada	64.0374, -131.7611
30344	2290	Snake Backbone *	1063	Canada	64.9373, -132.8257
30345	2296	Misty Mountain *	1063	Canada	64.1575, -131.4774
30349	1905	Hell Roaring Peak *	1059	Canada	61.8394, -126.6689
30352	2260	Mount Landreville	1057	Canada	65.1559, -132.8964
30354	2294	Painted Mountains Peak *	1056	Canada	62.9814, -126.2192
30357	2413	Orthogonal Mountain *	1055	Canada	64.8392, -131.7866
30360	1953	Snake River Ridge *	1054	Canada	65.2008, -133.2207
30367	1827	Cambrian Peak *	1052	Canada	65.1082, -129.2417
30368	1705	Caribou Range Peak *	1051	Canada	59.6819, -125.4948
30372	1990	Stewart Mountain *	1046	Canada	64.0931, -132.8294
30375	2290	Mount Ervin *	1045	Canada	64.6008, -135.3683
30377	2245	Mount Einarson *	1045	Canada	63.9028, -131.5212
30386	2201	Landry Mountain *	1038	Canada	62.6192, -125.5294
30394	2026	Nahanni Peak	1036	Canada	61.9869, -126.5761
30399	2195	Delthore Mountain	1033	Canada	63.5692, -128.1644
30405	2205	Mount Godlin *	1031	Canada	63.9808, -128.8219
30411	2052	Katherine Peak *	1029	Canada	64.8617, -127.7817
30415	2305	Lened Peak *	1027	Canada	62.3400, -128.5119
30420	2165	Sekwi Mountain	1026	Canada	63.4642, -128.6617
30421	2052	McEvoy Peak	1025	Canada	61.7195, -130.1018
30425	2352	Mount Orthogonal Red *	1023	Canada	64.7559, -131.6665
30426	1248	Nahanni Mountain	1023	Canada	62.0869, -123.3364
30427	2100	South Macmillan Mountain *	1023	Canada	62.8425, -131.6583
30430	2265	Ten Stone Range Peak *	1022	Canada	64.6247, -129.4083
30432	1955	Rackla Ridge *	1021	Canada	64.1400, -133.7403
30437	1933	Mount Dempster	1020	Canada	65.1390, -136.0743
30438	1750	Beaver River Peak *	1019	Canada	64.2139, -134.5061
30441	2444	Flat River Mountain *	1018	Canada	61.8636, -128.0814
30454	2435	Tsichu Peak *	1009	Canada	63.3675, -129.9182
30456	2306	Jata Eta Mountain	1008	Canada	63.8517, -127.6573
30462	2107	Mount Rackla *	1005	Canada	64.2955, -132.7099
30463	2015	Airfield Mountain *	1005	Canada	62.9325, -132.1203
30474	1268	Paynaychee Mountain	1000	Canada	62.5808, -123.6372
30475	2189	Caesar Mountain *	1000	Canada	61.3765, -127.9720

NA11 North America Arctic Islands

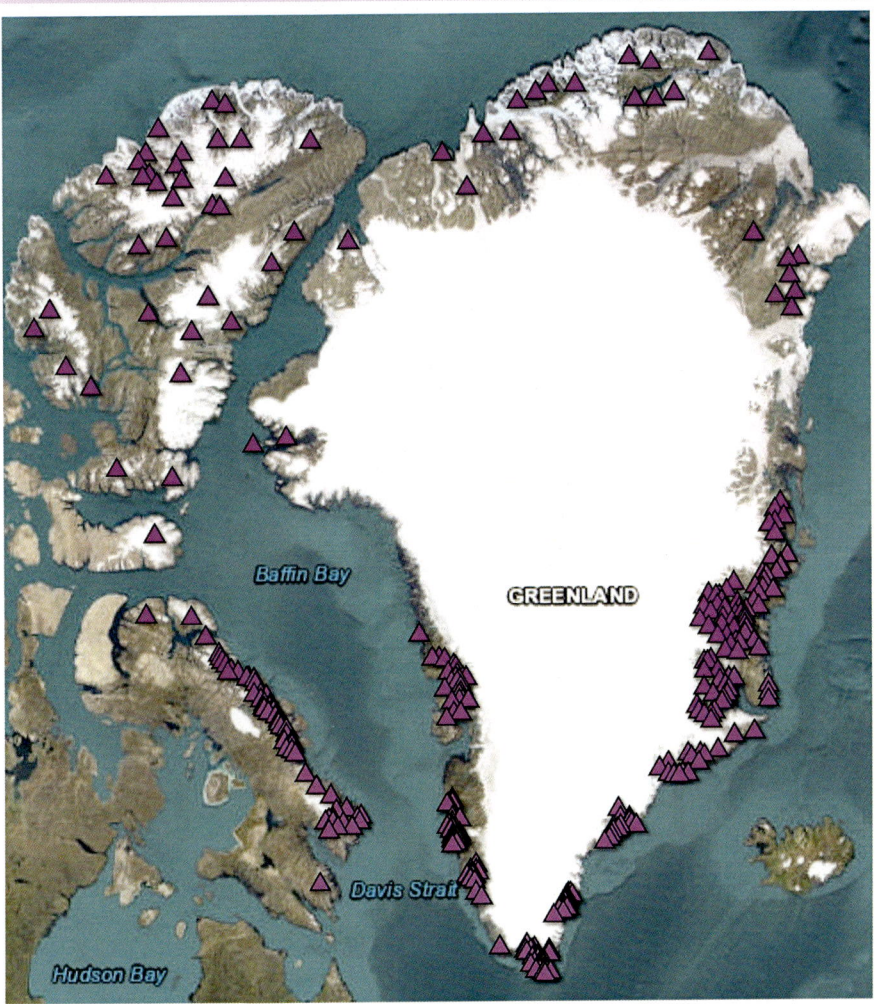

Greenland is an autonomous territory of the Kingdom of Denmark and is the largest island in the world. Its geographical names originate from English, Greenlandic and Danish (such as the symbol Ø meaning island). Its shape is distorted on the projection used for the map, as the northern part is exaggerated in size. The same is true of Ellesmere Island to the west, which is the tenth largest island, slightly smaller than the island of Great Britain. It is part of the Nunavut territory of Canada and its native name is Umingmak Nuna. Baffin Island is over twice the size of Ellesmere Island and is the fifth largest island in the world, with a population of around 13000 in 2021. Between Baffin Island and Ellesmere Island lies Devon Island, the 27th largest island. It is the largest uninhabited island in the world but it does receive periodic visitors from NASA, as its landscape and remoteness makes it ideal for testing vehicles and astronauts for expeditions on Mars or the Moon. However, these simulated lunar or Martian excursions do not include an ascent of the Devon Ice Cap.

NA110 Queen Elizabeth Islands

Id	Height	Name	Island	Drop	Country	Location
30602	2594	Barbeau Peak – First Peak East	Ellesmere	2594	Canada	81.9150, -75.0101
30613	2247	Beitstad Peak	Ellesmere	1931	Canada	78.8000, -79.5364
30621	2294	Agassiz Ice Cap	Ellesmere	1796	Canada	80.1378, -76.7750
30673	1901	Mount Eugene	Ellesmere	1482	Canada	82.4078, -66.6733
30695	1960	Mount Hare *	Ellesmere	1383	Canada	81.6395, -80.1475
30704	1430	Mount Mitchell *	Ellesmere	1359	Canada	82.2564, -82.7103
30708	1785	Wootton Peninsula	Ellesmere	1352	Canada	82.1511, -83.4297
30720	1882	Mount M'Clintock *	Ellesmere	1317	Canada	82.4250, -75.8017
30759	1405	Manson Icefield	Ellesmere	1226	Canada	76.6650, -80.2689
30763	1718	Mount Reeds	Ellesmere	1219	Canada	81.5183, -75.6158
30766	1590	Sven Hedin Mountain *	Ellesmere	1212	Canada	79.5756, -78.3156
30771	1420	Marvin Peninsula *	Ellesmere	1205	Canada	82.8947, -76.3617
30791	1604	Mount Phillips *	Ellesmere	1167	Canada	81.9425, -83.0906
30806	1640	Esayoo Peak *	Ellesmere	1145	Canada	81.0586, -80.9428
30824	1858	Kislingbury Peak *	Ellesmere	1121	Canada	80.6864, -70.4714
30825	1524	John Evans Peak *	Ellesmere	1120	Canada	79.7208, -74.5008
30831	1681	Per Ardua Peak *	Ellesmere	1118	Canada	81.5419, -76.3764
30842	1533	Ninnis Peak *	Ellesmere	1105	Canada	81.1347, -68.1678
30847	1643	Mount Otto *	Ellesmere	1097	Canada	81.8608, -81.7067
30851	1130	Purple Mountain *	Ellesmere	1089	Canada	82.5664, -81.5339
30865	1551	De Vries Peak *	Ellesmere	1078	Canada	81.9064, -79.1944
30871	2060	Commando Peak	Ellesmere	1073	Canada	82.2642, -79.2217
30877	1488	Van Royen Ridges	Ellesmere	1066	Canada	80.9544, -83.4628
30882	1695	Mount Yelverton *	Ellesmere	1061	Canada	82.1056, -79.8247
30888	1343	Sydkap Ice Cap	Ellesmere	1056	Canada	76.8728, -85.8378
30891	2022	Disraeli Mountain *	Ellesmere	1050	Canada	82.4286, -73.5464
30893	1488	Kulutingwak Qaqqaq *	Ellesmere	1048	Canada	81.9792, -82.5242
30900	1373	Fosheim Peninsula *	Ellesmere	1043	Canada	79.8594, -82.6717
30927	1240	Inlet Peak *	Ellesmere	1009	Canada	81.9372, -86.6961
30929	1280	Ootah Peak *	Ellesmere	1008	Canada	82.8611, -75.0292
30607	2102	White Crown Mountain	Axel Heiberg	2102	Canada	79.9261, -92.3067
30734	1820	Steachie Ice Cap	Axel Heiberg	1278	Canada	78.9425, -90.6997
30883	1336	Mount Gosling *	Axel Heiberg	1060	Canada	79.6178, -93.9475
30923	1110	Mount Skaare *	Axel Heiberg	1011	Canada	78.5711, -88.2283
30612	1933	Devon Ice Cap	Devon Island	1933	Canada	75.3453, -82.1400

Barbeau Peak – First Peak East, NA110

Barbeau Peak is the highest point on Ellesmere Island and in the Canadian Arctic. There is no higher land between it and the North Pole 900 kilometres away. It is named after Marius Barbeau, a Canadian anthropologist. Barbeau Peak was measured as 2616m in 1967 but is now thought to be slightly under 2600m. The summit name First Peak East comes from an Arctic Jubilee Expedition in 2012 during which several peaks were visited between the peak labelled Barbeau Peak on Canadian maps and Mount Whisler to the north-east.

The first peak east from Barbeau Peak on the map was measured as 47 metres higher and therefore the true summit of the Barbeau Peak area. A tobacco tin with a climbers' register was left here in 1967. Barbeau Peak on the map, which is of course the first peak west of First Peak East, is also known as Resolute. Along with several other peaks in the British Empire Range, it was named after famous ships used in Arctic exploration, during a 1982 expedition detailed in the American Alpine Journal. Second Peak East is also known as Griper Peak and at approximately 2519m is lower than Resolute, First Peak East and Whisler. First Peak East may or may not also be known as Victory. Different sources give wildly differing elevation figures for the various peaks here, but anyone finding a tobacco tin is probably on the highest summit.

NA112 Baffin Island

Id	Height	Name	Drop	Country	Location
30605	2143	Mount Odin	2143	Canada	66.5466, -65.4288
30626	1838	Ukpik Peak	1737	Canada	70.6881, -71.3247
30632	1835	Qiajivik Mountain	1659	Canada	72.1800, -75.9258
30635	1637	Sillem Island	1637	Canada	70.9781, -71.6767
30639	2020	Qilaut Mountain	1625	Canada	66.5303, -64.7013
30648	1830	Mount Kingnait *	1600	Canada	66.4584, -63.6697
30653	1858	Kisimngiuqtuq Peak	1581	Canada	70.7989, -71.6486
30659	1671	Cockscomb Mountain	1557	Canada	70.5492, -70.7828
30662	1722	McBeth Peak *	1532	Canada	69.6531, -69.3084
30666	1675	Inuk Mountain	1505	Canada	66.5311, -62.1094
30676	1640	Jameson Mountain *	1465	Canada	71.8719, -75.2836
30680	1542	Mount Nedlukseak	1444	Canada	67.8418, -66.3012
30688	1695	Coutts Mountain *	1414	Canada	72.0642, -75.8417
30697	1735	Clyde Mountain *	1382	Canada	70.2592, -70.3417
30699	1610	Duart Mountain *	1373	Canada	71.3247, -72.2756
30701	1715	Mount Henry Kater *	1372	Canada	69.3899, -69.3958
30702	1660	Ayr Mountain *	1372	Canada	70.4339, -70.4731
30707	1450	Mount Tingin *	1353	Canada	69.1017, -68.6928
30714	1790	Sam Ford Peninsula *	1333	Canada	70.5005, -71.3503
30741	1686	Mount Inugsuin *	1262	Canada	69.9029, -69.8291
30744	1420	Dexterity Mountain *	1257	Canada	71.3975, -72.3742
30748	1642	Mount Itirbilung *	1253	Canada	69.2908, -68.8003
30753	1871	Mount Pangnirtung *	1238	Canada	66.9531, -64.3375
30764	1670	Mount Maktak *	1218	Canada	67.4622, -64.8983
30774	1661	Kimmiaqtaqtujuq Qaqqaq *	1197	Canada	70.1507, -70.0079
30777	1485	Mount Morin South *	1193	Canada	72.6769, -77.1753
30790	1381	Mount Nudlung *	1168	Canada	68.2413, -67.3965
30799	1531	Mount Gilbert	1156	Canada	66.6583, -62.2169
30801	1191	Hall Peninsula Peak *	1155	Canada	63.9842, -65.8375
30805	1622	Mount Damocles	1145	Canada	70.4406, -70.6480
30810	1354	Mount Mermaid *	1140	Canada	66.3283, -62.6928
30812	1254	Elwin Mountain *	1138	Canada	73.2658, -83.0150

Id	Height	Name	Drop	Country	Location
30817	1636	The Tail Feathers	1132	Canada	70.5111, -70.5175
30820	1202	Mount Padle *	1129	Canada	66.9806, -63.3063
30826	1320	Perfection Pass Peak *	1120	Canada	69.8438, -69.2363
30827	1185	Drever Mountain *	1119	Canada	71.6511, -73.9681
30828	1386	Qulliqtaliujaq / Walker Citadel	1118	Canada	70.5694, -71.4792
30841	1440	Coutts Ridge *	1105	Canada	71.9486, -75.5031
30845	1620	Mount Nuuksatluguluk *	1097	Canada	69.3806, -68.8069
30846	1275	Mount Aarrujaup Qinngua *	1097	Canada	70.0403, -70.0177
30857	1830	Mount Fleming	1083	Canada	66.6856, -64.6819
30864	1498	Mount Nuuksuq *	1080	Canada	69.3386, -68.6669
30870	1445	Narwhal Mountain	1073	Canada	66.7203, -61.9567
30872	1154	Mount Pitchforth *	1071	Canada	68.9631, -68.4481
30880	2030	Tupeq Mountain	1064	Canada	66.5747, -65.0705
30885	1468	Mount Nallulik *	1059	Canada	69.1395, -69.2054
30898	1592	Bruce Mountains	1043	Canada	70.9547, -72.4111
30901	1230	Gibbs Fiord Peak	1042	Canada	70.9028, -71.2067
30903	1620	Utinatuk Peak *	1036	Canada	70.4027, -70.9975
30905	1327	Quernbiter Mountain *	1033	Canada	71.6633, -75.1392
30906	1688	Mount Aqairungnaq *	1031	Canada	66.2733, -64.1053
30920	1421	Kigut North *	1020	Canada	70.6322, -70.9214
30930	1355	Suilven Peak *	1007	Canada	71.1653, -74.6608
30935	1440	Qavarusiqtuuq Qaqqaq *	1000	Canada	66.1608, -64.9875
30611	1944	Angilaaq Mountain, Bylot Island	1944	Canada	73.2296, -78.6234
30751	1241	Adams Island Peak *, Adams Island	1241	Canada	71.4581, -73.0167
30832	1162	Ratcliffe Mountain *, Adams Island	1116	Canada	71.4931, -73.1492

NA113 Greenland
Grønland / Kalaallit Nunaat

Id	Height	Name	Drop	Country	Location
30601	3694	Gunnbjørn Fjeld	3694	Greenland	68.9195, -29.8985
30603	2842	Dansketinden	2255	Greenland	72.1258, -24.9525
30604	2370	Payer Tinde	2157	Greenland	73.1267, -26.3583
30609	2259	Perserajoq	2087	Greenland	71.4017, -51.8400
30610	2341	Tuttut Nunaat / Renland	2084	Greenland	71.3050, -26.7025
30617	2544	Klosterbjerge	1849	Greenland	72.1633, -26.1125
30618	1849	Paarnaqussuit Qaavat Peninsula	1823	Greenland	66.4758, -52.8467
30619	3340	Borgtinderne	1819	Greenland	68.8517, -28.2417
30620	1944	Johannes V Jensen Land	1802	Greenland	83.3183, -33.2025
30622	2000	Favre Bjerg	1781	Greenland	73.9508, -23.1725
30629	2580	Lauper Bjerg	1695	Greenland	66.5508, -36.6308
30630	1744	Prinsesse Caroline-Mathilde Alper	1688	Greenland	80.4325, -19.6883
30631	2144	Iterdlaup Qaqai	1679	Greenland	70.6967, -52.9708
30633	2163	Kloftbjerge	1657	Greenland	71.3425, -25.7567
30634	1679	Harder Bjerg	1644	Greenland	73.4242, -22.8608

30636	2360	Margaretatop	1628	Greenland	73.3692, -26.2750
30637	2470	Fraenkel Land	1627	Greenland	73.2933, -27.6517
30638	2140	Assaasat	1626	Greenland	65.8808, -52.1267
30640	1852	Takkerne	1621	Greenland	73.9158, -22.5192
30641	1860	Agdlerulik	1617	Greenland	61.0200, -45.1558
30643	1700	Ilivnera Bjerg	1615	Greenland	66.1200, -37.4442
30644	1971	Kilikilat Fjeld *	1611	Greenland	66.2017, -37.2233
30645	1650	Kînaussaq	1607	Greenland	64.4542, -50.5151
30647	1782	Qingagssat Qaqat	1602	Greenland	60.5650, -44.6958
30649	3391	Mont Forel	1596	Greenland	66.9350, -36.7875
30650	1829	Mågefjeld	1596	Greenland	71.9742, -53.6650
30651	2020	Paatuut	1588	Greenland	70.2967, -52.7008
30652	1763	Agdlerussakasit	1583	Greenland	60.1358, -44.5283
30654	2005	Johnstrup Bjerge	1575	Greenland	73.0033, -25.5333
30655	1810	Berzelius Bjerg	1573	Greenland	72.4683, -25.0742
30657	2070	Gaseland	1560	Greenland	70.3058, -27.2900
30658	2101	Akuliarusinguaq Qaqa *	1553	Greenland	71.7308, -52.5808
30661	3317	Ejnar Mikkelsen Fjeld	1545	Greenland	68.8950, -28.6283
30663	2220	Taateraat	1518	Greenland	66.0392, -52.2550
30664	2305	Andree Land	1508	Greenland	73.7175, -26.7706
30665	1525	Spath Plateau	1507	Greenland	73.8858, -21.4100
30667	1952	Skønheden	1499	Greenland	63.5758, -41.6675
30669	2470	Hagar Bjerg	1494	Greenland	72.8792, -27.7175
30668	2260	Lacroix Bjerge	1494	Greenland	73.4567, -26.9067
30670	2381	Forsblad Fjeld *	1493	Greenland	72.3275, -25.6400
30671	1845	Tuilissuaq	1490	Greenland	60.1842, -44.4975
30672	2051	Uiluit Qaqqaa	1482	Greenland	60.3850, -44.4658
30674	1665	Akuliarusersuaq	1470	Greenland	60.6892, -45.2158
30675	2210	Tupilak	1467	Greenland	66.3242, -36.5458
30677	1530	Nigsik Qaqa	1465	Greenland	64.3142, -50.8067
30678	1670	Iviangiusarsuit	1461	Greenland	63.5883, -50.6525
30679	1848	Nordkronen	1453	Greenland	82.8867, -32.8967
30681	1572	Prinsesse Elizabeth Alper	1441	Greenland	80.7450, -18.7533
30682	2030	Salliarutsip Qaqa *	1440	Greenland	71.8267, -52.7883
30683	1791	Qorqup Qaqa	1436	Greenland	61.1292, -45.0617
30684	2470	Snehætten	1433	Greenland	72.6142, -26.0817
30689	1973	Utsuggsuatsiatt	1414	Greenland	60.2883, -44.4275
30690	1597	Pisissarfik	1407	Greenland	67.1992, -52.9733
30698	2350	Ingolf Fjeld	1375	Greenland	66.4233, -35.6383
30705	1923	Faxa Fjeld *	1359	Greenland	70.2958, -28.8167
30706	1683	Rødebjerg	1355	Greenland	73.0567, -24.3183
30709	1936	Gravstenene	1348	Greenland	71.6008, -26.8950
30710	1519	Umataussaq	1348	Greenland	67.3358, -52.9883
30711	1720	Kaempekeglen	1341	Greenland	63.2742, -41.7583

30712	3620	Qaqqaq Paul Emile Victor	1339	Greenland	68.8117, -29.5583
30715	1768	Storborgen	1332	Greenland	75.5308, -21.8475
30716	2720	Lemon Bjerge	1331	Greenland	68.5900, -31.8450
30717	1430	Tvillingerne	1329	Greenland	70.6708, -21.9825
30718	2695	Louise Boyd Land	1327	Greenland	73.4333, -28.2842
30719	1783	Dronning Margrethe II Land	1318	Greenland	75.5858, -21.2225
30721	1639	Qoruarssuaq Qaqqaa *	1317	Greenland	66.4008, -53.1667
30723	2280	Akuliaruseq Peninsula *	1316	Greenland	71.5317, -52.3075
30722	1696	Tvillingespidser	1316	Greenland	62.9325, -42.1317
30724	1438	Nîniartivaraq	1313	Greenland	65.9425, -37.4842
30725	1933	Styrelse	1312	Greenland	70.0167, -27.6283
30726	1955	Geologfjord Fjeld *	1310	Greenland	73.8633, -26.0369
30727	1441	Ilimaussaq	1301	Greenland	60.9883, -45.8983
30729	1929	Helvetia Tinde	1295	Greenland	83.3750, -35.2733
30730	1380	Pythagoras Bjerg	1294	Greenland	71.3833, -25.2275
30731	1450	Qáqatoqaq	1292	Greenland	66.6342, -52.8600
30732	1627	Kværken	1283	Greenland	62.8433, -42.2858
30733	1465	Vesterport	1282	Greenland	75.3067, -21.2508
30735	1650	Qingârssuaq	1277	Greenland	71.3558, -52.2208
30737	1780	Fuchs Bjerg	1276	Greenland	73.7633, -22.7817
30739	2260	Kangerlussuaq Tinde	1271	Greenland	68.4292, -32.6975
30740	1413	Nansen Land	1265	Greenland	82.9925, -44.4133
30686	2069	Storebror	1262	Greenland	66.1758, -36.9967
30742	2225	Snepyramiden	1261	Greenland	71.4317, -52.4925
30747	1920	Ringhorne	1254	Greenland	63.0517, -42.1508
30750	1980	Qioqe Qaqa *	1241	Greenland	71.4183, -51.5167
30754	1350	Kinguleq	1238	Greenland	66.3039, -53.3789
30755	1785	Heinrich Wild Iskappe	1236	Greenland	82.9667, -30.9125
30757	1570	Kong Dan Halvo	1229	Greenland	63.1433, -41.9175
30756	1418	Kuunnaat	1229	Greenland	61.2108, -48.4217
30760	2330	Lancaster Fjeld *	1225	Greenland	71.5783, -28.3250
30761	1480	Qororssuaq Qaqa	1225	Greenland	64.1608, -51.1067
30762	2184	Commandment Peak	1222	Greenland	71.1233, -26.1908
30765	1332	Qáqarssuaralak	1215	Greenland	65.7500, -52.8300
30769	1465	Dombjerg	1208	Greenland	74.5525, -20.7975
30770	2595	Mellem Fjeld *	1206	Greenland	66.5542, -35.7583
30772	1470	Qatsingneq	1204	Greenland	72.0267, -54.8158
30773	1432	Langsø Bjerg *	1203	Greenland	75.8808, -21.1825
30775	1450	Avqutikitsoq	1196	Greenland	67.1092, -53.2050
30776	1646	Victor Madsen Bjerg	1195	Greenland	73.5733, -23.3075
30778	1510	Iterdlak	1192	Greenland	64.0950, -50.7483
30779	2948	Petermann Bjerg	1190	Greenland	73.0905, -28.6187
30780	1670	Balders Fjeld *	1189	Greenland	63.3108, -41.8425

30781	1206	Ivnajaugtoq	1188	Greenland	64.7500, -50.6958
30783	1300	Mjolner Peninsula	1183	Greenland	63.5008, -41.2600
30784	1752	Illerfissalik	1180	Greenland	61.0575, -45.2933
30786	1289	Mikis Fjeld *	1173	Greenland	68.1408, -31.3533
30787	1333	Illoqarajuttoq	1172	Greenland	62.8082, -42.4983
30788	1281	Natsersalik	1172	Greenland	60.0886, -44.7472
30792	2520	Oscar Wisting Bjerg	1166	Greenland	73.7692, -27.7842
30794	1559	Ivnatsiait	1165	Greenland	66.0692, -37.2650
30793	1220	Kitdlavât	1165	Greenland	60.8933, -45.7400
30796	2785	Rigny Bjerg	1160	Greenland	69.0483, -26.8217
30795	1959	Sorensen Land	1160	Greenland	71.0875, -28.2358
30797	1388	Ulungnaq	1159	Greenland	65.6475, -52.5583
30798	1581	Mørkebjerg	1157	Greenland	73.5450, -24.9300
30800	2201	West Gletsjer Fjeld *	1155	Greenland	71.8367, -28.2983
30803	1550	Alfefjeldane	1148	Greenland	66.3583, -53.2433
30802	1520	Karlenes Bjerg *	1148	Greenland	72.3842, -24.7508
30804	1241	Ungatdliup Qáqai	1146	Greenland	67.1283, -53.4367
30807	1272	Blosseville Bjerg	1143	Greenland	74.2633, -22.1425
30811	2039	Inip Nua	1138	Greenland	60.3350, -44.1667
30814	1414	Jordanhill	1137	Greenland	74.1275, -22.3275
30813	1314	Petermann Halvo	1137	Greenland	81.0025, -63.0150
30816	2055	Gletscher Land	1135	Greenland	72.6075, -26.8717
30819	2001	Hvidfjeld	1130	Greenland	63.3550, -41.8692
30818	1540	Pilerqit	1130	Greenland	63.1242, -41.9700
30821	2221	Stenmanden	1125	Greenland	73.5928, -26.4836
30822	2292	Igdlorssuit Qaqat	1124	Greenland	60.3925, -44.0000
30823	1212	Holm Bjerg	1124	Greenland	80.1092, -21.0217
30830	1340	Kindtaenderne	1118	Greenland	70.8883, -21.9525
30829	1330	Qaqortorssup Kangilia	1118	Greenland	66.5850, -52.2367
30834	2482	Lilloise Bjerge	1116	Greenland	68.5758, -28.8133
30833	1455	Daly Bjerge	1116	Greenland	83.4258, -27.5883
30835	1544	Heimdal Iskappe	1113	Greenland	82.8883, -34.8550
30836	1880	Illorsok	1110	Greenland	60.2425, -43.8950
30837	1720	Heinesen Fjeld *	1109	Greenland	62.5650, -43.0275
30838	1372	Zackenberg	1109	Greenland	74.4958, -20.7636
30840	2400	Púsugssivit Fjeld *	1107	Greenland	66.5217, -35.5958
30839	1170	Nunat Fjeld *	1107	Greenland	62.9242, -41.7350
30843	1350	Utorqanguit	1103	Greenland	65.9667, -52.9336
30850	2166	Iluileq Fjeld *	1092	Greenland	60.8725, -43.5775
30849	1755	Niaqornata Qula	1092	Greenland	65.7558, -52.6075
30848	1240	Ryberg Fjeld *	1092	Greenland	68.1733, -30.3525
30854	1922	Alfred Wegener Halvø Peninsula	1088	Greenland	71.1192, -52.0642
30855	1967	Rytterknægten	1087	Greenland	66.1500, -36.7117

30856	2062	Gasefjord Fjeld *	1085	Greenland	70.2097, -27.6606
30859	1523	Tagefjeldene	1083	Greenland	80.7033, -19.8975
30858	1122	Ingmikortilaq	1083	Greenland	71.8650, -27.9317
30861	1730	Siuterqut	1081	Greenland	71.9992, -54.0733
30863	1540	A.P. Olsen Land	1081	Greenland	74.7225, -21.6683
30866	1114	Piulip Nunaa	1078	Greenland	77.5450, -69.0800
30868	2206	Leicester Fjeld *	1075	Greenland	71.9008, -27.5241
30869	1819	Strindberg Land	1075	Greenland	74.0608, -25.3167
30867	1570	Umiiviit	1075	Greenland	63.4067, -50.1133
30873	1426	Qasingortorrsuaq	1070	Greenland	62.8800, -41.9000
30876	2010	Ketil	1067	Greenland	60.4167, -44.5108
30875	1908	Qingarssuk	1067	Greenland	65.8450, -52.4050
30878	1350	Strømø Fjeld *	1066	Greenland	68.1255, -30.7450
30879	1263	Adolf S. Jensen Land	1065	Greenland	76.0692, -20.6583
30881	2315	Spejderhatten	1063	Greenland	73.7192, -27.0108
30884	1150	Iviángit	1060	Greenland	64.5533, -50.6127
30886	1270	Agnete Sø Bjerg *	1059	Greenland	75.7133, -20.4650
30887	1172	Aettestub	1058	Greenland	81.7792, -51.1900
30889	2000	Kangerluluk Fjeld *	1054	Greenland	61.0156, -43.6306
30892	1209	Kirken	1050	Greenland	71.1175, -21.8917
30894	1975	Hjørnedal Fjeld *	1048	Greenland	70.1708, -28.3583
30895	1097	Andritup Qaqa	1047	Greenland	70.7442, -51.2592
30896	1120	Naqerdloq	1046	Greenland	66.1658, -53.1642
30899	1815	Hakkefjeld	1043	Greenland	63.5575, -41.4917
30904	1080	Ailsa Bjerg *	1036	Greenland	66.3200, -34.9925
30909	1290	Qínguata Qáqai	1030	Greenland	65.8050, -52.7550
30910	2235	Sylvia Maria Tinde	1026	Greenland	72.9192, -26.4575
30915	1470	Sêraq Fjeld *	1024	Greenland	66.3725, -35.5767
30913	1167	Jewell Bjerg *	1024	Greenland	83.0783, -43.3008
30914	1129	Hjertefjeld	1024	Greenland	81.1017, -23.1408
30917	1850	Sardloq	1023	Greenland	65.8542, -52.5717
30916	1116	Augpalârtorssivit	1023	Greenland	65.6842, -38.2242
30919	2159	Naajarsuit Saqqarliit Qaqqaat	1021	Greenland	60.7750, -44.6833
30918	1723	Pebermyntefjeld	1021	Greenland	70.4825, -28.9400
30922	1290	Natinguaq	1018	Greenland	61.2742, -45.6492
30926	1750	Rebild	1011	Greenland	72.7942, -24.1183
30925	1700	Troldfjeldene	1011	Greenland	66.3333, -52.9125
30924	1493	Sagdliata Portornga	1011	Greenland	64.3300, -50.9125
30928	1473	Alangua	1009	Greenland	70.2969, -52.0141
30931	1600	Qaqortorssuaq	1007	Greenland	66.2633, -52.9425
30932	1835	Dendrit Fjeld *	1005	Greenland	69.5533, -25.2483
30934	1312	Courtauld Bjerg	1001	Greenland	74.2842, -22.4867
30933	1123	Qaqatoqak	1001	Greenland	65.8150, -52.9433

Greenland Coastal Islands

Id	Height	Name	Island	Drop	Location
30606	2109	Ilimananngip Nunaa	Milne Land	2109	70.7008, -26.3808
30768	1972	Arabertoppe	Milne Land	1208	70.6183, -26.4633
30890	2085	Red Rose Mountain	Milne Land	1052	70.8700, -26.0900
30911	1546	Jytte's Fjeld *	Milne Land	1026	71.0367, -25.8467
30608	2101	Palup Qaqa	Upernivik	2101	71.3267, -52.9525
30691	1732	Qaarsorsuaq	Upernivik	1403	71.2900, -52.4058
30615	1910	Angelin Bjerg	Ymer	1910	73.1558, -24.3242
30656	1638	Hammeren	Ymer	1564	73.3817, -24.8717
30685	1830	Noa Sø Fjeld	Ymer	1431	73.2250, -25.1000
30693	1600	Blaskbjerg	Ymer	1385	73.3075, -24.0308
30844	1723	Scott Bjerg	Ymer	1102	73.2250, -24.6817
30614	1910	Pyramiden	Disko	1910	70.1192, -53.3883
30616	1884	Lunedal Topmøde	Traill	1884	72.6400, -24.2658
30758	1400	Svinhufvud Bjerge	Traill	1228	72.4233, -23.4067
30852	1352	Forchhammer Bjerg	Traill	1089	72.2442, -22.8550
30623	1765	Snehætten	Qeqertarssuaq	1765	71.5967, -53.1758
30624	1764	Kaasarip Nasaa	Storø	1764	70.8292, -27.4758
30625	1750	Pandebrasken	Skjoldungen	1750	63.4550, -41.8500
30627	1730	Svedenborg Bjerg	Geografisk Samfund	1730	72.9425, -24.3425
30628	1710	Agpalit	Appat	1710	70.9475, -51.9917
30642	1616	Qingaq	Qeqertarsuaq	1616	64.3908, -51.1117
30897	1180	Nákaigajugtoq	Qeqertarsuaq	1045	64.2358, -51.2233
30646	1604	Ortlerspids	Clavering	1604	74.3633, -21.1133
30660	1549	Christian IV Ø	Sammisoq	1549	60.0525, -43.9133
30696	1399	Kitdlavaat	Sammisoq	1383	59.9967, -43.7533
30687	1418	Inugsugtalik	Salliaruseq	1418	70.7192, -51.7950
30692	1388	Toornaarsuk	Ikeq	1388	59.9467, -44.1892
30694	1384	Gustav Thostrup Bjerge	Hovgaard	1384	79.8967, -19.5017
30700	1373	Anoraliuirsoq Topmøde	Pamialluk	1373	60.0508, -44.3517
30736	1340	Qaqqarsuaq Killeq	Pamialluk	1277	60.0700, -44.4292
30703	1367	Bastionen	Ella	1367	72.8392, -25.3135
30713	1335	Asingaleq	Angmagssalik	1335	65.8225, -37.5933
30728	1300	Takkerne	Timmiarmiit	1300	62.7325, -42.2433
30738	1275	Savtakkerne	Sermersoq	1275	60.3017, -45.2883
30743	1260	Niaqornaq	Ammalortoq	1260	60.3908, -45.0617
30745	1257	Qunnerit Topmøde	Qunnerit	1257	59.9667, -44.0808
30746	1256	Marasisoq	Qoornup Qeqertarsua	1256	64.5175, -51.2033
30749	1251	Kangersivasiip Qaqqaa	Eggers / Itilleq	1251	59.9183, -43.9650
30752	1240	Lynn Ø	Lynn	1240	80.1900, -19.1917
30767	1210	Sadlen	Sermitsiaq	1210	64.2942, -51.4933
30782	1187	Nares Peak *	Nares Land	1187	82.4975, -46.8942

30785	1180	Sverdrup Topmøde	Sverdrup	1180	82.8692, -46.2233
30789	1170	Uummannaq Ø	Uummannaq	1170	70.7092, -52.1333
30808	1142	Dragefjeld	Hendrik	1142	82.2300, -53.5767
30809	1141	Saqqaata Qaqqaa	Illorsuit	1141	71.0592, -53.6133
30815	1136	Schwarze Wand	Kuhn	1136	74.7725, -20.1242
30853	1089	Macmillan Ø	Macmillan	1089	83.0700, -40.6708
30860	1082	Kuttuulap Immikkeertiva	Søkongen	1082	68.2233, -29.8133
30862	1081	Qassit Qaqa	Qernertoq	1081	59.9708, -43.4217
30874	1070	Salleq Topmøde	Salleq	1070	70.9308, -52.2833
30902	1042	Sandersons Hope	Qaarsorsuaq	1042	72.7042, -56.0825
30907	1031	Sermersuut Topmøde	Sermersuut	1031	65.6158, -52.9933
30908	1030	Josephine Headland	Kiatak	1030	77.4000, -72.3650
30912	1025	Kraemer Topmøde	Kraemer	1025	68.2225, -31.8375
30921	1020	Immikkeertigajik	Turner	1020	69.6842, -23.3567
30936	1000	Stephenson Ø	Stephenson	1000	82.4633, -49.5483

Petermann Bjerg, NA113 (Petter Bjørstad)

NA12 Pacific Ranges

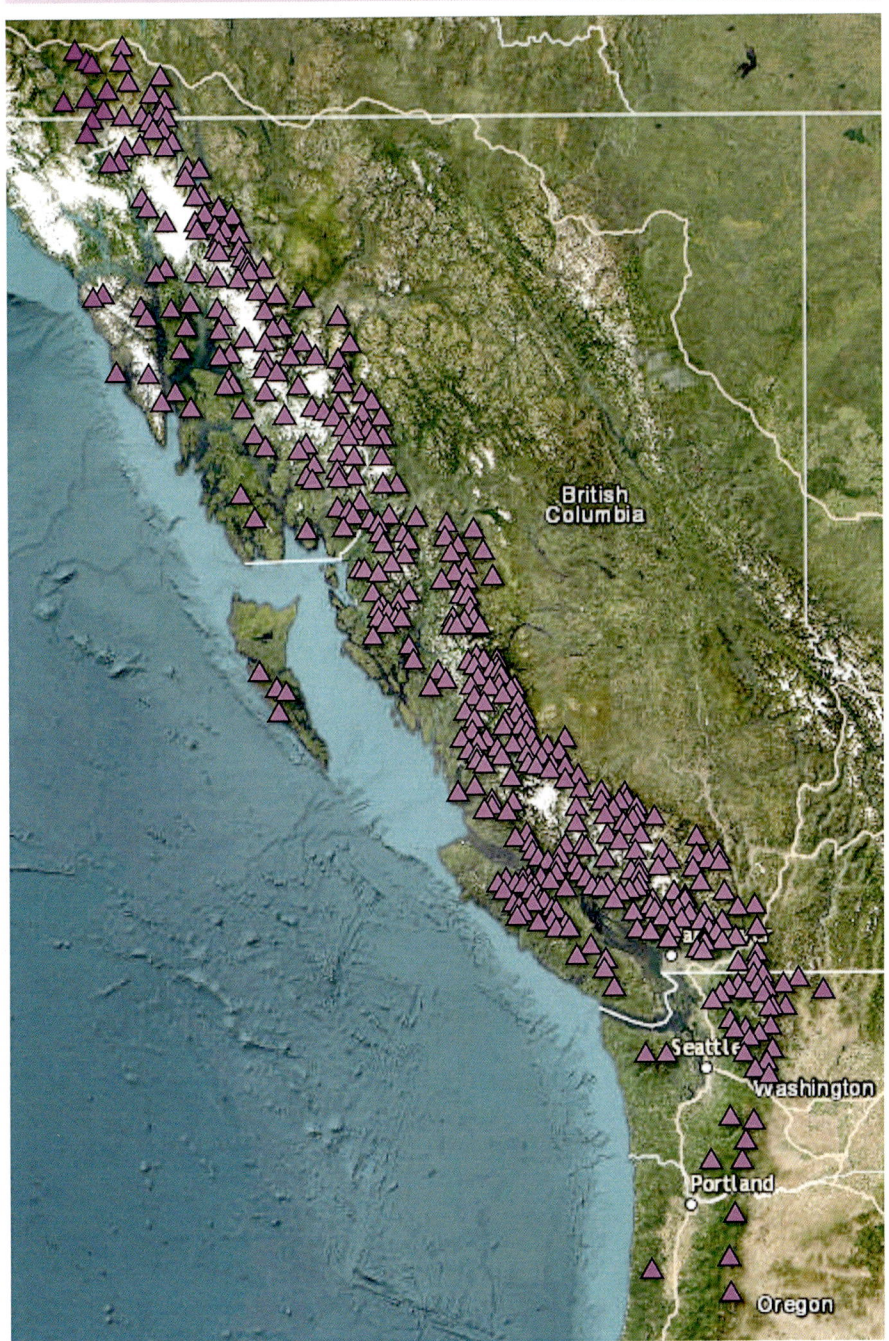

NA120 North-west Coast Islands

Id	Height	Name	Island	Drop	Country	Location
31019	2195	Golden Hinde	Vancouver Island	2195	Canada	49.6626, -125.7469
31038	2159	Victoria Peak	Vancouver Island	1826	Canada	50.0547, -126.1007
31071	1861	Rugged Mountain	Vancouver Island	1564	Canada	50.0253, -126.6778
31073	1671	Hkusam Mountain	Vancouver Island	1534	Canada	50.3350, -125.8407
31094	1766	Bonanza Peak	Vancouver Island	1442	Canada	50.3309, -126.6295
31098	1819	Mount Arrowsmith	Vancouver Island	1426	Canada	49.2238, -124.5946
31112	1639	Klitsa Mountain	Vancouver Island	1389	Canada	49.2540, -125.2313
31128	1874	Mount Sutton	Vancouver Island	1355	Canada	50.0411, -126.2352
31132	1767	Tsitika Peak	Vancouver Island	1345	Canada	50.3160, -126.3162
31135	1849	Crown Mountain	Vancouver Island	1337	Canada	49.9445, -125.8134
31145	1459	Tlakwa Mountain	Vancouver Island	1317	Canada	50.3115, -127.0510
31151	1822	Mount Abel	Vancouver Island	1306	Canada	50.2120, -126.3206
31197	1557	Mount Elliott	Vancouver Island	1228	Canada	50.2907, -126.4942
31199	1706	Naka Peak	Vancouver Island	1227	Canada	50.3736, -126.4939
31209	1765	Mount Palmerston	Vancouver Island	1219	Canada	50.4074, -126.3375
31212	1688	Mount Bate	Vancouver Island	1217	Canada	49.8899, -126.4732
31216	2093	Mount Albert Edward	Vancouver Island	1204	Canada	49.6777, -125.4317
31259	1542	Pinder Peak	Vancouver Island	1157	Canada	50.1953, -126.9302
31275	1419	Mount Hoy	Vancouver Island	1134	Canada	50.3795, -126.8491
31279	1556	Mount Joan	Vancouver Island	1131	Canada	49.4158, -124.9206
31321	1621	Mount McKelvie	Vancouver Island	1097	Canada	49.9884, -126.5808
31331	1325	Tahsis Mountain	Vancouver Island	1089	Canada	49.8436, -126.6111
31360	1983	Alexandra Peak	Vancouver Island	1061	Canada	49.7381, -125.4925
31373	1556	Mount Flannigan	Vancouver Island	1051	Canada	49.9203, -125.7316
31374	1249	Towincut Mountain	Vancouver Island	1049	Canada	48.8199, -124.3955
31385	1333	Newcastle Ridge	Vancouver Island	1043	Canada	50.4142, -126.0742
31389	1663	Mount Romeo	Vancouver Island	1038	Canada	50.2594, -126.2081
31403	1686	Mount Nora	Vancouver Island	1026	Canada	50.1541, -126.1140
31407	2194	Elkhorn Mountain	Vancouver Island	1024	Canada	49.7900, -125.8280
31409	1618	Big Baldy Mountain	Vancouver Island	1021	Canada	49.7606, -126.1336
31411	1232	Mount Menzies	Vancouver Island	1019	Canada	50.2303, -125.4967
31419	1550	Memekay Peak	Vancouver Island	1016	Canada	50.0593, -125.9723
31421	1454	Mount Spencer	Vancouver Island	1016	Canada	49.0587, -124.6468
31050	1679	Farquhar Peak	King Island	1679	Canada	52.3215, -127.3068
31378	1190	King Island Mountain	King Island	1048	Canada	52.1480, -127.6850
31431	1178	Jenny Peak *	King Island	1011	Canada	52.2692, -127.4781
31057	1643	Lacey Peak	Baranof Island	1643	USA-AK	57.0150, -134.9875
31136	1380	Mount Ada	Baranof Island	1336	USA-AK	56.6801, -134.6952
31067	1591	Mount Addenbroke	East Redonda	1591	Canada	50.2317, -124.6858

31234	1258	Mount Bunsen	East Redonda	1188	Canada	50.2683, -124.7547
31081	1484	Mount Read	Gilford	1484	Canada	50.7719, -126.2767
31084	1476	Kootznoowoo Peak	Admiralty Island	1476	USA-AK	57.7892, -134.4542
31154	1311	Randolph Peak	Admiralty Island	1299	USA-AK	57.8727, -134.0534
31337	1174	Bear Pass Mountain	Admiralty Island	1082	USA-AK	57.3119, -134.2500
31383	1059	Mount Robert Barron	Admiralty Island	1043	USA-AK	58.2262, -134.8401
31386	1159	Mount Distik	Admiralty Island	1041	USA-AK	57.5959, -134.1339
31106	1400	Mount Reid	Revillagigedo	1400	USA-AK	55.7063, -131.2464
31213	1362	Claude Peak *	Revillagigedo	1210	USA-AK	55.9045, -131.2384
31423	1196	Carroll Peak *	Revillagigedo	1016	USA-AK	55.7561, -131.4037
31211	1218	Neversummer Peak	Prince of Wales	1218	USA-AK	55.5370, -132.8769
31314	1194	Copper Mountain	Prince of Wales	1103	USA-AK	55.2382, -132.6045
31217	1204	Etolin Island	Etolin Island	1204	USA-AK	56.1192, -132.3242
31245	1195	Red Mountain	Etolin Island	1177	USA-AK	56.2584, -132.5611
31221	1200	Hawkesbury Island Peak *	Hawkesbury Island	1200	Canada	53.5581, -129.0842
31230	1191	Chichagof Island Peak *	Chichagof Island	1191	USA-AK	57.8142, -135.1800
31269	1162	Pegmatite Mountain	Chichagof Island	1142	USA-AK	57.9736, -136.0496
31352	1180	Corner Mountain *	Chichagof Island	1065	USA-AK	57.7087, -135.0262
31370	1101	Mount Raatikainen	Chichagof Island	1055	USA-AK	57.9311, -136.2745
31233	1189	Sherman Peak	Kupreanof Island	1189	USA-AK	56.8972, -133.0469
31384	1097	Portage Mountain	Kupreanof Island	1043	USA-AK	56.8681, -133.2374
31420	1128	De Long Peak	Kupreanof Island	1016	USA-AK	56.9761, -133.1558
31255	1164	Mount Moresby	Moresby Island	1164	Canada	53.0195, -132.0856
31347	1118	Mount de la Touche	Moresby Island	1076	Canada	52.7001, -132.0349
31283	1127	Mount La Pérouse	Graham Island	1127	Canada	53.2246, -132.5109
31309	1105	Gribbell Peak	Gribbell Island	1105	Canada	53.3767, -128.9614
31311	1104	Canoona Peak	Princess Royal	1104	Canada	53.0048, -128.5907
31319	1099	Heavenor Peak	Pitt Island	1099	Canada	53.7094, -129.9064
31323	1095	Tamgas Mountain	Annette Island	1095	USA-AK	55.0658, -131.4075
31328	1091	Mount Kermode	Louise Island	1091	Canada	52.9568, -131.8580
31371	1054	Douglas Island Peak *	Douglas Island	1054	USA-AK	58.2825, -134.6042
31346	1080	Kuiu Island Peak *	Kuiu Island	1080	USA-AK	56.8030, -134.3798
31377	1067	Kutlaku Peak *	Kuiu Island	1049	USA-AK	56.6108, -134.0375
31380	1048	Mount Perritt	West Redonda	1048	Canada	50.2700, -124.8914
31418	1017	Mount Buxton	Calvert Island	1017	Canada	51.5919, -127.9834
31432	1011	Crystal Mountain	Mitkof Island	1011	USA-AK	56.5850, -132.8667
31439	1008	Mount Edgecumbe / L'ux	Kruzof Island	1008	USA-AK	57.0514, -135.7603

On 1st April 1974 a prankster named Oliver Bickar decided to ignite 70 old tyres in the crater of Mount Edgecumbe, leading local residents to think the volcano was erupting. After considerable alarm, he spray-painted huge letters around the rim revealing that it had all been a joke. The official height of the mountain is 976 metres but satellite sources support Ribu status. It seems unlikely that Bickar's burnt tyres would have increased the mountain's height by over 24 metres, so the measurement mystery remains unsolved.

East ridge of Ashlu Mountain, NA121, from near the summit (Sean Caulfield)

Tetrahedron Peak, NA121 (Sean Caulfield)

NA121 Coast Mountains

Id	Height	Name	Drop	Country	Location
31002	4019	Mount Waddington	3304	Canada	51.3736, -125.2636
31005	3555	Monarch Mountain	2920	Canada	51.8995, -125.8761
31010	2968	Skihist Mountain	2463	Canada	50.1881, -121.9036
31011	3090	Mount Ratz	2430	Canada	57.3930, -132.3031
31013	3298	Mount Queen Bess	2354	Canada	51.2714, -124.5683
31016	2892	Wedge Mountain	2249	Canada	50.1331, -122.7933
31017	2692	Otter Mountain	2239	Canada	56.0066, -129.6928
31018	2283	Kwatna Peak	2220	Canada	52.0705, -126.9629
31020	2987	Scud Peak	2172	Canada	57.2412, -131.1678
31021	3183	Razorback Mountain	2153	Canada	51.5904, -124.6913
31023	2336	Oscar Peak	2101	Canada	54.9289, -129.0594
31024	2729	Mount Jancowski	2077	Canada	56.3374, -129.9816
31025	2219	Mount Valpy	2016	Canada	54.2750, -129.0565
31026	2365	Chatsquot Mountain	1981	Canada	53.1422, -127.4772
31027	2366	Mount Priestley	1968	Canada	55.2300, -128.8761
31028	2304	Sharks Teeth Peak	1907	Canada	53.0071, -127.2400
31032	2759	Howson Peak	1864	Canada	54.4185, -127.7441
31033	2747	Seven Sisters Peaks – Weeskinisht	1862	Canada	54.9678, -128.2322
31034	2003	Snow Tower	1858	USA-AK	58.1724, -133.4008
31035	2908	Mount Saugstad	1849	Canada	52.2542, -126.5148
31036	2507	Brian Boru Peak	1833	Canada	55.0739, -127.5743
31037	2758	Tsaydaychuz Peak	1829	Canada	53.0213, -126.6400
31039	2724	Atna Peak	1787	Canada	53.9398, -128.0456
31040	2506	Birkenhead Peak	1781	Canada	50.5111, -122.6211
31041	2910	Chutine Peak	1765	Canada	57.7753, -132.3367
31043	2793	Mount Edziza	1760	Canada	57.7156, -130.6347
31044	2595	Unuk Peak / Bowser River Peak	1725	Canada	56.3764, -130.1933
31045	2415	Sittakanay Peak	1710	Canada	58.4782, -133.3620
31047	2664	Thunder Mountain	1701	Canada	52.5531, -126.3697
31048	2593	Devils Paw	1701	Canada, USA-AK	58.7292, -133.8400
31049	2749	Overseer Mountain	1679	Canada	50.5289, -123.3808
31051	3037	Talchako Mountain	1675	Canada	52.0919, -126.0159
31052	2239	Faisal Peak	1671	Canada	56.8856, -130.5799
31053	2524	Whiting Peak	1669	Canada	58.1390, -132.9348
31054	2469	Lehua Mountain	1667	Canada	56.4910, -130.7710
31055	2408	Mount Lester Jones	1658	Canada	58.7174, -133.2307
31056	2532	Mount Porsild	1648	Canada	60.0842, -136.0142
31058	2262	Mount Judge Howay	1632	Canada	49.5072, -122.3219
31061	2727	Mount Pattullo	1617	Canada	56.2338, -129.6577
31062	1934	Corsan Peak	1608	Canada	51.0175, -126.4060
31063	3063	Mount Tatlow	1607	Canada	51.3842, -123.8642

31064	2589	Hudson Bay Mountain	1606	Canada	54.8117, -127.3397
31065	3182	Mount Monmouth	1602	Canada	50.9924, -123.7899
31068	1664	Estero Peak	1587	Canada	50.4622, -125.1858
31069	2859	Mount Seton	1584	Canada	50.6239, -122.2603
31072	2918	Whitecap Mountain	1538	Canada	50.7167, -122.5097
31074	1967	Mount Monkley	1529	Canada	54.8914, -129.6483
31075	2907	The Horn	1527	Canada	52.3191, -126.2362
31076	1801	Mount Van der Est	1502	Canada	50.5565, -125.2832
31077	2252	Robertson Peak	1502	Canada	49.6461, -122.2503
31078	1942	Kitlope Peak	1497	Canada	53.0383, -127.6413
31079	2953	Ambition Mountain	1496	Canada	57.3946, -131.4853
31080	3242	Good Hope Mountain	1485	Canada	51.1425, -124.1719
31082	2607	Wilderness Mountain	1482	Canada	51.9397, -125.5281
31083	2603	Mount Tantalus	1478	Canada	49.8183, -123.3297
31085	2439	Salient Mountain	1471	Canada	53.0506, -126.9880
31086	2306	Lavender Peak	1469	Canada	55.6513, -129.3186
31089	1984	Johnston Peak	1465	Canada	53.9239, -129.3564
31092	2566	Mount Elfrida	1455	Canada	51.9596, -126.3213
31093	2671	Big Mountain	1446	Canada	56.8822, -131.5761
31096	2666	Klokon Peak	1436	Canada	51.4768, -124.0931
31097	2360	Chechidla Peak	1436	Canada	58.3971, -132.8468
31099	2218	Stuhini Peak	1415	Canada	58.6221, -133.3705
31100	2317	Serb Peak	1412	Canada	54.6246, -127.7324
31101	1652	Endicott Mountain *	1409	USA-AK	57.6950, -133.2564
31102	2279	Kitwanga Peak	1408	Canada	55.1550, -128.2033
31103	2594	Glacier Mountain	1407	Canada	52.2129, -125.8945
31104	2469	Legate Peak	1406	Canada	54.7640, -128.0997
31107	2127	Pond Peak	1398	Canada	60.6222, -136.3869
31109	2062	Birch Mountain, Teresa Island	1394	Canada	59.4318, -133.8208
31110	2526	Kalone Peak	1390	Canada	52.6396, -126.6171
31111	1551	Mount Marten *	1389	USA-AK	55.2576, -130.3333
31113	2368	Tatsatua Peak	1389	Canada	58.2414, -132.6506
31114	1656	Niel Young Peak *	1388	Canada	51.9824, -127.3418
31115	2059	Goat Hollow Mountain *	1387	USA-AK	59.4847, -135.8917
31117	3053	Kates Needle	1379	Canada, USA-AK	57.0452, -132.0450
31118	2933	Migma Mountain	1379	Canada	51.9779, -125.8127
31119	2195	Tezwa Peak	1377	Canada	52.8862, -127.5902
31120	1433	Ecstall Peak	1373	Canada	53.8497, -129.5744
31121	2146	Three Finger Peak	1373	Canada	50.8396, -125.5109
31122	3132	Mount Raleigh	1372	Canada	50.9100, -124.2742
31123	2297	Melville Peak	1370	Canada	56.6269, -130.6322
31125	2325	Khawachen Mountain	1367	Canada	53.4411, -127.5508
31129	2019	Mount Pereleshin	1350	Canada	57.2344, -131.7267

31130	2881	Shulaps Peak	1346	Canada	50.9489, -122.5175
31131	2205	Montana Mountain	1346	Canada	60.0583, -134.6892
31137	2059	Corvus Peak	1335	Canada	56.6144, -131.2711
31139	2038	Marmor Peak	1328	Canada	53.1318, -128.2322
31140	2420	Mount Alfred	1321	Canada	50.2060, -124.0766
31141	2355	Hang Ten Peak	1320	Canada	58.8965, -133.6797
31142	2235	Alder Peak	1320	Canada	55.0194, -129.2044
31143	2257	Sandpiper Peak	1319	Canada	60.3018, -135.9321
31144	1559	Mount Antony	1319	Canada	50.6937, -126.1189
31146	2022	Greenpoint Mountain *	1314	USA-AK	56.0008, -130.3058
31147	2338	Telkwa Range	1313	Canada	54.4775, -127.1369
31148	1671	Cap Cone	1313	Canada	50.7122, -125.6263
31149	2101	Nass Peak	1312	Canada	55.2653, -129.4855
31150	1824	Kirby Crags	1307	Canada	54.1500, -129.2800
31152	2627	Tatsamenie Peak	1302	Canada	58.2682, -132.3842
31155	2415	Mount Ney	1298	Canada	53.8254, -127.4263
31156	1788	Brunswick Mountain	1294	Canada	49.4875, -123.1972
31157	2671	Mount Boardman	1291	Canada	50.4294, -123.8572
31158	2111	Racine Peak	1289	Canada	59.7255, -134.4091
31159	2249	Teepee Peak	1282	Canada	59.6784, -134.6252
31160	1928	Mount Anderson	1281	Canada	56.4783, -129.6813
31162	3063	Taseko Mountain	1277	Canada	51.2334, -123.4731
31163	2246	Chikamin Mountain	1277	Canada	53.3901, -127.0508
31164	2091	Grass Mountain	1274	Canada	57.9222, -131.4561
31165	1319	Kwatsi Peak *	1273	Canada	50.8722, -126.2948
31166	2456	Mount Algard	1267	Canada	50.65834, -124.6052
31167	2966	Snowside Mountain	1266	Canada	52.1068, -126.3884
31168	3008	Mount Vishnu	1264	Canada	51.6247, -125.1519
31169	2213	Mount Berhardt	1261	Canada	52.8384, -126.5622
31170	1372	Reflection Peak	1261	USA-AK	56.0765, -131.5941
31171	2691	Tremor Mountain	1261	Canada	50.0553, -122.8047
31172	2811	Mount Sampson	1261	Canada	50.6208, -123.1378
31173	2045	Surprise Mountain	1261	Canada	60.2542, -134.9067
31174	2020	Mount Lorne	1260	Canada	60.4613, -134.7051
31175	1735	Smoker Peak	1259	Canada	51.4914, -127.1884
31176	1314	Goat Island Peak	1259	Canada	50.0645, -124.3967
31177	3044	Mount Moore	1259	Canada	51.3375, -124.4160
31179	2123	The Cathedral	1256	Canada	59.3277, -134.1234
31180	2095	Mount Robie Reid	1253	Canada	49.4319, -122.3561
31181	2427	Mount McLean	1252	Canada	50.7164, -122.0356
31182	2622	Tahltan Peak	1252	Canada	57.9511, -132.0431
31183	1314	Mount Scriven	1250	Canada	50.6332, -125.8862
31184	1259	Spípiyus Peak	1249	Canada	49.6431, -123.8922

31185	1464	Mount Dent	1243	Canada	55.2053, -129.9547
31186	2137	Jack Peak	1241	Canada	59.8615, -134.6475
31187	2783	Mount Matier	1241	Canada	50.3264, -122.4436
31188	2031	Sky Pilot Mountain	1236	Canada	49.6353, -123.0864
31189	1469	Mount Calder	1236	Canada	49.8878, -123.9867
31190	2123	Bennett Peak	1235	Canada	59.9565, -134.9710
31191	1610	Sharp Peak	1235	Canada	55.0230, -129.7226
31192	1976	Eight Mile Mountain *	1234	Canada	54.4135, -128.3066
31193	2286	Gable Mountain	1230	Canada	53.1609, -126.9602
31194	2502	Mount Saunders	1229	Canada	52.4919, -126.9000
31195	2299	The Nipple	1229	Canada	49.9450, -121.5853
31196	1536	Mount Francis	1229	Canada	55.1611, -129.7864
31201	2378	Skuce Peak	1226	Canada	52.9169, -126.9150
31202	1798	Rousseau Peak *	1223	USA-AK	55.4242, -130.1528
31203	2132	The Old Settler	1222	Canada	49.5122, -121.6219
31204	2064	Neechantz Peak	1221	Canada	51.4664, -126.7133
31207	2182	Mount Kendall	1220	Canada	51.7898, -126.7377
31208	2779	Cheja Peak	1219	Canada	58.0067, -132.4758
31210	2524	Colwell Mountain *	1219	Canada	51.8219, -125.2106
31215	2882	Mount Olson	1207	Canada	51.2579, -123.8794
31218	1548	Walker Lake Mountain *	1202	USA-AK	55.7225, -130.6369
31219	1996	Mount Adams	1200	Canada	59.1008, -133.9075
31220	1981	Mount Patterson	1200	Canada	59.9933, -134.5425
31225	1494	Lincoln Peak	1197	USA-AK	57.2484, -133.1080
31226	2357	Big Snow Mountain	1196	Canada	52.2378, -126.6878
31227	2552	Mount Albert	1196	Canada	50.2339, -123.8769
31228	2192	Pillar Peak East	1196	Canada	54.2411, -127.8622
31229	2183	Grainger Peak	1193	Canada	49.5825, -122.0725
31231	2215	Kidprice Peak	1190	Canada	53.9178, -127.5658
31232	2562	Hankin Peak	1190	Canada	57.1892, -130.6358
31236	1706	Nascall Peak	1186	Canada	52.5781, -127.5553
31237	2070	Mount Cameron North	1185	Canada	59.4367, -134.0800
31239	2561	Ashlu Mountain	1183	Canada	50.0764, -123.5492
31240	2819	Mount Ethelweard	1182	Canada	50.7742, -123.3231
31241	1878	King Salmon Peak *	1182	Canada	58.6714, -132.9017
31242	2166	Mount Irma	1180	Canada	53.3741, -127.3566
31243	2043	Motherall Peak	1178	Canada	60.1690, -136.9141
31244	2953	Cloud Drifter Peak	1178	Canada	51.4522, -124.6752
31246	1649	Chakluk Mountain	1176	Canada	58.8717, -133.0639
31247	2288	Asteroid Peak	1172	Canada	52.8117, -127.3746
31248	2531	Nelles Peak	1171	Canada	58.8040, -133.9145
31249	1918	Treasure Mountain	1169	Canada	54.5291, -128.0336
31250	1316	Downie Range Peak *	1169	Canada	50.3845, -125.0104

31251	1293	Ayton Peak *	1168	Canada	54.1172, -129.6656
31256	1739	Tetrahedron Peak	1164	Canada	49.6078, -123.5675
31258	2435	Potlatch Peak	1159	Canada	59.9693, -136.2807
31260	2110	Munroe Peak	1156	Canada	60.0196, -135.1221
31261	2459	Euler Peak	1150	Canada	52.5763, -126.8849
31262	2454	Kalahin Mountain	1150	Canada	56.5669, -131.0081
31263	2045	Snowslide Range Peak *	1149	Canada	56.6774, -129.8848
31264	2146	Mount Willibert	1145	Canada	56.2397, -130.4458
31265	1923	Mount Bratnober	1145	Canada	60.7395, -136.6638
31266	2167	Mount Trapper *	1144	Canada	58.3599, -132.7162
31267	2189	Mount Haven	1144	Canada	53.2941, -127.0593
31268	2363	Mount Collins	1143	Canada	52.6566, -126.4505
31270	2201	Teigen Peak	1139	Canada	56.7816, -130.1103
31271	2481	Shaker Peak	1138	Canada	50.8600, -125.0936
31272	1762	Shakes Peak *	1138	USA-AK	56.7932, -132.3185
31273	2588	Mamquam Mountain	1138	Canada	49.7753, -122.8511
31274	2319	Mount Kelsall	1135	Canada	59.8337, -136.4275
31276	2048	Tenaiko Peak	1133	Canada	53.3082, -127.5521
31277	1376	Mitt Peak	1133	Canada	53.9251, -129.7630
31280	2225	Alligator Peak *	1131	Canada	60.3899, -135.4271
31281	2437	Valhalla Mountain	1130	Canada	57.5778, -131.9075
31282	1893	Gilt Peak	1128	Canada	53.9425, -129.2223
31284	1586	Kynoch Peak	1126	Canada	52.6860, -127.7859
31285	2566	Brucejack Peak	1126	Canada	56.5289, -130.1247
31287	1823	Kikahe Peak *	1123	USA-AK	56.5192, -131.8917
31288	1535	Khutze Peak	1122	Canada	53.2294, -128.3994
31291	2785	Aurora Tower	1116	Canada	52.1792, -126.1542
31292	2966	Mount Burkett	1116	USA-AK	57.1732, -132.3013
31293	2261	Smaby Peak	1116	Canada	53.2515, -127.1959
31294	1622	Dorothy Mountain *	1116	USA-AK	58.2207, -133.9215
31295	2324	Hanging Glacier Mountain	1116	Canada	53.9090, -127.8043
31298	1128	Mapalaklenk Peak *	1113	Canada	52.1183, -127.5122
31299	2808	Elaho Mountain	1112	Canada	50.5090, -123.8271
31300	2184	Mount Hadden	1111	Canada	54.7411, -129.1500
31301	2229	Bensins Peak	1110	Canada	52.1997, -127.0364
31302	2298	Sutlahine Peak	1110	Canada	58.5088, -132.8920
31303	2341	Hagens Peak	1110	Canada	52.4813, -126.4972
31304	1498	Chickamin Peak *	1109	USA-AK	55.8205, -130.6872
31305	2314	Kappan Mountain	1108	Canada	52.3193, -125.5074
31306	1891	Sloko Peak *	1108	Canada	59.1399, -133.7584
31307	2073	Sinclair Mountain	1108	USA-AK	59.0967, -135.1242
31310	3021	Mount Tisiphone	1104	Canada	50.7589, -123.9202
31312	1220	Mount Keyes	1103	Canada	52.3261, -127.8921

31313	2676	Castle Towers Mountain	1103	Canada		49.9400, -122.9428
31315	1938	Mount Campagnolo	1103	Canada		54.5161, -129.7533
31316	1370	Mount McNeil	1101	Canada		54.5781, -130.2261
31317	1154	Mount George	1101	Canada		50.4557, -125.7192
31318	2306	Chimai Mountain	1101	Canada		49.9717, -123.5794
31320	2494	Blackfin Peak	1098	Canada		50.4990, -124.0079
31324	2272	Tsaytis Peak	1094	Canada		53.3688, -127.6948
31325	3126	Mount Grenville	1094	Canada		50.9737, -124.5286
31326	2208	Iskut Peak *	1094	Canada		57.3731, -130.3892
31327	2779	Pendant Peak *	1093	Canada		57.5522, -132.1597
31329	1169	Hayward Creek Peak *	1090	Canada		54.0508, -129.7807
31330	1178	Work Peak	1089	Canada		54.2575, -129.9230
31332	2985	Whitemantle Mountain	1087	Canada		51.1642, -125.2389
31333	2047	Tutshi Peak	1086	Canada		59.8623, -134.8573
31334	1981	Mount Livingston	1086	USA-AK		58.8045, -134.6012
31335	2022	Chuunk Mountain	1083	Canada		58.7767, -133.4517
31336	2139	Mount Loring	1082	Canada		54.0534, -127.6774
31338	2362	Pastoral Peak	1082	Canada		53.8242, -128.0943
31339	1526	Grant Creek Peak *	1082	USA-AK		56.1494, -131.3807
31341	2271	Muscle Peak	1081	Canada		53.2585, -127.0016
31342	2079	Dawes Peak *	1081	USA-AK		57.4488, -132.8201
31343	2516	Todd Peak *	1081	Canada		56.2425, -129.8417
31348	2006	Herd Dome	1074	Canada		54.2028, -127.7055
31349	2511	Nourse Peak	1070	USA-AK		59.6701, -135.5377
31350	2105	Slide Mountain	1067	Canada		50.1733, -124.2989
31351	1202	Smith Inlet Mountain	1066	Canada		51.3964, -127.1658
31354	1909	Tentacle Peak	1064	Canada		54.0187, -129.3321
31355	1345	Enshesh Peak	1064	Canada		54.5758, -130.0721
31357	2212	Mount Arkell	1063	Canada		60.6043, -135.6212
31358	3138	Cerberus Mountain	1062	Canada		51.9391, -126.1887
31359	2112	Fire Mountain	1062	Canada		49.8603, -122.3653
31363	2650	Demeter Peak	1059	Canada		51.7408, -125.4875
31364	2575	Nusatsum Mountain	1059	Canada		52.3975, -126.3783
31365	2032	Mount Sumdum	1058	USA-AK		57.8064, -133.4369
31366	1238	Mount Berkeley	1058	Canada		50.5647, -125.7048
31367	2487	Mount Pitt	1057	Canada		49.8783, -122.7042
31368	2461	Mount MacAuley	1057	Canada		60.0264, -135.5522
31369	2235	Ishkheenickh Peak *	1056	Canada		54.6503, -129.4636
31372	1991	Mount Denman	1052	Canada		50.2803, -124.5191
31375	1871	Cloudburst Mountain	1049	Canada		49.9336, -123.2364
31376	1359	Mount Crickmer	1049	Canada		49.3206, -122.3772
31379	1962	Smokehouse Peak	1048	Canada		51.3206, -126.8269
31387	1250	Bartholomew Peak *	1039	USA-AK		55.3603, -130.7115

31388	1463	Boca de Quadra Peak *	1039	USA-AK	55.3384, -130.4095
31390	1592	Mount Stephens	1038	Canada	50.9708, -126.6636
31391	2352	Tsuniah Peak	1036	Canada	51.5628, -124.1252
31392	1141	Naysash Peak	1035	Canada	51.3564, -127.3494
31393	2891	Mount Brew	1035	Canada	50.5850, -121.9711
31394	2777	Taalkhunaxhk'u Shaa	1034	Canada, USA-AK	57.0913, -132.3694
31395	1252	Quatlena Mountain *	1034	Canada	52.0211, -127.5319
31396	2043	Elsfield Peak	1033	Canada	52.9836, -126.7414
31398	2554	Mount Frank Mackie	1031	Canada	56.3164, -130.3172
31399	1348	Saiak Peak	1029	Canada	52.4361, -127.6331
31400	2206	Chechidla Ridge *	1029	Canada	58.2869, -132.7042
31401	1791	Leduc Peak *	1029	USA-AK	56.0423, -130.6626
31402	2890	Mount Farrow	1029	Canada	51.0972, -124.1100
31404	2256	Ember Mountain	1026	Canada	49.7581, -122.4272
31408	1534	Mount McRae	1024	Canada	49.4764, -121.9556
31410	1960	Kusawa Mountain *	1020	Canada	60.5942, -136.2581
31412	2314	Rainbow Mountain	1019	Canada	50.1800, -123.0536
31413	2122	Mount Evindsen	1018	Canada	55.6579, -129.6257
31414	2208	Mount Jimmy Jimmy	1018	Canada	49.9100, -123.4869
31415	1863	Wright Peaks Ridge *	1018	Canada, USA-AK	58.4853, -133.4792
31422	2606	Mount Tinniswood	1016	Canada	50.3136, -123.8394
31424	1175	Berners Peak *	1015	USA-AK	58.9776, -135.0119
31425	1920	Mount Hayford	1015	USA-AK	55.7502, -130.2876
31426	1345	Big Falls Peak *	1014	Canada	54.0100, -129.5672
31427	2517	Mount Ada	1014	Canada	52.1282, -125.6488
31428	2531	Mount Goddard	1013	Canada	51.2037, -123.9521
31429	1877	Cub Lake Peak *	1013	Canada	60.7831, -135.5681
31430	2374	Huckleberry Mountain	1012	Canada	51.4608, -124.2772
31445	2163	Lawrence Peak	1011	Canada	57.0003, -130.5076
31433	1047	Sandell Peak	1010	Canada	51.6653, -127.5922
31434	2347	Paleo Peak	1010	Canada	54.8833, -127.9125
31435	2460	Traverse Peak	1010	Canada	49.7550, -121.9489
31436	1145	Chuck Peak *	1009	USA-AK	57.5493, -133.3875
31437	1172	Buschmann Peak *	1008	USA-AK	55.0961, -130.5700
31438	2086	Taiya Peak	1008	Canada	59.6869, -135.1832
31440	1778	Nares Mountain	1006	Canada	60.1896, -134.5896
31442	1079	Dahlgren Peak	1006	USA-AK	57.2331, -133.3669
31446	1878	Nakonake Peak *	1004	Canada	58.9692, -133.3792
31447	2073	McQuillan Ridge	1004	Canada	56.3767, -130.5794
31448	2231	Mount Smith	1004	Canada	50.8244, -125.0281
31455	2293	Kemano Peak	1002	Canada	53.8353, -127.9617
31451	1716	Golden Ears	1002	Canada	49.3631, -122.5075
31452	2258	Devilhole Peak	1001	Canada	60.2083, -136.4233
31453	2103	Ferebee Peak *	1000	USA-AK	59.5092, -136.4233

Niel Young Peak, NA121

There are 299 peaks in region NA121, more than in NA113 (Greenland) which has 244. Peak 31114 is 1656m high with 1388m drop. Its name is derived from the Niel Creek to the south and Young River to the north and east. Like many peaks in the region it has no recorded ascent, so at present nobody knows this is somewhere.

Southern part of NA12

NA122 North-west USA Coast Ranges

Id	Height	Name	Drop	Country	Location
31012	2429	Mount Olympus	2389	USA-WA	47.8013, -123.7107
31070	2751	Mount Eddy	1568	USA-CA	41.3199, -122.4794
31087	2467	South Yolla Bolly Mountain	1468	USA-CA	40.0365, -122.8542
31178	2374	Mount Deception	1257	USA-WA	47.8134, -123.2334
31223	2744	Thompson Peak	1200	USA-CA	41.0006, -123.0484
31296	1615	Brandy Peak	1114	USA-OR	42.5976, -123.8806
31405	1249	Marys Peak	1026	USA-OR	44.5044, -123.5525

NA123 Central and Southern California Ranges

Id	Height	Name	Drop	Country	Location
31007	3305	San Jacinto Peak	2539	USA-CA	33.8148, -116.6795
31008	3505	San Gorgonio Mountain	2528	USA-CA	34.0993, -116.8249
31030	3068	Mount San Antonio	1897	USA-CA	34.2894, -117.6464
31091	2692	Mount Pinos	1463	USA-CA	34.8128, -119.1454
31127	1787	Junipero Serra Peak	1356	USA-CA	36.1456, -121.4190
31134	1733	Santiago Peak	1340	USA-CA	33.7106, -117.5341
31200	2657	Toro Peak	1226	USA-CA	33.5234, -116.4257
31361	1597	San Benito Mountain	1060	USA-CA	36.3697, -120.6448
31382	1154	Loma Prieta	1046	USA-CA	37.1109, -121.8443

NA124 Baja California

Id	Height	Name	Drop	Country	Location
31022	3095	Picacho del Diablo	2135	Mexico	30.9927, -115.3751
31029	2080	Sierra La Laguna	1900	Mexico	23.5394, -109.9544
31060	1951	Volcán Las Tres Vírgenes	1631	Mexico	27.4700, -112.5919
31105	1800	Cerro La Sandía	1400	Mexico	28.4071, -113.4386
31116	1680	Cerro Giganta	1380	Mexico	26.1064, -111.5846
31206	1740	Cerro Las Palmas	1220	Mexico	26.8612, -112.4573
31322	1580	Sierra Agua Verde	1096	Mexico	27.5759, -113.0289
31344	1660	Sierra la Asamblea	1080	Mexico	29.3678, -114.0899
31397	1092	Cerro Pescadores	1032	Mexico	32.3676, -115.4459
31454	1140	Sierra Agua de Soda	1000	Mexico	28.7253, -113.2478
31153	1300	Monte Augusta, Guadalupe	1300	Mexico	29.0958, -118.3114
31222	1200	Isla Cedros	1200	Mexico	28.1295, -115.2207
31345	1080	Isla Ángel de la Guarda / Archangel	1080	Mexico	29.4562, -113.5163

NA125 Cascade Range

Id	Height	Name	Drop	Country	Location
31001	4392	Mount Rainier / Tahoma	4037	USA-WA	46.8529, -121.7604
31004	4319	Mount Shasta	2980	USA-CA	41.4090, -122.1949
31006	3284	Mount Baker	2684	USA-WA	48.7768, -121.8145

31009	3741	Mount Adams / Pah-To	2479	USA-WA	46.2025, -121.4907
31014	3426	Mount Hood / Wy'east	2349	USA-OR	45.3735, -121.6959
31015	3214	Glacier Peak / Dakobed	2297	USA-WA	48.1119, -121.1142
31031	2596	Silvertip Mountain	1871	Canada	49.1631, -121.2164
31042	3199	Mount Jefferson	1762	USA-OR	44.6744, -121.7996
31046	3157	South Sister	1705	USA-OR	44.1035, -121.7694
31059	2869	Mount Stuart	1628	USA-WA	47.4752, -120.9024
31066	3187	Lassen Peak	1594	USA-CA	40.4882, -121.5050
31088	2737	Mount Spickard	1466	USA-WA	48.9696, -121.2408
31090	1627	Round Mountain	1464	USA-WA	48.3266, -121.7509
31095	2431	Welch Peak	1441	Canada	49.1603, -121.6006
31108	2536	Mount Saint Helens	1399	USA-WA	46.1915, -122.1957
31124	2088	Three Fingers / Queest-Alb	1369	USA-WA	48.1700, -121.6879
31126	2895	Mount McLoughlin	1365	USA-OR	42.4445, -122.3159
31133	2781	Mount Shuksan	1342	USA-WA	48.8313, -121.6029
31138	2647	Remmel Mountain	1330	USA-WA	48.9234, -120.1969
31161	2763	Jack Mountain	1285	USA-WA	48.7729, -120.9563
31198	2334	Mount Prophet	1227	USA-WA	48.8487, -121.1628
31205	2730	North Gardner Mountain	1220	USA-WA	48.5152, -120.5017
31224	2459	Hozomeen Mountain	1199	USA-WA	48.9823, -121.0120
31235	2258	Ruby Mountain	1187	USA-WA	48.6944, -121.0430
31238	2388	Sloan Peak	1184	USA-WA	48.0415, -121.3401
31252	2811	Goode Mountain	1169	USA-WA	48.4831, -120.9116
31253	2276	Stoyoma Mountain	1166	Canada	49.9922, -121.2106
31257	2130	White Chuck Mountain	1159	USA-WA	48.2085, -121.4170
31278	2897	Bonanza Peak	1136	USA-WA	48.2382, -120.8664
31286	2463	Big Chiwaukum	1125	USA-WA	47.7025, -120.9348
31289	2461	Mount Outram	1121	Canada	49.2889, -121.1583
31290	2494	Gilbert Peak	1119	USA-WA	46.4885, -121.4081
31297	1902	Gunn Peak	1113	USA-WA	47.8162, -121.4480
31340	2138	South Twin	1082	USA-WA	48.7048, -121.9875
31362	2734	Black Peak	1066	USA-WA	48.5235, -120.8162
31353	2430	Mount Daniel	1065	USA-WA	47.5649, -121.1808
31381	1312	Lyman Hill	1047	USA-WA	48.5946, -122.1591
31406	2799	Mount Thielsen	1025	USA-OR	43.1528, -122.0665
31416	1575	Aeneas Mountain	1018	USA-WA	48.7431, -119.6224
31417	1905	Dirtyface Peak	1017	USA-WA	47.8714, -120.8252
31441	2341	Mount Blum	1006	USA-WA	48.7542, -121.4822
31444	2367	Mount Aix	1005	USA-WA	46.7951, -121.2559
31450	2127	Guanaco Peak	1002	Canada	49.6619, -121.1434
31449	2665	Mount Lago	1000	USA-WA	48.8293, -120.5375

NA126 Sierra Nevada

Id	Height	Name	Drop	Country	Location
31003	4419	Mount Whitney	3072	USA-CA	36.5786, -118.2924
31214	4009	Mount Ritter	1209	USA-CA	37.6891, -119.1995
31254	2433	Double Mountain	1165	USA-CA	35.0333, -118.4867
31308	3285	Mount Rose	1107	USA-NV	39.3437, -119.9179
31356	2574	Piute Peak	1064	USA-CA	35.4494, -118.3883
31443	2308	Breckenridge Mountain	1005	USA-CA	35.4512, -118.5870

Mount Whitney, NA126

Alastair Govan, June 2019

Mount Whitney is a long hike, 22 miles round trip with 1900 metres of ascent. Most of the time is spent above 3000 metres so you certainly feel the altitude. Most hikers either camp en route or start before dawn but we opted to do neither, starting around sunrise and getting back to the car at dusk, over fourteen hours later. My calculation of time using my standard formula did not adequately allow for altitude or for the snow cover, which was unusually extensive for the end of June.

There is a steep 500-metre snow slope which I knew would be a challenge, so we took ice axe and crampons. They were not essential but they certainly made progress safer and a little easier. Most hikers slid down this slope on their return, so it was a horrendous mess of steep mushy snow, footsteps and slide marks. The usual trail that zig-zags up the slope was invisible under the snow and no one had bothered to try and follow a similar line. We were almost the last ones off the summit and short of time and energy, so we opted to slither down, relying on our ice axes to control our descent. I was not normally keen to do this, partly to avoid ruining my Gore-Tex clothing, but trying to come down the steep slippery mess in an upright position would have been too slow.

We got back to the hotel in Lone Pine after dark, exhausted but rather pleased with ourselves. Then we discovered our eyes felt very dry and gritty. Having forgotten to take sunglasses, we both had a touch of snow blindness. The June sun reflected off snow at 4000 metres in California was much stronger than anything in the UK or even most of year in the Alps.

Mount Rainier, NA125

This is the third most prominent mountain in the USA, after Denali in Alaska and Mauna Kea in Hawaii. It is more prominent than K2, the second highest mountain on Earth, and one of only 22 peaks worldwide with a prominence of over 4000 metres. There is one in each of Canada, Mexico, Argentina, Chile, Ecuador, Tanzania, Indonesia, Malaysia, Iran, Pakistan and Antarctica. There is one on the border of France and Italy, two in Russia, and the other five are wholly or partly in China. All the 4000ers are listed in the table of the fifty most prominent Ribus on page 321.

Although Mount Rainier is not as high as Mount Whitney it is more prominent because its key col in Canada is much lower than the key col for Mount Whitney, which is to the south-east in New Mexico. The only Ribus in North America more prominent than Mount Rainier are Denali in Alaska, Mount Logan in Canada and Pico de Orizaba in Mexico. To the south (but north of the Panama Canal), the only Ribus more prominent than Mount Whitney are Pico de Orizaba, Volcán Tajumulco in Guatemala and Cerro Chirripó in Costa Rica.

As well as being more prominent, Mount Rainier is also snowier than Mount Whitney.

NA13 Inter-mountain West

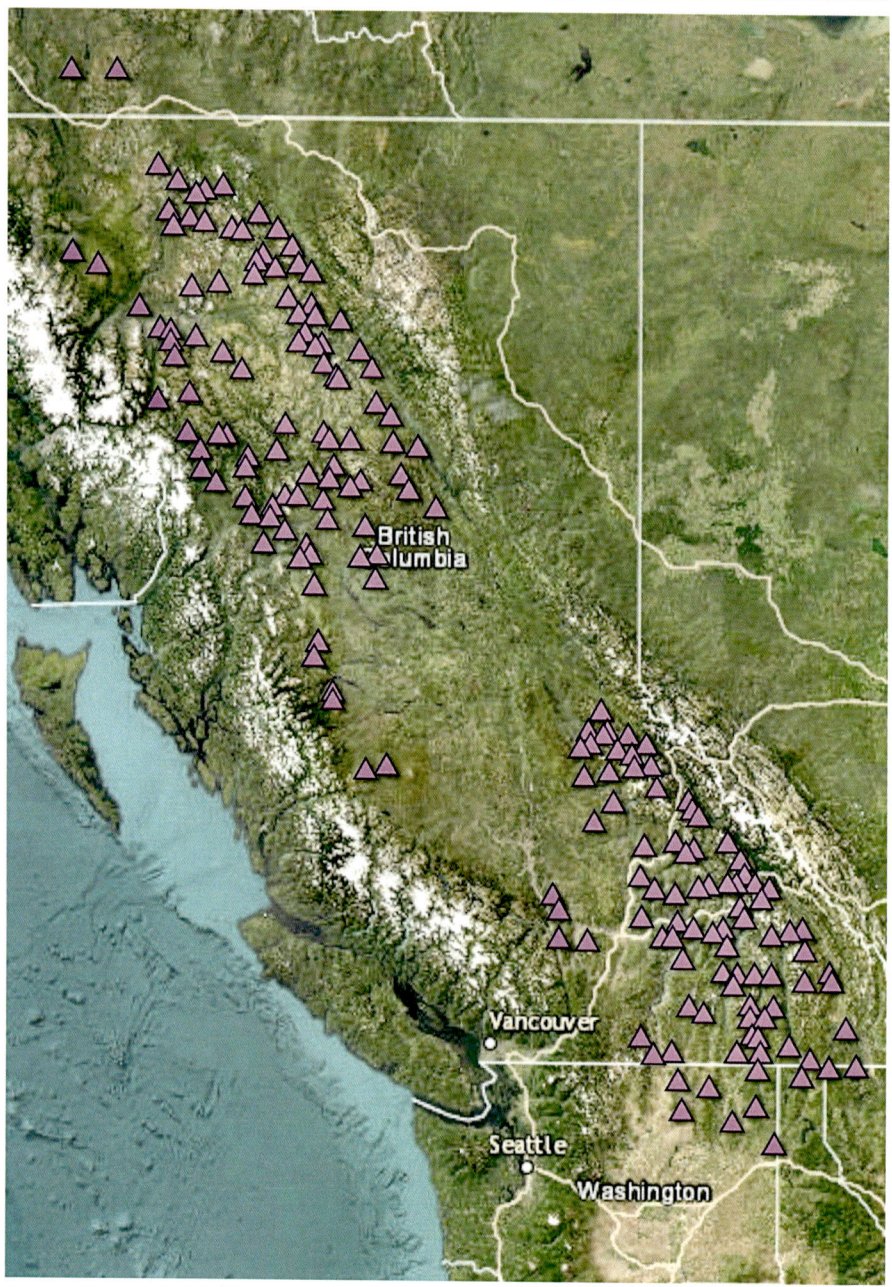

NA130 British Columbia Interior

Id	Height	Name	Drop	Country	Location
31518	2588	Shedin Peak	1800	Canada	55.9392, -127.4797
31523	2748	Thudaka Peak	1739	Canada	57.9272, -126.8486
31528	2553	Mount Perseus	1680	Canada	52.3540, -120.5327
31529	2451	Mount Thomlinson	1667	Canada	55.5439, -127.4863
31531	2668	Sharktooth Mountain	1653	Canada	58.5876, -127.9625
31542	2396	Mount Cronin	1573	Canada	54.9301, -126.8639
31545	2096	Kispiox Mountain	1563	Canada	55.3986, -127.9434
31546	2189	Vile Peak	1554	Canada	56.2711, -128.3397
31547	2597	Mount Wotzke	1539	Canada	52.7130, -120.6506
31550	2155	Mount Tod	1525	Canada	50.9166, -119.9408
31552	2334	Blustry Mountain	1484	Canada	50.6117, -121.6989
31558	2472	Shelagyote Peak	1464	Canada	55.9547, -127.2062
31568	2280	Mount Kerr	1411	Canada	51.1705, -121.7987
31573	2260	Michel Peak	1394	Canada	53.5707, -126.4791
31575	2369	Ramhorn Peak	1391	Canada	58.8261, -128.4017
31578	2276	Tuktsayda Mountain	1387	Canada	57.7953, -130.1072
31589	2219	Mount Henri	1360	Canada	56.5094, -124.7241
31593	2382	Mount Skook Davidson	1352	Canada	58.6817, -127.3321
31595	2268	Cormier Peak	1351	Canada	57.5567, -125.9503
31600	2641	Mount Cushing	1333	Canada	57.6152, -126.8502
31604	2302	Iverson Peak *	1327	Canada	59.5128, -130.1464
31607	2393	Ningunsaw Peak	1309	Canada	57.0254, -130.1503
31608	2644	Chukachida Peak	1308	Canada	57.6450, -126.7544
31613	1988	Shilahou Peak	1302	Canada	56.3956, -128.2739
31614	2342	Netalzul Mountain	1300	Canada	55.2782, -126.9412
31621	2535	Bower Peak	1279	Canada	57.2494, -126.3938
31622	2223	Horseranch Peak	1277	Canada	59.3189, -128.7975
31623	2247	Mount Patcha	1272	Canada	56.1941, -127.0190
31626	2519	Mount Will	1267	Canada	57.5452, -128.7987
31628	2431	Frog Peak	1264	Canada	57.9539, -127.2139
31629	2106	Barrier Peak	1264	Canada	56.8446, -125.3062
31630	2342	Major Hart Peak	1262	Canada	58.8604, -128.6452
31631	2247	Apex Mountain	1262	Canada	49.3594, -119.9103
31633	2221	Inspector Peak	1260	Canada	58.8542, -127.6711
31634	2005	Anvil Peak	1260	Canada	50.5939, -121.0619
31636	2609	Toodoggone Peak	1259	Canada	57.4289, -126.6728
31637	2124	Nadina Mountain	1255	Canada	54.0954, -126.8789
31648	2313	Delta Peak	1228	Canada	56.6522, -129.5697
31649	2410	Far Mountain	1226	Canada	52.7865, -125.3226

31652	2027	Spike Peak	1223	Canada	55.2469, -125.8844
31653	2138	Mount Tinsdale	1222	Canada	53.0219, -121.2651
31654	2425	King Mountain	1219	Canada	58.2828, -128.8844
31655	2481	Sustut Peak	1218	Canada	56.5867, -126.5817
31662	2108	Mount Porter South	1200	Canada	55.8258, -124.3375
31664	2175	Mount Forrest	1194	Canada	56.0243, -124.9137
31665	2304	Russel Range Peak *	1191	Canada	57.0039, -125.5782
31666	2381	Klappan Peak	1191	Canada	57.4922, -129.8128
31668	2165	Mount Pendleton	1190	Canada	59.2267, -129.3658
31670	1799	Mount Madely	1187	Canada	56.1061, -128.9456
31671	2593	Johiah Peak	1185	Canada	58.0472, -126.9744
31673	2240	Mount Stevenson	1184	Canada	52.6756, -121.1414
31675	2403	Mount Slocomb	1182	Canada	57.9031, -126.3472
31677	2291	Blunt Mountain	1180	Canada	55.2229, -127.1913
31678	2495	Tsitsutl Peak	1180	Canada	52.7237, -125.7792
31680	2286	Bait Peak	1176	Canada	55.6830, -126.6255
31681	2239	Denetiah Peak *	1163	Canada	58.4974, -127.2016
31682	2227	Mount Dalton	1162	Canada	58.9675, -129.5167
31685	2304	Mount Thoen	1160	Canada	55.3885, -127.0265
31686	2090	Nesabut Peak	1157	Canada	55.2678, -125.5442
31690	2410	Alma Peak	1148	Canada	56.7595, -127.5022
31693	2166	Meszah Peak	1146	Canada	58.4785, -131.4373
31694	2233	Notchtop Peak	1144	Canada	56.4583, -127.6675
31698	1935	Skeena Mountains	1139	Canada	55.7394, -128.2097
31701	2017	Hogem Ranges Peak	1134	Canada	55.0078, -125.6011
31707	2487	Mount Irving	1128	Canada	58.1200, -127.4456
31709	2438	Ferriston Peak	1127	Canada	56.1090, -125.9053
31710	2522	Geese Mountain *	1126	Canada	57.7568, -127.1054
31713	2041	Mount Ritchie	1121	Canada	56.4603, -129.2819
31714	2233	Kastberg Peak *	1121	Canada	56.1422, -126.5506
31715	2218	Chase Mountain	1120	Canada	56.5691, -125.2646
31716	2142	Pyramid Mountain	1120	Canada	58.8861, -129.8489
31718	1891	McDame Peak *	1118	Canada	59.2758, -129.1847
31723	2469	Delta Peak	1114	Canada	57.2883, -126.4200
31724	2194	Tweedsmuir Peak	1114	Canada	53.6611, -126.4705
31728	1806	Mount Wallensteen / Spa Mountain	1109	Canada	50.6558, -119.4966
31730	2125	Marker Peak	1107	Canada	60.4863, -131.0578
31733	2368	Cassiar Ridge *	1103	Canada	58.5269, -128.0839
31735	1932	Muskaboo Peak *	1100	Canada	56.6272, -128.6940
31742	2522	Mount McNamara	1093	Canada	57.6569, -127.2286
31743	1871	Mount Kobau	1093	Canada	49.1150, -119.6758
31747	2092	Cottonwood Mountain *	1090	Canada	59.0483, -129.9383

31748	2352	Sweeny Peak *	1089	Canada	57.0828, -129.5217
31750	2464	Dall Mountain *	1087	Canada	58.4497, -127.7076
31752	2315	Glacial Mountain	1085	Canada	58.2429, -129.4528
31757	2158	Big Timothy Mountain	1080	Canada	52.1022, -120.9314
31764	1823	Mount Morice	1066	Canada	54.2692, -126.7845
31765	1975	Mount Bennett	1065	Canada	57.3681, -125.7031
31770	2303	Zus Mountain	1053	Canada	59.3461, -129.7700
31771	2019	Shelf Ridge	1053	Canada	55.8375, -127.7475
31773	1961	Mount Meehaus	1051	Canada	58.0284, -130.5728
31777	1570	Mount Bell-Irving	1045	Canada	56.2472, -129.2250
31779	2410	Johanson Peak	1045	Canada	56.5778, -126.1092
31780	2159	Todagin Mountain	1043	Canada	57.6641, -129.8987
31781	2165	Axelgold Peak	1042	Canada	56.0522, -126.1128
31784	2273	Tsargoss Peak	1041	Canada	57.6983, -129.3778
31785	1956	Ehahcezetle Mountain	1041	Canada	57.7850, -129.9186
31787	1651	Cutoff Mountain	1041	Canada	55.7069, -127.8144
31788	1995	Sandpile Peak	1032	Canada	59.0181, -128.0731
31790	2322	Savage Mountain	1032	Canada	56.6536, -126.7008
31792	2186	Kechika Mountain *	1028	Canada	58.4131, -126.9531
31794	2027	Driftwood Range	1026	Canada	55.9019, -126.6731
31795	2286	Crescent Mountain	1026	Canada	57.3494, -128.4272
31797	2005	Sweetin Peak *	1022	Canada	55.9247, -128.3042
31798	2082	Tenakihi Range Peak *	1022	Canada	56.1997, -125.0756
31800	2226	Beale Mountain	1021	Canada	58.9225, -129.1997
31801	2240	Carruthers Mountain *	1021	Canada	56.2961, -126.4538
31803	2012	Heart Peak	1019	Canada	58.5989, -131.9630
31804	2089	Pavilion Mountain	1019	Canada	50.9736, -121.6847
31813	1881	Shanoss Ridge *	1013	Canada	56.6386, -128.8781
31816	2048	Mount Bodine	1011	Canada	55.5981, -125.8144
31819	2314	Tucho Mountain *	1007	Canada	58.3853, -128.1500
31821	2009	Englishmans Peak *	1002	Canada	60.4800, -132.0256

Mount Perseus, NA130

Rob Woodall, August 2023

Mount Perseus in British Columbia had assumed an almost legendary status since I first heard of it. The peak was listed by Washington-based John Stolk on a website detailing Canadian Ultras that seemed potentially doable by ordinary mortals, and it was the last to be climbed. There were records of exploratory forays along the ridge, including one by Chris Hood, who retreated owing to a difficult down-climb with lack of equipment and time. He returned in 2023 and managed to bypass the difficulties via a long contouring traverse. I was in Canada when I heard about this. Seizing a weather window, I made the long but straightforward drive in.

The approach was typical of British Columbia, with an old alder-choked road, mature forest and nice alpine pasture. After the first two tops there was a superb one-kilometre arete on good rock but often exposed. From the third top, the next was a false summit, which I bypassed on the right. I was using Chris's GPS track, which kept pretty level. The crux seemed to be a delicate and exposed section of steep grass. A steep ascent with a little scrambling then led up to an old cairn. It was a superb situation, with great views.

I almost returned over the false summit, but that section looked pretty messy. Chris's route down via Pegasus Creek didn't sound good so I retraced my outward route. It was warm and I was glad that my stashed can of fizzy drink had stayed cool. I didn't take the best line down through the forest, but was back at the vehicle in good time. With many wildfires around, I wasn't keen to spend a second night in this remote spot, so I drove back to the main (unpaved) road before sleeping.

Mount Odin, NA131
Rob Woodall, August 2017

Mount Odin is an obscure but impressive peak. The only ascents I was aware of had taken five or six days. I wasn't confident about keeping my food safe from bears for that long and was not an enthusiastic camper, so I decided to try to climb it in a long day from Big Peter Lake, which had a serviced camping ground with a bear-proof food hanger. I hiked in and made an afternoon diversion to Mount Fosthall (P600).

The next morning I started at first light and followed the route taken by previous parties. It was quite complex, linking valley systems, with numerous lakes and some rough bush-whacking. At long last there was a view of the peak and a choice of a glacier crossing or a scrambly rim. I chose the scramble, over an impressive ridge with several pinnacles.

By the time I reached the summit I was two hours past my turn-around time and resigned to finishing the walk in the dark. On the way back I gambled on a shortcut, a steep slope of stable grippy boulders, making for a rapid descent. Across the creek, the ascent was initially straightforward but then ran into cliffs. These held mature trees, and I judged correctly that I could scramble using the trees. A little more scrambling lay ahead, which I managed in the last of the light. My remaining problem was that my phone had failed to pick up satellites at the start so I had no GPS track to follow back, and the forest and water features weren't shown well on my digital mapping. This wasted an hour, but I made it back. It's sometimes said that you make your own luck, usually by those who have had lucky escapes rather than unlucky accidents. It doesn't do to push your luck too much. On this occasion I was lucky, and Mount Odin had been well worth the effort.

NA131 Columbia Mountains

Id	Height	Name	Drop	Country	Location
31501	3516	Mount Sir Wilfrid Laurier	2728	Canada	52.8016, -119.7315
31502	3519	Mount Sir Sandford	2703	Canada	51.6566, -117.8677
31504	2971	Mount Odin	2410	Canada	50.5518, -118.1294
31505	3274	Mount Monashee	2401	Canada	52.3853, -118.9400
31506	3094	Mount Cooper	2319	Canada	50.1797, -117.1991
31509	3493	Mount Farnham	2161	Canada	50.4889, -116.4872
31510	2830	Gladsheim Peak	2063	Canada	49.7867, -117.6272
31511	3377	Mount Dawson	2002	Canada	51.1516, -117.4205

31517	2456	Kootenay Mountain	1801	Canada	49.2407, -116.8226
31524	2801	Cond Peak	1716	Canada	49.7461, -117.1416
31525	2301	Pukeashun Mountain	1696	Canada	51.2047, -119.2356
31527	2245	Morton Peak	1690	Canada	50.7656, -118.8431
31530	2573	The Pinnacles	1667	Canada	50.1953, -118.2290
31535	2330	Upper Saddle Mountain	1645	Canada	50.1726, -117.9000
31540	2227	Abercrombie Mountain	1580	USA-WA	48.9283, -117.4598
31543	2543	Kaza Mountain	1573	Canada	53.0712, -121.0090
31548	2636	Dunn Peak	1531	Canada	51.4373, -119.9547
31555	2577	Trophy Mountain	1473	Canada	51.7993, -119.8759
31560	3045	Albert Peak	1459	Canada	51.0380, -117.8507
31561	3236	Iconoclast Mountain	1453	Canada	51.4545, -117.7594
31562	2176	Copper Butte	1444	USA-WA	48.7026, -118.4658
31564	3169	Mount Rogers	1439	Canada	51.3553, -117.5436
31566	2555	Probity Peak	1427	Canada	51.2849, -118.7307
31569	3038	Quanstrom Peak	1406	Canada	52.9348, -120.1681
31572	3201	Neptune Peak	1395	Canada	51.8751, -118.1367
31579	2843	Gold Peak	1385	Canada	51.7308, -119.0031
31580	2320	Siwash Mountain	1380	Canada	49.3533, -117.4508
31581	2964	Chevron Peak	1376	Canada	53.1617, -120.2495
31586	2371	Mount Ferrie	1363	Canada	50.1862, -117.5556
31587	2496	Capra Peak	1363	Canada	53.4641, -120.8248
31591	2937	Cougar Peak	1354	Canada	51.3059, -118.5280
31592	2348	Northwest Peak	1353	USA-MT	48.9640, -115.9680
31594	2090	Perry Peak	1352	Canada	49.6042, -117.6594
31596	2212	Mount Ingersoll	1349	Canada	50.0461, -117.9915
31597	1889	Silver Star Mountain	1348	Canada	50.3696, -119.0636
31603	2454	Mount Marion	1329	Canada	50.2189, -115.9728
31605	2462	Dunster Peak	1322	Canada	53.0565, -119.8193
31606	3094	Mount Moloch	1314	Canada	51.3382, -117.9422
31612	3205	Hallam Peak	1304	Canada	52.1808, -118.7613
31615	3412	Howser Spire	1299	Canada	50.7296, -116.8136
31617	2176	Mount Thompson	1286	Canada	49.0656, -116.3858
31618	2365	Ford Peak	1285	Canada	53.2246, -121.0906
31620	1726	Shuswap Mountain	1280	Canada	50.8431, -119.1761
31635	2065	Moses Mountain	1260	USA-WA	48.3718, -119.0612
31639	2881	Gordon Horne Peak	1253	Canada	51.7761, -118.8208
31646	1956	Mount Kelly	1240	Canada	49.1492, -117.4397
31657	2693	Vixen Peak	1213	Canada	53.1730, -120.7708
31672	2419	Mount Tanner	1184	Canada	49.6560, -118.5875
31674	2299	Mount Grohman	1183	Canada	49.6247, -117.3211
31679	1775	Huckleberry Mountain	1178	USA-WA	48.2111, -117.9774

31687	2367	Mount Allen	1153	Canada	50.0832, -115.9243
31688	2376	Old Glory Mountain	1151	Canada	49.1497, -117.9125
31691	2918	Mount Lunn	1147	Canada	52.9938, -120.4522
31700	2298	Robinson Mountain	1138	USA-MT	48.9671, -115.4121
31702	2487	Tsuius Mountain	1133	Canada	50.7041, -118.4222
31705	2762	Metis Peak	1130	Canada	52.5256, -119.6181
31717	3032	Pancake Peak	1118	Canada	52.2719, -118.8610
31720	2315	Big White Mountain	1115	Canada	49.7343, -118.9353
31729	2089	Calispell Peak	1107	USA-WA	48.4369, -117.5027
31731	1925	Blomley Peak	1105	Canada	51.2617, -119.6764
31739	2930	Mount Goodall	1098	Canada	52.7773, -120.0905
31744	2309	Baldy Mountain	1092	Canada	49.1661, -119.2542
31753	1573	Mount Ida East	1084	Canada	50.6400, -119.2772
31758	2212	Mount Bonaparte	1078	USA-WA	48.7854, -119.1222
31761	1663	Sentinel Mountain	1072	Canada	49.3792, -117.6156
31763	1793	Mount Spokane	1067	USA-WA	47.9237, -117.1121
31772	3035	Carnes Peak	1052	Canada	51.3453, -118.1116
31775	2544	Dasher Peak	1048	Canada	53.2349, -120.6720
31782	3181	Mount Findlay	1042	Canada	50.0819, -116.4950
31789	3074	Mount Templeman	1032	Canada	50.6897, -117.2050
31793	3176	Mount Ethelbert	1027	Canada	50.7761, -116.5444
31799	2351	South Selkirk Crest	1022	USA-ID	48.8457, -116.5544
31805	2838	Dogtooth Peak	1019	Canada	51.2936, -117.2243
31806	2206	Mount Baker	1019	Canada	49.4590, -115.6306
31818	2164	Groundhog Mountain	1008	Canada	51.8756, -119.2152
31822	2809	Blanket Mountain	1002	Canada	50.7581, -118.2281
31824	2680	Mount Darling	1000	Canada	50.9056, -117.7703

Mount Farnham, NA131

Rob Woodall, August 2017 and August 2023

Canada has over 930 Ribus, more than any other country and around 13% of the world total. Maybe one hundred are straightforward, including twenty Ultras. The remainder are difficult or remote or both. The Rockies have some inviting peaks and a few unstable ones. To their west the Purcells have some excellent rock, for instance the Bugaboo Spires. The highest point of the range, Mount Farnham, seems feasible but has plenty of steep, loose ground and some very brittle limestone, as Greg Slayden and I discovered in 2017. We had managed to find the start of the trail the previous evening, and next morning an early start helped us reach a small tarn in a couple of hours. This was surrounded by unfriendly steep ground. We understood that the alternatives were the south ridge (which looked complicated), a gully in the west face (but which one?) or a climb to the west col followed by a couloir. The third option seemed well defined so we chose that, but the gully leading up to the col was steep and loose. We escaped from it to the left and soon needed to use the rope, burning some valuable time.

Crossing to the right we found some decent scrambling, although we didn't fancy descending that way. Reaching the col, we enjoyed a steep and slabby scramble then a disturbingly brittle cliff. We gingerly traversed left below it, above steep scree, and found the key couloir leading to the summit, but it was filled with hard ice. We had no ice screws and could not climb it, so we retraced our steps across the top of the scree and found a steep gully that looked promising. However, we were up against our turn-around time and we had no decent descent route. While we were peering down a steep but solid-looking gully, a large rock detached itself from the brittle rock face and clattered down the gully. It would have killed us had we been down there. Returning the way we came seemed the least worst option. The slabby scramble was all right but the gully below was terrible. Descending into the start of it, Greg was left teetering on not much when a boulder he was about to stand on gave way. Getting across it, we discovered the scramble we had ascended wasn't so bad after all, and we made it down to the road before nightfall.

Amazingly, we found an online account of someone who had made a guided ascent the previous day. I tracked down the guide, Kirk, and he helped me up the peak in 2023. We ascended a nice and solid west-face gully then followed a short section of the south ridge to the summit. A couple of abseils brought us back down the gully. As we descended towards the little tarn, in a kind of replay from six years earlier, a large boulder detached itself from a cliff face and headed for the tarn. Keeping safely out of the fall line we made our way back to the vehicle after an exciting ten-hour day.

Canadian wildfires
Rob Woodall

Wildfires have been an increasing problem in the ten years I've been visiting Canada. On Golden Hinde on Vancouver Island we could barely see five miles, while Rugged Mountain was inaccessible. On Mount Assiniboine the sun was orange through a veil of smoke. Access to Mount Harrison involved a 100-kilometre detour due to a road closure. In 2023 on Blomley Peak I had to change my ascent route due to a fire. That afternoon my phone was pinged with an *Evacuate Immediately* message, but I had been on the safe side of the peak, and was miles away, on my next Ribu.

Around Lillooet there was smoke all the time I was there, compounded by low cloud. Shulaps Peak was inaccessible. The Peakbagger phone app provided easy access to the Active Fire Layer data and this was a big help with planning. On one peak I was quickly able to ascertain that the smoke which suddenly appeared on my route was from a fire that had started that morning. It was a few miles away and didn't endanger my hike, other than the smoke, which wasn't dense.

I have very much appreciated the courtesy of fire fighters, whether at road blocks or when responding to queries initiated via contact details available via the Fire Layer site. There are usually other peaks available nearby, and having to change one's plans is a very minor thing compared with the horror facing those having to leave their homes.

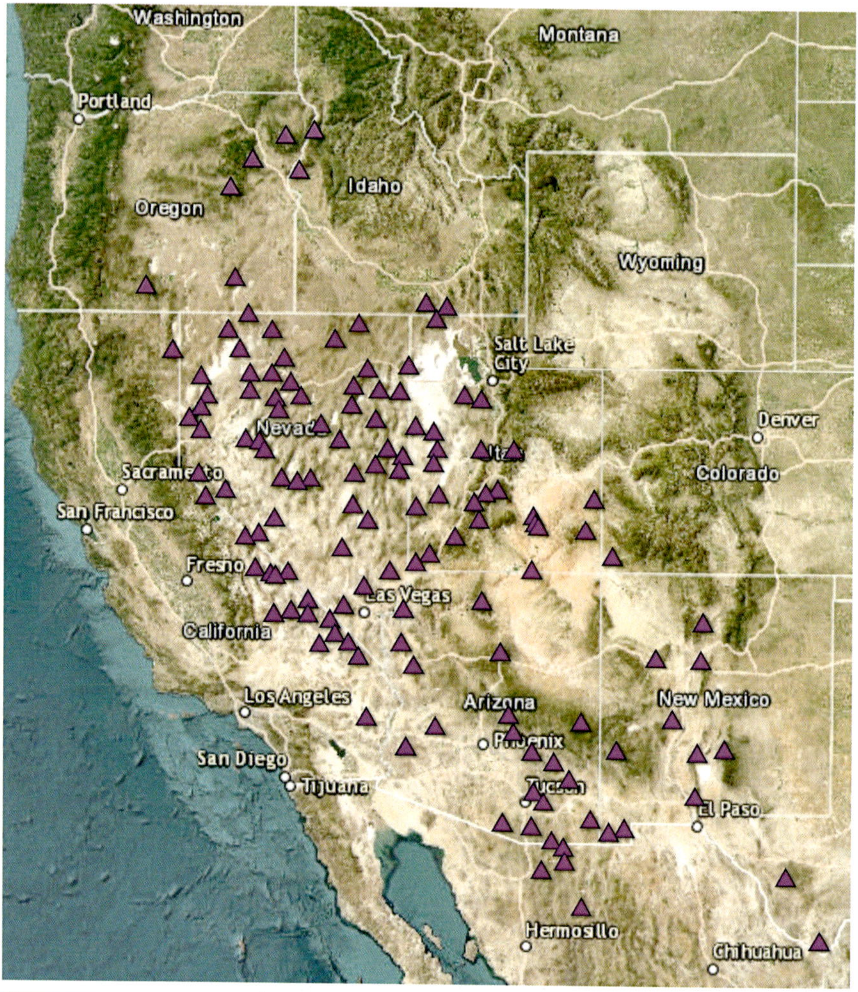

White Mountain Peak, NA133 (Deividas Valaitis)

NA132 Columbia Plateau

Id	Height	Name	Drop	Country	Location
31512	2999	Sacajawea Peak	1947	USA-OR	45.2450, -117.2929
31539	2861	She Devil	1584	USA-ID	45.3240, -116.5412
31588	2776	Rock Creek Butte	1360	USA-OR	44.8168, -118.1039
31642	2760	Strawberry Mountain	1249	USA-OR	44.3119, -118.7164
31776	2313	Sturgill Peak	1047	USA-ID	44.6200, -116.9434

NA133 Great Basin Ranges

Id	Height	Name	Drop	Country	Location
31503	3632	Charleston Peak	2518	USA-NV	36.2716, -115.6956
31507	3982	Wheeler Peak	2306	USA-NW	38.9858, -114.3139
31508	4344	White Mountain Peak	2195	USA-CA	37.6342, -118.2557
31514	3367	Telescope Peak	1899	USA-CA	36.1699, -117.0892
31519	3640	Mount Jefferson	1790	USA-NV	38.7519, -116.9267
31521	3362	Deseret Peak	1771	USA-UT	40.4595, -112.6264
31522	3266	Pilot Peak	1745	USA-NV	41.0212, -114.0774
31532	3021	Hayford Peak	1652	USA-NV	36.6578, -115.2008
31533	3622	North Schell Peak	1650	USA-NV	39.4132, -114.5999
31534	2998	Star Peak	1646	USA-NV	40.5225, -118.1709
31536	3237	Flat Top Mountain	1640	USA-UT	40.3725, -112.1889
31537	3684	Ibapah Peak	1608	USA-UT	39.8282, -113.9200
31538	3588	Arc Dome	1593	USA-NV	38.8328, -117.3531
31551	3678	Mount Moriah	1496	USA-NV	39.2733, -114.1988
31553	2772	Quinn Peak	1482	USA-NV	41.3033, -118.4164
31554	3446	Hole In The Mountain Peak	1478	USA-NV	40.9508, -115.1224
31556	2979	Mount Tobin	1472	USA-NV	40.3765, -117.5262
31557	3471	Ruby Dome	1469	USA-NV	40.6218, -115.4756
31559	3444	Troy Peak	1460	USA-NV	38.3194, -115.5019
31567	3303	Matterhorn	1426	USA-NV	41.8107, -115.3745
31574	3509	Currant Mountain	1394	USA-NV	38.9097, -115.4247
31576	2663	Grapevine Peak	1388	USA-NV	36.9652, -117.1497
31582	2947	Swasey Peak	1376	USA-UT	39.3881, -113.3164
31583	3159	Signal Peak	1371	USA-UT	37.3197, -113.4922
31584	3151	Cache Peak	1369	USA-ID	42.1856, -113.6612
31598	2966	Granite Peak	1340	USA-NV	41.6680, -117.5893
31599	2967	Steens Mountain	1338	USA-OR	42.6358, -118.5764
31601	3038	Mount Augusta	1332	USA-NV	39.5401, -117.9195
31602	3015	Eagle Peak	1329	USA-CA	41.2836, -120.2007
31609	2415	Clark Mountain	1308	USA-CA	35.5257, -115.5887
31610	2950	Mount Lewis	1307	USA-NV	40.4035, -116.8616
31624	3560	Mount Patterson	1268	USA-CA	38.4366, -119.3052

31625	3182	McAfee Peak	1268	USA-NV	41.5218, -115.9733
31632	2874	Duffer Peak	1262	USA-NV	41.6574, -118.7322
31644	2864	Black Pine Mountains Peak *	1245	USA-ID	42.1387, -113.1256
31645	2880	Piper Peak	1244	USA-NV	37.7044, -117.9089
31647	2260	Mormon Peak	1231	USA-NV	36.9740, -114.5006
31650	2944	Frisco Peak	1225	USA-UT	38.5202, -113.2876
31656	2729	Tin Mountain	1218	USA-CA	36.8867, -117.4562
31659	3392	Waucoba Mountain	1207	USA-CA	37.0218, -118.0079
31660	3445	Mount Grant	1205	USA-NV	38.5686, -118.7911
31661	3128	Spruce Mountain	1202	USA-NV	40.5521, -114.8218
31667	2678	Job Peak	1191	USA-NV	39.5832, -118.2355
31669	2864	Sonoma Peak	1189	USA-NV	40.8605, -117.6071
31684	2776	Lone Mountain	1161	USA-NV	38.0245, -117.4941
31692	3029	Bull Mountain	1146	USA-UT	41.9108, -113.3658
31695	2849	Bald Mountain	1142	USA-NV	37.4496, -115.7337
31697	2236	Kingston Peak	1140	USA-CA	35.7267, -115.9156
31699	3207	Cherry Creek Benchmark	1138	USA-NV	39.9662, -114.8958
31703	2960	Fool Creek Peak	1131	USA-UT	39.3926, -112.2071
31704	2043	Pyramid Peak	1130	USA-CA	36.3919, -116.6122
31706	2929	Goshute Peak	1129	USA-NV	40.4995, -114.2956
31711	3333	Ward Mountain	1125	USA-NV	39.1001, -114.9206
31712	2510	Kumiva Peak	1123	USA-NV	40.4062, -119.2632
31719	3319	Table Mountain	1116	USA-NV	38.8118, -116.5882
31721	2550	Virginia Peak	1115	USA-NV	39.7557, -119.4612
31722	2694	Maturango Peak	1114	USA-CA	36.1200, -117.4956
31725	2984	Indian Peak	1113	USA-UT	38.2670, -113.8753
31726	2341	West Mountain Peak	1111	USA-UT	37.1552, -113.8832
31732	2598	George H Hansen Peak	1104	USA-UT	39.7253, -113.4402
31736	3306	Pearl Peak	1099	USA-NV	40.2351, -115.5406
31738	2644	Dry Mountain	1098	USA-CA	36.9088, -117.5981
31740	3235	Diamond Peak	1095	USA-NV	39.5849, -115.8186
31745	1949	Nopah Range Peak *	1091	USA-CA	36.0064, -116.0806
31746	3089	Roberts Creek Mountain	1090	USA-NV	39.8699, -116.3107
31749	2645	Adam Peak	1089	USA-NV	41.1607, -117.3054
31755	2593	Orevada View Benchmark	1082	USA-NV	41.9793, -118.2232
31756	3040	Desatoya Peak	1081	USA-NV	39.3651, -117.7589
31760	2636	Mount Moses	1076	USA-NV	40.1471, -117.4156
31762	2494	Tohakum Peak	1070	USA-NV	40.1793, -119.4552
31767	2881	Mount Siegel	1060	USA-NV	38.8896, -119.5022
31768	2737	Granite Peak	1057	USA-NV	40.7911, -119.4333
31774	2551	Gearhart Mountain	1049	USA-OR	42.4961, -120.8774
31778	2659	Tule Peak	1045	USA-NV	39.9759, -119.7442
31786	2943	Notch Peak	1041	USA-UT	39.1432, -113.4093

Id	Height	Name	Drop	Country	Location
31807	2623	Seaman Range Peak *	1017	USA-NV	37.9807, -115.1016
31808	1946	Funeral Peak	1017	USA-CA	36.1031, -116.6238
31809	2296	New York Mountains Peak *	1015	USA-CA	35.2587, -115.3112
31810	2606	North Peak	1015	USA-NV	40.6750, -117.1325
31811	1325	Granite Mountain	1015	USA-CA	33.9702, -115.0729
31812	1756	Jumbo Peak	1014	USA-NV	36.2065, -114.1809
31814	2311	Eugene Mountains Peak *	1013	USA-NV	40.8361, -118.1851
31820	1876	Avawatz Peak	1005	USA-CA	35.5128, -116.3317

NA134 Colorado Plateau

Id	Height	Name	Drop	Country	Location
31515	3877	Mount Peale	1881	USA-UT	38.4384, -109.2293
31516	3851	Humphreys Peak	1841	USA-AZ	35.3464, -111.6780
31520	3512	Mount Ellen	1781	USA-UT	38.1090, -110.8136
31563	3476	Mount Baldy	1442	USA-AZ	33.9059, -109.5627
31565	3709	Delano Peak	1439	USA-UT	38.3692, -112.3715
31577	3463	Abajo Peak	1387	USA-UT	37.8394, -109.4625
31611	3524	Chicoma Mountain	1304	USA-NM	36.0074, -106.3846
31616	3153	Navajo Mountain	1290	USA-UT	37.0343, -110.8697
31627	3546	Fish Lake Hightop	1266	USA-UT	38.6081, -111.7394
31638	3423	Monroe Peak	1255	USA-UT	38.5361, -112.0734
31643	3445	Mount Taylor	1248	USA-NM	35.2387, -107.6085
31651	3042	Ute Peak	1225	USA-CO	37.2840, -108.7786
31689	3446	Brian Head	1150	USA-UT	37.6813, -112.8311
31737	3478	Mount Pennell	1098	USA-UT	37.9565, -110.7908
31741	2807	Kaibab Plateau Peak *	1094	USA-AZ	36.3958, -112.1510
31783	3365	Mount Dutton	1042	USA-UT	38.0203, -112.2168
31791	3440	South Tent Mountain	1029	USA-UT	39.3921, -111.3576
31796	3273	Mount Hillers	1024	USA-UT	37.8874, -110.6970

NA135 South-west Basins and Ranges

Id	Height	Name	Drop	Country	Location
31513	3267	Mount Graham	1925	USA-AZ	32.7016, -109.8714
31526	3649	Sierra Blanca Peak	1691	USA-NM	33.3743, -105.8088
31541	2791	Mount Lemmon	1577	USA-AZ	32.4430, -110.7885
31544	2975	Chiricahua Peak	1567	USA-AZ	31.8456, -109.2910
31549	2885	Miller Peak	1526	USA-AZ	31.3929, -110.2930
31570	2641	Mica Mountain	1404	USA-AZ	32.2199, -110.5434
31571	2881	Mount Wrightson	1400	USA-AZ	31.6962, -110.8481
31585	2385	Emory Peak	1367	USA-TX	29.2460, -103.3053
31590	2566	Hualapai Peak	1354	USA-AZ	35.0752, -113.8979
31619	2357	Baboquivari Peak	1281	USA-AZ	31.7711, -111.5958

31640	3255	Sandia Crest	1253	USA-NM	35.2101, -106.4495
31641	2393	Pinal Peak	1252	USA-AZ	33.2824, -110.8213
31658	2409	Mazatzal Peak	1209	USA-AZ	34.0626, -111.4615
31663	2554	Baldy Peak / Mount Livermore	1195	USA-TX	30.6357, -104.1737
31676	2620	Cerro Las Flores	1180	Mexico	30.9289, -109.9566
31683	3287	South Baldy	1161	USA-NM	33.9911, -107.1880
31696	2739	Organ Needle	1141	USA-NM	32.3453, -106.5620
31708	2548	Big Hatchet Peak	1128	USA-NM	31.6356, -108.3990
31727	2179	Mount Tipton	1111	USA-AZ	35.5389, -114.1929
31734	2733	Salinas Peak	1102	USA-NM	33.2985, -106.5316
31751	2524	Mount Turnbull	1086	USA-AZ	33.0740, -110.2610
31754	3321	Whitewater Baldy	1082	USA-NM	33.3239, -108.6423
31759	2360	Cerro San José	1077	Mexico	29.9452, -109.5247
31766	1487	Signal Peak	1061	USA-AZ	33.3593, -114.0828
31769	1732	Harquahala Mountain	1056	USA-AZ	33.8119, -113.3469
31802	2440	Cerro Azul	1020	Mexico	30.7400, -110.5729
31815	2611	Animas Mountains Peak *	1011	USA-NM	31.5697, -108.7890
31817	2334	Browns Peak	1009	USA-AZ	33.6842, -111.3257
31823	2540	Sierra San José	1000	Mexico	31.2574, -109.9898

Ribus of the Contiguous US States
Rob Woodall

The USA has over 640 Ribus. About half of them are in Alaska and most these are difficult to reach and difficult to climb. A handful are in Hawaii. Most of the remainder, in the Lower 48 States (also known as Contiguous US, or ConUS) are accessible and feasible. They include 57 Ultras, which make a good challenge for keen hikers and climbers. Bob Packard was the first to climb them all, and by 2023 at least twenty others had done so.

Many of these 57 can be climbed in day hikes with few formalities, but some require permits. In a few cases, such as Mount Whitney and Mount Cleveland, permits can be hard to obtain. Some peaks, such as Mount Olympus and Gannet Peak, are multi-day outings and involve glacier travel. Grand Teton involves low-grade rock climbing. Scenery varies from the rugged alpine peaks of Washington to the colourful desert peaks of Nevada. Three peaks on the outskirts of Los Angeles are close enough to be linked on foot by a 24-hour challenge route, though two of the ascents can be eased by using a cable car. There are just two Ultras in the eastern USA – forested Mount Mitchell in North Carolina and Mount Washington in New Hampshire, which can be reached by car or train or a variety of hiking routes. There used to be a 58th Ultra until Mount Saint Helens lost 300 metres of its elevation in the catastrophic eruption of May 1989. Two people who climbed it before then are known to have climbed the full set of 58.

A further 85 of the Ribus in the Contiguous US have over 4000 feet of prominence (1219 metres), including classic peaks such as Ruby Dome in Nevada and tough peaks in the north-west such as Jack Mountain. Edward Earl was the first person to climb all these, and at least three others have done so. The full set of Ribus in the Contiguous US would present quite a challenge, but climbers based in the USA tend to be more focused on peaks with 3000 feet of prominence (914 metres) rather than 1000 metres.

NA14 Rocky Mountains

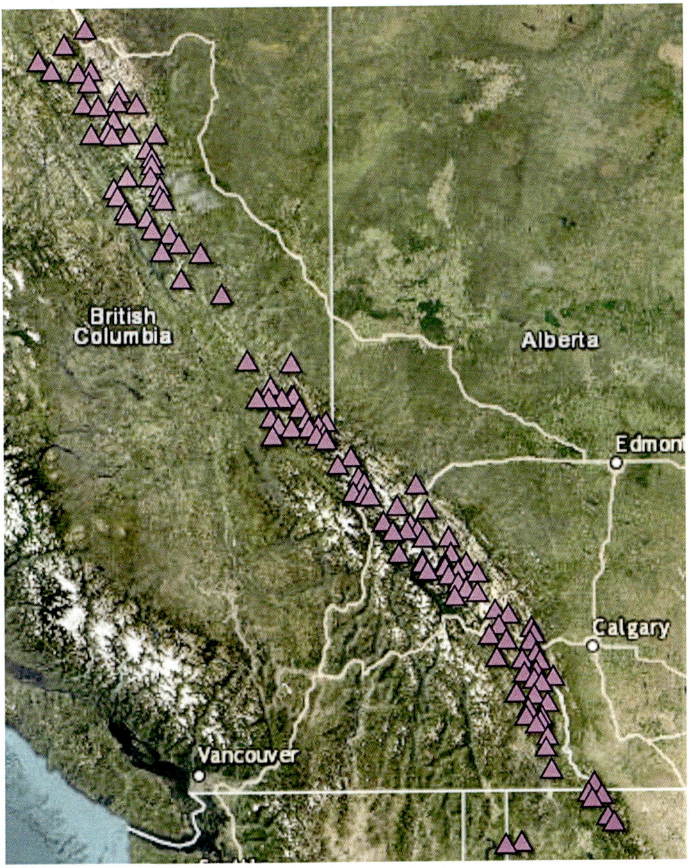

Garfield Mountain, NA143 (Rob Woodall)

NA140 Far Northern Rockies

Id	Height	Name	Drop	Country	Location
32004	3024	Ulysses Mountain	2299	Canada	57.3463, -124.0928
32029	2949	Mount Ovington	1600	Canada	54.1433, -120.5740
32032	2940	Mount Sylvia	1559	Canada	58.0820, -124.4686
32033	2429	Mount Crysdale	1554	Canada	55.9384, -123.4209
32035	2533	Gataga Peak	1515	Canada	58.0697, -125.7009
32043	2513	Sentinel Peak	1453	Canada	54.9080, -121.9608
32049	2785	Muskwa Peak	1374	Canada	57.7393, -124.6285
32050	2661	Limestone Peak	1362	Canada	54.4496, -120.9359
32058	2274	Deserters Peak	1325	Canada	56.9680, -124.9052
32060	2316	Brownie Mountain	1304	Canada	58.5905, -126.7536
32063	2678	Mount Kenny	1293	Canada	56.9258, -123.8178
32064	2384	Nonda Peak	1284	Canada	58.9514, -125.6453
32065	2095	Longworth Peak	1283	Canada	53.9283, -121.3575
32066	2470	Mount Vreeland	1280	Canada	54.5692, -121.4323
32070	2337	Ice Mountain	1267	Canada	54.4145, -121.1508
32083	2751	Toad Peak	1229	Canada	58.3278, -125.5594
32095	2938	Mount Lloyd George	1204	Canada	57.8958, -124.9980
32096	2899	Campobasso Mountain	1204	Canada	58.0911, -124.8792
32097	2032	McGregor Range	1202	Canada	54.0528, -121.2503
32101	2346	Gauvreau Peak *	1186	Canada	56.2808, -123.8794
32102	2299	Mount McCullagh South	1183	Canada	54.0389, -120.9481
32105	2574	Sikanni Chief	1175	Canada	57.2179, -124.1339
32107	2592	Mount McCusker	1168	Canada	57.0814, -123.9256
32110	2320	Blue Light Mountain *	1159	Canada	57.7039, -125.0344
32113	2506	Cloudmaker Mountain	1154	Canada	57.7607, -125.0939
32132	2076	Emerslund Peak	1121	Canada	56.2770, -123.0086
32134	2072	Chowika Mountain	1118	Canada	56.7485, -124.6605
32135	2278	Lafferty Peak *	1118	Canada	56.5682, -124.0846
32138	2127	Mount Monteith	1113	Canada	55.7434, -122.5085
32139	1974	Mount Charles	1112	Canada	54.1514, -121.4225
32142	2952	Great Snow Mountain	1101	Canada	57.4494, -124.0989
32146	2559	Mount Hanington	1088	Canada	54.1234, -120.1670
32149	2596	Weaver Peak	1083	Canada	54.4317, -120.9001
32153	2138	Split Top Ridge *	1078	Canada	58.4814, -126.4375
32155	2267	Ospika Peak *	1077	Canada	56.6939, -124.2439
32157	2028	Deserters Range	1071	Canada	56.7933, -124.7047
32158	1831	Mount Kenchuse	1069	Canada	54.4106, -121.7242
32161	2663	Crehan Peak *	1064	Canada	57.7239, -124.0169
32163	2030	Akie Mountain	1062	Canada	57.0689, -124.9925

Id	Height	Name	Drop	Country	Location
32165	2899	Keily Peak *	1060	Canada	57.5353, -124.2189
32169	2863	Dieppe Mountain	1054	Canada	58.4756, -125.4861
32172	2027	Roman Mountain	1043	Canada	54.8756, -120.9533
32174	2461	Otelsas Peak *	1043	Canada	58.7758, -126.1114
32176	2853	King Peak	1041	Canada	58.2239, -124.8567
32177	1965	Overland Peak	1040	Canada	54.4109, -121.4776
32183	2456	Aley Peak	1033	Canada	56.5200, -123.7058
32184	2108	Warneford Peak	1033	Canada	57.7164, -125.5294
32186	2432	Nabesche Peak *	1026	Canada	56.3808, -123.4883
32187	2678	Weissener Peak *	1023	Canada	58.0606, -125.3403
32193	2499	Mount Knudsen	1009	Canada	54.2844, -120.7506
32197	2505	Sidenius Peak *	1005	Canada	56.9744, -123.9131
32198	2339	Pesika Peak *	1003	Canada	57.2164, -124.6875
32200	2425	Gray Green Mountain *	1003	Canada	58.4453, -125.8175

NA141 Canadian Rockies

Id	Height	Name	Drop	Country	Location
32001	3959	Mount Robson	2829	Canada	53.1106, -119.1567
32003	3741	Mount Columbia	2383	Canada	52.1473, -117.4415
32007	3616	Mount Assiniboine	2082	Canada	50.8703, -115.6517
32008	3363	Mount Edith Cavell	2023	Canada	52.6670, -118.0539
32011	3567	Mount Goodsir	1925	Canada	51.2022, -116.3981
32013	3360	Mount Harrison	1778	Canada	50.0605, -115.2058
32014	3275	Mount Sir Alexander	1762	Canada	53.9360, -120.3867
32015	3394	Mount Hector	1759	Canada	51.5750, -116.2593
32016	3399	Whitehorn Mountain	1747	Canada	53.1369, -119.2669
32017	3316	Mount Chown	1746	Canada	53.3964, -119.4178
32022	3089	Jeannette Peak	1657	Canada	52.6358, -118.6175
32025	3617	Mount Forbes	1629	Canada	51.8603, -116.9319
32027	3361	Mount Fryatt	1608	Canada	52.5503, -117.9104
32031	3230	Mount Ida	1560	Canada	54.0581, -120.3275
32034	3545	Mount Temple	1540	Canada	51.3513, -116.2064
32036	3433	Mount Joffre	1505	Canada	50.5285, -115.2067
32037	2739	The Judge	1484	Canada	50.9092, -116.2205
32038	3664	Mount Clemenceau	1484	Canada	52.2474, -117.9579
32039	2633	Blue Knight Peak	1478	Canada	50.1739, -115.5472
32041	2995	Mount Girouard	1467	Canada	51.2364, -115.4033
32045	3120	Old Goat Mountain	1444	Canada	50.9447, -115.3731
32046	3470	Mount Brazeau	1420	Canada	52.5514, -117.3549
32052	3033	Mount Washburn	1343	Canada	49.7839, -115.0902
32055	3225	Mount Rae	1329	Canada	50.6231, -114.9746
32056	3413	Mount King George	1329	Canada	50.5965, -115.4050

32057	2850	Mount Bisaro	1325	Canada	49.6081, -115.1347
32067	3099	Karluk Peak	1279	Canada	52.3585, -118.4832
32068	2972	Mount Rundle	1277	Canada	51.1246, -115.4692
32069	2804	Sirdar Mountain	1274	Canada	52.9269, -117.8117
32071	3500	Mount Bryce	1264	Canada	52.0411, -117.3303
32072	3417	Tsar Mountain	1253	Canada	52.0964, -117.8067
32075	3313	Mount Mike	1245	Canada	50.0067, -115.2674
32079	3315	Mount St. Bride	1235	Canada	51.5078, -115.9554
32081	2430	Mount Broadwood	1233	Canada	49.2975, -114.9906
32085	3295	Howse Peak	1226	Canada	51.8137, -116.6814
32088	2643	Mount Aeolus	1223	Canada	53.2696, -118.0720
32089	3120	Mount Galatea	1220	Canada	50.8398, -115.2737
32093	2963	Mount Gagnebin	1213	Canada	49.9543, -115.3475
32094	2688	Indian Head Mountain	1205	Canada	50.3968, -115.7840
32099	3361	Mount Cline	1196	Canada	52.0700, -116.6836
32103	2736	Mount Buchanan	1183	Canada	53.8878, -120.1325
32106	3313	Simon Peak / Mount Fraser	1173	Canada	52.6566, -118.3190
32117	3312	Mount Stewart	1145	Canada	52.2196, -116.9449
32120	2823	Millstone Peak	1139	Canada	50.6735, -115.6314
32121	3411	Mount Sir Douglas	1136	Canada	50.7223, -115.3390
32123	2977	Celtic Peak	1133	Canada	53.1796, -119.5396
32125	3162	Mount Aylmer	1132	Canada	51.3238, -115.4335
32126	2870	Franklin Peak	1129	Canada	50.3794, -115.4054
32128	3294	Mount Ball	1126	Canada	51.1562, -116.0065
32129	3086	Majestic Mountain	1126	Canada	52.7574, -118.2156
32133	2804	Siberia Peak	1121	Canada	52.7753, -118.8378
32143	2650	Mount Pauline	1100	Canada	53.5352, -119.8991
32144	3362	Tusk Peak	1093	Canada	52.2081, -117.9381
32145	2966	Derr Peak	1093	Canada	52.9833, -118.5278
32150	2856	Kisano Mountain	1083	Canada	54.0318, -120.5382
32154	3498	Mount Lyell – Ernest Peak	1078	Canada	51.9567, -117.1039
32160	2689	Devout Peak	1064	Canada	53.2949, -119.2872
32162	3342	Mount Saskatchewan	1063	Canada	52.0999, -117.0980
32164	3002	Mount Hornickel	1062	Canada	50.2569, -115.0955
32168	2633	Wishaw Mountain	1055	Canada	53.9597, -120.2122
32173	2680	Mount Beechey	1043	Canada	53.6436, -119.5753
32188	2886	Frigate Mountain	1016	Canada	51.7407, -117.1999
32189	3315	Sunwapta Peak	1014	Canada	52.3494, -117.2758
32190	3690	North Twin	1014	Canada	52.2236, -117.4342
32192	2533	Shark Tooth Mountain	1010	Canada	50.0683, -115.5707

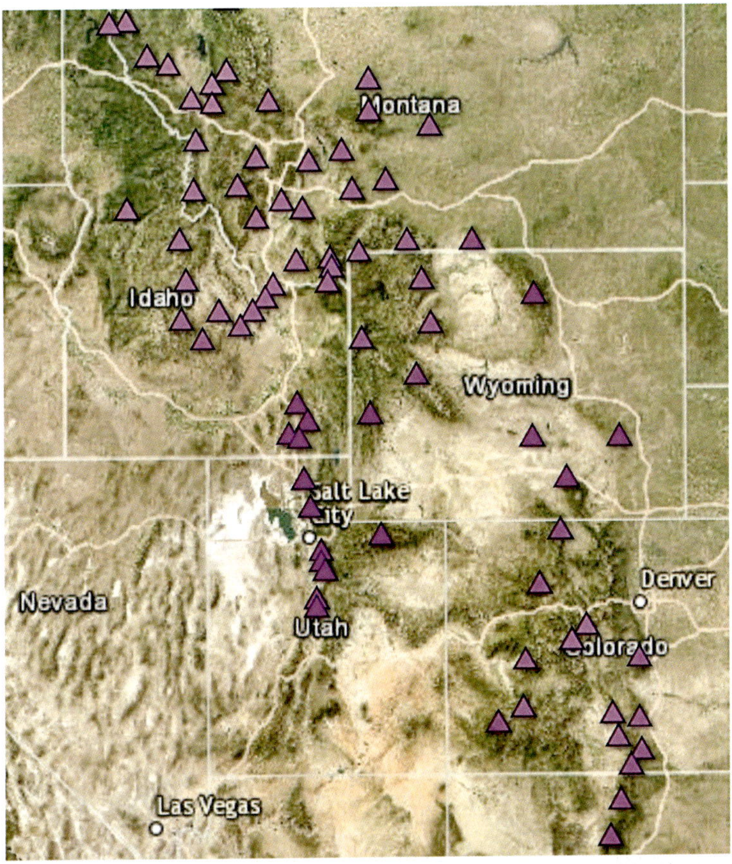

Mount Jefferson, NA143 (Rob Woodall)

NA142 Central Montana Rocky Mountains

Id	Height	Name	Drop	Country	Location
32018	3417	Crazy Peak	1742	USA-MT	46.0182, -110.2768
32019	2993	McDonald Peak	1719	USA-MT	47.3826, -113.9191
32023	2663	Snowshoe Peak	1651	USA-MT	48.2231, -115.6889
32030	3190	Mount Cleveland	1595	USA-MT	48.9246, -113.8481
32047	2138	Scotchman Peak	1419	USA-ID	48.1891, -116.0814
32051	3116	Table Mountain	1348	USA-MT	45.7426, -112.4618
32053	3079	Kintla Peak	1342	USA-MT	48.9437, -114.1714
32054	3091	Mount Stimson	1341	USA-MT	48.5142, -113.6104
32073	2894	Mount Edith	1249	USA-MT	46.4320, -111.1859
32074	2275	Baldy Mountain	1249	USA-MT	47.6214, -114.8247
32077	2646	Greathouse Peak	1237	USA-MT	46.7683, -109.3566
32087	2437	Ch-paa-qn Peak	1225	USA-MT	47.1578, -114.3559
32090	2852	Holland Peak	1220	USA-MT	47.5351, -113.5824
32092	3290	West Goat Peak	1214	USA-MT	45.9626, -113.3950
32098	2941	Sacagawea Peak	1199	USA-MT	45.8958, -110.9685
32100	3232	Hollowtop Mountain	1193	USA-MT	45.6117, -112.0082
32109	2870	Crow Peak	1160	USA-MT	46.2940, -111.9037
32111	3400	Tweedy Mountain	1158	USA-MT	45.4805, -112.9654
32112	2868	Red Mountain	1158	USA-MT	47.1167, -112.7388
32114	2932	Mount Blakiston	1149	Canada	49.0943, -114.0352
32118	2627	McLeod Peak	1144	USA-MT	47.0951, -113.9230
32119	3225	Sunset Peak	1143	USA-MT	44.8560, -112.1468
32122	3099	Mount Powell	1135	USA-MT	46.3499, -112.9797
32124	2264	Mount Headley	1133	USA-MT	47.7398, -115.2637
32141	3015	Rainbow Peak	1108	USA-MT	48.8786, -114.0974
32148	2797	Big Baldy Mountain	1084	USA-MT	46.9684, -110.6064
32179	3064	Mount Jackson	1038	USA-MT	48.6005, -113.7225
32191	2338	Highwood Baldy	1013	USA-MT	47.4423, -110.6309

Mount Cleveland, NA142

Rob Woodall, August 2012

Mount Cleveland is in Montana, just south of the Canadian border. It typically needs at least one night in a tent and permits are notoriously difficult to obtain. Petter and I failed to obtain a camping permit for the standard route via the south ridge, but we were instead offered the Western Bowl as an option. The ranger had, we imagined, never been there, or perhaps he didn't like Europeans. The start was civilised enough, with a ferry ride south from Canada down Waterton Lake, then the US Border officials alighted first so that they could stamp our passports. After two miles on a good trail, we faced a brutal three-hour bush-whack up through steep forest, including downed trees, slide alder and assorted other unfriendly vegetation.

At last we emerged into the Western Bowl, an undeniably fine scenic spot for a wild camp, although I ran into a practical problem when one of my socks, hung outside the tent to air, was missing in the morning. I blamed one of the marmots. Notably it didn't return for a second helping. Luckily I had spare socks.

Next morning Petter and I picked a way up awkward rubbly ledges, relieved to reach the summit plateau. We had no intention of reversing our steep, loose route. Instead we descended the standard south-ridge route, which was superb, and ranks among the finest I'd done anywhere. However, our tents were still in the Western Bowl. After hiking back almost to Waterton Lake we struggled up through the forest for the second time in two days, this time in the dark. Slide alder by head-torch soon lost its appeal, so we slept for a couple of hours in the trees before finishing in daylight, recovering our gear, then racing down to catch the ferry back to Waterton. Twenty-five hours in mountain boots cost me some foot damage, but even so I counted Mount Cleveland among my very best peaks.

NA143 Idaho-Bitterroot Rocky Mountains

Id	Height	Name	Drop	Country	Location
32012	3859	Borah Peak	1823	USA-ID	44.1374, -113.7811
32024	3718	Diamond Peak	1639	USA-ID	44.1417, -113.0827
32040	3660	Hyndman Peak	1474	USA-ID	43.7494, -114.1311
32062	3473	Scott Peak	1295	USA-ID	44.3536, -112.8213
32084	3601	Castle Peak	1227	USA-ID	44.0399, -114.5868
32116	3183	White Mountain West	1148	USA-ID	44.5749, -114.4958
32147	3096	Trapper Peak	1088	USA-MT	45.8898, -114.2978
32152	3073	Mount McGuire	1079	USA-ID	45.1743, -114.6020
32171	3377	South Lost River Peak *	1049	USA-ID	43.9292, -113.3352
32175	2724	Buffalo Hump	1042	USA-ID	45.6204, -115.6992
32180	2922	Saint Joseph Peak	1036	USA-MT	46.6017, -114.2552
32185	3110	Mount Jefferson	1027	USA-ID	44.5620, -111.5048
32199	3341	Garfield Mountain	1003	USA-MT	44.5203, -112.6211

NA144 Greater Yellowstone Rockies

Id	Height	Name	Drop	Country	Location
32005	4013	Cloud Peak	2171	USA-WY	44.3821, -107.1738
32006	4207	Gannett Peak	2156	USA-WY	43.1843, -109.6543
32009	4197	Grand Teton	1992	USA-WY	43.7413, -110.8024
32044	3901	Granite Peak	1450	USA-MT	45.1635, -109.8076
32059	2678	Big Pryor Mountain	1312	USA-MT	45.1606, -108.4694
32076	3449	Hilgard Peak	1238	USA-MT	44.9166, -111.4593
32078	4009	Francs Peak	1236	USA-WY	43.9613, -109.3394
32127	3732	Trout Peak	1126	USA-WY	44.6014, -109.5257
32136	3233	South Sheep Mountain / Sheep Point	1117	USA-MT	44.7632, -111.3906
32181	3343	Electric Peak	1035	USA-MT	45.0053, -110.8376
32196	3059	Ferris Peak	1007	USA-WY	42.2567, -107.2394

NA145 Western Rocky Mountains

Id	Height	Name	Drop	Country	Location
32010	4123	Kings Peak	1955	USA-UT	40.7763, -110.3729
32021	3636	Mount Nebo	1673	USA-UT	39.8219, -111.7604
32028	3581	Mount Timpanogos	1607	USA-UT	40.3909, -111.6461
32082	2837	Oxford Peak	1233	USA-ID	42.2675, -112.0964
32108	2917	Mount Ogden	1161	USA-UT	41.1999, -111.8820
32131	3047	Salt Benchmark	1124	USA-UT	39.6649, -111.7433
32137	3502	Twin Peaks West	1117	USA-UT	40.5518, -111.6567
32140	2794	Sedgwick Peak	1111	USA-ID	42.5158, -111.9234
32151	3468	Wyoming Peak	1080	USA-WY	42.6043, -110.6239
32159	2772	Elkhorn Peak	1066	USA-ID	42.3341, -112.3283
32166	2857	Box Elder Peak	1058	USA-UT	41.6357, -112.0146
32170	3374	Provo Peak	1050	USA-UT	40.2442, -111.5570
32182	2826	Bonneville Peak	1035	USA-ID	42.7633, -112.1411

NA146 Southern Rocky Mountains

Id	Height	Name	Drop	Country	Location
32002	4399	Mount Elbert	2767	USA-CO	39.1178, -106.4453
32020	4301	Pikes Peak	1684	USA-CO	38.8407, -105.0444
32026	4372	Blanca Peak / Sisnaajiní	1623	USA-CO	37.5775, -105.4855
32042	4282	Culebra Peak	1466	USA-CO	37.1223, -105.1857
32048	4357	Crestone Peak	1396	USA-CO	37.9669, -105.5856
32061	4361	Uncompahgre Peak	1303	USA-CO	38.0717, -107.4625
32080	3765	Flat Top Mountain	1234	USA-CO	40.0148, -107.0834
32086	4342	Mount Wilson	1226	USA-CO	37.8392, -107.9917
32091	3993	Truchas Peak	1219	USA-NM	35.9625, -105.6451
32104	4354	Mount Lincoln	1177	USA-CO	39.3515, -106.1115
32115	3763	Greenhorn Mountain	1148	USA-CO	37.8815, -105.0133
32130	4153	West Spanish Peak	1124	USA-CO	37.3756, -104.9934
32156	3877	Mount Gunnison	1076	USA-CO	38.8121, -107.3826
32167	3712	Mount Zirkel	1057	USA-CO	40.8313, -106.6632
32178	4011	Wheeler Peak	1039	USA-NM	36.5569, -105.4170
32194	3131	Laramie Peak	1009	USA-WY	42.2681, -105.4428
32195	3400	Elk Mountain	1008	USA-WY	41.6332, -106.5261

NA15 North America Plains

NA150 Canadian Shield

Canadian Arctic Shores

Id	Height	Name	Drop	Country	Location
32503	1576	Cap Mountain	1357	Canada	63.4064, -123.2061
32507	1470	Mount Clark	1233	Canada	64.4156, -124.2225

Torngat Mountains

Id	Height	Name	Drop	Country	Location
32502	1652	Mount Caubvick / Mont D'Iberville	1367	Canada	58.8873, -63.7127
32504	1568	Tallek Ridge *	1297	Canada	58.9300, -64.0461
32505	1347	Shittamat Peak	1291	Canada	59.5209, -63.9991
32509	1459	Nakvak Peak *	1149	Canada	58.6758, -63.9495
32510	1428	Saglek Peak *	1110	Canada	58.5625, -63.6792
32512	1524	Chasm Peak *	1100	Canada	59.1025, -64.1756
32513	1280	Ryans Peak *	1097	Canada	59.5264, -64.2422
32514	1356	Mount Tetragona	1045	Canada	59.3078, -63.9231
32515	1388	Mount Eliot	1022	Canada	59.1816, -63.8204

There are no Ribus in the Canadian province of Ontario but there is the deepest habitable hole on Earth. SNOLAB is located 2070 metres beneath the surface, which enables scientists to specialise in the study of dark matter and neutrinos. Particle detectors in the Kolar Gold Fields in India were a little deeper but are no longer in use. The Kola Superdeep Borehole in Russia is much deeper but extremely narrow and no longer open (see page 121).

Central and South Labrador

Id	Height	Name	Drop	Country	Location
32508	1230	Brave Mountain	1225	Canada	57.8814, -62.0267

Adirondack Mountains

Id	Height	Name	Drop	Country	Location
32501	1629	Mount Marcy / Tahawus	1502	USA-NY	44.1129, -73.9238

NA151 Great Plains

Id	Height	Name	Drop	Country	Location
32506	2108	Bearpaw Baldy / Baldy Mountain	1288	USA-MT	48.1487, -109.6509
32511	2128	West Butte	1108	USA-MT	48.9317, -111.5324

West Butte, NA151 (Rob Woodall)

Mount Washington, NA161 (Rob Woodall)

NA16 Appalachian Mountains

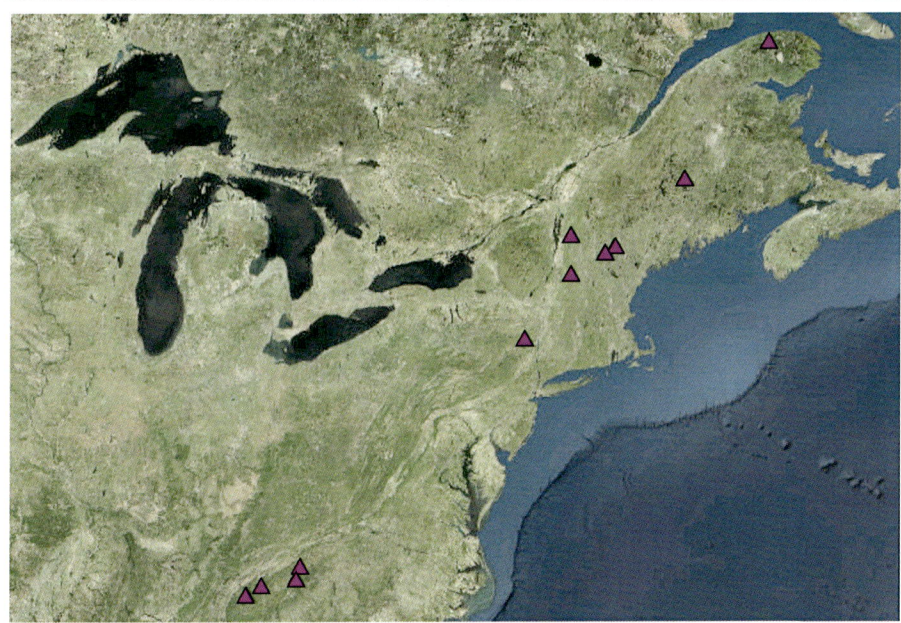

NA160 Canadian Appalachians

Id	Height	Name	Drop	Country	Location
33006	1276	Mont Jacques-Cartier	1096	Canada	48.9875, -65.9484

NA161 Northern USA Appalachians

Id	Height	Name	Drop	Country	Location
33001	1917	Mount Washington / Agiochook	1877	USA-NH	44.2705, -71.3034
33004	1606	Mount Katahdin	1311	USA-ME	45.9044, -68.9214
33005	1339	Mount Mansfield	1109	USA-VT	44.5438, -72.8144
33009	1600	Mount Lafayette	1022	USA-NH	44.1607, -71.6445
33010	1291	Killington Peak	1011	USA-VT	43.6047, -72.8202

NA162 Appalachian Plateaus

Id	Height	Name	Drop	Country	Location
33011	1274	Slide Mountain	1001	USA-NY	41.9991, -74.3860

NA164 Blue Ridge Mountains

Id	Height	Name	Drop	Country	Location
33002	2037	Mount Mitchell	1860	USA-NC	35.7649, -82.2651
33003	2025	Clingmans Dome / Kuwahi	1376	USA-NC/TN	35.5628, -83.4987
33007	1916	Roan High Knob	1072	USA-NC/TN	36.1048, -82.1225
33008	1695	Huckleberry Knob	1036	USA-NC	35.3221, -83.9939

NA17 Central Mexican Ranges

Volcán Iztaccíhuatl, NA174 (Rob Woodall)

NA170 Sierra Madre Occidental

Id	Height	Name	Drop	Country	Location
33534	3357	Cerro Gordo	1378	Mexico	23.2061, -104.9441
33536	2309	Cerro Los Algodones	1348	Mexico	25.8106, -107.6453
33539	1773	Cerro Sierra Alamos *	1314	Mexico	26.9731, -108.9903
33581	3148	Cerro El Toro	1109	Mexico	23.0322, -104.1961
33585	1460	Cerro Enmedio *	1097	Mexico	24.3269, -106.9410
33592	2440	Puerto La Cieneguita Sureste	1080	Mexico	30.5449, -109.1504
33595	2475	Cerro Cumbre de los Metates	1078	Mexico	26.5478, -107.7578
33596	3100	Cerro Alto de Promontorio	1060	Mexico	25.2106, -105.1323
33599	2400	Cerro La Placa	1060	Mexico	29.8444, -109.0276
33600	1920	Cerro El Cobre	1060	Mexico	29.0578, -109.5998
33608	3020	Cerro Los Altares	1040	Mexico	24.5876, -104.2721

NA171 Mexican Plateau

Id	Height	Name	Drop	Country	Location
33509	3020	Sierra La Madera	1890	Mexico	27.0343, -102.3919
33516	3120	Cerro El Centinela	1640	Mexico	25.1361, -103.2304
33526	3366	Cerro El Zamorano	1456	Mexico	20.9336, -100.1804
33537	3440	Cerro El Jabalín	1341	Mexico	25.1900, -101.3775
33544	3260	Cerro El Espolón	1290	Mexico	20.7908, -99.5648
33546	2660	Sierra El Pino	1280	Mexico	28.2574, -103.0620
33551	3160	Cerro La Pingüica	1245	Mexico	21.1600, -99.7005
33555	3174	Cerro Los Pelones	1242	Mexico	24.6441, -101.4666
33558	3180	Cerro Grande	1220	Mexico	23.6669, -100.8873
33560	2420	Sierra Los Organos	1210	Mexico	26.6901, -103.0411
33562	3172	Sierra El Astillero – Cerro El Refugio	1202	Mexico	24.5786, -101.0983
33574	2460	Sierra Mojada	1150	Mexico	27.2592, -103.6871
33575	2500	Cerro de la India	1140	Mexico	25.7894, -103.8054
33590	2400	Pico Norte de Sierra San Marcos *	1085	Mexico	26.7536, -102.0894
33598	2820	Cerro Santa Elena	1060	Mexico	25.6459, -103.9082
33606	2830	Cerro de Culiacán	1040	Mexico	20.3387, -100.9701
33609	3120	Cerro Agustinos	1030	Mexico	20.2140, -100.6415
33617	2400	Sierra Rica	1011	Mexico	29.1665, -104.1309

NA172 Sierra Madre Oriental

Id	Height	Name	Drop	Country	Location
33510	2640	Cerro Tía Chena	1890	Mexico	26.1194, -100.5565
33511	2940	Cerro La Joya	1885	Mexico	21.4309, -99.1325
33512	3720	Cerro El Potosí	1871	Mexico	24.8723, -100.2325
33515	3546	Picacho San Onofre	1646	Mexico	23.8006, -99.8464
33518	2403	Picachos El Fraile	1603	Mexico	25.8638, -100.6098

33523	2220	Sierra Gomas	1500	Mexico	26.3068, -100.4658
33524	1800	Cerro El Hongo	1490	Mexico	24.5725, -99.0757
33527	2620	Pico Sur de Sierra San Marcos *	1453	Mexico	26.4162, -101.7099
33532	3715	Cerro San Rafael / La Viga	1395	Mexico	25.3637, -100.5569
33533	2720	Cerro La Media Luna	1380	Mexico	29.0129, -102.6175
33535	1920	Cerro El Carrizal	1370	Mexico	26.7596, -100.5901
33540	2063	Sierra Las Mitras	1305	Mexico	25.7170, -100.4330
33543	1930	Cerro Pata de Gallo	1290	Mexico	27.0137, -100.8950
33548	2180	Sierra La Gloria	1270	Mexico	26.8454, -101.2564
33550	1830	Sierra La Rata	1250	Mexico	27.0506, -101.0764
33556	1460	Cerro Los Picachos	1240	Mexico	23.2529, -98.3970
33561	3502	Cerro El Viejo	1202	Mexico	23.9933, -99.7150
33564	3200	Cerro Grande	1200	Mexico	24.2592, -99.9543
33565	1810	Cerro de la Silla	1200	Mexico	25.6254, -100.2424
33569	3180	Cerro Banxú	1162	Mexico	20.6695, -99.2182
33570	2340	Cerro Los Picachos de Parreños	1161	Mexico	25.9603, -101.5974
33572	1320	Cerro Cruz Tepec	1160	Mexico	21.2392, -97.8891
33573	2976	Cerro Urbano	1156	Mexico	25.6318, -100.6553
33577	2660	Sierra Santa Maria	1134	Mexico	24.9533, -99.9853
33591	2960	Sierra El Pinal	1083	Mexico	23.4920, -99.7942
33593	1540	Sierra Lampazos	1080	Mexico	26.8686, -100.3756
33594	1880	Sierra de Enmedio	1080	Mexico	26.3159, -100.6386
33597	3160	Sierra Cieneguillas – Cerro El Infiernillo	1060	Mexico	24.4909, -99.9362
33601	2360	Cerro San Patricio	1060	Mexico	26.3108, -101.3081
33604	2780	Cerro Las Chinas	1041	Mexico	23.8517, -99.4407
33613	2320	Loma Casa Blanca	1020	Mexico	23.0688, -99.3080
33614	2800	Cerro Boludo	1019	Mexico	23.1628, -99.5967
33615	3714	Sierra de la Marta	1014	Mexico	25.2006, -100.3779
33619	2620	Cerro El Águila	1003	Mexico	20.8683, -98.9689

Cerro La Joya, NA172
Rob Woodall, January 2012

Our ten-Ultra trip consisted of five well-known high peaks, including the national high point Pico de Orizaba, and five lesser-known peaks. Volcán de Tequila involved a fixed rope, which later went missing. Cerro Tancítaro happened to be my 100th Ultra. Cerro La Joya we knew nothing about. It was approached via a nice block-paved road, passing upmarket houses. Bob, Adam and I speculated over how all this might have been funded and carried on, hoping for the best. The road ended at a more ordinary house, at the foot of the peak. The owner vaguely recalled that his uncle might had been up the peak once. He tracked down some folk with machetes, allowed us to camp in his yard, and we climbed Cerro La Joya the next day. It was steep but very doable.

NA173 Mexican West Coast Ranges

Id	Height	Name	Drop	Country	Location
33507	2880	Cerro Las Conchas	1942	Mexico	18.7219, -102.9742
33520	2880	Cerro Las Capillas	1580	Mexico	19.5552, -104.1473
33521	2940	Volcán de Tequila	1540	Mexico	20.7873, -103.8467
33525	2380	Cerros Santa Elena	1480	Mexico	18.6733, -102.5031
33538	2950	Cerro Viejo	1340	Mexico	20.3649, -103.4368
33541	2243	Cerro Alto	1304	Mexico	21.4485, -104.9746
33547	2760	Sierra Cacoma – Cerro El Torreón	1276	Mexico	20.3537, -104.9866
33549	2540	Cerro Grande	1261	Mexico	21.1763, -104.3395
33552	2340	Volcán de Sanganguey	1243	Mexico	21.4513, -104.7325
33557	2600	Cerro Grande de Ameca	1223	Mexico	20.6247, -104.0133
33589	2560	Sierra Manantlan	1086	Mexico	19.4914, -103.9600
33602	1050	Cerro Evermann, Isla Socorro	1050	Mexico	18.7902, -110.9757
33605	1840	Cerro Los Capulines	1041	Mexico	18.6441, -102.0633

NA174 Cordillera Neovolcanica

Id	Height	Name	Drop	Country	Location
33501	5636	Pico de Orizaba / Citlaltépetl	4922	Mexico	19.0303, -97.2698
33502	5413	Volcán Popocatépetl	3033	Mexico	19.0227, -98.6279
33503	4260	Nevado de Colima / Tzapotépetl	2702	Mexico	19.5631, -103.6085
33504	4688	Nevado de Toluca / Xinantécatl	2216	Mexico	19.1019, -99.7676
33508	4438	Volcán La Malinche / Matlalcuéyetl	1938	Mexico	19.2310, -98.0320
33513	3840	Cerro Tancítaro	1663	Mexico	19.4165, -102.3196
33517	1685	Sierra de Santa Martha	1615	Mexico	18.3465, -94.8574
33522	5213	Volcán Iztaccíhuatl	1530	Mexico	19.1762, -98.6408
33530	4282	Cofre de Perote / Naucampatépetl	1402	Mexico	19.4940, -97.1480
33531	3600	Cerro San Andrés	1400	Mexico	19.8057, -100.5962
33545	1680	Volcán San Martín Tuxtla	1284	Mexico	18.5575, -95.2005
33554	3937	Cerro Ajusco / Xitle	1242	Mexico	19.2076, -99.2581
33559	3928	Cerro Jocotitlán	1219	Mexico	19.7384, -99.7580
33563	3500	Cerro Grande	1200	Mexico	19.7538, -102.3387
33567	3420	Cerro La Nieve	1181	Mexico	19.4486, -101.4186
33579	2720	Sierra del Halo	1118	Mexico	19.2572, -103.1906
33580	3337	Cerro El Zirate	1116	Mexico	19.7299, -101.5159
33586	2760	Cerro Garcia	1096	Mexico	20.1692, -103.3482
33603	3640	Cerro El Campanario	1042	Mexico	19.5966, -100.2530
33607	1440	Cerro Tinoco / Mesa Los Caballos	1040	Mexico	18.3119, -100.5246
33610	2840	Cerro El Tigre / El Tecolote	1022	Mexico	19.8778, -102.9708
33611	2280	Cerro Frío	1022	Mexico	18.4622, -99.3139
33612	3480	Cerro Derrumbadas	1022	Mexico	19.2643, -97.4471
33620	2100	Cerro Tecaballo	1002	Mexico	18.0854, -98.8483

NA175 Sierra Madre del Sur

Id	Height	Name	Drop	Country	Location
33505	3540	Cerro Tiotepec	2180	Mexico	17.4682, -100.1367
33506	3712	Cerro el Nacimiento	2145	Mexico	16.2115, -96.1961
33514	2820	El Aguacate Oeste	1662	Mexico	16.5813, -95.8036
33519	3400	Cerro Zempoaltépetl	1580	Mexico	17.1324, -96.0125
33528	3360	Cerro La Muralla	1440	Mexico	17.1353, -97.6642
33529	3360	Cerro Yatin Noreste	1419	Mexico	17.1590, -96.4173
33542	3016	Cerro Tres Cruces	1296	Mexico	16.6143, -96.5927
33553	3200	Cerro Pelon	1242	Mexico	17.7928, -96.8303
33566	2145	Cerro La Neblina	1187	Mexico	16.4930, -97.4354
33568	2976	Cerro La Piedra del Sol	1170	Mexico	16.8719, -96.5241
33571	2700	Cerro El Billete	1161	Mexico	18.1537, -101.3325
33576	2960	Cerro Corral Cuate	1139	Mexico	17.6070, -99.8524
33578	2200	Cerro La Cruz	1125	Mexico	17.9094, -101.5329
33582	2461	Cerro El Volcán Negro	1102	Mexico	17.3930, -99.3215
33583	2980	Cerro de la Cebolla	1101	Mexico	17.2408, -98.5100
33584	2000	Cerro El Burro	1101	Mexico	16.6871, -97.7969
33587	2850	Puerto El Sapo	1090	Mexico	17.8579, -101.0267
33588	3320	Cerro Tlacatepec	1089	Mexico	17.4011, -100.0728
33616	3213	Cerro Negro	1013	Mexico	17.3256, -97.4270
33618	2766	Cerro El Encantado	1007	Mexico	16.2403, -97.0186

Volcán La Malinche, NA174 (Rob Woodall)

NA18 Central America Ranges

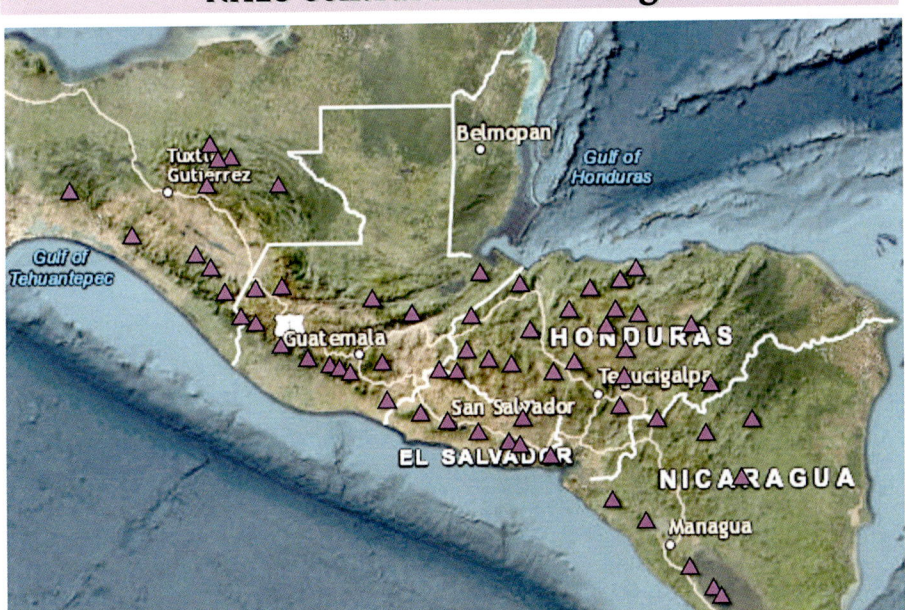

NA181 Chiapas Ranges

Id	Height	Name	Drop	Country	Location
34008	3520	Montaña Peña Blanca	1864	Guatemala	15.4996, -91.9151
34023	2300	Sierra El Cerro Azul – Atravesado	1520	Mexico	16.7647, -94.4517
34032	2909	Cerro Tzontehuítz	1381	Mexico	16.8185, -92.5805
34041	2480	Cerro Cavahlna	1304	Mexico	17.1675, -92.4172

34047	2550	Cerro Tres Picos	1251	Mexico	16.1969, -93.6136
34049	1864	Cerro Pando	1225	Mexico	15.9489, -92.7271
34055	3086	Cerro El Madrón	1150	Mexico	15.4478, -92.3244
34063	2060	Sierra Annover	1080	Mexico	17.1837, -92.2374
34068	4067	Volcán Tacaná	1037	Guatemala, Mexico	15.1325, -92.1085
34073	2160	Cerro Caballo Blanco	1015	Mexico	15.7711, -92.5331
34077	1680	Sierra Cruz de Plata	1000	Mexico	16.8225, -91.5927
34078	2100	Cerro Jolhuitz	1000	Mexico	17.3558, -92.5264

NA182 Guatemala Ranges

Id	Height	Name	Drop	Country	Location
34001	4220	Volcán Tajumulco	3980	Guatemala	15.0430, -91.9037
34005	3760	Volcán de Agua	1984	Guatemala	14.4654, -90.7428
34007	3837	Cerro de los Cuervos	1880	Guatemala	15.5182, -91.5446
34009	3976	Volcán de Acatenango	1853	Guatemala	14.5016, -90.8755
34013	3537	Volcán Atitlán	1740	Guatemala	14.5834, -91.1864
34025	3010	Cerro Raxón	1480	Guatemala	15.1500, -89.7308
34053	2710	Cerro Santiago Sureste	1200	Guatemala	14.5200, -90.1483
34060	1280	Cerro San Gil	1109	Guatemala	15.6700, -88.7875
34065	2645	Cerro Rocjá	1075	Guatemala	15.3383, -90.2750
34066	3771	Volcán Santa María / Gagxanul	1053	Guatemala	14.7571, -91.5518
34067	1662	Volcán Moyuta	1053	Guatemala	14.0275, -90.0958
34069	2580	Volcán de Pacaya	1030	Guatemala	14.3825, -90.6017

NA183 Central Central America

Id	Height	Name	Drop	Country	Location
34003	2744	Montaña de Santa Bárbara	2092	Honduras	14.9133, -88.1142
34004	2849	Cerro Las Minas / Pico Celaque	2072	Honduras	14.5342, -88.6800
34010	2130	Volcán de San Miguel	1842	El Salvador	13.4350, -88.2692
34012	2480	Montaña de Corozal	1747	Honduras	15.5575, -86.8758
34014	2241	Montaña San Ildefonso	1707	Honduras	15.5233, -88.2325
34015	1780	Volcán San Cristóbal	1702	Nicaragua	12.7033, -87.0061
34016	2381	Volcán de Santa Ana / Ilamatepec	1678	El Salvador	13.8550, -89.6284
34017	1610	Volcán Concepción, Ometepe	1579	Nicaragua	11.5384, -85.6226
34018	2182	Volcán de San Vicente	1579	El Salvador	13.5965, -88.8379
34019	2310	Pico Pijol	1568	Honduras	15.1765, -87.5734
34020	2354	Montaña de Babilonia	1534	Honduras	14.9575, -85.9167
34021	2730	Cerro El Pital	1533	El Salvador, HN	14.3842, -89.1292
34024	2406	Montaña de Comayagua	1501	Honduras	14.4950, -87.5083
34026	2220	Cerro Texiguat	1472	Honduras	15.4578, -87.2962
34029	2325	Montaña de la Florida	1415	Honduras	14.9610, -87.0749
34031	2418	Cerro Montecristo	1391	El Salvador, GT, HN	14.4206, -89.3561

34035	2285	Montaña del Cerro Azul	1344	Honduras	15.1083, -88.9183
34037	1960	Cerro El Picacho	1335	El Salvador	13.7442, -89.2567
34038	1370	Volcán Maderas, Ometepe	1333	Nicaragua	11.4463, -85.5149
34040	2106	Pico Mogotón	1321	Nicaragua, HN	13.7633, -86.3983
34042	1344	Volcán Mombacho	1288	Nicaragua	11.8275, -85.9600
34043	2195	Montaña El Chile	1287	Honduras	14.3038, -86.8450
34045	1675	Cerro El Toro	1274	Nicaragua	13.7370, -85.0676
34046	1745	Cerro Kilambé	1258	Nicaragua	13.5683, -85.7117
34048	1725	Cerro Azul	1244	Honduras	15.7167, -86.6592
34051	2459	Cordillera de Montecillos	1212	Honduras	14.3644, -87.8046
34052	1297	Volcán Momotombo	1202	Nicaragua	12.4239, -86.5398
34054	2153	Cerro El Volcán	1188	Honduras	14.6400, -86.8050
34056	1663	Cerro Cacahuatique	1145	El Salvador	13.7708, -88.2108
34057	1438	Cerro Musún	1139	Nicaragua	12.9850, -85.2425
34058	2064	Monte Mucupina	1120	Honduras	15.1150, -86.6392
34059	1250	Volcán Conchagua	1109	El Salvador	13.2758, -87.8450
34061	2390	Cordillera de Opalaca	1092	Honduras	14.4800, -88.3750
34062	2430	Cerro Erapuca	1089	Honduras	14.6650, -88.9817
34064	1930	Montaña de la Pimienta	1079	Honduras	15.1809, -86.9395
34072	1701	Cordillera Entre Ríos	1016	Honduras	14.1925, -85.6550
34074	1990	Cerro El Volcán	1010	Honduras	13.9317, -86.8958
34076	1650	Cerro El Tigre	1007	El Salvador	13.4675, -88.4275

NA184 Costa Rica-Panama Ranges

Id	Height	Name	Drop	Country	Location
34002	3819	Cerro Chirripó	3767	Costa Rica	9.4843, -83.4889
34006	3432	Volcán Irazú	1888	Costa Rica	9.9767, -83.8542
34011	1875	Cerro Tacarcuna	1770	Panama	8.1658, -77.2958
34022	2028	Volcán Miravalles	1528	Costa Rica	10.7470, -85.1505
34027	1559	Cerro Hoya	1470	Panama	7.3183, -80.6817
34028	2545	Cerro Sagui	1451	Panama	8.5822, -81.8469
34030	2906	Volcán Barva	1409	Costa Rica	10.1308, -84.1008
34033	1916	Volcán Santa María	1356	Costa Rica	10.8092, -85.3192
34034	3549	Cerro Kámuk	1346	Costa Rica	9.2708, -83.0325
34036	3474	Volcán Barú / Chiriquí	1342	Panama	8.8092, -82.5425
34039	1439	Cerro Chucanti	1325	Panama	8.8050, -78.4597
34044	1916	Volcán Tenorio	1277	Costa Rica	10.6683, -85.0117
34050	1954	Cerro Veraguas	1221	Panama	8.6164, -80.8838
34070	2260	Cerro Chorcha	1017	Panama	8.6458, -82.1212
34071	1665	Cerro Cacao	1016	Costa Rica	10.9325, -85.4475
34075	1756	Cerro Turrubares	1009	Costa Rica	9.7933, -84.4717

Peaks of Central America
Alastair Govan, January - February 2020

I love hiking in warm sunny weather and especially enjoy escaping the dark, cold Scottish winters for a few weeks. Many tourists travel independently in Central America but mainly between towns and cities and other attractions, mostly using shuttle buses which are easy to book online or in travel agencies. The local buses were very cheap but slow and uncomfortable. There was no timetable, they just left when they were full.

The roads were often congested and we saw a couple of serious accidents. We had police escorts on two of the mountains due to recent robberies. I found the people very friendly and polite and I never felt unsafe, but I avoided the big cities of Guatemala City and San Salvador, which had unsavoury reputations.

Central America is not a classic trekking destination due to the lack of dramatic ridges or valleys and the scarcity of views because of the extensive forest. The mountains are nearly all volcanoes. In Guatemala we reached the summit of six, including Volcán Tajumulco, the highest point in Guatemala and all of Central America at 4220m. The others were Volcán de Agua, Volcán de Acatenango, Volcán Atitlán, Volcán Santa María and Pico Zunil, which is not a Ribu as it has 832m prominence. Many of the summits involved quite strenuous days with 1200-1800 metres of ascent. The mountains were covered with dense forest almost to the top. The routes used well-trodden paths which were often steep, slippery and dusty in the dry season. Temperatures in the highlands were pleasant but the mountains get some cloud and were chilly at night. We had frost on our sunrise ascent of Volcán Tajumulco, and Volcán de Agua got a dusting of snow the day before we went up, but this was the first in at least three years and it soon disappeared.

The big attraction of the Guatemala volcanoes is that some are still highly active. Volcán Fuego is spectacular and the campsite on the adjacent slopes of Volcán de Acatenango provided stunning views, especially at night, of almost continuous eruptions. For this reason Volcán de Acatenango is probably the most popular mountain climb in Guatemala.

Later in the trip I climbed two Ultras in Nicaragua – Volcán San Cristóbal and Volcán Concepción. These are much lower (1780m and 1610m) so they are much hotter and drier and it is usual to set off before sunrise to partially avoid the heat. The route to Volcán San Cristóbal involved a bumpy ten-kilometre drive each way along an extremely rough dirt road, then a steep climb up loose ash direct to the summit, which was very hard going on the way up but very fast on the way down.

Volcan Concepción is an attractive mountain located on Ometepe Island in the middle of Lake Nicaragua. It's a popular hike though quite arduous, with 1400 metres of ascent, mostly on steep, dusty, slippery paths. The upper section is on rock and loose stones which my group, unused to mountain walking, found very tough. We took eleven hours for the round trip, starting before sunrise and returning at dusk.

During the trip we started to become aware of a new virus in other parts of the world, and had our temperatures checked at one of the border crossings. At the time I assumed it would be a storm in a tea cup, perhaps like bird flu or swine flu. How wrong I was.

NA19 Caribbean Area

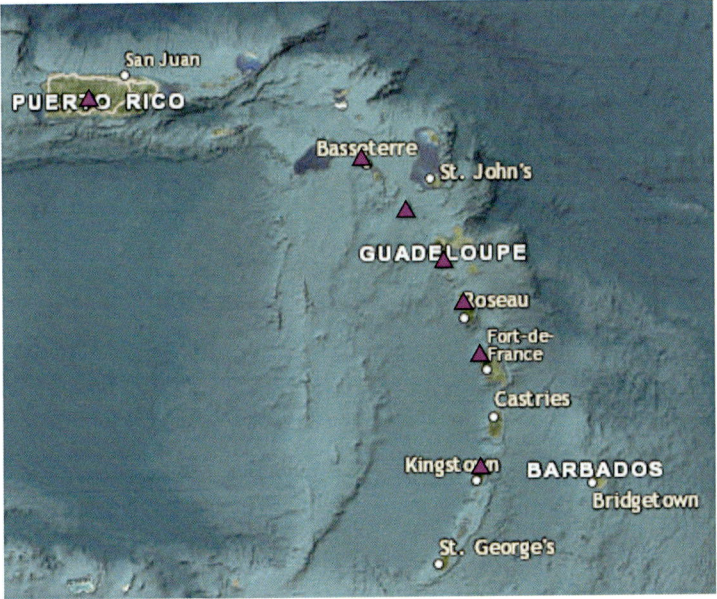

NA191 Cuba

Id	Height	Name	Drop	Country	Location
34505	1974	Pico Turquino	1974	Cuba	19.9898, -76.8360
34516	1140	Pico San Juan	1107	Cuba	21.9900, -80.1475
34519	1245	Pico del Cristal	1023	Cuba	20.5425, -75.4767

Pico Turquino, NA191
Andy M Dean, December 2014

After nine days of cycle touring in eastern Cuba, we arrived in Santiago de Cuba on 30th December. Instead of relaxing for a few days we decided to hike up Pico Turquino, Cuba's highest mountain, famous as the area of Che Guevara's bases before the revolution. The route from the south-west makes it possible to hike the peak in one day, but it requires 1850 metres of elevation gain. The climb was manageable and it was a great trail with fabulous views and interesting plants. It was the descent that killed us. We underestimated the strain on quadriceps muscles after the cycling. On new year's eve, back in the old square in Santiago de Cuba, we drank plenty of rum and tropical juice cocktails to ease the pain. The next day we could barely walk and the hosts at our casa were concerned that we had seriously hurt ourselves.

NA192 Jamaica

Id	Height	Name	Drop	Country	Location
34503	2256	Blue Mountain Peak	2256	Jamaica	18.0470, -76.5792

NA193 Hispaniola

Id	Height	Name	Drop	Country	Location
34501	3098	Pico Duarte	3098	Dominican Republic	19.0232, -70.9980
34502	2680	Pic La Selle	2646	Haiti	18.3602, -71.9766
34504	2347	Pic Macaya	2084	Haiti	18.3825, -74.0250
34506	2279	Loma Gajo en Medio	1780	Dominican Republic	18.6358, -71.5222
34507	2842	Loma Alto de la Bandera	1501	Dominican Republic	18.8125, -70.6267
34510	1788	Morne Bœuf	1430	Haiti	19.0725, -72.2500
34514	1370	Loma del Curro	1165	Dominican Republic	18.3808, -71.0267
34518	1249	Loma Diego de Ocampo	1049	Dominican Republic	19.5800, -70.7450
34520	1380	Morne Éloi	1008	Haiti	18.3342, -72.8258

NA194 Puerto Rico and Virgin Islands

Id	Height	Name	Drop	Country	Location
34512	1338	Cerro de Punta	1338	Puerto Rico	18.1723, -66.5917

NA196 Lesser Antilles

Id	Height	Name	Island	Drop	Country	Location
34508	1467	La Grande Soufrière	Basse-Terre	1467	France (Guadeloupe)	16.0450, -61.6639
34509	1447	Morne Diablotins	Dominica	1447	Dominica	15.5040, -61.3982
34511	1395	Montagne Pelée	Martinique	1395	France	14.8091, -61.1654
34513	1234	La Soufrière	Saint Vincent	1234	Saint Vincent and the Grenadines	13.3475, -61.1758
34515	1156	Mount Liamuiga	Saint Kitts	1156	Saint Kitts and Nevis	17.3687, -62.8030
34517	1050	Soufrière Hills	Montserrat	1050	Montserrat (UK)	16.7097, -62.1775

Descending the east ridge of Sacajawea Peak, NA132 (Rob Woodall)

Nevado de Toluca, NA174 (Rob Woodall)

Volcán Santa María, NA182 (James Stone)

Nevado Auzangate, SA213 (Sean Caulfield)

Volcán Parinacota, SA214 (James Stone)

Nevado Sajama, SA214 (James Stone)

South America

SA20 Coastal South America

SA200 Coastal Venezuela

Id	Height	Name	Drop	Country	Location
40003	2596	Cerro Tristeza	2455	Venezuela	10.0842, -63.9583
40004	2753	Pico Naiguatá	2443	Venezuela	10.5433, -66.7825
40014	2100	Cerro El Cerrón	1500	Venezuela	10.3225, -70.6308
40016	2447	Pico El Cenizo	1493	Venezuela	10.3767, -67.4292
40020	1929	Cerro Platillón	1400	Venezuela	9.8708, -67.5158
40022	2251	Cerro Negro	1373	Venezuela	10.2033, -63.5767
40032	1948	Cerro El Tigre	1263	Venezuela	10.4042, -68.8008
40040	1792	Cumbre de Capotillo	1190	Venezuela	10.2467, -68.3633
40044	1501	Sierra de San Luís	1145	Venezuela	11.1775, -69.7033
40047	1256	Cerro del Humo	1126	Venezuela	10.7033, -62.6308
40048	1700	Cerro Curucuti	1123	Venezuela	9.9917, -66.9358
40078	1675	Topo Cataurito	1010	Venezuela	10.0417, -67.3325

SA201 North Colombia Coast

Id	Height	Name	Drop	Country	Location
40001	5731	Pico Cristóbal Colón	5539	Colombia	10.8390, -73.6867
40005	3660	Cerro Pintado	2178	Colombia, Venezuela	10.3358, -72.9042
40011	2866	Cuchilla San Lorenzo / Cerro Kennedy	1522	Colombia	11.1128, -74.0343
40017	2618	Cerro Chiolaque	1423	Colombia	10.6575, -73.3850
40023	2860	Pico de la Cabeza Cortada *	1365	Colombia, Venezuela	9.4758, -73.1975

SA202 Coastal North-west South America

Id	Height	Name	Drop	Country	Location
40010	1730	Alturas de Nique	1557	Colombia, Panama	7.7017, -77.7275
40025	1551	Cerro Piña	1356	Panama	7.6833, -78.1525
40039	1788	Cerro Criterión	1192	Peru	-14.9892, -75.2500
40043	1613	Cerro Carrizal	1169	Peru	-4.1850, -80.6333
40070	1185	Cerro Dubaza *	1032	Colombia	5.4246, -77.2392

SA203 Chilean Coastal Range

Id	Height	Name	Drop	Country	Location
40007	2281	Cerro Alto de Cantillana	1784	Chile	-33.9667, -70.9658
40019	2222	Cerro El Roble	1401	Chile	-32.9767, -71.0133
40021	1530	Alto de Nahuelbuta	1396	Chile	-37.7867, -73.0333
40058	1968	Cerro Vizcachas	1089	Chile	-31.9872, -71.2286
40061	2326	Cerro de las Tetas	1072	Chile	-24.2033, -70.0725
40068	2515	Cerro Guatulame	1038	Chile	-30.8592, -70.8842
40072	2338	Cerro Chache	1027	Chile	-32.5633, -71.0508

SA204 Chilean Coastal Islands and Peninsula Taitao

Id	Height	Name	Island	Drop	Country	Location
40012	1520	Cerro Isla Wellington *	Isla Wellington	1520	Chile	-49.3207, -74.5012
40030	1410	Cerro Muscosa *	Isla Wellington	1318	Chile	-49.7892, -74.5050
40045	1319	Cerro Charteris *	Isla Wellington	1135	Chile	-49.5983, -74.5550
40049	1229	Isla Wallace	Isla Wellington	1118	Chile	-48.9757, -74.4934
40062	1250	Cerro Walkyren Stein Oeste *	Isla Wellington	1055	Chile	-48.9908, -74.7117
40063	1108	Monte Catedral	Isla Wellington	1054	Chile	-49.7675, -74.8275
40071	1168	Cerro Wellington Este *	Isla Wellington	1029	Chile	-49.6725, -74.4867
40079	1090	Monte Nuestra Señora	Isla Wellington	1008	Chile	-49.9592, -74.7658
40081	1051	Cerro Seno Kravel *	Isla Wellington	1004	Chile	-48.7606, -74.7350
40083	1240	Cerro Wellington Oeste *	Isla Wellington	1002	Chile	-49.2775, -74.7008
40031	1303	Cerro Cuptana	Isla Cuptana	1303	Chile	-44.6606, -73.7070
40041	1189	Isla Serrano	Isla Serrano	1189	Chile	-48.6192, -74.5850
40056	1150	Cerro Alemana *	Isla Serrano	1095	Chile	-48.3553, -74.6783
40042	1175	Isla Prat	Isla Prat	1175	Chile	-48.1833, -74.9967
40050	1115	Isla James	Isla James	1115	Chile	-44.8960, -74.1118
40057	1092	Isla Nalcayec	Isla Nalcayec	1092	Chile	-46.0934, -73.7134
40060	1075	Monte Lucia Norte	Diego de Almagro	1075	Chile	-51.5316, -75.2147
40064	1053	Isla Humos	Isla Humos	1053	Chile	-45.6199, -74.0285
40065	1048	Isla Angamos	Isla Angamos	1048	Chile	-49.1436, -74.9736
40067	1040	Isla Rennell Sur	Isla Rennell Sur	1040	Chile	-52.0350, -73.9183
40069	1035	Isla Traiguén	Isla Traiguén	1035	Chile	-45.7098, -73.6432
40073	1025	Isla Contreras	Isla Contreras	1025	Chile	-51.9839, -74.9336
40074	1020	Isla Saumarez	Isla Saumarez	1020	Chile	-49.5708, -74.3767
40075	1012	Isla Melchor	Isla Melchor	1012	Chile	-45.1071, -73.9672
40076	1012	Isla Rivero	Isla Rivero	1012	Chile	-45.7579, -74.4098
40084	1002	Isla Knorr	Isla Knorr	1002	Chile	-48.6517, -74.7975

Peninsula Taitao

Id	Height	Name	Drop	Country	Location
40035	1253	Cerro Wickham *	1250	Chile	-45.9754, -74.5249
40054	1155	Cerro Ultima Esperanza *	1110	Chile	-45.9403, -74.2303
40055	1125	Cordón Sisquelán	1102	Chile	-46.2442, -73.8496
40059	1250	Cerro del Salto *	1075	Chile	-46.0878, -74.4928
40066	1065	Cerro Presidente Rios *	1044	Chile	-46.2694, -74.1881

Isla Wellington

This large and mountainous island with ten Ribus but no roads is largely unexplored. It is one of the wettest places on Earth, with rain almost every day. It includes part of the largest glacier in South America, Pio XI Glacier in Bernardo O'Higgins National Park, one of the few glaciers on Earth that is not shrinking. The only inhabited place on the island, Puerto Edén, had a population of under 200 at the start of the century. Few of the mountains are named on any map. Many of the smaller islands nearby are also unexplored and the peaks have no recorded ascents. Isla Wallace is in the north of Wellington Island but is not an island.

SA205 Tierra del Fuego

Isla Grande de Tierra del Fuego

Id	Height	Name	Drop	Country	Location
40002	2595	Monte Shipton	2595	Chile	-54.6628, -69.5921
40006	2187	Monte Sarmiento	2062	Chile	-54.4500, -70.8313
40013	1864	Cerro Navarro	1519	Chile	-54.5650, -70.4292
40018	1746	Cerro Rudolphy / Monte Buckland	1421	Chile	-54.3756, -70.3625
40029	2279	Monte Bove	1374	Chile	-54.8647, -69.0875
40024	1425	Muela	1360	Chile	-54.3992, -69.0267
40037	1366	Serka	1251	Chile	-54.8043, -68.7780
40038	2275	Cerro Dalla Vedova	1200	Chile	-54.7285, -69.1785
40053	1565	Cerro Hernán Cubillos	1138	Chile	-54.8908, -68.9558
40051	1517	Monte Giordano	1112	Chile	-54.4542, -70.2003
40085	1455	Cerro Carbajal *	1000	Argentina	-54.7093, -68.4237

Cape Horn Islands

Id	Height	Name	Island	Drop	Country	Location
40027	1341	Cerro Santa Inés *	Isla Santa Inés	1341	Chile	-53.7932, -72.6488
40036	1276	Monte Wharton	Isla Santa Inés	1243	Chile	-53.5075, -72.9775
40028	1335	Punto Alto	Isla Hoste	1335	Chile	-55.1508, -69.6600
40033	1279	Peninsula Dumas	Isla Hoste	1257	Chile	-55.0358, -68.5608
40077	1077	Peninsula Pasteur	Isla Hoste	1012	Chile	-55.2196, -68.6375
40082	1050	Peninsula Rous	Isla Hoste	1003	Chile	-55.2600, -69.5658
40034	1251	Isla Gordon	Isla Gordon	1251	Chile	-54.9591, -69.2325
40046	1128	Monte Hart Dyke	Isla Desolación	1128	Chile	-53.0475, -74.0658
40052	1111	Picacho Diente de Navarino	Isla Navarino	1111	Chile	-55.0144, -67.6519
40080	1005	Isla Capitán Aracena	Isla Capitán Aracena	1005	Chile	-54.1655, -71.0711

SA206 Galapagos Islands

Id	Height	Name	Island	Drop	Country	Location
40008	1707	Volcán Wolf	Isabela	1707	Ecuador	0.0425, -91.3350
40009	1689	Volcán Cerro Azul	Isabela	1669	Ecuador	-0.9283, -91.4100
40015	1494	Volcán La Cumbre	Fernandina	1494	Ecuador	-0.3542, -91.5242

SA207 South-eastern Pacific Islands

Id	Height	Name	Island	Drop	Country	Location
40026	1350	Cerro de los Inocentes	Alexander Selkirk	1350	Chile	-33.7842, -80.8033

SA21 Andes North

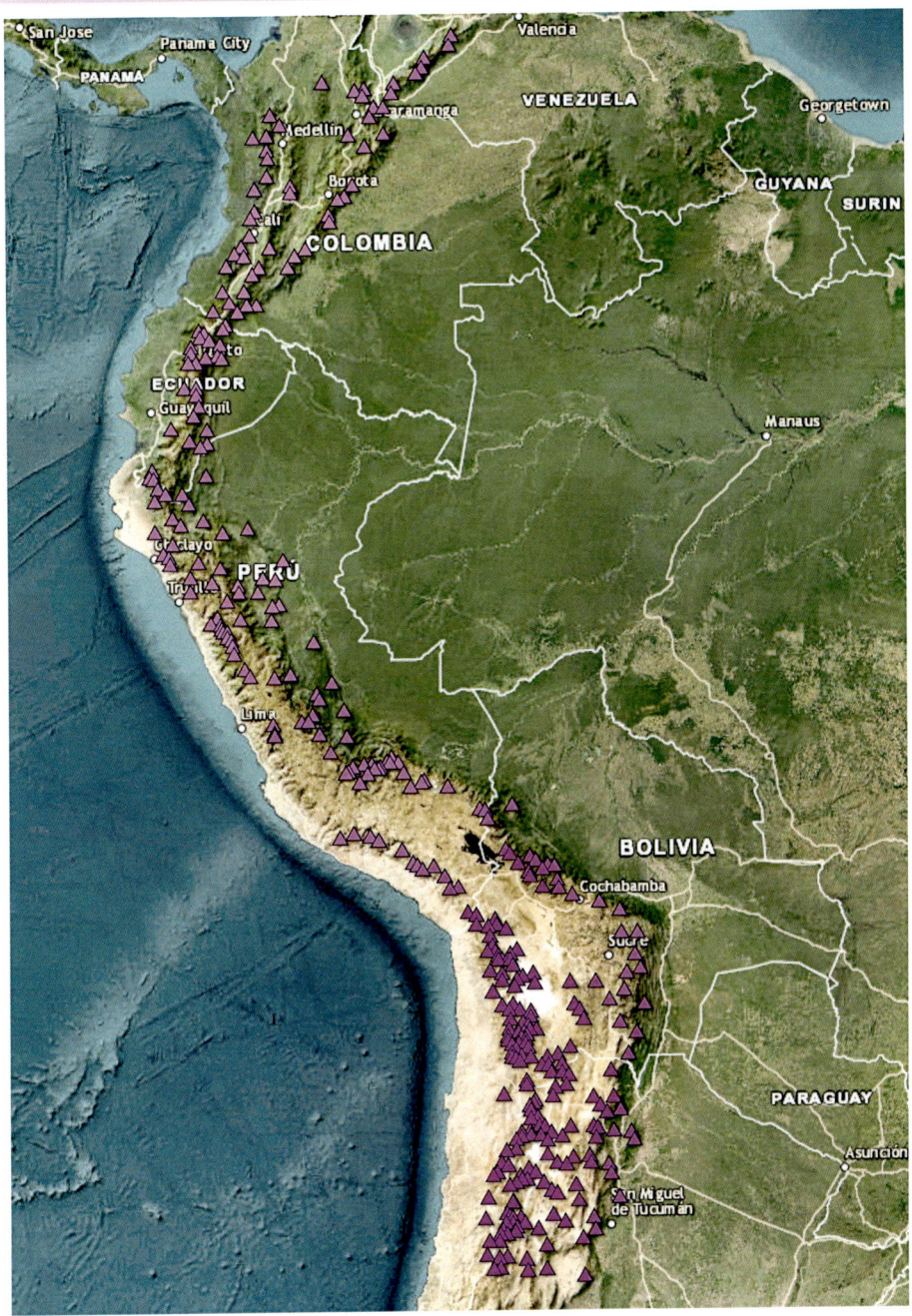

SA210 Cordillera de Merida

Id	Height	Name	Drop	Country	Location
40502	4988	Pico Bolívar	3964	Venezuela	8.5408, -71.0483
40589	3560	Páramo Cende	1543	Venezuela	9.5275, -70.1133
40610	3140	Fila Los Recostaderos	1437	Venezuela	9.2308, -70.1858
40617	3912	Pico El Púlpito	1422	Venezuela	8.0722, -71.9223
40720	4748	Pico Piedras Blancas	1169	Venezuela	8.8583, -70.9517
40801	1963	Cerro Poncho	1061	Venezuela	7.7625, -72.0158
40850	3648	Páramo de Acequias - Pico Las Lajas	1022	Venezuela	8.3633, -71.2333

SA211 Colombian Andes

Id	Height	Name	Drop	Country	Location
40504	5398	Ritacuba Blanco	3629	Colombia	6.4946, -72.2965
40508	5390	Nevado del Huila	2649	Colombia	2.9242, -76.0292
40509	4100	Cerro Tatamá	2574	Colombia	5.1617, -76.0917
40515	4070	Pico Pance	2329	Colombia	3.3442, -76.6958
40518	4020	Farallones de Citará - Cerro San Nicolas	2249	Colombia	5.7590, -76.0618
40516	3840	Cerro Calima	2241	Colombia	4.0692, -76.5233
40529	5311	Nevado del Ruiz	2046	Colombia	4.8917, -75.3233
40537	3950	Páramo de Frontino	1949	Colombia	6.4567, -76.1225
40543	3860	Cerro Napí	1837	Colombia	2.3783, -77.4342
40544	4180	Saliente del Rio Guape	1834	Colombia	3.7150, -74.0425
40556	3630	Cerro Leiva / Cordillera Los Pichachos	1705	Colombia	2.9133, -74.8500
40558	2270	Cerro San Lucas	1701	Colombia	8.1117, -74.2725
40566	2820	Cerro Torrá	1659	Colombia	4.7825, -76.4950
40567	3420	Cordillera de los Cobardes	1655	Colombia	6.4625, -73.4442
40585	3730	Cerro Paramillo	1565	Colombia	7.1033, -75.9692
40590	4250	Nevado Sumapaz	1531	Colombia	3.9350, -74.1100
40602	3370	Alto Mora	1469	Colombia	6.7783, -75.6925
40611	3710	Alto Concordia	1437	Colombia	6.0033, -76.0958
40621	4280	Páramo Guantiva La Rusia	1416	Colombia	6.0983, -72.9242
40626	4646	Volcán Puracé	1396	Colombia	2.3092, -76.3950
40640	3475	Cerro Miraflores Suroeste	1351	Colombia	2.3067, -75.4100
40685	5215	Nevado del Tolima	1236	Colombia	4.6583, -75.3300
40686	4400	Volcán Sotará	1236	Colombia	2.1092, -76.5917
40689	4180	Volcán Las Animas	1227	Colombia	1.5675, -76.8567
42012	2740	Cerro Cantor	1211	Colombia	5.1050, -72.9117
40703	3560	Cerro Palado	1192	Colombia	7.8467, -73.2258
40708	4210	Cerro Tigre	1185	Colombia	0.5225, -77.4675
40711	4005	Paramo Bagueche	1182	Colombia	7.6592, -72.9633
40730	3350	Cerro Azul / Cerro Naya	1146	Colombia	2.9933, -76.9275

40733	1490	Cerro San Juan de Micay *	1134	Colombia	2.7625, -77.1725
40735	4051	Cerro San Luis	1131	Colombia	4.4498, -73.7643
40738	4525	Cerro Piedra Molino	1128	Colombia	6.9925, -72.7258
40748	4256	Volcán Galeras	1116	Colombia	1.2194, -77.3536
40750	1570	Cerro El Mojauro	1115	Colombia	6.3967, -76.5375
40756	2615	Cerro Cristalina *	1112	Colombia	3.8483, -76.6525
40758	2731	Cuchilla Cerro Negro / Cuchilla de Chivor	1107	Colombia	4.8725, -73.3050
40760	3260	Alto Cresta Del Gallo	1104	Colombia	2.6942, -75.1708
40765	3140	Cerro El Almendro	1099	Colombia	2.6983, -76.8717
40768	3609	Cerro Soto Mayor *	1095	Colombia	1.5775, -77.5758
40773	3855	Chimichagua	1089	Colombia	4.5067, -73.5758
40784	3923	Cerro Patascoy de Santa Lucía	1077	Colombia	0.9433, -77.0725
40787	2485	Serrania de los Churumbelas	1075	Colombia	1.1592, -76.4783
40790	3265	Cuchilla El Espartillo	1073	Colombia	7.9025, -72.9008
40834	3655	Cerro La Lejía *	1033	Colombia	7.3342, -72.5792
40838	3545	Cerro El Dorado *	1029	Colombia	1.1438, -76.7860
40853	3640	Páramo de Tama	1019	Colombia	7.3192, -72.2975

Ritacuba Blanco, SA211
Rob Woodall, January 2014

Many of my most prominent South American peaks were climbed with Adam Helman. He was an enthusiastic organiser, a great proponent of topographic prominence and a Spanish speaker. This was our last trip together, on this occasion just us two. We met in Bogota, admired the street art and found the minibus we needed, which we shared with a guided group on a similar itinerary to ours. We explored the lower part of the route, getting used to the altitude, watching the Colombians enjoying the snow – possibly the only place in their country where they could see it. We reached the summit, but sadly the peak was closed to climbers soon afterwards and Adam is no longer with us. Poignant memories.

Volcán Cotopaxi, SA212
Alan Dawson, December 1996

The aim was to climb three high volcanoes. Antisana was ruled out before we left the high hut, after the guide assessed the snow and ice conditions as too dangerous. Fair enough, it can happen. Cotopaxi was a chaotic circus of overlapping ropes and overtaking parties. Our local guide was in a hurry as we weaved our way past groups struggling with altitude or gradient. It was good fun at times but caused tension and sharp exchanges with slower parties. My stomach was misbehaving, so reaching the magnificent summit provided more satisfaction than exhilaration. Chimborazo was another farce. I sought assurances that we could split our party if some wanted to go down early, but it seemed our English guide had little drive to reach the summit. Somewhere around the 6000m contour our group waited for about an hour while those up ahead faffed around and assessed it too cold and windy to continue. Conditions were not that bad but they had had enough. A party led by renowned mountaineer Alan Hinkes stormed past us with no hesitation. Nothing was going to stop him and his group. I could not join them or carry on without ropes due to occasional small crevasses. I was reminded of the saying that if you are not making your own decisions then you are not mountaineering. I did not go on another guided trip for 28 years.

SA212 Ecuador Andes

Id	Height	Name	Drop	Country	Location
40501	6267	Volcán Chimborazo	4120	Ecuador	-1.4678, -78.8170
40513	5897	Volcán Cotopaxi	2403	Ecuador	-0.6806, -78.4380
40525	5790	Volcán Cayambe	2075	Ecuador	0.0250, -77.9892
40526	5319	Volcán Altar	2072	Ecuador	-1.6850, -78.4233
40528	2988	Cordillera del Condor	2049	Ecuador	-3.2852, -78.3184
40547	4939	Volcán Cotacachi	1832	Ecuador	0.3604, -78.3488
40562	5758	Volcán Antisana	1732	Ecuador	-0.4842, -78.1417
40554	5241	Volcán Iliniza	1727	Ecuador	-0.6633, -78.7158
40563	2868	Cerro Paramo	1662	Peru	-5.0792, -78.7008
40569	4784	Volcán Pichincha	1642	Ecuador	-0.1745, -78.6007
40573	5300	Volcán Sangay	1588	Ecuador	-2.0050, -78.3419
40579	3832	Volcán Sumaco	1579	Ecuador	-0.5412, -77.6272
40580	4764	Volcán Cumbal	1578	Colombia	0.9558, -77.8867
40587	5023	Volcán Tungurahua	1560	Ecuador	-1.4700, -78.4450
40596	4621	Volcán Imbabura	1505	Ecuador	0.2543, -78.1805
40604	3100	Huachaurco	1463	Ecuador	-4.0375, -79.8717
40634	4143	Loma Picacho	1380	Ecuador	-3.1092, -78.6800
40635	2510	Cordillera Cutucu Occidental	1379	Ecuador	-2.7783, -78.1108
40673	3515	Cerro Guagra-Urcu	1261	Ecuador	-0.4325, -77.7192
40674	3205	Hito Tres Cumbres	1258	Ecuador, Peru	-4.7800, -78.9150
40680	4524	Cerro Patul	1249	Ecuador	-2.7450, -79.2633
40691	2210	Cerro Cenepa *	1211	Peru	-4.1950, -78.1158
40698	4730	Cerro Soroche	1203	Ecuador	-2.3358, -78.5455
40707	4457	Atacazo	1185	Ecuador	-0.3603, -78.6204
40744	3468	Montañas Muralla	1122	Ecuador	0.3800, -77.5800
40757	4279	Fuya Fuya	1109	Ecuador	0.1336, -78.2941
40761	2450	Cerro Yawa Naint	1103	Ecuador	-3.2225, -78.1008
40775	3562	Volcán Reventador	1086	Ecuador	-0.0808, -77.6592
40786	1778	Jujal	1076	Ecuador	-4.2742, -79.9867
42022	1440	Cordillera Campanquis	1061	Peru	-4.1692, -77.5675
40836	2620	Cerro Collona	1032	Ecuador	-4.3017, -79.8417

Volcán Sangay

This is an active stratovolcano, regularly producing ash, lava and pyroclastic flows. Its latest phase of eruptions began in March 2019 and was still continuing five years later. It was climbed in 1929 but there have been few recorded ascents since then and none in recent years.

Volcán Chimborazo, SA212 (James Stone)

Ojos del Salado, SA215, from Vicuñas (Rob Woodall)

Cerro Malcante, SA215 (Deividas Valaitis)

SA213 Peruvian Andes

Id	Height	Name	Drop	Country	Location
40506	6768	Nevado Huascarán	2795	Peru	-9.1212, -77.6046
40510	6264	Nevado Salcantay	2538	Peru	-13.3333, -72.5450
40517	6425	Volcán Coropuna	2228	Peru	-15.5458, -72.6608
40523	4185	Cordillera Vilcabamba Norte	2112	Peru	-12.3758, -73.6175
40524	6372	Nevado Auzangate	2086	Peru	-13.7883, -71.2292
40527	5505	Nevado Sara Sara	2059	Peru	-15.3300, -73.4458
40530	6617	Nevado Yerupajá	2025	Peru	-10.2683, -76.9050
40533	6288	Nevado Ampato	1992	Peru	-15.8200, -71.8800
40535	6057	Nevado Chachani	1963	Peru	-16.1942, -71.5317
40539	5818	Nevado Sahuasiray / Nevado Colque Cruz	1920	Peru	-13.2142, -71.9883
40545	4118	Cerro Mishahuanga	1824	Peru	-6.3733, -79.2375
40546	4025	Cerro Ignacio	1794	Peru	-6.0242, -77.5975
40549	5822	Volcán Misti	1785	Peru	-16.2967, -71.4108
40552	3605	Abra La Esperanza	1743	Peru	-10.4308, -75.4225
40555	5988	Volcán Tacora	1721	Chile	-17.7208, -69.7725
40561	6395	Nevado Huandoy	1680	Peru	-9.0275, -77.6633
40571	6369	Nevado Huantsán	1632	Peru	-9.5150, -77.3108
40583	5558	Cerro Jallacata / Waytapallana	1572	Peru	-11.9075, -75.0542
40584	3970	Cerro Bravo	1571	Peru	-5.5333, -79.2450
40586	2450	Pico Sira	1564	Peru	-9.4517, -74.6783
40594	5735	Nevado Champará	1510	Peru	-8.6850, -77.7908
40597	6241	Nevado Santa Cruz	1491	Peru	-8.8942, -77.7092
40605	6093	Nevado Solimana	1462	Peru	-15.4075, -72.8917
40608	5723	Nevado Tarata / Waqurunchu	1451	Peru	-10.5308, -75.9317
40619	6188	Nevado Copa	1416	Peru	-9.2697, -77.4809
40637	5682	Nevado Verónica / Huaycay Huilque	1358	Peru	-13.1650, -72.3267
40647	5991	Pumasillo	1341	Peru	-13.2500, -72.8200
40650	3675	Cerro La Flor *	1314	Peru	-5.6350, -78.2133
40651	6309	Nevado Rurichinchay	1311	Peru	-9.3825, -77.3300
40652	4496	Cerro Rumi Rumi	1311	Peru	-7.5608, -77.9700
40658	5664	Pichu Pichu	1304	Peru	-16.4425, -71.2375
40659	1982	Cerro Alto Huantachiri	1300	Peru	-11.2225, -74.4792
40660	3960	Cerro Viejo	1294	Peru	-4.7792, -79.4408
40662	5897	Nevado Ticlla	1288	Peru	-12.2592, -75.9592
40666	5928	Nevado Tucarhuay	1283	Peru	-13.3608, -72.5942
40670	5235	Nevado Ampay	1273	Peru	-13.5567, -72.9317
40688	4962	Cerro Luichopata *	1267	Peru	-12.3167, -74.5000
40681	5815	Volcán Tutupaca	1249	Peru	-17.0250, -70.3717
40690	5680	Nevado Panta	1215	Peru	-13.2317, -73.0911
40697	2595	Cerro Sangapillo Aspuzana	1203	Peru	-8.7336, -76.0162

40700	4333	Cerro Chin Chin	1195	Peru	-7.4267, -78.6725
40701	3681	Cerro Negro	1193	Peru	-4.9917, -79.7883
40706	4735	Cerro Vicuña	1187	Peru	-13.4867, -73.6608
40709	4781	Cerro Negrococha	1184	Peru	-8.7175, -77.0425
40717	3685	Cerro Cataripango *	1170	Peru	-11.5492, -73.7083
40721	1970	Cerro Huatata	1167	Peru	-11.0700, -74.5608
40724	4842	Pachatusan	1162	Peru	-13.5167, -71.7917
40726	4945	Cerro Chupon *	1158	Peru	-13.3058, -73.4508
40728	4990	Cerro Cantahuire	1157	Peru	-13.7817, -73.1950
40732	4954	Cerro Razuhuilca	1139	Peru	-12.8725, -74.1492
40734	5800	Allincapac / Schio	1133	Peru	-13.9083, -70.4150
40736	5758	Nevado Pariachaca / Azulcocha	1130	Peru	-11.9942, -75.9933
40737	1334	Cerro Chumillan	1129	Peru	-6.6775, -79.5250
40759	5637	Volcán Ubinas	1123	Peru	-16.3483, -70.9025
40747	6110	Callangate / Collpa Ananta	1119	Peru	-13.7317, -71.1600
40752	3275	Cerro Chorrera	1114	Peru	-5.7575, -78.9508
40762	5312	Nevado Lalaccotuna	1101	Peru	-11.8975, -74.8500
40764	4985	Cerro Acuyac	1099	Peru	-13.9046, -71.5688
40767	5688	Nevado Mururaju / Nevado Pongos Sur	1098	Peru	-9.8081, -77.2442
40772	4608	Cerro Achatayhua	1091	Peru	-15.4392, -73.8767
40833	4913	Cerro Azulcocha *	1090	Peru	-11.6900, -74.7050
40777	5181	Coñocranra	1085	Peru	-8.8417, -78.0058
40780	4295	Cerro de la Piedra Caballera *	1081	Peru	-7.8583, -78.6533
40785	3039	Cerro Chacas	1076	Peru	-4.6008, -79.6992
40792	5771	Nevado Padreyoc / Kiswar	1069	Peru	-13.3783, -72.7417
40796	5954	Nevado Contrahierbas / Nevado Ruricocha	1064	Peru	-9.1061, -77.4908
40797	1720	Cerro Santa Catalina *	1063	Peru	-6.9033, -75.6258
40800	5780	Nevado Llongote	1061	Peru	-12.3333, -75.9500
40804	2310	Cerro Paranapura *	1060	Peru	-5.8983, -76.7750
40807	1533	Cerro Alumbral	1057	Peru	-6.7708, -79.3733
40812	1212	Cerro Pompurre	1048	Peru	-5.9826, -79.8123
40813	1800	Cerro Panya *	1047	Peru	-7.5033, -75.9025
40816	2460	Cerro Challuazapa *	1045	Peru	-8.3158, -76.0017
40819	5706	Nevado Santa Rosa	1043	Peru	-10.4858, -76.7233
40820	2333	Cerro Larga *	1043	Peru	-8.2675, -75.7817
40843	4379	Cerro Antacaray	1027	Peru	-13.4408, -73.5458
40844	5367	Nevado Halancoma	1026	Peru	-13.1842, -72.2533
40846	1566	Cerro Conquis	1024	Peru	-6.9917, -79.3042
40847	2215	Cerro Shironpeveni	1023	Peru	-10.7097, -74.0896
40849	4250	Cerro Quinua Pampa	1023	Peru	-6.9300, -78.4033
40851	3575	Cerro Abiseo *	1021	Peru	-7.6746, -77.14168
40858	5615	Nevado Larjanco	1015	Peru	-16.9875, -70.0950

40860	5330	Nevado Terijuay	1009	Peru	-13.0071, -72.1926
40861	4718	Cerro Apushalla	1009	Peru	-8.1642, -77.4617
40862	1888	Cerro Yuracyacu *	1008	Peru	-7.4294, -76.2933
40864	4696	Nevado de Bolivar	1005	Peru	-7.1200, -77.6883
40865	2115	Cerro Chupichontal *	1005	Peru	-7.8828, -76.4594
40867	5597	Nevado Hipocapac	1001	Peru	-16.6233, -70.5433
40869	3623	Cerro Juscusbamba *	1000	Peru	-7.8708, -77.0864

SA214 Bolivian Andes

Id	Height	Name	Drop	Country	Location
40511	6438	Nevado Illimani	2451	Bolivia	-16.6550, -67.7836
40512	6542	Nevado Sajama	2428	Bolivia	-18.1083, -68.8833
40519	6176	Cerro Aucanquilcha	2164	Chile	-21.2208, -68.4683
40531	6145	Volcán San Pedro	2024	Chile	-21.8877, -68.3914
40534	6342	Volcán Parinacota	1989	Bolivia, Chile	-18.1658, -69.1417
40538	6040	Cerro Palpana	1947	Chile	-21.5467, -68.5225
40542	6427	Nevado Ancohuma	1897	Bolivia	-15.8542, -68.5408
40551	5748	Cerro Gigante / Jachacunocollo	1768	Bolivia	-16.9783, -67.3483
40553	5995	Alto Toroni / Cerro Sillajguay	1734	Bolivia, Chile	-19.7525, -68.6967
40560	5868	Volcán Ollagüe	1686	Bolivia, Chile	-21.3025, -68.1792
40564	4480	Cumbre Salto del Fraile	1661	Bolivia	-16.7417, -66.8883
40568	5960	Cerro Paniri	1654	Chile	-22.0592, -68.2283
40575	5321	Cerro Tunupa	1601	Bolivia	-19.8325, -67.6458
40576	5900	Cerros de Cañapa	1596	Bolivia	-21.4483, -68.0708
40577	5840	Cerro Tomasamil	1592	Bolivia	-21.2925, -67.9683
40578	5869	Cerro Cabaraya	1590	Bolivia	-19.1458, -68.6983
40581	5555	Cerro Chorolque	1577	Bolivia	-20.9177, -66.0360
40588	6044	Chaupi Orco	1555	Bolivia, Peru	-14.6558, -69.2292
40591	4284	Cerro Photulo Punta	1519	Bolivia	-19.5417, -64.6600
40598	5965	Cerro Caquella	1487	Bolivia	-21.4908, -67.9317
40600	5800	Cerro Puquintica	1476	Bolivia, Chile	-18.7392, -68.9775
40606	5393	Cerro Caltama	1460	Bolivia	-20.6358, -68.1092
40613	6063	Volcán Guallatiri	1430	Chile	-18.4225, -69.0892
40614	5728	Nevado Paroma	1430	Bolivia, Chile	-20.9383, -68.4125
40620	5504	Cerro Llixar	1416	Bolivia	-20.9908, -68.0458
40623	5301	Cerro Chiguana	1408	Bolivia	-21.1042, -67.8642
40624	4430	Cerro Sipe	1398	Bolivia	-21.0000, -64.8683
40630	5075	Cerro Kolligi	1388	Bolivia	-20.6617, -67.7558
40631	5644	Cerro Chela	1388	Chile	-21.4067, -68.5017
40632	3450	Cerro Garrapatas *	1386	Bolivia	-21.9258, -64.5792
40633	6008	Uturuncu	1384	Bolivia	-22.2645, -67.1869
40636	4765	Cerro Lique	1365	Bolivia	-20.3414, -65.2329
40639	5079	Cerro Pucara	1353	Bolivia	-19.6233, -68.0317

40641	5929	Nuevo Mundo / Cerro Lipez Sur	1348	Bolivia	-21.9333, -66.8792
40642	3300	Cerro Agua Milagro	1346	Bolivia	-16.1908, -67.5933
40643	4604	Cerro Condoriri	1344	Bolivia	-20.0650, -64.7508
40645	5382	Cerro Khala Katin	1342	Bolivia	-21.2183, -67.6075
40648	5760	Cerro del León	1329	Chile	-22.1415, -68.1064
40649	5390	Cerro Cariquima	1323	Chile	-19.5433, -68.6700
40655	5450	Nuevo Mundo	1307	Bolivia	-19.8025, -66.4792
40656	5665	Cerro Boneta	1306	Bolivia	-21.7525, -66.4808
40657	5227	Cerro Chascos	1305	Bolivia	-21.1883, -67.8000
40661	5899	Cerro Sonequera	1289	Bolivia	-22.0092, -67.2183
40665	4683	Cerro Infiernillos *	1283	Bolivia	-17.4258, -65.5267
40667	4155	Cerro Volcán	1275	Bolivia	-17.6662, -64.8422
40668	5860	Volcán Taapacá	1275	Chile	-18.1128, -69.5078
40671	5846	Cerro del Azufre	1272	Chile	-21.7833, -68.2400
40676	5688	Cerro Araral	1253	Bolivia, Chile	-21.6042, -68.1808
40678	5269	Cerro Tata J'achura	1251	Chile	-19.4967, -69.1025
40682	5838	Cerro Pastos Grandes	1248	Bolivia	-21.7500, -67.8392
40683	4910	Cerro Vila Pucarani	1243	Bolivia	-19.3242, -68.3142
40684	5631	Cerro Lliscaya	1242	Bolivia, Chile	-18.8908, -68.9117
40687	5868	Nevado Mururata	1231	Bolivia	-16.5200, -67.8167
40692	5060	Cerro Pirhuata	1210	Bolivia	-17.2137, -66.3996
40693	5164	Cerro Ubina	1210	Bolivia	-20.4575, -66.3667
40695	5006	Cerro Tetivilla	1208	Bolivia	-19.7183, -68.1883
40696	5171	Cerro Sapajo	1207	Bolivia	-19.9473, -68.3115
40699	5430	Cerro Tata Sabaya	1202	Bolivia	-19.1358, -68.5233
40710	6088	Nevado Huayna Potosí	1183	Bolivia	-16.2625, -68.1542
40712	3355	Cerro San José *	1176	Bolivia	-16.4159, -67.3595
40716	5949	Cerro Polapi	1170	Chile	-21.6483, -68.3933
40719	5888	Cerro Loromayu	1169	Bolivia	-22.4853, -67.1058
40727	5239	Cerro Yarvicoya	1157	Chile	-20.1167, -69.0083
40729	3440	Cerro Achachi	1150	Bolivia	-19.0042, -64.3892
40742	5815	Cerro Tapaquilcha	1123	Bolivia	-21.6008, -67.9542
40743	5601	Cerro Chuquiananta	1123	Chile	-18.9158, -69.1517
40746	5852	Nevado Callijon / Nevado Ananea Grande	1119	Peru	-14.6130, -69.3799
40754	5071	Cerro Cunurana	1114	Bolivia	-19.8019, -65.6532
40755	3506	Cumbre Huacayo	1112	Bolivia	-21.3117, -64.3564
40769	5572	Nevado de Chuquiananta	1094	Chile	-17.7923, -69.4999
40770	4859	Cerro Coracora	1094	Bolivia	-19.5742, -67.6600
40774	2746	Cerro Cruz Pata	1088	Bolivia	-16.0408, -67.7492
40781	5082	Cerro Planadita Plata	1081	Bolivia	-20.4675, -68.3367
40782	5696	Cerro Granada Segundo	1079	Argentina	-22.5575, -66.5450
40788	5915	Nevado Cololo	1074	Bolivia	-14.8867, -69.1125

40789	4988	Cerro Caral	1073	Bolivia	-20.8248, -67.7852
40791	5170	Cerro Napa	1073	Bolivia, Chile	-20.5167, -68.6667
40798	5551	Volcán Isluga	1062	Chile	-19.1550, -68.8200
40802	5610	Cerro El Volcán	1061	Bolivia	-22.2175, -66.7483
40803	3076	Cerro Rodeo	1060	Bolivia	-18.3600, -64.8092
40806	5306	Cerro Ocaña	1058	Bolivia	-20.6250, -68.4492
40808	6104	Nevado de Chiaraco	1056	Bolivia	-15.9625, -68.4108
40815	5550	Cerro Curumaya	1045	Bolivia	-19.0050, -68.8325
40817	3430	Cerro Enseñada de Meñique *	1044	Bolivia	-16.2950, -67.1800
40818	4792	Cerro Incacamachi	1043	Bolivia	-18.8533, -68.2117
40823	2325	Cerro Parapeti *	1040	Bolivia	-20.4708, -64.0575
40824	5374	Cerro Inti Pasto	1038	Bolivia	-21.3917, -67.9058
40825	5781	Cerro Salle	1037	Argentina	-22.4875, -66.7742
40826	2561	Cerro Paraiso *	1037	Bolivia	-14.4600, -68.3375
40827	5090	Paryani	1036	Bolivia	-19.1258, -68.4200
40830	4820	Volcán Pumire	1034	Bolivia	-18.9975, -68.4283
40832	3410	Cerro Kanamarca *	1033	Bolivia	-16.3461, -66.9819
40837	4340	Cerro Huanakkota	1032	Bolivia	-17.0125, -66.8575
40839	5740	Cerro Kapina	1029	Bolivia	-22.0083, -67.7767
40840	5060	Cerro Tazna	1028	Bolivia	-20.6283, -66.2008
40842	5628	Cerro Inacaliri	1027	Bolivia, Chile	-21.9789, -68.0714
40855	5106	Cerro Laram Khaua	1018	Bolivia	-18.2175, -68.5333
40857	3060	Cerro Bufete	1016	Bolivia	-19.4208, -64.1850
40863	4881	Cerro Carcanal	1005	Chile	-22.0178, -68.3598
40866	2985	Cerro La Ojada	1002	Bolivia	-18.3530, -64.2825
40868	5560	Nevado Anallajsi	1000	Bolivia	-17.9275, -68.9100

SA215 Puna de Atacama

Id	Height	Name	Drop	Country	Location
40503	6893	Ojos del Salado	3680	Argentina, Chile	-27.1092, -68.5408
40505	5550	Cerro Bolsón de los Cerrillos	3250	Argentina	-27.2132, -66.0937
40507	4575	Cerro El Manchao	2713	Argentina	-28.2550, -66.0358
40514	6739	Volcán Llullaillaco	2343	Argentina, Chile	-24.7200, -68.5367
40520	6380	Nevado de Cachi / Cerro El Libertador	2146	Argentina	-24.9317, -66.3900
40521	6792	Monte Pissis	2140	Argentina	-27.7550, -68.7992
40522	5896	Nevado de Chañi	2131	Argentina	-24.0629, -65.7458
40532	6051	Volcán Socompa	2015	Argentina, Chile	-24.3960, -68.2455
40536	6440	Volcán Antofalla	1957	Argentina	-25.5625, -67.8808
40540	5093	Cerro Malcante	1903	Argentina	-25.0776, -65.8513
40541	6233	Cerro Pular	1898	Chile	-24.2008, -68.0667
40548	6095	Cerro Aracar	1792	Argentina	-24.2900, -67.7833
40550	6012	Cerro Laguna Blanca	1777	Argentina	-26.5300, -67.0594
40557	6052	Cerro Copiapó	1702	Chile	-27.3058, -69.1308

40559	4740	Cumbres Calchaquies	1688	Argentina	-26.6148, -65.7214
40565	6414	Cerro El Cóndor	1659	Argentina	-26.6317, -68.3617
40570	2600	Cerros de Pereyra	1640	Argentina	-24.2070, -64.5140
40572	6140	Nevado Quehuar	1635	Argentina	-24.3083, -66.7323
40574	6046	Pili / Cerro Acamarachi	1608	Chile	-23.2925, -67.6175
40582	5810	Cerro Tebenquicho	1576	Argentina	-25.3508, -67.6467
40592	6239	Cerro de los Patos / Tres Quebradas	1519	Argentina, Chile	-27.3000, -68.8083
40593	6621	Cerro de Incahuasi	1514	Argentina, Chile	-27.0333, -68.2964
40595	2480	Cerro Castillejos	1505	Argentina	-26.0658, -64.8917
40599	6029	Cerro Salin	1483	Argentina, Chile	-24.3284, -68.0673
40601	6759	Cerro Bonete Chico	1473	Argentina	-28.0186, -68.7562
40603	4866	Cerro Negro de Rodriguez	1465	Argentina	-28.1183, -67.9150
40607	5129	Alto del Manantial / Serranía de Hornocal	1452	Argentina	-23.2200, -65.0725
40609	5920	Volcán Licancábur	1438	Bolivia, Chile	-22.8333, -67.8858
40612	5920	Cerro Luracatao	1436	Argentina	-25.1383, -66.6225
40615	5912	Cerro Galán	1429	Argentina	-25.9395, -66.9218
40616	5489	Cerro del Azufre	1427	Chile	-25.3742, -68.8825
40618	6748	Nevado Tres Cruces Sur	1419	Argentina, Chile	-27.0983, -68.7783
40622	3218	Cerro Crestón	1416	Argentina	-25.3950, -65.1833
40625	5127	Cerro Tipara / Cerro Aguilar	1397	Argentina	-23.1858, -65.7250
40627	5897	Volcán Puntas Negras	1395	Chile	-23.7458, -67.5400
40628	5842	Cerro Peinado	1394	Argentina	-26.6225, -68.1158
40629	5590	Cerro Piedra Sonada	1393	Argentina	-24.3642, -65.6558
40638	6141	Sierra Nevada de Lagunas Bravas	1353	Argentina	-26.4908, -68.5600
40644	6145	Volcán El Ermitaño	1343	Chile	-26.7842, -68.6008
40646	5733	Cerro Mojones	1342	Argentina	-25.6542, -67.3567
40653	5910	Cerro Miñiques	1311	Chile	-23.8166, -67.7581
40654	5314	Cerro Tultul	1310	Argentina	-24.1917, -67.1075
40663	5658	Cerro Tumisa	1287	Chile	-23.4600, -67.8100
40664	5265	Cerro de la Pena / Lozería	1283	Chile	-25.0716, -68.7139
40669	5629	Cerro Archibarca	1274	Argentina	-25.2375, -67.8650
40672	5704	Cerro Casliri	1265	Chile	-24.0250, -67.5175
40675	5760	Cerro Aguas Blancas	1254	Argentina, Chile	-25.7058, -68.4783
40677	5971	Cerro Sairecábur	1252	Bolivia, Chile	-22.7190, -67.8907
40679	2966	Sierra de Vinquis	1251	Argentina	-28.0583, -67.2667
40694	5793	Cerro Lejía	1208	Chile	-23.5551, -67.7643
40702	5878	Nevado Jotabeche	1192	Chile	-27.6975, -69.2183
40704	5334	Sierra de los Ratones	1191	Argentina	-25.0725, -66.9358
40705	5310	Bravo Alto	1188	Chile	-26.6730, -69.2612
40713	5924	Volcán Simba	1176	Chile	-23.3650, -67.6817
40714	5475	Cerro de la Carpa	1175	Argentina	-24.6842, -68.2312
40715	6100	Cerro Vallecitos	1170	Argentina	-26.2108, -68.3167

40718	5013	Cerro Negro de Zucho	1170	Argentina	-23.6300, -65.2850
40722	5819	Cerro Lila	1167	Argentina	-25.5567, -68.0733
40723	2380	Cerro Negro	1162	Argentina	-25.1079, -65.2640
40725	5050	Cerro Fundición	1161	Argentina	-22.4500, -65.1892
40731	5606	Cerro del Rincón	1142	Argentina, Chile	-24.0333, -67.3225
40739	5415	Cerro Chuscha	1127	Argentina	-26.1492, -66.2308
40740	6436	Cerro Veladero	1125	Argentina	-28.0727, -68.9773
40741	5540	Cerro Macón	1123	Argentina	-24.4658, -67.2550
40745	5730	Cerro Rosario	1122	Argentina	-22.8358, -66.6275
40749	6027	Nevado San Francisco	1116	Argentina, Chile	-26.9192, -68.2625
40751	5205	Cerro Hermoso	1115	Argentina	-23.4367, -65.5275
40753	4278	Cerro El Iruchal	1114	Argentina	-27.7913, -67.9486
40763	5187	Punta de la Casa del Alto	1100	Argentina	-26.9258, -67.5392
40766	5792	Cerro Ojo Antofalla	1098	Argentina	-25.4483, -68.0942
40771	3333	Cerro Nuñorco Grande	1093	Argentina	-26.9811, -65.7148
40776	5785	Toconquis	1086	Argentina	-25.5858, -67.0842
40778	2572	Cerro Ceibal	1083	Argentina	-24.4442, -64.4408
40779	5050	Cerro Río Blanco	1081	Argentina	-24.8983, -65.8875
40783	5167	Pampa Pajonal del Chaco	1077	Chile	-25.4608, -69.0025
40793	5850	Nevado de San Pedro	1069	Argentina	-22.9367, -66.9650
40794	5895	Cerro Chucula / Negro Muerto	1066	Argentina	-26.7667, -67.9975
40795	2340	Cerro Centinela	1064	Argentina	-24.1725, -65.0733
40799	5075	Volcán Doña Inés	1061	Chile	-26.0800, -69.1842
40805	6119	Volcán Barrancas Blancas	1059	Chile	-26.9908, -68.6658
40809	5706	Volcán Azufre o Lastarria	1052	Argentina, Chile	-25.1683, -68.5067
40810	5500	Cerro Tuzgle	1050	Argentina	-24.0558, -66.4792
40811	5203	Cerro Guanaquero	1050	Argentina	-24.2892, -67.4483
40814	5917	Cerro Laguna Escondida	1047	Argentina	-26.6033, -68.4800
40821	6080	Cerro Colorados	1043	Argentina, Chile	-26.1783, -68.3808
40822	4276	Cerro del Quimal	1041	Chile	-23.1125, -68.6567
40828	3646	Cerro Amarillo	1036	Argentina	-23.5567, -64.8583
40829	5421	Cerro Quebrada Honda	1036	Argentina	-25.6342, -68.2425
40831	5906	Morro Peñón Al Norte del Falso Azufre	1033	Argentina, Chile	-26.8000, -68.3625
40835	5105	Cerro Bayo Grande	1033	Argentina	-26.7308, -66.6558
40841	5764	Cerro Negro de la Laguna Verde	1028	Argentina	-27.7075, -68.5458
40845	4982	Cerro Azul / Médano Blanca	1026	Argentina	-24.1042, -65.6267
40848	3815	Cerro Cuevas	1023	Argentina	-25.7250, -66.3267
40852	5398	Cerro Curutú	1020	Chile	-23.1765, -67.0594
40854	5568	Cerro Leoncito	1019	Chile	-24.1625, -67.8173
40856	5070	Cerro de Navarro	1016	Argentina	-24.8642, -67.2517
40859	4920	Cerro Alto del Volcán / Cerro Tolar	1014	Argentina	-27.3967, -67.2850
40870	5730	Volcán Quetena	1000	Bolivia	-22.2607, -67.4156

SA22 Andes South

SA220 Central Argentina / Chile Andes

Id	Height	Name	Drop	Country	Location
41001	6963	Cerro Aconcagua	6963	Argentina	-32.6533, -70.0108
41003	6717	Cerro Mercedario	3356	Argentina	-31.9789, -70.1128
41006	4150	El Mela	2906	Argentina	-28.8675, -67.1275
41007	6097	Cerro General Manuel Belgrano / Famatina	2765	Argentina	-29.0142, -67.8267
41008	6573	Cerro Tupungato	2764	Argentina, Chile	-33.3583, -69.7700
41009	3491	Cerro Tronador	2662	Argentina, Chile	-41.1608, -71.8883
41010	3747	Volcán Lanin	2631	Argentina, Chile	-39.6375, -71.5025
41011	3160	Mogote Corralitos	2467	Argentina	-31.3158, -67.9233
41012	3810	Cerro Nevado	2281	Argentina	-35.5808, -68.4900
41015	4709	Volcán Domuyo	2228	Argentina	-36.6375, -70.4325
41017	5887	Cordillera de Ansilta	2204	Argentina	-31.6258, -69.8767
41019	6120	Cerro Marmolejo	2115	Argentina, Chile	-33.7348, -69.8780
41020	6280	Cerro de la Majadita	2113	Argentina	-30.4200, -69.7808
41022	4380	Cerro Pircas	2070	Argentina	-31.7075, -69.1567
41026	3838	Cerro Payún Liso	1954	Argentina	-36.5142, -69.2858
41028	2015	Volcán Calbuco	1946	Chile	-41.3300, -72.6183
41029	5189	Cerro Sosneado	1936	Argentina	-34.7533, -69.9717
41030	6168	Cerro del Toro	1911	Argentina, Chile	-29.1300, -69.7867
41032	2652	Volcán Osorno	1889	Chile	-41.1042, -72.4958
41037	3125	Volcán Llaima	1818	Chile	-38.6958, -71.7317
41038	3535	Cerro Sierra Velluda	1784	Chile	-37.4642, -71.4150
41040	5174	Cerro Picos del Barroso	1749	Chile	-34.2867, -70.0333
41045	3980	Volcán Tromen	1721	Argentina	-37.1400, -70.0500
41051	5460	Cerro Castillo	1626	Argentina, Chile	-33.9758, -69.8817
41053	5680	Cerro del Tambillo	1624	Argentina	-32.3042, -69.6808
41060	4999	Cerro Risco Plateado	1601	Argentina	-34.9183, -69.9942
41063	2422	Volcán El Mocho	1585	Chile	-39.9317, -72.0300
41064	4084	Volcán Azufre / Volcán Peteroa	1575	Argentina, Chile	-35.2725, -70.5817
41065	2860	Volcán Villarrica	1575	Chile	-39.4208, -71.9392
41066	2493	Volcán Puntiagudo	1574	Chile	-40.9742, -72.2658
41070	6122	Colangüil	1548	Argentina	-29.5888, -69.4494
41075	2364	Cerro Carreras	1531	Argentina	-41.5042, -71.2358
41078	6070	Nevado del Plomo	1525	Argentina, Chile	-33.1033, -70.0658
41079	2865	Volcán Lonquimay	1524	Chile	-38.3792, -71.5858
41085	5803	Cordillera de la Totora	1490	Argentina	-31.4458, -70.0317
41086	2284	Cerro Piltriquitrón	1489	Argentina	-41.9793, -71.4423
41095	5264	Volcán Maipo	1469	Argentina, Chile	-34.1642, -69.8317
41096	4049	Cerro Campanario	1466	Argentina, Chile	-35.9233, -70.3658
41099	5968	Cerro El Plata	1460	Argentina	-33.0158, -69.4550

41100	4990	Cerro Alto de los Arrieros	1455	Chile	-34.6508, -70.3725
41103	5993	Cerro de las Polleras	1437	Argentina, Chile	-33.2458, -69.9183
41104	1744	Cerro Bonete	1436	Chile	-41.1783, -72.1975
41105	2467	Cerro Azul	1435	Argentina	-40.2458, -71.2067
41107	2257	Cerro Hielo Azul	1435	Argentina	-41.8775, -71.6642
41108	3212	Nevado de Chillán	1434	Chile	-36.8292, -71.4100
41109	5685	Cerro de la Ortiga	1434	Argentina	-29.2667, -69.8017
41111	5864	Cerro del Potro	1429	Argentina, Chile	-28.3942, -69.6300
41118	3164	Volcán Callaqui	1408	Chile	-37.9275, -71.4467
41120	3953	Volcán Decabezado Grande	1403	Chile	-35.5900, -70.7467
41122	2785	Cerro Las Chacras	1398	Argentina	-31.1067, -67.4433
41125	6160	Cerro Las Tórtolas	1392	Argentina, Chile	-29.9394, -69.9069
41129	2258	Cerro Aucá Mahuida	1384	Argentina	-37.7383, -68.9242
41130	5014	Morro del Cuero	1377	Argentina	-34.3983, -69.5800
41131	4178	Cerro de las Minas	1374	Argentina	-35.3500, -69.9942
41132	4883	Nevado Flores	1374	Chile	-34.1400, -70.1658
41137	1592	Cerro Maltusado	1352	Chile	-39.8325, -72.2158
41139	3621	Volcán San Pedro	1342	Chile	-35.9933, -70.8517
41141	3386	Sierras Altas	1341	Argentina	-29.6317, -67.6158
41143	5645	Cerro Doña Ana	1338	Chile	-29.7617, -70.1100
41144	5080	Lagunas	1334	Argentina	-34.1108, -69.6275
41148	4841	Cerro Guanaquero	1318	Argentina	-34.5442, -69.9050
41149	4961	Cerro de la Bolsa	1317	Argentina	-29.5867, -69.0300
41152	5404	Cerro Loma Larga	1311	Chile	-33.6873, -69.9883
41154	2325	Cerro Falkner	1305	Argentina	-40.4958, -71.5358
41156	6216	Nevado Olivares	1304	Argentina, Chile	-30.2983, -69.9008
41158	1648	Cerro Lumaco	1294	Chile	-39.7183, -72.1158
41161	5545	Cerro del Volcán	1287	Chile	-30.4813, -70.2669
41162	1902	Mogote Los Quesillos	1285	Argentina	-30.7433, -66.5758
41163	3242	Nevado Longaví	1282	Chile	-36.1967, -71.1633
41164	3047	Sierra de Maz	1282	Argentina	-29.3400, -68.4467
41165	5411	Cortadera	1279	Argentina	-30.5583, -70.0333
41166	3710	Cerro Villalón	1277	Argentina	-31.0958, -69.2158
41173	4929	Cordillera de Lucho	1242	Argentina	-30.9800, -70.1492
41177	3826	Cerro Mary	1239	Argentina	-36.1667, -70.1592
41178	4405	Sierra de Umango	1239	Argentina	-29.0308, -68.5867
41179	4921	Cerro Picos del Río Bayo	1237	Argentina, Chile	-34.2842, -69.8992
41181	2229	Cerro Cuyín Manzano	1231	Argentina	-40.7967, -71.4025
41197	6384	Cerro La Ramada	1207	Argentina	-32.0825, -70.0175
41194	3478	Cerro Tulahuén	1204	Chile	-30.9517, -70.6833
41203	3081	Cerro El Toro	1191	Chile	-35.9850, -71.1258
41205	5467	Cerro Imán	1189	Argentina	-29.2337, -69.4721

41208	2199	Cerro Granitico	1188	Argentina	-41.3825, -71.6592
41212	5352	Cerro Piramidal del Potrero Escondido	1185	Argentina	-33.0075, -69.9292
41216	2554	Sierra Nevada	1178	Chile	-38.5758, -71.5892
41219	4771	Cerro Volcán Overo	1173	Argentina	-34.5667, -70.0083
41223	2296	Cerro Rucachoroi	1163	Argentina	-39.2958, -71.2183
41224	4681	Cerro del Molino	1162	Argentina, Chile	-32.3042, -70.2567
41226	2076	Cerro El Maitén	1159	Argentina	-42.0683, -71.3208
41227	5598	Cerro San Lorenzo	1156	Argentina	-30.4175, -69.9567
41228	5587	Los Amarillos	1155	Argentina, Chile	-29.2933, -70.0008
41229	3001	Volcán Copahue	1152	Argentina, Chile	-37.8583, -71.1833
41230	5612	Cerro Fandango	1152	Argentina	-28.3050, -69.0150
41237	3114	Cerro La Mocha	1149	Argentina	-35.9166, -69.5304
41238	1289	Cerro Ille	1146	Chile	-40.2900, -72.2242
41241	2294	Cerro Grande O Venzano	1140	Argentina	-41.7425, -71.6517
41250	2280	Cerro La Sierra	1133	Argentina	-41.8075, -71.3050
41251	2839	Cerro Chachil	1132	Argentina	-39.1067, -70.6167
41258	5216	Cordillera de la Punilla	1129	Chile	-29.7200, -70.2333
41272	5740	Pico 7 de Ansilta	1103	Argentina	-31.7642, -69.9083
41279	1605	Cerro Las Quemas *	1098	Chile	-41.1875, -72.3475
41280	2236	Volcán Puyehue	1097	Chile	-40.5933, -72.1183
41282	6090	Cerro Negro / Pabellón de Santa Clara	1092	Argentina	-33.4500, -69.7025
41284	2120	Cerro Riyunco *	1089	Argentina	-40.5708, -71.5800
41289	1596	Cerro Chuquilcura	1086	Chile	-39.2150, -71.9175
41290	3680	Cerro Payún Matru	1085	Argentina	-36.4217, -69.2417
41292	2130	Cerro Currhué	1082	Argentina	-39.8492, -71.3883
41300	3640	Cerro Blanco	1076	Argentina	-30.4875, -68.9725
41301	2124	Cerro Ezpeleta	1075	Argentina	-40.4017, -71.3775
41302	3460	Cerro Negro	1074	Argentina	-35.9100, -70.1350
41305	1526	Cerro Cuadrado	1071	Chile	-41.5500, -72.4150
41308	4308	Cerro La Aspereza	1069	Argentina	-28.8942, -68.7025
41309	1815	Cerros Cululies	1069	Chile	-41.4575, -72.4075
41310	2105	Cerro Torrecillas	1067	Chile	-41.4764, -72.1549
41313	2388	Cerro Catedral	1063	Argentina	-41.2167, -71.4983
41319	2091	Cerro Padre Laguna	1058	Argentina	-41.4008, -71.5300
41321	4648	Cerro Carnicería *	1056	Argentina	-31.6833, -70.3925
41322	2618	Cerro El Manzano	1056	Argentina	-29.0650, -66.8108
41323	4614	Cerro de las Mulas	1055	Argentina	-30.8483, -70.1558
41325	2382	Cerro Geda	1054	Argentina	-41.4191, -71.3241
41329	3540	Cerro Quebrada de Cosme	1052	Argentina	-29.3000, -67.8492
41331	4691	Cerro Alto del Azufre	1050	Argentina, Chile	-34.7658, -70.3083
41333	2342	Cerro Tabaco	1049	Chile	-32.6450, -70.8200
41339	2120	Cerro Bastión Norte *	1043	Argentina	-41.5108, -71.7450

41340	2206	Cerro Crespo	1040	Argentina, Chile	-40.4375, -71.7408
41344	2806	Volcán Tolhuaca	1036	Chile	-38.3150, -71.6483
41355	1955	Cerro Chachín	1019	Argentina	-40.1675, -71.6917
41358	5480	Chollay	1017	Argentina, Chile	-29.1883, -69.9492
41361	1940	Cerro Colorado	1014	Argentina	-41.4308, -71.6992
41367	2427	Cerro Zapallo	1007	Chile	-30.7983, -70.7183
41371	2146	Cerro Colo Huincull	1003	Argentina	-39.9475, -71.3550
41372	2174	Cerro El Manzanar	1000	Chile	-35.7933, -71.0375

Cerro Aconcagua, SA220
Rob Woodall, January 2011

We thought we'd been so smart. Instead of sitting around at base camp for several days, acclimatising, we started in Bolivia, climbed a few progressively higher Ultras, then drove to Ojos del Salado, second highest in the Andes but a straightforward two-day outing. Then Greg, Adam and I flew to Mendoza hoping to make short work of the near-7000m peak by hiking to base camp in a day, with our bags carried by mule. Then we had to sit around for a week, waiting for the weather. We stashed a tent at 5500 metres then returned to base camp intending to return and reach the summit. Instead we spent a couple of days watching lenticular clouds and checking weather forecasts. We went back up, struggled to locate our tent under half a metre of new snow, pitched it and sat inside for another couple of days, playing cards. I had to return to base camp for a fresh gas canister. On the last possible day the weather relented, we reached the highest point in the Andes in nice conditions, then headed for Santiago and home.

High camp on Cerro Aconcagua, SA220 (Rob Woodall)

SA221 Patagonian Andes

Id	Height	Name	Drop	Country	Location
41002	4058	Cerro San Valentín	3695	Chile	-46.5958, -73.3450
41004	3600	Volcán Lautaro	3322	Chile	-49.0200, -73.5058
41005	3706	Monte San Lorenzo / Cerro Cochrane	3319	Argentina, Chile	-47.5917, -72.3100
41013	2440	Cerro Melimoyu	2272	Chile	-44.0758, -72.8600
41014	2390	Cerro Yelcho Chico *	2238	Chile	-43.2942, -72.5250
41016	2700	Monte Zeballos	2228	Argentina	-47.0350, -71.6983
41018	2884	Cerro Paine Grande	2195	Chile	-50.9989, -73.0953
41021	2675	Cordillera Castillo	2088	Chile	-46.0643, -72.2073
41023	2300	Volcán Macá	2066	Chile	-45.1050, -73.1692
41024	2216	Cerro Balmaceda	2065	Chile	-51.4183, -73.1883
41025	3340	Cerro Mellizo Sur	1985	Chile	-48.5550, -73.1408
41027	3405	Cerro Fitzroy	1951	Argentina, Chile	-49.2717, -73.0433
41031	3446	Cerro Arenales	1909	Chile	-47.1958, -73.4692
41033	2160	Cerro Pináculo	1877	Argentina	-50.7600, -72.2558
41034	2100	Macizo Nevado	1835	Chile	-43.5425, -72.2017
41035	2515	Cerro Dos Picos	1834	Argentina	-42.4402, -71.9278
41036	2158	Cerro Elefantes	1829	Chile	-44.7600, -72.4242
41039	2366	Cerro Cristal	1782	Chile	-46.5183, -72.4383
41041	2050	Cerro Tres Frailes	1748	Chile	-48.6642, -72.6858
41042	2300	Nevado Queulat	1738	Chile	-44.3913, -72.3795
41043	2250	Pascua / Mellizo Este	1731	Chile	-48.6564, -72.9226
41044	3485	Cordón Mariano Moreno	1730	Argentina, Chile	-49.3208, -73.4167
41046	3293	Cerro Bertrand / Cerro Agassiz Norte	1717	Argentina, Chile	-49.9658, -73.5033
41048	2636	Cerro Mesón	1688	Argentina	-49.7567, -73.0150
41049	2286	Cerro Barros Arana	1645	Chile	-43.8883, -72.1858
41050	1910	Cerro Huemules	1634	Chile	-45.7358, -72.4492
41052	2730	Cerro Norte	1624	Argentina	-49.7833, -73.1067
41054	1780	Cordón Los Ñadis	1621	Chile	-47.5425, -72.9417
41056	1925	La Dama Blanca	1619	Chile	-51.8023, -73.3841
41057	2943	Cerro Penitentes	1611	Argentina	-47.6733, -72.2508
41058	2250	Cerro Situación	1610	Argentina	-42.9550, -71.6608
41059	1640	Gran Campo Nevado	1609	Chile	-52.7983, -73.0925
41061	2850	Cerro Pietrobelli	1600	Chile	-50.5350, -73.3575
41062	2200	Cerro Puño	1590	Chile	-47.2964, -73.1124
41269	2360	Cerro Michael *	1572	Chile	-46.6150, -72.9358
41067	2230	Cerro Aguja Sur	1563	Argentina, Chile	-42.1625, -71.8342
41068	1995	Cerro de la Paloma / Cerro Sombrero	1559	Chile	-45.8467, -72.2092
41069	2150	Cordón Soler	1557	Chile	-47.0533, -73.0658
41071	2271	Cerro Cónico	1544	Argentina, Chile	-43.2608, -71.7472

41072	1830	Cerro Mañihuales *	1541	Chile	-45.1983, -72.2633
41073	1590	Cerro Tenerife	1538	Chile	-51.3792, -72.8500
41074	1580	Peninsula Videau	1534	Chile	-48.1042, -73.3800
41076	2300	Cerro Desfiladero	1528	Chile	-47.4250, -73.1917
41077	2460	Volcán Michinmahuida	1527	Chile	-42.7992, -72.4458
41080	2010	Cerro Tres Hermanos	1514	Chile	-44.0708, -72.0167
41082	2200	Sierra de Sangra	1507	Argentina	-48.4692, -72.3917
41083	1520	Monte Burney	1493	Chile	-52.3250, -73.3800
41084	1810	Cerro Cuatro Puntas	1491	Chile	-45.5792, -72.3325
41087	2210	Cordón de Esquel	1488	Argentina	-42.7617, -71.2525
41088	2230	Cerro Desnudo	1487	Argentina	-44.1025, -71.6908
41089	2480	Cerro Campanario	1483	Chile	-50.4003, -73.7733
41090	2475	Cerro de las Nieves *	1478	Chile	-46.6681, -72.1272
41091	1590	Cerro Gualas *	1478	Chile	-46.4625, -73.6283
41092	2911	Cerro O'Higgins	1477	Chile	-48.8028, -73.1586
41093	1538	Cerro Monumento Moore	1472	Chile	-51.6459, -72.8578
41094	2090	Cerro Cay	1470	Chile	-45.0600, -72.9858
41097	1630	Cerro de los Huemules *	1465	Chile	-45.8100, -73.2067
41098	1727	Nevado Cóndor	1464	Chile	-45.6123, -72.9102
41101	1985	Cerro Christie *	1455	Chile	-48.1925, -72.4917
41102	2100	Cerro Emperador Guillermo	1443	Chile	-45.3100, -72.1825
41106	2440	Cordón de las Pirámides	1435	Argentina	-42.9048, -71.9228
41110	2122	Cerro Bonete	1433	Argentina	-49.1425, -72.8250
41112	2200	Volcán Corcovado	1424	Chile	-43.1942, -72.7933
41113	2007	Cerro Huina *	1424	Chile	-46.1975, -73.0692
41115	1440	Cerro Elefantes *	1415	Chile	-46.1009, -73.5227
41116	1930	Cerro Salto *	1414	Chile	-47.3783, -72.5467
41117	1510	Cerro Blanco Encalada *	1412	Chile	-49.2942, -74.2450
41119	2031	Cerro Wood	1405	Chile	-47.1150, -72.1392
41123	2279	Cerro Árido	1396	Argentina	-47.8200, -72.3008
41124	2153	Cerro Nahuel Pan	1396	Argentina	-42.9892, -71.2500
41126	1601	Cerro Mitre	1389	Argentina	-50.4342, -72.8458
41127	1883	Cerro Epuyén *	1389	Argentina	-42.1700, -71.4808
41128	2322	Cerro Hornopirén *	1387	Chile	-41.9336, -72.2003
41133	2254	Cerro Mie	1371	Argentina	-47.9242, -72.1500
41134	1425	Cerro Leal *	1368	Chile	-48.0367, -73.1975
41136	2288	Cerro Año Nuevo *	1355	Chile	-47.9508, -72.7900
41138	2334	Cerro Las Tablas *	1347	Chile	-47.5658, -72.7825
41140	2852	Cerro Gorra Blanca	1341	Argentina, Chile	-49.1342, -73.0825
41142	2035	Cerro Negro	1339	Chile	-45.1133, -71.9669
41145	1385	Volcán Huaqui	1334	Chile	-42.3883, -72.5450
41146	1595	Cerro Malito *	1326	Chile	-43.6167, -72.0750

41147	2405	Cerro Kristine	1324	Chile	-46.8874, -72.2788
41150	1614	Peninsula Maipu	1316	Argentina	-49.0383, -72.4842
41151	1362	Cerro Cordón	1313	Chile	-45.4408, -72.6642
41153	2270	Cerro El Victor *	1311	Chile	-46.4033, -72.2800
41155	1795	Cerro Iglesia	1304	Chile	-45.8242, -72.3183
41157	1370	Cerro Yelcho *	1294	Chile	-43.0188, -72.5857
41159	2103	Cerro Steffen	1290	Argentina, Chile	-44.4036, -71.6422
41160	1894	Cerro Vargas *	1289	Chile	-48.3183, -72.7025
41167	2020	Cerro Pueyrredón *	1276	Argentina	-47.3992, -72.0725
41168	2677	Cerro Huemul	1275	Argentina	-49.4237, -73.0345
41169	1392	Cerro Boxer *	1266	Chile	-48.5542, -74.2367
41170	1850	Cerro Tuerto	1256	Chile	-47.8232, -73.2171
41171	1324	Aguja Este *	1253	Chile	-51.9842, -73.2025
41172	3078	Cerro Hyades	1247	Chile	-46.8480, -73.2395
41174	1875	Cerro Martinez de Rozas *	1242	Argentina	-48.9925, -72.6417
41175	1350	Cerro Meseta	1241	Chile	-51.1300, -72.7250
41176	2705	Cerro La Torre	1240	Chile	-46.8313, -73.0802
41180	2235	Cerro Tigre *	1234	Chile	-43.2082, -72.0690
41182	1301	Monte Partido	1230	Chile	-47.2492, -74.1275
41183	1405	Cerro Alejandro *	1229	Chile	-47.4778, -73.9725
41184	3102	Cerro Torre	1227	Argentina, Chile	-49.2917, -73.0986
41185	2013	Cerro Cuche	1220	Argentina	-43.4792, -71.1650
41186	2570	Cerro Campana	1218	Argentina	-49.6589, -73.1539
41187	1655	Cerro Codo *	1216	Chile	-48.2258, -74.0628
41188	1906	Cerro Barrientos *	1215	Chile	-45.0533, -72.7200
41189	2072	Cerro Techado Blanco	1214	Argentina	-42.7367, -71.8817
41190	2085	Cerro El Toqui	1207	Argentina, Chile	-44.9150, -71.9792
41191	2187	Volcán Yate	1206	Chile	-41.7589, -72.3989
41192	1585	Cerro Figueroa *	1205	Chile	-44.1361, -72.3091
41193	1220	Monte Muela	1205	Chile	-53.3500, -72.2800
41195	1817	Cerro Moraga	1202	Chile	-43.3342, -72.3342
41196	2305	Cerro Ap Iwan	1199	Argentina, Chile	-46.1573, -71.8665
41198	1300	Cerro Estrecha *	1197	Chile	-51.5375, -73.1625
41199	2177	Cerro Claro Solar *	1197	Chile	-43.9483, -72.0808
41200	1887	Cerro Turbio *	1197	Chile	-44.3175, -72.2892
41201	1327	Cerro Celebes *	1195	Chile	-51.6325, -73.3367
41202	1200	Cerro Castillo de Dynevor	1192	Chile	-52.5825, -72.4867
41204	1205	Cerro Barranco *	1190	Chile	-44.1104, -73.1592
41206	1873	Cerro Viedma *	1189	Argentina	-49.6325, -72.9733
41207	1198	Cerro Garrao *	1189	Chile	-46.2657, -73.6255
41210	2140	Cerro Áspero	1187	Argentina	-47.8667, -72.3600
41211	1321	Cerro La Silueta	1187	Chile	-52.3275, -72.1050

41213	2490	Cordón del Pico Alto	1185	Argentina, Chile	-42.1217, -72.0650
41214	1980	Cerro Cisnes *	1180	Chile	-44.6019, -71.9719
41215	2050	Cerro Cuadrado	1178	Argentina, Chile	-43.1442, -71.8417
41217	1491	Cerro Chacabuco	1178	Argentina	-48.9783, -72.3058
41222	1820	Cerro Alto del Petizo	1169	Argentina	-42.6658, -71.7450
41225	1330	Cerro Rio Negro *	1160	Chile	-45.4028, -73.1968
41231	2411	Cerro Hermoso	1151	Argentina	-47.5583, -72.2233
41232	1740	Cerro Redondo	1151	Chile	-44.6061, -72.4931
41233	1410	Cerro Cascadas Escondidas *	1151	Chile	-42.6853, -72.6306
41234	1295	Cerro El Altar	1150	Chile	-50.6218, -73.8502
41235	1979	Cerro Nef *	1150	Chile	-47.0108, -73.1400
41239	2820	Cerro Largo	1141	Chile	-46.9590, -73.3758
41242	1190	Cerro Pilcomayo *	1137	Chile	-45.2214, -73.3590
41243	1948	Cerro Enredaderas	1137	Chile	-43.5125, -71.9983
41244	1955	Cerro El Desparramado *	1135	Chile	-45.9417, -72.6667
41245	2113	Cerro Central	1135	Argentina	-43.7192, -71.4733
41247	2588	Pico Triangular Sur	1134	Argentina, Chile	-46.9850, -71.9183
41248	1329	Cerro Torrejón Oeste *	1134	Chile	-47.2883, -73.9592
41249	1170	Cerro Abbé	1134	Chile	-43.8101, -72.8626
41252	1722	Cerro Tamango	1131	Chile	-47.1658, -72.5775
41253	1347	Cerro Caldera	1131	Chile	-44.0175, -72.2567
41254	2215	Cerro Tetris	1130	Argentina	-48.1917, -72.1200
41255	1678	Nevado Acantilado	1130	Chile	-45.3700, -72.8983
41256	2250	Cerro T	1130	Argentina, Chile	-47.7458, -72.4425
41259	1510	Cerro Cute *	1122	Chile	-47.8525, -73.4075
41260	2053	Cerro Mayer	1122	Argentina, Chile	-48.3540, -72.3102
41261	1935	Cerro Engaño *	1120	Chile	-46.4267, -72.9775
41262	1763	Cerro César	1118	Chile	-44.2775, -72.4842
41263	1735	Cerro Katalalixar *	1116	Chile	-47.6471, -73.8334
41264	2095	Cerro Congelado *	1115	Chile	-43.9942, -71.8908
41265	1215	Cerro Baker *	1114	Chile	-48.0242, -74.0900
41266	1176	Cerro Luisa *	1112	Chile	-47.9392, -73.5275
41267	2498	Cerro Anexo	1112	Argentina	-42.3711, -71.7663
41268	1961	Cerro Cascada	1110	Chile	-43.1233, -72.5333
41270	1655	Cerro Copa *	1107	Chile	-44.8883, -72.7108
41271	1280	Cerro Julián *	1105	Chile	-47.3883, -74.0675
41273	2205	Cerro Barrancos *	1103	Chile	-47.6133, -72.5683
41274	1625	Cerro Chico *	1102	Chile	-48.9575, -73.0967
41275	1130	Monte Olvidado	1099	Chile	-52.4908, -72.7475
41276	1940	Cerro Sin Nombre	1099	Argentina, Chile	-48.9392, -72.9142
41277	2045	Cerro Fantasma	1098	Argentina	-50.4150, -73.2642
41278	1927	Cerro Langueley	1098	Argentina	-43.2367, -71.2775

41081	2300	Cerro Gran Chileno	1088	Chile	-46.5692, -73.0783
41285	1802	Cerro Teta	1088	Chile	-43.1708, -71.9650
41286	1300	Cerro Rodriguez *	1087	Chile	-43.7987, -72.7748
41287	2150	Cerro Palena *	1086	Chile	-43.9367, -71.8942
41288	1875	Cerro del Torrente *	1086	Chile	-43.7194, -72.0381
41291	1220	Cerro Denmon *	1083	Chile	-48.8539, -74.2680
41293	1838	Cerro Colorado	1082	Chile	-45.2875, -71.9850
41294	1322	Cerro Chano	1080	Chile	-42.7375, -72.6592
41295	1344	Cerro Mocho	1077	Chile	-51.4825, -72.6333
41296	2273	Cerro La Leona	1077	Chile	-46.9917, -72.1225
41297	2244	Cerro Los Nadis *	1077	Chile	-47.8342, -72.8092
41298	2253	Cerro Torrecilla	1077	Argentina	-42.6460, -71.9404
41299	1210	Cerro Claro *	1077	Chile	-43.9592, -72.3183
41303	2174	Cerro La Quemada	1073	Argentina	-42.8017, -71.5275
41304	2697	Almirante Nieto	1072	Chile	-50.9721, -72.9640
41306	1485	Cerro Michimahuida *	1071	Chile	-43.0508, -72.4130
41307	1080	Cerro Valdés *	1070	Chile	-52.1300, -72.9225
41311	1144	Cerro Gaviota *	1066	Chile	-44.2267, -73.1383
41312	1083	Cerro Grappler *	1064	Chile	-49.5708, -74.0267
41314	1310	Cerro Puyuhuapi *	1063	Chile	-44.4117, -72.7250
41315	1925	Cerro Rebalse *	1061	Chile	-47.1292, -73.2175
41318	1125	Cerro Estero Nef *	1058	Chile	-48.1125, -74.1683
41320	1545	Cerro Colorado	1057	Argentina	-47.3800, -71.6167
41326	1879	Cerro Trono	1054	Chile	-51.8367, -73.3883
41327	1771	Cerro Daudet	1054	Argentina, Chile	-50.7900, -73.0700
41328	1125	Cerro Santa Lucía	1053	Chile	-47.3325, -74.2917
41330	1854	Cerro Castillo de Aysén	1052	Chile	-45.4233, -72.3092
41332	1860	Cerro Cajón *	1049	Chile	-46.1133, -72.6325
41334	1599	Cerro Ferrier	1048	Chile	-51.1517, -73.1986
41335	2050	Cordón de Cholila	1046	Argentina	-42.3050, -71.4250
41336	2105	Cerro Salton *	1045	Chile	-47.4658, -73.1033
41338	1555	Cerro Rosselot *	1043	Chile	-44.1108, -72.3933
41341	2083	Cerro Barros Luco	1039	Chile	-43.8400, -72.2775
41342	1885	Cerro Álvarez	1036	Argentina	-48.8314, -72.3775
41343	1585	Pico Alto	1036	Chile	-44.6983, -72.2908
41345	1560	Cerro Sorpresa *	1034	Chile	-44.1875, -72.1417
41346	1050	Peninsula Swett	1032	Chile	-48.1067, -74.3992
41347	2016	Cerro Mineral	1031	Argentina, Chile	-44.7800, -71.4067
41348	1918	Cerro Blanco *	1030	Chile	-41.9117, -72.3267
41349	2125	Cerro de las Golondrinas *	1029	Chile	-43.9669, -71.9816
41350	1114	Cerro Gamero *	1024	Chile	-52.3708, -73.1500
41351	1175	Cerro Bernardo *	1023	Chile	-48.6208, -73.9408

Id	Height	Name		Drop	Country	Location
41353	2150	La Gloria		1020	Chile	-46.8008, -72.1808
41354	2105	Cerro Sin Nombre *		1019	Chile	-46.2150, -72.5742
41356	1535	Cerro Riesco *		1019	Chile	-45.6219, -72.7346
41357	1250	Cerro Pomar *		1018	Chile	-48.4917, -74.1642
41359	1195	Morro Gacitúa		1016	Chile	-43.9133, -72.3392
41360	1930	Cerro Rivadavia		1015	Argentina	-42.6203, -71.6076
41362	1065	Cerro Guala *		1012	Chile	-43.7050, -72.9217
41363	1760	Cerro Vera *		1011	Chile	-45.7289, -72.7497
41364	1992	Cerro Bordali *		1010	Chile	-44.2500, -72.3975
41365	1155	Cerro El Altar Norte *		1010	Chile	-50.5810, -73.8320
41366	1170	Cerro Sombrero		1008	Chile	-43.0392, -72.6958
41368	1835	Cerro Correntoso *		1006	Chile	-43.0503, -72.2800
41369	2642	Cerro Pirámide		1004	Chile	-49.0677, -73.2665
41370	1154	Cerro Cascajal		1004	Chile	-41.9975, -72.5308
41373	1952	Cordón Esperanza		1000	Argentina	-42.2250, -71.9683
41374	1195	Cerro San Bernabe *		1000	Chile	-53.6700, -71.6794

Patagonian Islands

Islands in Tierra del Fuego are in region SA205 and other coastal islands are in SA204.

Id	Height	Name	Island	Drop	Country	Location
41047	1705	Cerro Ladrillero	Isla Riesco	1705	Chile	-52.9508, -72.5958
41114	1600	Cerro Gajardo *	Isla Riesco	1420	Chile	-52.8892, -72.8583
41240	1183	Monte Wyndham	Isla Riesco	1141	Chile	-53.3010, -72.8927
41324	1230	Cerro Alacalufes *	Isla Riesco	1055	Chile	-53.1189, -72.5486
41055	1620	Monte Mentolat	Magdalena	1620	Chile	-44.6967, -73.0758
41135	1398	Cerro Colmillo	Magdalena	1357	Chile	-44.5783, -72.9158
41209	1400	Cerro Gaviota *	Magdalena	1187	Chile	-44.8775, -73.2008
41220	1210	Cerro Los Mallines *	Magdalena	1170	Chile	-44.5283, -73.0725
41317	1240	Cerro Pangal *	Magdalena	1059	Chile	-44.7548, -73.2245
41121	1402	Isla Farquhar	Isla Farquhar	1402	Chile	-48.4508, -74.3442
41218	1175	Cerro Portales	Diego Portales	1175	Chile	-51.9567, -73.0017
41221	1170	Isla Golondrina	Isla Golondrina	1170	Chile	-48.2183, -74.4008
41236	1150	Cerro Martinez *	Isla Merino Jarpa	1150	Chile	-47.8642, -73.9833
41316	1095	Cerro Sierralta *	Isla Merino Jarpa	1060	Chile	-47.9017, -74.2725
41246	1135	Cerro Calzoncillo	Llancahué	1135	Chile	-42.1342, -72.5308
41257	1130	Isla Ofhidro	Isla Ofhidro	1130	Chile	-48.4133, -74.0583
41281	1095	Isla Refugio	Isla Refugio	1095	Chile	-43.9883, -73.1608
41283	1091	Cerro Ester	Isla Ester	1091	Chile	-45.1099, -73.3978
41337	1045	Isla Atilio	Isla Atilio	1045	Chile	-44.3652, -73.2574
41352	1020	Isla Caldeleugh	Isla Caldeleugh	1020	Chile	-48.3233, -74.3225

SA23 Guiana Highlands

Piedra Maverick, summit of Roraima-tepui, SA230 (Sean Caulfield)

Kukenan-tepuí and Roraima-tepui, SA230 (Sean Caulfield)

SA230 La Gran Sabana

Id	Height	Name	Drop	Country	Location
41502	2810	Roraima-tepuí - Piedra Maverick	2335	Venezuela	5.1408, -60.7633
41511	2634	Aprada-tepuí	1709	Venezuela	5.4192, -62.4417
41512	2515	Auyan-tepuí	1687	Venezuela	5.7517, -62.4625
41514	2692	Chimata Tepuy	1675	Venezuela	5.3700, -62.0792
41517	2777	Ilú-tepuí	1549	Venezuela	5.3983, -61.0050
41519	2500	Kamarkarawai-tepuí	1419	Venezuela	5.8658, -61.9983
41520	2260	Upuigma-tepuí	1410	Venezuela	5.0858, -61.9492
41523	2460	Ptari-tepuí	1364	Venezuela	5.7675, -61.8117
41525	1754	Cerro Guaiquinima	1353	Venezuela	5.8717, -63.7600
41530	2240	Angasima-tepuí	1315	Venezuela	5.0442, -62.1092
41536	1775	Cerro Topochí	1221	Venezuela	6.2497, -62.6922
41548	2052	Ayanganna Mountains	1097	Guyana	5.3850, -59.9900
41557	1535	Cerro Puruê *	1027	Venezuela	3.7142, -62.8508

SA231 Western Guiana Highlands

Id	Height	Name	Drop	Country	Location
41503	2832	Cerro Marahuaca	2287	Venezuela	3.6600, -65.4067
41504	2392	Serranía Yutajé	2025	Venezuela	5.7658, -66.1917
41508	2350	Sierra Maigualida	1789	Venezuela	5.5808, -65.2492
41510	2080	Cerro Cerbatana	1712	Venezuela	6.6600, -66.2375
41513	2070	Cerro Raya	1687	Venezuela	5.4167, -66.3667
41516	2395	Cerro Jaua	1569	Venezuela	4.7558, -64.5075
41522	2015	Cerro Sipapo	1384	Venezuela	4.9617, -67.3350
41524	1972	Cerro Maigualida *	1355	Venezuela	5.9975, -65.6867
41526	2775	Cerro Huha	1351	Venezuela	3.8299, -65.4727
41529	2425	Cerro Duida / Cerro Yennamadi	1329	Venezuela	3.3533, -65.7075
41531	1775	Cerro Huachamacari	1308	Venezuela	3.8558, -65.7583
41533	1625	Cerro Yagua *	1244	Venezuela	3.8023, -66.1660
41539	1990	Cerro Guanay	1182	Venezuela	5.8038, -66.3672
41540	2188	Cerro Asisa *	1174	Venezuela	4.3325, -65.6900
41542	1790	Cerro Corobo	1138	Venezuela	5.5525, -65.6408
41546	1220	Cerro Yapacana	1103	Venezuela	3.6917, -66.7708
41547	1245	Cerro Ventuari *	1098	Venezuela	4.7253, -66.3933
41549	1210	Cerro Candelaria *	1077	Venezuela	7.2150, -65.4392
41553	1150	Cerro Mocho *	1045	Venezuela	6.6392, -65.0750
41556	2460	Wataba Siru	1036	Venezuela	3.5925, -65.4792
41561	1978	Cerro Ovana	1015	Venezuela	4.5839, -66.7530
41562	2251	Cerro Yaví	1014	Venezuela	5.7058, -65.9067

SA232 Southern Guiana Highlands

Id	Height	Name	Drop	Country	Location
41501	2993	Pico da Neblina / Yaripo	2885	Brazil	0.7983, -66.0075
41505	2140	Serra Tulu Tuloi	1949	Brazil	1.1958, -63.8000
41506	2475	Serra Imeri	1926	Brazil	0.4906, -65.3330
41507	1980	Serra da Mocidade	1832	Brazil	1.7467, -61.7925
41509	1880	Serra do Pacu	1714	Brazil	1.5289, -62.1736
41515	1780	Tulu Tuloi II	1585	Brazil	0.9600, -63.3400
41518	2005	Serra Tapirapeco	1431	Brazil, Venezuela	1.2233, -64.7492
41521	2140	Cerro Castanhal *	1397	Brazil	0.4617, -65.5917
41527	1490	Pico Apiaú *	1351	Brazil	2.4433, -61.4442
41528	1910	Cerro Marari *	1335	Brazil, Venezuela	1.1583, -64.9810
41532	1706	Cerro Preto *	1244	Brazil	1.3025, -64.0392
41534	1540	Pico Mucajaí *	1238	Brazil	2.6000, -62.5142
41535	1890	Pico Marechal Mascarenhas de Moraes	1236	Brazil	0.7271, -65.6039
41537	1360	Cerro Ananaluia *	1213	Brazil	1.5542, -62.8442
41538	1820	Cerro Ariapo *	1211	Brazil, Venezuela	1.2958, -64.6617
41543	1740	Pico Ocamo *	1131	Brazil, Venezuela	3.2033, -64.1683
41544	1238	Serra do Padre	1124	Brazil	0.6192, -66.4175
41545	1250	Cerro Mafi *	1122	Brazil	0.4192, -65.9775
41550	1172	Pico Paulo *	1052	Brazil	2.3533, -61.3583
41551	1885	Pico Matacuni *	1047	Venezuela	3.3887, -64.6755
41552	2295	Cerro Abuera *	1046	Brazil	0.4158, -65.3775
41554	1270	Cerro Maia *	1042	Brazil	0.5425, -65.8600
41555	1600	Cerro Aracamuni	1041	Venezuela	1.6275, -65.8717
41558	1335	Pico Tabatinga	1026	Brazil	1.3308, -62.1867
41559	1175	Serra do Opikhteri	1025	Brazil	1.7608, -62.1808
41560	1940	Cerro Bacati *	1025	Brazil, Venezuela	1.2629, -64.7857

SA233 Eastern Guiana Highlands

Id	Height	Name	Drop	Country	Location
41541	1230	Juliana Top	1145	Suriname	3.6825, -56.5358

Roraima-tepui, SA230
Sean Caulfield, May 2016

The campsites on top of Roraima are all called hotels. These include Hotel Indio, Hotel Arenal, Hotel Uno and Hotel Coati. I stayed for three nights in Hotel Arenal, which was in a small cave under an overhung rock and looked directly at Piedra Maverick, the highest point on Monte Roraima, around 500 metres away. Our guide took us to some rock pools which were known as the 'jacuzzi', so there are many amenities on top of Roraima!

SA24 Brazilian Highlands

SA245 East-Central Brazilian Highlands

Id	Height	Name	Drop	Country	Location
42001	2891	Pico da Bandeira	2640	Brazil	-20.4344, -41.7962
42004	2033	Serra do Barbado	1395	Brazil	-13.2967, -41.9075
42009	1751	Pico do Pitengo	1334	Brazil	-18.5067, -41.1708
42010	2039	Pico Forno Grande	1294	Brazil	-20.5200, -41.1025
42013	2000	Pico do Soares	1141	Brazil	-20.6625, -42.4200
42016	2080	Pico do Sol	1123	Brazil	-20.1117, -43.4442
42018	2062	Pico do Itambé	1099	Brazil	-18.3992, -43.3483
42023	1409	Pedra Riscada	1051	Brazil	-18.3642, -41.3350
42024	1570	Pico Caratinga *	1049	Brazil	-19.2458, -41.5883
42025	1380	Serra do Caparaó	1035	Brazil	-19.7425, -40.9800
42027	1798	Pico do Sucuriú *	1025	Brazil	-15.2383, -42.8208

SA246 Southern Brazilian Highlands

Id	Height	Name	Drop	Country	Location
42002	2798	Pico Pedra da Mina	2066	Brazil	-22.4283, -44.8433
42003	2366	Pico Maior de Friburgo / Pedra dos Três Picos	1946	Brazil	-22.3413, -42.7254
42006	2275	Pedra do Sino - Morro da Agulha do Diablo	1356	Brazil	-22.4620, -43.0315
42007	2088	Morro Tira Chapéu	1349	Brazil	-22.7700, -44.6592
42008	1416	Serra dos Itatins	1344	Brazil	-24.3783, -47.2375
42011	2421	Pico dos Marins	1221	Brazil	-22.5025, -45.1208
42014	2257	Serra dos Órgãos - Pico da Caledônia	1137	Brazil	-22.3535, -42.5871
42015	1877	Pico Paraná	1126	Brazil	-25.2527, -48.8088
42017	2791	Pico das Agulhas Negras	1103	Brazil	-22.3808, -44.6617
42019	1470	Torre da Prata - Morro Grande	1092	Brazil	-25.6271, -48.6886
42020	1761	Pedra do Desengano	1077	Brazil	-21.9000, -41.9117
42021	1926	Pico da Maria Comprida	1070	Brazil	-22.4011, -43.2092
42028	1078	Morro Taquari	1032	Brazil	-25.1442, -48.1558
42029	1660	Morro das Lajes	1019	Brazil	-22.9275, -44.1942
42030	1824	Morro da Bela Vista do Guizoni	1018	Brazil	-27.9083, -49.3200
42005	1378	Pico de São Sebastião, São Sebastião	1378	Brazil	-23.8758, -45.3792
42026	1031	Pico da Pedra D'Água, Ilha Grande	1031	Brazil	-23.1517, -44.2300

Brazil

The Brazilian Highlands region contains 28 Ribus stretching over 2000 kilometres from Serra do Barbado in the north to Morro da Bela Vista do Guizoni in the south. This region of Ribus is isolated from all others, with the next nearest Ribus being almost 2000 kilometres away to the west in Bolivia and Argentina. Brazil's other cluster of Ribus is in the Guiana Highlands region, which is approximately 3000 kilometres to the north-west and therefore not much closer to Rio de Janeiro or São Paulo than the supremely isolated Ribu of Queen Mary's Peak, Tristan da Cunha in the middle of the southern Atlantic Ocean.

A keen hiker in Rio de Janeiro or São Paulo (both cities conveniently located in the middle of the region) might in theory attempt to climb all 28 Ribus in an incredibly active month, but would probably choose to spread them out with two or three Ribus a month.

Ribu baggers would find far more opportunities in Chile, though most of its peaks are high and challenging or awkward to reach. Brazil is the fifth largest country, with 5.6% of the Earth's land mass but less than 1% of its Ribus, whereas Chile is the 38th largest country and less than 10% of the size of Brazil, but its 381 Ribus represent over 5% of the total. The Ribu density per square kilometre is therefore over 50 times as high in Chile as in Brazil. Canada and China have a huge number of Ribus but their density is not as high as in other large countries such as Iran, Indonesia and Greenland. Ribu density in Chile is almost four times as high as in any of the twenty largest countries, but some smaller countries do even better. Nepal has 78 Ribus packed into its 147000 square km (60% of the size of the UK) but Tajikistan does even better with 77 Ribus in 143000 square km. Greece and Bhutan also have high Ribu density – not as high as Chile, Nepal or Tajikistan, but those in Greece are much easier to climb than those in the Andes, Himalaya or Pamir. Some of the smaller European countries are more mountainous than Greece, as shown in the table on page 337.

The largest countries with no Ribus are Mauritania and Mali. Libya is even larger and has only one, which is shared with Sudan, while Australia also has very low Ribu density.

SA25 South-east South America

SA252 Sierras de Cordoba

Id	Height	Name	Drop	Country	Location
42502	2770	Cerro Champaquí	2207	Argentina	-31.9875, -64.9367
42504	2220	Sierra de San Luís	1315	Argentina	-33.0653, -66.2070

SA253 Pampas

Id	Height	Name	Drop	Country	Location
42508	1239	Cerro Tres Picos	1076	Argentina	-38.1583, -61.9517

SA256 South-west Atlantic Islands

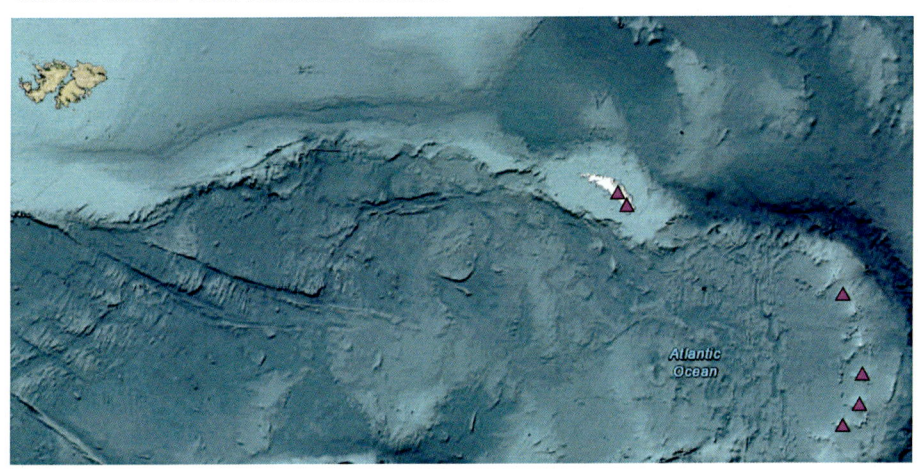

Id	Height	Name	Island	Drop	Country	Location
42501	2934	Mount Paget	South Georgia	2934	South Georgia (UK)	-54.4498, -36.5253
42503	2331	Mount Carse	South Georgia	1688	South Georgia (UK)	-54.7100, -36.1075
42505	1210	Mount Hodson	Visokoi	1210	South Georgia (UK)	-56.7094, -27.2080
42506	1160	Mount Darnley	Bristol Island	1160	South Georgia (UK)	-59.0406, -26.4990
42507	1139	Mount Belinda	Montagu Island	1139	South Georgia (UK)	-58.4344, -26.3841
42509	1115	Mount Harmer	Cook Island	1115	South Georgia (UK)	-59.4372, -27.1811

South Georgia and the South Sandwich Islands is one of fourteen current British Overseas Territories. Given its height, Mount Paget is the highest British peak anywhere in the world. It is more than twice as high and more than twice as prominent as Ben Nevis (1345m), the highest peak in the United Kingdom. In recent years South Georgia has had a population of around thirty people during the summer months, though this number halves over the winter.

The Antarctic Peninsula of the West Antarctica Ranges has multiple overlapping claims of sovereignty from Chile, Argentina and the United Kingdom. If the claims of the UK were recognised and it became another British Overseas Territory then 3239m Mount Hope would be the highest British peak anywhere and the second most prominent. Mount Paget would remain the most prominent as Mount Hope has a prominence of 2193 metres, well below the 2934 metres of Mount Paget.

Grytviken in South Georgia, SA256 (Anne Gray)

——— Europe ———

EU30 Scandinavia – European Arctic

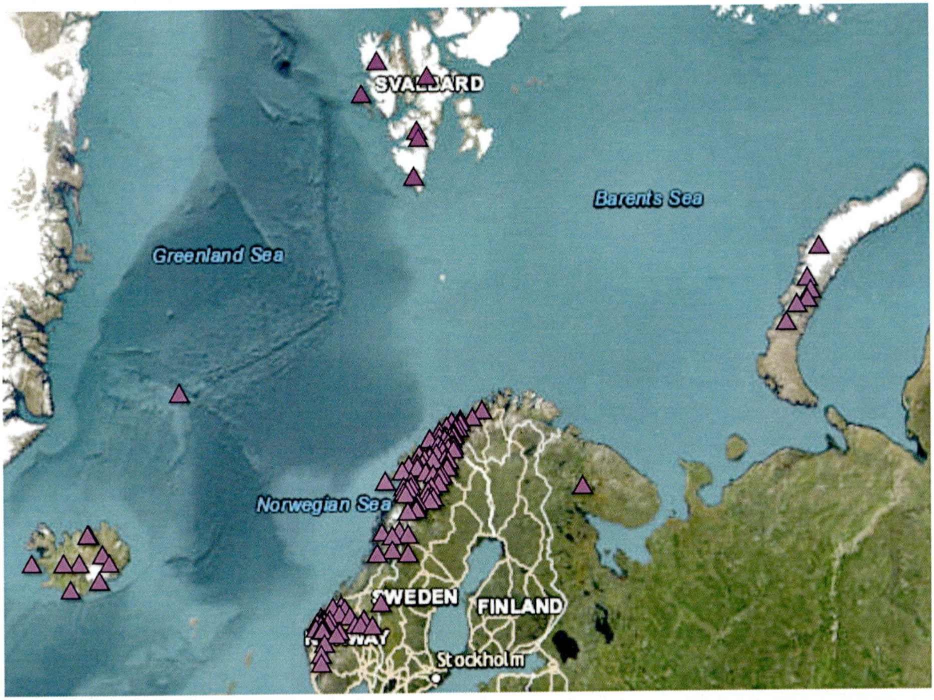

Beerenberg, EU302 (Petter Bjørstad)

EU300 Svalbard

Id	Height	Name	Island	Drop	Country	Location
50006	1710	Newtontoppen	Spitsbergen	1710	Norway	79.0103, 17.4931
50020	1433	Hornsundtind	Spitsbergen	1288	Norway	76.9199, 16.1405
50050	1457	Kongen	Spitsbergen	1132	Norway	79.2917, 12.4776
50066	1223	Gustavfjellet	Spitsbergen	1078	Norway	77.9333, 16.4460
50088	1221	Aspelintoppen	Spitsbergen	1039	Norway	77.7696, 16.6555
50064	1082	Monacofjellet	Prins Karls Forland	1082	Norway	78.6580, 10.9245

EU301 Western Russian Arctic Islands

Id	Height	Name	Island	Drop	Country	Location
50009	1547	Gora Kruzenshtern	Novaya Zemlya – Severny	1547	Russia	75.1762, 57.8285
50032	1285	Gora Gol'covoe *	Novaya Zemlya – Severny	1217	Russia	74.0300, 56.8800
50051	1163	Gora Mityushikha *	Novaya Zemlya – Severny	1129	Russia	73.6040, 55.4723
50073	1293	Gora Lednikovoe *	Novaya Zemlya – Severny	1063	Russia	74.3446, 56.5936
50100	1107	Gora Mullera *	Novaya Zemlya – Severny	1026	Russia	73.7658, 56.6033
50023	1279	Gora Pervosvotrennaya *	Novaya Zemlya – Yuzhny	1279	Russia	73.1204, 54.5657

EU302 Norwegian Sea Islands

Id	Height	Name	Island	Drop	Country	Location
50002	2277	Beerenberg – Haakon VII Topp	Jan Mayen	2277	Norway	71.0818, -8.1786
50003	2110	Hvannadalshnúkur	Iceland	2110	Iceland	64.0141, -16.6774
50021	1446	Snæfellsjökull – Miðþufa	Iceland	1283	Iceland	64.8033, -23.7758
50122	1214	Grjótskálarhnjúkur	Iceland	1087	Iceland	65.9337, -17.9978
50091	1639	Eyjafjallajökull	Iceland	1036	Iceland	63.6199, -19.6150
50092	1792	Hofsjökull	Iceland	1035	Iceland	64.8095, -18.8648
50104	1671	Eiríksjökull	Iceland	1021	Iceland	64.7721, -20.3990
50108	1687	Herðubreið	Iceland	1014	Iceland	65.1750, -16.3451
50113	1833	Snæffel	Iceland	1010	Iceland	64.7969, -15.5606

Beerenberg, EU302
Petter Bjørstad, June 2019

Jan Mayen is located at 71 degrees north and home to the northernmost volcano in the world, which had its most recent eruption in 1985. In 2019 there was a permanent base with eighteen people working on a six-month rotation on the island. Jan Mayen is about 55 kilometres long, with Beerenberg volcano reaching 2277 metres at its northern end.

I chartered a boat from Seil Norge with a crew of three for a two-week trip from Longyearbyen on Svalbard. With four Norwegians, four from the UK, one from Finland and one from the USA, we were a team of ten. All non-Norwegians needed prior approval, but this was straightforward. The crossing, a little over 1000 kilometres of the North Atlantic, took about four days each way. There is no harbour, so we had to jump into the shallow water and wade ashore. We had six full days to climb the mountain and explore several smaller peaks. We had excellent weather and the climb of Beerenberg was a successful three-day excursion from the boat. All ten of us reached the summit. The mountain has glaciers running all the way into the ocean, so experience with glacier ascents was needed.

Eyjafjallajökull, EU302

This volcano caused a lot of trouble in 2010. The eruption began in March and continued for several weeks, producing vast volumes of ash that disrupted air travel and affected the economic, political and cultural activities in Europe and around the world. Several major events were cancelled or delayed because those due to attend were unable to travel.

EU303 Scandinavian Mountains

Id	Height	Name	Drop	Country	Location
50001	2469	Galdhøpiggen	2372	Norway	61.6365, 8.3125
50004	2097	Kebnekaise Nordtoppen	1738	Sweden	67.9044, 18.5273
50005	1831	Jiehkkevárri	1734	Norway	69.4693, 19.8785
50007	2287	Snøhetta	1676	Norway	62.3200, 9.2672
50008	1625	Store Lenangstind	1577	Norway	69.7101, 20.0859
50010	2089	Sarektjåkkå	1526	Sweden	67.4314, 17.7231
50011	1670	Blånibba / Gjegnen	1462	Norway	61.8038, 5.8212
50012	1404	Hamperokken	1395	Norway	69.5620, 19.3570
50013	1916	Oksskolten	1386	Norway	66.0142, 14.3375
50014	1542	Skårasalen	1383	Norway	62.1657, 6.4858
50015	1572	Botnafjellet	1338	Norway	61.6603, 6.3104
50016	1700	Kvitegga	1312	Norway	62.0947, 6.7021
50017	1640	Nummestolane	1304	Norway	61.0498, 6.6886
50018	1717	Njunis	1304	Norway	68.7492, 19.4880
50019	1631	Store Smørskredtind	1303	Norway	62.1998, 6.7322
50022	1842	Store Trolla	1282	Norway	62.6834, 8.7423
50025	1527	Lille Russetinden	1267	Norway	69.1341, 19.5626
50027	1320	Stortinden	1242	Norway	69.4525, 19.1783
50028	1662	Folgefonnen	1233	Norway	60.0675, 6.3892
50029	2178	Rondslottet	1232	Norway	61.9149, 9.8513
50031	1445	Daurmål	1220	Norway	61.6511, 6.4731
50033	1381	Hjerttinden	1213	Norway	68.9954, 18.2270
50034	1810	Kallaktjåkkå / Gállaktjåhkkå	1190	Sweden	67.7219, 17.7933
50035	1894	Storsteinsfjellet	1185	Norway	68.2316, 17.8769
50036	1351	Helldalisen	1184	Norway	67.6664, 15.3803
50038	1237	Tromsdalstind	1169	Norway	69.6071, 19.1458
50039	1203	Vassbruntinden	1165	Norway	69.2999, 18.4567
50040	1432	Kolåstinden	1164	Norway	62.2589, 6.3111
50041	1699	Kvigtinden	1161	Norway	65.2262, 13.7949
50042	1659	Rohkunborri	1160	Norway	68.5558, 19.3538
50043	1306	Skittendalstinden	1160	Norway	68.5789, 16.9542
50044	2016	Bálgattjåhkkå	1160	Sweden	67.1778, 17.6125
50045	1187	Sjunkhatten	1149	Norway	67.4792, 15.1276
50047	1379	Blåtindan	1147	Norway	69.1870, 18.8275

50049	1797	Helagsfjället	1133	Sweden	62.9040, 12.4529
50052	1925	Ahpartjåkkå	1124	Sweden	67.3300, 17.9792
50053	1191	Øksfjordjøkelen	1120	Norway	70.1799, 22.0602
50054	1768	Norra Sytertoppen	1116	Sweden	65.8923, 15.2697
50055	1986	Kåtotjåkkå / Godučohkka	1113	Sweden	68.1450, 18.6247
50056	1556	Geittinden	1109	Norway	65.7762, 13.7533
50057	1964	Kleneggen	1104	Norway	62.3965, 8.2062
50058	1228	Litlforra	1102	Norway	67.9493, 15.7167
50059	1351	Hjortahorgi	1101	Norway	60.5279, 6.3545
50060	1491	Istinden	1101	Norway	69.6146, 20.1109
50061	2011	Akkavare	1098	Sweden	67.5785, 17.4862
50062	1755	Midtre Sølen	1091	Norway	61.8841, 11.5171
50067	1751	Ølfjellet	1077	Norway	66.7893, 15.2521
50069	1983	Akkatjåkkå	1068	Sweden	67.3256, 17.4891
50070	1609	Fedalsnibba	1067	Norway	61.9819, 6.9833
50071	1241	Løksetinden	1066	Norway	68.9323, 17.5601
50072	1261	Reitetinden	1066	Norway	68.8223, 17.6298
50074	1549	Mannfjellet	1059	Norway	69.2002, 20.0324
50075	1509	Biellogaisa	1055	Norway	69.3063, 19.7819
50076	1059	Heilhornet	1053	Norway	65.0772, 12.1390
50077	1169	Bentsjordtinden	1053	Norway	69.5120, 18.6185
50078	1723	Frostisen	1053	Norway	68.2475, 17.1790
50079	1214	Søre Reinviktinden	1053	Norway	67.7215, 15.6194
50080	1297	Glitregga	1052	Norway	61.9075, 6.3728
50082	1827	Storsølnkletten	1047	Norway	61.9799, 10.2921
50085	1391	Tverrbakktinden	1042	Norway	69.8504, 20.2775
50086	1603	Šalmmečohkat	1042	Sweden	68.4328, 19.3564
50087	1483	Eidskyrkja	1040	Norway	62.0171, 6.2624
50089	1718	Årjep Sávllo / Södra Saulo	1039	Sweden	66.8924, 16.1486
50090	1215	Lavangstinden	1038	Norway	69.5648, 19.6110
50093	1457	Spanstinden	1034	Norway	68.6999, 17.8683
50095	1768	Nuortta Sávllo / Nordre Saulo	1031	Norway, Sweden	66.9807, 16.1923
50096	1128	Skåla	1029	Norway	62.7387, 7.6179
50098	1095	Sætertinden	1027	Norway	68.5866, 16.3617
50099	1175	Smisetnebba	1026	Norway	62.8034, 8.4343
50101	1441	Trollvasstinden	1025	Norway	69.6479, 19.9705
50102	1677	Kirkestinden	1022	Norway	68.7881, 19.1020
50103	2405	Store Skagastølstinden	1022	Norway	61.4615, 7.8719
50106	1249	Stormauken	1021	Norway	69.0619, 18.9667
50107	1576	Vassdalsfjellet	1015	Norway	69.1003, 19.9554
50109	1046	Kråktindan	1011	Norway	67.7144, 14.9539
50111	1792	Gielasčohkka – Nordvästtoppen	1011	Sweden	68.2068, 18.8006

50114	1224	Rasmustinden	1008	Norway	69.3615, 19.5281
50116	1630	Eidshornet	1006	Norway	62.1524, 7.1461
50117	1666	Tron	1006	Norway	62.1744, 10.6949
50118	1908	Suliskongen	1006	Norway	67.1468, 16.3773
50119	1020	Eidetinden	1003	Norway	67.5589, 14.9493
50120	1590	Marsfjället	1002	Sweden	65.1066, 15.3797
50121	1285	Trollvasstinden	1001	Norway	62.0395, 5.9934

Norwegian Islands

Id	Height	Name	Island	Drop	Country	Location
50024	1276	Langlitinden	Andørja	1276	Norway	68.8679, 17.3874
50026	1262	Møysalen	Hinnøya	1262	Norway	68.5260, 15.4522
50030	1229	Store Kågtinden	Kågen	1229	Norway	70.0002, 20.7984
50037	1169	Arnøyhøgda	Arnøya	1169	Norway	70.1533, 20.7001
50046	1148	Higravtindan	Austvågøy	1148	Norway	68.3567, 14.7924
50048	1139	Blåtinden	Uløya	1139	Norway	69.8437, 20.6106
50065	1078	Seilandstuva	Seiland	1078	Norway	70.4463, 23.0951
50068	1072	Botnkrona	Alsta	1072	Norway	65.9617, 12.6282
50081	1049	Soltindan	Ringvassøya	1049	Norway	69.8896, 19.3340
50084	1044	Store Blåmann	Kvaløya	1044	Norway	69.7350, 18.5916
50094	1031	Vanntinden	Vanna	1031	Norway	70.0985, 19.7829
50097	1027	Hermannsdalstinden	Moskenesøy	1027	Norway	67.9420, 12.9376
50105	1021	Drangen	Rolla	1021	Norway	68.7923, 17.0368
50110	1011	Nona	Grytøya	1011	Norway	68.9216, 16.4506
50112	1010	Trollfjellet	Tjeldøya	1010	Norway	68.4769, 16.2739
50115	1007	Breitinden	Senja	1007	Norway	69.4518, 17.6561

EU304 Finland – Kola – Karelia Area

Id	Height	Name	Drop	Country	Location
50083	1198	Gora Yudychvumchorr	1046	Russia	67.7258, 33.4747

Gora Yudychvumchorr, EU304

Gora Yudychvumchorr is the only Ribu on Russia's Kola Peninsula, which is one of Europe's largest peninsulas and lies mostly in the Arctic Circle. This remote region is home to the Kola Superdeep Borehole which since 1979 has been the deepest man-made hole in the world, at an astonishing 12262 metres deep. That is considerably deeper than Everest is high, and with more than enough anti-prominence to count as a rather bizarre man-made negative Ribu. Financial constraints meant that the project was abandoned in 1995, with the original superstructure covering the hole now destroyed and the hole itself welded shut. The hole is only 23 centimetres wide, but it would be theoretically possible for a very small creature to reach the base of the hole if it were protected against the dangerously hot temperatures and provided with sufficient breathing apparatus.

There are several other incredibly deep man-made holes on Earth. These include mines, which are much easier for human beings to get into. The Bingham Canyon Mine in Utah, USA, is over 1210 metres deep so it counts as another man-made negative Ribu.

EU31 North-west Europe

EU310 Ireland

Id	Height	Name	Drop	Country	Location
20001	1039	Carrauntoohil	1039	Ireland	51.9992, -9.7428

EU311 Great Britain

Id	Height	Name	Drop	Country	Location
278	1345	Ben Nevis	1345	United Kingdom	56.7969, -5.0036
803	1183	Carn Eighe	1147	United Kingdom	57.2876, -5.1154
1963	1085	Snowdon / Yr Wyddfa	1039	United Kingdom	53.0685, -4.0762

Ben Nevis, EU311, the highest peak in Great Britain (James Stone)

Carrauntoohil, EU310
Martin Richardson, August 1995

The plan was to do the full Macgillycuddy's Reeks ridge from the eastern end. I arranged to be picked up at the Glencar Inn. All went well until I reached Carrauntoohil, when heavy rain clouds rolled in from the Atlantic. I took a compass bearing from the summit cross and came to a steep drop, not shown on the map. After returning to the cross I decided to try to get round the drop and then lost my way. The rain had rendered my map to a pulp and the light was fading. In the distance I could see lights and decided to head for them.

It was quite dark when I came to a little two-roomed cottage. Inside were four adult sisters and their mother, watching the annual Rose of Tralee contest on TV. There was no telephone so one of the sisters offered me a lift, but not until the winning Rose had been crowned. It was close to midnight when I reached the phone box and realised I was on the wrong side of the mountain. I tried several times to ring the Glencar Inn, but their phone was continuously engaged, so I rang the gardai (police). The phone at the inn had been engaged because it was the mountain rescue centre and the team were busy calling out volunteers. I was picked up and taken to a police station, where at 2am my lift managed to reach me. If it hadn't been for the Rose of Tralee, I would probably have been headline news in the local paper. I later read that the OS map for the Reeks was notoriously unreliable.

EU312 North France - West Rhine Area

Id	Height	Name	Drop	Country	Location
50503	1721	Crêt de la Neige – J1	1266	France	46.2728, 5.9442
50505	1423	Grand Ballon	1071	France	47.9008, 7.0983

EU314 Massif Central

Id	Height	Name	Drop	Country	Location
50501	1885	Puy de Sancy	1575	France	45.5283, 2.8142

Crêt de la Neige, EU312

Until September 2024, there was uncertainty over which was the highest peak in the Jura Mountains, a sub-alpine range straddling France and Switzerland. Older French maps from IGN gave 1717.6m for Crêt de la Neige ('snow crest') and 1717.4 metres for Le Reculet, 2km to the south-west. More recent maps gave 1718 metres for both, but 1720 for a less well-known point 400 metres north-east of the popular summit of Crêt de la Neige.

Researchers for the Ribus project were confident that the highest point was near the 1720 spot height on the modern French IGN map, but two of the team planned a visit to the area to conduct a survey to confirm the exact highest point of the massif. However, a team of researchers from the University of Lausanne announced that they had conducted a survey of these peaks in July 2024. They concluded that the highest point was not one of the two main candidates but was a less-visited peak that they named J1, with J standing for Jura. Its height was given as 1720.83m but the exact location was not disclosed due to it being part of the Haute Chaîne du Jura national nature reserve. However, a J1 label soon became visible in this area on the open-source Outdoors terrain map.

Jonathan de Ferranti was able to assess Lidar data for the area and determine the exact location of the highest Lidar cell, given as 1720.52m, which was consistent with 1720.83m from the Lausanne team. Both figures round up to 1721m. As expected, the location is about 400 metres north-east of the most popular summit of Crêt de la Neige.

This story demonstrates that, with sufficient high-quality data, the highest point of a mountain can often be located without the need for a visit.

EU32 Iberian Peninsula

EU320 Portugal – Galicia

Id	Height	Name	Drop	Country	Location
51013	1993	Serra da Estrela – Torre	1204	Portugal	40.3219, -7.6129
51025	2183	Teleno	1088	Spain	42.3459, -6.3938

EU321 Cordillera Cantabrica

Id	Height	Name	Drop	Country	Location
51003	2649	Torrecerredo	1933	Spain	43.1977, -4.8529
51017	2596	Peña Santa de Castilla	1133	Spain	43.2019, -4.9623
51021	2414	Pico del Fontán Sur	1118	Spain	43.0336, -5.9607

Torrecerredo, EU321

David Jamieson, July 2022

It was with some excitement that we managed to grab a bargain flight to Santander on Spain's Bay of Biscay and from there hired a van – weirdly cheaper than a car – to get us into the heart of the Picos de Europa. It was our first time to this small but perfectly formed limestone massif, a hidden gem for the scrambler, climber and peak bagger. This small national park is often overlooked by hill walkers dazzled by the higher summits of the Pyrenees or Western Alps, but it has ten summits over 2000 metres high and countless smaller peaks. It's not just the density of peaks that draws the eye, but also their sheer serrated beauty fashioned by karst, water and ice.

Our initial objective was Torrecerredo, the highest summit at 2649m. The guidebook had advised rope and harness for the final stretch, so I took the liberty of hiring a local guide. Juanluis was thirty years younger than us, with physique and facial features honed on rock faces and mountain air. He met us for dinner at Refugio de Urriellu, right under a stunning and sheer 500m vertical cliff of the same name. He had guided someone up that very cliff that afternoon and settled any misgivings by suggesting that the ascent of Torrecerredo would be a nice 'day off' for him by comparison.

Rising at 6am we set off into a cloudless dawn that promised success. After crossing a couple of barren cols and cirques, with only inquisitive rebeco (chamois) for company, we arrived at the base of the first technical challenge. It was a good scramble to start with, then the route up the east side of Torrecerredo became increasingly steep and ever more exposed, so we elected to rope up for the final few metres.

The views from the summit were spectacular in all directions. Immediately below us fanned out long lines of saw-toothed limestone that warded off all but the best mountaineers. On the horizon lay the azure blue Cantabrian sea to the north and the parched khaki lands of Castile and León to the south. The summit provided limited space to sit and drink in these vistas, but a small-walled wind shelter of loosely piled rock gave us the chance to celebrate in relative safety with blood-dark chorizo made by our guide's grandfather. I wished I had brought whisky from home to complement it.

We reversed our route, diminishing any hazard by use of the rope and stopping only so that Juanluis could admonish another climber for ascending in shorts and sandals, with a plastic bag to carry any essentials. He almost went apoplectic at the bikinied woman we passed a little further along. Back at the refugio by noon, we had time for a couple of cold cervezas before a sun-drenched and energy-sapping descent to our van near the wonderfully characteristic village of Sotres in the distant valley below.

EU322 Pyrenees

Id	Height	Name	Drop	Country	Location
51002	3404	Pico de Aneto	2811	Spain	42.6311, 0.6566
51008	2910	Puigmal d'Er	1331	France, Spain	42.3833, 2.1167
51011	3144	Pica d'Estats	1275	France, Spain	42.6669, 1.3979
51014	2912	Cotiella	1195	Spain	42.5119, 0.3197
51019	3369	Posets	1130	Spain	42.6546, 0.4352
51020	1706	Turó de l'Home	1122	Spain	41.7765, 2.4348
51024	2884	Pic du Midi d'Ossau	1089	France	42.8431, -0.4381
51026	2669	Bisaurín	1038	Spain	42.7885, -0.6400
51027	3298	Vignemale	1026	France, Spain	42.7740, -0.1473
51029	2492	El Turbón	1020	Spain	42.4167, 0.5050
51030	2368	Pic de Soularac	1007	France	42.8180, 1.7811
51031	2321	Cap de la Gallina Pelada	1007	Spain	42.1894, 1.7381
51032	2921	Pic Carlit	1001	France	42.5699, 1.9322

Torreceredo, EU321 (Alastair Govan)

Pic du Midi d'Ossau, EU322 (Oscar Argudo)

Pic du Midi d'Ossau, EU322

Rob Woodall, September 2022

Pic du Midi d'Ossau was the one Pyrenean Ribu I had not managed on my previous visit. It is at the west end of the range and, by all accounts, was challenging. I was on my own but packed a rope in case I needed to abseil on the descent. From the pass it looked impressive, from the refuge more so. The approach path was busy, with several parties ascending the steep ridge which leads to the foot of the east face, so there was little danger of losing the route. The first pitch was reasonably easy scrambling, with a few metal pegs in place for footholds. Pitch two was either a gully or a wall to the right, both pretty steep. Above this the ground became more broken and easier. I reached the summit with two Frenchmen. One was a master baker, so I got to taste his wares. They had tiny backpacks and no rope so were obviously not intending to abseil. I descended with them. The first one confidently climbed down the wall. It was pretty vertical but the rock was excellent, the holds small but good. I enjoyed it despite the 60-metre rope on my back.

The same thing happened a couple of days later on Monte Viso, where James and I enjoyed climbing down three chimneys of the great peak. The rope stayed in the pack again.

EU323 Castile Ranges

Id	Height	Name	Drop	Country	Location
51004	2532	Pico Almanzor	1627	Spain	40.2461, -5.2976
51016	2427	Canchal de la Ceja	1153	Spain	40.3044, -5.7289
51023	2428	Peñalara	1112	Spain	40.8500, -3.9560

EU324 Sistema Iberico

Id	Height	Name	Drop	Country	Location
51010	2314	Moncayo	1297	Spain	41.7870, -1.8396
51022	2271	Cerro San Lorenzo	1117	Spain	42.2425, -2.9726
51028	2028	Peñarroya	1020	Spain	40.3901, -0.6651

EU325 Balearic Islands

Id	Height	Name	Drop	Country	Location
51006	1436	Puig Major, Mallorca	1436	Spain	39.8075, 2.7942

EU326 Andalucian Ranges

Id	Height	Name	Drop	Country	Location
51001	3479	Mulhacén	3289	Spain	37.0533, -3.3115
51005	1918	Torrecilla	1467	Spain	36.6760, -4.9963
51007	2381	La Sagra	1408	Spain	37.9501, -2.5654
51009	2247	Morrón de Mariné / Morrón de la Lagunilla	1322	Spain	36.9030, -2.8271
51012	2073	Sierra de Tejeda	1241	Spain	36.9041, -4.0383
51015	2269	Calar de Santa Bárbara	1153	Spain	37.3805, -2.8420
51018	2164	Pico Mágina	1132	Spain	37.7259, -3.4642

EU33 Alps

EU330 Western Alps

Id	Height	Name	Drop	Country	Location
51501	4806	Mont Blanc / Monte Bianco	4693	France, Italy	45.8325, 6.8650
51510	3841	Monte Viso	2062	Italy	44.6675, 7.0901
51512	4102	Barre des Écrins	2044	France	44.9225, 6.3600
51516	4061	Gran Paradiso	1890	Italy	45.5179, 7.2671
51519	3257	Dents du Midi – Haute Cime	1796	Switzerland	46.1610, 6.9233
51520	2082	Chamechaude	1769	France	45.2878, 5.7879
51523	2210	Pointe d'Arcalod	1712	France	45.6817, 6.2283
51531	2750	Pointe Percée	1643	France	45.9558, 6.5558
51537	2789	Grande Tête de l'Obiou	1541	France	44.7750, 5.8400
51541	2351	La Tournette	1508	France	45.8271, 6.2861
51545	2857	Le Taillefer	1492	France	45.0395, 5.9243
51553	3506	Aiguille de Scolette / Pierre Menue	1421	France, Italy	45.1600, 6.7683
51574	3297	Monte Argentera	1306	Italy	44.1780, 7.3053
51577	3855	La Grande Casse	1290	France	45.4050, 6.8267
51581	3131	Mont Chaberton	1282	France	44.9642, 6.7517
51584	2709	Pic de Bure	1271	France	44.6267, 5.9350
51587	1863	Le Môle	1254	France	46.1067, 6.4547
51607	3695	La Dent Parrachée	1178	France	45.2892, 6.7558
51610	3465	Pic Bayle	1174	France	45.1380, 6.1357
51612	2341	Grand Veymont	1165	France	44.8700, 5.5267

51615	2063	Dent de Cons	1155	France	45.7292, 6.3508
51620	1910	Mont Ventoux	1142	France	44.1742, 5.2783
51624	3779	Mont Pourri	1127	France	45.5282, 6.8601
51633	2597	Catogne	1103	Switzerland	46.0544, 7.1108
51636	2045	Mont Colombier	1095	France	45.6442, 6.1192
51643	3514	Aiguille Méridionale d'Arves	1081	France	45.1230, 6.3345
51644	2244	Le Roc d'Enfer	1080	France	46.1892, 6.6103
51651	2023	Mont Lachat	1064	France	45.9276, 6.3507
51655	2977	Grand Pic de Belledonne	1055	France	45.1708, 5.9917
51657	2432	Les Cornettes de Bise	1054	France, Switzerland	46.3326, 6.7846
51663	2016	Pic de Céüse	1040	France	44.5083, 5.9617
51669	2995	Le Roignais	1028	France	45.6431, 6.6887
51673	3320	Pic de Rochebrune	1021	France	44.8223, 6.7875
51675	2389	Le Tabor	1021	France	44.9769, 5.8555
51681	3752	Pointe de Charbonnel	1011	France	45.2805, 7.0556

Grande Tête de l'Obiou, EU330
Rob Woodall, August 2020

On a fine evening the peak was a striking fortress of gleaming limestone. I needed an early start as heavy rain was forecast from early afternoon. Oscar said to be sure to take the chatiéres route (cat-flaps) and had sent a link to an annotated photo. The details were not entirely obvious but I reckoned all would become clear. The route started up a grassy ridge then bent right and entered a grassy sheepy combe, with huge cliffs ahead. A scree path led to a scrambly head-wall. Once above this, a cairn marked the point where my route diverged right, leading through a couple of natural tunnels with scrambly exits. It was fascinating, entertaining, promising. An ascending line then traversed right, below a cliff.

I found myself at a promontory above a sensational drop. Where next? A ledge traversed left but looked unlikely. I wandered along it – sensational but not summit-bound. A young couple appeared at the promontory, evidently climbers, but in scrambling mode for the day. She knew the route so I tagged along. We reversed our approach route a few metres along the foot of the cliff then entered a deep cleft, which ascended improbably steeply. Soon we exited left into another cleft, squeezed under a chock-stone, then my new friends climbed over a big boulder while I squeezed through a gap beside it. Beyond, I scrambled right, up a fairly obvious cleft, and in a couple of minutes popped out beside the summit cairn, where my friends were starting on their pique-nique.

All around were impressive, shapely limestone peaks. Distant veils of rain signalled the approach of the deluge, probably a few hours away. It was time to find the usual route, which had plenty of exposure and a little steep scrambling but no cat-flaps. The French couple went ahead, lost the route then followed me down for a while. I searched briefly for a cave then followed them down a steep head-wall and a rubbly scree path. I explored a shapely ridge below, reminiscent of the English limestone Dales, but this one was at the foot of a 300-metre cliff.

There was a little rain on the walk out but I reached the car half an hour before the deluge started. This ascent had been planned for a few days, and I could not have wished for a better coda to part one of my long Alpine trip. Three years and half a thousand peaks later it was still my all-time favourite.

Grande Tête de l'Obiou, EU330 (Alastair Govan)

Monte Rosa, EU332 (Alastair Govan)

EU331 Northern Alps

Id	Height	Name	Drop	Country	Location
51503	4274	Finsteraarhorn	2279	Switzerland	46.5373, 8.1262
51506	2941	Hochkönig	2181	Austria	47.4204, 13.0624
51513	2502	Säntis	2015	Switzerland	47.2495, 9.3433
51521	2962	Zugspitze	1746	Austria, Germany	47.4212, 10.9846
51529	2634	Birnhorn	1665	Austria	47.4748, 12.7336
51534	3613	Tödi / Piz Russein	1569	Switzerland	46.8113, 8.9147
51535	2749	Birkkarspitze	1567	Austria	47.4112, 11.4376
51536	2344	Wilder Kaiser – Ellmauer Halt	1556	Austria	47.5617, 12.3025
51547	3631	Dammastock	1468	Switzerland	46.6436, 8.4210
51549	2805	Haldensteiner Calanda	1458	Switzerland	46.9000, 9.4675
51564	2299	Hochiss	1359	Austria	47.4583, 11.7649
51565	2384	Gamsberg	1357	Switzerland	47.1353, 9.3743
51569	3168	Hoher Riffler	1341	Austria	47.1161, 10.3711
51570	2348	Brienzer Rothorn	1340	Switzerland	46.7871, 8.0468
51573	2511	Großes Ochsenhorn	1309	Austria	47.5383, 12.6608
51580	1797	Rigi Kulm	1287	Switzerland	47.0567, 8.4854
51582	1972	Untersberg	1278	Germany	47.6942, 12.9875
51586	2370	Tschirgant	1264	Austria	47.2419, 10.7966
51591	3036	Parseierspitze	1243	Austria	47.1743, 10.4781
51594	2340	Daniel	1233	Austria	47.4328, 10.8805
51602	2768	Hochplattig	1189	Austria	47.3531, 10.9888
51605	2185	Kreuzspitze	1182	Germany	47.5265, 10.9181
51606	1961	Sonntagshorn	1181	Austria, Germany	47.6823, 12.6958
51614	2086	Krottenkopf	1156	Germany	47.5445, 11.1914
51618	1808	Geigelstein	1143	Germany	47.7075, 12.3350
51619	2194	Guffertspitze	1143	Austria	47.5463, 11.7892
51625	2286	Stadelhorn	1124	Austria, Germany	47.5929, 12.7951
51632	2389	Vanil Noir	1116	Switzerland	46.5285, 7.1483
51638	2363	Geißstein	1089	Austria	47.3374, 12.4952
51639	2238	Köllenspitze	1088	Austria	47.4992, 10.6300
51653	1782	Hinterstaufen – Zwiesel	1060	Germany	47.7558, 12.8150
51658	2558	Kreuzjoch	1051	Austria	47.2517, 11.9826
51666	4193	Aletschhorn	1036	Switzerland	46.4652, 7.9936
51670	3410	Piz Linard	1027	Switzerland	46.7989, 10.0715
51674	3698	Balmhorn	1021	Switzerland	46.4250, 7.6936
51676	2376	Knittelkarspitze	1017	Austria	47.3756, 10.6511
51678	1773	Unterberghorn	1013	Austria	47.6207, 12.4365
51679	3051	Grand Muveran	1013	Switzerland	46.2372, 7.1261
51682	1828	Hohe Salve	1010	Austria	47.4651, 12.2041
51683	1852	Großer Traithen	1007	Germany	47.6467, 12.0377

| 51686 | 2196 | Große Arnspitze | 1007 | Austria, Germany | 47.3976, 11.2227 |
| 51684 | 2548 | Le Tarent | 1002 | Switzerland | 46.3822, 7.1475 |

EU332 Southern Alps

Id	Height	Name	Drop	Country	Location
51505	4049	Piz Bernina	2234	Switzerland	46.3824, 9.9080
51507	4634	Monte Rosa – Dufourspitze	2165	Switzerland	45.9368, 7.8667
51514	3905	Ortler / Ortles	1953	Italy	46.5090, 10.5449
51515	2218	Monte Baldo – Cima Valdritta	1944	Italy	45.7265, 10.8439
51517	3050	Pizzo di Coca	1878	Italy	46.0715, 10.0117
51526	2410	Grigna Settentrionale	1687	Italy	45.9534, 9.3877
51527	2180	Monte Bondone – Cornetto	1685	Italy	45.9881, 11.0318
51528	3558	Cima Presanella	1675	Italy	46.2199, 10.6639
51540	4314	Grand Combin – Combin de Grafeneire	1517	Switzerland	45.9376, 7.2991
51543	3151	Cima Brenta	1501	Italy	46.1796, 10.8996
51544	3418	Piz Kesch / Piz d'Es-cha	1501	Switzerland	46.6213, 9.8728
51546	2299	Monte Togano	1477	Italy	46.0898, 8.3947
51552	2254	Monte Cadria	1434	Italy	45.9386, 10.6982
51557	1686	Monte San Primo	1407	Italy	45.9155, 9.2097
51558	1962	Monte Tamaro	1406	Switzerland	46.1039, 8.8660
51567	2980	Aroser Rothorn	1348	Switzerland	46.7378, 9.6139
51571	3402	Rheinwaldhorn / Adula	1337	Switzerland	46.4936, 9.0402
51572	1701	Monte Generoso	1330	Italy, Switzerland	45.9313, 9.0199
51589	2186	Gridone / Monte Limidario	1246	Italy, Switzerland	46.1234, 8.6479
51592	4506	Weisshorn	1236	Switzerland	46.1013, 7.7161
51597	1976	Monte Caplone	1218	Italy	45.8024, 10.6412
51598	3439	Cima de' Piazzi	1212	Italy	46.4172, 10.2867
51603	4013	Weissmies	1183	Switzerland	46.1277, 8.0120
51613	3279	Pizzo Tambò	1165	Italy, Switzerland	46.4970, 9.2835
51622	1491	Mottarone	1131	Italy	45.8818, 8.4540
51623	3554	Monte Leone	1129	Italy, Switzerland	46.2495, 8.1100
51630	3678	Monte Disgrazia	1116	Italy	46.2692, 9.7492
51631	3392	Piz Platta	1116	Switzerland	46.4871, 9.5618
51634	2124	Paganella – Cima Roda	1099	Italy	46.1433, 11.0375
51641	3397	Piz Calderas	1085	Switzerland	46.5364, 9.6960
51645	3374	Cima Viola	1074	Italy	46.3833, 10.1958
51654	4546	Dom	1056	Switzerland	46.0941, 7.8590
51656	3204	Piz Sesvenna	1055	Switzerland	46.7060, 10.4027
51659	1636	Pizzo Formico	1050	Italy	45.8475, 9.9238
51664	1803	Monte Misone	1040	Italy	45.9552, 10.8335
51665	4478	Matterhorn / Cervino / Mont Cervin	1038	Italy, Switzerland	45.9765, 7.6584
51668	1378	Monte Torrezzo	1031	Italy	45.7583, 9.9633
51671	2574	Stätzerhorn / Piz Raschil	1027	Switzerland	46.7559, 9.5123

Alpine summits by train

David Jamieson, 2023

Climbing hills and mountains without the use of a car or van is not particularly easy. Their topography does not favour trains and buses, and even where this handicap can be overcome with bridges, tunnels, switchbacks, cogs and cable cars, public transport stops are often several miles from otherwise useful road heads, mountain refuges or accessible footpaths. Nevertheless, many relative hills across Europe can be reached by train, bus and even boat, so long as you are willing to plan ahead, travel lightly, succumb to local transport timetables and walk or cycle the extra necessary distance to get to the climb.

Monte San Primo (1686m, EU332) was a logistical problem. It is a straightforward walk from a car park at the nearby ski resort but we had no car. We took an early-morning bus from Lecco to the lakeside village of Vassena, then simply headed upwards on our feet along a mix of ancient tracks and modern roads, meeting only deer and goats. This took several hours but eventually got us the start of the hill climb. A muddy track running alongside a grassy ridge led to a high point, where the views over Lake Como towards the snow-covered Alps were stupendous. In order to retain these views as long as possible we headed northwards along paths and minor roads until eventually we reached the beautiful lakeside town of Bellagio, home to the rich and famous. We had time for celebratory gelato cones before boarding the last boat back to Lecco, a truly glorious way to end the day's adventure and rest sore legs that had clocked up thirty kilometres, none of it on the flat.

A looming train strike drove us back up north sooner than we planned, this time to Lake Lugano and Lake Maggiore in Switzerland, where we knew that many more mountains were reachable by train and accessible to walkers in April. Perhaps the simplest is Monte Generoso (1701m) as it has an impressive rack railway to a restaurant and visitor centre just below the summit. We opted to walk from Mendrisio train station, which meant following an ever-steeper series of suburban streets up to a glorious woodland path that climbed steadily up the mountain's south-west flank. The summit views were outstanding, taking in Lake Lugano below, Monte Viso in the west and an extensive range of snow-capped 4000-metre peaks from Monte Rosa to Lagginhorn in the north. We had lots of time left so returned via the pristine Valle di Muggio, Switzerland's southernmost valley and surely one of its most perfect. Charming rustic villages clinging to the steep sides of the valley are linked by myriad ancient mule paths, giving easy walking amongst a perfect patchwork of terraced pasture and ancient forest of elm, chestnut, birch and beech.

Before heading to Vienna we had time for one more nearby mountain. The highest within range of a train station turned out to be Monte Tamaro (1962m) from Rivera Bironico, but what we thought would be a standard hike turned into a more adventurous day out. We arrived early at the Monte Tamaro cable car station to get advice on routes, to be told that the summit area was 'closed' due to snow and ice (it was mid April). Somewhat disheartened, we decided to take the cable car up to its highest station (1530m) and do some walking beneath the snow-line, from where there were plenty of marked paths. We initially contoured southwards around the bulk of a hill called Mugia, which eventually brought us to the lovely Val Duragno and within sight of the southern side of the Tamaro summit ridge. The ridge above looked free of snow so we decided to climb the well-worn path up the valley and join the ridge at Motto Rotondo (1928m). However, as we climbed it became ever more apparent that the narrow kilometre-long section between Rotondo and Tamaro did indeed contain snow and ice, and this definitely restricted access along the traditional ridge path to those without winter gear.

After a quick discussion, Deana decided to wait at Rotondo whilst I carefully picked my way up and down the mini rock pinnacles above the iced footpath, which was no more than a rock scramble but had significant exposure in places. After a few summit photos I reversed the route, but this time in the company of a nervous and uncertain German mother and her son. We were all glad of the safety in numbers.

Peak bagging by train across Europe is certainly feasible if you have the additional time required and the stamina to cover the extra necessary walking. Buses and boats can further help in getting to those summits even farther off the rail network. There is also the self-satisfaction in reducing your personal carbon-miles. After a final two weeks in Bavaria and Luxembourg, taking in the summit of Großer Arber (EU351, 1456m) we had taken 130 trains to cover 7968 kilometres.

EU333 Eastern Alps

Id	Height	Name	Drop	Country	Location
51502	3798	Großglockner	2428	Austria	47.0745, 12.6939
51504	3768	Wildspitze	2261	Austria	46.8858, 10.8675
51508	2995	Hoher Dachstein	2136	Austria	47.4750, 13.6050
51509	3343	Marmolada – Punta Penia	2131	Italy	46.4344, 11.8513
51511	2864	Triglav	2052	Slovenia	46.3783, 13.8366
51518	2336	Cima Dodici / Ferozzo	1874	Italy	45.9976, 11.4680
51522	3264	Monte Antelao	1734	Italy	46.4520, 12.2618
51524	2558	Grintovec	1706	Slovenia	46.3572, 14.5353
51525	2515	Großer Priel	1703	Austria	47.7171, 14.0633
51530	2472	Col Nudo	1645	Italy	46.2274, 12.4034
51532	2753	Jôf di Montasio	1597	Italy	46.4358, 13.4337
51533	2784	Polinik	1580	Austria	46.8951, 13.1581
51538	2369	Hochtor	1520	Austria	47.5618, 14.6329
51539	2351	Grimming	1518	Austria	47.5207, 14.0172
51542	2396	Zirbitzkogel	1502	Austria	47.0636, 14.5675
51548	2430	Raucheck	1463	Austria	47.4992, 13.2267
51550	1775	Monte Grappa	1456	Italy	45.8733, 11.7993
51551	3220	Monte Civetta	1454	Italy	46.3800, 12.0533
51554	2706	Cima dei Preti	1420	Italy	46.3423, 12.4211
51555	3221	Monte Cristallo	1416	Italy	46.5757, 12.2007
51556	2587	Kanin	1409	Italy, Slovenia	46.3601, 13.4392
51559	3145	Dreischusterspitze	1393	Italy	46.6690, 12.3173
51560	1642	Matajur	1392	Italy, Slovenia	46.2125, 13.5292
51561	2371	Reißkofel	1390	Austria	46.6858, 13.1474
51562	3244	Tofana di Mezzo	1369	Italy	46.5510, 12.0657
51563	2224	Großer Buchstein	1363	Austria	47.6103, 14.5968
51566	2076	Schneeberg – Klosterwappen	1348	Austria	47.7670, 15.8045
51568	2110	Mirnock	1343	Austria	46.7589, 13.7155
51575	1763	Col Visentin	1295	Italy	46.0562, 12.2822

51576	1862	Großer Höllkogel	1294	Austria	47.7975, 13.6783
51578	2244	Großer Pyhrgas	1290	Austria	47.6526, 14.3981
51579	2588	Monte Terza Grande	1290	Italy	46.5273, 12.6221
51583	3192	Cima della Vezzana	1274	Italy	46.2899, 11.8299
51585	2236	Latschur	1268	Austria	46.7383, 13.3967
51588	2240	Piz di Mezzodi	1248	Italy	46.2187, 12.0359
51590	2770	Große Sandspitze	1245	Austria	46.7664, 12.8119
51593	2166	Dobratsch / Villacher Alpe	1233	Austria	46.6035, 13.6709
51595	2187	Ameringkogel	1232	Austria	47.0734, 14.8082
51596	3476	Olperer	1230	Austria	47.0533, 11.6590
51599	1505	Monte San Simeone	1202	Italy	46.3436, 13.1064
51600	3666	Großvenediger	1199	Austria	47.1090, 12.3465
51601	3168	Monte Pelmo	1191	Italy	46.4200, 12.1347
51604	2259	Cima Carega	1185	Italy	45.7245, 11.1307
51608	2547	Sass de Mura	1178	Italy	46.1636, 11.9252
51609	1782	Schafberg	1178	Austria	47.7765, 13.4338
51611	2417	Geierhaupt	1172	Austria	47.3746, 14.6359
51616	3436	Hochgall / Collalto	1148	Italy	46.9108, 12.1400
51617	2780	Monte Coglians / Hohe Warte	1144	Austria, Italy	46.6070, 12.8825
51621	3146	Croda Rossa d'Ampezzo / Hohe Gaisl	1133	Italy	46.6350, 12.1433
51626	3181	Sassolungo / Langkofel	1124	Italy	46.5249, 11.7355
51627	1914	Monte Verzegnis	1124	Italy	46.3632, 12.9052
51628	2862	Hochgolling	1124	Austria	47.2662, 13.7608
51629	2195	Zuc del Bôr	1118	Italy	46.4495, 13.2585
51635	2842	Latemar – Diamantiditurm	1097	Italy	46.3811, 11.5753
51637	1774	Gamsstein – Hochkogel	1094	Austria	47.7286, 14.7774
51640	3205	Punta Sorapiss	1085	Italy	46.5069, 12.2116
51642	1975	Hoher Sarstein	1084	Austria	47.6022, 13.6988
51646	1919	Kräuterin – Hochstadl	1072	Austria	47.6857, 15.0749
51647	2139	Obir – Hochobir	1071	Austria	46.5059, 14.4878
51648	2027	Gamsfeld	1070	Austria	47.6232, 13.4811
51649	2232	Pasubio – Cima Palon	1069	Italy	45.7922, 11.1766
51650	2679	Veliki Mangart	1068	Italy, Slovenia	46.4396, 13.6544
51652	1738	La Marzola	1060	Italy	46.0319, 11.1875
51660	2277	Hochschwab	1045	Austria	47.6183, 15.1425
51661	2119	Spitzegel	1045	Austria	46.6550, 13.4106
51662	2145	Wöllaner Nock	1042	Austria	46.7766, 13.8294
51667	3507	Zuckerhütl	1033	Austria	46.9644, 11.1533
51672	2236	Hochstuhl / Veliki Stol	1021	Austria, Slovenia	46.4340, 14.1737
51677	2548	Monte Brentoni	1017	Italy	46.5117, 12.5650
51680	1970	Monte Tamai	1012	Italy	46.4906, 12.9368

Monte Pelmo, EU333
Rob Woodall, July 2020

Being in the Dolomites, Monte Pelmo is steep and challenging. It is a huge tower of a mountain, broadly triangular, with cliffs on all sides. Most climbers stay at the hut at the foot of the route. The usual route, the Ball Ledge, is known as the ordinary route, but it's pretty extraordinary. It's named after John Ball, a Dubliner who was the first to reach the top. My plan was for a solo day hike, possibly turning back if the ledge was too terrifying. It is about a metre wide, with a few very narrow sections, and is encountered soon after leaving the hut. After starting at first light I was through the forest in an hour or so, with the early sun turning the cliffs gold.

The way to the start of the Ball Ledge wasn't marked, wasn't easy and wasn't promising. However, once attained, the ledge was excellent, taking a sensational line across the cliffs. I knew the so-called catwalk would be a different matter, as it is very narrow and forces you out of balance. In fact there were several such sections. To my surprise there were sections of fixed rope, seemingly of reasonable quality. The choice was to trust it or reach into the crevice behind and try to find handholds. Either way you end up leaning out above a death fall. I did a bit of both. Eventually a ramp led up to the right, then there was a zigzag trail interspersed with mostly easy scrambling ascended a huge combe before reaching the summit ridge. Unusually for me I examined the summit register, to find my smugness at having got up the thing tempered by the realisation that it was climbed on most days, whenever the weather was reasonable. It was a fantastic outing, to be recommended for those who enjoy an adventure.

Parângu Mare, EU353 (Rob Woodall)

EU34 Italian Peninsula and Islands

Corno Grande, Gran Sasso, EU340, from the south-east (Rob Woodall)

EU340 Apennines

Id	Height	Name	Drop	Country	Location
52003	2912	Gran Sasso – Corno Grande	2476	Italy	42.4692, 13.5658
52005	2793	Monte Amaro	1810	Italy	42.0864, 14.0859
52006	2267	Serra Dolcedorme	1715	Italy	39.8944, 16.2158
52007	1956	Aspromonte – Montalto	1710	Italy	38.1585, 15.9197
52008	2165	Monte Cimone	1577	Italy	44.1937, 10.6989
52010	2476	Monte Vettore	1463	Italy	42.8244, 13.2750
52012	2486	Monte Velino	1385	Italy	42.1473, 13.3816
52014	1899	Monte Cervati	1344	Italy	40.2848, 15.4838
52015	1928	Sila Grande – Monte Botte Donato	1312	Italy	39.2833, 16.4520
52016	2050	Monte Miletto	1306	Italy	41.4497, 14.3719
52023	2458	Monte Gorzano	1183	Italy	42.6182, 13.3957
52026	1947	Monte Pisanino	1167	Italy	44.1342, 10.2136
52027	1669	Monte Cairo	1165	Italy	41.5419, 13.7598
52028	2217	Monte Terminillo	1163	Italy	42.4739, 12.9978
52029	2005	Monte Sirino – Monte Papa	1159	Italy	40.1322, 15.8317
52030	1598	Monte Toppole	1159	Italy	40.9775, 14.6883
52031	1809	Monte Cervialto	1129	Italy	40.7817, 15.1307
52032	1394	Monte Taburno	1115	Italy	41.0927, 14.6036
52033	1482	Monte San Vicino	1102	Italy	43.3317, 13.0609
52035	1701	Monte Catria	1066	Italy	43.4611, 12.7042
52039	2285	Monte Greco	1005	Italy	41.7975, 13.9942
52040	2348	Monte Sirente	1000	Italy	42.1451, 13.6109

EU341 Western Italy

Id	Height	Name	Drop	Country	Location
52009	1733	Monte Amiata	1485	Italy	42.8874, 11.6235
52011	2156	Monte Viglio	1422	Italy	41.8848, 13.3739
52013	1533	Monte Petrella	1370	Italy	41.3223, 13.6655
52017	1444	Monte San Michele	1248	Italy	40.6475, 14.5059
52018	1281	Vesuvio / Vesuvius	1232	Italy	40.8229, 14.4291
52019	1536	Monte Semprevisa	1231	Italy	41.5699, 13.0918
52038	1017	Monte Capanne, Elba	1017	Italy	42.7717, 10.1675

EU342 Tyrrhennian Islands

Id	Height	Name	Island	Drop	Country	Location
52002	2706	Monte Cinto	Corse	2706	France	42.3800, 8.9458
52020	1767	Monte San Petrone	Corse	1208	France	42.3963, 9.3271
52022	2352	Monte Renoso	Corse	1191	France	42.0597, 9.1336
52025	2622	Monte Rotondo	Corse	1170	France	42.2158, 9.0575
52034	1535	Monte Astu	Corse	1071	France	42.5813, 9.2100
52004	1833	Gennargentu – Punta la Marmora	Sardegna	1833	Italy	39.9879, 9.3246

| 52024 | 1236 | Monte Línas - Punta Perda de sa Mesa | Sardegna | 1182 | Italy | 39.4482, 8.6176 |
| 52036 | 1359 | Monte Limbara | Sardegna | 1066 | Italy | 40.8525, 9.1767 |

EU343 Sicilia

Id	Height	Name	Drop	Country	Location
52001	3323	Etna / Mongibello	3323	Italy	37.7505, 14.9948
52021	1979	Pizzo Carbonara	1196	Italy	37.8941, 14.0253
52037	1613	Rocca Busambra	1049	Italy	37.8556, 13.3945

Vesuvio and Monte San Michele, EU341

Alan Dawson, September 2011

Hills were not on the agenda for a holiday based in the resorts of Sorrento and Praiano, so I packed shorts and sunglasses but not boots or maps. My partner at the time was not a hill walker but was good at talking to people, so we met a couple with a car who fancied a trip to Vesuvius and invited us for the ride. We joined the throng of other tourists for the stroll from high car park to crater rim, where numerous stall holders were doing brisk business. The guard at the end of the line of shops made it clear that access to the summit was very much forbidden, but it looked easy enough to reach. I retreated and stared down into the smoking crater then seized the chance to squeeze between two stalls and kept my head down for an easy circuit. I was in full view of the guards on my way down and knew I would get caught, but I was more worried about the reaction from my partner. Luckily she also had a rebellious streak and so I got away with no more than a severe telling off from both.

In Praiano I negotiated a day off from boat trips and beaches to go for a walk up what seemed to be the highest hill in the area. My soles had no grip but I weaved a way from sea level along paths and grassy slopes to a more barren summit area, with fabulous views and weather and no shops or people. Some years later I learned that both peaks qualify as Ribus.

Nearing the summit of Monte San Michele, EU341 (Alan Dawson)

EU35 Eastern Europe Ranges

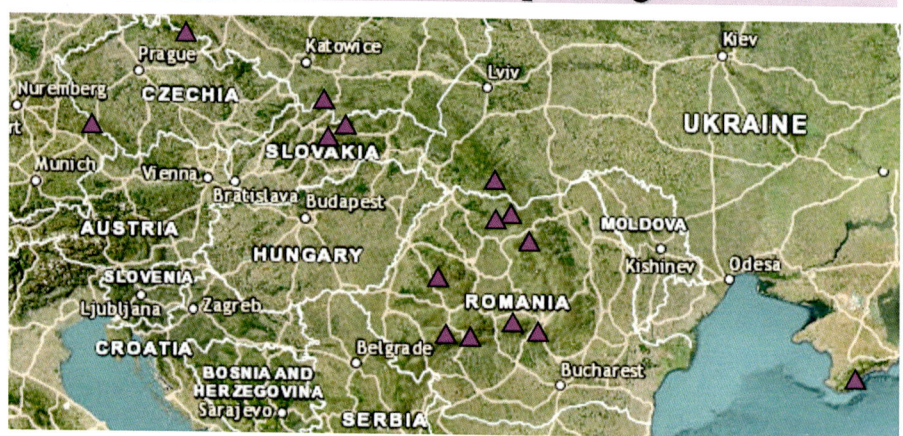

EU351 Bohemian Ranges

Id	Height	Name	Drop	Country	Location
52510	1603	Sněžka	1183	Czechia, Poland	50.7360, 15.7398
52514	1456	Großer Arber	1025	Germany	49.1125, 13.1358

EU352 Carpathian Mountains

Id	Height	Name	Drop	Country	Location
52501	2655	Gerlachovský štít	2354	Slovakia	49.1640, 20.1339
52505	2303	Pietrosul Rodnei	1568	Romania	47.5972, 24.6338
52509	2100	Pietrosul Călimanilor	1194	Romania	47.1249, 25.1857
52511	2046	Ďumbier	1181	Slovakia	48.9364, 19.6403
52512	1723	Babia Góra – Diablak	1071	Poland, Slovakia	49.5731, 19.5294
52513	1840	Bran	1067	Romania	47.5159, 24.2699
52515	1881	Blyznytsya / Близниця	1001	Ukraine	48.2225, 24.2313

EU353 Southern Carpathians

Id	Height	Name	Drop	Country	Location
52502	2518	Parângu Mare	2102	Romania	45.3401, 23.5392
52503	2544	Moldoveanu	2046	Romania	45.6000, 24.7358
52504	2509	Peleaga	1757	Romania	45.3653, 22.8929
52507	1849	Curcubăta Mare	1478	Romania	46.4408, 22.6889
52508	2514	Omu	1354	Romania	45.4456, 25.4563

EU354 Ukrainian Plains

Id	Height	Name	Drop	Country	Location
52506	1545	Roman-Kosh / Роман-Кош	1539	Ukraine / Russia	44.6128, 34.2428

Roman-Kosh, EU354

The war between Ukraine and Russia means that the Crimean peninsula has been occupied by Russia since 2014. Roman-Kosh faces an uncertain future along with the rest of Ukraine. Over previous centuries the region has been controlled by numerous empires and forces.

EU36 Balkan Peninsula

EU360 Dinaric Alps

Id	Height	Name	Drop	Country	Location
53007	2694	Maja e Jezercës	2036	Albania	42.4425, 19.8125
53031	2523	Durmitor – Bobotov Kuk	1480	Montenegro	43.1284, 19.0349
53035	2017	Pančićev vrh / Maja Pançiq	1444	Kosovo, Serbia	43.2683, 20.8258
53037	1988	Maja e Pashtrikut	1425	Albania, Kosovo	42.2107, 20.5240
53046	2227	Čvrsnica – Pločno	1350	Bosnia	43.5992, 17.5642
53058	2238	Ljubišnja – Dernečište	1256	Bosnia, Montenegro	43.3200, 19.0858
53063	2394	Veliki Vitao	1215	Montenegro	43.2254, 18.7571
53070	1764	Sveti Jure	1168	Croatia	43.3420, 17.0540
53072	2112	Nadkrstac	1142	Bosnia	43.9566, 17.7166

53074	2487	Komovi – Kom Kučki	1131	Montenegro	42.6817, 19.6425
53076	1796	Veliki Snežnik	1122	Slovenia	45.5885, 14.4476
53078	2115	Zelena Glava	1117	Bosnia	43.5497, 17.9039
53081	1492	Velika Đulica / Велика Ђулица	1103	Serbia	43.3917, 21.4433
53086	1509	Svilaja – Bat	1066	Croatia	43.7906, 16.4848
53087	1758	Vaganski vrh	1059	Croatia	44.3672, 15.5047
53088	1913	Troglav	1051	Bosnia	43.9455, 16.5967
53093	1895	Orjen – Zubački Kabao	1035	Montenegro	42.5697, 18.5438
53097	2656	Gjeravica	1026	Kosovo	42.5330, 20.1406
53098	1943	Vlašić – Paljenik	1022	Bosnia	44.2925, 17.6365

Gjeravica, EU360

Alastair Govan, August 2014

Kosovo is one of the poorest countries in Europe, without a seat at the United Nations but recognised by over 100 countries. The population is mainly ethnic Albanian (Muslim), but 10% are Serbian (Orthodox Christian) and this has predictably led to several years of tension. However, the Kosovans we met were incredibly friendly and hospitable and we thoroughly enjoyed our short visit in 2014. At that time Gjeravica, in the Prokletje ('accursed') mountains on the Albanian border, was considered to be the highest point of Kosovo, but this was subsequently moved to the Sharr Mountains as a result of remapping the border with North Macedonia. The Prokletje mountains are remote and rugged, but the hike up Gjeravica was straightforward once we had reached the start of the route, which was in a small summer settlement a few kilometres to the south-east. The logging road to the start was extremely rough, requiring a tough vehicle and confident driving (not least to pass the logging vehicles). To guarantee success we hired a local guide to drive us there and also guide us on an enjoyable circuit of the mountain. The guide wasn't strictly necessary but we learned a lot about this little-known part of Europe.

Nemërçka, EU361

Rob Woodall, September 2016 and October 2020

On the 2016 trip we failed to reach the summit of the southernmost of six Ultras in Albania. Four years later I was in Greece, climbing Ribus, but this missing peak was playing on my mind. There was a good paved road to the foot of the peak from the Greek side but access, by vehicle or on foot, was for locals only. From the Albanian side it was an awkward drive on sometimes muddy unpaved roads. It was a longish day hike from the south, with several nice summits en route and a few sheep flocks. A couple of dogs came close but picking up a stone ready to throw did the trick. Just before the summit was a deep notch, which I recalled from my previous attempt, but fortunately there was an easy gully as well.

EU361 Greek - Albanian Ranges

Id	Height	Name	Drop	Country	Location
53003	2918	Olympus / Ólimbos – Mýtikas	2354	Greece	40.0857, 22.3587
53005	2764	Maja e Korabit / Golem Korab	2166	Albania, N Macedonia	41.7907, 20.5466
53010	1978	Kíssavos – Profítis Ilías	1854	Greece	39.7957, 22.6852
53012	2482	Nemërçka – Maja e Papingut	1792	Albania	40.1242, 20.4327

53015	2521	Óros Voras – Kajmakčalan	1749	Greece, N Macedonia	40.9308, 21.7867
53017	2637	Smólikas / Σμόλικας	1736	Greece	40.0888, 20.9249
53018	2510	Gióna / Γκιώνα	1712	Greece	38.6473, 22.2518
53019	2540	Solunska Glava / Солунска Глава	1670	North Macedonia	41.7041, 21.4041
53020	2121	Maja e Këndrevicës	1666	Albania	40.2864, 19.8504
53024	2457	Parnassós – Liákoura	1591	Greece	38.5350, 22.6220
53027	2044	Mali i Çikës	1563	Albania	40.1982, 19.6399
53028	2373	Valamara – Maja e Valamarës	1526	Albania	40.7941, 20.4653
53029	2601	Baba Planina – Pelister	1516	North Macedonia	41.0033, 21.1842
53030	1589	Psilí Koryfí / Ψηλή Κορυφή	1514	Greece	38.7588, 20.9956
53033	1610	Pílio – Pourianós Stavrós	1473	Greece	39.4374, 23.0464
53034	2416	Tomorr – Çuka e Partizanit	1449	Albania	40.7067, 20.1425
53040	2244	Maja e Dejës	1401	Albania	41.6979, 20.1649
53041	2392	Maja e Pikëllimës / Koritnik	1395	Albania, Kosovo	42.0804, 20.5568
53042	1923	Maja e Trebeshinës	1370	Albania	40.3425, 20.1050
53043	1937	Tómaros / Τόμαρος	1364	Greece	39.4896, 20.7913
53044	2052	Vérmio – Chamítis	1361	Greece	40.6273, 21.9377
53047	2253	Maja e Shebenikut	1317	Albania	41.2167, 20.4625
53048	2155	Maja e Lalucit	1308	Albania	40.1325, 20.2508
53049	2523	Gramoz / Tsoúka Pétsik	1303	Albania, Greece	40.3483, 20.7792
53052	1748	Paliovoúna	1287	Greece	38.2991, 22.8811
53053	2495	Vardoúsia – Kórakas	1287	Greece	38.6808, 22.1442
53055	2383	Maja e Ostrovicës	1272	Albania	40.5589, 20.4403
53056	2497	Týmfi – Gamíla	1267	Greece	39.9885, 20.8083
53059	1806	Maja e Murganës / Μουργκάνα	1240	Albania, Greece	39.7883, 20.3917
53060	1852	Aëtoí / Αετοί	1232	Greece	39.2378, 21.2829
53069	2188	Piéria Óri – Flámbouro	1177	Greece	40.2270, 22.1548
53071	2101	Maja e Kreshtës	1143	Albania	41.5334, 20.2160
53073	1866	Voúrinos – Drisiníkos	1136	Greece	40.1760, 21.6727
53075	1413	Párnitha – Karavóla	1127	Greece	38.1745, 23.7168
53077	2288	Pllaja e Pusit / Vir	1118	Albania	40.8817, 20.8400
53079	2313	Tymfristós / Τυμφρηστός	1114	Greece	38.9444, 21.8243
53082	1658	Gorílas / Paramythías	1103	Greece	39.4734, 20.5474
53083	1726	Gerakovoúni	1098	Greece	39.0178, 22.7076
53085	1653	Ramno / Рамно	1087	North Macedonia	42.1915, 21.4460
53094	1990	Mali i Munellës	1034	Albania	41.9751, 20.0979
53095	1365	Geráneia – Makryplági	1032	Greece	38.0189, 23.1231
53096	1650	Xerovoúni – Sklávi	1029	Greece	39.3948, 20.9916
53102	2172	Kožuf / Tzéna	1006	Greece	41.1597, 22.2092
53103	2184	Schizokáravo	1003	Greece	39.3117, 21.5575
53104	1991	Mali i Zepës	1001	Albania	41.9294, 20.2338
53106	1520	Kanála / Báltou	1000	Greece	39.0031, 21.3456

A Greek Ultra Odyssey

Alastair Govan, September 2020

Greece is a mountainous country, with 59 Ribus, including eighteen Ultras. The mountains are mostly rocky but not technically demanding. I had climbed six of the Greek Ultras on previous trips and planned to climb the remaining twelve during a four-week stay in between Covid restrictions. September is an ideal time to visit as it is not too hot but the sea is still warm and most places are relatively quiet.

Weather is unlikely to present a serious obstacle in Greece, but in recent years the Mediterranean has had an autumn 'medicane' season, analogous to the hurricane season in other parts of the world, with some disruptive winds and rain. I was lucky, as a severe but short-lived medicane struck western Greece and Crete late in my trip, while I was in the largely unscathed east side of the country. The biggest risk in Greece, particularly on the mainland, seems to be semi-feral packs of dogs, which can be very scary, especially as the locals don't seem bothered about them. With a few exceptions the Greek mountains are quiet and unfrequented, but almost all of my twelve target peaks had paths with some form of markings, though they were not always easy to follow. Reaching the start of the routes often involved some quite rough driving. However, armed with digital maps and route descriptions, all this could be readily negotiated.

In the first week I did a circuit from Athens taking in five mountains, four of which were rather dull while the other, Smólikas, was the outstanding exception. It is located in the north-west of Greece, in a beautiful area of canyons, forests and alpine meadows. Apart from a shepherd with his flock, there was no one else around. There was a well-built mountain refuge near the start of the route but, as with many of these in Greece, it seemed to be deserted. The second week, on Crete, was a very different experience. All three Ultras are much more arid than the hills of northern Greece. All have marked paths and good views and the highest, Tímios Stavrós, is quite popular. The most dramatic scenery on Crete is in the numerous gorges such as the Samaria Gorge, which we also hiked during our visit.

The final part of my journey, from Thessaloniki in north-eastern Greece, provided the two most interesting summits of the trip. Samothráki is a remote and rugged island halfway between Greece and Turkey, somewhat off the tourist trail, so facilities are fairly basic. It is an island of rocky ridges, waterfalls, gorges and deserted but windswept sandy coves. The highest summit, Óros Fengári, has sections of ridge a little reminiscent of the Cuillin hills on Skye, especially in the damp mist enveloping it while I was there.

The ultimate highlight of the trip was Mount Athos, an isolated and rugged finger of land protruding 50 kilometres into the Aegean Sea. The territory operates as a semi-autonomous Greek Orthodox community with restricted access – strictly no women, and for non-Orthodox men only ten permits per day are issued, allowing stays of up to three nights. The peninsula is listed as a UNESCO World Heritage site, home to over twenty spectacular monasteries which are up to a thousand years old, and these provide the only accommodation (for pilgrims, not tourists). Although there is a land border, access is only by sea (with a customs check on the return trip) and the boat ride is superbly scenic, stopping at several monasteries en route. The highest peak, Ágion Óros, has a prominent position near the end of the peninsula, in an area remote from most of the monasteries and with no vehicle access. During my two-night stay I came across only one other non-Orthodox pilgrim, while the rest were all Greek, Romanian and Moldovan. So I managed to climb all eighteen Greek Ultras, which was satisfying.

The upper part of Olympus, EU361 (Alastair Govan)

View en route to Smólikas, EU361 (Alastair Govan)

EU362 Balkan Mountains

Id	Height	Name	Drop	Country	Location
53026	2376	Botev / Ботев	1567	Bulgaria	42.7169, 24.9173
53032	2169	Midzhur / Миџор	1480	Bulgaria, Serbia	43.3952, 22.6775
53065	1808	Trem / Трем	1209	Serbia	43.1832, 22.1712
53092	1560	Šiljak / Шиљак	1039	Serbia	43.7758, 21.8933

EU363 Macedonia – Thrace

Id	Height	Name	Drop	Country	Location
53001	2925	Musala / Мусала	2474	Bulgaria	42.1792, 23.5852
53008	2033	Ágion Óros / Άγιον Όρος	2018	Greece	40.1584, 24.3274
53013	2914	Vihren / Вихрен	1779	Bulgaria	41.7667, 23.3996
53014	1956	Pangaíon Óros – Koútra	1771	Greece	40.9138, 24.0909
53025	2030	Radomir / Kerkíni	1589	Bulgaria, Greece	41.3206, 23.1207
53038	2251	Ruen / Руен	1411	Bulgaria, N Macedonia	42.1580, 22.5163
53039	2229	Falakró / Chionótripa	1409	Greece	41.2938, 24.0946
53057	2290	Cherni Vrah / Черни връх	1259	Bulgaria	42.5631, 23.2793
53091	2212	Slavyanka / Órvilos	1040	Bulgaria, Greece	41.3771, 23.6207
53100	1401	Achlát Tsál / Αχλάτ Τσάλ	1011	Greece	41.1747, 24.8016
53107	1924	Ogreyak / Kadijca	1010	Bulgaria, N Macedonia	41.7895, 22.9634
53101	1201	Chortiátis / Χορτιάτης	1009	Greece	40.5818, 23.1168

EU364 Greek Islands and Peloponnesus

Id	Height	Name	Island	Drop	Country	Location
53002	2456	Psilorítis – Tímios Stavrós	Kríti	2456	Greece	35.2267, 24.7708
53006	2453	Páchnes / Πάχνες	Kríti	2038	Greece	35.2926, 24.0331
53011	2148	Óros Díkti – Spathí	Kríti	1800	Greece	35.1181, 25.4973
53045	1476	Thryptí – Aféntis	Kríti	1351	Greece	35.0801, 25.8754
53050	1777	Kédros / Κέδρος	Kríti	1300	Greece	35.1825, 24.6175
53016	1743	Dírfi / Δίρφη	Euboea	1743	Greece	38.6270, 23.8410
53021	1628	Óros Aínos / Όρος Αίνος	Kefalonia	1628	Greece	38.1366, 20.6710
53023	1611	Óros Fengári / Óros Sáos	Samothráki	1611	Greece	40.4618, 25.5878
53036	1433	Óros Kérkis – Vígla	Sámos	1433	Greece	37.7264, 26.6221
53051	1297	Óros Pelinaío – Koryfí Agía Triás	Khíos	1297	Greece	38.5568, 26.0050
53054	1398	Óchi / Όχη	Euboea	1283	Greece	38.0599, 24.4668
53062	1216	Óros Attávyros – Ágios Joánnis	Ródos	1216	Greece	36.2100, 27.8644
53064	1215	Óros Lástos – Káli Limní	Kárpathos	1215	Greece	35.5896, 27.1253
53066	1204	Ipsárion / Υψάριον	Thásos	1204	Greece	40.7034, 24.7056
53068	1182	Stavrotás / Eláti	Lefkada	1182	Greece	38.6991, 20.6248
53090	1043	Óros Aithéras – Efanós	Ikaría	1043	Greece	37.6136, 26.2536
53105	1002	Zas / Ζας	Náxos	1002	Greece	37.0305, 25.5023

Peloponnesus peninsula

Id	Height	Name	Drop	Country	Location
53004	2405	Taÿgetos – Profítis Ilías	2345	Greece	36.9530, 22.3503
53009	2374	Kyllíni / Zíria	1868	Greece	37.9393, 22.3958
53061	1981	Ménalo – Profítis Ilías	1216	Greece	37.6437, 22.2798
53067	2223	Erýmanthos – Granítis	1202	Greece	37.9882, 21.8345
53080	1935	Megáli Toúrla / Μεγάλη Τούρλα	1112	Greece	37.2781, 22.6130
53084	1928	Panachaïkó / Παναχαϊκό	1094	Greece	38.1963, 21.8706
53089	2355	Chelmós – Psilí Korifí	1043	Greece	37.9725, 22.2006
53099	1208	Agios Konstantinos	1014	Greece	37.1867, 21.7142

EU37 Ural Mountains

EU371 Pre-polar Urals

Id	Height	Name	Drop	Country	Location
53501	1895	Gora Narodnaya / Гора Народная	1771	Russia	65.0350, 60.1142
53503	1376	Netempe / Нэтемпэ	1216	Russia	68.0625, 65.6833
53504	1620	Gora Telpoziz / Гора Телпозиз	1206	Russia	63.9194, 59.1585
53506	1472	Gora Payer / Гора Пайер	1154	Russia	66.7208, 64.3917
53507	1333	Gora Khanmey / Гора Ханмей	1093	Russia	67.1658, 66.0925
53508	1646	Gora Neroyka / Гора Неройка	1068	Russia	64.5602, 59.5545
53509	1344	Gora Vysochayshiy	1064	Russia	67.6783, 65.9958
53510	1489	Gora Sablya / Гора Сабля	1024	Russia	64.7758, 58.8875

EU372 Northern Urals

Id	Height	Name	Drop	Country	Location
53505	1570	Gora Konzhakovskiy Kamen'	1170	Russia	59.6317, 59.1342

EU374 Southern Urals

Id	Height	Name	Drop	Country	Location
53502	1640	Gora Yamantau' / Гора Ямантау	1337	Russia	54.2550, 58.1042

EU38 Caucasus Mountains

On the way up Elbrus, EU381 (Alastair Govan)

EU380 Western Caucasus

Id	Height	Name	Drop	Country	Location
54014	2850	Fishta / Фишта	1374	Russia	43.9537, 39.9029
54016	3237	Chugush / Чугуш	1322	Russia	43.7975, 40.2108
54019	2665	Dzishra / ძიშრა	1265	Georgia	43.3247, 40.6831
54020	4046	Dombai-Ulgen / Домбай-Ульген	1265	Georgia, Russia	43.2439, 41.7258
54031	3313	Khojali / ხოჯალი	1203	Georgia	42.9845, 41.8677
54032	3256	Agepsta / Аҕьаҧсҭа	1201	Georgia, Russia	43.5477, 40.4818
54037	3026	Shkhapizga / შხაპიზგა	1145	Georgia	43.2488, 41.3992
54043	2809	Akiba / აკიბა	1093	Georgia	42.8742, 41.9058
54044	3235	Chilik Pervyy / Чилик Первый	1089	Russia	43.6492, 41.1175
54045	3346	Tsakhvoa / Цахвоа	1081	Russia	43.6717, 40.5775
54048	3790	Pshish / Пшиш	1042	Russia	43.4092, 41.1600

EU381 Central Caucasus

Id	Height	Name	Drop	Country	Location
54001	5642	Elbrus / Mingi Taw	4741	Russia	43.3525, 42.4375
54003	5054	Kazbek / Mkinvartsveri	2369	Georgia, Russia	42.6967, 44.5183
54006	5205	Dykhtau / Дыхтау	2002	Russia	43.0517, 43.1325
54011	4646	Uilpata / Уилпата	1462	Russia	42.7750, 43.8042
54012	4009	Lailchala / ლაილო	1395	Georgia	42.9207, 42.5564
54015	5193	Shkhara / შხარა / Шхара	1357	Georgia, Russia	42.9993, 43.1131
54024	2990	Tbaukhokh / Тбаухох	1250	Russia	42.8673, 44.3950
54027	3438	Karivkhokh / Каривхох	1229	Russia	42.8724, 44.2373
54028	4705	Ushba / უშბა	1222	Georgia	43.1240, 42.6585
54030	3603	Shoda / შოდა	1206	Georgia	42.6977, 43.4710
54033	4491	Gyul'chi / Гюльчи	1197	Russia	42.9936, 43.3957
54034	3646	Karakaya / Каракая	1184	Russia	43.2675, 43.2455
54035	2002	Khvamli / ხვამლი	1180	Georgia	42.5025, 42.7150
54036	4431	Tepli / Тепли	1156	Russia	42.7337, 44.1317
54039	3938	Khalatsa / Халасхох	1115	Georgia, Russia	42.5983, 43.8350
54041	4454	Babis / Donguzorun	1100	Georgia, Russia	43.1948, 42.5142
54042	2863	Lebeuris / ლებურისები	1095	Georgia	42.4595, 43.6517
54050	2823	Chizdzhinkhokh / Чиздджинхох	1028	Russia	42.8592, 44.4785

Elbrus, EU381

Alastair Govan, June 2016

In 2016 Elbrus was the last major obstacle to my reaching the highest point in every country in Europe. The Caucasus mountains are high, rugged and snowy, a bit like the Alps without the infrastructure. The main watershed ridge is a sensitive border area with difficult access. Fortunately, Elbrus sits a little north of the watershed, fully in Russia, and access was straightforward in spite of a UK government travel advisory notice.

I opted for the easier southern approach which has ski infrastructure up to about 4400 metres, starting at the small resort of Terskol, including the option of an early morning snow-cat ride taking me steeply up the last 700 metres from the highest 'huts', which are actually metal storage containers. There is very limited trekking in the immediate area so acclimatisation consisted largely of walking up and down the ski areas. Summit temperature in June was around -15C with occasional storms. There are frequent fatalities due to poor weather or poor route finding on the descent. Success is not guaranteed, even with a two or three day window, but luckily my summit day was perfect. With good acclimatisation, it was not overly demanding.

EU382 Eastern Caucasus

Id	Height	Name	Drop	Country	Location
54002	4466	Bazardüzü / Базардюзю	2461	Azerbaijan, Russia	41.2208, 47.8583
54004	4493	Tebulos / ტებულოს	2145	Georgia, Russia	42.5742, 45.3150
54007	4127	Dyultydag / Дюльтыдаг	1834	Russia	41.9592, 46.9217
54009	4152	Addala-Shukhgelmeer	1799	Russia	42.3390, 46.2489
54010	4452	Shani / შანი	1774	Georgia, Russia	42.6742, 44.7575
54021	4285	Diklo / დიკლოსმთა	1263	Georgia, Russia	42.4883, 45.7758
54022	4016	Deavgay / Kyelbid Ban	1251	Russia	41.4968, 47.3261
54025	3171	Gaykomd / Гайкомд	1247	Russia	42.8390, 44.8318
54029	4142	Shalbuzdag / Шалбуздаг	1209	Russia	41.3270, 47.7992
54038	2806	Kashkerlam / Кашкерлам	1138	Russia	42.7984, 46.0701
54040	4255	Şahdağ	1113	Azerbaijan	41.2691, 48.0064
54046	3890	Makhismagali / Магисмабали	1054	Georgia, Russia	42.7041, 45.0703
54049	3569	Chodoridag / Чодоридаг	1028	Russia	41.9592, 46.3925

EU383 Lesser Caucasus

Id	Height	Name	Drop	Country	Location
54005	4090	Aragats / Արագած	2142	Armenia	40.5232, 44.1941
54008	3905	Kaputjugh / Qapıcıq	1820	Armenia, Azerbaijan	39.1592, 46.0033
54013	3724	Gamış Dağı	1393	Azerbaijan	40.2792, 46.3583
54017	3300	Didi Abuli / დიდი აბული	1314	Georgia	41.4370, 43.6458
54018	3597	Azhdahak / Աժդահակ	1268	Armenia	40.2248, 44.9501
54023	3616	Dəlidağ	1250	Azerbaijan	39.9175, 46.0417
54026	3016	Bovak'ar / Բովքար	1235	Armenia	40.7941, 44.6980
54047	2412	İlandağ	1044	Azerbaijan	39.1375, 45.7158
54051	3196	Ach'k'asar / Աչքասար	1027	Armenia	41.1563, 43.9591

——— Asia West ———

AS40 Anatolia

Dedegol Tepesi, AS403 (Deividas Valaitis)

AS400 Western Anatolia

Id	Height	Name	Drop	Country	Location
60008	3070	Bey Dağları – Kizlar Sivrisi	1970	Türkiye	36.6050, 30.1208
60011	1969	Babadağ	1762	Türkiye	36.5302, 29.1809
60014	3016	Uyluk Tepesi	1665	Türkiye	36.5440, 29.5679
60016	2156	Boz Dağ	1578	Türkiye	38.3238, 28.1023
60017	2800	Barla Dağı	1575	Türkiye	38.0533, 30.7017
60019	2637	Davraz Tepe	1557	Türkiye	37.7542, 30.7250

60023	2546	Uludağ Tepe	1507	Türkiye	40.0729, 29.2166
60031	2325	Alacadağ	1396	Türkiye	36.4154, 29.9988
60034	1773	Kaz Dağı / Kirklar Tepe	1366	Türkiye	39.6999, 26.8653
60039	2602	Gelincikana Tepesi	1342	Türkiye	38.5044, 31.0981
60044	2449	Kıraç Tepe	1307	Türkiye	38.3008, 29.9575
60045	2089	Akdağ	1297	Türkiye	39.2669, 28.8104
60049	1601	Kartepe	1264	Türkiye	40.6425, 30.1004
60050	2283	Kara Dağ	1257	Türkiye	37.3994, 33.1471
60053	2421	Boz Dağ	1245	Türkiye	37.3012, 29.2008
60054	1517	Spil Dağı / Manisa Dağı	1245	Türkiye	38.5670, 27.4548
60055	2528	Esler Dağı / Honaz Dağı	1244	Türkiye	37.6786, 29.2847
60058	2295	Emiroğlu Tepesi	1205	Türkiye	38.8246, 31.2369
60063	2366	Tahtali Dağı	1178	Türkiye	36.5364, 30.4419
60064	2308	Babadağ / Gok Tepe	1178	Türkiye	37.7322, 28.8783
60065	1212	Bozdağ	1168	Türkiye	38.5566, 26.5014
60068	2399	Köroğlu Dağlan	1153	Türkiye	40.5159, 31.8740
60071	2469	Susuz Dağı / Mancarli Dağı	1136	Türkiye	36.5319, 29.9142
60072	1163	Bozdağ Tepesi	1135	Türkiye	36.7309, 27.5817
60075	2300	Çiçekbaba Tepe / Sandras Dağı	1118	Türkiye	37.0824, 28.8368
60080	2305	Murat Dağı	1101	Türkiye	38.9332, 29.7097
60092	1509	Nif Dağı / Nifkarlığı Tepe	1058	Türkiye	38.3879, 27.3565
60093	1896	Göktepe	1052	Türkiye	37.3429, 28.3729
60095	2120	Saphane Daği	1046	Türkiye	39.0479, 29.2744
60097	1982	Çeledoruğu Tepesi	1036	Türkiye	40.8653, 31.7022
60099	1240	Dilik Tepe	1030	Türkiye	37.6611, 27.1504
60101	2334	Kestel Dağı / Katranci Dağı	1023	Türkiye	37.4678, 30.3245
60104	2274	Gelincik Dağı / Ak Dağ	1005	Türkiye	37.6883, 30.5750
60106	2250	Kumalar Dağı	1003	Türkiye	38.4015, 30.4189

AS401 Pontic Mountains

Id	Height	Name	Drop	Country	Location
60005	3937	Kaçkar Dağı	2280	Türkiye	40.8350, 41.1617
60018	3555	Kesis Dağı	1571	Türkiye	39.7911, 39.7700
60022	2587	Ilgaz Dağları / Büyükhacet Tepe	1546	Türkiye	41.1000, 33.8633
60025	3328	Aptalmusa Dağı / Gümüşhane Dağları	1445	Türkiye	40.3952, 39.0648
60035	3438	Karçal Dağları	1359	Türkiye	41.3471, 41.9832
60038	2080	Akdağ / Konacık Tepe	1350	Türkiye	40.8155, 35.8767
60066	3255	Mescit Tepesi	1163	Türkiye	40.3562, 41.1767
60073	3107	Karagöl Dağı	1127	Türkiye	40.5225, 38.1539
60087	3196	Kisir Dağı	1068	Türkiye	40.946, 43.0792
60091	3135	Ala Dağ	1061	Türkiye	40.1850, 42.8367
60107	3165	Arsiyan / Göze Dağı	1002	Türkiye	41.3908, 42.5193

Ilgaz Dağlari, AS401

Rob Woodall, July 2018

Turkey and the Balkans are notorious for their sheep dogs – big fierce brutes, trained to intimidate, not to bite, in my experience. My strangest dog encounter was on Ilgaz Dağları. I had misunderstood the driving directions, which left me hiking in the dog zone. On the way down I was met by five of the barking, lunging brutes. The shepherd was nearby but didn't intervene. I headed down the road with my canine escort snapping at my heels and passed the shepherd's house, but again no intervention. It occurred to me that I might as well get some video footage. I turned the phone on them ... and they slunk away. It may be that they were spooked by the infra-red range finder. I wished I had tried it sooner.

AS402 Central Anatolia

Id	Height	Name	Drop	Country	Location
60003	3917	Erciyes Dağı	2420	Türkiye	38.5317, 35.4467
60009	3268	Hasan Dağı	1924	Türkiye	38.1267, 34.1650
60012	2260	Uludaz / Uzunziyaret Tepesi	1746	Türkiye	37.4500, 36.6548
60020	3081	Killi Tepe / Nurhak Daği	1554	Türkiye	38.0275, 37.4842
60027	3080	Bey Daği	1439	Türkiye	38.2917, 36.0533
60032	3020	Karagölyatağı Tepesi / Berit Daği	1395	Türkiye	38.0021, 36.8557
60042	2605	Türkdağı Tepesi	1323	Türkiye	38.1240, 38.4718
60043	2816	Engizek Daği	1304	Türkiye	37.8272, 37.0742
60047	2240	Bozdağ Daği / Migir	1271	Türkiye	36.8083, 36.3900
60062	2958	Binboğa Dağları – Işık Daği	1197	Türkiye	38.2475, 36.5186
60070	2737	Yama Daği / Çalgan Daği	1145	Türkiye	39.0974, 38.0627
60069	1800	Kizil Dağ / Susuz Tepe	1143	Türkiye	36.3033, 36.0025
60074	3025	Köse Daği / Kizildağ	1130	Türkiye	39.9217, 38.3550
60076	2805	Bey Daği	1117	Türkiye	39.6840, 37.8787
60086	2963	Melendiz Daği	1073	Türkiye	38.0713, 34.5265
60088	1962	Sakarat Daği / Cami Tepe	1068	Türkiye	40.6005, 36.2965
60089	2535	Tucak Daği / Ulubaba Tepe	1062	Türkiye	37.9502, 38.1555
60026	3623	Kūh-e Avarīn-e Bozorg / کوه اورین بزرگ	1446	Iran	38.5542, 44.5742
60096	2510	Akdağ	1044	Türkiye	38.0216, 38.3310

AS403 Taurus Mountains

Id	Height	Name	Drop	Country	Location
60004	3767	Kızılkaya	2347	Türkiye	37.7975, 35.1558
60007	3524	Medetsiz Tepe	2060	Türkiye	37.3930, 34.6313
60015	2988	Dedegol Tepesi	1663	Türkiye	37.6658, 31.3008
60021	2881	Geyik Daglari	1549	Türkiye	36.8892, 32.1717
60037	2554	Sarp Daği	1351	Türkiye	37.4776, 31.1168
60061	2420	Akdağ	1198	Türkiye	37.4101, 34.9418
60078	2490	Hacıbaba Daği	1104	Türkiye	37.1892, 32.8892
60102	2504	Kuyucak Daği / Bozburun Daği	1013	Türkiye	37.3040, 31.0565

| 60105 | 2450 | Manaşır Tepe / Seytan Dağı | 1004 | Türkiye | 37.2962, 31.5309 |
| 60109 | 3059 | Karanfıl Dağı | 1000 | Türkiye | 37.6001, 35.0410 |

AS404 South-east Anatolia

Id	Height	Name	Drop	Country	Location
60001	5137	Büyük Ağrı Dağı / Greater Ararat	3610	Türkiye	39.7021, 44.2984
60002	4136	Cilo Dağları – Uludoruk	2482	Türkiye	37.4867, 44.0033
60006	4058	Süphan Dağı	2189	Türkiye	38.9267, 42.8275
60010	3810	Mor Dağı	1807	Türkiye	37.7517, 44.3208
60013	3811	Samdi Dağ	1727	Türkiye	37.3092, 44.2508
60024	3462	Akbaba Tepesi	1508	Türkiye	39.5360, 39.5407
60026	3623	Kūh-e Avarīn-e Bozorg / کوه اورین بزرگ	1446	Iran	38.5542, 44.5742
60028	3431	Büyükköse Dağı	1432	Türkiye	39.8954, 42.6437
60029	3640	İhtiyarşahap Dağı	1417	Türkiye	38.0600, 42.9533
60030	2620	Akdağ	1404	Türkiye	38.6373, 40.1478
60033	3609	Kūh-e Bardehrash	1383	Iran	37.5158, 44.6767
60036	3470	Kūh-e Bozsīnā	1353	Iran	37.1142, 44.8800
60040	2978	Aydin Tepesi / Mereto Dağı	1342	Türkiye	38.3825, 41.5431
60041	2940	Kenek Tepesi	1326	Türkiye	38.7025, 40.8942
60046	3292	Bagirpasa Dağı	1275	Türkiye	39.4833, 40.1200
60048	3752	Kara Dağ	1265	Türkiye	37.6998, 43.6828
60051	2218	Chiya-e Gara	1256	Iraq	36.9769, 43.4825
60052	3543	Hüdavendigar Dağı	1252	Türkiye	39.3401, 43.4469
60056	2960	Gora Kherakul / Herakol Dag	1242	Türkiye	37.7475, 42.5567
60057	3010	Ziyaret Tepesi / Karz Dağı	1241	Türkiye	38.4037, 42.4546
60059	3925	Küçük Ağrı Dağı / Little Ararat	1202	Türkiye	39.6483, 44.4133
60060	3446	Kartal Tepe / Beyaz Tepe	1198	Türkiye	38.1675, 43.3117
60067	1957	Karaca Dağ	1153	Türkiye	37.7120, 39.8288
60077	2348	Hazar Dağı / Karaoğlan Dağı	1112	Türkiye	38.3604, 39.2350
60081	2068	Jabal Birādawst / جبل برادوست	1099	Iraq	36.7342, 44.3892
60079	3196	Dağkale Tepesi / Serpulas Dagi	1098	Türkiye	39.3599, 41.3825
60082	2331	Qimmat Pīrsiyah	1096	Iraq	37.1358, 43.5308
60083	3679	Baset Tepesi	1091	Türkiye	38.2022, 43.6444
60084	3180	Eğerli Dağı / Karakaya Tepesi	1084	Türkiye	39.7842, 41.2293
60085	3250	Hama Dağ	1079	Türkiye	39.7183, 43.9512
60090	2878	Sülbüs Dağı	1059	Türkiye	39.2596, 40.0199
60094	2933	Nemrut Dağı	1052	Türkiye	38.6547, 42.2555
60098	2897	Sultanbaba Dağı	1029	Türkiye	39.3226, 39.4932
60100	3537	Çadir Dağı / Artos Dağı	1012	Türkiye	38.2467, 43.1067
60103	3470	Kara Dağ	1006	Türkiye	37.3425, 43.8017
60108	2819	Tosun Dağı	1001	Türkiye	38.5976, 41.2582

AS41 Levant Ranges

AS410 Cyprus

Id	Height	Name	Drop	Country	Location
60503	1952	Ólimbos / Chionístra	1952	Cyprus	34.9367, 32.8642

AS411 Northern Levant Coastal Ranges

Id	Height	Name	Drop	Country	Location
60502	3088	Qurnat as Sawdā / القرنة السوداء	2393	Lebanon	34.3008, 36.1158
60504	2814	Jabal ash Shaykh / Mount Hermon	1810	Lebanon, Syria	33.4167, 35.8567
60506	2629	Ouâdi Hajar	1284	Lebanon, Syria	34.0492, 36.4925
60507	1728	Kel Dağı / Jabal al-Aqra	1276	Türkiye	35.9520, 35.9691
60511	1562	Jabal Mattá / جبل متى	1050	Syria	35.5908, 36.2183

AS412 Sinai-Palestine Ranges

Id	Height	Name	Drop	Country	Location
60501	2653	Gabal Katrîne / Mount Catherine	2448	Egypt	28.5094, 33.9556
60512	2070	Jebel Serbal / جبل سربال	1047	Egypt	28.6450, 33.6525
60514	2439	Gebel Yithmid el-Qibli	1008	Egypt	28.2617, 34.0167

AS413 Syrian Desert

Id	Height	Name	Drop	Country	Location
60505	2556	Jabal al Lawz / جبل أللوز	1598	Saudi Arabia	28.6540, 35.3040
60508	1966	Jabal az Zuhd / جبل الزهد	1140	Saudi Arabia	28.3100, 35.2983
60509	1804	Tall Ḥawrān	1093	Syria	32.6675, 36.7192
60510	1463	Çêl Mêra	1076	Iraq	36.3950, 41.8567
60513	2160	Jabal Neom *	1015	Saudi Arabia	28.1994, 35.5972

Gabal Katrîne, AS412

Rob Woodall, November 2012

Egypt has ten Ribus, of which two are Ultras, straddling the Red Sea. Gabal Katrîne (Mount Catherine) is a pretty straightforward outing. There was a fair bit of terrorist activity in Sinai, but we heard that kidnap victims were generally treated very well, and soon released after the captors had made their point to their target audience. We had to settle for the peak, some impressive rock scenery, finishing on the iconic Mount Sinai at sunset.

AS42 Zagros Mountains

AS420 Northern Zagros

Id	Height	Name	Drop	Country	Location
61009	3360	Kūh-e Parau / پراو	1832	Iran	34.4186, 47.2442
61010	3587	Kūh-e Ḥājī Ebrāhīm / حاجی ابراهیم	1800	Iran, Iraq	36.5474, 45.0069
61011	3630	Kuh-e Garin / گرین	1781	Iran	33.9592, 48.4817
61012	3350	Shahu / شاهو	1714	Iran	34.9975, 46.4725

Id	Height	Name	Drop	Country	Location
61014	2975	Kūh-e Takht / تخت	1675	Iran	35.2380, 46.2195
61015	3586	Alvand Kūh / الوند	1670	Iran	34.6642, 48.4864
61019	3611	Cheekha Dar / چیخادار	1575	Iran, Iraq	36.7761, 44.9188
61027	2624	Shak-i Pira Magrūn	1493	Iraq	35.7732, 45.2295
61028	2672	Jabal Kārūkh	1490	Iraq	36.5295, 44.6747
61030	3320	Dalakhani / دالاخانى	1465	Iran	34.6867, 47.6250
61036	3080	Qolleh-ye Gorbeh'ī	1418	Iran	33.6642, 48.0350
61037	2545	Kurkur	1405	Iraq	36.0161, 45.2195
61038	2810	Kan Seifi	1385	Iran	33.3933, 46.7808
61041	2810	Kūh-e Sefīd	1372	Iran	34.0542, 47.3867
61043	3260	Kūh-e Nakhowd Chāl	1352	Iran	34.6308, 47.7358
61048	3290	Kūh-e Badr / کوه بدر	1297	Iran	35.0317, 47.7792
61055	3381	Kūh-e Kal Borj / Shahbaz	1250	Iran	33.8524, 49.4364
61059	2930	Avalan	1209	Iran	35.0081, 46.8659
61062	2560	Kūh-e Chālāb	1190	Iran	34.5317, 47.4450
61067	3195	Kūh-e Qolī Zoleykhā	1161	Iran	35.8192, 46.5367
61071	2990	Kūh-e Hashtādpahlū	1139	Iran	33.2250, 48.4100
61073	2980	Kūh-e Narāmān	1138	Iran	34.5492, 47.1358
61078	2955	Kūh-e Korreh Meyāneh	1120	Iran	35.3297, 46.4510
61082	2650	Kūh-e Mānasht	1107	Iran	33.6883, 46.4500
61090	3215	Kūh-e Ālā Dāgh / آلاداغ	1073	Iran	34.0825, 49.1850
61091	3230	Kūh-e Do Tūreh	1071	Iran	33.9692, 49.2917
61093	2560	Kasheh Kūh	1058	Iran	34.8008, 46.2733
61094	2640	Kūh-e Hanjas	1055	Iran	33.7292, 47.6433
61097	2200	Jabal Kajlī	1037	Iraq	35.6150, 45.6725
61099	2980	Takht Kūh	1027	Iran	33.4850, 48.9433
61104	2280	Loven	1012	Iran	33.1017, 48.6100
61107	1862	Qimmat Qal'at Kīlānāwah	1010	Iraq	35.2867, 45.3035

AS421 North Central Zagros

Id	Height	Name	Drop	Country	Location
61002	4221	Zard Kūh / زردکوه	2115	Iran	32.3646, 50.0775
61006	4150	Oshtoran Kūh / اشتوران کوه	1997	Iran	33.3403, 49.3044
61013	3480	Kūh-e Sefīd Māfārūn / مافارون	1689	Iran	32.1242, 49.9950
61025	3750	Kūh-e Menār / Keyno	1510	Iran	32.5687, 49.5634
61026	3900	Kūh-e Darabshah	1494	Iran	32.9626, 50.5133
61033	4078	Qalikuh / قالى کوه	1439	Iran	33.0586, 49.4866
61035	4038	Shahankuh / Asiab Badineh	1427	Iran	32.8035, 49.9821
61051	3692	Kūh-e Ādel Fārs	1276	Iran	33.1558, 50.3225
61056	3858	Kūh-e Hashtād	1236	Iran	33.0142, 49.9642
61060	2680	Kūh-e Chelī	1204	Iran	32.8050, 48.9083

Id	Height	Name	Drop	Country	Location
61074	2590	Kūh-e Garīveh	1135	Iran	32.9917, 48.8558
61077	3640	Kūh-e Zarrāb	1121	Iran	32.3517, 50.2650
61084	2890	Kūh-e Mālū	1099	Iran	33.0858, 48.9283
61102	3920	Kūh-e Garah / Kūh-e Ferdan	1019	Iran	32.7475, 49.9392
61103	3127	Kūh-e Alvand	1015	Iran	33.5442, 50.2092

AS422 South Central Zagros

Id	Height	Name	Drop	Country	Location
61001	4435	Dena / دنا	2630	Iran	30.9510, 51.4362
61008	3190	Kūh-e Khāmī / خامی	1945	Iran	30.4925, 50.8992
61016	3880	Kūh-e Hezār Darreh / کوه هزار دره	1620	Iran	31.6749, 51.0285
61017	3661	Kūh-e Rag / رگ	1608	Iran	31.3367, 50.9717
61021	3943	Kūh-e Bol / بل	1563	Iran	30.7775, 52.7500
61022	3990	Kūh-e Haft Cheshmeh / هفت چشمه	1560	Iran	31.8908, 50.3795
61024	3120	Kuhsefid / کوه سفید	1510	Iran	31.1258, 50.2758
61032	3613	Kūh-e Mūngasht / Qarun	1457	Iran	31.4675, 50.2675
61049	3510	Kūh-e Nīl	1293	Iran	30.8900, 50.8600
61050	3720	Kūh-e Jey Qod	1289	Iran	31.4958, 51.7183
61057	3730	Kūh-e Barm Fīrūz	1221	Iran	30.4017, 51.9475
61066	3030	Kūh-e Āb Zālū	1164	Iran	30.5542, 51.1600
61068	2390	Kūh-e Māqer	1154	Iran	31.0458, 50.1200
61070	1970	Kūh-e Golestan *	1140	Iran	29.5708, 51.5850
61072	3280	Vol	1139	Iran	29.8917, 53.6617
61075	3340	Kūh-e Jahān Bīn	1134	Iran	32.2000, 50.6933
61076	3520	Kūh-e Kalāh Qāzī	1134	Iran	30.5075, 52.6467
61083	3910	Kūh-e Mili	1106	Iran	32.0992, 50.2783
61086	3040	Kūh-e Āb Bāgh	1081	Iran	31.6258, 50.9092
61089	3820	Kūh-e Kalar	1075	Iran	31.8450, 50.9025
61092	4280	Pazane Pir	1067	Iran	30.7883, 51.6492
61095	3470	Kūh-e Bavanat *	1042	Iran	30.4050, 53.6250
61105	2870	Kūh-e Qollat Sefid	1011	Iran	29.8725, 53.1967
61108	3020	Kūh-e Lamush	1005	Iran	31.8350, 52.0808
61109	3055	Kūh-e Tabask	1005	Iran	29.8539, 51.8219
61112	3230	Siah Kūh	1001	Iran	31.2000, 50.8892

AS423 Southern Zagros

Id	Height	Name	Drop	Country	Location
61003	2681	Kūh-e Shab / شب	2100	Iran	27.4317, 55.1342
61004	3240	Kūh-e Fāreghān / Homag	2085	Iran	27.8867, 56.3474
61005	2350	Genu / گنو	2035	Iran	27.4258, 56.1725
61007	2650	Kūh-e Poshtkūh / پشتکوه	1967	Iran	27.6133, 56.6692

61018	2846	Kūh-e Namak / نمک	1600	Iran	28.7005, 53.2493
61020	2980	Kūh-e Jā'īn / جائین	1571	Iran	28.0950, 55.9900
61023	2209	Kūh-e Par-e Lavar / لاور	1530	Iran	27.1942, 54.5392
61029	2180	Kūh-e Gāvbast Gap / گاوبست	1469	Iran	27.3433, 53.8717
61031	2475	Baz / باز	1464	Iran	27.7775, 55.8683
61034	3185	Kharman Kūh	1433	Iran	29.2150, 53.5783
61039	2840	Kūh-e Sefīd	1384	Iran	28.8700, 54.2608
61040	2080	Kūh-e Dār Modān	1373	Iran	27.7517, 55.5142
61042	2670	Kūh-e Chāhū	1370	Iran	28.3775, 53.7775
61044	2480	Kūh-e Mārūn	1347	Iran	27.9083, 55.8475
61045	1690	Kūh-e Gīshū	1344	Iran	27.3217, 55.7550
61046	2220	Kūh-e Zarhedūn	1338	Iran	27.4567, 54.3983
61047	3190	Kūh-e Sefidar	1308	Iran	28.9392, 52.8783
61052	2940	Kūh-e Kahdān	1268	Iran	29.1150, 53.0183
61053	2910	Kūh-e Pīdank	1268	Iran	28.8233, 52.7042
61054	1954	Kūh-e Bayramī	1257	Iran	28.7200, 51.4683
61058	1810	Kūh-e Z̧ālemī	1220	Iran	27.5350, 53.0517
61061	2980	Kūh-e Khāneh Ket	1197	Iran	29.4284, 53.5938
61063	2820	Kūh-e Sūr	1172	Iran	28.8092, 52.9150
61064	2110	Kūh-e Holū	1172	Iran	27.6150, 54.0642
61065	1927	Kūh-e Devīn	1169	Iran	27.6843, 56.0576
61069	2060	Kūh-e Bandūbast	1141	Iran	28.1892, 53.4033
61079	2240	Kūh-e Panj Shir *	1118	Iran	28.5367, 52.5342
61080	3126	Qollāt-e Sārdū	1114	Iran	28.7608, 54.7817
61081	3120	Kūh-e Dalī	1111	Iran	29.3742, 52.2767
61085	2180	Kūh-e Bardowmeh	1084	Iran	27.7783, 54.5750
61087	1776	Kūh-e Bībī Shahr Bānū	1080	Iran	27.6634, 56.4246
61088	2800	Kūh-e Qashqeh	1080	Iran	28.3425, 55.3150
61096	2970	Kūh-e Barg Sīb	1042	Iran	29.1175, 53.8058
61098	1570	Kūh-e Nīmvar	1033	Iran	27.7200, 52.4325
61100	2210	Kūh-e Sīāh	1025	Iran	27.5158, 54.7867
61101	2590	Kūh-e Khar	1020	Iran	29.4733, 53.8658
61106	3060	Kūh-e Posht Pahn	1010	Iran	29.5008, 52.0358
61110	1480	Kūh-e Khowrgū	1003	Iran	27.5842, 56.3775
61111	2855	Kūh-e Bejishk *	1003	Iran	29.1467, 53.3450

AS43 Iranian Plateau

Kūh-e Damāvand, AS431 (Rob Woodall)

AS430 North-west Iran Ranges

Id	Height	Name	Drop	Country	Location
61502	4794	Kūh-e Sabalan / سبلان	3266	Iran	38.2670, 47.8368
61515	3695	Kūh-e Sahand / سهند	1813	Iran	37.7295, 46.5003
61536	3332	Kūh-e Belqeys / بلقیس	1493	Iran	36.6697, 47.2991
61538	3347	Kīyāmakī Dāgh / کیاماکی داغ	1489	Iran	38.7858, 45.8567
61551	3131	Kūh-e Alamdar / کوه علمدار	1346	Iran	38.3458, 45.5300
61557	3302	Bouzghoush	1302	Iran	37.7558, 47.4458
61570	3230	Kūh-e Arjaneh Qarah Gol	1209	Iran	37.9367, 48.5875
61583	2493	Kūh-e Oveystī	1164	Azerbaijan	38.7361, 48.2429
61589	2940	Kūh-e Gishtasar	1126	Iran	38.8225, 47.2217
61630	2195	Ilandag	1011	Iran	38.8178, 46.1803

AS431 Elburz

Id	Height	Name	Drop	Country	Location
61501	5610	Kūh-e Damāvand / دماوند	4667	Iran	35.9550, 52.1100
61510	3932	Kūh-e Shāhvār / شاهوار	1923	Iran	36.5800, 54.7650
61512	4826	Alam Kūh / علم کوه	1848	Iran	36.3756, 50.9616
61525	3321	Agh Dagh / آق داغ	1625	Iran	37.3858, 48.5500
61534	3730	Kūh-e Nozva / نیزوا	1513	Iran	35.9429, 53.3250
61548	4072	Kūh-e Dowbarār / دوبرار	1381	Iran	35.7658, 52.2308
61550	2687	Kūh-e Qebleh	1364	Iran	36.3500, 55.6283
61564	2805	Kūh-e Qowrkhūd	1245	Iran	37.4533, 56.4850
61569	2452	Kūh-e Molḥadū	1210	Iran	35.9525, 55.9417
61576	3840	Kūh-e Gūkeshān	1176	Iran	36.5233, 54.4558
61579	4160	Sialan / سیالان	1170	Iran	36.5117, 50.6983
61580	4015	Parchenan / Vion	1168	Iran	35.9617, 52.5933
61582	3964	Tochal / توچال	1164	Iran	35.8842, 51.4200
61601	3240	Shahdarkuh	1092	Iran	36.3137, 53.9779
61612	2523	Kuh-e Bahār	1066	Iran	37.2238, 56.7141
61619	2568	Kūh-e Khvajeh Qanbar	1047	Iran	37.0933, 55.6314
61621	3200	Bādeleh Kūh	1032	Iran	36.4025, 53.9683
61622	3540	Kūh-e Qadamgāh / قدمگاه	1032	Iran	35.8637, 53.0697
61625	3120	Kūh-e Māsūleh Dāgh	1027	Iran	37.2092, 48.8992
61627	4108	Yaskhar	1022	Iran	36.1083, 51.0408

AS432 Central Iranian Plateau

Id	Height	Name	Drop	Country	Location
61504	4500	Kūh-e Hezār / هزار	2740	Iran	29.5117, 57.2717
61507	4050	Shir Kūh / شیرکوه	2271	Iran	31.6058, 54.0683
61508	4229	Kūh-e Palvār / پلوار	1970	Iran	30.0700, 57.4658
61509	2960	Nayband / نایبند	1967	Iran	32.4408, 57.3692
61518	3856	Kūh-e Khabr / خبر	1758	Iran	28.7959, 56.3967
61519	3150	Kūh-e Kharanaq / دربید	1733	Iran	32.1145, 54.5794
61521	3870	Kūh-e Karkas / کرکس	1698	Iran	33.4558, 51.8000
61524	3775	Kūh-e Bagh-e Bala / باغ بالا	1636	Iran	30.5625, 57.1617
61527	4150	Jupar / جوپار	1598	Iran	29.9108, 57.2017
61529	3592	Kūh-e Mohammadabad / Madvar	1584	Iran	30.5808, 54.8663
61531	2777	Kūh-e Denband / دنبند	1538	Iran	31.5925, 57.0333
61539	3205	Kūh-e Gerdū	1453	Iran	30.5550, 56.3567
61540	3750	Jebale-Barez / جبال بارز	1441	Iran	28.5671, 58.2291
61542	4384	Kūh Shāh	1409	Iran	29.3900, 56.7467
61545	3503	Domir	1385	Iran	33.9267, 51.0432
61547	2415	Kūh-e Darreh Anjir / کوه دره انجیر	1383	Iran	33.3442, 53.6442
61554	1980	Kūh-e Kalmard	1323	Iran	28.0117, 57.5083
61559	2420	Kūh-e Gargīn	1296	Iran	33.3958, 54.6817
61561	3545	Kūh-e Cheshmeh Rowghanī	1262	Iran	31.2703, 56.4814
61562	3120	Kūh-e Sīneh Ābastan	1261	Iran	34.6799, 50.1139
61565	3320	Marshenan	1241	Iran	32.8817, 52.4017
61567	2300	Jūrkas Gelīj	1224	Iran	34.0361, 52.1055
61571	3360	Kūh-e Kamar Kangū	1204	Iran	28.7842, 56.8358
61572	3280	Kūh-e Dāvdūn	1204	Iran	31.5350, 56.2325
61574	2370	Sāghand Kūh	1185	Iran	32.8884, 55.5648
61575	3000	Kūh-e Īnjeh Qāreh	1183	Iran	35.2883, 49.8125
61577	2190	Rashidkuh	1173	Iran	33.9050, 54.7092
61578	2980	Kūh-e Sūr	1173	Iran	31.0437, 57.0993
61584	2964	Kūh-e Sendān Dāghī	1159	Iran	36.4317, 49.1042
61587	2731	Kūh-e Sefīd Bāgh Chenār	1134	Iran	28.1713, 56.8455
61588	3895	Bahr Aseman	1128	Iran	29.1586, 57.3230
61590	3000	Kūh-e Hāmāneh	1124	Iran	32.3835, 54.5567
61592	3452	Kamar-e Sardkash	1118	Iran	30.3531, 55.3147
61593	2860	Kūh-e Dārestān	1118	Iran	31.2908, 54.7433
61594	3300	Kūh-e Gūshk	1116	Iran	28.7603, 56.6670
61596	2130	Kūh-e Rabatkhan *	1108	Iran	33.4833, 56.1996
61598	1920	Siāh Kūh	1107	Iran	34.7017, 52.2067
61599	2110	Kūh-e Kach	1106	Iran	33.9733, 56.5300
61602	2560	Kūh-e Khaṭkī	1091	Iran	31.4929, 54.9829

61607	3351	Kūh-e Valījā	1080	Iran	34.1150, 50.9050
61611	3850	Kūh-e Kheybar	1066	Iran	31.4788, 54.2884
61617	2910	Kūh-e Qāfel	1051	Iran	29.1333, 55.6225
61618	2878	Kūh-e Damīrlū	1049	Iran	36.6792, 47.9683
61624	3560	Kūh-e Dorān	1028	Iran	30.5067, 57.4208
61631	2220	Kūh-e Sāghand	1009	Iran	32.5267, 55.1800

AS433 Eastern Iranian Ranges

Id	Height	Name	Drop	Country	Location
61511	3314	Shirbad / شیرباد	1870	Iran	36.2808, 59.0492
61513	2920	Kūh-e Shotorī / شتری	1830	Iran	33.5333, 57.2275
61517	3120	Kūh-e Hezār Masjed / هزارمسجد	1760	Iran	36.9733, 59.3567
61520	2950	Kūh-e Gar / گر	1710	Iran	36.5033, 56.9617
61522	2888	Kūh-e Shāskūh / شاسکوه	1686	Iran	33.7550, 59.8583
61523	2887	Kūh-e Mīrzā ʿArab	1657	Iran	33.2200, 60.2475
61530	2958	Molkooh / ملکوه	1560	Iran	35.5202, 58.8342
61535	3070	Kūh-e Pātū / Aladagh	1510	Iran	37.0333, 57.9000
61552	2850	Kūh-e Pārof	1346	Iran	33.1050, 57.4967
61560	2710	Kūh-e Shāh	1274	Iran	31.6255, 59.2696
61568	2820	Kūh-e Kūmīsh	1219	Iran	35.8708, 57.6733
61603	2140	Kūh-e Karbalāʾī ʿAbdollāh ʿAlī	1087	Iran	34.8575, 57.3667
61606	2981	Kūhhā-ye Salūk / سالوک	1081	Iran	37.2567, 57.1383
61608	2960	Kūh-e Kalīlāq	1077	Iran	35.3564, 60.0269
61613	2020	Qolleh-ye Shāh Neshīn	1061	Iran	34.3309, 59.6523
61614	2970	Kūh-e Rīzeh	1059	Iran	37.7892, 58.0875
61623	2860	Kūh-e Sīāh	1030	Iran	34.0325, 58.6150
61626	2610	Kūh-e Tahūdarreh	1022	Iran	34.9583, 60.1058
61629	2750	Kūh-e Shusef *	1014	Iran	31.7617, 59.9092

AS434 Baluchistan

Id	Height	Name	Drop	Country	Location
61506	4755	Sikaram Sar / سیکرم	2297	Afghanistan, Pakistan	34.0387, 69.9034
61514	3452	Obasta Tsukai / Takht-i-sulaiman	1823	Pakistan	31.6833, 69.9367
61516	3003	Ras Koh	1797	Pakistan	28.8283, 65.1950
61526	3111	Mizri Ghar	1617	Pakistan	31.3400, 70.0292
61528	3578	Zarghun Ghar – Loe Nekan	1593	Pakistan	30.2625, 67.3017
61533	4280	Kūh-e Soltan Saheb	1522	Afghanistan	34.1447, 69.4052
61537	3300	Chiltan	1490	Pakistan	30.0150, 66.8283
61541	2386	Malik Naro Koh	1413	Pakistan	29.3383, 63.4525
61543	3475	Khalifat	1409	Pakistan	30.3117, 67.6850
61544	3274	Koh-i-Maran	1396	Pakistan	29.4392, 66.8075

Id	Height	Name	Drop	Country	Location
61549	3515	Pre Ghar	1373	Pakistan	32.6036, 69.7038
61553	3472	Koh-i-Takatu / کوہ تکتو	1323	Pakistan	30.4000, 67.1217
61556	2334	Koh-i-Sultan	1305	Pakistan	29.1183, 62.8050
61558	3850	Ghumbur Khole / Tōr Ghuṯ	1299	Afghanistan	33.4342, 69.2800
61566	2813	Chapraizai / Maland	1228	Pakistan	31.7867, 69.9292
61573	1580	Dhrun	1198	Pakistan	26.0304, 65.5623
61585	2454	Hazargat	1156	Pakistan	30.7717, 70.0058
61586	2569	Kambaran	1135	Pakistan	28.8264, 64.9284
61591	2321	Suroh	1121	Pakistan	30.3608, 70.1283
61595	3331	Koh Kand	1111	Pakistan	30.8017, 67.5333
61600	2098	Koh-i-Duki *	1092	Pakistan	29.8775, 68.3208
61604	2354	Koh-i-Kocha *	1087	Pakistan	27.5158, 66.0292
61605	2264	Zardak	1085	Pakistan	27.8783, 67.0817
61609	3165	Nodgwar	1072	Pakistan	30.0133, 67.2892
61610	3000	Ziruk	1070	Pakistan	28.9575, 66.7275
61615	3179	Murdar Ghar	1057	Pakistan	30.1633, 67.1000
61616	1734	Gorakh	1051	Pakistan	26.8633, 67.1508
61620	3388	Pēl Ghar	1040	Afghanistan	34.4250, 69.4392
61632	1275	Koh-i-Harian Kaur *	1002	Pakistan	25.6344, 65.3353

AS435 South-east Iran

Id	Height	Name	Drop	Country	Location
61503	3947	Kūh-e Taftān / تفتان	2907	Iran	28.6001, 61.1326
61505	3503	Kūh-e Bazman - Zendeh	2399	Iran	28.0758, 60.0108
61532	2995	Geli Kūh / Siahan	1534	Iran	28.1396, 61.8268
61546	1920	Kūh-e Benūshī	1384	Iran	26.1108, 58.4225
61555	2185	Kūhran	1322	Iran	26.7733, 58.1992
61563	2708	Kūh-e Bīrak	1246	Iran	27.5892, 61.3350
61581	1750	Kūh-e Meyha	1167	Iran	26.3258, 58.6933
61597	2160	Kūh-e Garān 'Īsá	1107	Iran	28.1270, 59.3699
61628	2870	Kūh-e Bon Gar	1020	Iran	28.0942, 61.6867

Kūh-e Damāvand, AS431

Rob Woodall, August 2009

Iran has a long list of prominent peaks (212 Ribus including 55 Ultras), and a huge span of history as is clear from a visit to the many excellent museums in Tehran. The politics, of course, make access awkward, but once inside the country it's a friendly place. On our ascent we met a large group of soldiers on Damavand who were quite surprised to meet Westerners up there and seemed pleased to meet us. It would be wonderful to explore more peaks in this fascinating country.

AS44 Arabian Peninsula

Jebel Shams, AS443 (Rob Woodall)

AS440 Hejaz

Id	Height	Name	Drop	Country	Location
62005	2300	Jabal Jar / جبل جار	1664	Saudi Arabia	24.5550, 38.2150
62009	2393	Jabal Warjān / جبل ورقان	1471	Saudi Arabia	23.9767, 39.2825
62011	2204	Jabal Shadā Āl Zahrān / جبل شدا آل زهران	1388	Saudi Arabia	19.8458, 41.3200
62012	1865	Jabal Shār / جبل شار	1372	Saudi Arabia	27.6383, 35.7450
62014	2287	Jabal Dabbāgh	1314	Saudi Arabia	27.8592, 35.7417
62015	1983	Jabal Harb	1307	Saudi Arabia	27.9608, 35.6575
62016	1898	Jabal Sabah / جبال صبح	1305	Saudi Arabia	23.6342, 39.1208
62021	1800	Jabal Helah *	1211	Saudi Arabia	19.2008, 41.6700
62022	3002	Jabal Ferwa	1205	Saudi Arabia	17.9286, 43.2655
62025	1910	Jabal Aba Alghryr	1127	Saudi Arabia	24.6970, 37.9423
62030	1915	Jabal Al Anagen	1090	Saudi Arabia	24.2858, 38.9008
62032	2161	Jabal Idqis / جبل ادقس	1073	Saudi Arabia	23.5750, 39.4942
62033	2485	Jabal Ḥarūb	1069	Saudi Arabia	17.5442, 42.9317
62035	1804	Jabal Al Hadabah / جبال الهضبة	1064	Saudi Arabia	23.2325, 39.6383
62036	2125	Shyban / شيبان	1058	Saudi Arabia	27.6442, 36.7192
62038	1380	Jabal Banī Ayyūb	1046	Saudi Arabia	23.3100, 39.0417
62041	2096	Jabal Al-Ward / جبل الورد	1025	Saudi Arabia	26.4125, 37.2175
62045	1840	Jabal Lahah	1002	Saudi Arabia	20.7919, 40.2269

AS441 Central Arabia

Id	Height	Name	Drop	Country	Location
62037	2093	Jabal Abyad / جبل الراس الابيض	1054	Saudi Arabia	25.6608, 39.9700
62044	1598	Jabal Nahr	1016	Saudi Arabia	26.0467, 38.1417

AS442 Yemen Highlands

Id	Height	Name	Drop	Country	Location
62001	3666	Jabal an Nabī Shuʻayb / جبل آلنبي شعيب	3326	Yemen	15.2803, 43.9781
62006	2920	Jabal Raymah / جبل ريمى	1635	Yemen	14.6817, 43.6567
62008	3006	Jabal Ṣabir / جبل صبر	1587	Yemen	13.5170, 44.0517
62010	2528	Jibal Milhan	1456	Yemen	15.3725, 43.3592
62013	2940	Jabal Shibām	1358	Yemen	15.0559, 43.7289
62018	2900	Jabal ʻĀniz	1302	Yemen	14.9299, 43.8303
62019	2679	Jabal al Gharbī	1289	Yemen	16.2025, 43.6625
62023	2230	Jabal Naʻmān	1196	Yemen	14.8942, 43.4825
62024	3092	Jabal at Taʻkar	1133	Yemen	13.8825, 44.1275
62027	3515	Jabal Ṭiyāl / Jabal Adiyah	1125	Yemen	15.3986, 44.5511
62028	2485	Jabal al ʻAdhar / Jibal Hufash	1101	Yemen	15.3658, 43.4467
62034	1874	Jabal Ḥūrīyah	1066	Yemen	13.4358, 44.9900

Id							
62040	2795	Jabal Al-Husn Jaar / جبل الحصن جعر		1027	Yemen	14.3203, 43.8717
62042	1996	Jabal Mubarakah *		1021	Yemen	14.1033, 47.4558
62043	2780	Sorq		1021	Yemen	13.7314, 44.3467

AS443 South-east Arabia

Id	Height	Name	Drop	Country	Location
62002	3018	Jebel Shams / جبل شمس	2896	Oman	23.2380, 57.2630
62003	2087	Jebel al Harim / جبال حارم	1794	Oman	25.9762, 56.2325
62004	2730	Jebel Kawr / جبل الكور	1719	Oman	23.1387, 57.0140
62007	2211	Jebel Khadar	1611	Oman	22.6095, 59.1913
62017	1961	Jabal Serin	1305	Oman	23.1733, 58.6767
62020	2030	Jabal Dhawi / جبل ضوي	1224	Oman	23.3253, 57.3898
62026	1810	Jabal Haymir	1126	Oman	23.2765, 57.6658
62029	2090	Jebel Misht / جبل مشط	1098	Oman	23.2574, 56.9992
62031	1317	Jabal Ja'alān	1073	Oman	22.1950, 59.3683
62039	2100	Jabal al Jaru	1044	Oman	23.2392, 57.4739

Jebel Shams, AS443

Rob Woodall, March 2018

Oman is a fascinating country with spectacular desert scenery. It has ten Ribus including four Ultras, three of which are problematic (the fourth, Jebel Kawr is just a very long day hike). Jebel Shams, the highest point in the country, is in a military base. Custom and practice amongst those seeking to reach the highest point in every country seems to be to reach the highest legal ground, although opinions vary widely. There are a few Shams stories. Here is mine.

As of 2018, a new fence had been built, with large signs in English prohibiting access. Before that it had been a construction site, where some people had been able to wander up and get invited in for coffee. In Britain we have a convention whereby you don't have to stand on a summit but your head needs to be higher than it. Overseas it is common to apply more latitude. If it would be a trivial walk from the fence to the summit I would typically regard that as acceptable and count it. Having visited the highest point of the fence I went round to the gate and was contemplating going inside when a pick-up truck drove out containing local workmen. I asked if I could go to the summit. They said no but offered me a lift down. It was an offer I couldn't refuse.

Jebel Khadar, AS443

Rob Woodall, March 2018

Jebel Khadar has two summits ten kilometres apart. The north-west summit is the accepted one, but for some reason OpenStreetMap favours the south-east summit. It would be a very long, hard and thirsty day to combine them in one walk. I had a day to spare, no realistic possibility of getting to Jebel al Harim in the time available, and a high probability of arrest if I tried to get close as it's another military site. So I found my way to Jebel Khadar south-east summit. Based on hand levelling and other available evidence, the north-west summit is probably higher. Both are excellent, long day hikes.

AS45 Central Asia Ranges

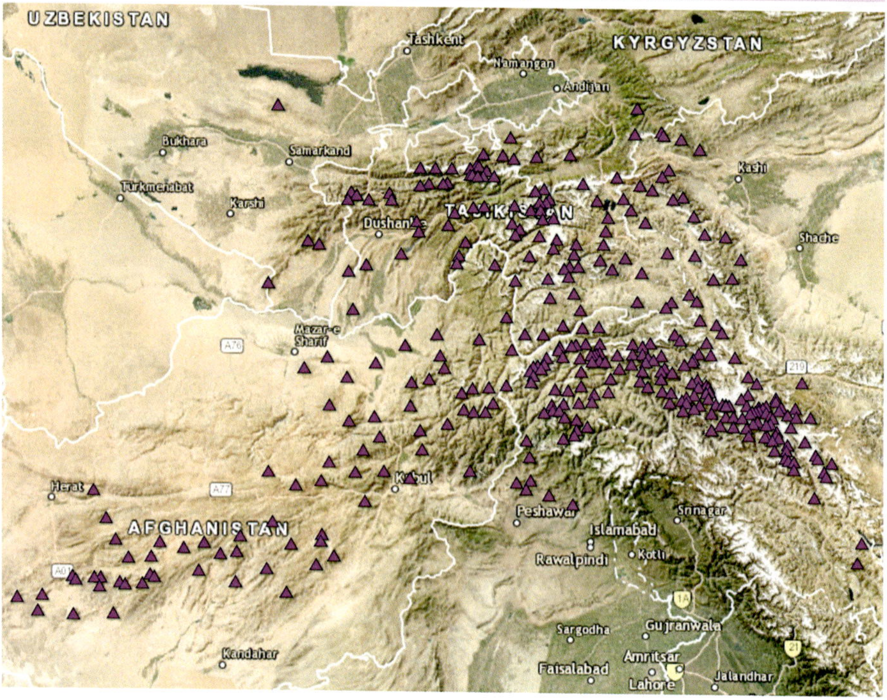

AS450 Aral-East Caspian Area

Id	Height	Name	Drop	Country	Location
62553	1880	Gora Arlan / Uly Balkan Gerşi	1748	Turkmenistan	40.3467, 54.4825

Gora Arlan, AS450

This peak sits alone in Turkmenistan, just about connected topographically to the Urals in Europe, though nearly 2000 kilometres south, near the Caspian Sea. But Turkmenistan is an Asian country and Gora Arlan's closest Ribus are in the neighbouring countries of Iran and Uzbekistan. As the continents of Europe and Asia are part of the same land mass, there are several factors to consider when drawing a line between them, including historical, cultural, topographical and tectonic. It is legitimate to claim that both Europe and Asia are subcontinents of Eurasia, but any credible division into Europe and Asia leaves Gora Arlan sitting on the edge of both. It is so far from its nearest Ribu that it is not shown above, as all the other peaks would be squeezed together in the eastern part of the image, as shown below.

AS451 Central Turkestan Ranges

Id	Height	Name	Drop	Country	Location
62523	5489	Chimtarga	2267	Tajikistan	39.1975, 68.1950
62531	5621	Pik Skalistyy / Пик Скалистый	2097	Kyrgyzstan	39.6206, 70.7193
62546	5416	Pik MGU	1824	Tajikistan	39.3311, 70.0463
62561	5544	Pik Tandykul	1682	Kyrgyzstan, Tajikistan	39.4491, 71.0832
62565	3137	Aýrybaba	1640	Turkmenistan, Uzbekistan	37.7891, 66.5563
62566	5230	Koktutau	1639	China	40.0400, 74.8292
62592	2290	Zarkossa Togʻ	1474	Uzbekistan	37.9850, 68.1700
62604	5140	Pik Samarkand	1426	Tajikistan	39.2986, 69.5965
62605	5570	Schurovskogo / Щуровского	1422	Tajikistan	39.5742, 70.5975
62607	4767	Pik Zamin-Karor	1418	Tajikistan	39.1750, 68.9808
62609	5428	Ajlama	1411	Kyrgyzstan	39.7175, 71.4867
62616	3812	Gory Chul'bair	1400	Uzbekistan	38.3850, 67.5583
62618	5051	Pik Skobeleva	1388	Kyrgyzstan	39.7925, 72.6167
62619	2170	Gora Khayatbashi	1385	Uzbekistan	40.4967, 66.7200
62630	3920	Gory Khodzha-Gurgur-Ata	1329	Uzbekistan	38.4433, 67.3525
62635	4948	Gory Oybala	1320	Kyrgyzstan	40.1092, 73.9125
62641	4365	Karabyoktertag	1315	China	39.8850, 75.2075
62643	4775	Koktutau	1307	China, Kyrgyzstan	40.0892, 74.4792
62646	5509	Pik Piramidalny	1299	Kyrgyzstan, Tajikistan	39.5658, 70.2208
62652	5176	Korgon	1284	Kyrgyzstan	39.5350, 70.9317
62659	4328	Gory Chetin Tash	1273	Kyrgyzstan	39.7992, 70.8558
62663	5307	Bolshaya Ganza	1261	Tajikistan	39.1508, 68.3183
62671	5303	Gory Tutek *	1246	Kyrgyzstan	39.4583, 70.8550
62696	3375	Gory Katranbashi	1206	Kyrgyzstan	40.0458, 71.4092
62714	2963	Kŭhi Darvoz	1178	Tajikistan	38.6033, 69.5742
62729	2310	Gory Sanglak	1148	Tajikistan	38.2617, 69.2192
62734	5101	Kŭhi Oqchuqur	1145	Kyrgyzstan, Tajikistan	39.5717, 69.5848
62745	5021	Gora Golova	1135	Tajikistan	39.4767, 70.6042
62755	5170	Pik Siob *	1114	Tajikistan	39.3452, 70.1364
62756	5239	Gory Darapioz *	1114	Kyrgyzstan, Tajikistan	39.4600, 70.7625
62763	4887	Qulla Gaznok	1108	Tajikistan	39.0725, 68.5617
62776	4896	Dukdon	1090	Tajikistan	39.0742, 68.1433
62778	4318	Gory Chakan-Tash	1088	Kyrgyzstan	40.4892, 73.9608
62779	5147	Pik Kolcova	1082	Kyrgyzstan	39.7669, 71.2649
62790	5223	Gora Ahun *	1071	Tajikistan	39.4775, 70.6492
62791	1636	Kŭhi Kaypiaztoí	1069	Tajikistan	37.3800, 68.2558
62795	4635	Pik Tagrich *	1063	Tajikistan	39.0872, 69.0211
62799	5282	Pik Sabakh	1060	Kyrgyzstan, Tajikistan	39.5737, 69.9021
62805	2303	Khrebet Gardaniushti	1050	Tajikistan	38.0742, 68.5158

62822	5140	Pik Utren *	1039	Kyrgyzstan	39.6125, 70.7725
62827	3585	Kŭhi Sorbo *	1030	Tajikistan	38.7572, 69.5155
62829	4690	Gora Savoyardy	1029	China, Kyrgyzstan	40.1502, 74.4394
62852	5058	Pik Jindon *	1002	Tajikistan	39.3358, 69.7533
62853	5226	Suuk Jailoo	1001	Kyrgyzstan	39.7608, 71.9483

AS452 Central Afghanistan Ranges

Id	Height	Name	Drop	Country	Location
62529	5075	Shāh Fuladi	2138	Afghanistan	34.6433, 67.6250
62554	4803	Shāh Ṭūs Āqā Ghar	1730	Afghanistan	33.6217, 67.0475
62579	4780	Kūh-e Sefīd	1534	Afghanistan	33.6617, 67.6258
62591	4171	Kūh-e Jang Qal'eh	1476	Afghanistan	33.1075, 64.2008
62594	2553	Kōh-e Bala Boluk *	1471	Afghanistan	32.4375, 62.6367
62603	2967	Kōh-e Safēd	1426	Afghanistan	33.0545, 63.1965
62640	4763	Kūh-e Nafe Dunya	1315	Afghanistan	34.8058, 68.8783
62658	4572	Kōh-e Zard Qadaḥ	1274	Afghanistan	33.4383, 67.8908
62660	3507	Zāghān	1266	Afghanistan	34.0150, 63.2950
62661	3168	Kōh-e Zūl	1266	Afghanistan	33.4575, 65.6283
62677	2175	Kūh-e Khak-e Sefid	1235	Afghanistan	32.7592, 62.0117
62678	2101	Kūh-e Bidak	1234	Afghanistan	36.6297, 67.7514
62679	3849	Kōh-e Chihil Abdālān	1233	Afghanistan	33.6292, 64.4008
62680	1929	Kūh-e Bībīcheh Bāṛān	1232	Afghanistan	32.4850, 61.9142
62682	3815	Kōh-e Biland	1230	Afghanistan	33.6708, 63.4967
62685	3598	Kōh-e Sang-e Zard	1223	Afghanistan	34.4667, 63.0333
62693	3407	Sang-e Āsmān	1212	Afghanistan	32.9658, 63.5850
62697	2386	Kōh-e Khwājah Sarbur	1205	Afghanistan	33.0608, 62.6300
62703	3750	Kōh-e Ribat *	1190	Afghanistan	32.9375, 63.7075
62730	3935	Ghālkhugā	1147	Afghanistan	33.5342, 64.8867
62731	2755	Kōh-e Safandow	1146	Afghanistan	32.4542, 63.4492
62736	4098	Siyāh Tōp-e Badqāq	1143	Afghanistan	35.6192, 68.1817
62738	3507	Kōh-e Nōl	1142	Afghanistan	33.3833, 63.7642
62740	4635	Band-e Zirak	1140	Afghanistan	34.7992, 68.3042
62748	4380	Tōr Tsūk / Spinah Kadah	1131	Afghanistan	34.3300, 68.5217
62749	4530	Katah Kōh	1130	Afghanistan	34.8033, 66.5742
62753	4120	Kōh-e Jūgī	1120	Afghanistan	33.2150, 66.5658
62757	4120	Sar-e Rōbah / Siah Nilan	1113	Afghanistan	33.9708, 66.6625
62758	4215	Lōyah Zīnah / Kuh-e Kalnilu	1110	Afghanistan	32.8275, 66.9442
62764	4090	Kōh-e Surkh Lāṣh	1107	Afghanistan	33.7442, 66.0208
62770	2547	Kūh-e Absib	1099	Afghanistan	33.0450, 63.0608
62773	3690	Lajar	1096	Afghanistan	33.3867, 64.2358
62775	3265	Kōh-e Lejay *	1094	Afghanistan	33.1667, 65.1992

Id	Height	Name	Drop	Country	Location
62777	3978	Kōh-e Sang-e Bād	1088	Afghanistan	33.4783, 65.9542
62780	2955	Khalilay Ghar / خلیلی غر	1081	Afghanistan	32.9817, 65.9400
62782	2463	Kōh-e Āq Gunbad	1077	Afghanistan	36.3108, 68.1350
62785	4629	Kōh-e Gulī	1075	Afghanistan	34.5850, 67.1217
62801	1921	Kūh-e Hazrat-e Sheykh	1058	Afghanistan	32.7183, 61.4942
62802	2764	Bukah Mazār	1058	Afghanistan	36.4558, 67.2750
62807	4373	Miānah Band-e Ghōr wa Gulistān	1050	Afghanistan	34.9633, 67.7842
62809	2267	Narkhar Kōh	1049	Afghanistan	33.0150, 62.6900
62815	4592	Kōh-e Safēd	1045	Afghanistan	33.7852, 67.6611
62823	2596	Kōh-e Kanak	1035	Afghanistan	32.8925, 63.1808
62824	3748	Ghūkah-ye Kalān	1033	Afghanistan	33.0708, 64.3000
62831	1735	Kūh-e Qarah Batur	1027	Afghanistan	36.5367, 68.7175
62832	2665	Kōh-e Dorumbak	1026	Afghanistan	35.6858, 68.6767
62837	3771	Kōh-e Shangali	1018	Afghanistan	33.6364, 65.2944
62845	3774	Sar-e Kūy	1009	Afghanistan	32.9567, 64.0400
62848	3487	Kūh-e Shelbatu / Kōh-e Ghirjow	1006	Afghanistan	35.8717, 67.7850
62857	4050	Kōh-e Caragah	1000	Afghanistan	33.2908, 67.5514

AS453 Hindu Kush

Id	Height	Name	Drop	Country	Location
62502	7708	Tirich Mīr / ترچ میر	3918	Pakistan	36.2551, 71.8428
62506	6864	Kūh-e Bandaka / Tirgaran	2890	Afghanistan	36.1791, 70.9831
62508	6542	Būni Zom	2842	Pakistan	36.1542, 72.3275
62513	6872	Koyo Zom / کویو زوم	2560	Pakistan	36.7308, 73.2408
62515	5325	Kūh-e Safed Khers / کوه سفید خرس	2470	Afghanistan	38.0947, 71.0942
62516	5467	Kōh-e Chūk Shākh / کوه چوک شاخ	2443	Afghanistan	36.7782, 71.4512
62530	6530	Daspar / Ghamubar Zom	2126	Pakistan	36.5905, 73.3418
62533	7492	Noshaq / نوشاخ	2017	Afghanistan, Pakistan	36.4325, 71.8292
62538	7349	Saraghrar / سراغرار	1957	Pakistan	36.5475, 72.1158
62543	5135	Hoja-Sari-Ab	1880	Afghanistan	36.2936, 69.7875
62544	6416	Chiantar Sar	1849	Pakistan	36.7292, 73.8908
62545	5190	Kōh-e Tīshal Darah	1847	Afghanistan	37.8600, 71.5314
62547	6035	Shayuz Zom	1812	Pakistan	36.6484, 72.8285
62548	6318	Shah Dok	1810	Pakistan	36.4370, 72.8604
62549	6031	Thalo Zom	1800	Pakistan	35.8172, 72.2880
62551	6310	Kōh-e Mondi	1770	Afghanistan	35.7900, 70.9200
62563	6902	Lunkho-e-Dosare	1663	Afghanistan, Pakistan	36.7758, 72.3950
62570	7108	Udren Zom	1604	Pakistan	36.5358, 71.9883
62576	5950	Falak Sar	1582	Pakistan	35.6775, 72.7800
62577	7038	Kōh-e Urgunt	1560	Afghanistan, Pakistan	36.6592, 72.1617
62587	5126	Kūh-e Kokzaro Zaghicha	1484	Afghanistan	35.4858, 69.6100

62593	4331	Kōh-e Mughulān	1474	Afghanistan		36.2458, 69.4417
62596	2474	Kahmohr Sar	1449	Pakistan		34.6525, 71.5592
62598	5845	Kōh-e Koran / Kūh-e Shakaraw	1440	Afghanistan		36.0800, 70.4467
62600	4945	Godar Sar	1438	Pakistan		35.3775, 72.5192
62602	6045	Yajun	1433	Afghanistan		35.7751, 70.6764
62610	5090	Kōh-e Talkhīān	1411	Afghanistan		35.3692, 68.7950
62614	4879	Safēd Shākh / Kūh-e Doab	1405	Afghanistan		36.4733, 70.0975
62615	5980	Thoi Zom *	1404	Pakistan		36.6167, 73.2433
62620	5820	Kōh-e Khākistarak Dahānak	1381	Afghanistan		36.1517, 70.6700
62621	2250	Ziarat Shankot Sar / Mahaban	1381	Pakistan		34.3000, 72.7083
62623	5730	Mankial Tsukai	1372	Pakistan		35.4175, 72.7192
62629	6553	Raho Zom	1342	Pakistan		36.8425, 72.6550
62636	3105	Showgār Ghar	1320	Afghanistan		34.7050, 69.4067
62648	6507	Kōh-e Baba Tungi	1288	Afghanistan, Pakistan		36.8767, 72.9592
62653	4812	Gory Astandara	1280	Afghanistan		37.2758, 71.3408
62657	6445	Nohbaiznoh Zom	1276	Pakistan		36.4668, 72.0451
62662	6537	Thui Zom II	1262	Pakistan		36.6983, 73.0650
62665	5729	Batain	1256	Pakistan		35.5075, 72.7625
62666	6849	Kūh-e Hevad	1253	Afghanistan		36.8292, 72.4292
62667	2835	Kōh-e Khwājah Sar	1252	Afghanistan		37.0067, 69.9433
62676	5786	Kūh-e Mir Samir	1238	Afghanistan		35.5867, 70.1650
62681	6225	Sararich Zom	1232	Pakistan		36.6658, 72.4867
62683	5798	Asambar / Shawaran	1228	Pakistan		36.4850, 73.6358
62684	5970	Sharang Bar	1225	Pakistan		35.9442, 72.8208
62687	5552	Mastuj Zom *	1218	Pakistan		36.1342, 72.5950
62690	6191	Blatts Yoz Zom / Zhang Tek	1213	Pakistan		36.5983, 73.0892
62691	6249	Ghochhar Sar	1213	Pakistan		35.9117, 72.2667
62694	1930	Anbar Kuh	1207	Afghanistan		36.8342, 69.3017
62695	4300	Khwājah-Kānshayr-e Walī	1207	Afghanistan		35.8708, 69.4042
62706	5570	Masher Zom *	1190	Pakistan		36.3342, 73.4575
62708	6244	Garmush Zom	1186	Pakistan		36.7105, 73.5855
62710	5315	Hamaran Zom *	1184	Pakistan		36.1175, 73.4075
62711	5748	Mandlash / Poshkari	1184	Pakistan		35.7842, 72.1217
62719	3310	Tajoka / Shiklai Sar	1160	Pakistan		35.0683, 71.8250
62720	5390	Pingal Zom *	1159	Pakistan		36.0850, 73.1308
62725	3852	Takht-e Sulaīmān	1153	Afghanistan		36.6600, 70.0083
62732	6317	Kukunha / Kohanha-e Sarqi	1146	Afghanistan, Pakistan		36.8550, 72.7525
62733	2109	Deolai Sar	1146	Pakistan		34.6833, 71.8458
62735	4270	Deo Zhazh / Guneh Ghar	1144	Pakistan		35.3292, 71.7583
62739	5907	Shiniki	1142	Pakistan		36.5692, 73.8825
62746	5340	Karang Sar *	1134	Pakistan		35.5758, 72.9892

Id	Height	Name	Drop	Country	Location
62747	3303	Kōh-e Surkh Kōh	1131	Afghanistan	36.9350, 70.7917
62766	2056	Paija / Padja	1105	Pakistan	34.4483, 72.2325
62768	6290	Kūh-e Shashgal	1101	Afghanistan	35.9306, 71.0808
62769	5940	Golukmuli Tori Zom *	1100	Pakistan	36.2142, 72.8692
62774	5854	Dadal Bahu	1096	Pakistan	35.9192, 72.5058
62783	4993	Kōh-e Sūrgul	1076	Afghanistan	35.1542, 68.4767
62793	1903	Bagh Banda / Hazar Nau	1065	Pakistan	34.5433, 71.7667
62797	4365	Kachar Kand / Kond Ghar	1062	Afghanistan	34.8250, 70.6158
62800	6670	Thui I / Karol Zom	1060	Pakistan	36.7258, 73.1733
62803	5714	Thinik	1057	Pakistan	35.9592, 73.0917
62804	7403	Istor-o-Nal	1054	Pakistan	36.3763, 71.8974
62806	6026	Shaye Anjuman	1050	Afghanistan	35.8183, 70.4958
62811	5871	Kharakhali	1047	Pakistan	35.8233, 72.4133
62814	5933	Gharqab	1045	Afghanistan, Pakistan	36.8833, 73.2425
62817	5795	Kōh-e Gōy Bāz	1044	Afghanistan	36.2122, 71.3525
62825	5690	Dherai Khun Sar	1032	Pakistan	35.7058, 72.5217
62834	6628	Kōh-e Mandaras	1025	Afghanistan, Pakistan	36.5025, 71.8883
62836	6280	Ghaireroom Zom *	1020	Pakistan	36.6975, 73.1263
62854	4955	Kūh-e Gardaneh	1001	Afghanistan	35.1817, 69.6442

AS454 Pamir

Id	Height	Name	Drop	Country	Location
62503	7649	Kongur Shan / 公格尔峰	3580	China	38.5933, 75.3125
62504	7495	Pik Imeni Ismail Samani	3403	Tajikistan	38.9433, 72.0158
62507	6690	Chakragil / 阿依拉尼什雪山	2866	China	38.8667, 75.1075
62510	7134	Pik Lenin / Qulla'i Abûalî Ibni Sino	2791	Tajikistan	39.3433, 72.8775
62511	7509	Muztagh Ata / 慕士塔格峰	2697	China	38.2758, 75.1167
62512	6723	Pik Karla Marksa	2690	Tajikistan	37.1600, 72.4817
62518	6940	Qullai Istiqlol / Pik Revolyutsii	2409	Tajikistan	38.5011, 72.3583
62519	6613	Gora Kurumdy	2350	Kyrgyzstan, Tajikistan	39.4558, 73.5667
62520	5920	Pik Sat	2320	Tajikistan	39.2367, 71.9108
62532	6386	Kōh-i Pamir	2106	Afghanistan	37.1350, 73.2600
62534	6233	Pik Sovetskikh Ofitserov	1981	Tajikistan	38.4242, 73.3025
62537	6083	Pik Patkhor	1962	Tajikistan	37.8891, 72.1883
62539	5735	Gora Radzhi-Bek / Kudara	1944	Tajikistan	38.4255, 72.7600
62555	7160	Pik Korzhenevskoy / Pik Ozodi	1716	Tajikistan	39.0575, 72.0100
62558	4573	Gora Imeni Fuchika / Kuhifrush	1707	Tajikistan	38.1258, 70.3400
62562	6361	Lyavirdyr Tag	1665	China	37.5633, 75.1617
62564	5925	Pik Agashidze	1644	Tajikistan	39.0142, 71.5042
62569	5890	Pik Sarez *	1605	Tajikistan	38.2675, 72.7133
62575	4755	Gory Petra Pervogo	1584	Tajikistan	38.9983, 70.8792

62578	5992	Qullai Arnavad	1553	Tajikistan	38.5654, 71.5227
62583	5779	Gora Bakchigir	1505	Tajikistan	37.6658, 72.7083
62585	6132	Qullai Vudor	1499	Tajikistan	38.2346, 71.8016
62586	5707	Pik Skalistyy / Пик Скалистый	1492	Tajikistan	37.6008, 72.2267
62588	6028	Pik Gorbunova	1482	Tajikistan	38.8308, 72.2933
62590	5135	Tashkurgan Shan *	1480	China	37.9242, 75.8775
62595	5535	Markanta	1465	China	39.3400, 74.0250
62597	6130	Buduk Seltau	1443	China	39.1242, 74.6867
62612	5963	Qullai Tekharv	1406	Tajikistan	38.6483, 71.6192
62613	5931	Kŭhi Kulin	1406	Tajikistan	38.0892, 72.6200
62626	5951	Pik Sarezskiy	1358	Tajikistan	38.1917, 73.2425
62631	5650	Bostanterek Shan *	1327	China	39.1692, 74.8917
62633	5909	Sari Kolskiy	1324	China, Tajikistan	39.1217, 73.7058
62634	5312	Kushan Shan *	1323	China	38.5667, 75.7433
62638	6601	Pik Garmo / Pik Kaganovicha	1319	Tajikistan	38.8108, 72.0717
62650	5704	Kŭhi Qizildangí	1286	Tajikistan	37.4008, 72.8433
62656	5564	Khrebet Kukjigit *	1280	Tajikistan	37.5383, 73.9892
62669	5567	Khrebet Pshartskiy	1249	Tajikistan	38.2275, 73.7358
62670	4334	Siyohkuh	1247	Tajikistan	38.2383, 70.3733
62672	6620	Pik Karpinski	1243	Tajikistan	39.0567, 72.1392
62674	6095	Pik Mayakovski / Пик Маяковского	1242	Tajikistan	37.0207, 71.7153
62675	5541	Pik Kashkasu *	1240	Kyrgyzstan, Tajikistan	39.2733, 72.0944
62688	4470	Khamtarma	1218	Tajikistan	38.4458, 70.5183
62698	5820	Kŭhi Marjanay *	1205	Tajikistan	38.0867, 72.8042
62699	5990	Lyapnazar / Pik Avzashalo Olimov	1200	Tajikistan	38.3669, 72.2945
62700	5950	Pas Kurgan	1198	China	37.2717, 75.2350
62701	3511	Bakhmalon	1194	Tajikistan	38.6975, 70.1533
62704	5600	Jilikkadir	1190	China	37.9108, 75.4950
62705	4700	Khrebet Kazykart	1190	China	39.5683, 74.6025
62707	5880	Mazorskiy Khrebet	1187	Tajikistan	38.7358, 71.4542
62709	5846	Trezubets / Трезубец	1185	Tajikistan	38.0450, 73.4717
62716	6785	Pik Moskva	1173	Tajikistan	38.9484, 71.8343
62723	5940	Kŭhi Bardara *	1157	Tajikistan	38.0558, 72.5017
62724	5661	Xin Gun He Shan *	1154	China	37.6642, 75.0242
62741	5507	Gori Dzhilmatau	1140	China	38.7717, 74.1417
62742	5247	Gori Mamek	1140	Tajikistan	38.3125, 74.5742
62744	6138	Pik Sovetskoi Armii	1135	Tajikistan	37.0267, 72.0833
62759	5670	Kōh-i Tashy *	1110	Afghanistan	37.1325, 72.8733
62765	4955	Khrebet Archabel	1105	China	39.4725, 74.4692
62767	5298	Aksai / Aghbai Oqsoy	1104	Tajikistan	37.5483, 74.6667
62771	4870	Korumdu Shan	1098	China	38.2158, 76.0558

Id	Height	Name	Drop	Country	Location
62772	5888	Kul Dzhilgatau	1097	China, Tajikistan	38.9525, 73.8542
62794	6128	Severnyy Muzkol	1064	Tajikistan	38.6308, 73.3533
62796	3700	Gory Kamchirak *	1063	Tajikistan	38.8858, 70.2900
62808	4744	Gory Novobastakho *	1050	Tajikistan	38.9705, 70.6647
62812	5520	Khrebet Kara-Kul'	1047	Tajikistan	39.1003, 73.1620
62816	5214	Gory Kar Beles Bashi	1045	Tajikistan	37.9967, 74.0700
62819	5356	Buryukurmes Khrebet *	1040	Tajikistan	37.4583, 74.5450
62838	5052	Urtabuz	1014	Tajikistan	38.8442, 73.3933
62839	5588	Vysoki Yazgulem	1012	Tajikistan	38.5508, 72.0133
62842	6289	Gora Muzdzhilga	1010	Tajikistan	39.1205, 72.1914
62849	5550	Kŭhi Taskil *	1005	Tajikistan	37.9241, 72.6083
62850	6120	Aksaibash	1004	China	39.2733, 74.2600

AS455 Karakoram

Id	Height	Name	Drop	Country	Location
62501	8611	K2 / Chogori	4015	China, Pakistan	35.8816, 76.5127
62505	7795	Batura Sar / بتورا سر	3120	Pakistan	36.5103, 74.5232
62509	7788	Rakaposhi / راکاپوشی	2800	Pakistan	36.1425, 74.4900
62514	7885	Disteghil Sar / دستاغل سر	2512	Pakistan	36.3258, 75.1883
62517	7821	Masherbrum / K1	2416	Pakistan	35.6417, 76.3058
62521	7672	Saser Kangri	2310	India	34.8668, 77.7533
62522	7397	Haramosh I	2273	Pakistan	35.8400, 74.8975
62524	7457	Malubiting / مالونیتنگ	2248	Pakistan	36.0033, 74.8758
62525	6977	Karun Kuh / قارون کوه	2236	Pakistan	36.6110, 75.0802
62526	8080	Gasherbrum I / Hidden Peak / K5	2155	China, Pakistan	35.7248, 76.6960
62527	6725	Kangju Kangri	2148	India	33.7250, 78.5275
62528	7742	Saltoro Kangri I / K10	2147	Pakistan, India	35.3993, 76.8486
62535	7428	K12	1970	Pakistan, India	35.2958, 77.0225
62536	6760	Surukwat Kangri	1963	China	36.2875, 76.3867
62540	7282	K6 / Baltistan Peak	1925	Pakistan	35.4183, 76.5517
62541	7295	Huang Guan Shan / The Crown	1910	China	36.1067, 76.2058
62542	7285	Baintha Brakk I / The Ogre	1892	Pakistan	35.9481, 75.7534
62550	7516	Mamostong Kangri	1791	India	35.1417, 77.5775
62552	7852	Kunyang Chhish / کنیانگ چھیش	1751	Pakistan	36.2050, 75.2067
62556	6407	Mintaka Sar / Kharchanai	1710	Pakistan	36.9507, 74.8357
62557	7276	Muztagh Tower	1710	China, Pakistan	35.8295, 76.3619
62559	8051	Broad Peak / K3	1701	China, Pakistan	35.8134, 76.5652
62560	7464	Teram Kangri I / 特拉木坎力	1694	China, India	35.5798, 77.0789
62567	7760	Kanjut Sar I / کنجت سر	1630	Pakistan	36.2058, 75.4167
62568	7668	Chogolisa I / Bride Peak	1613	Pakistan	35.6133, 76.5747
62571	6134	Bilchhar Dobani / بلچھار دوبانی	1597	Pakistan	35.9559, 74.6332
62572	5880	B21	1594	Pakistan	35.5333, 75.4708

62573	7060	Kezhen Peak / Karpogo Sar I	1589	China	35.9256, 76.1748
62574	6824	Durbin Kangri	1588	China	35.9967, 76.7675
62580	8034	Gasherbrum II / K4	1531	China, Pakistan	35.7578, 76.6532
62581	6534	Chakula / Gangra Ri	1520	India	33.3975, 78.4417
62582	6860	Kaimuk Kangri	1505	China	35.9133, 76.8867
62584	6461	Ganchen	1502	Pakistan	35.8083, 75.4850
62589	7401	Ghent Kangri	1481	Pakistan, India	35.5183, 76.8008
62599	6720	Burnag Kangri	1438	China	35.8592, 76.8333
62601	6820	Ayakebagela	1435	China	35.7525, 77.4850
62606	7385	Rimo Kangri I	1420	India	35.3553, 77.3688
62608	7518	Saser Kangri II	1413	India	34.8044, 77.8058
62611	7168	Kampire Dior	1406	Pakistan	36.6250, 74.3175
62617	6745	Marpo Kangri	1389	China	35.7392, 77.1967
62622	7145	Latok I	1375	Pakistan	35.9266, 75.8249
62624	6677	Koz Sar I	1372	Pakistan	36.7208, 74.0900
62625	7530	Yukshin Gardan Sar / یکشن گردن سر	1365	Pakistan	36.2501, 75.3736
62627	6272	Sakar Sar	1351	Afghanistan, Pakistan	36.8960, 74.2435
62628	6050	Chongtash Kangri *	1350	India	35.0083, 77.9075
62632	6986	Laila	1327	Pakistan	35.9567, 74.9617
62637	6300	Chapchingal Sar I	1320	Pakistan	36.7412, 75.2039
62639	7269	Diran / دیرن	1318	Pakistan	36.1219, 74.6609
62642	6769	Choricho	1310	Pakistan	35.7267, 76.0867
62644	6950	Hachindar Chhish	1301	Pakistan	36.4500, 74.4692
62645	5920	Khaltar / Shani	1300	Pakistan	36.2917, 74.0583
62647	6666	Dansam / K13	1293	Pakistan	35.2027, 76.7605
62649	7315	Chongtar Kangri I	1286	China	35.9117, 76.4292
62651	6413	Sosbun Brakk	1285	Pakistan	35.9358, 75.5641
62654	6810	Ghandogoro Ri / Biarchedi I	1280	Pakistan	35.6717, 76.4058
62655	6608	Makrong Chhish	1280	Pakistan	36.0883, 75.1208
62664	5920	Qalandar Zom	1260	Afghanistan, Pakistan	36.8800, 73.8917
62668	6106	Tupopdan / Passu Cathedral	1250	Pakistan	36.5572, 74.9337
62673	5886	Chari Khand / Pallo	1242	Pakistan	36.2158, 74.1967
62686	7027	Spantik / Golden Peak	1221	Pakistan	36.0567, 74.9658
62689	7611	Shispare Sar / Pasu	1216	Pakistan	36.4408, 74.6808
62692	6220	Kapaltang Kun	1213	Pakistan	35.8642, 75.1200
62702	6828	La Yongma Ri	1192	India	35.0267, 77.1475
62712	6288	Mango Gusor	1181	Pakistan	35.5775, 75.9183
62713	6568	Yashkuk Sar	1181	Pakistan	36.6758, 74.2092
62715	6960	Baintha Brakk II / The Ogre II	1178	Pakistan	35.9325, 75.7658
62717	6230	Tang-I-Dur Kangri I	1171	China	36.3892, 76.1983
62718	5475	Mazarbashitag	1168	China	37.1892, 75.5542

62721	7340	Baltoro Kangri	1158	Pakistan	35.6386, 76.6727
62722	6140	Khunjerab Sar I	1158	Pakistan	36.9143, 75.3626
62726	7410	Skilbrum	1152	China, Pakistan	35.8508, 76.4283
62727	6634	Dizma Kangri / Shaskumbatag	1151	China	35.8850, 77.1775
62728	7016	Skyampoche Ri / Aq Tash I	1150	India	35.0776, 77.6367
62737	6820	Durbin Kangri II	1143	China	36.0433, 76.7675
62743	7303	Sherpi Kangri I	1139	Pakistan	35.4667, 76.7817
62750	7545	Skyang Kangri / Staircase	1125	China, Pakistan	35.9240, 76.5647
62751	6620	Gharkun	1122	Pakistan	35.0833, 76.9675
62752	6523	Pastan Kangri	1121	India	34.9083, 77.1467
62754	6745	Thyor	1116	China, Pakistan	35.8433, 76.2992
62760	5911	Karachukar Sar *	1109	China, Pakistan	37.0358, 74.7242
62761	5900	Maiun Chhish	1109	Pakistan	36.3358, 74.4650
62762	6243	Alchori Sar	1108	Pakistan	36.0300, 75.4050
62781	5990	Yarkand Sar *	1080	China	36.6883, 75.9292
62784	6772	Biale Kangri	1076	Pakistan	35.8033, 76.2383
62786	6680	Sa Kangri	1075	China	35.7750, 77.0250
62787	6230	Purzin-Wa-Dasht / Spe Syngo Sar	1075	Pakistan	36.6567, 75.1125
62788	6831	Kanjut Sar II	1073	Pakistan	36.1400, 75.4400
62789	6771	Skamri Sar	1073	China, Pakistan	36.0242, 76.0725
62792	6400	Hispar Sar	1067	Pakistan	36.1153, 75.3619
62798	6754	Chumik Kangri	1061	Pakistan, India	35.2108, 76.9892
62810	5900	Sar Taghdumbash *	1048	China	37.0708, 75.6825
62813	6293	Purian Sar	1046	Pakistan	36.4600, 74.0908
62818	6320	Khor Kangri	1041	Pakistan	35.3692, 76.7100
62820	7041	Link Sar	1040	Pakistan	35.4481, 76.5982
62821	6005	Kero Sar *	1040	Pakistan	35.9184, 75.2371
62826	6320	Yarkand Kangri	1030	China	36.3008, 77.3083
62828	6510	Mangma Kangri	1029	Pakistan	35.5608, 76.1683
62830	6459	Honboro Kangri	1028	Pakistan	35.4442, 76.2150
62833	6520	Tusa Kangri *	1026	India, Pakistan	35.0392, 77.0375
62835	6422	Uzun Brakk	1020	Pakistan	35.9408, 75.6900
62840	6273	Karambar Sar	1011	Pakistan	36.6025, 74.1586
62841	6279	Gama Sokha Lumbu	1010	Pakistan	35.7517, 75.7525
62843	6050	Koser Gunge	1010	Pakistan	35.5966, 75.6539
62844	7650	Trivor	1010	Pakistan	36.2882, 75.0845
62846	6082	Lupsuk Sar	1008	Afghanistan, Pakistan	36.8381, 74.0915
62847	6294	Bullah	1008	Pakistan	35.7431, 75.9258
62851	6258	Yawash Sar I	1003	China, Pakistan	36.7208, 75.4591
62855	6295	Khalsar Kangri	1001	India	34.4569, 77.5719
62856	6156	Chapursan Sar *	1000	Pakistan	36.7101, 74.4642

Biale Kangri, AS455 (Oscar Argudo)

Biarchedi, AS455 (Oscar Argudo)

AS46 Tien Shan

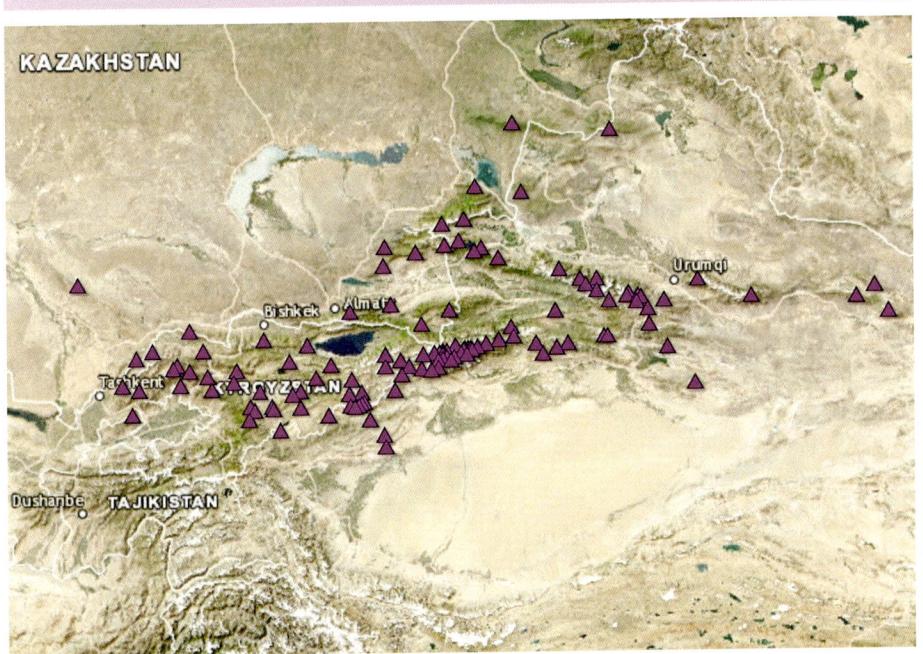

AS461 Tarbagatay-Jungarskiy

Id	Height	Name	Drop	Country	Location
63003	3840	Sauyr Zhotasy / Muz Tau	3252	China	47.0492, 85.5667
63009	4622	Gora Alagordy / Köketau	2480	China, Kazakhstan	45.0432, 80.2559
63010	3282	Kertau	2365	China	45.7425, 82.7575
63021	2993	Gora Tastau / Гора Тастау	1679	Kazakhstan	47.1883, 82.4658
63043	3460	Khrebet Keskenterek *	1340	Kazakhstan	44.4467, 79.3925
63057	4359	Panfilova	1236	Kazakhstan	44.5975, 80.3208
63065	2880	Gora Matay	1185	Kazakhstan	44.1529, 78.3880
63072	2551	Bolshoi Shagan / Большой Шаған	1150	Kazakhstan	44.5708, 78.4467
63074	2385	Gora Qarasay *	1147	Kazakhstan	45.8683, 81.2892
63104	4350	Gory Saricheku	1065	China	44.6986, 80.7800
63107	4127	Gora Qiziltentek *	1062	China, Kazakhstan	45.1522, 80.9267

AS462 Western Tien Shan

Id	Height	Name	Drop	Country	Location
63006	4979	Talgar / Талғар	2984	Kazakhstan	43.1183, 77.3413
63011	4895	Semionova Tien-Shanskogo	2226	Kyrgyzstan	42.5205, 74.5710
63018	3728	Karatau I	1721	Kazakhstan	43.1733, 80.4538
63025	3770	Gora Boboiob	1529	Tajikistan	40.8490, 70.3435

Id	Height	Name	Drop	Country	Location
63026	2876	Gora Bozbu-Too	1524	Kyrgyzstan	41.4950, 71.8925
63029	4501	Gora Manas / Гора Манас	1487	Kyrgyzstan	42.3092, 71.0275
63033	2176	Bessaz Biigi	1443	Kazakhstan	43.8106, 68.6533
63041	4503	Khrebet Chatkalskiy	1344	Kyrgyzstan	41.8883, 71.6775
63044	4360	Gory Karakokty	1332	Kyrgyzstan	42.0208, 75.3992
63056	4080	Zekir-bobo	1242	Kyrgyzstan, Uzbekistan	41.4258, 70.5700
63063	4920	Gory Archaly *	1211	Kyrgyzstan	41.5992, 77.3967
63066	4450	Gory Nura	1174	Kyrgyzstan	41.6258, 76.2400
63081	4763	Kara-Kyungey / Terskey Alatau	1118	Kyrgyzstan	41.9400, 76.7242
63082	3310	Gora Bol'shoy Chimgan	1116	Uzbekistan	41.4955, 70.0583
63087	2471	Gora Karagayly	1100	Kazakhstan	43.2841, 78.6008
63090	3820	Gora Manas	1092	Kazakhstan	42.7600, 72.2158
63093	3897	Atoynaskiy Khrebet	1084	Kyrgyzstan	41.8442, 72.2233
63100	4377	Talasskiy Atalau	1068	Kyrgyzstan	42.2917, 72.6242
63108	5275	Pik Karakol	1059	Kyrgyzstan	42.1694, 78.4641
63109	4236	Pik Sayramskiy	1058	Kazakhstan	42.1376, 70.4808
63110	3483	Gora Alabasshoky	1057	Kazakhstan	42.8308, 79.6033
63111	4430	Gora Eshenkul *	1052	Kyrgyzstan	41.9650, 71.7950
63119	3184	Gori Kizilombil	1020	Kyrgyzstan	42.3917, 75.9725
63122	3470	Gory Suuk-Tyube	1003	Kyrgyzstan	41.8267, 73.6867

AS463 Central Tien Shan

Id	Height	Name	Drop	Country	Location
63001	7439	Jengish Chokusu / Pik Pobeda	4137	China, Kyrgyzstan	42.0363, 80.1208
63005	6627	Xuelian Feng / 雪莲峰	3068	China	42.2625, 80.8892
63007	5982	Pik Dankova	2679	Kyrgyzstan	41.0592, 77.6833
63013	6590	Muzart / 木扎提	1881	China	42.0375, 80.5033
63016	6357	Yanamax	1737	China	42.2850, 81.0433
63017	7020	Khan Tengri Shyngy / Hantengri Feng	1726	Kazakhstan, Kyrgyzstan	42.2109, 80.1744
63019	4428	Gora Baubashata	1711	Kyrgyzstan	41.4117, 72.9125
63022	5281	Khrebet Kuylyutau	1667	Kyrgyzstan	42.0363, 78.9081
63023	5650	Yekeaqia Shan *	1581	China	42.3533, 80.6283
63024	5318	Kokshaltau	1560	Kyrgyzstan	41.6894, 78.9755
63027	5140	Gory Uch-Chat	1505	Kyrgyzstan	41.8931, 79.2019
63028	4737	Gory Dzhamantau	1489	Kyrgyzstan	40.9308, 74.8733
63031	4405	Gora Karasura *	1470	Kyrgyzstan	40.6983, 74.1133
63034	5940	Kosmos / космос	1424	China, Kyrgyzstan	41.0067, 77.6158
63035	6873	Pik Vojennich Topografov	1416	China, Kyrgyzstan	42.0526, 80.2505
63036	4037	Khrebet Ak-Shyyrak	1399	Kyrgyzstan	41.3450, 74.4550
63037	4351	Khrebet Kekirimtau	1372	Kyrgyzstan	41.5700, 73.6225

63038	5155	Borkoldoy Khrebet *	1365	Kyrgyzstan	41.2983, 77.6958
63039	6735	Chuelebos Feng / 却勒博斯	1361	China	42.2342, 80.3658
63040	6347	Pik Kashkar / Koxkar Feng	1345	China	41.8858, 80.1342
63042	5361	Maibashtau Khrebet *	1340	China, Kyrgyzstan	41.8492, 79.5850
63045	4966	Khrebet Kekkyya	1328	China, Kyrgyzstan	40.7663, 76.6480
63048	6443	Vostochnyy Pik Druzhby *	1301	China	42.1125, 80.3658
63049	5126	Khrebet Ak-Shyyrak	1301	Kyrgyzstan	41.8933, 78.4325
63050	4067	Khrebet Kara-Tau	1295	Kyrgyzstan	41.2817, 75.5017
63052	5108	Mustyr	1273	Kyrgyzstan	40.4492, 75.0875
63053	4314	Gora Aktash	1260	Kyrgyzstan	40.9033, 74.2742
63054	4410	Narat Shan *	1257	China	43.1200, 83.8117
63055	5870	Pik Petrovskogo	1246	Kyrgyzstan	42.1875, 79.9639
63058	5842	Kyzyl-Asker	1234	China, Kyrgyzstan	41.0275, 77.3350
63059	4795	Atbashi	1225	Kyrgyzstan	40.9742, 75.7633
63062	3925	Kuche Shan *	1214	China	42.1700, 83.4192
63064	4165	Dalong Shan *	1199	China	42.3817, 83.1992
63067	5510	Yakuotan Shan *	1168	China	42.0967, 80.6150
63068	5445	Silangda Shan *	1165	China	42.2550, 81.1567
63069	6000	Kaliktag	1164	China	41.7992, 79.9008
63070	5843	Akeqihe Shan *	1155	China	42.1817, 80.8042
63071	5816	Pik Koroleva	1154	Kyrgyzstan	41.0800, 77.7692
63075	5270	Halik Shan	1145	China	42.3325, 81.3583
63076	4684	Koekteketau	1133	China	42.3992, 84.2192
63077	5720	Fersmana Shan	1126	China	40.9642, 77.4725
63078	2710	Kelpinchyoltag	1125	China	40.0300, 78.4450
63079	6296	Dongbei Xuelian Feng *	1124	China	42.2892, 80.9642
63080	4050	Gora Tashkurochoky	1122	China	40.6853, 77.9503
63083	2534	Gora Aktash	1112	Kyrgyzstan	41.6967, 72.7708
63085	5697	Pik Nansena	1105	Kyrgyzstan	42.1483, 79.6311
63091	3100	Karayalpaktag	1087	China	40.3200, 78.3875
63094	5170	Simuta Si Shan *	1075	China	42.4033, 81.5942
63095	4500	Piyazi Like Shan *	1072	China	42.3094, 83.8536
63097	4325	Gora Tyuyekuyruk	1071	Kyrgyzstan	41.0103, 74.8488
63099	4835	Akekule Shan *	1069	China	42.5458, 82.4917
63098	4380	Gory Viik	1069	China	42.7917, 82.3775
63101	3877	Gora Akmeke	1066	Kyrgyzstan	41.0168, 74.1233
63102	5510	Etam Likonggai Shan *	1065	China	42.1642, 80.9808
63103	4995	Qie Bute'er Shan *	1065	China	42.4800, 81.9975
63106	4860	Zmea	1064	Kyrgyzstan	41.2675, 77.2908
63112	3563	Gora Karacha	1050	Kyrgyzstan	41.3461, 75.7489

Id	Height	Name	Drop	Country	Location
63114	6637	Pik Shater	1049	China, Kazakhstan	42.2188, 80.2504
63113	6360	Pik Demchenko / Pik Thorez	1049	China, Kyrgyzstan	42.1625, 80.2617
63116	4790	Baldyrtag	1040	China	41.3592, 78.7375
63121	5340	Ding Shan *	1014	China	42.3025, 81.1042

AS464 Eastern Tien Shan

Id	Height	Name	Drop	Country	Location
63002	5445	Bogeda Feng / 博格达峰	4122	China	43.8000, 88.3350
63004	4886	Tomort Feng / 托木尔提峰	3243	China	43.0742, 94.3467
63008	5289	Heyuan Feng / 河源峰	2615	China	43.4380, 86.0855
63012	4300	Barkol Shan / 月牙山	2084	China	43.3817, 93.3558
63014	5248	Borgora / 博罗科努山	1871	China	43.5800, 85.1183
63015	4830	Sarmin-Ula Shan	1826	China	42.5433, 85.3442
63020	3963	Dahei Shan / 大黑山	1693	China	43.6492, 93.9200
63030	2800	Sita Shan	1470	China	41.4731, 88.2547
63032	3698	Daheyanzi Shan *	1467	China	44.3100, 81.9842
63047	4900	Kuytun Shan *	1320	China	43.8367, 84.6033
63046	4850	Hustai Gol Shan *	1320	China	43.3700, 85.5233
63051	3580	Kyzemchek Shan	1290	China	44.5311, 81.4831
63060	4490	Haidutau	1220	China	42.8050, 86.7992
63061	4710	Jirgalang Shan *	1214	China	44.0708, 83.9442
63073	4600	Moxun Xiare Shan *	1150	China	43.3342, 86.4175
63084	4435	Hutubi Shan *	1107	China	43.4625, 86.4283
63086	4560	Sa'Er Tuosi Shan *	1102	China	43.8194, 85.1377
63088	2760	Tsagan-Tyunge Shan	1098	China	42.3025, 87.3558
63089	4940	Irentau	1097	China	43.6975, 84.7575
63092	4755	Hara-Daban Shan	1086	China	42.5442, 85.4942
63096	4170	Santun Shan *	1072	China	43.4258, 86.5300
63105	3951	Kaiken Shan *	1065	China	43.4200, 90.0633
63115	4560	Tengger Feng	1047	China	43.1808, 86.7558
63117	4970	Taipu Qike Shan *	1036	China	43.5258, 86.1208
63118	3470	Dongbaiyangshugou Shan *	1029	China	43.3700, 87.2633
63120	3350	Sayram Shan *	1017	China	44.4567, 81.2517

AS47 Tibet and Central China

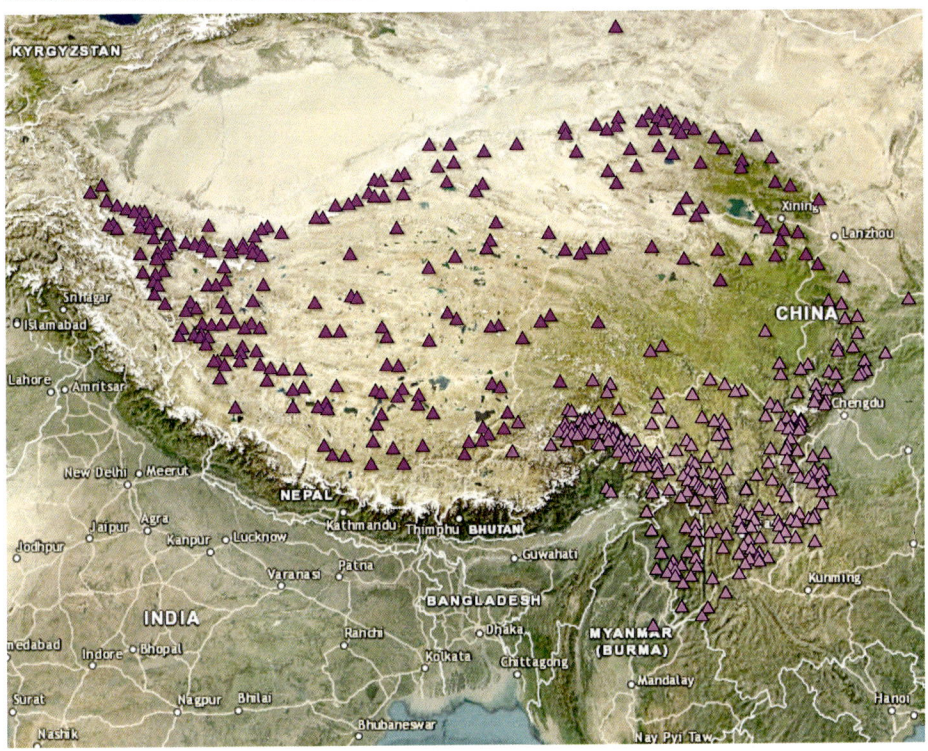

AS470 Kunlun

Id	Height	Name	Drop	Country	Location
63308	5465	Tekilik Shan / 铁克勒克山	2330	China	36.5217, 80.3150
63320	6973	Muztag Feng / Ulugh Muztagh	1949	China	36.4125, 87.3842
63322	7167	Liushi Shan / 昆仑女神峰	1946	China	35.3142, 80.9167
63332	6860	Bukadaban Feng / Bokalik Tagh	1849	China	36.0242, 90.8658
63338	6167	Ayaliktag	1770	China	37.3883, 87.6067
63355	6542	Mazar Shan	1666	China	36.4517, 76.8633
63357	6691	Selik Gulam Muztag / Kashitashi	1661	China	36.2167, 82.0358
63358	6200	Yushu Feng / Sob Gangri	1654	China	35.6525, 94.2508
63361	6638	Mush Muztagh	1630	China	36.0475, 80.1192
63373	6546	Karakash Tagh	1564	China	35.7225, 78.6875
63381	6472	Togras Kangri	1535	China	36.6892, 77.7350
63383	6596	Kotaklik Shan / Liushen Tag	1520	China	35.9950, 81.5925
63386	6962	Chung Muztagh I / 琼木孜塔格	1510	China	35.6517, 82.3117
63394	6802	Qierlizuoke Feng	1477	China	36.0200, 79.4608
63400	6120	Keriya Shan *	1461	China	36.4133, 82.3150

63410	5640	Rebute Shan *		1430	China	37.5092, 75.8650
63412	5400	Atsalatag		1423	China	37.2483, 76.4483
63417	6320	Kaiyinggou Shan *		1414	China	36.5458, 76.5542
63441	6248	Sanju Daban		1361	China	36.6767, 78.3583
63444	5685	Tanbei Xuofeng		1353	China	37.6933, 90.6183
63451	6388	Kukushili		1341	China	35.6633, 85.6175
63459	5670	Kayakdigtag		1329	China	37.7450, 89.2642
63468	6544	Bostan Shan *		1318	China	35.9450, 81.1217
63473	6315	Kangzhag Ri / 岗扎日		1301	China	35.5567, 89.5783
63479	6644	Tuán Jié Fēng		1287	China	35.2000, 78.6383
63483	5421	Karaliktag		1279	China	36.9442, 77.7300
63485	5740	Xiu Shan *		1276	China	35.8794, 95.1292
63501	6442	Toghra Su Shan *		1258	China	36.5056, 77.7200
63512	6350	Yurungkash Shan *		1249	China	35.7350, 81.1658
63513	6536	Nanpingsher Shan		1243	China	35.8508, 78.6933
63517	6280	Kangxiwa Shan *		1239	China	35.9692, 78.8708
63519	5050	Kazinake Shan *		1234	China	36.9617, 77.5408
63520	6280	Uzatag		1232	China	36.3292, 83.0425
63526	6324	Polu Shan *		1230	China	35.8667, 81.6258
63527	5340	Syrogaztag		1229	China	37.0108, 77.2258
63543	6470	Ajila Shan *		1207	China	36.2950, 78.7558
63544	6827	Moshi		1204	China	35.7950, 80.3908
63560	6110	Chokri		1188	China	36.4808, 82.5475
63562	5520	Burhan-Budda Shan		1184	China	35.8267, 96.9492
63566	6210	Chalu Kou Shan *		1180	China	35.6950, 77.7458
63574	6481	Puxiya Shan *		1172	China	36.2683, 78.8125
63577	4970	Kawake Shan *		1169	China	37.7325, 76.2708
63579	5940	Shen Gou Shan *		1167	China	35.7575, 93.6833
63585	6079	Tatirang Jilega Shan *		1161	China	36.6500, 78.0708
63610	6153	Taiping Kate Shan *		1135	China	36.6100, 76.7408
63622	6236	Kawak Shan *		1125	China	36.1558, 78.2625
63627	5580	Qimantag Shan *		1120	China	37.4917, 90.3625
63631	5410	Wenquan Shan *		1118	China	35.7906, 95.0111
63641	6222	Satman		1104	China	35.9792, 79.8183
63650	5935	Keriya Shan *		1094	China	35.7642, 82.1333
63653	5480	Muztag		1092	China	35.9231, 80.1236
63681	6437	Kara Tagh		1069	China	35.7308, 78.4075
63696	6386	Saitula Shan *		1059	China	36.4400, 78.1142
63707	5350	Xiari Kende Shan *		1053	China	35.7811, 94.4822
63708	4250	Halastan Shan *		1053	China	37.1408, 76.8458
63713	5980	Tahetuobanri		1050	China	36.5775, 91.1092

Id	Height	Name	Drop	Country	Location
63715	6340	Takhta Ri *	1049	China	35.5592, 78.4458
63716	6381	Chorten Ri	1048	China	35.5508, 78.3400
63721	6220	Iksu Shan *	1044	China	35.8808, 81.9717
63746	6340	Ketasi Jilegan Shan *	1026	China	35.6942, 81.9750
63748	6040	Malan Shan / 马兰山	1025	China	35.8350, 90.7450
63778	5630	Kaimu Shan *	1006	China	36.2442, 93.0833
63781	4830	Argiuliutag	1002	China	36.9525, 77.8967

AS471 Altun Shan

Id	Height	Name	Drop	Country	Location
63306	5829	Altun Shan / 阿尔金山	2527	China	39.2508, 93.6967
63316	6245	Sulamutag Feng / 苏拉木塔格峰	2029	China	37.9133, 87.3892
63325	6064	Yusupu Aleketag Shan / Altintag	1922	China	38.1900, 88.9083
63326	6748	Ak Tag / 四岔雪峰	1921	China	36.7242, 84.6017
63367	4790	Kogantag	1602	China	38.6317, 90.6400
63397	5766	Muzluktag	1468	China	37.3483, 86.8933
63403	6300	Jianxia Shan I	1457	China	37.2433, 85.8850
63431	4651	Su Wushijie Shan *	1381	China	38.8125, 89.3892
63440	5710	Keke Enge Shan *	1361	China	37.3283, 86.5308
63443	5821	Tokuzdavantag	1359	China	37.7950, 86.8108
63463	6135	Manda Laike Shan *	1320	China	36.7283, 84.3225
63545	5010	Kasayi Shan *	1201	China	38.0008, 87.6850
63587	5380	Sileka Zitakuo Shan *	1157	China	37.8267, 86.5125
63608	5846	Paxialeke Sayi Shan *	1136	China	38.3108, 89.5108
63619	4340	Niubi Ziliang Shan *	1128	China	38.8314, 91.9078
63643	5250	Muztag	1104	China	37.0967, 85.0742
63691	4700	Deleji Shan *	1060	China	39.3375, 94.8800
63728	5610	Kangsayi Shan *	1037	China	37.4267, 86.2892
63732	4240	Yunmukuang Shan *	1035	China	38.8067, 88.6142
63744	5935	Yongbogou Shan *	1027	China	37.1333, 85.5783
63755	4995	Jiaole Sayi Shan *	1023	China	39.1025, 93.7350

AS472 Qilian Shan

Id	Height	Name	Drop	Country	Location
63310	5825	Kangze'gyai / Shule Nanshan	2248	China	38.5008, 97.7250
63366	5561	Qilian Shan / 祁连山	1606	China	39.2033, 98.5442
63374	5376	Nahei Shan *	1564	China	39.3475, 98.2017
63379	4905	Nan Shan / Yenui Shan	1556	China	36.3375, 101.2008
63387	5025	Amisyatsian Shan	1503	China	35.5417, 101.5033
63389	5759	Qaidam Shan / 柴旦峰	1500	China	38.0383, 95.3242
63390	5254	Lenglong Ling / Gangshika Feng	1499	China	37.6933, 101.5050

63391	5120	Tsilian Shan	1496	China	38.3158, 100.2767
63398	4930	Emanan Shan	1467	China	39.3067, 95.6092
63408	3650	Dongda Shan / 东大山	1433	China	39.0083, 100.8267
63425	5480	Daxue Shan / 大雪山	1390	China	39.4350, 96.5725
63426	3985	Yanzhi Shan	1388	China	38.3850, 101.3642
63445	5675	Yugete Baileqi Erguole Shan *	1350	China	39.1942, 95.2950
63449	2740	Iryk	1346	China	42.0492, 95.6464
63456	4574	Sarlik-Ula Shan *	1335	China	36.9125, 97.9375
63484	5621	Betulan Daban Shan *	1278	China	38.6525, 96.1558
63487	5720	Daken Laban	1271	China	38.1692, 96.3900
63493	5205	Jingtie Shan	1267	China	39.3858, 97.8358
63496	4605	Shenbaoja Shan	1264	China	35.9833, 101.6675
63515	4572	Saishit	1242	China	38.5983, 94.1517
63534	4490	Machang Shan / 马场山	1216	China	36.2231, 102.3642
63546	5375	Tulai Nanshan	1201	China	39.2033, 97.0858
63559	4368	Mǔtàizǐ Shān / 母太子山	1190	China	35.2733, 103.0825
63563	5550	Long'e'a'Edang Shan *	1182	China	38.7175, 97.2083
63581	4640	Kecuo Shan *	1163	China	36.9658, 98.7717
63583	4625	Riyue Shan / 恰和日山	1163	China	36.5613, 100.9972
63586	4665	Aderganlin Shan	1159	China	37.2133, 98.2350
63588	5373	Tsagat Obot Shan	1156	China	35.4625, 98.1450
63623	5170	Tulai Shan	1124	China	39.1933, 97.8633
63625	4285	Erlun Shan	1120	China	39.6442, 96.8583
63636	5165	Beida Shan *	1110	China	39.0858, 98.0467
63638	4635	Wòbǎoqí Shān / 渥宝琪山	1108	China	35.5550, 102.6483
63639	5305	Ziussa Shan / 岗格尔肖合力山	1108	China	38.2400, 98.7292
63649	4074	Ximaomao Shan / 西毛毛山	1097	China	37.1750, 103.1517
63654	4895	Xiaobai Shan *	1091	China	38.6517, 99.5867
63659	4580	Yuaomo Shan	1090	China	39.7058, 97.2892
63674	4560	Jupar Shan	1078	China	35.4383, 100.4142
63675	4415	Nantianshengquan Shan *	1078	China	39.6233, 97.5267
63697	4630	Niú Xīn Shān / 牛心山	1058	China	38.1142, 100.2317
63720	4720	Keke Dawu Shan *	1044	China	36.6916, 98.5629
63725	4960	Hamir Daban Shan *	1040	China	37.6700, 95.6108
63743	5110	Huoshixia Shan *	1027	China	38.9450, 99.2858
63765	5020	Shiyou Shan *	1017	China	39.4483, 97.3767
63767	4880	Lenglungling	1016	China	37.5717, 102.1017
63770	4415	Ganhetan Shan *	1011	China	36.2733, 101.8300
63774	4770	Emashan Shan *	1009	China	39.5350, 95.7311
63777	5325	Wakhun Shan	1006	China	35.7111, 99.3758
63779	4625	Baishuwan Shan *	1005	China	39.5425, 97.1608

AS473 Central Tibetan Plateau

Id	Height	Name	Drop	Country	Location
63327	6297	Lhari Qiasadong / Bangong	1915	China	33.4833, 79.3367
63328	6822	Shakangshan / Xiakangjian	1914	China	31.6975, 85.0617
63337	6720	Nganglong Kangri / 昂龙岗日	1772	China	32.8083, 81.0008
63349	6934	Shahi Kangri	1699	India	35.1708, 77.8300
63350	6320	Kailas Kangri *	1680	China, India	33.2317, 79.1833
63353	6223	Gyoinmaixoi'og Kangri / 君麦雪外岗日	1672	China	33.2958, 79.7667
63382	6876	Kataklik Kangri	1522	China, India	34.9022, 78.2076
63402	6610	Kuhanbo Kang I	1460	China	31.5950, 83.4425
63409	6260	Zhalong Kang *	1430	China	31.6617, 83.8300
63415	6610	Targo Gangri I	1417	China	30.4708, 86.5575
63416	6513	Zangser Gangri I	1414	China	34.3942, 85.8492
63435	6336	Qinbaiganglung	1378	China	31.4533, 86.7575
63437	6790	Zangqung Kangri	1373	China	34.0958, 79.8400
63442	6710	Charbagh Kangri	1360	India	34.5258, 78.2875
63461	6282	Dareyog	1323	China	33.3425, 85.2158
63465	5970	Anglacuo Kangri *	1318	China	33.6292, 80.0700
63471	6289	Muggargoibo	1308	China	32.3025, 87.3875
63475	6315	Buren Kangri *	1297	China	32.9725, 80.1842
63489	6237	Beilong Kang *	1270	China	31.8817, 82.4667
63491	5925	Dorenza	1269	China	32.7475, 81.5325
63498	6120	Jang Kar	1262	China	31.3375, 87.3742
63500	6040	Jialong Kang *	1258	China	33.1950, 79.9908
63502	6444	Gyagang	1253	China	30.8167, 88.6617
63506	6209	Yaria	1251	China	32.4683, 81.4892
63510	6601	Reheba Baicao Kang *	1249	China	34.2717, 80.8517
63511	6075	Qomo Ri	1249	China	33.1842, 86.9500
63514	6535	Sirengou	1242	China	34.7858, 80.2892
63521	6536	Chang Chenmo Kangri	1230	India	34.2233, 78.6575
63528	6198	Zhaya Kang *	1229	China	33.6683, 81.2733
63531	6220	Tagdedomsing	1224	China	31.5375, 86.5417
63553	6266	Mayer Kangri	1197	China	33.4633, 86.7758
63554	6356	Tozê Kangri	1196	China	34.7742, 82.3642
63555	6390	Fuye	1194	China	33.4642, 81.6658
63557	6074	Gangmo Shan	1190	China	32.3783, 82.2300
63558	6418	Tagchagpu Ri	1190	China	33.4858, 82.2242
63572	6625	Yunfengjian	1174	China	34.0017, 79.4458
63576	5980	Syemar	1169	China	31.3825, 88.1592
63580	5755	Aweng Kang *	1164	China	32.9025, 81.5542
63584	6613	Gyabgochaggar	1161	China	34.2667, 79.6383
63591	6451	Luotuo Kangri *	1154	China	34.2950, 81.9617

Id	Height	Name	Drop	Country	Location
63609	5926	Xiaga Kang *	1136	China	32.2050, 83.7250
63615	6806	Galwan Kangri I	1131	China	34.7841, 78.4166
63618	6224	Pengta	1128	China	32.2008, 83.0850
63620	6050	Pozarmalung	1127	China	33.3425, 84.6725
63630	5860	Dogotamtsog	1118	China	31.5600, 87.5317
63662	5850	Qionglong Kang *	1089	China	31.6042, 91.2458
63665	5590	Nawu Kang *	1085	China	32.7553, 82.0914
63678	6045	Dari Ga	1076	China	31.0867, 88.1225
63686	5900	Ouna Kang *	1066	China	33.5908, 80.4242
63690	6125	Chawutuodie	1060	China	32.3108, 86.9733
63700	5970	Chaluo Kang *	1058	China	33.3067, 80.0233
63702	6436	Purog Kangri	1056	China	34.4130, 85.6338
63704	5760	Goreja	1055	China	31.7292, 90.9050
63706	5870	Kanlong Kang *	1054	China	33.2225, 80.2683
63722	6030	Laerjyakashan	1043	China	30.7992, 86.7500
63724	6148	Chagdo Kangri	1042	China	34.2517, 84.2717
63727	6360	Rehepan Kang *	1038	China	34.1008, 81.0100
63741	6264	Rongye Ri *	1028	China	33.6000, 81.8975
63742	5966	Yagen Shan *	1027	China	32.2542, 82.6033
63745	6035	Rola Kangri	1026	China	35.2600, 88.5500
63749	6476	Dayuan	1025	China	35.1042, 78.2992
63753	5958	Jiongcang Kang *	1024	China	33.5925, 80.7800
63754	6269	Gozha Kang *	1023	China	34.9067, 80.9275
63761	6273	Xinxing Kang *	1020	China	34.7842, 80.6125
63775	5855	Chari	1008	China	31.1558, 84.6758

AS474 Tanggula Shan

Id	Height	Name	Drop	Country	Location
63354	6328	Bu'gyai Kangri / 布加岗日	1668	China	31.8066, 94.7197
63380	6621	Geladaindong / 各拉丹冬	1543	China	33.4958, 91.1675
63432	6482	Purog Kangri / 普若岗日	1381	China	33.9250, 89.2475
63457	5200	Dayadi Kang *	1332	China	30.9081, 95.6867
63486	6100	Chudanzhen	1274	China	31.6950, 95.3725
63492	6304	Zaqungngomar / 扎琼鄂玛	1268	China	33.0650, 88.5400
63505	5720	Luohelong Kang *	1252	China	31.4275, 95.2250
63535	5650	Jipo Shan *	1215	China	32.7067, 96.8558
63567	5875	Qiajajima	1179	China	33.5717, 94.9308
63669	6513	Gar Kangri	1081	China	33.4667, 90.8733
63729	5180	Ninjin Shan	1037	China	32.8383, 97.2750
63730	6110	Medu-Kun	1037	China	33.1033, 92.0658
63731	5740	Dorzy / Parronglangna	1036	China	33.6294, 92.7542
63747	5739	Xeqag Ri	1026	China	33.7933, 93.1092

| 63760 | 5750 | Dongqiong Ri * | 1020 | China | 31.7600, 93.4692 |
| 63783 | 6242 | Mejekanggain | 1001 | China | 33.7392, 89.5933 |

AS475 Gangdisi Shanmai

Id	Height	Name	Drop	Country	Location
63323	7095	Lunpo Gangri / 冷布岗日	1944	China	29.8325, 84.6100
63418	6300	Jantang	1410	China	29.2475, 86.3400
63429	6670	Godong Kangri / Kading Kangri	1383	China	31.0392, 83.4417
63462	6638	Kangrinboqe Feng / Kailash	1321	China	31.0667, 81.3125
63480	6085	Bangliechazu	1287	China	30.9850, 84.7217
63499	6050	Duogule Kang *	1262	China	32.4858, 80.6608
63541	6436	Dobzebo	1209	China	29.9533, 86.4442
63605	5912	Chalamuyu / 察拉木育	1140	China	31.0383, 84.3725
63613	5656	Yakshi Ri	1132	China	29.2275, 87.5642
63657	6170	Goicangdoi Kang *	1090	China	31.9658, 80.7350
63676	5930	Bugong Kang *	1078	China	32.4825, 80.4967
63710	5810	Lower Zoco Kang *	1052	China	32.3433, 80.8867
63750	6405	Gurkiang	1025	China	29.4781, 85.4011
63769	5645	Degong Kang *	1012	China	29.5292, 84.9150

AS476 Nyainqêntanglha Shan

Id	Height	Name	Drop	Country	Location
63303	7294	Gyalha Peri / 加拉白垒	2936	China	29.8150, 94.9708
63311	7162	Nyainqêntanglha Feng / 念青唐古拉峰	2242	China	30.3827, 90.5755
63313	6956	Sepu Kangri / 色浦岗日	2214	China	30.9042, 93.7867
63321	6870	Nenang / 乃朗	1949	China	30.3033, 93.6508
63352	6310	Pulongu	1675	China	30.1819, 94.6063
63365	6590	Samdain Kangsang / 桑丹康桑	1614	China	30.8367, 91.4883
63369	6240	Dojiza	1575	China	29.9867, 95.4650
63370	6630	Cuo Dui Feng	1574	China	30.2000, 94.1792
63372	6275	Beu-tse / 巴次普	1568	China	29.9525, 90.5383
63376	6842	Chugo	1561	China	30.3433, 93.9133
63392	6692	Lei Pu	1491	China	30.5783, 94.4692
63399	6846	Tiba Kangri / Langmon Zhabaran	1466	China	29.8325, 94.8675
63405	6488	Kongga	1448	China	30.6075, 94.7542
63422	6209	Taxilanlung / 塔西朗隆	1434	China	30.3211, 94.3200
63436	5496	Kyamuna	1377	China	29.9352, 95.2869
63438	6304	Saamareze Bei *	1373	China	30.1467, 93.9167
63439	7048	Qiongmo Kangri	1364	China	29.9033, 90.0242
63446	6420	Jalong Kangri I	1350	China	30.3925, 95.1242
63453	6691	Qang Dhen / Birutaso	1339	China	30.2075, 93.4217
63454	6168	Tatsekangpu	1336	China	30.3396, 95.3083

Id	Height	Name	Drop	Country	Location
63460	6240	Maoqie Kang *	1327	China	30.2683, 95.5692
63466	5900	Xue Ba Ri	1318	China	29.9019, 93.7513
63482	6550	Duo Ga	1281	China	30.5775, 94.2083
63494	6284	Golingka	1266	China	29.7942, 93.1083
63509	6316	Jieqinnalagabu	1250	China	30.1033, 94.1166
63529	6605	Jonlamapu	1226	China	30.6150, 94.3800
63536	5927	Pumobunju Dongfang *	1211	China	30.1625, 94.7408
63552	6502	Yi Xi Duo Ji	1199	China	30.4800, 93.6317
63556	6108	Yuri / Ren Yu Feng	1192	China	30.3008, 95.4283
63561	6619	Mawo Kangri	1187	China	30.8567, 93.9133
63570	6216	Ou Bu *	1177	China	30.1983, 93.7424
63571	6452	Long Ba Ha Zhen	1176	China	30.4524, 94.4087
63582	6100	Tanglai Kang *	1163	China	29.5467, 89.8683
63590	6378	Kona Kangri I	1154	China	30.6233, 94.5802
63594	5610	Kongoing Kang *	1151	China	30.7992, 94.9167
63600	6414	Yóu Lóong	1145	China	30.1758, 94.0483
63604	5900	Qucun Kang *	1142	China	30.0933, 95.2950
63611	6115	Potamolam	1134	China	30.5092, 91.8783
63629	6040	La Bu Da Zan Men *	1119	China	30.2767, 94.3978
63634	5720	Marong Kang *	1116	China	30.1508, 90.8083
63645	6570	Jongpo Po Rong	1102	China	30.5436, 94.4400
63648	5720	Rigagong Kang *	1099	China	30.3500, 91.3417
63663	6100	Womo Kangri *	1087	China	29.7167, 87.1733
63664	6648	Ya Ning Zuo Pu	1087	China	30.3522, 94.0147
63677	6310	Xoilapu Kangri	1077	China	29.7908, 88.2850
63684	6368	Hayungarpo	1067	China	30.3403, 94.9356
63699	6001	You Kang *	1058	China	30.1814, 95.5681
63705	5844	Dongdong Kang *	1055	China	30.2133, 95.4558
63718	5745	Leja	1046	China	29.6092, 91.6575
63734	6364	Zepu Kangri	1032	China	30.3022, 95.0891
63759	6382	Jiongpu Kangri *	1020	China	30.5583, 94.5317

AS477 Parallel Gorges Area

Id	Height	Name	Drop	Country	Location
63302	5596	Yulongxue Shan / Shanzidou	3202	China	27.0992, 100.1767
63307	6882	Bairiga / Ruoni	2471	China	29.1667, 96.7233
63312	6740	Moirigkawagarbo / 卡瓦格博	2235	China	28.4383, 98.6842
63329	3677	Hkaru Bum	1914	Myanmar	27.1450, 98.1517
63331	5770	Geuzong / 茸棍	1856	China	28.9033, 98.3833
63333	4580	Yang Zhiyang	1846	China	27.5767, 100.3108
63336	4300	Xuebang Shan / 雪邦山	1774	China	26.4800, 99.4975
63339	6324	Damyon / 大米勇	1760	China	29.1800, 98.4617

63340	6200	Jelungba	1741	China		29.1975, 96.9692
63343	3680	Dabaicao Ling	1730	China		26.1408, 101.1808
63345	6146	Chagelazi / 查格腊子	1725	China		28.8233, 98.0600
63346	4930	Mode Shan *	1710	China		28.5992, 98.5025
63362	3411	Bumhpa Bum / ဘွမ်ဖာဘွမ်	1630	Myanmar		26.6783, 97.2383
63363	6135	Dinpernalason / 顶彭朗拉松	1629	China		29.9422, 95.7456
63364	4578	Dapha Bum	1620	India		27.6610, 96.7000
63368	3585	Finchuiyanou Shan *	1590	China		25.4892, 99.0750
63371	4513	Jinsichang / 金丝厂	1570	China		26.8833, 99.6108
63384	6347	Kone Kangri / 格尼岗日	1515	China		29.6183, 96.0550
63388	4122	Mǎlóng Fēng / 马龙峰	1502	China		25.6490, 100.0980
63393	5780	Kanjanaripa	1478	China		29.8047, 95.6702
63396	5590	Yangla Shan *	1470	China		28.8917, 98.9667
63404	5881	Hkakabo Razi	1449	Myanmar		28.3279, 97.5352
63406	2640	Lopula Range	1440	China		24.5733, 97.9617
63414	3747	Laojashan	1420	China		25.5450, 98.3008
63419	5950	Dorje Shan *	1409	China		29.9358, 95.9767
63420	6054	Mianzimu / Maicomo	1409	China		28.3358, 98.7517
63424	5976	Renqingjiankar	1392	China		29.5375, 97.0600
63452	5951	Chudan Zhen *	1340	China		30.4472, 96.9022
63455	5600	Kargang Shan *	1335	China		30.4917, 97.6617
63458	6177	Geni	1330	China		29.1142, 97.0775
63467	6011	Kangruma	1318	China		28.9800, 97.5058
63477	3260	Tudinuan Shan	1290	China		26.0208, 100.8625
63478	3958	Namo Shan / 南无山	1289	China		26.2808, 100.0983
63481	2029	Layang Pum *	1284	Myanmar		25.7550, 97.7542
63488	5725	Gongriga Shan *	1270	China		29.1058, 96.3850
63490	3410	Tabu Bum	1270	China, Myanmar		25.3050, 98.0100
63497	5150	Gawa Gapu *	1264	China		28.0092, 98.4808
63503	5410	Langyachi Shan *	1253	China		29.9317, 98.1542
63504	6082	Sangyi Chu Shan *	1253	China		29.1258, 96.5558
63507	6606	Gemsongu	1251	China		29.3767, 96.5075
63508	5470	Gu Bu Shen Shan / 谷布神山	1250	China		31.3750, 97.1025
63518	5950	Buzong Shan *	1237	China		29.2258, 96.4775
63525	1539	Loingu Pum / Singleng Bum	1230	Myanmar		25.5492, 97.7417
63530	5698	Shingikangla	1225	China		29.7473, 95.8039
63538	5460	Zogang Shan *	1210	China		29.6050, 97.7694
63540	1760	Hpunrang Pum *	1210	Myanmar		26.0425, 97.6442
63542	2569	Wuraw Bum	1208	Myanmar		25.7938, 97.0521
63547	3785	Phimaw Bum *	1200	Myanmar		25.8983, 98.5225
63549	3210	Kinye	1200	India		28.3117, 95.3658

63550	6090	Dungri Garpo		1199	China	29.2767, 98.3458
63551	1540	Nhkai Pum		1199	Myanmar	25.6700, 97.4300
63564	2907	Shao Wei		1180	China	24.2642, 98.7000
63565	3320	Muxiangping Shan *		1180	China	25.9625, 100.3100
63568	6080	Anmu Shan *		1179	China	29.5814, 96.6479
63575	2700	Bumpa		1170	Myanmar	26.3208, 97.2167
63578	5230	Du Dakhru		1168	India	28.2649, 96.8825
63595	5010	Za Ge Duo A / 杂哥朵阿		1151	China	27.7542, 98.8733
63597	6045	Kangxiao Kangri		1150	China	29.6267, 95.8942
63599	5800	Duomuge / 多木格		1146	China	30.0139, 95.7406
63603	3352	Tawang Bum		1142	Myanmar	27.0398, 96.8748
63606	4002	Tongdian Shan *		1140	China	27.0800, 99.2733
63607	5820	Namu Shan *		1138	China	29.4683, 96.0483
63612	5730	Barong Shan *		1134	China	29.9300, 96.2250
63614	3472	Shan-ngaw Bum		1132	Myanmar	26.3508, 98.1725
63621	5390	Zai Mi Di		1127	China	31.3517, 98.4033
63624	6280	Engkong Chu Shan *		1121	China	29.4317, 96.3617
63626	3220	Zhongying Shan *		1120	China	26.1408, 100.8125
63632	5450	Nai Bo		1116	China	30.6417, 98.7450
63635	5150	Bumpa Shan *		1115	China	29.3792, 98.9092
63637	5466	Baimang Xueshan		1109	China	28.3058, 98.9731
63644	4870	Khambi Madin		1104	Myanmar	28.1058, 97.9642
63646	4435	Nu Shan		1100	China	26.9742, 99.0100
63647	3032	Daxue Shan		1100	China	24.5150, 98.9142
63651	5500	La Qu Shan *		1093	China	28.8733, 97.1075
63652	5320	Qiu Ri		1093	China	29.7467, 98.3325
63655	2450	Dirang		1091	India	28.4117, 95.1750
63660	4075	Imaw Bum		1090	Myanmar	26.1606, 98.4622
63668	5320	Kazamiyo Shan *		1082	China	28.4258, 96.9058
63671	5380	Ang Zong Nong Ba Shan *		1080	China	29.3967, 95.8708
63672	3630	Madiqing Shan *		1080	China	26.5550, 100.2633
63680	6509	Cogar Laka		1071	China	28.5133, 98.6067
63689	2860	Si Jiao Shan		1060	China	26.1325, 100.4925
63692	2890	Xiaowan Shan *		1060	China	25.0058, 99.5875
63695	1254	Tangte		1060	Myanmar	23.9308, 96.9125
63701	5700	Yaqie Shan *		1057	China	28.9575, 98.2100
63714	1482	Inzutzut Pum *		1050	Myanmar	25.8958, 97.5550
63717	6005	Mukong Xueshan		1046	China	28.6333, 98.2142
63738	2560	Tunbau Pum		1030	Myanmar	25.9184, 97.9721
63739	3335	Maga Hpawng		1030	Myanmar	27.2733, 98.4717
63740	5402	Nyenchen Kangri		1028	China	29.5925, 95.6233

Id	Height	Name	Drop	Country	Location
63766	5221	Di She Er La Ka / 滴舍尔腊卡	1017	China	28.3042, 98.1625
63768	5420	Ormaika Shan *	1016	China	30.9350, 97.1292
63771	3610	Tarāngsha	1010	Myanmar	26.7002, 98.5079
63772	3920	Kritaw Razi	1010	Myanmar	27.0342, 98.4867
63782	5800	Demo La Shan *	1002	China	29.3033, 97.0433

AS478 West Sichuan Ranges

Id	Height	Name	Drop	Country	Location
63301	7556	Minya Konka / Gongga Shan	3646	China	29.5958, 101.8792
63304	4989	Shīzǐwáng Fēng / 狮子王峰	2825	China	31.5433, 103.8533
63305	6250	Siguniang Shan – Yaomei Feng	2562	China	31.1087, 102.9044
63309	4791	Huatou Jian / 铧头尖	2271	China	28.7292, 102.3792
63314	6070	Tianhaizi Shan – Lamo-She	2092	China	29.9492, 102.0508
63315	5588	Xuěbǎo Dǐng / 雪宝顶	2061	China	32.6760, 103.8468
63317	6204	Ge'nyen / 格聂峰	1997	China	29.8075, 99.6075
63318	5950	Kawarani / 卡瓦洛日	1974	China	31.4517, 100.2242
63319	6282	Dradullungshog / Amnye Maqen	1959	China	34.7967, 99.4625
63324	4076	Shizi Shan / Dalyandun Shan	1939	China	27.8942, 103.2367
63330	6032	Xiannairi / Shenrezig	1876	China	28.3950, 100.3500
63334	4360	Luobin Shan	1824	China	27.5508, 102.3567
63335	5396	Haba Xueshan / 哈巴雪山	1794	China	27.3208, 100.1042
63341	3480	Da'an Shan *	1740	China	26.7350, 100.4617
63342	5314	Jiankho Shan	1733	China	31.4525, 103.3992
63344	5412	Dapin Shan	1728	China	30.2083, 102.3325
63347	4500	Jinping Shan / 锦屏山	1704	China	28.2928, 101.7406
63348	6168	Que Er Shan – Chola Shan I	1704	China	31.7858, 99.0725
63351	5734	Jiaojin Shan	1679	China	30.5875, 102.1683
63356	3045	Jiàozǐ Dǐng / 轿子顶	1661	China	32.3569, 104.8461
63359	4288	Ma'an Shan / 马鞍山	1652	China	28.9583, 102.9367
63360	6079	Ren Zhong Feng / 人中峰	1646	China	29.2987, 101.9065
63375	5744	Lianhua Xueshan / 莲花雪山	1563	China	30.2692, 101.9633
63377	5800	Haizi Shan / Zhara Lhatse	1560	China	30.3800, 101.7000
63378	3590	Yaoji Shan	1559	China	28.9783, 103.2658
63385	5521	Beri Shan *	1514	China	30.9544, 101.5536
63395	5300	Laha Shan *	1474	China	29.6308, 101.2742
63401	3450	Baipo Shan	1461	China	26.9925, 101.8350
63407	4269	Cuiyu Shan *	1435	China	27.3725, 100.6758
63411	5330	Poktak Shan *	1429	China	30.4792, 102.4158
63413	4040	Dafeng Ding / 摸罗峨觉	1423	China	28.5875, 103.2442
63421	3900	Yuelyanyan	1407	China	27.5417, 102.9250
63423	3610	Lungchao Shan	1393	China	26.7900, 102.2058

63427	3941	Lùgǔ Shān / 露骨山	1387	China		34.8875, 104.0617
63428	4706	Bailianguo / 白连果	1386	China		27.6625, 100.1308
63430	5527	Xuelongbao / 雪隆包	1382	China		31.6181, 103.0019
63433	4920	Cuòměi Fēng / 措美峰	1380	China		34.1833, 103.4786
63434	5540	Ba La Ge Zong Xue Shan / 巴拉格宗	1380	China		28.3442, 99.4067
63447	4070	Yantyanwo	1349	China		28.0925, 101.8842
63448	2180	Lijiayuanzi Shan *	1348	China		31.9117, 104.6317
63450	5695	Zhuo Da La Shan	1342	China		31.4175, 99.9875
63464	4800	Kaixiang Shan *	1320	China		28.2375, 99.4458
63469	5310	Yan Shan	1315	China		30.5733, 102.4267
63470	3410	Xi Yao Zi Liang Zi	1310	China		26.2992, 100.8425
63472	3970	Baoding Shan	1307	China		31.0192, 103.3308
63474	5812	Garrapunsum	1298	China		30.5783, 99.4942
63476	5960	Yangmaiyong	1290	China		28.3567, 100.3558
63495	6060	Yangmolong / 央莫龙	1265	China		30.0592, 99.3100
63516	3865	Dalao Ling / Pukui	1241	China		27.4192, 102.7208
63522	3020	Guantou Shan	1230	China		26.7992, 101.5867
63523	4267	Yanyuan Shan *	1230	China		27.3350, 101.5450
63524	5922	Dahuang Feng / 大黄峰	1230	China		31.3155, 103.0175
63532	4135	Gengda Shan *	1221	China		31.1417, 103.3783
63533	3552	Jiao Ding Shan	1217	China		29.3983, 102.8667
63537	4021	Haiji Shan	1211	China		29.5658, 102.3167
63539	4080	Jinmian Shan *	1210	China		27.1533, 100.5458
63548	3954	Guangmao Shan	1200	China		26.7933, 100.9008
63569	6618	E-Konka / Mount Edgar	1178	China		29.7342, 101.9133
63573	4740	Waluo Shan *	1172	China		32.0400, 103.4992
63589	5833	Xiashe / Haizi	1155	China		30.3933, 99.5692
63592	3180	Luji Shan *	1153	China		26.6742, 102.9208
63593	2118	Zhujia Shan / 朱家山	1153	China		31.9915, 104.7433
63596	5369	Golog Shan / Nyainbo Yuze	1150	China		33.2875, 101.1033
63598	4820	Ribu Shan *	1146	China		32.2883, 101.6608
63601	4769	Chāqí Shān / 插旗山	1144	China		31.9575, 103.7483
63602	4890	Rangkou Shan *	1144	China		32.1158, 102.4433
63633	5096	Se Jiu Hai Zi / 色旧海子	1132	China		28.5576, 99.3906
63616	2350	Xiaoqingwanli	1129	China		32.0592, 104.9117
63617	5950	Chaigunlungshe	1129	China		30.1505, 99.4783
63628	5320	Xieqingnong Shan *	1120	China		30.5092, 99.1900
63640	5270	Ze'er Shan	1107	China		29.0375, 102.1617
63642	5590	Shangtuan Shan *	1104	China		29.1825, 101.2117
63656	4233	Woluo Shan *	1090	China		27.6683, 101.1967
63658	3600	Zemulong Shan *	1090	China		27.1958, 101.5900

63661	5482	Heihaizi Shan *		1089	China	30.6060, 101.9029
63666	3440	Maotsao Ping		1085	China	27.3617, 102.0567
63667	5175	Gourd Haizi Shan *		1084	China	31.3931, 102.2946
63670	5250	Changdegou Shan *		1081	China	32.2553, 102.7092
63673	2738	Tòumǎjū / 透马驹		1078	China	34.2508, 106.5400
63679	4890	Morang Shan *		1073	China	28.9967, 99.6708
63682	4187	Xiónghuáng Shān / 雄黄山		1069	China	33.1975, 104.6100
63683	5080	Zhollung Shan *		1069	China	28.8300, 99.1725
63685	5540	Xieda		1066	China	31.6542, 99.5675
63687	3099	Wànfú Dǐng / 万佛顶		1065	China	29.5108, 103.3325
63688	4510	Baiyanzi / 白岩子		1065	China	27.5392, 100.5750
63693	3150	Changlingji		1060	China	27.3042, 102.2617
63694	4950	Muni Shan *		1060	China	28.8008, 100.7833
63698	4946	Ba Sigeiya Shan *		1058	China	31.9658, 101.6867
63703	5330	Jia Mi Feng		1056	China	30.3517, 102.0458
63709	3400	Golo Shan		1052	China	28.7508, 102.8083
63711	5005	Wodi Shan *		1051	China	30.6925, 101.1075
63712	3325	Bai Fo Tai / 拜佛台		1050	China	26.4475, 100.5608
63719	3970	Shaonaomenchehe		1045	China	28.2658, 103.2425
63723	3340	Huama Shan *		1042	China	33.7342, 104.5917
63726	5281	Muti Konka		1039	China	28.6592, 101.3367
63733	5070	Kya'gyu Shan		1034	China	30.3183, 102.4067
63735	3820	Lugu Shan *		1030	China	27.8075, 100.8725
63736	3000	Jinbin Shan		1030	China	28.3092, 103.5308
63737	1708	Lóngchí Shān / 龙池山		1030	China	32.5700, 105.6292
63752	4625	Gonba Shan *		1024	China	33.6641, 104.1091
63756	3992	Biji Shan / 碧鸡山		1022	China	28.7042, 102.6833
63757	4167	Shenta Shan *		1022	China	28.0600, 99.4500
63758	4020	Guoewaju Shan *		1021	China	28.5217, 102.8942
63762	4206	Jiāgǎ / 加尔		1018	China	34.0725, 103.9733
63763	3680	Baoguping Shan *		1018	China	27.4217, 102.8600
63764	5470	Xia Qiang Ia / 夏羌拉		1017	China	31.0467, 101.3050
63773	3910	Wahou Nenghe / 瓦侯能和		1009	China	28.8275, 103.1300
63776	4060	Baima Shan *		1008	China	32.7700, 104.4192
63780	5010	Hóngxīng Yán / 红星岩		1002	China	32.8565, 103.7837

Ribu Shan, AS478

The 4820-metre high Ribu Shan is so named not because it has a prominence of over 1000 metres but because the closest village happens to be called Ribu. The settlement lies at an elevation of approximately 2700 metres and a track appears to snake up from Ribu village to as high as 3900 metres on the south-western slopes of the Ribu mountain range.

AS48 Himalaya

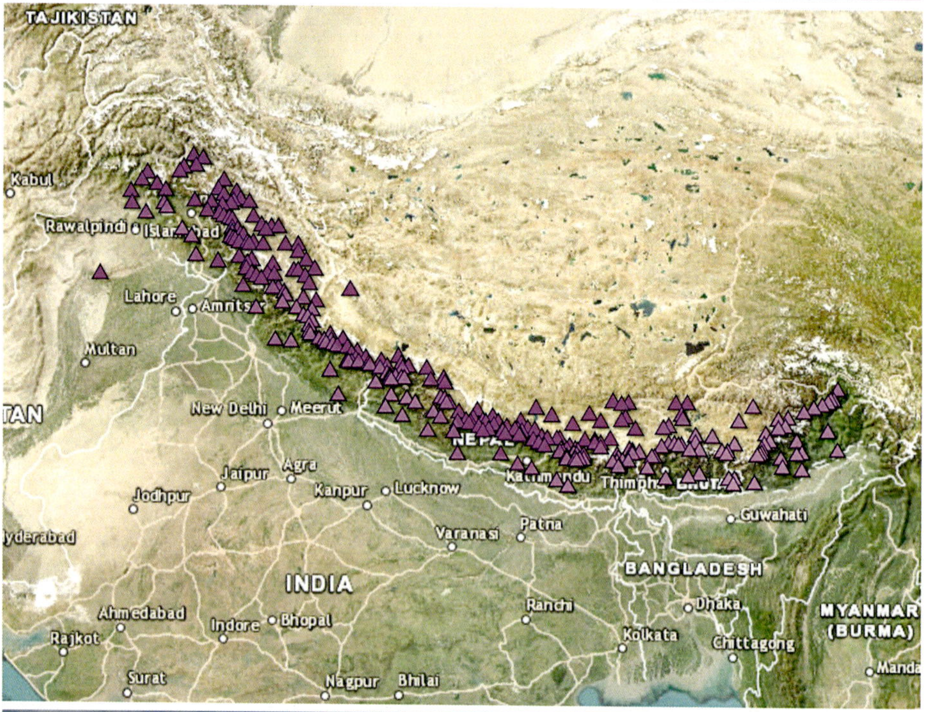

Pumori, AS483 (Oscar Argudo)

AS480 Punjab Himalaya

Id	Height	Name	Drop	Country	Location
64002	8125	Nanga Parbat / Diamer	4614	Pakistan	35.2385, 74.5893
64014	7135	Nun	2404	India	33.9817, 76.0233
64020	6200	Shikar Beh	2238	India	32.4333, 77.0544
64023	6632	Parvati Parbat	2099	India	32.0900, 77.7325
64027	6818	Reo Pargial	1981	China, India	31.8844, 78.7353
64029	5940	Dofana	1953	Pakistan	35.5456, 74.8839
64030	4745	Sanset	1923	India	33.6800, 74.5408
64032	6794	Gya / 盖亚山	1910	China, India	32.5257, 78.4002
64033	2981	Miranjani	1908	Pakistan	34.1042, 73.4075
64035	5608	Shingo Sar *	1851	India, Pakistan	34.5558, 75.8358
64044	6593	Manirang	1700	India	31.9536, 78.3655
64049	6657	Hagshu	1674	India	33.5448, 76.4644
64059	6086	Machu Kangri	1618	India	34.0292, 76.7942
64061	5720	Karapchu Sar *	1601	Pakistan	34.9050, 75.8325
64064	6517	Mulkila	1589	India	32.5457, 77.4117
64067	5980	Machai Sar	1580	India	34.2900, 75.7908
64068	5425	Kolahoi	1573	India	34.1649, 75.3258
64072	5373	Jhunkar	1555	India	34.6225, 76.2458
64073	6574	Bharanzar / Sickle Moon	1550	India	33.6036, 76.1320
64081	4398	Kāla Pahār	1500	India	34.2292, 74.0275
64086	4920	Dhaula Trishul	1479	India	32.2519, 76.4825
64087	4688	Sukai Sar / Khapero Sokai	1477	Pakistan	34.9159, 73.2354
64088	6666	Thalda Kurmi – Lungser Kangri	1474	India	32.9325, 78.4575
64090	5148	Haramukh	1470	India	34.4005, 74.9086
64091	6550	Doda	1469	India	33.6758, 76.3042
64095	6394	Kang Yatse I	1440	India	33.7483, 77.5567
64098	5499	Nindam	1410	India	34.3692, 76.6558
64099	6443	Menthosa	1406	India	32.9200, 76.7108
64101	6485	Brammah II	1390	India	33.4550, 76.1553
64107	6416	Brammah I	1376	India	33.5067, 76.0508
64108	2587	Ranibat / Bhingra	1376	Pakistan	34.3450, 72.9708
64109	6390	Spangnak Ri	1375	India	33.1258, 78.1750
64110	30356	Dandai Sar	1371	Pakistan	34.6333, 72.8983
64112	5290	Malika Parbat	1358	Pakistan	34.8233, 73.7250
64113	6420	Barnaj II	1357	India	33.5775, 76.3800
64116	5499	Bod Gumar Sar *	1353	India	34.3700, 75.4494
64123	4341	Kaplas	1314	India	32.8633, 75.6825
64124	6200	Agyasol	1307	India	33.3508, 76.3542
64135	6385	Pologongka	1273	India	33.3067, 781983

64139	6248	Pyramid	1261	India	31.8583, 77.7125
64143	4725	Brahmasakli	1241	India	33.4883, 74.8250
64144	6221	Indrasan	1238	India	32.2136, 77.3963
64147	5850	Satrabat	1230	Pakistan	35.4558, 75.1700
64148	6302	Baihāli Jot	1225	India	32.8419, 76.5866
64149	6495	Qiu Ri	1224	China	32.1783, 79.8158
64151	6325	Toshe Ri I / Sarwali Peak	1218	Pakistan	35.1308, 74.4375
64152	5971	Shansha Sar *	1216	India	34.1025, 75.7208
64155	6392	Kiar Ri / N8	1213	India	33.7342, 76.1175
64166	6126	Ukharpu	1200	India	33.7808, 77.0175
64167	6302	Z1	1200	India	33.9433, 76.1100
64168	5934	Chhobrak	1197	India	34.3275, 76.0483
64173	5994	Dumgol	1182	India	32.6808, 76.5339
64178	5562	Naktul	1177	India	34.4133, 76.1725
64180	5919	Pangmur	1172	India	33.3191, 77.7788
64181	6100	Zumlung Sar *	1170	India	33.6797, 77.1490
64188	5280	Moi Sar	1150	Pakistan	34.7158, 75.6850
64191	6486	Kishtwar Kailash	1144	India	33.3188, 76.6263
64192	6053	Goplang / Dilburi	1141	India	32.5658, 77.2042
64195	6113	Goutam Parbat / Tent Peak	1134	India	32.5783, 76.7117
64199	6331	Lingdi Ri *	1123	India	32.6452, 78.0463
64201	5291	Spat Sar *	1123	Pakistan	35.0908, 73.4475
64205	2051	Duk *	1110	India	31.7075, 76.8467
64210	6322	Chomochior	1103	India	33.3730, 76.5904
64211	6138	Barmal Sar *	1100	India	34.0058, 75.8425
64215	5718	Kinebari	1098	Pakistan	35.2900, 74.9700
64218	6451	Papsura	1091	India	32.2125, 77.5542
64222	6120	Yunam	1088	India	32.8183, 77.4042
64223	5944	Khurna Sar *	1086	India	33.7608, 77.3642
64224	5135	Biachuthusa	1084	India	34.4392, 76.3642
64228	6436	Korlomshe Tokpo Sar *	1076	India	33.3669, 76.7932
64236	2705	Trikta / Suaj Kund	1066	India	33.0275, 74.9632
64238	4370	Shamshabari – Koni Rāwal	1060	India	34.3550, 73.9458
64244	5999	Cha	1059	India	33.3200, 77.0917
64245	6045	Sanakdeik Jot	1055	India	32.5112, 76.8747
64249	6255	Nishing Lungpa Ri *	1047	India	32.6531, 78.1831
64261	6507	Dibibokri Parvat	1027	India	32.0258, 77.7883
64264	5322	Cheni / Dharampap	1023	India	32.9725, 76.3400
64272	6060	Wangar Gad Sar *	1019	India	31.6950, 78.1333
64274	6250	Arjuna	1015	India	33.4467, 76.1925
64277	1521	Sakesar	1013	Pakistan	32.5425, 71.9345

64279	3938	Kalang		1010	India	34.6625, 74.0175
64283	6410	Seru'ur Ri		1004	India	32.7086, 78.7272
64287	6657	Bargaon Kangri		1001	China	32.3153, 78.5481

AS481 Garwhal Himalaya

Id	Height	Name	Drop	Country	Location
64006	7816	Nanda Devi	3139	India	30.3759, 79.9706
64011	7756	Kāmet	2820	India	30.9195, 79.5929
64050	6727	Hāthi Parvat	1670	India	30.6837, 79.7063
64058	7120	Trisūl	1620	India	30.3117, 79.7767
64060	6904	Panch Chuli II	1610	India	30.2142, 80.4258
64062	6861	Nanda Kot	1593	India	30.2818, 80.0684
64063	7138	Badrīnāth / Chaukhamba	1590	India	30.7499, 79.2887
64075	6553	Rangrik Rang	1540	India	31.3527, 78.6097
64096	6968	Kedarnath	1420	India	30.7975, 79.0675
64117	7066	Dūnagiri	1350	India	30.5156, 79.8663
64136	7151	Hardeol	1270	India	30.5600, 80.0108
64141	6474	Jorkanden	1250	India	31.4923, 78.3735
64150	6387	Kalanag / Bandarpunch	1220	India	31.0275, 78.5725
64159	6309	Nanda Ghunti	1210	India	30.3483, 79.7183
64160	6559	Chiring We	1210	India	30.4267, 80.2969
64161	6596	Nilkantha	1210	India	30.7300, 79.4058
64174	6672	Gangotri I	1180	India	30.9183, 78.8442
64182	3090	Musa Ka Kotha	1160	India	30.0842, 79.1925
64198	3071	Kharamba Choti	1126	India	30.8108, 77.9392
64206	6932	Sri Kailas	1110	India	31.0175, 79.1775
64226	6349	Phawararang	1080	India	31.4533, 78.4842
64230	7075	Satopanth	1070	India	30.8458, 79.2133
64231	6227	Mandab Nadi *	1070	India	30.1558, 80.7248
64232	6295	Gang Chua	1070	India	31.6675, 78.6250
64239	6279	Jupkia	1060	India	31.2358, 78.5333
64241	6537	Rajrambha	1060	India	30.2548, 80.3754
64248	3648	Churdhar	1049	India	30.8700, 77.4800
64250	6855	Mrigthuni	1045	India	30.2900, 79.8283
64258	6773	Bhrigupanth	1033	India	30.8811, 79.0029
64268	6252	Swargarohini I / Surgnalin	1020	China	31.1000, 78.5158
64269	2638	Naina	1020	India	29.4067, 79.4392
64276	6904	Thalaiyasgar / Phating Pithwara	1014	India	30.8605, 78.9946

AS482 Western Nepal Himalaya

Id	Height	Name	Drop	Country	Location
64005	8167	Dhaulagiri I / धौलागिरी	3358	Nepal	28.6973, 83.4933
64012	7694	Naimonanyi / Gurla Mandhata	2787	China	30.4383, 81.2950
64016	7751	Dhaulagiri II	2390	Nepal	28.7633, 83.3883
64026	7132	Api	2030	Nepal	30.0050, 80.9292
64034	6883	Kānjirobā / कान्जिरोबा	1868	Nepal	29.3758, 82.6375
64037	7031	Sāipāl	1820	Nepal	29.8873, 81.4928
64046	6850	Kaqur Kangri / Kubi Gangri	1690	China, Nepal	29.7658, 82.7519
64051	5425	Bhalu Lek	1670	Nepal	28.9983, 82.3967
64052	4390	Deora	1670	Nepal	29.3533, 81.5533
64054	6721	Changla	1657	China, Nepal	30.1367, 82.1992
64070	6850	Jethi Bahurani	1558	Nepal	29.8817, 81.0408
64105	5911	Hiūnchuli Pātan	1380	Nepal	28.8275, 82.6167
64120	6564	Surmasarawar	1330	Nepal	29.8500, 81.0876
64122	6612	Kanjeralwa	1322	Nepal	29.2325, 82.8742
64128	6530	Sunpani Dada	1301	Nepal	29.8608, 81.3675
64129	2895	Dhirkamandaun *	1300	Nepal	29.0967, 80.9117
64130	6808	Bobaye Chuli	1300	Nepal	29.9576, 81.0197
64169	7246	Putha Hiunchuli	1190	Nepal	28.7475, 83.1458
64175	6647	Rongla Kangri	1180	China	29.8600, 82.7050
64185	4485	Pugclimai	1150	Nepal	29.2183, 81.8075
64186	6402	Jakriojagga Lek	1150	Nepal	29.0213, 83.7587
64187	6403	Sangdachhe Himal – Peak Europa	1150	Nepal	28.8626, 83.6279
64207	3310	Maikathan *	1110	Nepal	29.4117, 81.0817
64212	5605	Yari *	1100	Nepal	30.1458, 81.4425
64213	6553	Tripurā Thumbā	1100	Nepal	29.3263, 82.7352
64214	4043	Surtibang Lenh	1098	Nepal	28.4697, 83.0070
64219	3240	Dokhame Dhar	1090	Nepal	29.7817, 80.5975
64220	2539	Kumak	1090	Nepal	28.4883, 82.2017
64221	6034	Chyoro Ri	1090	Nepal	30.1992, 81.6217
64234	6180	Tinkar *	1070	Nepal	30.1791, 80.9416
64240	6920	Tukche Ri / Tukuche	1060	Nepal	28.7460, 83.5586
64242	2277	Mulabari *	1059	Nepal	27.8917, 83.1633
64247	6107	Dolpo Himal	1050	Nepal	28.9800, 83.1817
64253	6444	Kanchauni Lekh	1040	Nepal	29.2371, 82.7896
64254	6024	Bhandar Lek	1040	Nepal	29.8242, 82.2975
64267	6600	Khorchak *	1020	China	30.2508, 81.3733
64270	2003	Mālikā Ḍāḍā	1020	Nepal	28.8658, 81.4192
64285	6480	Sangthang	1004	China, India	30.3533, 80.7867
64286	6015	Karko Lek – Kapkot	1003	Nepal	29.9203, 81.2174

Ama Dablam, AS483 (Oscar Argudo)

Kangtega, AS483 (Oscar Argudo)

AS483 Central Nepal Himalaya

Id	Height	Name	Drop	Country	Location
64001	8849	Mount Everest / Chomolungma / Sagarmāthā	8849	China, Nepal	27.9879, 86.9248
64007	8163	Manaslu / मनास्लु	3103	Nepal	28.5500, 84.5600
64009	8095	Annapūrna I / अन्नपूर्णा	2987	Nepal	28.5958, 83.8202
64010	8027	Shisha Pangma / Gosainthan	2909	China	28.3550, 85.7786
64013	7937	Annapūrna II	2437	Nepal	28.5350, 84.1217
64015	8485	Makalu / मकालु	2393	China, Nepal	27.8895, 87.0886
64017	8188	Cho Oyu / 卓友	2349	China, Nepal	28.0942, 86.6608
64018	7422	Yangra Kangri / Ganesh I	2336	China, Nepal	28.3917, 85.1267
64024	7165	Chamar	2080	Nepal	28.5550, 84.9442
64028	7367	Labuche Kang / 拉布吉康	1956	China	28.3042, 86.3508
64031	7140	Nemjung	1923	Nepal	28.7365, 84.4180
64043	6495	Tsanglha Ri / 藏拉	1720	China	28.9333, 86.0808
64055	7893	Himalchuli	1643	Nepal	28.4367, 84.6392
64056	6620	Pangpoche I	1631	Nepal	28.6283, 84.6817
64065	7135	Gauri Shankar / 赤仁玛峰	1589	China, Nepal	27.9658, 86.3350
64069	7181	Melungtse	1564	China	27.9717, 86.4325
64077	7227	Lāngtāng Lirung	1522	Nepal	28.2564, 85.5170
64080	2140	Chhimkeshwari	1503	Nepal	27.8800, 84.4958
64084	6648	Langbo Kangri / 朗勃岗日	1488	China, Nepal	28.4983, 85.1567
64085	6758	Tutse	1480	China, Nepal	27.7725, 87.0992
64093	6981	Kangaru Himal	1456	Nepal	28.6583, 84.3017
64094	2959	Naraun Than / Gode Chuli	1451	Nepal	27.4911, 85.4905
64111	7281	Gang Benchhen	1370	China	28.5517, 85.5450
64118	6525	Zarong Ri *	1332	China	28.7583, 85.1408
64125	7321	Chamlang	1304	Nepal	27.7771, 86.9808
64131	6958	Numbur	1293	Nepal	27.7547, 86.5733
64138	6993	Māchhāpuchhare	1262	Nepal	28.4980, 83.9459
64142	2391	Phukal Danda	1246	Nepal	27.1825, 86.2767
64145	2345	Nametar *	1236	Nepal	27.0200, 86.6142
64153	6938	Tengi Ragi Tau / Agole	1216	Nepal	27.8580, 86.5541
64165	6404	Pulha Ri	1202	China	28.9667, 87.2783
64171	6895	Lunag Ri / Raungsiyar	1188	China, Nepal	28.0525, 86.5510
64183	7118	Ganesh II	1158	Nepal	28.3792, 85.0567
64184	7138	Pumori / 普莫里山	1157	China, Nepal	28.0158, 86.8275
64189	5927	Quli	1147	China	29.1308, 85.6025
64190	6717	Kabang Ri	1144	China	28.5892, 85.3608
64193	6495	Taboche	1138	Nepal	27.8975, 86.7792
64197	2596	Ṭhosne Ḍāḍā	1127	Nepal	27.6125, 85.0275

64200	6770	Kyashar – Kangtega	1123	Nepal	27.7550, 86.8225
64202	6426	Lajo Dada	1120	Nepal	28.5458, 85.0533
64217	6470	Mera	1093	Nepal	27.7092, 86.8683
64225	5487	Yo Ri	1083	China	28.2833, 87.4358
64227	6484	Khatung Kang	1080	Nepal	28.7778, 83.9183
64233	6378	Dorje Himal – Ganchenpo	1070	Nepal	28.1694, 85.6785
64235	6637	Phurbi Chachu	1067	China, Nepal	28.1300, 85.8692
64237	6814	Ama Dablam	1064	Nepal	27.8608, 86.8617
64246	6899	Lugula Himal	1051	China, Nepal	28.8967, 84.2600
64256	6584	Chulu East	1036	Nepal	28.7366, 84.0349
64260	6985	Colangma	1028	China	28.3150, 86.2850
64265	7871	Ngadi Chuli / Peak 29	1021	Nepal	28.5033, 84.5667
64278	6140	Gyasêb	1011	China	28.2742, 87.1250
64280	6280	Ronxar Ri *	1010	China	28.0225, 86.4058
64282	5605	Tsipri	1005	China	28.6975, 86.7542
64284	6260	Dutang	1004	China	28.3025, 85.9408

AS484 Sikkim – Eastern Nepal Himalaya

Id	Height	Name	Drop	Country	Location
64004	8586	Kānchenjunga / कञ्चनजङ्घा	3923	India, Nepal	27.7025, 88.1475
64025	7128	Pauhunri	2038	China, India	27.9531, 88.8427
64036	6750	Nyönno Ri	1833	China	28.2050, 87.6083
64042	6691	Pandim	1745	India	27.5775, 88.2167
64071	6829	Chomo Yummo / 确母约母清	1557	China, India	28.0340, 88.5458
64083	6887	Siniolchu	1490	India	27.7117, 88.3175
64089	6889	Khangchengyao	1471	India	27.9858, 88.6542
64102	5731	Xiabu Shan *	1387	China	28.8983, 88.4250
64104	6457	Hlako / Lhagoi Kangri	1382	China	28.7650, 87.6358
64121	7462	Jongsang Ri / 琼桑峰	1327	China, India, Nepal	27.8818, 88.1349
64127	6669	Ama Drime	1301	China	28.0850, 87.6067
64132	6105	Kawu Shan *	1291	China	28.8050, 88.2775
64154	6435	Phuriga / Khinge	1214	China	28.2000, 87.4442
64156	7362	Kirat Chuli	1213	Nepal	27.7876, 88.1944
64157	5252	Meizhong / 美种	1210	China	29.2850, 88.5092
64163	5868	Lamo Angdang	1206	India	27.7337, 88.4932
64177	5664	Jonang Shan *	1179	China	29.3183, 88.0325
64209	5111	Geding Shan *	1104	China	29.2467, 88.3075
64255	7711	Jannu / Kumbhakarna	1036	Nepal	27.6817, 88.0442
64259	6362	Chombu	1032	India	27.8992, 88.6450
64263	5560	Guwa Shan *	1024	China	28.3000, 87.9492

AS485 Bhutan Himalaya

Id	Height	Name	Drop	Country	Location
64008	7570	Gangkhar Puensum / 冈嘎本孙	2997	Bhutan, China	28.0474, 90.4550
64019	7326	Chomolhari / ཇོ་མོ་ལྷ་རི	2334	Bhutan, China	27.8277, 89.2677
64022	7206	Norin Kang / 宁金抗沙	2160	China	28.9475, 90.1792
64039	7207	Tongshanjiabu	1779	Bhutan	28.1862, 89.9563
64045	6777	Tarlha Ri / 打拉日	1694	China	28.3633, 91.1350
64053	7538	Kula Kangri / 库拉岗日峰	1659	China	28.2267, 90.6167
64057	4735	Tarka La Kang *	1622	Bhutan	27.2500, 89.7042
64074	4940	Durshingang	1541	Bhutan	27.2764, 90.3791
64078	6678	Kangcheda I	1514	Bhutan, China	28.1030, 89.5473
64092	6674	Kalurong	1459	China	28.8508, 90.2075
64097	6720	Masang Kang	1414	Bhutan	28.1692, 89.7690
64100	6441	Garula Kang	1401	Bhutan, China	28.0067, 91.4658
64106	6085	Chomo Kara	1378	China	29.2530, 90.3425
64114	7047	Zongophu Kang	1353	Bhutan	28.1658, 90.1825
64140	5820	Sāng Duō Bái Rì	1254	Bhutan, China	27.9092, 91.5925
64158	6155	Lhaqensangrang	1210	China	28.5733, 88.7083
64162	5695	Changgu Kang	1210	Bhutan, China	27.5438, 89.1162
64164	7204	Kangphu Kang I / Shimo Kangri	1204	Bhutan	28.1556, 90.0762
64176	4600	Burgang Kang *	1179	Bhutan	27.3775, 90.7450
64208	5862	Min Kang *	1108	China	28.6358, 89.7775
64243	5740	Karru Kang *	1059	China	29.2792, 89.9825
64257	6425	Moinda Kangri	1034	China	28.4350, 90.6092
64266	5765	Nyang Kang *	1020	China	28.6242, 89.5958
64271	6200	Mena Kang	1020	China	28.0017, 91.6292
64275	6809	Jichu Drake / 吉楚椎柯雪山	1015	Bhutan	27.8447, 89.3347
64281	6330	Chura Kang	1007	Bhutan, China	28.0515, 90.7498

AS486 Assam Himalaya

Id	Height	Name	Drop	Country	Location
64003	7782	Namcha Barwa / 南迦巴瓦峰	4093	China	29.6317, 95.0550
64021	7060	Kangtö / Kanggardo Rizê	2199	China, India	27.8658, 92.5308
64038	6636	Yarla Shampo	1807	China	28.8008, 91.9642
64041	7047	Nyegyi Kansang	1746	China, India	27.9368, 92.6665
64047	5641	Milin Shan *	1684	China	29.0458, 94.0142
64048	3752	Dafla Ri *	1677	India	27.5542, 93.3300
64040	5889	Pa Su Ting Na / 怕苏挺纳	1656	China	29.3222, 94.7493
64066	6520	Kazi Razi	1583	China	28.1967, 91.8658
64076	6215	Bobo Lang Feng	1524	China	28.8517, 93.2017
64079	5840	Pé Shan *	1507	China	29.3983, 94.9000
64082	5361	Sirapatang Shan *	1493	China	29.1508, 94.2917

64103	6151	Palung Ri	1387	China	29.1958, 92.3992
64115	6045	Xi Ri Ka	1355	China	28.9015, 93.5141
64119	3018	Ladu	1332	India	27.9005, 93.7608
64126	3435	Miri Ri *	1302	India	27.8167, 93.2817
64133	2940	Puriperti Ri *	1286	India	27.4958, 93.9600
64134	2160	Lumna	1276	India	28.0300, 95.0625
64137	6883	Tui Kangri	1263	China	28.0617, 92.6642
64146	6890	Khyari Satam / Chiumo	1234	China, India	27.9100, 92.6258
64170	4050	Qoidengarbo Ri	1189	India	28.2667, 93.7692
64172	5944	Kyimmapu Ri *	1186	China	28.4600, 92.7925
64179	5593	Lugong Shan *	1176	China	29.3775, 94.8175
64194	5670	Dakpa Shiri	1135	China	28.6000, 93.2267
64196	5220	Ringon Shan *	1133	China, India	29.2283, 94.5558
64203	5885	Tsoga Ri *	1119	China	28.6675, 93.4475
64204	6654	Takpa Shiri	1113	China	28.1767, 92.7675
64216	5771	Tron Ri *	1096	China, India	28.2633, 92.9583
64229	3060	Moling	1074	India	28.5458, 94.7592
64251	4012	Chenla Neychen *	1043	Bhutan	27.0858, 91.7817
64252	3005	Romta	1041	India	27.9675, 93.9692
64262	4520	Merak Ri *	1025	Bhutan	27.2367, 91.8250
64273	4110	Dangling Ri *	1015	Bhutan	27.2517, 91.6875
64288	3275	Jungpam Ri *	1000	India	27.1325, 92.4408

Makalu and Taboche, AS483 (Oscar Argudo)

AS49 Indian Subcontinent

Gombaniya, AS495 (Petter Bjørstad)

AS490 Central India

Id	Height	Name	Drop	Country	Location
64508	1722	Guru Shikhar	1396	India	24.6500, 72.7767
64514	1145	Girnar – Gorakhnāth	1130	India	21.5280, 70.5275
64522	1366	Parasnāth	1017	India	23.9636, 86.1289

AS491 Western Ghats

Id	Height	Name	Drop	Country	Location
64503	2636	Doddabetta	2257	India	11.4022, 76.7371
64504	2088	Elivāl Malai	1539	India	10.9400, 76.6325
64506	2339	Vavul Mala	1479	India	11.4275, 76.1308
64509	2059	Banasuram	1306	India	11.6938, 75.9080
64513	1925	Mullayanagiri	1176	India	13.3910, 75.7215
64519	1646	Kalsūbai	1079	India	19.6012, 73.7107
64520	1892	Kudremukh	1052	India	13.1290, 75.2653

AS493 Eastern Ghats

Id	Height	Name	Drop	Country	Location
64510	1680	Ārma Konda	1306	India	18.2278, 82.7228
64511	1649	Sholaikaradu	1192	India	11.8308, 78.2258
64512	1500	Pāla Malai	1176	India	11.6925, 77.7350
64515	1515	Singaraju Parbat	1126	India	19.0139, 84.3472
64521	1416	Kollaimalai	1049	India	11.3758, 78.3125

AS494 Cardamom Hills / Yela Mala

Id	Height	Name	Drop	Country	Location
64502	2695	Anamudi	2478	India	10.1700, 77.0608
64505	1869	Agastya Malai	1510	India	8.5858, 77.2675
64517	2018	Kottai Malai	1120	India	9.5210, 77.4020
64518	1379	Musalpārai Medu	1081	India	10.2438, 77.9869
64524	1633	Nelliyampathy	1007	India	10.5374, 76.7278

AS495 Sri Lanka

Id	Height	Name	Drop	Country	Location
64501	2524	Pidurutalagala / පිදුරුතලාගල	2524	Sri Lanka	7.0010, 80.7754
64507	1906	Gombaniya / ගොම්බානි යා	1415	Sri Lanka	7.4534, 80.7508
64516	1385	Beralagala / බෙරලගල	1125	Sri Lanka	6.4367, 80.5775
64523	2036	Namunukula / නමුනුකුල	1012	Sri Lanka	6.9325, 81.1133

Gombaniya, AS495
Petter Bjørstad, May 2023

We drove to the small town of Huluganga and stayed in a small but nice guest-house called Knuckles Barefoot Inn. The next morning we drove along an interesting narrow road that served the tea plantation. Whenever we met a vehicle, time was needed to find a suitable place wide enough to pass. A young boy named Ich had been mobilized to act as a guide.

We started walking and left the plantation trail after less than 30 minutes. From here it was pretty easy, despite all the bamboo overhead, to reach the first summit point. The ridge continued higher straight ahead but the trail ended here. I realized that most people only would hike to this point and not to the summit. I had read a couple of online trip reports implying they had climbed the peak, but their hiking times clearly indicated they had turned around here. I realized that this hike might be a much harder trip than anticipated. My driver might have to wait much longer than I had estimated.

I pointed to the summit skyline and indicated to Ich that we had to find a way up there through the vegetation. After quite some effort we reached this point only to find another, higher ridge top ahead. More jungle struggle, and again there was a higher point ahead. Ich looked rather discouraged. However, he now understood that there was no easy way out. He carried on without complaining. Finally we reached a small rocky summit that looked like it might be the highest point. A short and fairly horizontal ridge remained.

I told Ich that we might as well complete the entire ridge, in order to guarantee that we had passed over the highest point. The landscape was quite nice and rugged, with good views. Arriving at the north end of the summit ridge, it did seem that our previous high point was the summit. Once we were back at the trail, it was clear that the jungle section of the climb had taken longer than the up and down to the viewpoint. A ten-minute rest, some water and a careful check for leeches were needed before heading down to the car.

Doddabetta, AS491

Petter Bjørstad, May 2023

I had been to Sri Lanka and noticed that Doddabetta in southern India could be visited via a small detour to the city of Coimbatore. My first ever visit to India would be rather short – two nights at the Marriott airport hotel in Coimbatore. The visit went according to plan and I spent the day travelling round to Doddabetta, a peak which had a road to the top.

The check-in at the airport was normal, with friendly people that helped to get my bag checked all the way to Bergen, despite the two separate tickets. Passing through security, they wanted to look in my carry-on bag. They took out my Garmin GPS device and asked me about it. *Did it receive signals from the GPS satellites? Any device receiving such signals must be confiscated – it is highly illegal to have such a device in India*, they said. I tried to explain that all mobile phones did the same. No, this they did not believe. By now, five or six security officials had assembled, mostly in uniform. It was decided the case had to be investigated by the Coimbatore police. I suggested that they could just take the device, but that would not resolve the issue. I had, in violation of Indian law, carried this device, apparently a serious crime. I realised that I would miss my flight. My bag had to come off the plane.

What they did not notice was that I had a Garmin InReach Mini as well. I succeeded in hiding this device in my checked bag as they pulled it from my flight. Next, I was driven to the police station in Coimbatore. This was a bad start to my journey home. I was told that the police chief would have to interview me but that he would not be present until later. Eventually he showed up and informed me that the GPS would be confiscated and that I would have to write and sign an official letter of apology. OK, with a seven-hour connection in Chennai, there was still a slim chance I could catch my flight to Europe. I was driven back to the airport by the police. Fortunately, another airline had a flight that I was able to catch with a few minutes to spare and I made my connection in Chennai.

I regarded this as an example of state-sponsored hassle and robbery, with a total cost of about 800 US dollars, not reimbursed by travel insurance. All officials behaved politely and there was no hint of corruption, but I did not expect it to happen in India in 2023.

Asia East

AS50 Central Siberia

AS500 Byrranga

Id	Height	Name	Drop	Country	Location
65024	1151	Lednikovaya Gora	1120	Russia	75.8967, 107.7042

AS501 Kuznetskiy Alatau

Id	Height	Name	Drop	Country	Location
65006	2217	Khrebet Kharatas – Staraya Krepost	1398	Russia	53.8600, 89.3000
65038	1872	Gora Bol'shoy Kanym	1024	Russia	54.2833, 88.4775

AS502 Central Siberian Plateau

Id	Height	Name	Drop	Country	Location
65007	1678	Gora Kamen / Гора Камень	1383	Russia	69.1200, 95.3296
65026	1621	Gory Ayan *	1102	Russia	69.2375, 93.0200
65040	1135	Gora Bershina Ekekoy	1022	Russia	69.1808, 90.0775

AS503 Gory Sayan

Id	Height	Name	Drop	Country	Location
65001	3491	Munku-Sardyk	1578	Mongolia, Russia	51.7190, 100.5970
65002	2922	Pik Grandiozniyy / Пик Грандиозный	1560	Russia	53.8933, 96.0076
65003	2522	Khrebet Baldyrgannyg	1509	Russia	52.5800, 94.2700
65004	3162	Khrebet Kropotkina – Khoyto-Ula	1485	Russia	52.8464, 99.6946
65005	2939	Khrebet Bol'shoy Sayan – Pik Tofalaria	1470	Russia	53.6417, 97.2358
65008	2491	Gora Bedelig / Гора Беделиг	1357	Russia	51.7892, 92.4758
65009	2505	Khrebet Ergak-Targak-Tayga	1353	Russia	53.3233, 95.4250
65010	3284	Strelnikova	1336	Russia	51.8882, 101.9814
65011	2650	Gora Figuristyy Belok	1253	Russia	54.0248, 95.4337
65012	3196	Ospin-Ulan-Sardyk	1223	Russia	52.1708, 101.4250
65013	2606	Khrebet Ulug-Tayga	1212	Russia	52.0267, 97.5592
65014	2810	Gora Etomen-Ekhin-Sardyk	1195	Russia	52.9165, 100.2439
65015	2319	Khrebet Borus – Gora Poylova	1191	Russia	52.7892, 91.5425
65016	3105	Gora Kyzyl-Tayga	1171	Russia	51.4751, 89.9437
65017	3263	Dornod Sayan	1156	Russia	51.9800, 99.5100
65018	2467	Khrebet Aradanskiy	1146	Russia	52.5625, 93.0958
65019	1883	Gora Bazybayskiy Belok	1144	Russia	53.8000, 94.9883
65020	2824	Gora Bol'shoy Kadraus *	1135	Russia	51.5550, 97.6592
65021	2739	Khrebet Khertesh-Tayga	1131	Russia	52.2317, 94.7100
65022	2180	Elobyy	1122	Russia	51.8683, 88.1667
65023	3089	Pik Topografov / пик Топографов	1121	Russia	52.4934, 98.8169
65025	3106	Khoyt Agaya Uul	1116	Mongolia	51.5590, 98.6633
65027	2726	Skalistyy Khrebet	1100	Russia	54.0675, 96.8433
65028	1779	Khrebet Chebulak	1069	Russia	54.2492, 94.0633
65029	2931	Gora Karakosh / Гора Карагош	1068	Russia	51.7325, 89.4067
65030	2312	Gora Dukgu-Khol' *	1067	Russia	52.8942, 97.8592
65031	2683	Agul'skie-Belki – Korona	1050	Russia	54.0642, 96.4592
65032	2713	Okinskiy Khrebet	1043	Russia	53.1128, 99.4888
65033	2338	Gora Vysokaya / Гора Высокая	1043	Russia	53.4875, 95.9317
65034	1733	Khrebet Turbat	1040	Russia	53.6900, 93.7675
65035	2711	Utkhumiyskiy Khrebet	1032	Russia	53.1300, 99.1308
65036	2737	Kara-Khem / Кара-Хем	1030	Russia	52.0158, 95.3833
65037	2423	Gora Bol'shoy Kyzyrsuk *	1026	Russia	51.8217, 88.4642
65039	1983	Khrebet Abakan – Khrebet Choochek	1023	Russia	52.0933, 88.5200
65041	1588	Khariusovyi Belok	1018	Russia	54.0958, 94.4150
65042	3102	Tunkinskiye Goltsy Zapadnyy	1013	Russia	51.7475, 101.0625
65043	1828	Gora Moskva / Гора Москва	1003	Russia	54.3517, 93.9192
65044	3038	Khrebet Kheltesiyn-Tayga	1002	Mongolia	51.8744, 98.9614

AS51 Eastern Siberia

On Wrangel Island, AS510 (Anne Gray)

AS510 Wrangel Island

Id	Height	Name	Drop	Country	Location
65649	1096	Gora Sovetskaya / Berry Peak	1096	Russia	71.0974, -179.3528

AS511 Stanovoy Khrebet and Khrebet Dzhugdzhur

Id	Height	Name	Drop	Country	Location
65522	2380	Stanovoy Khrebet – Tokinskiy Stanovik *	1683	Russia	55.8975, 130.4533
65539	2243	Aldano Uchurskiy Khrebet	1428	Russia	57.9558, 129.2658
65556	1890	Khrebet Ketkap – Gora Konus	1333	Russia	57.5325, 131.8158
65575	2287	Gora Ningam / Гора Нингам	1259	Russia	56.4950, 129.4358
65593	2230	Goltsy Bilibina	1206	Russia	57.0775, 127.9783
65612	1925	Khrebet Dzhugdzhur Yuzhnyy	1168	Russia	57.0633, 137.3275
65625	2007	Khrayazh Zvereva	1145	Russia	56.6008, 123.6183
65631	2258	Khrebet Geran	1123	Russia	55.9225, 134.6617
65663	1903	Khrebet Dzhugdzhur Severnyy	1075	Russia	56.3542, 137.2275
65704	1623	Khrebet Ul'inskiy – Gora Gogda	1027	Russia	57.7483, 139.4558

AS512 Verkhoyanskiy Khrebet

Id	Height	Name	Drop	Country	Location
65512	2973	Mus-Khaya / Мус-Хая	1936	Russia	62.6046, 140.9409
65521	2409	Khrebet Orulgan / Хребет Орулган	1690	Russia	67.5825, 128.1425
65532	2615	Gora Khakandya / Гора Хакандя	1545	Russia	61.6000, 142.8375
65537	2766	Suntar Khayata Khrebet – Gora Druza	1452	Russia	61.9472, 143.0255
65558	2032	Gora Sobopol *	1326	Russia	67.0725, 127.8383
65559	2230	Gora Dzhelindzha / Гора Джелинджа	1314	Russia	61.2075, 138.7050
65565	2158	Khrebet Kommunar *	1296	Russia	64.1592, 133.6225
65580	2161	Uzmlyakhskie Gol'tsy	1237	Russia	60.7308, 138.4992
65581	1981	Gora Rosomakha *	1234	Russia	63.2342, 138.0292
65582	2331	Golets Khalyinskiy	1234	Russia	61.9708, 138.9417
65583	2193	Khrebet Sergeya Obrucheva	1233	Russia	61.1133, 144.5392
65584	1784	Gora Gadakchan / Гора Гадакчан	1231	Russia	60.8867, 142.6042
65585	2934	Gora Beriya	1230	Russia	62.3967, 141.3275
65595	2077	Gora Perm / Гора Пермь	1205	Russia	61.2067, 142.6192
65603	2448	Gora Yuryakh *	1189	Russia	62.6217, 139.5008
65606	1622	Mat' Gora	1178	Russia	67.4242, 134.8683
65609	2078	Kyutyr	1171	Russia	65.5850, 128.8392
65611	2120	Gora Khannakh *	1169	Russia	64.4558, 131.7650
65624	1788	Gora Yudoma Yuzhnyy *	1149	Russia	60.0675, 138.8033
65634	1928	Gora Kantakan *	1122	Russia	61.7500, 138.5108
65637	2156	Gora Kharan / Гора Харан	1118	Russia	62.1174, 146.1789
65640	2095	Gora Boguchan	1115	Russia	61.0225, 139.0333
65646	2410	Peresal'kyy	1099	Russia	63.2658, 139.4050
65647	1616	Gora Bilyakh *	1097	Russia	62.1500, 137.4892
65648	2130	Skalistyy Khrebet	1097	Russia	62.5356, 138.2972
65655	2247	Amkynda	1087	Russia	68.4150, 128.6367
65656	1800	Tirekhtyakhskiy Khrebet	1087	Russia	66.6717, 135.4033

Id	Height	Name	Drop	Country	Location
65658	2229	Gora Burgali / Гора Бургали	1084	Russia	61.1295, 141.4999
65660	1961	Khrebet Byrandya – Vidimost'	1081	Russia	66.6796, 127.2746
65662	2306	Khalkanskiy Khrebet	1076	Russia	62.7633, 145.3550
65665	2391	Pik Komandnaya *	1072	Russia	61.4117, 144.2308
65667	2018	Karskie Gol'tsy	1070	Russia	60.2517, 138.5133
65669	2144	Gora Astra / Гора Астра	1067	Russia	61.4975, 143.5800
65674	2369	Gora Yudoma Severnyy *	1061	Russia	62.0425, 140.3500
65685	2444	Gora Troynoy Zubets	1046	Russia	61.7967, 142.5908
65689	1836	Ketandinskiy	1043	Russia	60.4823, 141.4032
65694	2238	Gora Tobandya *	1039	Russia	61.8967, 139.7442
65696	1869	Gora Perekhod / Гора Переход	1038	Russia	60.8742, 144.0675
65699	1727	Gora Kheydzhan *	1034	Russia	60.2142, 144.5367
65705	2184	Tarbagannakhskie Gol'tsy	1025	Russia	61.1857, 138.3945
65707	2058	Gora Muus-Attyk *	1023	Russia	67.3758, 127.8475
65709	1916	Tagindyanskiy Khrebet	1021	Russia	64.7550, 128.3175
65710	2019	Gora Kuren / Гора Курень	1021	Russia	61.1092, 142.7533
65714	1785	Gora Akanzha *	1016	Russia	59.8725, 137.1175
65717	1646	Gora Khizindzha	1014	Russia	60.7825, 142.1300
65724	2206	Gora Menkyule *	1006	Russia	63.3000, 138.8817
65727	1520	Gora Khandyga *	1003	Russia	62.9508, 137.5117

AS513 Khrebet Cherskogo

Id	Height	Name	Drop	Country	Location
65506	3003	Gora Pobeda / Гора Победа	2442	Russia	65.1767, 146.0100
65516	2480	Momskiy Khrebet / Момский хребет	1761	Russia	66.5950, 144.7792
65519	2690	Khrebet Silyapskiy – Gora Chen	1734	Russia	65.2842, 141.8025
65524	2021	Khrebet Saltaga-Tas	1622	Russia	68.2750, 140.2233
65527	2400	Khrebet Arga-Tas	1600	Russia	65.2150, 149.0800
65536	2155	Tuonnakh	1481	Russia	63.1058, 151.3800
65538	2426	Gora Yechenka *	1433	Russia	65.2342, 143.6733
65540	2546	Gora Yelau / Гора Елау	1426	Russia	64.6017, 146.4567
65541	2617	Chibagalakhskiy Khrebet	1400	Russia	66.0033, 140.1750
65542	2387	Mus-Khaya / Мус-Хая	1399	Russia	64.7625, 143.0508
65544	2389	Momskiy Khrebet	1390	Russia	65.1842, 147.8650
65546	2484	Porozhnyy Khrebet – Gora Berga	1375	Russia	65.4450, 142.0675
65548	2394	Ozhogos	1365	Russia	65.5035, 142.8304
65550	2259	Khrebet Tas-Khayakhtakh	1353	Russia	67.5533, 139.1742
65552	2287	Pik Aborigen / Пик Аборигён	1350	Russia	61.9833, 149.3313
65562	2022	Khrebet Arga-Tas Yuzhnyy	1307	Russia	65.0483, 149.1892
65563	2622	Khrebet Silyapskiy Yuzhnyy *	1302	Russia	65.1617, 141.9458
65568	2552	Nakhatta	1286	Russia	66.7317, 140.2017
65571	2350	Gora Myurele Vostochnyy *	1271	Russia	65.7867, 141.3008

65577	2340	Gora Ocharon	1249	Russia	65.3608, 143.7828
65579	2295	Gora Chubuka-Tala	1246	Russia	65.9408, 146.7289
65586	2371	Erikitskiy Khrebet Zapadnyy *	1230	Russia	65.2067, 144.3683
65588	1921	Verkhneye	1223	Russia	66.7800, 138.7758
65594	2442	Erikitskiy Khrebet Yuzhnyy *	1206	Russia	64.9008, 145.3992
65596	2353	Gory Vysokiy *	1201	Russia	63.3500, 144.7942
65597	2274	Gora Chergekh	1196	Russia	63.4233, 148.2197
65599	2243	Yelersyubyut	1195	Russia	67.2983, 138.8267
65601	1739	Tiganir Gol'tsy *	1191	Russia	68.2183, 141.6592
65607	2523	Gory Porozhnyy *	1178	Russia	65.4667, 141.6025
65608	1972	Gora Malykh Porogov	1172	Russia	61.7908, 148.9492
65614	2457	Khrebet Ulakhan-Chistay Yuzhnyy *	1167	Russia	64.1167, 147.7333
65615	2149	Khrebet Khadaran'ya	1161	Russia	67.9942, 138.7550
65616	1451	Ryazhandrey-Tas	1158	Russia	67.6783, 141.9192
65617	2134	Sibekki	1158	Russia	66.5558, 138.7033
65622	1296	Gora Ploskaya / Плоская	1151	Russia	59.3880, 146.9369
65626	1492	Gora Vetrenaya / Гора Ветренная	1144	Russia	59.7683, 144.8592
65627	2527	Gora Erikit Vostochnyy *	1144	Russia	65.1033, 145.5708
65628	2190	Gora Kuobakh-Baga *	1142	Russia	64.9325, 143.4675
65629	2041	Gory Bol'shoi Tuonnakh – Gora Ezop	1141	Russia	63.3004, 151.1070
65741	2107	Gora Nyulkandya	1127	Russia	66.3259, 138.4552
65633	2637	Gora Myurele Zapadnyy*	1122	Russia	65.7733, 140.9467
65635	2127	Gora Mordzhet / Гора Морджот	1118	Russia	62.7174, 148.5281
65636	2418	Tuos	1118	Russia	66.4550, 141.1767
65641	2059	Gora Mayak / Гора Маяк	1107	Russia	62.8198, 149.4835
65650	2412	Gora Burkatyndya *	1095	Russia	66.8492, 144.5308
65651	2230	Gora Kysyl-Tas	1091	Russia	64.9067, 146.3208
65652	1241	Gora Shan' / Гора Шань	1090	Russia	59.3755, 146.1736
65664	2461	Khrebet Ulakhan-Chistay	1073	Russia	64.6933, 146.8900
65673	2337	Khrebet Okhandya	1063	Russia	63.7350, 147.7950
65681	2271	Erikitskiy Khrebet Severnyy *	1053	Russia	65.1733, 144.6333
65687	2380	Khrebet Ulakhan-Chistay Severnyy *	1045	Russia	64.8325, 146.5617
65693	1875	Gora Charky *	1040	Russia	66.3933, 138.6108
65695	2109	Gora Erikit Zapadnyy *	1039	Russia	65.1100, 144.9000
65701	1527	Khangas	1032	Russia	67.8158, 140.1233
65702	2090	Gora Munnakan *	1030	Russia	67.3508, 139.7558
65703	1869	Nel'kobinskaya Gryada	1027	Russia	61.0567, 148.0050
65711	2179	Gora Albyn *	1021	Russia	65.6675, 141.2083
65715	1873	Omulevskoye Srednegor'ye	1016	Russia	64.0842, 148.1658
65718	2237	Ulakhan	1014	Russia	67.0664, 139.8767
65720	2408	Papon'ka	1010	Russia	65.4117, 145.3192

AS514 Khrebet Kolymskiy

Id	Height	Name	Drop	Country	Location
65533	2222	Bol'shoy Mandychan	1519	Russia	61.6867, 150.4450
65534	1548	Gora Skalistaya / Гора Скалистая	1497	Russia	59.0675, 151.5317
65551	1484	Khrebet Taygonotskiy	1350	Russia	61.8417, 161.9392
65555	1604	Eguyya	1337	Russia	59.2154, 152.9033
65561	1815	Gory Peshenskiy *	1308	Russia	66.0250, 163.2367
65569	2042	Bakhapchinskiy Gory	1286	Russia	61.5600, 151.0217
65574	1785	Gora Dvukh Tsirkov	1260	Russia	67.5392, 168.1383
65578	1884	Gora Omolon *	1249	Russia	62.7433, 157.4858
65598	2005	Omsukchanskiye Gory	1196	Russia	61.4867, 155.3142
65604	2189	Gora Obinskaya	1184	Russia	61.8008, 150.0942
65605	1779	Pik Blokhina	1179	Russia	67.1017, 166.8558
65610	2068	Siverdin	1170	Russia	61.5333, 150.0092
65632	1156	Pik Larikh	1123	Russia	59.2550, 155.0108
65644	1597	Gryada Bilibinya	1100	Russia	59.9517, 152.2350
65654	1614	Pik Nuvanay	1089	Russia	67.5208, 166.9075
65657	1929	Briz	1085	Russia	60.4983, 149.8358
65666	2020	Yaryga	1071	Russia	61.4867, 149.5242
65672	1893	Kilganskiy Gory	1066	Russia	61.0542, 154.4475
65678	1649	Gora Belaya / Гора Белая	1056	Russia	68.1586, 168.8330
65684	1759	Pik Sovetskoy Gvardii	1047	Russia	66.8400, 166.5883
65690	1596	Gora Kelil'vun	1043	Russia	68.7891, 166.9697
65698	1652	Gory Komandnaya	1035	Russia	68.3433, 165.8667
65700	1828	Gora Nukh	1033	Russia	60.4514, 151.6234
65712	1815	Nayakhanskiy Khrebet	1018	Russia	62.3219, 158.0255
65719	1764	Tumanskiy Gory	1010	Russia	61.2608, 155.5600
65721	1814	Gora Namalinga	1008	Russia	63.1075, 158.3067
65723	1873	Granitnyy Verkhniy	1008	Russia	60.8017, 152.7583
65725	1685	Khrebet Ushurzkchzi	1005	Russia	65.5608, 161.3067
65728	1699	Gora Vys' / Гора Высь	1003	Russia	62.1742, 154.5983
65729	1787	Khrebet Korbzndya	1002	Russia	62.5750, 158.9458
65639	1116	Ostrov Zav'yalova, Zavyalov	1116	Russia	59.1017, 150.7242

AS515 Chukotskiy Khrebet

Id	Height	Name	Drop	Country	Location
65535	1887	Iskhodnaya / Исходная	1495	Russia	67.8175, 178.2942
65590	1849	Zasblachnyy	1214	Russia	68.0233, 177.7408
65613	1525	Gora Velikaya	1167	Russia	66.8246, -178.2401
65618	1636	Gora Past'	1156	Russia	68.2574, 179.6397
65643	1621	Gora Rubinovaya	1104	Russia	68.7450, 176.7350
65645	1468	Gora Bol'shoy Matachingay	1099	Russia	66.4767, -179.4100

Id	Height	Name	Drop	Country	Location
65661	1794	Gora Nedostupnaya	1077	Russia	68.6075, 177.1625
65675	1194	Khrebet Pryamoy	1061	Russia	64.8555, -173.4355
65680	1393	Khrebet Televeyem *	1053	Russia	66.0700, 174.9867
65686	1592	Greben'	1046	Russia	68.9625, 176.0958
65697	1397	Gory Ploskaya Vostochnyy *	1035	Russia	66.7975, -177.9433
65706	1709	Gora Konus	1024	Russia	67.5433, 178.2308
65708	1440	Malyy Matachinay / Малый Матачинай	1023	Russia	66.5692, -179.4050
65732	1360	Gora Kolyuchaya / Гора Колючая	1000	Russia	66.6147, 175.4011

AS516 Koryakskiy Khrebet

Id	Height	Name	Drop	Country	Location
65507	2453	Gora Ledyanaya / Ледяная	2337	Russia	61.8883, 171.1700
65560	1898	Khrebet Unzlayat Vostochnyy	1312	Russia	61.7414, 172.1094
65573	1484	Dikiy Khrebet	1262	Russia	62.9142, 176.5158
65576	2038	Khrebet Unzlayat Zapadnyy	1254	Russia	61.8050, 171.3950
65591	1574	Khrebet Vatyna*	1209	Russia	61.4550, 171.5925
65592	1357	Khrebet Pylginskiy	1207	Russia	60.4975, 167.1992
65600	1429	Khrebet Pakhachinskiye	1194	Russia	60.9958, 169.8567
65642	1522	Gora Greben'	1105	Russia	61.0683, 171.5483
65676	1339	Gory Unneytynup	1059	Russia	61.1258, 165.1417
65677	1319	Khrebet Kayrytgyngzgty	1058	Russia	62.7300, 176.1442
65682	1772	Snegovoy Khrebet	1050	Russia	61.5525, 172.0308
65683	1248	Gora Yastreb	1048	Russia	63.3275, 177.1667
65730	1059	Talovskiye Gory	1002.0	Russia	61.7475, 164.9917

AS517 Kamchatka

Id	Height	Name	Drop	Country	Location
65501	4753	Klyuchevskaya Sopka / Ключевская сопка	4653	Russia	56.0558, 160.6417
65502	3307	Vulkan Shiveluch / Шивелуч	3168	Russia	56.6533, 161.3642
65503	3607	Vulkan Ichinskaya Sopka / Ичинская Сопка	3125	Russia	55.6783, 157.7183
65504	3456	Sopka Koryakskaya	2999	Russia	53.3208, 158.7125
65505	3527	Vulkan Kronotskaya Sopka / Кроноцкая Сопка	2736	Russia	54.7527, 160.5326
65508	2923	Sopka Zhupanovskaya / Жупановская Сопка	2210	Russia	53.5883, 159.1483
65509	3672	Gora Ostry Tolbachik / Толбачик	2190	Russia	55.8308, 160.3258
65510	2460	Sopka Opala / Опальская сопка	2069	Russia	52.5433, 157.3392
65511	2161	Vulkan Kambal'nyy / Камбальная Сопка	1976	Russia	51.3058, 156.8758
65513	2616	Gora Khuvkhoitun / Хувхой	1920	Russia	57.9208, 160.6758
65514	2598	Gora Alney / Гора Алней	1825	Russia	56.6925, 159.6450
65515	2089	Sopka Khodutka / Ходутка	1810	Russia	52.0623, 157.7107
65517	2322	Sopka Mutnovskaya / Мутновская сопка	1750	Russia	52.4483, 158.1975
65518	2578	Gora Gamchen / Гора Гамчен	1740	Russia	54.9742, 160.7033
65520	1957	Vulkan Zheltovskaya Sopka	1730	Russia	51.5767, 157.3283
65523	2920	Gora Bol'shaya Udina / Гора Большая Удина	1630	Russia	55.7583, 160.5267

65525	2276	Gora Bakening / Гора Бакенинг	1611	Russia	53.9042, 158.0700
65526	2173	Sopka Vilyuchinskaya / Вилючинская сопка	1610	Russia	52.7050, 158.2817
65528	3080	Gora Oval'naya Zimina / Малая Зимина	1576	Russia	55.8609, 160.6056
65530	2354	Sopka Taunshits / Тауншиц	1551	Russia	54.5283, 159.8042
65531	2741	Sopka Avachinskaya / Авачинская Сопка	1550	Russia	53.2558, 158.8367
65529	2380	Gora Shish / Шиш	1535	Russia	55.7525, 161.1767
65543	2376	Vulkan Kizimen / Кизимен	1396	Russia	55.1308, 160.3200
65545	1400	Vulkan Kharchinskaya / Харчинский	1381	Russia	56.4258, 160.8242
65547	4057	Proskaya Blizhnaya / Krestovsky	1369	Russia	56.1133, 160.5083
65549	2192	Vulkan Unana / Унана	1359	Russia	54.6433, 159.7183
65553	2526	Gora Shishel' / Гора Шишель	1344	Russia	57.4392, 160.3767
65554	1872	Gory Lenayge Tunup *	1339	Russia	59.1783, 161.4833
65557	2029	Gora Tupaya	1333	Russia	54.8850, 157.6133
65564	4580	Gora Kamen' / Камень	1298	Russia	56.0183, 160.5942
65566	1831	Khrebet Inzchvinzi Tunup *	1292	Russia	59.4800, 161.8450
65567	1298	Gora Snezhnaya / Гора Снежная	1288	Russia	56.1400, 163.0050
65570	1707	Gora Zhupanovskiye Vostryaki	1276	Russia	53.7875, 159.3050
65572	1853	Vulkan Kosheleva / Вулкан Кошелева	1268	Russia	51.3558, 156.7542
65587	2175	Sredinnyy Khrebet *	1226	Russia	55.6225, 158.1583
65589	1909	Sopka Asacha / Асача	1220	Russia	52.3550, 157.8300
65602	1501	Gora Ketepana / Гора Кетепана	1189	Russia	57.0425, 158.3792
65619	2539	Gora Ostraya	1155	Russia	58.1842, 160.8283
65620	1557	Gora Vachkazhets	1152	Russia	53.0458, 157.9300
65621	1962	Gora Vershinnaya	1151	Russia	54.0258, 157.4375
65623	1577	Vulkan Il'inskiy / Ильинская Сопка	1150	Russia	51.4983, 157.2042
65630	1863	Valaginskiy Khrebet Yuzhnyy	1136	Russia	54.5750, 158.9842
65638	1211	Gora Nachikinskaya / Гора Начикинская	1118	Russia	57.8400, 162.6933
65653	1869	Gora Khrebtovaya	1089	Russia	53.5508, 157.1633
65659	1857	Vulkan Krasheninnikova	1084	Russia	54.5958, 160.2692
65668	1616	Gory Lamkayling / Горы Ламкайлинг	1070	Russia	59.5992, 162.0625
65670	1901	Valaginskiy Khrebet Severnyy *	1067	Russia	54.8833, 159.9325
65671	1798	Gora Vershinskaya / Гора Вершинская	1067	Russia	53.6033, 158.6817
65692	1876	Tsentral'naya	1066	Russia	55.1112, 157.3298
65716	2172	Sopka Tylele	1066	Russia	58.5617, 161.0325
65679	1735	Sopka Anangravnen / Сопка Анангравнен	1053	Russia	59.2234, 161.9332
65688	1563	Vulkan Malyy Semyachik	1043	Russia	54.1350, 159.6742
65691	1893	Vulkan Konradi	1042	Russia	55.0925, 160.5533
65713	1828	Gora Anaun / Гора Анаун	1017	Russia	56.3067, 158.8433
65722	1571	Shvazh *	1008	Russia	58.9192, 161.5333
65726	1700	Gora Kornilovskaya / Корнильская	1003	Russia	54.2042, 158.7542
65731	1146	Gora Khaylyulya	1002	Russia	58.0417, 161.6200

AS52 Baikal Area Ranges

AS520 Baykalskiy Khrebet

Id	Height	Name	Drop	Country	Location
66007	2588	Gora Cherskogo / Гора Черского	1596	Russia	55.0592, 108.6842
66035	2202	Baykalskiy Khrebet Zapovednik	1063	Russia	54.3500, 108.4258
66041	1906	Vysokiy Khrebet	1026	Russia	56.3225, 108.9067

AS521 Northern Buryatia Ranges

Id	Height	Name	Drop	Country	Location
66002	3067	Muyskiy Gigant / Муйский Гигант	2107	Russia	55.9737, 114.4392
66011	2641	Verkhneangarskiy Khrebet	1818	Russia	56.3561, 111.6475
66005	2841	Barguzinskiy Khrebet – Pik Baikal	1724	Russia	54.6225, 110.4567
66010	1878	Gora Markova, Svyatoy Nos	1427	Russia	53.6375, 108.8092
66012	2546	Severo-Muyskiy Khrebet Vostochnyy *	1405	Russia	56.4058, 113.9083
66003	2629	Verkhneangarskiy Khrebet Zapadnyy	1393	Russia	56.2175, 111.2217
66013	2581	Ikatskiy Khrebet	1380	Russia	53.8758, 111.0058
66014	2537	Severo-Muyskiy Khrebet Zapadnyy	1352	Russia	55.7892, 111.6792
66015	2503	Gory Babanty	1313	Russia	54.4317, 114.8408
66016	2514	Golets Inyaptuk / Голец Иняптук	1287	Russia	56.3732, 110.0757
66018	2654	Nos Pokoynika	1240	Russia	55.7742, 110.4908
66020	2995	Gora Bayshint Ula	1200	Mongolia, Russia	51.4533, 101.7217
66021	2273	Gora Kamennyy *	1190	Russia	56.7392, 115.2575
66023	1717	Golets Davydov	1160	Russia	52.5492, 107.4397

Id		Name	Drop	Country	Location
66025	2645	Barguzinskiy Khrebet Severnyy	1142	Russia	55.2167, 110.9125
66026	2473	Muyakanskiy Khrebet	1137	Russia	55.8450, 112.5425
66027	1676	Pik Amalyk *	1134	Russia	57.5267, 116.3300
66028	1994	Delyun-Uranskiy Khrebet	1128	Russia	56.3725, 112.6508
66029	2574	Yugo-Zapadnyy Muyskiy Khrebet	1117	Russia	55.1058, 111.8733
66031	2034	Gora Soli *	1096	Russia	56.5317, 111.0483
66033	2062	Gora Karalon *	1066	Russia	57.1050, 115.6608
66036	2421	Gora Inoragda	1061	Russia	55.6650, 111.3217
66038	2440	Gora Tompuda *	1055	Russia	55.2417, 110.2850
66044	2661	Yuzhno Muyskiy Khrebet – Bushueva	1046	Russia	55.4967, 112.6867
66043	2537	Gora Namama *	1017	Russia	55.4942, 111.1242
66047	2284	Gora Bol'shoy Khapmon	1006	Russia	55.0892, 112.8683
66048	2025	Gora Dzhyalokan *	1005	Russia	56.6117, 112.7942
66050	2217	Gora Yanchuy *	1002	Russia	56.1283, 112.5997

AS522 Stanovoy and Patom Highlands

Id	Height	Name	Drop	Country	Location
66001	3073	Pik BAM / Пик БАМ	2231	Russia	56.8640, 117.5770
66004	2966	Muskunakh / Мускунах	1810	Russia	57.1222, 117.9875
66006	2363	Gora Shaman / Гора Шаман	1597	Russia	56.0692, 115.8617
66024	2604	Khrebet Udokan / Хребет Удокан	1535	Russia	56.7408, 118.8767
66009	2351	Gora El'ger *	1442	Russia	57.2817, 117.4383
66017	2355	Pik Tri Ozera *	1252	Russia	56.5058, 117.2200
66019	2533	Gora Chara *	1224	Russia	57.2017, 118.5475
66022	2024	Gora Shirik *	1174	Russia	57.6358, 117.3342
66008	2570	Khrebet Udokan Vostochnyy	1116	Russia	56.6725, 119.1250
66030	2208	Khrebet Yankan	1112	Russia	55.8608, 118.4308
66032	1921	Gora Taksima *	1068	Russia	56.1975, 115.9550
66034	2519	Skalistyy Golets	1064	Russia	56.4017, 119.0950
66039	1989	Gora Bakhtatnak *	1050	Russia	56.6375, 115.7517
66046	2229	Khrebet Kodar Vostochny *	1042	Russia	57.4358, 118.7500
66040	2309	Gora Evonokit *	1035	Russia	57.2317, 119.8525
66042	1829	Gora Nechera *	1019	Russia	57.7800, 116.7425
66045	2195	Gora Sygykta *	1016	Russia	57.2750, 117.2192
66049	2829	Khrebet Kodar Zapadnyy *	1005	Russia	57.0508, 117.5183

Gora Markova, Svyatoy Nos, AS521

Svyatoy Nos is a large peninsula, over 50km long, on the eastern shore of Lake Baikal, part of Zabaykalsky National Park. Tourism is permitted but there are no recorded ascents of Gora Markova, the highest point in a steep-sided and well-forested mountain range.

Pik BAM, AS522

This peak is named after the Baikal Amur Mainline railway, which runs through a valley to the south but also crosses some cold, rugged and mountainous territory.

AS53 Mongolia Ranges

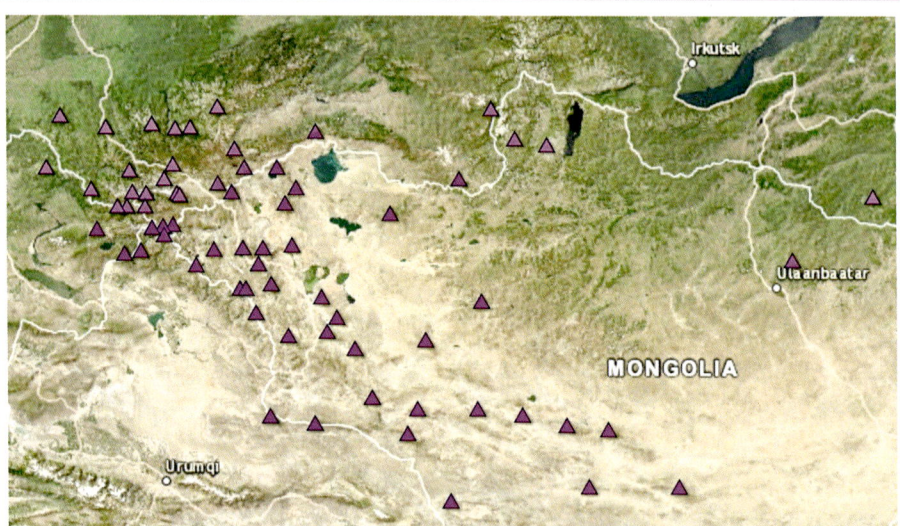

Myangan Yamaat, AS530 (Deividas Valaitis)

Bumbat Khairkhan Uul, AS530 (Deividas Valaitis)

AS530 Altai Mountains

Id	Height	Name	Drop	Country	Location
66501	4506	Gora Belukha / Белуха	3343	Kazakhstan, Russia	49.8071, 86.5899
66502	3796	Jargalant Khairkhan	2352	Mongolia	47.6878, 92.5637
66503	4356	Khüiten Uul	2326	China, Mongolia	49.1496, 87.8252
66505	3802	Ikh Ovoo	2132	Mongolia	44.7992, 95.2400
66506	3315	Dünkheger	2075	Mongolia	45.1933, 90.9056
66507	3957	Tergun Bogd	1979	Mongolia	44.9950, 100.2308
66509	4070	Kharkhiraa Uul – Möst Uul	1838	Mongolia	49.5700, 91.3858
66508	4207	Sutai Uul	1836	Mongolia	46.6176, 93.5943
66510	4177	Severo-Chuyskiy Khrebet	1804	Russia	50.0628, 87.5676
66512	4203	Tsast Uul	1768	Mongolia	48.6819, 90.7249
66511	4193	Munkh Khairkhan – Sukhbaatar	1757	Mongolia	46.8900, 91.4733
66513	3578	Khasagt Khairkhan Uul	1749	Mongolia	46.7892, 95.8014
66514	3620	Myangan Yamaat / Bogdin Tergun Uul	1745	Mongolia	44.8954, 101.5774
66515	3351	Altan Hohiy	1688	Mongolia	48.7500, 91.6200
66516	3970	Mungun-Taiga	1685	Russia	50.2792, 90.1192
66517	3470	Bumbat Khairkhan Uul	1664	Mongolia	47.2883, 93.0308
66518	4029	Ikh Türgen Uul – Deglii Tsagaan	1579	Mongolia	49.7992, 89.7542
66519	3085	Dzhata	1563	China	48.6308, 86.8392
66520	2927	Khrebet Terektinskiy	1550	Russia	50.2443, 86.4894
66521	3984	Baatar Khairkhan Uul	1541	Mongolia	46.9689, 92.7237
66525	3914	Ondor Khairkhan Uul	1424	China, Mongolia	48.3380, 88.6041
66526	4019	Khokh Serkh Uul – Takhilt	1423	Mongolia	47.9600, 90.9467
66527	3981	Sajryn Uul	1416	Mongolia	48.3775, 90.5525
66528	2784	Khrebet Listvyaga Zapadnyy *	1390	Russia	49.8633, 85.2333
66530	3944	Tsengel Khairkhan	1359	Mongolia	48.6483, 89.1567
66532	3604	Gora Ak-Oyuk	1317	Russia	50.6575, 89.8267
66533	3772	Erdene Uul *	1314	Mongolia	45.3517, 97.4117
66534	2775	Vorosilova	1296	Kazakhstan	50.2982, 83.8341
66535	3353	Gora Ploskogor'ye Ukok *	1287	Russia	49.5250, 86.9567
66536	2777	Gora Ushkurmynker	1287	Kazakhstan	48.5625, 86.3050
66537	3374	Burkitauyl Tau	1261	Kazakhstan	49.0576, 85.4291
66538	3842	Sartam Uul *	1256	China	48.9467, 87.5658
66539	2912	Shuurgat Uul	1213	China, Mongolia	45.0125, 92.3433
66540	3452	Bayan Tsagaan Uul	1211	Mongolia	45.2208, 98.8542
66541	3871	Ülken Buqtirma Gory *	1200	China	49.1083, 87.1983
66542	3821	Tolbo Uul *	1186	Mongolia	48.6767, 90.0900
66543	2651	Gora Chokurtayga	1184	Russia	51.0382, 87.9343
66550	3905	Ikh Shiver Uul *	1181	Mongolia	47.8800, 90.1658
66544	2508	Gora Sarlyk / Гора Сарлык	1163	Russia	51.0775, 85.7350
66545	3446	Verkhove Ortolyka	1156	Russia	50.3417, 87.8667
66546	3739	Alag Khairkhan Uul	1154	Mongolia	45.5808, 94.1183
66547	3110	Gora Kurkurebazhi	1151	Russia	51.0575, 88.4058

Id	Height	Name	Drop	Country	Location
66548	3885	Kayierte Uul *	1147	China, Mongolia	47.8735, 90.0212
66549	2756	Khrebet Sumul'tinskiy	1145	Russia	51.1137, 87.1942
66551	3876	Dushin Uul	1139	China, Mongolia	47.3574, 90.4992
66554	3496	Tsagaan Shuvuut Uul	1131	Mongolia	50.2983, 91.1533
66556	3967	Irbistu	1130	Russia	49.7592, 88.0867
66557	2423	Bashchelakskiye Khrebet	1122	Russia	51.2792, 84.2958
66558	3234	Ikh-Tayangiin Nuruu Uul *	1112	Mongolia	45.3258, 95.5258
66560	3888	Gora Shenelyu	1065	Russia	49.7858, 87.0133
66561	3764	Gora Ake Kule *	1053	China	49.1186, 87.5485
66562	3220	Gora Tavan-Arkhag	1046	Mongolia	49.8892, 91.7533
66563	2968	Khrebet Zapadnyy Tannu-Ola	1041	Russia	50.9800, 92.3908
66564	3506	Gora Talduair / Гора Талдуаир	1035	Russia	49.9729, 89.3049
66565	2721	Gora Berel *	1031	Kazakhstan	49.5142, 86.3775
66566	2691	Khrebet Listvyaga Vostochnyy *	1023	Kazakhstan, Russia	49.5258, 86.0883
66567	3922	Gora Dzhaniktu	1015	Russia	49.7817, 87.9625
66568	3026	Khrebet Eri-Tayga	1008	Russia	51.4433, 89.2858

AS531 Khangai Mountains

Id	Height	Name	Drop	Country	Location
66504	4010	Otgon Tenger Uul	2269	Mongolia	47.6083, 97.5525
66524	3352	Belchir Uul	1427	Mongolia	50.8475, 98.6135
66531	3277	Khrebet Erzinskiy *	1324	Russia	50.0600, 96.8692
66553	2928	Khan Khökhii	1133	Mongolia	49.3783, 94.6892
66555	2817	Gora Chongyz-Tayga	1131	Russia	51.4242, 97.8583
66559	3178	Sneznyj Stol	1107	Mongolia	50.7350, 99.6408

AS532 Gobi Desert Ranges

Id	Height	Name	Drop	Country	Location
66522	2830	Dund Saikhany Nuruu	1531	Mongolia	43.6342, 103.7794
66523	2799	Asralt-Khairkhan	1438	Mongolia	48.4658, 107.4125
66529	2695	Atas Bogd	1364	Mongolia	43.3117, 96.5900
66552	2768	Nemegt Uul	1138	Mongolia	43.6383, 100.9483
66037	2519	Gora Burun-Shibertuy	1055	Russia	49.7108, 109.9708

Dund Saikhany Nuruu, AS532, and Jargalant Khairkhan, AS530
Rob Woodall, June 2022

Mongolia has 42 Ribus including eighteen Ultras. Due to the low rainfall there is very little forest and few fenced fields, so it is easy to drive to the base of the peaks in the east and climb them. We targeted the non-glaciated peaks and climbed eight, none of which had previous ascents on Peakbagger.com. The locals in their yurts seemed unconcerned. On Dund Saikhany Nuruu we were initially pursued by a man on a motorbike (they don't seem to use horses much nowadays). Having decided we posed no threat to his goats he left us to our mysterious but apparently harmless pursuit. At the foot of Jargalant Khairkhan, having set up camp for the night, we received another motorcycle visitation, this time by an older couple. We chatted for a while despite having no common language. They examined our Landcruiser and found my tiny tent very amusing. Our vehicle got stuck just twice, once on mud while off route, once in sand while on route.

AS54 East China

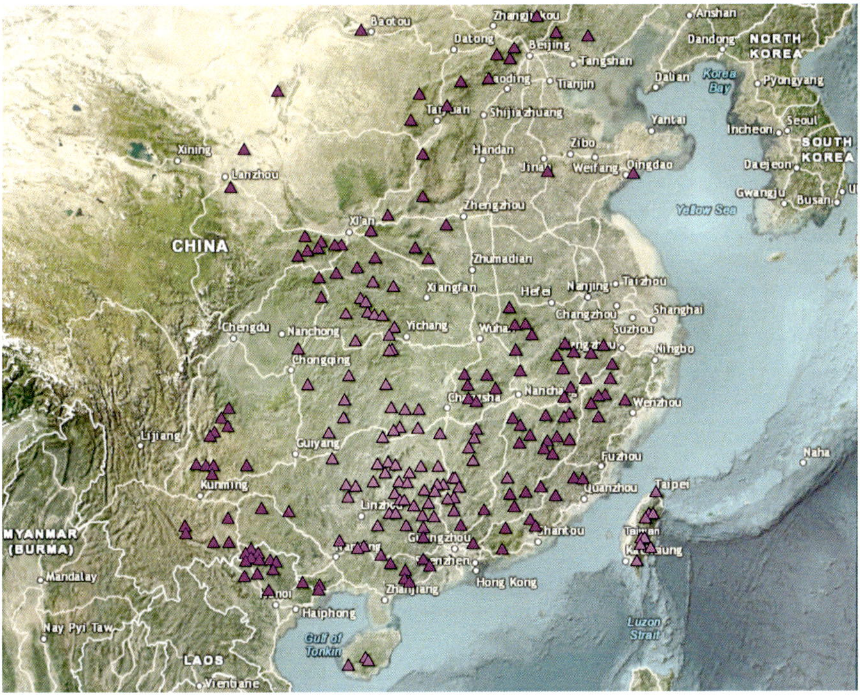

Liánhuā Fēng, AS546 (Mark Trengove)

AS540 North China

Id	Height	Name	Drop	Country	Location
67005	3556	Hèlán Shān / 贺兰山	2119	China	38.8333, 105.9508
67037	2118	Wùlíng Shān / 雾灵山	1527	China	40.5983, 117.4808
67079	1846	Du Shan / 都山	1272	China	40.5150, 118.7933
67143	2039	Yunwu Shan	1112	China	41.1033, 116.6967
67185	2343	Dahuabei	1040	China	40.7008, 109.4050
67200	1629	Guangdi Shan / 广地山	1020	China	40.1617, 115.7408

AS541 North Central China

Id	Height	Name	Drop	Country	Location
67013	3061	Wǔtái Shān / Běitái Dǐng	1784	China	39.0808, 113.5667
67029	2882	Xiǎowǔtái Shān - Dōngtái	1565	China	39.9417, 115.0433
67030	2567	Niújiǎo Ān / 牛角鞍	1551	China	36.8175, 111.9717
67044	2831	Guāndì Shān / 关帝山	1454	China	37.8983, 111.4917
67067	3670	Mǎxián Shān / 马衔山	1325	China	35.7308, 103.9850
67075	2784	Heyeping	1279	China	38.7275, 111.8383
67101	1993	Xuehua Shan	1216	China	34.8050, 110.5233
67105	2322	Li Shan / 厉山	1199	China	35.4167, 111.9625
67108	3018	Dàmǎohuái Shān / 大茆槐山	1198	China	37.0000, 104.5486
67129	2035	Baicaopan / 白草畔	1149	China	39.8133, 115.5825
67135	2096	Báishí Shān / 白石山	1131	China	39.2100, 114.6958
67201	2098	Liulinjian Shan / 柳林尖山	1018	China	38.3567, 112.9650

AS542 Hua Shan-Daba Shan

Id	Height	Name	Drop	Country	Location
67003	3106	Shénnóng Dǐng / 神农顶	2276	China	31.4400, 110.3075
67004	3767	Tàibái Shān / 太白山	2255	China	33.9551, 107.7653
67026	2128	Tiěwǎdiàn / 铁瓦殿	1604	China	32.8650, 108.3725
67048	2534	Jiàngān Shān / 箭杆山	1444	China	32.7364, 107.6804
67059	2917	Huàlóng Shān / 化龙山	1383	China	32.0233, 109.3583
67061	3015	Bīngjīng Dǐng / 冰晶顶	1376	China	33.8383, 108.5900
67064	2358	Nanyang Shan / 南羊山	1337	China	33.0750, 109.2642
67066	2646	Caolian Ling	1328	China	34.2908, 109.8258
67071	1704	Gāodēng Shān / 高登山	1301	China	30.3008, 106.8075
67099	1512	Song Shan	1219	China	34.4758, 112.9358
67104	1901	Wulong Jian / 五龙尖	1205	China	32.5917, 109.9233
67095	2512	Guāngdǐng Shān / 光顶山	1198	China	31.9250, 109.5958
67107	2074	Tianzhu Shan / 天竺山	1196	China	33.3967, 110.0092
67119	2645	Guāngtóu Shān / 光头山	1166	China	33.4858, 106.8058
67121	1700	Wuduo Shan	1165	China	33.3592, 112.2025

Id	Height	Name	Drop	Country	Location
67126	2184	Laojun Shan	1153	China	33.7200, 111.6433
67137	2819	Yùhuáng Shān / 玉皇山	1127	China	34.1225, 107.1050
67147	3071	Hūnrénpíng Liáng / 昏人坪梁	1105	China	33.7175, 107.6083
67150	2280	Zhonghua Shan *	1096	China	31.5075, 108.7433
67157	2796	Yintiao Ling / 阴条岭	1079	China	31.4825, 109.9350
67163	2025	Jiangjia Shan *	1070	China	31.0017, 110.8025
67172	1907	Qīngpíng Zhài / 清坪寨	1055	China	32.0533, 107.7333
67173	1722	Putuo Shan / 菩陀山	1054	China	32.4311, 110.7570
67188	2603	Mótiān Lǐng / 摩天岭	1039	China	33.6692, 107.1808
67190	2996	Guāngtóu Shān / 光头山	1035	China	33.8492, 108.3133
67217	2610	Dàguān Shān / 大官山	1007	China	31.5558, 109.7067

AS543 Shangdong Ranges

Id	Height	Name	Drop	Country	Location
67021	1777	Báimǎ Jiān / 白马尖	1658	China	31.1135, 116.1858
67039	1533	Tài Shān / 泰山	1491	China	36.2558, 117.1050
67068	1729	Tiantangzhai / 天堂寨	1322	China	31.1058, 115.7717
67087	1584	Jingangtai Shan / 金岗台	1244	China	31.7050, 115.5533
67140	1133	Jù Fēng / 巨峰	1122	China	36.1750, 120.6258
67144	1244	Luanni Tan / 乱泥滩	1112	China	30.2258, 115.8042
67156	1488	Tianzhu Feng / 天柱峰	1085	China	30.7450, 116.4508

From summit to airport

Chongqing Wushan Airport, formerly Wushan Shannufeng, is located on what used to be a Ribu in a range that appears to be called Taohua. It was blown up with dynamite then flattened with bulldozers to create an airport runway. Before demolition and construction began in 2015, the mountain was over 1800 metres high (at 31.0642, 109.7053) and possibly as high as 1868m, with a prominence of at least 1000 metres, possibly as much as 1055 metres. The atlas of Sichuan Province from 1981 gives the name Motian Ling and a figure of 1769 metres, but this seemed to refer to a lower peak on the range, not the summit. After the airport buildings and runway were completed in 2019, a very different scene emerged. The mountain summit was demolished in order to benefit tourists flying in to visit the nearby Goddess Peak and Three Gorges Dam, demolishing one peak so that people could fly in to visit another. Recent satellite data suggest that the highest ground at the 3.3km long runway development is about 1762 metres, which broadly supports the height of 1771 metres shown on Chinese Wikipedia and means a prominence of 958 metres.

It is presumed that the runway now marks the highest point of the mountain, which is unclear from the videos of the site available online and may be an artificial bump over to one side. The terminal building roof is apparently designed in the style of an uneven mountain top, perhaps in a vain attempt to make up for the real mountain top having been obliterated.

So it is now not even a Sub-Ribu, but it may be the easiest of all mountain summits to reach in China, assuming that the highest point is not on the runway itself or in some other off-limits zone for pedestrians. It is unclear whether landing at the airport would count as a valid summit ascent.

AS544 Greater Guizhou Ranges

Id	Height	Name	Drop	Country	Location
67002	4344	Gǒngwáng Shān – Xuělǐng	2484	China	26.1492, 102.9133
67006	4042	Yào Shān / 药山	1988	China	27.2133, 103.0775
67011	4017	Dàgǔniú Shān / 大牯牛山	1823	China	26.1583, 103.2358
67014	2572	Fènghuángjīn Dǐng / 凤凰金顶	1772	China	27.8805, 108.6802
67019	2320	Hēifēng Jiān / 黑峰尖	1655	China	30.2345, 110.5772
67020	2142	Māo'ér Shān / 猫儿山	1649	China	25.8667, 110.4125
67027	2402	Chiêu Lầu Thi	1574	Vietnam	22.6617, 104.6031
67031	1760	Lóngtóu Shān / 龙头山	1543	China	23.3858, 108.5033
67033	2997	Báozhú Shān / 薄竹山	1526	China	23.3617, 103.9067
67043	3364	Kèchē Liángzi / 课车梁子	1458	China	27.3708, 103.2825
67046	2123	Zhenbao Ding / 真宝顶	1447	China	26.1358, 110.8225
67047	1934	Subao Ding / 苏宝顶	1445	China	27.1758, 110.3058
67050	1592	Tam Đảo Bắc	1438	Vietnam	21.5733, 105.5442
67052	1587	Núi Chạm Chu	1427	Vietnam	22.2042, 105.0950
67051	3301	Fēngmào Lǐng / 风帽岭	1419	China	26.1917, 102.5450
67056	1977	Núi Pia Ya	1402	Vietnam	22.7275, 105.5908
67058	2276	Núi Pu Tha Ca	1387	Vietnam	22.9500, 105.1358
67060	1622	Jiulongchi / 九龙池	1383	China	28.1575, 111.2300
67062	2086	Yuánbǎo Shān / 元宝山	1375	China	25.4117, 109.1792
67069	2123	Māo'ér Liáng / 猫儿梁	1313	China	30.5558, 109.1417
67070	1450	Núi Cai	1304	Vietnam	22.0867, 104.5620
67073	2178	Leigong Shan / 雷公山	1294	China	26.3872, 108.2032
67076	2063	Cénwánglǎo Shān / 岑王老山	1279	China	24.4925, 106.3975
67081	2068	Yúntáihuāng / 云台荒	1252	China	30.7667, 110.5717
67082	1541	Phia Mè	1251	Vietnam	21.8433, 106.9800
67080	3198	Shānmù Lǐng / 杉木岭	1249	China	27.5631, 103.8363
67086	1514	Yueping Feng / 岳坪峰	1246	China	27.4992, 111.7408
67089	1470	Ban Ma	1242	Vietnam	22.7050, 105.1508
67097	1938	Mótiān Lǐng / 摩天岭	1220	China	25.4317, 108.7850
67100	2238	Jīnfó Shān / 金佛山	1217	China	29.0350, 107.1933
67106	1507	Khoang Nam Chau Lanh	1197	Vietnam	21.5667, 107.6117
67109	2431	Tây Côn Lĩnh	1194	Vietnam	22.8017, 104.8058
67115	3295	Huāshítóu / 花石头	1176	China	25.8250, 103.1817
67116	2530	Xiǎo Shào Shān / 小哨山	1173	China	23.6983, 102.0992
67118	1565	Pia Bioc / Núi Lăng Phai	1167	Vietnam	22.3537, 105.7475
67114	2749	Liánhuā Shān / 莲花山	1159	China	23.3667, 103.2200
67125	1300	Zhùróng Fēng / 祝融峰	1155	China	27.2975, 112.6892
67130	1940	Nanshan Ding / 南山顶	1147	China	26.1892, 110.0858
67138	1780	Baima Shan / 白马山	1124	China	27.4033, 110.7525

Id	Height	Name	Drop	Country	Location
67142	1939	Huīqiān Liángzi / 灰千梁子	1113	China	29.3308, 108.9092
67146	1931	Núi Pia Oac Sud	1107	Vietnam	22.6158, 105.8633
67159	1425	Qīngmíng Shān / 青明山	1091	China	24.9950, 108.8350
67148	2858	Gān Shān Wūjī Dàshān / 甘山屋基大山	1089	China	26.1485, 104.6436
67169	1431	Mǎhuáng Shān / 蚂蟥山	1085	China	28.1650, 111.7900
67166	2579	Lǎojūn Shān / 老君山	1069	China	22.9517, 104.5742
67175	1462	Shǔliáng Lǐng / 薯良岭	1053	China	21.7650, 107.6592
67168	2259	Bēngjiānzi / 崩尖子	1047	China	30.2708, 110.7075
67177	1869	Fódǐng Shān / 佛顶山	1046	China	27.3275, 108.0683
67189	2021	Erbaoding / 二宝鼎	1038	China	26.2667, 110.5425
67191	1528	Qīxīng Shān / 七星山	1034	China	29.0333, 110.4283
67186	2288	Dàhēi Shān / 大黑山	1033	China	23.1283, 104.8075
67195	2445	Tuanjie Shan *	1023	China	28.2375, 103.9025
67198	2502	Yángxióng Shān / 羊雄山	1022	China	24.2658, 103.8575
67197	1663	Jiàozi Dǐng / 轿子顶	1019	China	28.5150, 108.7242
67192	2614	Mòpán Shān / 磨盘山	1017	China	23.9675, 102.0267
67204	3189	Jìngzǐ Shān / 镜子山	1013	China	27.8808, 103.5900
67210	1355	Shengren Shan / 圣人山	1006	China	28.2442, 110.6675
67213	1951	Dǒuhōng Pō / 斗烘坡	1006	China	24.5908, 105.2517
67211	1492	Gaoshuiping / 高水坪	1005	China	27.5267, 111.0117

AS545 Nan Ling

Id	Height	Name	Drop	Country	Location
67009	2120	Nánfēngmiàn / 南风面	1902	China	26.3140, 114.0413
67012	1979	Shèngtáng Shān / 圣堂山	1829	China	23.9754, 110.0991
67015	2009	Jiǔcài Lǐng / 韭菜岭	1739	China	25.5150, 111.3292
67017	1918	Wugong Shan – Jīndǐng	1723	China	27.4545, 114.1729
67018	1959	Běnjī Wō / 畚箕窝	1633	China	25.2475, 112.0033
67022	1794	Jiǔlǐng Jiān / 九岭尖	1629	China	28.8810, 114.9507
67023	1902	Shíkēng Kōng / 石坑崆	1622	China	24.9279, 112.9912
67024	1704	Dàtián Dǐng / 大田顶	1606	China	22.2908, 111.2150
67124	1885	Yíndiàn Shān / 银殿山	1600	China	24.8875, 110.9958
67032	1936	Bǎojiè Lǐng / 宝界岭	1536	China	25.5592, 110.9617
67042	1657	Lǎoyā Jiān / 老鸦尖	1468	China	29.3603, 114.5949
67045	1844	Tiāntáng Dǐng / 天堂顶	1453	China	24.7000, 111.5890
67049	1957	Shīzǐ Kǒu / 狮子口	1444	China	25.6908, 113.2133
67053	1473	Dàhànyáng Fēng / 大汉阳峰	1415	China	29.5010, 115.9565
67065	1625	Wàngfú Tái / 望佛台	1330	China	26.1167, 111.8974
67078	1596	Yīfēng Jiān / 一峰尖	1272	China	28.9875, 113.8266
67083	1608	Qīxīng Lǐng / 星岭	1248	China	28.4395, 114.1657
67092	1654	Èrjiān Fēng / 二尖峰	1238	China	25.4416, 112.8278

Id	Height	Name	Drop	Country	Location
67098	1659	Sān Jiāngjūn / 三将军	1219	China	24.7681, 112.1789
67102	1338	Éhuáng Zhàng / 鹅凰嶂	1213	China	21.8433, 111.4142
67110	1274	Qīxīngyán Dǐng / 七星岩顶	1192	China	23.5383, 111.9625
67113	1251	Tiānlù Shān / 天露山	1185	China	22.4658, 112.2492
67028	1857	Běiqiǎ Dǐng / 北卡顶	1174	China	24.8925, 111.1667
67117	1275	Liánhuā Dǐng / 莲花顶	1172	China	22.8600, 110.2033
67123	1680	Gǒuwěi Zhàng / 狗尾嶂	1158	China	24.9535, 113.2352
67127	1428	Sānjiǎo Píng / 三角坪	1151	China	26.1205, 112.5851
67132	1594	Xiānghuā Lǐng / 香花岭	1144	China	25.4374, 112.5371
67145	1808	Wèiqīng Lǐng / 蔚青岭	1140	China	25.5525, 109.9192
67133	1757	Yázi Shí / 崖子石	1137	China	25.3725, 113.4700
67141	1391	Qiū Shān / 秋山	1121	China	27.1317, 114.0642
67153	1620	Wàngjūn Shān / 望军山	1090	China	24.3191, 112.3481
67155	1335	Dàjiào Dǐng / 大轿顶	1085	China	21.9833, 111.1725
67158	1586	Chuándǐ Dǐng / 船底顶	1076	China	24.4813, 113.2608
67160	1253	Lítóu Dǐng / 犁头顶	1075	China	23.9547, 111.2856
67162	1261	Sānxiān Tǎn / 三仙坦	1074	China	29.3959, 113.6860
67164	1711	Tiāntáng Lǐng / 天堂岭	1069	China	25.1874, 112.4432
67165	1627	Jiguanxi	1068	China	25.1142, 110.7833
67167	1356	Zhūtóu Shān / 猪头山	1066	China	24.4108, 110.5608
67171	1170	Dàshèng Shān / 大圣山	1057	China	23.1350, 109.2458
67174	1344	Shífēng Xiān / 石峰仙	1054	China	26.7733, 113.8475
67176	1293	Shīzǐ Shān / 狮子山	1053	China	24.4108, 110.8175
67179	1158	Dàpíngtiān Shān / 大平天山	1051	China	23.1892, 109.5025
67180	1600	Xiǎoliányún Shān / 小连云山	1050	China	28.5360, 113.8508
67193	1691	Yáogǎngxiān Shān / 瑶岗仙山	1031	China	25.6676, 113.3109
67194	1274	Wàngjūn Dǐng / 望君顶	1025	China	22.5537, 110.6223
67202	1311	Xiānrén Táng / 仙人塘	1017	China	25.8875, 111.4008
67203	1175	Dǎng Shān / 党山	1015	China	23.8968, 111.9552
67206	1571	Zhǎngchōng Dǐng / 长冲顶	1011	China	24.3346, 111.9086
67214	1140	Dayunwu Shan	1005	China	22.7042, 111.9558

AS546 Wuyi Shan

Id	Height	Name	Drop	Country	Location
67007	2161	Huánggāng Shān / 黄岗山	1956	China	27.8597, 117.7832
67016	1865	Liánhuā Fēng / 莲花峰	1735	China	30.1271, 118.1655
67025	1820	Yùjīng Fēng / 玉京峰	1605	China	28.9092, 118.0587
67035	1929	Huángmáo Jiān / 黄茅尖	1524	China	27.8932, 119.1866
67034	1787	Qīngliáng Fēng / 清凉峰	1517	China	30.1008, 118.8619
67036	1761	Jūnfēng Shān / 军峰山	1511	China	27.2192, 116.3583
67038	1857	Báishí Dǐng / 白石顶	1497	China	26.7573, 116.9302

67040	1856	Dàiyún Shān / 戴云山	1486	China	25.6828, 118.1860
67057	1560	Tónggǔ Zhàng / 铜鼓嶂	1395	China	24.1748, 116.3505
67063	1630	Liùgǔ Jiān / 六股尖	1350	China	29.5635, 117.7500
67072	1494	Dàyáng Shān / 大洋山	1297	China	28.4704, 120.2959
67074	1523	Móxīn Jiān / 磨心尖	1293	China	29.2287, 118.6389
67077	1728	Gǔniúdà Gǎng / 牯牛大岗	1273	China	30.0495, 117.4579
67084	1667	Kǔsǔnlín Jiān / 苦笋林尖	1247	China	25.0510, 117.4093
67085	1811	Gǒuzi Nǎo / 狗子脑	1246	China	25.3805, 116.8146
67091	1803	Shígǔ Jiě / 石谷解	1238	China	25.6493, 118.5380
67093	1714	Éméi Fēng / 峨嵋峰	1234	China	27.0083, 117.0808
67094	1312	Dàpán Jiān / 大盘尖	1232	China	29.2338, 119.6623
67096	1281	Fēiyún Dǐng / 飞云顶	1221	China	23.2830, 114.0165
67111	1724	Jiǔlóng Shān / 九龙山	1189	China	28.3587, 118.8774
67112	1587	Lóngwáng Shān / 龙王山	1187	China	30.3835, 119.3985
67120	1498	Fènghuáng Shān / 凤凰山	1166	China	23.9116, 116.5970
67122	1910	Tóngluó Xíng / 铜锣形	1160	China	27.9996, 117.9925
67128	1620	Lóngxī Shān / 龙溪山	1150	China	26.5538, 117.2727
67131	1560	Niútóu Shān / 牛头山	1145	China	28.6423, 119.4510
67134	1621	Báimǎ Shān / 白马山	1136	China	28.6250, 119.1642
67136	1337	Liánhuā Shān / 莲花山	1132	China	23.0610, 115.2317
67139	1538	Liángshān Dǐng / 梁山顶	1123	China	25.1807, 116.1718
67149	1218	Yàpó Jì / 亚婆髻	1098	China	23.9641, 113.5233
67151	1247	Guānyīn Jiān / 观音尖	1092	China	29.7236, 119.7437
67152	1496	Tiāntī Fēng / 天梯峰	1091	China	28.5800, 117.7929
67154	1384	Guōyán Shān / 郭岩山	1089	China	27.0534, 117.9863
67161	1455	Línghuà Shān / 灵华山	1075	China	26.9542, 115.9275
67178	1341	Shíwáng Fēng / 十王峰	1051	China	30.4635, 117.8182
67181	1524	Sāwǎng Shān / 撒网山	1049	China	27.1633, 117.4558
67182	1319	Qīmù Zhàng / 七目嶂	1049	China	23.8501, 115.3659
67183	1169	Yùhuá Shān / 玉华山	1044	China	27.8313, 115.6500
67184	1445	Jīlóng Zhàng / 鸡笼嶂	1041	China	25.0828, 115.5288
67199	1312	Píngkēng Shān / 屏坑山	1020	China	25.6942, 115.4239
67205	1363	Bǐjià Fēng / 笔架峰	1013	China	27.9180, 117.0204
67207	1219	Xiāng Shān / 相山	1009	China	27.5550, 115.9558
67208	1430	Huángniú Shí / 黄牛石	1009	China	24.5096, 114.4562
67209	1348	Luànluō Zhàng / 乱罗嶂	1008	China	24.6450, 115.7258

Huáng Shān

Mark Trengove

Canada is the only country with more Ribus than China. A visit to the peaks of the Huáng Shān (Yellow Mountains), a World Heritage Site in Anhui Province, can provide an introductory experience of mountain hiking unlike any other, except within China.

Situated in eastern China, and reachable by fast public transport links from Shanghai and the other major conurbations of the eastern Yangtse valley, these mountains are a major tourist destination for Chinese visitors. They come to admire the scenery of granite pinnacles, pine trees, cloud inversions, waterfalls and sunsets, but not for peak-bagging purposes. The summits of the major peaks are accessible to hikers without the use of ropes and hands, due to the extensive network of stone stairs and pathways that have been constructed around the massif. The summit of Liánhuā Fēng (Lotus Flower Peak, AS546) can be visited without difficulty from the top station of the Yuping cableway by winding stone steps off the main trail – when this trail is open.

It is possible to hike to the summits from the valleys, but most people use the modern Swiss-constructed cable car systems to access the heights. The Huáng Shān massif really needs two days to explore, and there are a number of comfortable hotels nestling between the peaks. To avoid the worst of the crowds it is best to visit between the major annual festivals (spring festival in February, autumn festival in September or October). Late in the year trails to the summits can be closed for safety reasons when there is snow or ice, as happened to our party on Liánhuā Fēng in late November 2019. Trails also may be closed for extended periods due to renovation work, so it is best to check before booking.

There are no topographic Chinese maps available to the public for any part of the country, although sketch maps (in Chinese) of the Huáng Shān can be bought from various stalls near the bottom cable car stations. Online mapping such as OpenTopoMap can give some idea of the lay-out of the peaks, but access to these is likely to be blocked when in the country, and it is advisable not to have a copy on a device while in China.

Unless you speak Mandarin Chinese, it is not easy to arrange a visit to the massif as a foreign visitor by yourself. English is not widely spoken outside Shanghai, so it is best to engage the services of a travel agency in China to arrange a package for you.

AS547 Taiwan

Id	Height	Name	Drop	Country	Location
67001	3952	Yù Shān / 玉山	3952	Taiwan	23.4700, 120.9573
67008	3886	Xuě Shān / 雪山	1938	Taiwan	24.3834, 121.2318
67054	1682	Máláolòu Shān / 麻荖漏山	1413	Taiwan	23.1397, 121.3222
67055	3092	Beidawushan / 北大武山	1409	Taiwan	22.6275, 120.7617
67090	3742	Nanhu Dashan / 南湖大山	1241	Taiwan	24.3617, 121.4392
67103	3342	Baigou Dashan / 白姑大山	1212	Taiwan	24.2025, 121.1092
67170	1118	Qīxīng Shān / 七星山	1059	Taiwan	25.1708, 121.5533
67196	3825	Xiùgūluán Shān / 秀姑巒山	1022	Taiwan	23.4967, 121.0575
67212	3668	Guanshan / 關山	1005	Taiwan	23.2283, 120.9117

AS548 Hainan

Id	Height	Name	Drop	Country	Location
67010	1867	Wǔzhǐ Shān / 五指山	1867	China	18.8983, 109.7042
67041	1812	Yīnggē Lǐng / 鹦哥岭	1472	China	19.0358, 109.5425
67088	1412	Jianfeng Ling / 尖峰岭	1243	China	18.7172, 108.8721

AS55 Korea – Amur Area

AS550 Bureiskiy-Jagdy

Id	Height	Name	Drop	Country	Location
67504	2370	Yam-Alin Khrebet	1915	Russia	53.6075, 134.5767
67506	1573	Omel'dinskiy Khrebet	1478	Russia	52.4342, 137.6617
67508	2240	Badgalskiy Khrebet *	1403	Russia	50.5742, 134.5942
67510	1374	Gora Listvennichnyy *	1276	Russia	53.0642, 137.8942
67511	1796	Gora Eleor / Гора Элеор	1257	Russia	50.0292, 135.1033
67516	2167	Gora Amnunna *	1161	Russia	51.1842, 133.9192
67517	1462	Gora Kilanda *	1160	Russia	51.6625, 138.3117
67522	2298	Gora Gorod-Makit / Город-Макит	1139	Russia	52.9517, 134.6575
67527	1470	Gora Bekel'deul' / Гора Бекельдеуль	1078	Russia	53.9442, 127.7183
67534	2175	Gora Levaya Bureya *	1045	Russia	52.1092, 134.8933
67537	1748	Gora Sagdy *	1011	Russia	49.9042, 134.8067

AS551 Xiao Hinggan Ling

Id	Height	Name	Drop	Country	Location
67532	1429	Pingding Shan / 平顶山	1051	China	46.6325, 128.4650

AS552 Southern Manchuria Ranges

Id	Height	Name	Drop	Country	Location
67512	1694	Lǎo Ye Lǐng / 老爷岭	1216	China	44.1019, 128.0381
67536	1390	Nanlou Shan	1025	China	43.4117, 126.6550

AS554 Sikhote-Alin

Id	Height	Name	Drop	Country	Location
67502	2090	Gora Tardoki-Yani / Гора Тардоки-Яни	1989	Russia	48.8967, 138.0542
67507	1855	Gora Oblachnaya / Гора Облачная	1431	Russia	43.6958, 134.1992
67514	2004	Gora Ko / Гора Ко	1196	Russia	47.1158, 136.5683
67523	1758	Gora Bol'shaya Lugovaya *	1136	Russia	46.1150, 137.0200
67528	1182	Gora Shaman / Гора Шаман	1076	Russia	51.4508, 139.9125
67529	1671	Sestra / Гора Сестра	1068	Russia	43.5306, 134.0597

AS555 Hamgyong Sanmaek

Id	Height	Name	Drop	Country	Location
67501	2744	Paektu-san / 백두산	2592	North Korea	41.9933, 128.0775
67509	2522	Puksubaek-san / 북수백산	1359	North Korea	40.7108, 127.7492
67515	1994	Sungjŏk-san / 숭적산	1188	North Korea	40.5742, 126.2108
67518	1909	Myohyang-san / 묘향산	1151	North Korea	40.0189, 126.3335
67520	2541	Kwanmo-bong / 관모봉	1144	North Korea	41.7050, 129.2400
67530	2270	Wagal-bong / 와갈봉	1059	North Korea	40.7558, 126.9625
67535	1876	Paek-san / 백산	1042	North Korea	40.4497, 126.4613
67539	2355	Yonhwa-san / 연화산	1002	North Korea	40.7792, 127.3775

AS556 Taebaek Sanmae

Id	Height	Name	Drop	Country	Location
67503	1947	Halla-san, Cheju-do / 한라산	1947	South Korea	33.3614, 126.5294
67505	1915	Jiri-san / 지리산	1696	South Korea	35.3369, 127.7307
67513	1708	Seorak-san – Daecheongbong / 설악산	1201	South Korea	38.1192, 128.4658
67519	1614	Deogyu-san / 덕유산	1145	South Korea	35.8600, 127.7467
67521	1468	Hwaak-san / 화악산	1142	South Korea	37.9948, 127.5034
67524	1241	Gaji-san / 가지산	1111	South Korea	35.6200, 129.0025
67525	1638	Kumgang-san / 금강산	1111	North Korea	38.6567, 128.1050
67526	1218	Baegun-san / 백운산	1089	South Korea	35.1064, 127.6216
67531	1278	Taegak-san / 대각산	1051	North Korea	38.8317, 126.5808
67533	1485	Haram-san / 하람산	1049	North Korea	39.1275, 126.7483
67538	1187	Mudeung-san / 무등산	1011	South Korea	35.1242, 127.0092

AS56 Japanese Archipelago

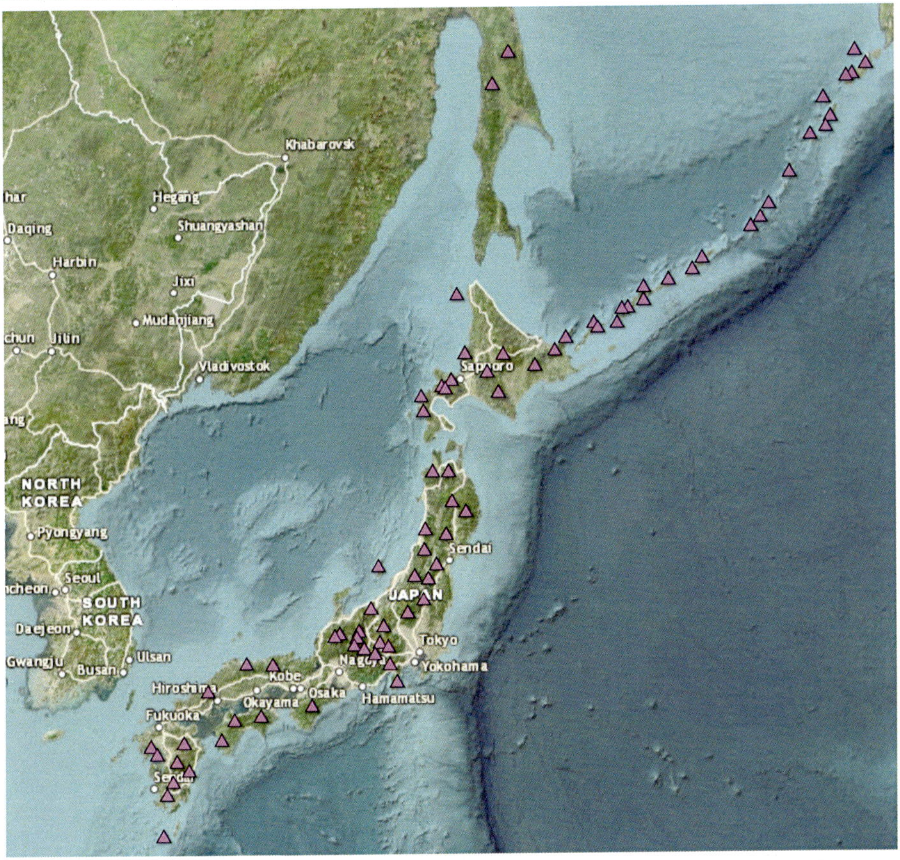

Vulkan Alaid, Ostrov Atlasova, AS561 (Anne Gray)

AS560 Sakhalin

Id	Height	Name	Drop	Country	Location
68025	1609	Gora Lopatina / Гора Лопатина	1609	Russia	50.8517, 143.1417
68056	1327	Gora Onor / Гора Онор	1168	Russia	50.1228, 142.5534

AS561 Kuril Islands

Id	Height	Name	Island	Drop	Country	Location
68002	2339	Vulkan Alaid / Алаид	Ostrov Atlasova	2339	Russia	50.8608, 155.5650
68012	1816	Vulkan Chikurachki / Чикурачки	Paramushir	1816	Russia	50.3233, 155.4608
68021	1772	Vulkan Fussa / вулкан Фусса	Paramushir	1637	Russia	50.2675, 155.2467
68075	1183	Gora Vernadskogo	Paramushir	1028	Russia	50.5492, 155.9633
68014	1772	Vulkan Tyatya / Тятя	Kunashir	1772	Russia	44.3533, 146.2533
68068	1486	Gora Ruruy / Гора Руруй	Kunashir	1093	Russia	44.4542, 146.1400
68022	1634	Gora Stokap / Гора Стокап	Iturup	1634	Russia	44.8392, 147.3442
68028	1585	Gora Bogdan Khmel'nitskiy	Iturup	1551	Russia	45.3375, 147.9208
68042	1322	Gora Kamuy / Гора Камуй	Iturup	1307	Russia	45.5158, 148.8067
68051	1205	Vulkan Atsonupuri	Iturup	1181	Russia	44.8075, 147.1308
68061	1220	Vulkan Berutarube	Iturup	1144	Russia	44.4616, 146.9323
68066	1211	Vulkan Machekha	Iturup	1096	Russia	45.0283, 147.9175
68029	1539	Gora Mil'na / Гора Мильна	Simushir	1539	Russia	46.8150, 151.7867
68043	1360	Vulkan Prevo / Вулкан Прево	Simushir	1299	Russia	47.0142, 152.1167
68033	1446	Pik Sarychev / Вулкан Сарычева	Matua	1446	Russia	48.0900, 153.2000
68035	1425	Gora Vysokaya	Urup	1425	Russia	45.7550, 149.6717
68049	1328	Vulkan Kolokol / Колокол	Urup	1205	Russia	46.0442, 150.0483
68041	1325	Vulkan Krenitsyna	Onekotan	1325	Russia	49.3533, 154.7083
68054	1170	Vulkan Ekarma / Вулкан Экарма	Ekarma	1170	Russia	48.9475, 153.9408
68055	1169	Gora Makanrushi	Makanrushi	1169	Russia	49.7850, 154.4283
68057	1166	Vulkan Pallasa / Вулкан Палласа	Ketoy	1166	Russia	47.3408, 152.4392
68059	1157	Pik Severgin / Вулкан Севергина	Kharimkotan	1157	Russia	49.1150, 154.5117

AS562 Hokkaido

Id	Height	Name	Drop	Country	Location
68004	2291	Asahi-dake, 朝日岳	2291	Japan	43.6636, 142.8541
68011	1898	Yotei-zan, 羊蹄山	1878	Japan	42.8266, 140.8115
68018	1721	Rishiri-zan, Rishiri-tō, 利尻岳	1721	Japan	45.1785, 141.2420
68034	1520	Kariba-san	1435	Japan	42.6133, 139.9406
68036	2052	Horoshiri-dake, 幌尻岳	1409	Japan	42.7194, 142.6829
68038	1492	Shokambetsu-dake	1388	Japan	43.7159, 141.5229
68040	1661	Rausu-dake / 羅臼岳	1348	Japan	44.0759, 145.1223
68048	1726	Ashibetsu-dake	1208	Japan	43.2357, 142.2835
68052	1499	Meakan-dake	1175	Japan	43.3864, 144.0087

Id	Height	Name	Drop	Country	Location
68060	1488	Yoichi-dake	1150	Japan	43.0327, 141.0198
68064	1277	Yurappu-dake	1124	Japan	42.2189, 140.0102
68069	1547	Shari-dake / 斜里岳	1090	Japan	43.7657, 144.7178
68071	1308	Niseko-Annupuri / ニセコアンヌプリ	1064	Japan	42.8751, 140.6590

AS563 Honshu

Id	Height	Name	Drop	Country	Location
68001	3776	Fuji-san / 富士山	3776	Japan	35.3608, 138.7275
68003	3190	Hotaka-dake / 穂高岳	2313	Japan	36.2892, 137.6475
68005	3193	Kita-dake / 間ノ岳	2238	Japan	35.6458, 138.2283
68008	2899	Aka-dake	1922	Japan	35.9708, 138.3700
68009	2702	Hakusan Okumiya / Gozengamine / 白山	1912	Japan	36.1550, 136.7717
68010	2220	Chokai-zan / 鳥海山	1882	Japan	39.0994, 140.0489
68015	2038	Iwate-san / 岩手山	1753	Japan	39.8526, 141.0010
68016	2956	Kisokomaga-take	1751	Japan	35.7892, 137.8050
68017	1915	Hakken-san – Hachikyoga-take	1736	Japan	34.1733, 135.9067
68019	3067	Ontake-san / 御嶽山	1712	Japan	35.8942, 137.4767
68020	2462	Hiuchi-yama / 火打山	1639	Japan	36.9225, 138.0683
68023	1729	Dai-sen – Kengamine / 大山	1632	Japan	35.3717, 133.5458
68024	2578	Shirane-san / 日光白根山	1615	Japan	36.7983, 139.3758
68026	2128	Dainichi-dake	1595	Japan	37.8328, 139.6603
68030	1917	Hayachine-san / 早池峰山	1489	Japan	39.5584, 141.4887
68031	1984	Gassan / 月山	1487	Japan	38.5492, 140.0269
68039	1625	Iwaki-san / 岩木山	1362	Japan	40.6559, 140.3031
68044	1841	Zaō-san – Kumano-dake / 蔵王山	1294	Japan	38.1439, 140.4398
68045	2568	Asama-yama	1271	Japan	36.4067, 138.5233
68046	3026	Kengamine / Norikura / 乗鞍岳	1236	Japan	36.1042, 137.5517
68047	2601	Kitaoku-Senjodake	1231	Japan	35.8687, 138.6708
68050	1627	Kurikoma-yama	1199	Japan	38.9609, 140.7883
68053	1172	Kimpoku-san, Sadoga-shima	1172	Japan	38.1038, 138.3498
68062	1585	Hakkōda-san – Odake / 八甲田山	1142	Japan	40.6589, 140.8772
68063	1346	Osorakan-zan / 恐羅漢山	1127	Japan	34.5956, 132.1297
68072	2035	Nishi-Azuma-yama / 吾妻山	1062	Japan	37.7383, 140.1408
68073	1406	Amagi-san	1046	Japan	34.8629, 139.0018
68076	1875	Sarugabamba-yama	1013	Japan	36.2261, 136.9426
68077	1917	Sanbonyari-dake	1009	Japan	37.1500, 139.9617
68078	1510	Hyono-sen	1002	Japan	35.3533, 134.5142

Hotaka-dake ascent, AS563 (Rob Woodall)

Dainichi-dake, AS563 (Rob Woodall)

Summit ridge of Kisokomaga-take, AS563 (Rob Woodall)

Dai-sen and Chokai-zan, AS563
Rob Woodall, September 2019

Japan has 54 Ribus including 21 Ultras, of which Dai-sen was promising to be a stopper, due to an extremely loose ridge. Denise and Richard had chanced on a retired professor from Osaka who turned out to be the key. Tsutomu ('Tom') did some research and identified a safe route. The route worked well. It was exposed but clearly well used.

I emailed Tom to thank him. He emailed back to say he would quite like to meet up. Pete was due to head home, so he was swapped for Tom and my trip continued, mostly climbing Ribus rather than Ultras. The routes were fairly short but the weather was wet and windy at times. Tom was in his seventies but fit and determined (I was barely in my sixties). The one Ultra on our schedule, Chokai-zan, was however a long day. The weather was poor – not terrible, but we were passing a lot of people who had turned back. They were presumably locals and could come back another day. We weren't, and so we kept going. After reaching a minor summit the route descended a fixed chain then entered a chaos of boulders and tunnels. We reached the summit and hiked down feeling ridiculously pleased with ourselves. The old men had put the youngsters to shame.

AS564 Shikoku

Id	Height	Name	Drop	Country	Location
68006	1982	Ishizuchi-san – Tengu-dake / 石鎚山	1982	Japan	33.7667, 133.1158
68027	1955	Tsurugi-san / 剣岳	1559	Japan	33.8542, 134.0950
68070	1229	Takatsuki-yama / 高月山	1071	Japan	33.1883, 132.6358

AS565 Kyushu

Id	Height	Name	Drop	Country	Location
68013	1791	Nakadake / 中岳	1791	Japan	33.0858, 131.2492
68032	1483	Unzen-dake – Heisei Shinzan	1465	Japan	32.7617, 130.2983
68037	1700	Karakuni-dake / Kirishima-yama	1391	Japan	31.9342, 130.8608
68058	1739	Kunimi-dake	1164	Japan	32.5475, 131.0183
68065	1405	Osuzu-yama	1102	Japan	32.2992, 131.4258
68067	1117	Sakurajima	1093	Japan	31.5892, 130.6575
68074	1076	Kyoga-dake / 経ヶ岳	1034	Japan	32.9875, 130.0764

AS566 Outlying Japanese Islands

Id	Height	Name	Drop	Country	Location
68007	1936	Miyanoura-dake / 宮之浦岳, Yakushima	1936	Japan	30.3358, 130.5042

AS57 Southeast Asia

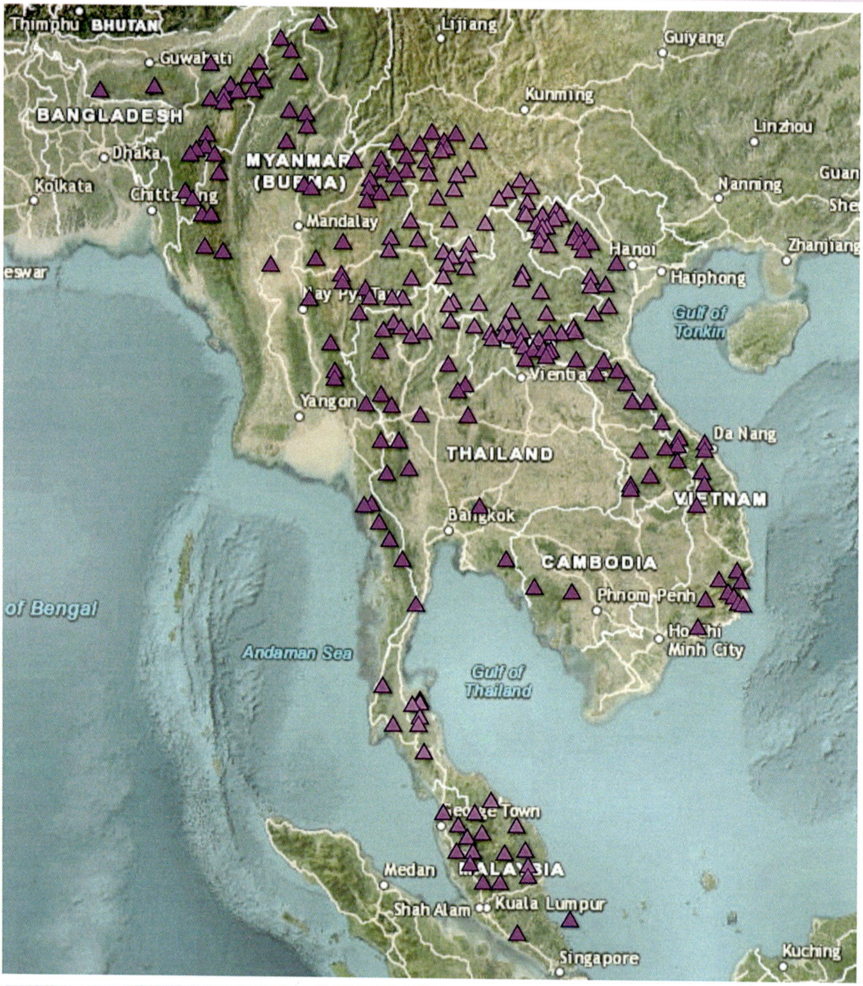

Gunung Jerai, AS573 (Daniel Patrick Quinn)

AS570 Nagaland Hills

Id	Height	Name	Drop	Country	Location
68501	3826	Saramati	2894	India, Myanmar	25.7400, 95.0375
68503	3070	Nat Ma Taung / Mount Victoria	2148	Myanmar	21.2333, 93.9033
68515	3088	Mol Len	1739	India, Myanmar	25.4942, 94.7517
68523	2692	Sangpang Bum	1667	Myanmar	26.4908, 95.8458
68524	2832	Laikot	1665	India	25.3567, 93.8992
68530	2780	Pakhain Parvat	1593	India, Myanmar	26.8157, 95.5236
68535	1874	Mawhpung Bum	1561	Myanmar	25.9550, 96.0708
68536	3014	Jāpvo	1556	India	25.5975, 94.0667
68538	2703	Kennedy Peak	1510	Myanmar	23.3175, 93.7617
68544	1708	Taungthonlon	1479	Myanmar	24.9592, 95.8025
68550	1695	Maingthon Taung	1432	Myanmar	24.1692, 95.7300
68558	1965	Shillong Parvat	1371	India	25.5442, 91.8817
68607	2700	Yakkō	1225	India	26.1942, 94.9142
68608	2157	Phawngpui / Blue Mountain	1223	India	22.6310, 93.0393
68617	1375	Khunbaman Parbat / Mikir Hills	1189	India	26.1467, 93.5067
68627	2521	Boinu Taung *	1159	Myanmar	22.2442, 93.2833
68636	1550	Loi Maw	1130	Myanmar	24.8858, 96.2667
68641	2670	Chingkhu	1122	India	25.8233, 94.5992
68647	2607	Sangu Lok Parvat *	1111	India	25.4333, 94.2967
68653	1717	Tuivai Parvat *	1100	India	23.9350, 93.1233
68654	1378	Loi Maw	1100	Myanmar	24.5574, 96.3421
68655	2600	Kindang Bum	1100	Myanmar	27.2092, 96.6342
68671	2704	Aika Taung *	1076	Myanmar	22.2375, 93.5458
68676	1410	Nokrek	1070	India	25.4617, 90.3217
68682	2172	Pawn Zung	1062	Myanmar	21.3683, 93.3692
68690	2012	Kailam Dakshin Parvat *	1052	India	24.3186, 93.4237
68692	2375	Manipur Taung *	1050	Myanmar	23.8125, 93.6458
68714	1904	Buhban Parvat *	1019	India	23.7975, 92.9458
68717	2188	Magulong Parvat	1018	India	25.2450, 93.5333
68723	2685	Tampaba	1009	India	25.1683, 93.9100
68726	2015	Lunglen	1006	Myanmar	23.9995, 93.3886
68729	1555	Sairep	1000	India	22.8167, 92.8208

The relative height of trees

The Massenerhebung Effect describes differences in tree-line according to mountain size and location. Mountains close to higher mountains tend to have higher tree-lines than more isolated mountains, due to heat retention and shadowing. This is well-illustrated in the tropics where moss forest exists at low altitudes on peaks such as Gunung Ledang (Malay Peninsula, Malaysia) and Gunung Palung (Kalimantan, Indonesia) that do not have higher neighbours for considerable distances. The same ecosystems that exist at under 1000 metres of elevation on these isolated peaks are not found below 1800 metres on Gunung Kinabalu in Borneo, the highest mountain in Malaysia.

AS572 Shan – Western Thailand

Id	Height	Name	Drop	Country	Location
68507	3510	Daxue Shan / 大雪山	2051	China	24.1117, 99.6400
68512	2565	Doi Inthanon / ดอยอินทนนท์	1835	Thailand	18.5883, 98.4875
68513	2673	Loi Leng	1823	Myanmar	22.6425, 98.0742
68517	3435	Hunhua Shan	1730	China	23.9575, 100.2608
68518	2623	Nattaung	1726	Myanmar	18.8100, 97.0375
68520	2080	Mela Taung	1708	Myanmar	17.2024, 98.0796
68525	2079	Phou Khe / ภูเข้	1623	Lao, Thailand	19.3240, 101.2414
68527	2641	Měnglín Shān / 猛林山	1620	China, Myanmar	23.3300, 98.8775
68531	2563	Loi Pangnao	1590	Myanmar	21.3033, 100.3133
68532	2519	Mong Pawn Bum *	1589	Myanmar	20.6858, 97.3417
68537	2995	Mengding Shan *	1543	China	23.4300, 99.2158
68543	2030	Mulayit Taung	1479	Myanmar	16.1833, 98.5275
68547	2285	Doi Pha Hom Pok / ดอยผ้าห่มปก	1461	Thailand	20.0708, 99.1417
68548	2490	Mong Maw Bum *	1441	Myanmar	22.9458, 99.0017
68552	3105	Stoe-Shan	1420	China	24.4583, 99.9758
68553	2321	Loi Lung	1420	Myanmar	21.6706, 98.7877
68563	2152	Khao Kacheu La / เขากะเจอลา	1356	Thailand	16.1708, 99.0367
68565	2031	Doi Lang Ka / Doi Mae Tho / ดอยแม่โถ	1350	Thailand	19.0025, 99.4050
68566	2299	Taungme	1350	Myanmar	22.9717, 96.4694
68567	2363	Ashae Myim Anauk Myim Taung	1340	Myanmar	21.0917, 96.6008
68571	1811	Khao Tai Pa / เขาใต้ป่า	1329	Thailand	15.2683, 98.7125
68572	1518	Popa / ပုပ္ပားတောင်	1324	Myanmar	20.9208, 95.2542
68573	3233	Daxue Shan	1322	China	23.7042, 99.7892
68582	2031	Loi Hpwi	1280	Myanmar	21.3492, 98.7250
68585	1865	Mawn Hpa-hsat	1266	Myanmar	21.1742, 100.5975
68586	2603	Ánglǎng Shān / 昂朗山	1263	China, Myanmar	22.1067, 99.3633
68587	2360	Loi Hsong	1262	Myanmar	23.7042, 97.6967
68588	1965	Kawng Pu-sang	1261	Myanmar	21.5117, 101.0733
68589	2267	Loi Maw	1260	Myanmar	22.8561, 98.4744
68590	2167	Loi Hsanhtong	1260	Myanmar	23.1992, 98.1842
68591	2452	Laomiandi Shan	1260	China	22.1442, 100.5192
68592	2491	Loi Sang	1260	Myanmar	21.5550, 97.3925
68598	2179	Loi Lan	1252	Myanmar	19.6448, 97.8859
68599	2175	Doi Chiang Dao / ดอยหลวง เชียงดาว	1249	Thailand	19.3969, 98.8896
68601	1621	Phou Phaxang	1236	Lao	19.1442, 101.7492
68602	1801	Supaliko Taung	1231	Myanmar	17.8333, 97.1600
68606	1720	Doi Phu Kha / ดอยภูคา	1218	Thailand	18.2700, 100.5033
68610	1870	Loi Sā-lü	1210	Myanmar	20.2845, 98.0490
68611	1891	Shweudaung	1210	Myanmar	23.0200, 96.2225

Id	Height	Name	Drop	Country	Location
68612	2978	Xuezhulin Dashan / 雪竹林大山	1205	China	23.7908, 99.2117
68615	1752	Doi Chi / ยอดดอยจี่	1191	Thailand	19.4158, 100.5400
68622	2540	Wuhuazhai Shan *	1180	China	22.6967, 100.1517
68623	1629	Doi Soi Malai / ดอยสอยมาลัย	1176	Thailand	17.1508, 98.8450
68625	2630	Shi Zhulin Shan	1170	China	24.1483, 98.9558
68643	2243	Loi Panglom	1120	Myanmar	23.7063, 98.4704
68644	1244	Khao Luang / ยอดเขาหลวง	1117	Thailand	16.8700, 99.6633
68645	1694	Doi Luang / ยอดดอยหลวง	1117	Thailand	19.1333, 99.7592
68656	1996	Loi Hpa-tan	1100	Myanmar	22.9417, 98.1225
68658	1884	Yomakyo	1092	Myanmar	18.0550, 97.1625
68659	1906	Byingye Taung	1091	Myanmar	20.0199, 96.4306
68662	1801	Loi Pangsè	1090	Myanmar	20.0442, 98.1808
68663	1718	Doi Chom Hot / ยอดดอยจอมหด	1089	Thailand	19.2817, 99.0925
68666	1740	Doi Pha Mon / ดอยผาหม่น	1086	Lao, Thailand	19.8833, 100.5008
68669	2780	Lake Shan *	1080	China	24.2000, 100.3158
68672	3000	Qingping Shan *	1075	China	23.3675, 99.8950
68675	2280	Lancang Shan *	1070	China	24.0400, 100.4058
68677	1991	Monghsat Bum *	1070	Myanmar	20.6000, 99.3958
68681	2005	Doi Khun Mae Ya / ดอยแม่ยะ	1066	Thailand	19.2042, 98.5575
68691	1554	Khao Yai / เขาใหญ่	1050	Thailand	15.4108, 99.3417
68693	2244	Loi Mi	1050	Myanmar	21.6000, 99.5617
68694	2469	Loi Maw	1047	Myanmar	20.4529, 97.3989
68697	1584	Phou Phông	1043	Lao	18.9958, 101.7667
68706	1909	Loi Hpa-chitwe	1030	Myanmar	20.9717, 100.4433
68715	1929	Doi Mon Chong / ดอยม่อนจอง	1019	Thailand	17.4542, 98.5283
68722	2183	Loi Ping-ye	1010	Myanmar	23.4355, 98.5311
68725	1979	Loi Kyi-lek	1006	Myanmar	20.0417, 98.8233

AS573 Malay Peninsula

Id	Height	Name	Drop	Country	Location
68504	2187	Gunung Tahan	2133	Malaysia	4.6330, 102.2350
68508	2183	Gunung Korbu	1993	Malaysia	4.6897, 101.2973
68509	2107	Gunung Benum	1950	Malaysia	3.8230, 102,0943
68511	2072	Myinmoletkat Taung	1856	Myanmar	13.4667, 98.8050
68519	1780	Khao Luang / ยอดเขาหลวง	1714	Thailand	8.4942, 99.7300
68534	1862	Gunung Bintang	1566	Malaysia	5.4292, 100.8667
68541	1657	Gunung Bubu	1494	Malaysia	4.6821, 100.8072
68570	1571	Gunung Teranu Indah Abadi *	1334	Malaysia	4.7305, 102.8514
68574	1397	Khao Phanom Bencha	1320	Thailand	8.2792, 98.9342
68579	1519	Gunung Lawit	1292	Malaysia	5.4250, 102.5883
68580	1395	Khao Langkha Tuek / เขาหลังคาตึก	1289	Thailand	9.3425, 98.6158

68597	1355	Khao Ron / เขาร้อน	1255	Thailand	7.5033, 99.8333
68603	1531	Ngayanni Kyauk Taung	1231	Myanmar, Thailand	12.8800, 99.1883
68605	1512	Gunung Tapis	1227	Malaysia	4.0125, 102.9101
68613	1276	Gunung Ledang / Mount Ophir	1204	Malaysia	2.3733, 102.6083
68618	1564	Nwalabo Taung	1186	Myanmar	13.9325, 98.4792
68620	1217	Gunung Jerai	1184	Malaysia	5.7867, 100.4342
68648	1159	Paungchon Taung	1110	Myanmar	14.3942, 98.0358
68660	1324	Gunung Ulu Soh	1090	Malaysia	5.0833, 101.0975
68665	1374	Khao Nan Yai / ยอดเขานันใหญ่	1088	Thailand	8.8825, 99.6967
68667	1307	Khao Men / เขาเหมน	1086	Thailand	8.2975, 99.6625
68668	1234	Gunung Bujang Melaka	1083	Malaysia	4.3333, 101.2017
68674	1530	Khao Nong: เขาหนอง	1070	Thailand	8.8333, 99.4942
68685	1533	Gunung Ulu Titi Basah	1059	Malaysia, Thailand	5.7998, 101.3166
68687	1400	Huingye Taung	1055	Myanmar	14.4183, 98.2400
68698	2171	Gunung Chamah	1041	Malaysia	5.2275, 101.5742
68702	1280	Khao Nang / เขานาง	1036	Thailand	8.9750, 99.6950
68707	1391	Gunung Ulu Bakar / Gunung Palas	1029	Malaysia	4.3033, 102.9175
68713	1933	Gunung Liang	1020	Malaysia	3.8025, 101.5920
68716	1191	Khao Ta We / เขาตะเว	1018	Thailand	6.1225, 101.8050
68728	1251	Khao Luang / ยอดเขาหลวง	1005	Myanmar, Thailand	11.6517, 99.5792
68701	1038	Gunung Kajang, Pulau Tioman	1038	Malaysia	2.7700, 104.1542

Gunung Benum, AS573

Gunung Benum is also spelt Benom and the name allegedly originates from the Khmer word Phnom (or Phnum) meaning hill or mountain. Gunung Benum therefore means Mount Mountain.

Gunung Bintang, AS573
Rob Woodall, June 2022

If you like bureaucracy, rain and leeches, you'll love Malaysia. Gunung Bintang (star mountain) was a truly unpleasant ascent. Some people have climbed it in a day, avoiding a rainy camp. Deividas and I took a mandatory guide. We were met at Penang airport and taken to the start of the route. The trail is poor and obscure in places, but better higher up. It rained heavily for much of our ascent and even more heavily on the way down. Our guide suggested we camp low down on an old level platform. We looked at the several dozen leeches craning upwards from the ground and on our shoes, and opted to camp higher up. Leeches are small in their unfed state and not easy to detect. They inject an anaesthetic and an anti-coagulant, meaning that bleeding continues for quite a while after they have left. I react badly to them, with wounds itching and weeping for several days before eventually healing. The effect seems to be the same whether they are removed or leave of their own accord. The best chance is to pick them off before they have got started, but this is not always easy. This first time I used leech socks, but this just gave them more places to hide. Tucking trousers into socks worked better but they still got into the shoes. Guides prefer shorts and flip-flops for better visibility but not great traction. Preventive measures seem to include soap, washing powder, salt and tobacco.

AS574 Red River – Mekong Area

Id	Height	Name	Drop	Country	Location
68510	2979	Tà Chì Nhù	1933	Vietnam	21.5707, 104.3065
68516	3076	Phu Si Lùng	1732	China, Vietnam	22.6258, 102.7875
68522	2540	Phu Tra	1677	Vietnam	22.1683, 103.5892
68528	3143	Fan Si Pan / Đỉnh Phan Xi Păng	1613	Vietnam	22.3034, 103.7754
68540	2124	Phu Nam Tong	1499	Vietnam	22.3000, 102.7308
68546	2109	Phu Tả Tổng	1470	Vietnam	22.3667, 102.6833
68557	1870	Phou Phakhao	1371	Lao	20.7392, 102.6375
68560	2178	Phu Huổi Long	1361	Vietnam	21.6358, 103.1417
68561	3370	Ulyan Shan	1359	China	24.3892, 100.6883
68562	1685	Núi Bù Luông / Fafong	1358	Vietnam	20.4775, 105.0883
68568	2913	Núi Lang Cung	1340	Vietnam	21.9024, 104.2308
68593	2960	Aylao Shan	1259	China	23.0267, 102.8825
68596	1637	Núi Lop / Bu	1256	Vietnam	21.5908, 104.6458
68614	1296	Núi Tản Viên – Đỉnh Vua	1193	Vietnam	21.0582, 105.3672
68619	2094	Phou Thonglat *	1186	Lao	20.8733, 100.9808
68621	1977	Phou Chakhuen *	1180	Lao	21.1952, 100.9897
68624	1895	Tam Fuk	1173	Vietnam	21.4842, 103.4133
68631	3096	Phu Ta Leng	1147	Vietnam	22.4231, 103.6036
68632	1781	Núi Khe Ho	1143	Vietnam	21.7592, 104.5192
68635	2750	Hapu Shan *	1135	China	23.2017, 102.5800
68638	1890	Pha Luong	1127	Lao, Vietnam	20.6725, 104.6350
68642	3150	Ailao Shan	1120	China	24.2175, 101.3250
68646	1981	Phu Kiu Han / Nam He	1113	Vietnam	22.0492, 103.0342
68649	2900	Ulyan Shan	1110	China	23.4875, 101.0233
68650	1980	Maosaofeng / Ngai Thầu	1107	Vietnam	22.3117, 103.2217
68652	2085	Jiahe Shan *	1101	China	22.7258, 101.9408
68661	2610	Nauda Shan	1090	China	23.3283, 100.7433
68664	1661	Phou Phaphaniang	1088	Lao	19.9633, 100.6417
68670	2504	Núi Tà Cay Đắng	1078	Vietnam	21.6925, 104.1367
68678	2150	Yunxian Shan *	1069	China	22.9417, 100.6517
68680	1935	Phou Dông-Ngon	1069	Lao	19.9371, 101.3800
68689	1807	Nam Quan	1054	Vietnam	21.9983, 103.3758
68700	2640	Qimaba Shan *	1040	China	22.9183, 102.2325
68705	1867	Núi Pú Nhung	1033	Vietnam	21.9975, 103.2317
68709	2765	Phu Chiem Ban	1027	Vietnam	21.3542, 104.4300
68712	1670	Phou Bakha	1021	Lao	20.6367, 100.3142
68718	2025	Phou Kheukhanliam	1017	China	22.0617, 101.5758
68721	1975	Nui Sa Long *	1011	Vietnam	21.8208, 103.1675

AS575 Annamite Mountains

Id	Height	Name	Drop	Country	Location
68502	2598	Ngoc Linh	2208	Vietnam	15.0692, 107.9750
68505	2830	Phou Bia	2079	Lao	18.9808, 103.1517
68506	2420	Chư Yang Sin	2055	Vietnam	12.4063, 108.4242
68526	2720	Phou Xai Lai Leng	1622	Lao, Vietnam	19.1975, 104.1817
68529	2286	Rao Co	1602	Lao, Vietnam	18.1575, 105.4125
68539	2051	Chư Mư	1505	Vietnam	12.6947, 108.9431
68542	2625	Phou Sansoum	1490	Lao	19.1283, 103.8055
68545	1716	Phou Phiamay	1475	Lao	15.3017, 106.4017
68549	2051	Phou Xe Xap *	1436	Lao	16.0583, 106.8517
68554	2212	Phou Pha Banh	1397	Lao	19.7133, 102.3392
68555	1860	Phou Sè	1390	Lao	18.7652, 102.7043
68556	2452	Phu Hút	1389	Vietnam	19.6992, 104.7133
68559	2585	Phou Sao	1365	Lao	19.1558, 103.4667
68564	2066	Dông Be	1350	Lao	16.1176, 107.1997
68569	2461	Phou Mieng	1337	Lao	19.1750, 102.6383
68575	1563	Núi Cho	1318	Vietnam	19.8953, 105.1774
68577	1701	Động Voi Mẹp	1293	Vietnam	16.7692, 106.7130
68578	1654	Phou Sang	1292	Lao	18.4542, 102.7467
68583	1361	Hòn Bà	1278	Vietnam	12.3992, 109.0517
68584	2017	Phou Kopi	1272	Lao, Vietnam	17.8133, 105.6800
68594	2071	Phou Katta II	1256	Lao	18.6283, 103.3975
68595	1981	Phou Nagning *	1256	Lao	18.6800, 102.9583
68600	2287	Núi Bi Doup	1238	Vietnam	12.0908, 108.6625
68604	1528	Núi Bạch Mã	1231	Vietnam	16.1937, 107.9684
68609	2280	Phou Loi	1215	Lao	20.2717, 103.1967
68616	2220	Phou Patang *	1190	Lao	15.7058, 107.1808
68626	1994	Phou Larek	1159	Lao	18.6892, 103.2575
68628	1451	Hao Chu Hi	1156	Vietnam	11.7848, 108.9900
68629	1915	Phou Hindam *	1155	Lao, Vietnam	20.4317, 104.6158
68630	1853	Phou Ko	1153	Lao	18.9283, 102.6167
68633	1538	Phou Huasua	1143	Lao	18.6975, 103.4925
68634	1671	Phou Ho	1142	Lao	18.5350, 103.3692
68637	1774	Động Ngai	1127	Vietnam	16.3467, 107.2250
68639	1623	Co Ta Roun	1123	Lao, Vietnam	17.2944, 106.3000
68640	1773	Chu Mom Ray	1122	Vietnam	14.4583, 107.7392
68651	1616	Pha Lay	1105	Lao	19.1092, 102.0850
68657	1821	Phou Chomvoy	1099	Lao	18.4112, 105.0206
68673	1490	Bà Nà	1071	Vietnam	15.9982, 107.9857
68679	2118	Lao Pi	1069	Lao	19.4117, 102.1708
68686	2218	Phou San	1056	Lao	19.6758, 103.3579
68688	1560	Pha Kouang	1055	Lao	20.5878, 102.6138

Id		Name		Country	Location
68695	1731	Phou Houa Sang	1047	Lao	19.0675, 102.3608
68696	1636	Núi Marrai	1045	Vietnam	11.9642, 108.8517
68699	1265	Phou Houang	1040	Lao	15.9542, 106.0700
68704	1397	Phou Louang	1033	Lao	17.2942, 105.8758
68708	1578	Phou Ônghôn	1028	Lao	18.0754, 104.8119
68710	1865	Ngok Gle Iang	1024	Vietnam	15.3975, 107.8917
68711	1380	Phou Chomgnôk-Gnai	1022	Lao	18.4267, 104.2183
68719	1302	Núi Ông	1013	Vietnam	11.0808, 107.7917
68720	1039	Núi Chúa	1012	Vietnam	11.7325, 109.1283
68724	1982	Tadung	1009	Vietnam	11.8580, 108.0356
68727	2194	Núi Muong Xen *	1006	Vietnam	19.3042, 104.1320

AS576 Central Southeast Asia

Id	Height	Name	Drop	Country	Location
68514	1813	Phnom Aural / ភ្នំឱរ៉ាល់	1744	Cambodia	12.0325, 104.1708
68521	2120	Phu Soi Dao / ภูสอยดาว	1686	Lao, Thailand	17.7312, 101.0072
68533	1759	Phnom Samkos / ភ្នំសំកុស	1580	Cambodia	12.1558, 103.0433
68551	1633	Khao Sai Dao Tai / เขาสอยดาวใต้	1420	Thailand	12.9283, 102.2017
68576	1445	Phu Kao	1312	Lao	14.8967, 105.8000
68581	1794	Phu Thap Boek / ภูทับเบิก	1285	Thailand	16.9067, 101.0867
68683	1351	Khao Rom / เขาร่ม	1061	Thailand	14.3833, 101.4225
68684	1656	Doi Phu Miang / ดอยภูเมี่ยง	1059	Thailand	17.5583, 100.7467
68703	1286	Phou Malông	1036	Lao	15.0242, 105.8283

Phnom Samkos, AS576
Rob Woodall, July 2023

The highest point in Cambodia, Phnom Aural, is climbed quite frequently, usually in two days. Our guide was happy to arrange a one-day climb. Sensing an open door, I asked about the other Ultra in Cambodia, Phnom Samkos. He checked with some contacts then confirmed it was possible. We asked him to come up with an itinerary including the amazing Angkor Wat temple complex. Phnom Samkos was assigned a mere half day, which sounded promising. We met our guides in the late morning and were taken off on two motorbikes. Deividas was on a powerful dirt bike but I was on the back of the other one. Our easy farm track soon deteriorated. We dismounted to wade a river. I dismounted several more times, as the bike I was on couldn't handle the more serious obstacles with two people. At one point my bike fell spectacularly into a large muddy puddle. Our drivers eventually gave up. From the height and distance remaining, it was clearly going to take several hours more. The half-day estimate had not factored in how difficult the tracks can become outside the dry season. A few kilometres of muddy, swampy track-walking led to a camp site, and from there a reasonably well-defined hiking trail led to the summit. We were already using head torches by the time we got back down to the camp site. From there the four hours of slippery, boggy, leechy tracks were purgatory and the subsequent motorbike ride down was pretty terrifying. After dismounting a couple of times for difficult sections, I jogged down and waited for the bikes beyond the river crossing. It was midnight before we were cleaned up and in bed. It was a long 'half day', but worth it for a new Ultra with no previous logged ascents.

AS58 Malay Archipelago

Gunung Lewotolo, AS585 (Daniel Patrick Quinn)

The Malay Archipelago

The Malay Archipelago is the chain of islands between mainland Southeast Asia and Australasia. There is more than one definition, as the island of New Guinea is sometimes considered to be part of Oceania, as in this publication (region OC70). The Philippines are also listed separately (AS59) as they are an archipelago of their own, though often regarded as a sub-division of the Malay Archipelago.

The term is most strongly associated with British naturalist Alfred Russel Wallace and his publication *The Malay Archipelago* (1869). The Wallace Line is a faunal boundary line separating Asia from Wallacea, which is a transitional zone or sub-division in eastern Indonesia between Asia and Australasia. The line runs north-south through the archipelago between Borneo and Sulawesi and Bali and Lombok. It is one of several boundaries drawn up by naturalists.

The floral and faunal division can be explained by the nature of the environment during the Last Glacial Maximum around 20000 years ago, when sea level was over 100 metres lower than today. Given the much lower sea level, areas which today are separate islands either side of the Wallace Line were in many instances connected to each other, forming larger islands. In the west was the ancient land mass of Sunda (mainland Southeast Asia as far eastwards as Borneo and Bali), while Wallacea was a mini-archipelago to the east (from Sulawesi and Lombok). The larger land mass of Sahul was across another faunal boundary line further to the east, comprising the Aru Islands, New Guinea, the Australian mainland and Tasmania.

Back during the Last Glacial Maximum and the days of Sunda and Sahul, species could spread throughout areas which were once connected but are now different islands. Yet crossing the Wallace Line, over deep parts of the ocean, was impossible and this prevented species from making the jump across from one side to the other. For example, this is probably the reason that tigers were never known to have existed further east than Bali. There is no conclusive evidence of tigers having been in Borneo, although given the geography of Sunda it is possible that a long-extinct Bornean tiger did once exist.

The vast changes in the environment over the last 20000 years have affected the landscape as well as the flora and fauna. Several key cols which are now submerged would have been well above sea level during the Last Glacial Maximum. The summits of some islands which are today less than 1000 metres above sea level would at that time have been Ribus connected to larger land masses. These ancient ex-Ribus probably include the 995-metre high Gunung Manukoko in Timor-Leste, the 990-metre Gunung Samlor near western Indonesian Papua, and the 986-metre Gunung Maru on the island of Pura, but probably do not include the 913-metre Pulau Besar near Flores or Wawo Lantambaga, on what is today the 909-metre high island of Wawonii.

AS580 Borneo

Id	Height	Name	Drop	Country	Location
69001	4095	Gunung Kinabalu – Low's Peak	4095	Malaysia	6.0751, 116.5583
69035	2376	Gunung Mulu	2025	Malaysia	4.0463, 114.9304
69036	2300	Bukit Raya	2017	Indonesia	-0.6600, 5112.6889
69038	2423	Gunung Murud	1964	Malaysia	3.9049, 115.4883
69046	1901	Gunung Besar – Halau-halau	1801	Indonesia	-2.7106, 115.6260
69058	2643	Gunung Trusmadi	1702	Malaysia	5.5525, 116.5158

69067	1682	Gunung Niut	1639	Indonesia	1.0025, 109.9333
69072	2040	Bukit Batu	1574	Malaysia	2.2500, 113.7183
69076	2250	Batu Jumak	1558	Indonesia	1.8196, 115.2725
69077	1741	Gunung Saran	1558	Indonesia	-0.4242, 111.2958
69080	1570	Gunung Berumput – Gunung Kanyi	1539	Indonesia, Malaysia	1.7208, 109.6686
69085	1906	Bukit Sapat Hawung	1428	Indonesia	0.4454, 114.1304
69091	2195	Gunung Belayan	1408	Indonesia	1.5258, 115.9958
69101	1577	Gunung Beturan	1369	Indonesia	-0.0579, 112.4421
69102	2219	Gunung Curam *	1368	Indonesia	2.2741, 115.9607
69104	2240	Gunung Liangpran	1366	Indonesia	1.0446, 114.3671
69111	1428	Gunung Bawang	1320	Indonesia	0.9117, 109.3850
69115	1644	Gunung Berangin	1315	Indonesia	-0.4967, 111.0675
69116	1805	Gunung Lotung	1313	Malaysia	4.8700, 116.9825
69117	1830	Gunung Monkobo	1303	Malaysia	5.8200, 116.9550
69118	2024	Gunung Kujat	1295	Indonesia	2.4830, 116.4938
69120	1578	Gunung Kanamu	1280	Indonesia	-0.7307, 113.1469
69123	1421	Gunung Merdai / Gunung Bentuang	1263	Indonesia	0.8776, 110.2506
69131	1552	Gunung Pemancung	1232	Indonesia	-0.7254, 112.1755
69135	1325	Gunung Beriun	1221	Indonesia	1.3164, 117.4678
69138	1506	Gunung Rangga	1218	Indonesia	-0.6862, 111.2371
69141	1890	Gunung Kelembit	1202	Indonesia	2.8605, 115.9179
69142	1321	Gunung Biwa	1201	Indonesia	-0.6000, 110.8233
69146	1580	Gunung Batutenobong	1191	Indonesia	0.4508, 113.1992
69148	1377	Gunung Sebayan	1175	Indonesia	-1.1063, 110.9888
69150	1490	Gunung Imbak *	1168	Malaysia	5.0700, 117.2067
69149	1311	Bukit Bulud Tawai	1168	Malaysia	5.5183, 117.1242
69153	1220	Gunung Tutoop	1156	Indonesia	0.9133, 111.6283
69155	1600	Gunung Kalulong	1149	Malaysia	3.2200, 114.6708
69156	1461	Banjaran Dulit	1148	Malaysia	3.1583, 114.3200
69158	2005	Gunung Kerihun	1140	Indonesia	1.0354, 113.8896
69159	1516	Gunung Kongpas	1139	Indonesia	2.0533, 116.6325
69160	2064	Gunung Latuk	1135	Indonesia	2.8808, 115.6833
69164	2050	Gunung Mudung Dadu	1131	Indonesia, Malaysia	1.5772, 114.6138
69166	1767	Gunung Lawit	1128	Indonesia	1.3420, 112.9558
69168	1252	Gunung Kundas	1125	Indonesia	2.4758, 116.8883
69169	1593	Bukit Meliat	1117	Malaysia	4.4142, 116.9525
69170	1151	Gunung Palung	1115	Indonesia	-1.2334, 110.1448
69174	1964	Gunung Kayan *	1104	Indonesia	2.1754, 115.2996
69176	1923	Gunung Melatai	1104	Indonesia, Malaysia	1.3105, 113.5680
69177	1210	Gunung Kehuma	1102	Indonesia	0.9350, 111.3383
69178	1308	Gunung Kujau	1101	Indonesia	-0.2258, 111.2667

Id	Height	Name	Drop	Country	Location
69179	1770	Gunung Batuensambang	1098	Indonesia	0.1387, 113.1088
69184	1290	Gunung Nyapa	1081	Indonesia	1.7714, 117.4257
69185	2169	Gunung Harun	1076	Indonesia	4.1256, 115.8071
69187	1312	Gunung Magdalena	1065	Malaysia	4.4980, 117.9282
69190	1159	Gunung Kenepai	1062	Indonesia	0.7100, 111.7175
69191	1236	Gunung Lumut	1059	Indonesia	-1.3962, 115.9903
69193	1660	Gunung Nyaan	1053	Indonesia	1.0080, 115.0049
69194	1285	Gunung Kahung	1052	Indonesia	-3.6904, 115.0307
69198	1609	Gunung Antulai	1043	Malaysia	4.6767, 116.3475
69201	1642	Gunung Batuayau	1037	Indonesia	0.7454, 114.8796
69209	1208	Gunung Ular	1021	Indonesia	-1.5833, 111.5908
69212	1626	Gunung Murud Kecil	1020	Malaysia	3.3342, 115.1367
69213	1235	Gunung Beratus	1019	Indonesia	-1.0211, 116.3362
69214	1073	Bukit Kana	1019	Malaysia	2.6667, 112.8567
69202	1035	Gunung Ranai, Natuna Besar	1035	Indonesia	3.9756, 108.3362
69207	1030	Gunung Cabang, Pulau Karimata	1030	Indonesia	-1.6034, 108.9038

AS581 Sulawesi

Id	Height	Name	Drop	Country	Location
69005	3440	Latimojong – Bulu Rantemario	3440	Indonesia	-3.3851, 120.0243
69013	2886	Moncong Lompobatang	2868	Indonesia	-5.3536, 119.9347
69020	2890	Fuyu Sojol	2573	Indonesia	0.5774, 120.2048
69026	2870	Bulu Kandela / Buyu Kondorung	2250	Indonesia	-1.2991, 121.5429
69027	2650	Gunung Mekongga	2221	Indonesia	-3.6644, 121.2367
69028	3074	Tanete Gandangdewata	2140	Indonesia	-2.7480, 119.3685
69033	2565	Gunung Tumpu	2054	Indonesia	-1.0643, 122.1903
69040	2590	Pegunungan Pompangeo	1883	Indonesia	-1.6836, 120.9986
69041	1990	Gunung Klabat	1847	Indonesia	1.4533, 125.0313
69048	2253	Bukii Galang	1794	Indonesia	1.0626, 120.9345
69051	2403	Buyu Lumut	1756	Indonesia	-1.2036, 121.8034
69052	1964	Huidu Matabulawa	1756	Indonesia	0.4902, 123.6735
69059	2495	Bulu Torompupu	1681	Indonesia	-1.4248, 119.8563
69071	3016	Buyu Tolangi-Balease	1588	Indonesia	-2.4057, 120.5419
69075	2227	Huidu Tentolomatinan	1561	Indonesia	0.9388, 121.7765
69083	2410	Ibuyule Malino	1476	Indonesia	0.7058, 120.8876
69086	1809	Gunung Soputan	1425	Indonesia	1.1125, 124.7350
69095	2593	Gunung Tokala	1392	Indonesia	-1.6124, 121.6708
69098	1772	Gunung Ambang	1374	Indonesia	0.7571, 124.4160
69113	1540	Gunung Tompotika	1319	Indonesia	-0.6812, 123.1108
69129	1694	Bulu Tondongkarambu	1243	Indonesia	-4.7586, 119.8080
69130	2421	Osu Nando'oto	1235	Indonesia	-3.3861, 121.5577

Id	Height	Name		Drop	Country	Location
69132	2072	Gunung Boliohutu – Huido Ileile		1228	Indonesia	0.8864, 122.5069
69140	2730	Buntu Tinangko		1210	Indonesia	-2.1025, 119.8112
69144	2855	Gunung Kambuno / Bulu Lantangunta		1199	Indonesia	-2.3547, 120.0717
69143	1930	Gunung Batui		1199	Indonesia	-1.3610, 122.0814
69147	1808	Gunung Masamba		1180	Indonesia	-1.7545, 121.2525
69151	1694	Gunung Dapi		1167	Indonesia	0.7000, 122.0324
69206	1681	Buttu Tinaungan		1030	Indonesia	-2.7367, 119.0458
69208	2242	Bulu Mopeaanooleo		1026	Indonesia	-3.2233, 121.1950
69217	1971	Buntu Ambeso		1005	Indonesia	-3.2137, 119.8034
69219	2324	Bulu Nti		1002	Indonesia	-1.0868, 119.8007
69042	1827	Gunung Karangetang, Pulau Siau		1827	Indonesia	2.7755, 125.4062
69074	1570	Gunung Sabampolulu, Pulau Kabaena		1570	Indonesia	-5.3086, 121.9559
69109	1340	Gunung Awu, Pulau Sangihe Besar		1340	Indonesia	3.6883, 125.4477
69189	1063	Kabawo Wani, Pulau Buton		1063	Indonesia	-4.4866, 122.9699
69205	1031	Gunung Tombia, Pulau Peleng		1031	Indonesia	-1.3650, 122.9600

AS582 Maluku

Id	Height	Name	Island	Drop	Country	Location
69010	3030	Gunung Binaiya – Puncak Siale	Seram	3030	Indonesia	-3.1733, 129.4556
69203	1334	Gunung Toplana	Seram	1034	Indonesia	-3.3835, 128.5000
69220	1473	Solita Batu	Seram	1002	Indonesia	-3.0565, 128.6326
69018	2700	Gunung Kapalatmada	Buru	2700	Indonesia	-3.3007, 126.2199
69167	1750	Gunung Batakbual	Buru	1127	Indonesia	-3.5141, 127.1482
69032	2085	Buku Sibela	Pulau Bacan	2085	Indonesia	-0.7370, 127.5244
69163	1155	Buku Rica / Buku Raroang	Pulau Bacan	1132	Indonesia	-0.4922, 127.6119
69053	1750	Gunung Kiematubu	Pulau Tidore	1750	Indonesia	0.6620, 127.4030
69056	1715	Gunung Gamalama	Pulau Ternate	1715	Indonesia	0.8091, 127.3330
69068	1611	Pulau Obi	Pulau Obi	1611	Indonesia	-1.5381, 127.6687
69073	1571	Gunung Gamkonora	Halmahera	1571	Indonesia	1.3784, 127.5341
69094	1442	Bukit Watowato	Halmahera	1397	Indonesia	1.0134, 128.1089
69181	1250	Buku Rogirogi / Bukit Uwatcain	Halmahera	1092	Indonesia	-0.2660, 127.7569
69183	1377	Gunung Ibu	Halmahera	1089	Indonesia	1.4907, 127.6305
69218	1030	Gunung Jailolo	Halmahera	1005	Indonesia	1.0804, 127.4393
69089	1415	Lida Godo	Pulau Taliabu	1415	Indonesia	-1.7939, 124.7248
69105	1357	Gunung Kie Besi	Pulau Makian	1357	Indonesia	0.3189, 127.3911
69136	1220	Gunung Sabatai	Pulau Morotai	1220	Indonesia	2.2291, 128.4337
69161	1135	Gunung Loku	Pulau Mangole	1135	Indonesia	-1.8318, 126.0525
69200	1038	Gunung Salahutu	Pulau Ambon	1038	Indonesia	-3.5457, 128.2558

Gunung Karangetang, AS581
Rob Woodall, October 2022

Deividas and I weren't planning to go to Siau, but our new friend, guide and volcano junkie Aris was keen to take us up Karangetang, so in a change of plan we flew to North Sulawesi and caught the fast ferry to Ulu, the main town of Pulau Siau. The highest point was currently the south summit, which was smoking enthusiastically, so it was just as well we had brought gas masks. Next morning we took an early motorbike taxi ride to the start of the route and hiked up to the local guide's house. We set off through steep soggy forest, then up striking rocky lichen-covered slopes. The last part of the ascent was typically unstable volcanic terrain. We put on our gas masks and explored a few pinnacles, unclear exactly where the highest point was. After deciding we were close enough, we left this unfriendly place and headed down in heavy rain, which continued all the way down. This, it turned out, was the start of a typhoon that prevented us from travelling to our next planned volcano, Gunung Awu. A few days later Karangetang erupted properly, so the summit will have relocated again. It was an amazing experience to be up there.

Gunung Ibu, AS582
Daniel Patrick Quinn, 2021

I climbed Gunung Ibu (mother mountain) one night in 2021, setting out at 9pm along the plantation tracks with a couple of villagers. Many local men were still working there late into the night, preparing raw coconut husks to be sold for various purposes. Once through the plantations we started to hear rockfall every few minutes. These rocks were being ejected during eruptions. When you are wandering up a dry creek filled with black volcanic sand, hearing boulders hurtling down the mountainside above you at night is both disconcerting and exhilarating. I was exhausted, having had only a couple of hours of rest, but we finally made it up onto the rim well before sunrise and could see what looked like glowing orange embers down below in the crater. This vision was accompanied by the frequent eerie sounds of what could be mistaken for a bull in a china shop knocking plates and bottles over every thirty seconds. Every few minutes came an eruption from the main cone, with orange jets spraying out and a large cloud of fine ash drifting across the night sky. It is an incredible memory, even though I didn't manage to reach the highest point of the rim due to dense vegetation and lack of a trail.

AS583 Sumatera

Id	Height	Name	Drop	Country	Location
69002	3805	Gunung Kerinci	3805	Indonesia	-1.6966, 101.2642
69012	3466	Gunung Leuser – Puncak Tanpa Nama	2940	Indonesia	3.7976, 97.2193
69021	3173	Gunung Dempo	2450	Indonesia	-4.0155, 103.1280
69025	2919	Gunung Talamau	2329	Indonesia	0.0789, 99.9839
69030	2891	Gunung Marapi – Puncak Garuda	2116	Indonesia	-0.3804, 100.4736
69044	3085	Gunung Kurik	1811	Indonesia	4.2517, 97.4206
69047	2457	Gunung Sibuatan	1800	Indonesia	2.9183, 98.4235
69049	2933	Gunung Masurai	1789	Indonesia	-2.5025, 101.8578
69054	2877	Gunung Singgalang	1723	Indonesia	-0.3900, 100.3308
69055	2315	Gunung Hulumasen	1723	Indonesia	5.04410, 95.6334

69063	3011	Gunung Bandahara	1642	Indonesia	3.7492, 97.7817
69064	2850	Gunung Patah	1635	Indonesia	-4.2576, 103.3057
69069	1810	Seulawah Agam	1610	Indonesia	5.4471, 95.6559
69078	2885	Bur ni Geureudong	1551	Indonesia	4.8106, 96.8163
69079	2493	Bukit Daun – Gunung Hulu Palik	1541	Indonesia	-3.3920, 102.3425
69082	2801	Peuet Sague – Gunung Kemiki	1492	Indonesia	4.9151, 96.3288
69087	2199	Gunung Malea	1422	Indonesia	0.8600, 99.7684
69096	2102	Gunung Tanggamus	1383	Indonesia	-5.4271, 104.6748
69097	2262	Gunung Sago	1379	Indonesia	-0.3241, 100.6732
69099	2230	Gunung Pesagi	1373	Indonesia	-4.9233, 104.1467
69100	2274	Gunung Hijau	1369	Indonesia	0.1425, 100.2417
69103	2173	Gunung Kulabu	1366	Indonesia	0.4717, 99.8975
69121	2543	Gunung Raya	1273	Indonesia	-2.2283, 101.4300
69122	1682	Gunung Pesawaran-Ratai	1265	Indonesia	-5.5134, 105.0952
69125	1281	Gunung Rajabasa	1258	Indonesia	-5.7816, 105.6274
69127	2732	Gunung Tujuh	1250	Indonesia	-1.7014, 101.4403
69137	2690	Gunung Pantaicermin	1219	Indonesia	-1.2783, 100.8017
69154	2115	Gunung Tangkit Tebak	1150	Indonesia	-5.0084, 104.5754
69162	2450	Gunung Sinabung	1133	Indonesia	3.1714, 98.3906
69165	2448	Gunung Gedang	1130	Indonesia	-2.7362, 101.9195
69175	2985	Gunung Abong-Abong	1104	Indonesia	4.2416, 96.7950
69180	2635	Bur ni Kelieten	1093	Indonesia	4.5522, 96.9576
69188	2507	Gunung Sumbing	1063	Indonesia	-2.4149, 101.7292
69192	1796	Gunung Gumai	1057	Indonesia	-3.8837, 103.2784
69195	1440	Dolok Gongonan	1051	Indonesia	1.1529, 99.3301
69196	2597	Gunung Talang	1047	Indonesia	-0.9789, 100.6816
69204	2215	Gunung Pangulubao	1031	Indonesia	2.5899, 99.0792
69216	2015	Dolok Nabibong	1010	Indonesia	1.7517, 99.3858
69152	1165	Gunung Daik, Pulau Lingga	1165	Indonesia	-0.1959, 104.5501

Gunung Tangkit Tebak, AS583
Daniel Patrick Quinn

Most of my hiking experiences in Indonesia have been excellent adventures. When I lived in Jakarta, Tangkit Tebak in Sumatra's southernmost province of Lampung was my closest unclimbed Ribu and there was almost no information on anyone having climbed it. The Indonesian word 'tebak' actually means 'guess' and I was left guessing for several years on how to approach this. My first trip to the area did not prove fruitful, though I visited an ancient megalithic site. Some time later, after having found a Sumatran hiker who had been to the top and was willing to guide, I convinced a friend with a car to attempt it with me. We took the ferry over from Java to Sumatra and were treated to a clear view of Rakata island, the highest remnants of the original Krakatau volcano that famously erupted in 1883.

Once in Sumatra and with our guide, it emerged that he had injured his hand quite badly with a machete and would therefore be hiking one-handed, with the injured hand kept in a tied rag inside a plastic bag. Given how challenging the terrain turned out to be, with spiny plants, pathless sections of steep mud full of leeches, narrow crumbly ridges, unstable rocks and crevices, and mossy overhangs that could collapse at any moment, it was a wonder he contemplated going ahead with this mission. Indeed, it was one of the most difficult Ribus I have attempted. We camped on a mossy overhang as there was nowhere more suitable.

The last few metres before the summit involved a short vertical cliff with nothing to hold on to except some shrubbery and a rope so thin it was more like a shoelace, held by the guide's friend. My friend managed it, against my wishes, as I sat and wondered what I was going to have to tell his family. He made it to the top but I didn't. One of my few summit failures. Better to live another day.

I was disappointed and exhausted and it rained heavily on the descent. This brought out the leeches in great numbers. We were glad to be approaching the end of our ordeal when we reached the edge of the plantations to find several uniformed officials waiting for us, with at least one recording us on video. Back down at the village, representatives from immigration, police, army and forestry had congregated, along with local journalists. Either they were all bored and in need of a weekend event to attend or they believed that we were up to no good. We wanted desperately to get changed out of our muddy, wet and leech-ridden clothes but were not allowed to until we had been questioned and our vehicle searched. The forestry guy would not believe that we were hiking. He was convinced that we were poaching or doing some other illegal activity, and he accused me of smelling of alcohol. We were told that we needed a permit to enter the forest at all, a common Asian inverse of the European idea that you can wander anywhere unless specifically told not to. If there's no official trail and you don't have the 'paperwork' then you shouldn't be in there at all.

The officials seemed disappointed at having found no tiger skins, rare wood, mining equipment or even empty beer cans. They would have to put things right somehow, and what better way than to have us sign letters of apology and then form a circle with all the uniformed men and outstretch our right fists in a bizarre display of solidarity.

We finally got permission to get changed out of our clothes and boots but were then hauled to the nearest immigration office, where a mean-faced and permanently smoking boss sat outside trying to look like it happened all the time. The whole team were in on a Sunday evening for this 'incident' of a couple of foreigners going for a walk in the forest. After the obligatory selfies with staff members keen to share photos of foreigners on their social media profiles, several cups of unfiltered black coffee and more apology letters, we were free to drive back to the ferry terminal for an overnight ferry back to Java. No sleep. It was traumatic, and for months afterwards I was paranoid that towards the end of a hike there would be more uniformed officials waiting to capture us at the forest's edge. Thankfully the local journalists got our names, nationalities and professions completely mixed up so we appeared in the local press simply as two anonymous palefaces who had not got the proper permission to go for a walk in the country in which they lived.

AS584 Jawa

Id	Height	Name	Drop	Country	Location
69004	3676	Gunung Semeru	3676	Indonesia	-8.1079, 112.9227
69006	3428	Gunung Slamet	3284	Indonesia	-7.2391, 109.2200
69007	3265	Gunung Lawu	3118	Indonesia	-7.6273, 111.1946
69008	3332	Gunung Raung – Puncak Sejati	3069	Indonesia	-8.1256, 114.0467
69014	3339	Gunung Arjuno	2811	Indonesia	-7.7654, 112.5902
69015	3078	Gunung Ciremai	2792	Indonesia	-6.8930, 108.4069
69016	3088	Gunung Argopuro	2745	Indonesia	-7.9644, 113.5664
69019	3371	Gunung Sumbing – Puncak Rajawali	2627	Indonesia	-7.3834, 110.0712
69022	3145	Gunung Merbabu – Puncak Triangulasi	2432	Indonesia	-7.4542, 110.4397
69023	3020	Gunung Pangrango	2427	Indonesia	-6.7701, 106.9650
69029	2563	Gunung Liman	2130	Indonesia	-7.8204, 111.7569
69031	2821	Gunung Cikuray	2105	Indonesia	-7.3226, 107.8600
69050	3153	Gunung Sindoro	1764	Indonesia	-7.3005, 109.9972
69057	1778	Gunung Karang	1705	Indonesia	-6.2686, 106.0491
69060	2211	Gunung Salak	1679	Indonesia	-6.7161, 106.7336
69061	2868	Gunung Butak	1673	Indonesia	-7.9553, 112.4651
69070	1610	Gunung Muria – Puncak Songolikur	1602	Indonesia	-6.6162, 110.8903
69106	2930	Gunung Merapi	1356	Indonesia	-7.5397, 110.4470
69107	2215	Gunung Bukittunggul	1350	Indonesia	-6.8111, 107.7264
69110	2675	Gunung Papandayan – Gunung Malang	1339	Indonesia	-7.3289, 107.7159
69112	2050	Gunung Ungaran – Puncak Botak	1320	Indonesia	-7.1872, 110.3445
69124	2240	Gunung Galunggung – Gunung Beuticanar	1261	Indonesia	-7.2345, 108.0691
69139	2803	Gunung Ijen-Merapi	1218	Indonesia	-8.0627, 114.2620
69172	1684	Gunung Tampomas	1109	Indonesia	-6.7637, 107.9606
69173	1667	Gunung Lamongan – Gunung Tarub	1107	Indonesia	-7.9754, 113.3463
69199	1764	Gunung Sawal	1040	Indonesia	-7.1892, 108.2717
69210	1265	Gunung Baluran	1021	Indonesia	-7.8456, 114.3629
69211	1653	Gunung Penanggungan	1020	Indonesia	-7.6156, 112.6200

Gunung Galunggung, AS584

This is a huge, complex mountain massif consisting of Talaga Bodas lake and Kawah Saat crater in the north, Galunggung crater in the south and the highest peak, Gunung Beuticanar, lying in between, amongst a long ridge of forested peaks. The most recent large eruption was in 1982, when a British Airways flight from Kuala Lumpur in Malaysia to Perth in Australia was forced to make an emergency landing in Jakarta after all four of its engines failed, having filled with ash after dark. The first sign the pilots got that something was wrong was when St Elmo's Fire flickered across the windscreen, soon accompanied by the odour of smoke and then sulphur. The windscreen ended up blasted and pitted by the volcanic ash. Since then the main crater on Galunggung has been relatively calm, certainly compared with lively Gunung Papandayan nearby.

Gunung Papandayan, AS584

Daniel Patrick Quinn, August 2011

One weekend I took a friend who was new to living in Indonesia on a hike up Gunung Papandayan. The weather had been perfect. The plan had been to meet up with a local guide who had told me he knew the way to the mountain's highest point, Gunung Malang. There had been no confirmed reports of anyone having reached this peak, probably because it is covered in dense vegetation, but I fancied another try.

As often happens in Southeast Asia, it emerged that the guide didn't actually know the way to the summit, because there was no trail whatsoever, as I had previously concluded. Having anticipated this, I was happy enough hiking up to the peak known as Gunung Papandayan, which is the second highest peak of the range. It was quite a tough one and took quite a long time to reach – not many people go to this peak though the views of Tegal Alun and the main active craters were fantastic. Several years later I did make it back for a successful hike up to Gunung Malang, but both of the highest peaks were later closed to the general public.

We got back down to Pondok Salada where we had already set up tents to spend the night. Our guide wished us a pleasant evening and headed back down to the tourist office at the car park. The views in the late afternoon were excellent – quite a lot of smoke rising from one side of the crater walls and a large, full moon present in the sky from about 4.30pm. One thing that was rather strange was that another group of hikers who had planned to camp at Pondok Salada too were still not there.

All was fine until about 9pm, when we were settled into the tents to try to sleep. We then started to hear howling, presumably from wild dogs. They got closer and closer to us. Soon they were snarling at the tents and rummaging through our rubbish bag, which I had stupidly left open on the ground rather than tied to a tree branch. We tried not to attract their attention and stayed as still and as quiet as possible. Neither of us wanted to leave the tents. It was very eerie – we were the only people there, it was a full moon, there was all this howling going on and it got me recalling how it is known that a handful of big cats live in the Papandayan mountain area, in addition to a large number of wild pigs. I hadn't heard of the wild dogs here before. It was a very sleepless night as the beasts just wouldn't leave us alone – not a pleasant camping experience by any standard.

To add insult to injury, I received two text messages at just before 3am – both sent at around 4pm the day before and only just received due to the poor signal in the mountains. The first was from our guide who had reached the tourist office and found out that the alert level for Papandayan had been raised to Level 3 – standby for eruption. That was just one level below currently erupting. He told us we should come down for safety. Obviously this was impossible as I had only just received the message. We had another message from someone else saying the same thing. We had noticed some rather large plumes of smoke above the crater on Saturday afternoon and it now made sense why the other hiking group had not camped here too, but we didn't know about the increased frequency of volcanic earthquakes or that the gases rising from the crater were particularly lethal. We both had coughs and sore throats the following morning.

As soon as it was light we ventured outside to see if any beasts were still lurking and to pack up very quickly and head down the other side of the mountain in the direction of Pangalengan. This was something we had planned anyway but it made even more sense now given that to walk back through the main active crater area would have been pretty hazardous. All was quiet outside, apart from a few wild pigs grunting in the distance, and we set off at a great pace, stopping only for a few photos over the main crater with Cikuray beyond rising above the early morning mists. The trail down towards Cileuleuy and Pangalengan made a very pleasant stroll down a wide farm track but it was a very long way out. Luckily we found some crazy farm workers with off-road farm motorbikes who offered to take us all the way to Pangalengan. It turned out to be one of the most spectacular routes in West Java, despite the appalling nature of the tracks and road surfaces. We sped and weaved our way through tea plantations and were in Pangalengan in less than two hours. My new friend never came hiking with me again after this outing.

Gunung Raung, AS584
Rob Woodall, June 2007

Bob, Adam and I were making our way through Southeast Asia. After Gunung Kinabalu and Gunung Rinjani we arrived in East Java. Gunung Raung was less well known in 2007, but arriving at the base of the mountain we found guides – a man and his two sons who would take us up. It soon became apparent that they didn't know the way. They found a field worker who did, and so we continued. After some disagreement the trio abandoned us, leaving us carrying all the gear. Eventually we reached the rim of a spectacular, smoking mile-wide crater. Unfortunately the highest point was on the far side, and it was not the kind of crater rim you can walk around. That was the closest I got. Subsequent trips failed before they started, due to Covid 19, an eruption, and a damaged trail.

AS585 Nusa Tenggara

Id	Height	Name	Island	Drop	Country	Location
69003	3726	Gunung Rinjani	Lombok	3726	Indonesia	-8.4117, 116.4581
69009	3031	Gunung Agung	Bali	3031	Indonesia	-8.3407, 115.5036
69182	2276	Gunung Batukaru	Bali	1091	Indonesia	-8.3349, 115.0884
69011	2963	Ramelau – Foho Tatamailau	Timor	2963	Timor-Leste	-8.9065, 125.4935
69034	2372	Gunung Matebean Mane	Timor	2045	Timor-Leste	-8.6417, 126.5958
69037	2417	Gunung Mutis	Timor	1970	Indonesia	-9.5605, 124.2276
69134	1763	Gunung Mundo Perdido	Timor	1223	Timor-Leste	-8.7233, 126.3225
69145	1942	Foho Leohitu	Timor	1195	Timor-Leste	-9.0858, 125.2308
69157	1774	Fatu Timau	Timor	1143	Indonesia	-9.5806, 123.9400
69171	1929	Foho Leolako	Timor	1113	Timor-Leste	-8.9583, 125.2750
69215	2459	Foho Kabalaki	Timor	1014	Timor-Leste	-8.9525, 125.5983
69017	2722	Gunung Tambora	Sumbawa	2722	Indonesia	-8.2466, 117.9588
69045	1871	Olet Sangenges / Puncak Ngengas	Sumbawa	1804	Indonesia	-8.5803, 117.1222
69081	1628	Doro Dindi	Sumbawa	1514	Indonesia	-8.3939, 118.5424
69119	1433	Doro Pundunence	Sumbawa	1289	Indonesia	-8.4825, 118.9242
69024	2367	Poco Ngandonalu / Poco Pajung	Flores	2367	Indonesia	-8.6517, 120.4480
69065	2227	Gunung Inerie	Flores	1625	Indonesia	-8.8781, 120.9544
69084	1708	Gunung Egon	Flores	1453	Indonesia	-8.6759, 122.4550
69092	1484	Ili Mandiri	Flores	1401	Indonesia	-8.3143, 122.9678
69093	1703	Gunung Lewotobi	Flores	1398	Indonesia	-8.5545, 122.7819
69114	2137	Gunung Ebulobo	Flores	1315	Indonesia	-8.8171, 121.1905
69126	1754	Keli Lepembusu	Flores	1250	Indonesia	-8.6727, 121.8111

69186	1992	Gunung Curunumbeng / Poco Desu	Flores	1065	Indonesia	-8.7173, 120.3271
69197	1431	Ili Wukoh	Flores	1046	Indonesia	-8.5709, 122.6550
69039	1949	Sangeang Api	Pulau Sangeang	1949	Indonesia	-8.1959, 119.0698
69043	1821	Dola Koyakoya	Pulau Alor	1821	Indonesia	-8.2212, 125.0206
69062	1658	Ili Boleng	Pulau Adonara	1658	Indonesia	-8.3456, 123.2563
69066	1621	Ili Labalekang	Pulau Lembata	1621	Indonesia	-8.5445, 123.3843
69088	1455	Gunung Lewotolo	Pulau Lembata	1421	Indonesia	-8.2741, 123.5078
69128	1523	Ili Uyelewun	Pulau Lembata	1246	Indonesia	-8.2136, 123.7758
69090	1412	Gunung Lalaitu	Pulau Wetar	1412	Indonesia	-7.6842, 126.5133
69108	1344	Gunung Sirung – Kukka Taupekki	Pulau Pantar	1344	Indonesia	-8.5192, 124.1054
69133	1225	Gunung Wanggameti	Sumba	1225	Indonesia	-10.1164, 120.2364

Pantar, Lembata and Adonara
Daniel Patrick Quinn

Nusa Tenggara is home to some of the most mystical people and traditions on the planet – and some excellent Ribus. After spending a few days getting to the remote island of Pantar, we were surrounded by a group of village men chomping on betel nuts who prevented us from hiking up Gunung Sirung because such actions could apparently endanger the cashew nut harvest. Regrettably we withdrew. On Gunung Lewotolo on the neighbouring island of Lembata, we were told a story about ancient elephant tusks. Allegedly these tusks mated during the night to create tiny wriggling tusks that could sometimes be seen on the village roads beneath the volcano early in the morning. On Pulau Adonara we were forbidden from talking about maritime topics, including salt and fish, at any point during the hike up Ili Boleng, in case it brought bad luck on us.

Moncong Lompobatang, AS581 (Daniel Patrick Quinn)

AS59 Philippines

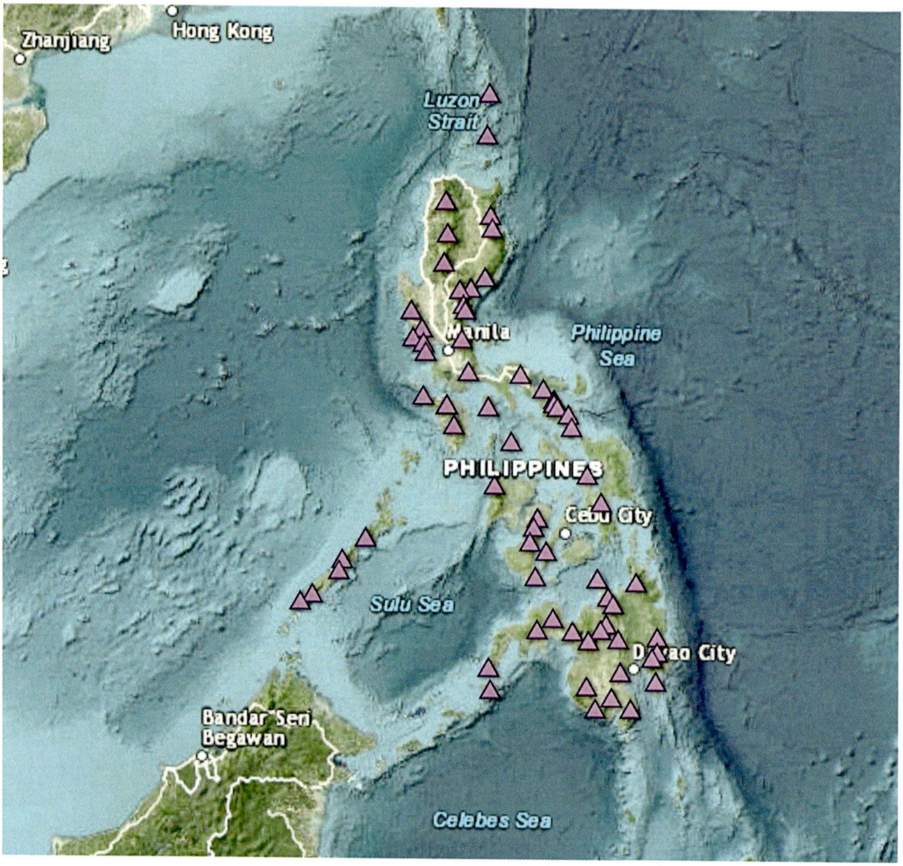

Mount Apo, AS592 (Deividas Valaitis)

AS590 Luzon

Id	Height	Name	Drop	Country	Location
69502	2926	Mount Pulag	2926	Philippines	16.5975, 120.8992
69506	2462	Mayon Volcano	2447	Philippines	13.2558, 123.6858
69512	2044	Mount Tapulao	2020	Philippines	15.4820, 120.1205
69513	2000	Mount Isarog	1950	Philippines	13.6592, 123.3733
69515	2169	Mount Banahaw	1918	Philippines	14.0675, 121.4925
69522	1901	Mount Mingan	1596	Philippines	15.4808, 121.4050
69524	2361	Mount Sicapoo	1582	Philippines	18.0133, 120.9392
69527	1565	Bulusan Volcano	1548	Philippines	12.7692, 124.0567
69528	1544	Mount Labo	1523	Philippines	14.0133, 122.7875
69533	1657	Mount Malinao	1368	Philippines	13.4025, 123.6075
69534	1844	Mount Dikatayan *	1367	Philippines	17.4108, 122.0767
69538	1841	Mount Anacuao	1334	Philippines	16.2542, 121.8892
69539	2618	Mount Cauitan	1302	Philippines	17.2475, 120.9925
69540	1421	Mount Bataan	1274	Philippines	14.5192, 120.4658
69541	1530	Mount Caladang	1250	Philippines	14.8092, 121.3367
69547	1584	Mount Negron	1154	Philippines	15.0925, 120.3675
69549	1280	Mount Natib	1121	Philippines	14.7117, 120.4008
69554	1950	Mount Guiwan	1061	Philippines	15.9451, 121.2865
69556	1102	Pocdol / Rock Dome	1049	Philippines	13.0492, 123.9608
69558	1100	Mount Balingkilat / Pointed Peak	1039	Philippines	14.8583, 120.1267
69559	1833	Mount Cetaceo	1018	Philippines	17.7042, 122.0533
69560	1750	Mount Cagayan *	1018	Philippines	16.0158, 121.5567
69564	1328	Mount Masaraga	1003	Philippines	13.3100, 123.5975
69565	1885	Mount Calaanan *	1002	Philippines	15.6183, 121.3625
69552	1088	Mount Pangasun, Babuyan Island	1088	Philippines	19.5250, 121.9525
69562	1009	Mount Iraya, Batan Island	1009	Philippines	20.4667, 122.0117

AS591 Central Philippines Islands

Id	Height	Name	Island	Drop	Country	Location
69503	2582	Mount Halcon	Mindoro	2582	Philippines	13.2625, 120.9950
69526	2364	Mount Baco	Mindoro	1560	Philippines	12.8208, 121.1733
69531	1520	Mount Calavite	Mindoro	1462	Philippines	13.4817, 120.4033
69505	2465	Mount Kanlaon	Negros	2465	Philippines	10.4100, 123.1300
69532	1862	Cuernos de Negros – Mount Talinis	Negros	1442	Philippines	9.2442, 123.1775
69537	1885	Mount Mandalagan	Negros	1340	Philippines	10.6375, 123.2358
69555	1492	Mount Irene	Negros	1053	Philippines	10.0367, 123.0633
69509	2117	Mount Madjaas	Panay	2117	Philippines	11.3892, 122.1625
69510	2085	Mount Mantalingajan	Palawan	2085	Philippines	8.8183, 117.6750
69521	1709	Victoria Peaks	Palawan	1617	Philippines	9.3650, 118.3342
69525	1603	Cleopatra Needle	Palawan	1577	Philippines	10.1242, 118.9950
69551	1338	Anepahan Peaks	Palawan	1093	Philippines	9.6183, 118.4475
69566	1036	Escapardo Peak	Palawan	1000	Philippines	8.6042, 117.3708
69511	2058	Mount Guiting-guiting	Sibuyan	2058	Philippines	12.4167, 122.5692

69520	1630	Mount Mambajao	Camiguin	1630	Philippines	9.1783, 124.7275
69535	1349	Mount Lobi	Leyte	1349	Philippines	11.0125, 124.8125
69536	1346	Mount Naliwatan	Biliran	1346	Philippines	11.6500, 124.4617
69546	1168	Mount Malindig / Mount Marlanga	Marinduque	1168	Philippines	13.2408, 122.0133
69553	1073	Mount Labalasan	Cebu	1073	Philippines	9.8367, 123.4508

AS592 Mindanao

Id	Height	Name	Drop	Country	Location
69501	2954	Mount Apo / Apo Sandawa	2954	Philippines	6.9873, 125.2710
69504	2670	Mount Tagubud	2575	Philippines	7.4450, 126.2267
69507	2938	Mount Dulang-dulang	2539	Philippines	8.1167, 124.9233
69508	2404	Mount Malindang	2287	Philippines	8.2175, 123.6367
69514	2286	Mount Matutum	1948	Philippines	6.3600, 125.0758
69516	1920	Mount Hilonghilong	1838	Philippines	9.0967, 125.7050
69517	2480	Mount Mangabon	1802	Philippines	8.5983, 125.0983
69518	2064	Mount Busa	1694	Philippines	6.1092, 124.6858
69519	1816	Kioto Mountains	1639	Philippines	6.1067, 125.5700
69523	2815	Mount Piapayungan / Mount Ragang	1590	Philippines	7.6908, 124.5075
69529	2880	Mount Kalatungan	1502	Philippines	7.9550, 124.8025
69530	1620	Mount Hamiguitan	1497	Philippines	6.7400, 126.1817
69542	2450	Mount Balatukan	1244	Philippines	8.7492, 124.9767
69543	1363	Mount Pasonanca *	1244	Philippines	7.0733, 122.0233
69544	1532	Mount Pinukis	1219	Philippines	7.9758, 123.2283
69545	1652	Mount Agtuuganon	1184	Philippines	7.7975, 126.2033
69548	2102	Mount Mabugnao *	1151	Philippines	7.3183, 126.0625
69550	1889	Gurain Mountains	1111	Philippines	7.9075, 124.1117
69557	1904	Mount Daguma Bagumbayan	1046	Philippines	6.6054, 124.4700
69563	1679	Mount Tangulang	1007	Philippines	7.7658, 125.2292
69561	1011	Basilan Peak, Basilan Island	1011	Philippines	6.5483, 122.0733

The Tagalog word for mountain, bundok, is not often used in the names of mountains in the Philippines because English is the country's second official language. The word 'bundok' has given rise to the American English word 'boondocks', meaning an inaccessible or unsophisticated place. In the southern Philippines, 'bukid' is more likely to be used than 'bundok', and is almost identical to the Indonesian and Malay word 'bukit', meaning hill.

Mindanao, Luzon and Panay
Rob Woodall, April 2023

The Philippines is a big archipelago with 66 Ribus (including 29 Ultras) on fifteen islands. Mindanao is quite troubled but its highest point, Mount Apo, is a popular climb, with an overnight camp and a scenic crater. We caught a spectacular rain storm on the way down, luckily finding shelter from the worst of it. We managed Mount Matutum too then flew to Luzon, where the peaks are more accessible. Transport was varied, including motor trikes, ancient charabancs and modern coaches. The highest point in Luzon, Mount Pulag, was another easy, popular hike. It has been surveyed to within a few millimetres, as a team spent a fortnight up there employing a range of techniques from traditional line survey to differential GNSS. Mount Madjaas on Panay was busy – we shared the campsite with a large group of Adventists. We also caught another rain storm, this time on summit day.

Africa

AF60 Atlas Mountains

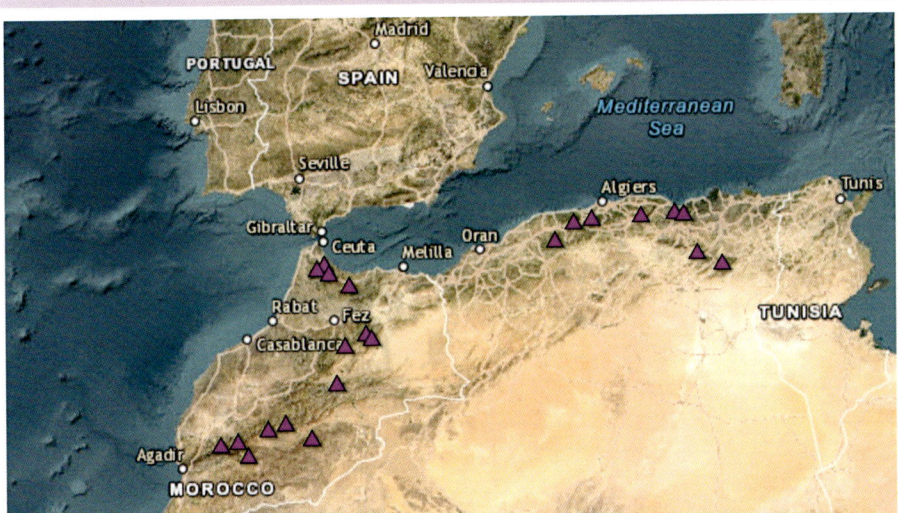

Djebel Tidirhine, AF600 (Deividas Valaitis)

AF600 North-western Atlas

Id	Height	Name	Drop	Country	Location
70003	2456	Djebel Tidirhine / جبل تدغين	1900	Morocco	34.8433, -4.5100
70005	3340	Adrar Bou Nacer / بوناصر	1642	Morocco	33.5627, -3.8860
70008	1926	Djebel Kelti	1479	Morocco	35.3583, -5.2750
70011	2170	Djebel Lakraa / Djebel Khmes	1168	Morocco	35.1317, -5.1467
70014	3172	Moussa ou Salah	1110	Morocco	33.6917, -4.0625
70020	2794	Djebel Tichoukt – Oum el Bent	1046	Morocco	33.3933, -4.6583
70022	1658	Djebel Kareha	1009	Morocco	35.2500, -5.4975

AF601 Maritime Atlas

Id	Height	Name	Drop	Country	Location
70004	2308	Lalla Khedidja / لالة خديجة	1720	Algeria	36.4475, 4.2283
70013	2004	Djebel Babor / جبل البابور	1149	Algeria	36.5013, 5.4743
70015	1985	Djebel Ouarsenis / جبل وارسنيس	1105	Algeria	35.8743, 1.6321
70018	1604	Djebel Mouzaïa / جبل موزة	1071	Algeria	36.3750, 2.7225
70019	1579	Djebel Zaccar Rherbi / جبل زكار الرحبي	1051	Algeria	36.3312, 2.2128
70021	1896	Djebel Takoucht / دجيبل طقوسهة	1042	Algeria	36.5185, 5.2113

AF602 High Atlas

Id	Height	Name	Drop	Country	Location
70001	4167	Djebel Toubkal / توبقال	3758	Morocco	31.0600, -7.9150
70002	4071	Ighil m'Goun	1904	Morocco	31.5083, -6.4442
70006	3619	Jebel Igdet	1614	Morocco	30.9645, -8.4433
70009	3609	Jebel Anghomer	1424	Morocco	31.3367, -6.9975
70010	3747	Djebel Ayachi / جبل العياشي	1403	Morocco	32.4767, -4.9275

AF603 Saharan Atlas

Id	Height	Name	Drop	Country	Location
70007	2328	Djebel Chélia / جبل شيليا	1612	Algeria	35.3184, 6.6368
70017	2170	Djebel Refaa / دجيبل رفاء	1090	Algeria	35.5589, 5.8677

AF604 Anti-Atlas

Id	Height	Name	Drop	Country	Location
70012	2712	Djebel Saghro – Amalou n'Mansour	1167	Morocco	31.1452, -5.6495
70016	3305	Djebel Siroua / جبل سيروا	1096	Morocco	30.7042, -7.6217

Ighil m'Goun, AF602, and Djebel Tidirhine, AF600
Rob Woodall, April 2017

On my first trip to Morocco we had two restauranteurs literally fighting for our custom, and a car repair involving two palm trees and a block and tackle. Driving to Ighil m'Goun we found the road blocked by a delivery of hay. The local accommodation provider assured us that it was impossible to drive further and so we should stay with him. He seemed quite impressed the next day when we completed the 50-kilometre round trip to the peak in twelve hours, followed by a large quantity of very sweet mint tea.

The cannabis farm slopes on Djebel Tidirhine offered a different kind of adventure. We were intercepted by a man in a fancy black Mercedes, questioned, then fixed up with a guide who escorted us up through the crops in safety.

Lalla Khedidja, AF601
Rob Woodall, October 2023

The Atlas Mountains extend to the Algerian coastal range. We had a blue-light police escort for the whole of our trip. Assembling the security forces required for Lalla Khedidja took so long that we nearly didn't have time for the hike. The peaks were generally easy, and clothed in beautiful cedars, related to the Cedar of Lebanon.

AF61 Sahara Desert Ranges

Jabal Tahat, AF611 (Deividas Valaitis)

AF611 Central Sahara Desert

Id	Height	Name	Drop	Country	Location
70503	2908	Jabal Tahat / جبل تاهات	2332	Algeria	23.2887, 5.5336
70511	2002	Mont Idoûkâl-n-Taghès / Mont Bagzane	1307	Niger	17.8386, 8.7202
70516	2262	Aheggar / أهقار	1191	Algeria	24.7171, 5.6443
70517	1613	Mont Mourgué	1154	Chad	11.9034, 18.1907
70524	1988	Adrar Tamgak	1066	Niger	19.0137, 8.6013
70525	2327	Garet el Djenoun / جرت إل دجنن	1064	Algeria	25.0799, 5.4165
70526	1946	Mont Gréboun	1051	Niger	19.9910, 8.5896
70532	2052	Taourirt Ta-n-Afella / تاوريرت تان أفلا	1000	Algeria	24.0560, 5.0323

AF612 Tibesti

Id	Height	Name	Drop	Country	Location
70501	3447	Emi Koussi	2936	Chad	19.7939, 18.5521
70507	3302	Pic Toussidé	1580	Chad	21.0408, 16.4726
70510	3069	Tarso Tiéroko	1314	Chad	20.7145, 17.8496
70514	3135	Mouskorbé	1257	Chad	21.3464, 18.6015
70515	3072	Tarso Kobour	1224	Chad	20.5644, 17.4648

AF613 Libyan Desert

Id	Height	Name	Drop	Country	Location
70502	3012	Jabal Marrah – Deriba / جبل مرہ	2478	Sudan	12.9340, 24.2296
70513	1895	Jabal Uweinat / جبل العوينات	1266	Libya, Sudan	21.9161, 25.0000
70519	2341	Jabal Gurgei / جبل جورجي	1135	Sudan	13.8319, 24.3137
70521	2009	Jabal Ubbor / جبل عبر	1106	Sudan	15.3086, 26.5496
70527	1708	Jabal Kissū / جبل قبلة	1047	Sudan	21.5827, 25.1407

AF614 Eastern Desert

Id	Height	Name	Drop	Country	Location
70504	2227	Jabal Oda	1805	Sudan	20.3435, 36.6704
70505	2187	Jabal Shayib el Banat / جبل شائب البنات	1760	Egypt	26.9773, 33.4894
70506	2198	Jabal Asoteriba / جبل أسوتيريبا	1601	Sudan	21.8650, 36.5075
70508	2196	Jabal Erba	1491	Sudan	20.7451, 36.8390
70509	1977	Jabal Hamata / جبل حماطة	1483	Egypt	24.2043, 35.0060
70512	1850	Jebel Is	1279	Sudan	21.8179, 35.6598
70518	1750	Gebel Gharib	1145	Egypt	28.1133, 32.9033
70520	1844	Jabal Shendib	1117	Egypt	22.0150, 36.2742
70522	1778	Jebel Hadalawer / جبل هدلاور	1072	Sudan	21.8708, 35.3775
70523	1965	Jabal al Qaṭṭār / جبل القطار	1070	Egypt	27.0908, 33.3633
70528	1802	Jabal Arit / جبل عريت	1037	Sudan	21.6142, 36.3917
70529	1688	Jabal Abū Ḥarbah	1034	Egypt	27.2883, 33.2133
70530	1732	Jabal Hadayu *	1023	Sudan	21.6025, 36.3300
70531	1274	Jabal al Jalālah al Baḥariyyah	1012	Egypt	29.3375, 32.3842

Jabal Tahat, AF611 and Jabal Shayib el Banat, AF614
Rob Woodall, October 2023

Jabal Tahat is the highest point in Algeria. We flew to tiny Tamanrasset airport for a three-day trip, with a police escort for the first day. It seemed they didn't get many tourists and were keen to look after them. The first night was spent at Refuge de l'Assekrem. Watching the sun rise over the Sâlek spires was quite special. On the second day we completed the rough and slow drive to the start of the route and climbed the peak, then drove out on the next day, enjoying some great rock scenery en route.

The only information on Jabal Shayib el Banat was from a 1950s ascent by John Hunt, perhaps in training for his 1953 Everest expedition. It was unclear what route he took or what equipment was needed. We found a man with a Landcruiser and headed off into the desert. After a brief stop to visit his village and try our hands at camel riding, we enjoyed a camp amidst impressive rocky peaks. Next morning our route headed up a wide rocky gully, including a short, easy roped pitch.

AF62 West Africa Mountains

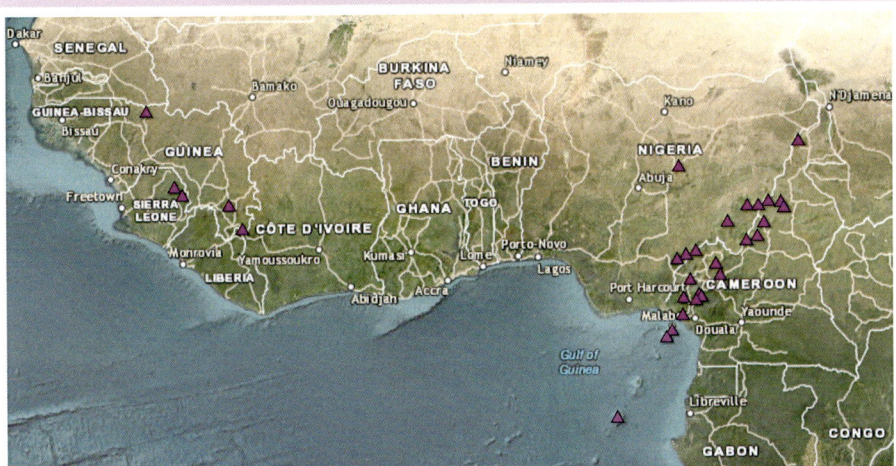

Mount Cameroon, AF622 (Deividas Valaitis)

On Pico de São Tomé, AF623 (Deividas Valaitis)

AF620 Guinea Highlands

Id	Height	Name	Drop	Country	Location
71005	1945	Bintumani / Loma Mansa	1666	Sierra Leone	9.2271, -11.1150
71012	1752	Nimba / Mont Richard-Molard	1294	Guinea, Côte d'Ivoire	7.6220, -8.4085
71013	1715	Sankan Biriwa	1198	Sierra Leone	8.9332, -10.8099
71018	1656	Pic de Fon	1104	Guinea	8.5392, -8.9043
71026	1534	Mont Loura	1045	Guinea	12.1119, -12.2638

AF621 Niger River Area

Id	Height	Name	Drop	Country	Location
71010	1776	Shere Hills	1324	Nigeria	9.9340, 9.0346
71017	1481	Hosséré Oupay	1106	Cameroon	10.8877, 13.7807

AF622 Cameroon Mountains

Id	Height	Name	Drop	Country	Location
71001	4045	Mount Cameroon – Fako	3919	Cameroon	4.2180, 9.1735
71003	3008	Mount Oku	2487	Cameroon	6.2000, 10.5185
71007	2049	Hosséré Vokré	1490	Cameroon	8.3399, 13.2398
71008	2396	Mont Manengouba – Eboga	1433	Cameroon	5.0220, 9.8421
71009	1847	Monts Alantika	1388	Cameroon	8.5716, 12.5918
71011	1768	Mont Rata	1308	Cameroon	4.8861, 9.2418
71014	1374	Afi Mountain	1195	Nigeria	6.3561, 8.9762
71015	2426	Chappal Waddi / Gangirwal	1165	Cameroon, Nigeria	7.0367, 11.7159
71016	1893	Oshie Ridge	1145	Nigeria	6.5350, 9.3068
71019	1615	Hosséré Godé	1070	Cameroon	8.5357, 13.1035
71020	1295	Nda Ali	1068	Cameroon	5.5617, 9.5021
71021	2391	Tchabal Mbabo	1067	Cameroon	7.2455, 12.1573
71022	1443	Mumum-Buyu	1066	Nigeria	6.6813, 9.7064
71023	2263	Massif du Nkogam	1061	Cameroon	5.7368, 10.6707
71024	1567	Hosséré Banglang	1061	Cameroon, Nigeria	8.3952, 12.2359
71025	1687	Mount Dimlang / Vogel Peak	1049	Nigeria	8.3949, 11.7769
71027	2064	Mont Koupé	1044	Cameroon	4.8013, 9.7076
71028	1271	Bali Hill	1038	Nigeria	7.8064, 10.9885
71029	1836	Mont Nlonako	1030	Cameroon	4.9064, 9.9501
71030	1697	Hosséré Guenfalabo	1001	Cameroon	7.7613, 12.4582

AF623 Bight of Benin

Id	Height	Name	Island	Drop	Country	Location
71002	3011	Pico Basilé / Pico de Santa Isabel	Bioko	3011	Equatorial Guinea	3.5883, 8.7616
71006	2261	Gran Caldera de Luba	Bioko	1517	Equatorial Guinea	3.3583, 8.5401
71004	2024	Pico de São Tomé	São Tomé	2024	Sao Tome and Principe	0.2693, 6.5415

AF63 Ethiopian Highlands

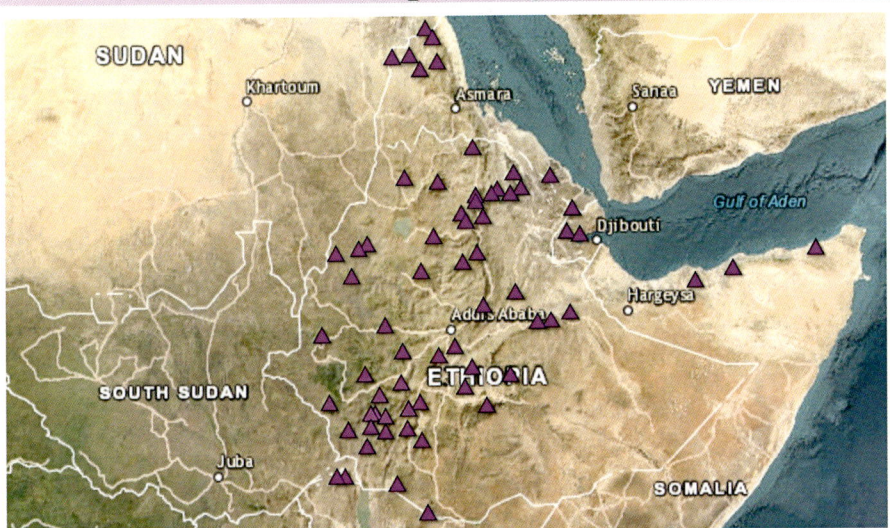

Ascent of Ras Dashen, AF630 (Alastair Govan)

AF630 Northern Ethiopian Highlands

Id	Height	Name	Drop	Country	Location
71501	4543	Ras Dashen	3989	Ethiopia	13.2367, 38.3725
71503	4100	Choke Terara / Birhan	2225	Ethiopia	10.7142, 37.8500
71505	4280	Ābune Yosēf	2071	Ethiopia	12.1417, 39.1833
71515	2731	Beleya Terara	1600	Ethiopia	11.4750, 36.1942
71518	3941	Tigray Terara *	1540	Ethiopia	12.8592, 39.4983
71520	4120	Guna Terara	1510	Ethiopia	11.7117, 38.2383

Id	Height	Name	Drop	Country	Location
71523	2780	Jabal Hamoyet / جبل حمويات	1393	Sudan	17.5625, 38.0058
71532	2597	Aighet Tada	1222	Eritrea	17.3167, 38.2375
71534	2605	Culan Sancai	1221	Ethiopia	10.5933, 35.7475
71537	3300	Alekeye	1182	Ethiopia	14.2158, 39.4167
71538	3705	Ts' Erk' Aba *	1174	Ethiopia	12.6700, 39.4958
71539	2964	Adenna	1174	Ethiopia	13.3675, 37.3625
71540	2685	Enghershatu	1168	Eritrea	16.6267, 38.3617
71544	3777	Baylamt'u Terara / Biala	1116	Ethiopia	12.3533, 39.0633
71545	1663	Jabal Rabussom	1110	Eritrea	16.7467, 37.0117
71548	2460	Dangvur Terara	1095	Ethiopia	11.3525, 35.9325
71549	1865	Badisilu	1089	Ethiopia	11.2383, 35.2350
71555	1815	Ma Alalta / Gar Uli	1051	Ethiopia	13.0125, 40.1850
71558	2350	Magalle	1033	Ethiopia	12.8892, 39.9933
71560	1877	Sceccai Reba	1031	Eritrea	16.4275, 37.8250
71562	1737	Adercale	1028	Eritrea	16.7992, 37.5308
71566	2434	Rama	1002	Ethiopia	12.2533, 39.7392

AF631 Central Ethiopian Highlands

Id	Height	Name	Drop	Country	Location
71504	3418	Argun	2207	Ethiopia	6.1067, 36.7442
71506	3568	Guje	2013	Ethiopia	6.2042, 37.3892
71507	4270	Amba Farit	1919	Ethiopia	10.9508, 39.1042
71509	3280	Tulu Welel	1720	Ethiopia	8.8742, 34.8167
71510	2560	Demegerfa Terara * / Mount Smith	1684	Ethiopia	6.2333, 36.2992
71511	3358	Aggio	1631	Ethiopia	7.1500, 36.5458
71514	3405	Aeledaba Terara *	1605	Ethiopia	6.5508, 36.7275
71516	3359	Mai Gudo	1589	Ethiopia	7.4917, 37.2058
71526	2535	Maji	1299	Ethiopia	6.1458, 35.6008
71527	2380	Gura Farda Ye'Terara Senselet	1261	Ethiopia	6.9100, 35.0125
71528	2435	Benkira	1259	Ethiopia	6.6258, 36.4392
71529	3611	K'ech'a Terara / Gurage	1254	Ethiopia	8.2717, 38.3617
71533	3165	Ch'alchīs Terara	1221	Ethiopia	9.1367, 36.7275
71541	2080	Bunanta Terara *	1168	Ethiopia	6.6317, 36.3125
71542	3010	Zuqualla	1150	Ethiopia	8.5358, 38.8583
71543	1753	Lorienetom / Nawakaiya	1150	Kenya, South Sudan	4.7793, 35.5038
71546	3467	Kuta Ber *	1102	Ethiopia	11.2325, 39.5400
71547	2899	Dabo Bota *	1100	Ethiopia	6.7650, 37.4575
71554	3705	Uoti	1062	Ethiopia	9.7267, 39.7292
71556	2954	Damota Terara	1039	Ethiopia	6.9075, 37.7883
71557	3025	Egan	1039	Ethiopia	8.4083, 37.2683
71563	3025	Gorgota	1019	Ethiopia	7.7550, 36.1075
71564	1701	Kathiren	1017	Kenya	4.7853, 35.2653
71567	1661	Dara	1000	Ethiopia	5.6442, 36.1492

AF632 Southern Ethiopian Highlands

Id	Height	Name	Drop	Country	Location
71502	4385	Tullu Dimtu	2512	Ethiopia	6.8267, 39.8192
71512	4210	Bada	1629	Ethiopia	7.9092, 39.3933
71519	3240	Delo / Ye'Terara Senselet	1516	Ethiopia	5.8217, 37.8408
71525	2698	Abul Casim	1322	Ethiopia	7.7125, 40.5133
71535	4185	K'ech'a Terara	1209	Ethiopia	7.3642, 39.1583
71550	2130	Īnch'īnī Terara	1082	Ethiopia	4.5842, 37.0708
71551	1890	Forole / Monte Wickenburg	1075	Ethiopia, Kenya	3.7173, 38.0141

AF633 Danakil

Id	Height	Name	Drop	Country	Location
71508	2248	Ramlo	1914	Eritrea	13.3917, 41.7283
71513	2021	Mousa Ali / موسى علي	1606	Djibouti, Eritrea, Ethiopia	12.4688, 42.4045
71530	1688	Garbi / Mêgo Aroug	1229	Djibouti	11.8367, 42.2483
71531	1785	'Êli Dâba	1226	Djibouti	11.7533, 42.6383
71536	1295	Āfrēra Terara	1191	Ethiopia	13.0883, 40.8533
71553	1031	Ale Bagu / Ummuna	1084	Ethiopia	13.5100, 40.6292
71552	1505	Alayta / Urīkomam Terara	1073	Ethiopia	12.8883, 40.5725

Ale Bagu, AF633

The Danakil Depression in Ethiopia is an unrelentingly hot and usually bone-dry plain so low-lying that it is tens of metres below sea level. Three tectonic plates meet here, causing considerable volcanic activity at Erta Ale as the continents of Africa and Asia move slowly apart. Widely regarded as one of the world's most inhospitable places, it is also home to the only known Ribu on our planet with a key col below sea level. The height of Ale Bagu (1031m) is lower than its prominence (1084m) due to its key col being at a height of minus 53 metres. Given this great novelty, reaching the top of this Ribu is a unique occasion, to be enjoyed with a bag of ale at the highest point, or perhaps a bottle of good Ethiopian wine. However, nobody is known to have climbed Ale Bagu yet. If it were only 950 metres high, the volcano would still just about qualify as a Ribu, despite having an elevation of less than a thousand metres above sea level. In theory, there could be a Ribu only one metre above sea level if its key col was located at least 999 metres below sea level. There surely will be such a mountain on a far-distant planet somewhere.

AF634 Ahmar-Somali

Id	Height	Name	Drop	Country	Location
71517	2107	Buurta Baxaya	1585	Somalia	11.3262, 49.7484
71521	3405	Gara Muleta Terara	1502	Ethiopia	9.2567, 41.7308
71522	2445	Buurta Shimbiris	1470	Somaliland	10.7356, 47.2443
71524	2145	Āyelu Terara	1383	Ethiopia	10.0842, 40.7033
71559	3028	Serīta Terara	1031	Ethiopia	9.4975, 42.3125
71561	3126	Gara-Tima	1029	Ethiopia	9.2142, 41.3317
71565	1682	Buuraha Gubane	1007	Somaliland	10.3892, 46.1068

AF64 East Africa Mountains

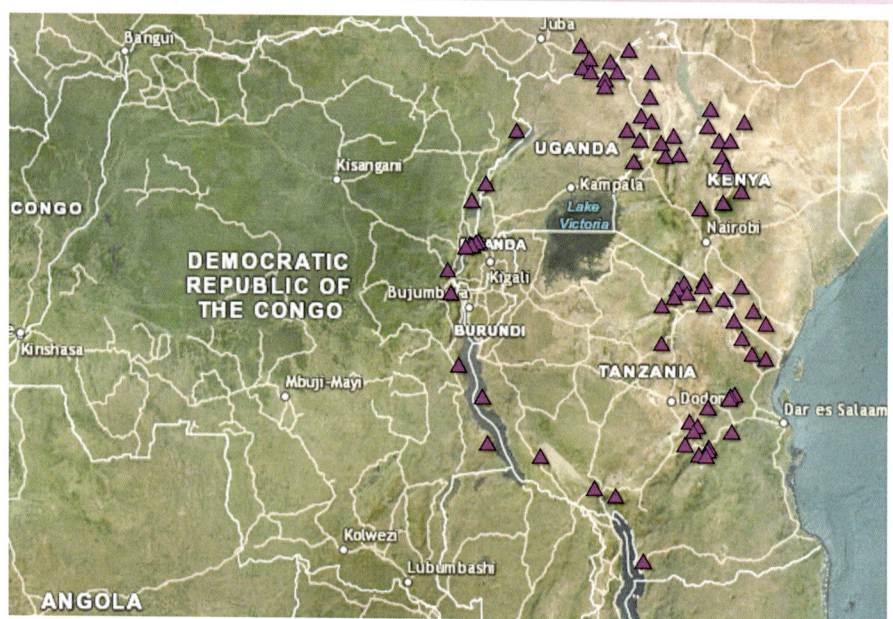

Mount Stanley, AF641 (Rob Woodall)

AF640 West Rift Valley Ranges

Id	Height	Name	Drop	Country	Location
72021	2725	Kabobo	1601	DR Congo	-5.1365, 29.0535
72022	3480	Mont Mohi	1592	DR Congo	-2.9533, 28.7842
72023	3095	Wuhevi / Mont Tschiaberimu	1567	DR Congo	-0.1417, 29.4258
72029	2480	Marungu – Kitumbi Mountain	1466	DR Congo	-7.5042, 29.9867
72034	2444	Aburo	1393	DR Congo	2.0100, 30.8650
72044	3308	Kahuzi	1271	DR Congo	-2.2500, 28.6883

AF641 East Rift Valley Ranges

Id	Height	Name	Drop	Country	Location
72002	5109	Mount Stanley / Ngaliema	3924	DR Congo, Uganda	0.3856, 29.8729
72004	4507	Volcan Karisimbi	3310	DR Congo, Rwanda	-1.5058, 29.4500
72025	4127	Mount Muhabura	1534	Rwanda, Uganda	-1.3830, 29.6778
72031	3470	Volcan Nyiragongo	1443	DR Congo	-1.5192, 29.2542
72040	2475	Nkungwe	1319	Tanzania	-6.1105, 29.7817
72049	4437	Volcan Mikeno	1193	DR Congo	-1.4640, 29.4198
72066	3669	Sabinyo	1046	DR Congo, Rwanda, Uganda	-1.3878, 29.5920
72067	2451	Mibizi	1044	Tanzania	-7.8658, 31.6576

Mount Kadam, AF642
Rob Woodall, January 2024

Kadam is a spectacular peak. Our ascent was more exciting than expected. We had hiked up to a low camp, quite scrambly in places, in an hour, but our guides were reluctant to hike another hour to a higher camp, although we had enough daylight. Next morning we found out why. We woke at 5am to the sound of machine-gun fire and an explosion. We later learned that this was a 'disarmament' operation – the security forces were arresting someone who had an illegal gun. It was apparently quite an issue. Tribesmen needed to be able to defend their cattle from marauders and were not keen to give up their weapons. All went quiet, then a fire started – presumably the home in question (a basic shelter) had been torched. So our own lights and breakfast fire were extinguished and we had an extra hour in bed.

The trail climbed steeply through pleasant forest, passing two basic tarpaulin shelters, one containing a family, apparently quite cheerful despite the morning's security operation. After an interesting rock ledge traverse we were at high camp in an hour, level with a big buttress we had been admiring from the low camp. There was more scrambling higher up, then a plateau, then the summit cairn perched above an impressive drop.

Nabato, ten kilometres to the north-east, looked as high as our summit. However, a careful sighting with a hand-level suggested it was lower, probably by about ten or twenty metres. Our local guide, who had taken people up it, reckoned it was lower. Satellite data of the highest cells for the two summits indicated 3058m for Kadam and 3016m for Nabato. Nabato could perhaps be up to twenty metres higher than the satellite figure but probably not 40 metres higher. Anyway, the summit of Kadam was safely in the bag and we got safely back down the mountain. Apparently no more armed operations were planned for the day.

AF642 Central East Africa Plateau

Id	Height	Name	Drop	Country	Location
72006	4321	Mount Elgon – Wagagai	2457	Uganda	1.1180, 34.5272
72008	3187	Kinyeti	2119	South Sudan	3.9458, 32.9100
72010	3420	Hanang	2046	Tanzania	-4.4342, 35.4017
72011	3648	Loolmalasin	2006	Tanzania	-3.0492, 35.8208
72013	3083	Moroto – Sokdek	1817	Uganda	2.5252, 34.7722
72015	3336	Mtelo	1768	Kenya	1.6598, 35.3820
72018	2623	Emogadong / Dongotona	1722	South Sudan	4.1972, 33.1302
72019	3063	Mount Kadam	1689	Uganda	1.7595, 34.7084
72027	3530	Nakugen / Kamelogon / Kakwa Ard	1521	Kenya	1.2672, 35.4996
72030	2795	Jabal Lotuke	1463	South Sudan	4.1250, 33.8017
72033	2749	Morungole	1400	Uganda	3.8149, 34.0317
72036	2962	Ol Doinyo Lengai	1370	Tanzania	-2.7635, 35.9142
72039	2538	Napak	1330	Uganda	2.0783, 34.3033
72042	2773	Kachagalau	1285	Kenya	2.3133, 35.0525
72043	1939	Jabal Lodio	1284	South Sudan	4.6036, 32.8688
72051	2285	Loma Hills	1160	Kenya	3.0963, 35.0203
72056	2087	Kailongol	1136	Kenya	1.8783, 35.7751
72059	2382	Rom	1095	Uganda	3.3917, 33.6133
72061	2190	Mount Tereteinia	1090	South Sudan	3.8233, 33.1975
72063	2351	Tiati	1069	Kenya	1.2968, 35.9339
72064	1794	Pelekech	1054	Kenya	3.8025, 35.0775
72069	2320	Kaleri	1028	Uganda	3.5901, 33.5996
72072	3228	Oldeani	1016	Tanzania	-3.2749, 35.4392
72074	1698	Mogila	1009	Kenya	4.4752, 34.3835

Napak, AF642
Rob Woodall, January 2024

Napak was conveniently situated at the end of our East Africa itinerary. Our tour operator in Kenya knew little about it but their local contacts said it was feasible to climb it in a day. It apparently involved some steep scrambling so we carried some climbing gear. Our local guides didn't, but they tended to be very agile.

The north face is a wall of cliffs and we were heading straight for them. We passed through a village of traditional round thatched huts, then several smaller settlements. Our local guide stopped at each one for a chat – not very efficient but I imagine it helped ease our passage up the mountain. The highest such settlement, we learned, was a single household comprising a man with four wives, each with several children. They subsisted on maize supplemented by a few items traded at the market (a substantial hike away).

Above the settlements, the mostly well-defined trail angled left beneath the cliffs. Ten metres of steep grippy slabs made a nice scramble, with an awkward move at the top. The remaining scrambling was in forest, rather green, some of the holds rather small, generally quite easy on the way up, requiring care in descent, definitely to be avoided in damp conditions. Our climbing rope remained unused. Above, a mile of easy plateau led to the unmarked level tussocky summit. Napak is easily accessible from the main paved highway and fits into an unhurried eight-hour day. Now that it has GPX tracks and trip reports readily available, perhaps this fine peak will gain wider popularity.

Mount Elgon, AF642
Alastair Govan, January 2024

Mount Elgon is the remnant of an ancient volcano in the Elgon National Park on the border of Kenya and Uganda. It has been described as the largest mountain crater in the world, but there is no flat crater floor, just a ring of modest-looking hills surrounding an area of valleys and ridges.

The closest approach is from an attractive campsite just inside the Chorlim gate in Kenya. An early start and a rough one-hour drive got us to the start of the route at 3500 metres around daybreak. A reasonable trail rises to the crater 'rim' just below Koitoboss, the highest point in Kenya, but the main summit is a further ten kilometres across rough, undulating ground at around 4000 metres altitude. This crosses the border, so a Ugandan official arranged to meet us on the summit to deal with border formalities. It was a long walk for him. The round trip was about 30 kilometres – a tough twelve-hour day.

Ng'iro, AF643
Rob Woodall, December 2023

When I climbed my 800th Ribu I wasn't sure which peak it was. This is due to measurement uncertainty and three ways of assessing prominence. Clean prominence gives a minimum figure as it assumes that if there are no spot heights then the summit height is equal to the highest contour ring and the col is the same height as the contour directly above the col. This is not usually the case. Optimistic prominence gives the maximum possible figure, so average (interpolated) prominence is typically the best way to identify the correct figure. Checking the data, this means that my 800th Ribu was Ng'iro, on 29th December 2023.

Ng'iro is a steep, forested peak served by two good trails from the village of Tuum. There is rich pasturage up on the ridge, so the villagers graze their cattle up there. However, at the time of our visit there was still adequate grass lower down, so the mountain pasture was lush and ungrazed, an unexpected sight at nearly 3000m in a rather arid part of Kenya. But there's a problem, as Ng'iro has two summits 0.6km apart, roughly equal in elevation. Our GPS devices couldn't distinguish them, and clouds prevented levelling. Naturally we visited both, so whichever it was, my 800th Ribu had been climbed.

Kilimanjaro, AF644
Alan Dawson, August 1989

My first attempt to climb a hill higher than 1345 metres was successful but not without cost. Point Lenana on Mount Kenya provided a great walk and valuable acclimatisation for Kilimanjaro. We then set off for a circuit of Mount Kenya. Our English leader warned us to take care as it was rough and remote territory, before he stumbled down a scree slope and broke an ankle. We sent a 69-year-old runner to get help but it took ages to arrive. The rest of us supported our leader with our shoulders and an improvised stretcher, but when I got home I was ill and found I had an umbilical hernia caused by stretcher carrying.

Kilimanjaro was easy by comparison, after we had found a new leader to navigate the bureaucracy and bribery. Our party left the top hut far too early, at midnight, along with most groups. I rebelled against the crazily slow pace and stepped out of line, so four of us went on ahead. The ascent route was superb but would have been much better in daylight. We reached the summit an hour before sunrise and had to run around trying to keep warm until the sun finally appeared to cast a shadow over the African plains and then set them alight. Great experience overall though.

AF643 East Central Kenya

Id	Height	Name	Drop	Country	Location
72003	5199	Mount Kenya – Batian	3825	Kenya	-0.1523, 37.3089
72009	4001	Oldoinyo Lesatima	2082	Kenya	-0.3108, 36.6158
72012	2948	Gelai	1925	Tanzania	-2.6125, 36.1050
72014	2871	Kitumbeine	1783	Tanzania	-2.8794, 36.2117
72024	2285	Mount Kulal	1542	Kenya	2.7303, 36.9276
72028	2848	Ng'iro	1502	Kenya	2.1908, 36.8150
72032	2688	Warges	1423	Kenya	0.9504, 37.3987
72045	2625	Ndoto Mountains – Naro Onyeki	1270	Kenya	1.7570, 37.1615
72047	2629	Mount Longido	1250	Tanzania	-2.6967, 36.7142
72052	1705	Mount Marsabit / Karantin	1157	Kenya	2.3172, 37.9620
72053	1751	Baio	1144	Kenya	1.7665, 37.5426
72055	2548	Oldoinyo Orok	1138	Kenya	-2.4933, 36.7508
72057	2513	Nyambene Hills – Ntiene	1123	Kenya	0.2342, 37.8783
72068	2321	Kichich / Ldoinyo Lenkiyio	1029	Kenya	1.2683, 37.2533

AF644 North-east Tanzania

Id	Height	Name	Drop	Country	Location
72001	5895	Kilimanjaro – Kibo – Uhuru	5885	Tanzania	-3.0764, 37.3540
72005	4565	Mount Meru	3169	Tanzania	-3.2434, 36.7498
72007	2656	Lukwangule Peak	2124	Tanzania	-7.0909, 37.6209
72016	2464	Shengena	1746	Tanzania	-4.2678, 37.9316
72017	2301	Sungwi	1736	Tanzania	-4.7308, 38.2333
72035	2392	Mlima Dibago *	1371	Tanzania	-6.0814, 37.5098
72037	1978	Mlima Kanga *	1354	Tanzania	-5.9873, 37.7155
72038	2356	Lugunga	1350	Tanzania	-6.7867, 36.3183
72041	2209	Mragua / Vuria	1296	Kenya	-3.4151, 38.2922
72050	2102	Kindoroko	1167	Tanzania	-3.7380, 37.6505
72054	1875	Chonwe	1139	Tanzania	-7.5830, 36.9336
72058	2295	Mangalisa	1098	Tanzania	-7.1147, 36.4403
72065	1653	Kasigau	1048	Kenya	-3.8274, 38.6622
72070	2222	Iputa	1025	Tanzania	-6.9424, 36.5623
72073	1518	Mlima Mkundi *	1011	Tanzania	-4.8623, 38.6527
72075	2164	Chyulu Hills	1008	Kenya	-2.6817, 37.8942
72076	2026	Mlima Msolokelo *	1008	Tanzania	-5.9901, 37.5686
72077	2269	Mamwera	1000	Tanzania	-6.3542, 36.8892

AF645 Southern Tanzania

Id	Height	Name	Drop	Country	Location
72020	2980	Mtorwi	1686	Tanzania	-9.0775, 34.0225
72026	2279	Karenga	1521	Tanzania	-7.6856, 36.8817
72046	2563	Luhombero	1270	Tanzania	-7.7821, 36.6046
72048	2107	Mlima Tukuzi *	1232	Tanzania	-11.0109, 34.9097
72060	2099	Mwanihana	1092	Tanzania	-7.8239, 36.8258
72062	2458	Selegu	1075	Tanzania	-7.4902, 36.1553
72071	2809	Mbeya / Loleza	1020	Tanzania	-8.8398, 33.3686

AF65 Southern Africa

View from Seweweekspoortpiek, AF657 (Rob Woodall)

AF650 Angola Plateau

Id	Height	Name	Drop	Country	Location
72506	2489	Serra da Neve	1615	Angola	-13.7840, 13.1812
72509	2620	Morro de Môco	1513	Angola	-12.4627, 15.1735
72518	2390	Tchivira	1298	Angola	-14.3221, 13.8915
72521	2057	Gandarengo	1238	Angola	-14.7378, 13.0962
72523	2044	Cafema	1216	Angola	-17.1288, 12.5137
72524	2060	Maluco	1215	Angola	-14.9768, 13.0740
72544	1819	Chai	1053	Angola	-13.6469, 12.9988
72550	2286	Chimboa	1032	Angola	-12.9511, 14.5646

AF652 Malawi Highlands

Id	Height	Name	Drop	Country	Location
72502	3002	Sapitwa / Mulanje	2323	Malawi	-15.9494, 35.5930
72504	2419	Monte Namuli	1755	Mozambique	-15.3584, 37.0611
72510	2065	Chiperone	1486	Mozambique	-16.4792, 35.7121
72511	2607	Nganda	1375	Malawi	-10.4477, 33.8645
72512	2086	Malumbe Peak	1375	Malawi	-15.3494, 35.2739
72525	1803	Serra Mitúcuè	1211	Mozambique	-14.7488, 36.6866
72529	1771	M'pàluwé	1167	Mozambique	-14.8863, 38.3087
72530	1846	Serra Macuta	1164	Mozambique	-12.8100, 35.1475
72531	2289	Mchese	1162	Malawi	-15.8188, 35.7044
72533	2198	Dedza Mountain	1120	Malawi	-14.3389, 34.3329
72542	1526	Serra Rupé	1063	Mozambique	-14.5199, 38.4382
72545	1764	Serra Mancuni	1043	Mozambique	-14.9987, 37.1927
72546	1710	Monte Mabu	1035	Mozambique	-16.2991, 36.3955
72549	1418	Montes Eráti	1033	Mozambique	-14.0567, 39.3957
72556	1603	Serra Nampatiua	1008	Mozambique	-14.6412, 37.5627

AF653 Kalahari

Id	Height	Name	Drop	Country	Location
72503	2573	Dâures / Brandberg – Königstein	1770	Namibia	-21.1499, 14.5775
72515	2482	Moltkeblick	1342	Namibia	-22.6497, 17.1831
72522	2202	Lord Hill	1226	Namibia	-27.1808, 18.7290
72540	2319	Hohenstein	1074	Namibia	-21.7283, 15.5283
72557	2060	Chowagasberg	1004	Namibia	-25.2708, 15.7544

AF654 Zimbabwe Plateau

Id	Height	Name	Drop	Country	Location
72508	2593	Mount Nyangani	1521	Zimbabwe	-18.3007, 32.8418
72513	2437	Mount Binga	1350	Mozambique, Zimbabwe	-19.7764, 33.0621
72516	1863	Gogogo	1336	Mozambique	-18.4299, 34.0385

AF655 South Africa Plateau

Id	Height	Name	Drop	Country	Location
72553	2088	Marakele Peak *	1017	South Africa	-24.4710, 27.5891

AF656 Drakensberg

Id	Height	Name	Drop	Country	Location
72501	3482	Thabana Ntlenyana	2392	Lesotho	-29.4681, 29.2692
72537	3039	Quthing Peak *	1094	Lesotho	-30.4302, 28.1079
72543	2126	Iron Crown	1056	South Africa	-23.9991, 29.9464
72552	2051	Blouberg – Ga-Monnaasenamoriri	1021	South Africa	-23.0715, 28.9886

AF657 Cape Ranges

Id	Height	Name	Drop	Country	Location
72505	1995	Du Toit's Peak / Dutoitspiek	1740	South Africa	-33.7540, 19.1886
72507	2325	Seweweekspoortpiek	1545	South Africa	-33.3982, 21.3678
72514	2249	Matroosberg	1345	South Africa	-33.3821, 19.6688
72517	1458	Zebrakop	1302	South Africa	-32.7381, 18.7701
72519	1758	Cockscomb	1282	South Africa	-33.5713, 24.7848
72520	2132	Tierberg	1264	South Africa	-33.3421, 22.2621
72526	2085	Blesberg	1199	South Africa	-33.4176, 22.6868
72527	1674	Riviersonderendberge	1197	South Africa	-33.9808, 19.4855
72528	2078	Groot-Winterhoek	1188	South Africa	-33.1062, 19.1460
72532	2027	Sneeuberg	1139	South Africa	-32.5074, 19.1532
72534	1637	Grootberg	1120	South Africa	-33.9184, 20.8752
72535	2072	Keeromsberg	1118	South Africa	-33.5620, 19.6028
72536	1955	Mannetjiesberg	1116	South Africa	-33.6176, 22.9386
72538	2070	Sneeukop	1089	South Africa	-32.8235, 19.3925
72539	2059	Buffelshoekpiek	1080	South Africa	-33.4808, 19.4055
72541	1085	Table Mountain / Tafelberg	1068	South Africa	-33.9668, 18.4256
72547	2369	Groot-Winterberg	1034	South Africa	-32.3637, 26.4038
72548	1500	Roodezandsberg	1034	South Africa	-33.2133, 19.0753
72551	1710	Misty Point	1024	South Africa	-33.9577, 20.4361
72554	2502	Kompasberg	1012	South Africa	-31.7593, 24.5400
72555	1390	Simonsberg	1011	South Africa	-33.8840, 18.9274

AF66 Mid-Atlantic Islands

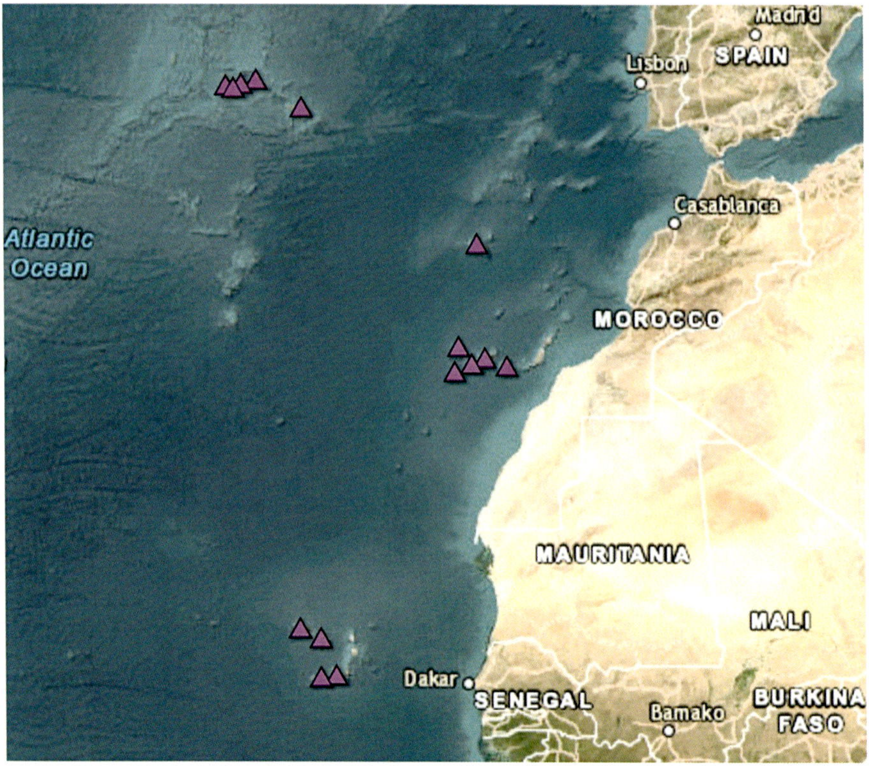

Queen Mary's Peak on Tristan da Cunha is in the south Atlantic and not shown above

Pico Ruivo de Santana on Madeira, AF660 (Alastair Govan)

AF660 North Atlantic Islands

Id	Height	Name	Island	Drop	Country	Location
73001	3718	Pico del Teide	Tenerife (Canarias)	3718	Spain	28.2728, -16.6423
73003	2423	Roque de los Muchachos	La Palma (Canarias)	2423	Spain	28.7542, -17.8848
73007	1956	Morro de la Agujereada	Gran Canaria (Canarias)	1956	Spain	27.9609, -15.5712
73009	1499	Malpaso	El Hierro (Canarias)	1499	Spain	27.7292, -18.0404
73010	1484	Alto de Garajonay	La Gomera (Canarias)	1484	Spain	28.1098, -17.2483
73002	2829	Pico do Fogo / Pico de Cano	Fogo	2829	Cabo Verde	14.9504, -24.3424
73006	1982	Tope da Caroa	Santo Antão	1982	Cabo Verde	17.0371, -25.2916
73011	1394	Pico da Antónia	São Tiago	1394	Cabo Verde	15.0509, -23.6353
73012	1312	Monte Gordo	São Nicolau	1312	Cabo Verde	16.6210, -24.3548
73008	1862	Pico Ruivo de Santana	Madeira	1862	Portugal	32.7586, -16.9422
73004	2350	Montanha do Pico	Pico (Açores)	2350	Portugal	38.4687, -28.3993
73013	1105	Pico da Vara	São Miguel (Açores)	1105	Portugal	37.8096, -25.2113
73014	1053	Pico da Esperança	São Jorge (Açores)	1053	Portugal	38.6506, -28.0741
73015	1043	Cabeço Gordo	Faial (Açores)	1043	Portugal	38.5760, -28.7131
73016	1021	Serra de Santa Bárbara	Terceira (Açores)	1021	Portugal	38.7298, -27.3186

AF661 South Atlantic Islands

Id	Height	Name	Island	Drop	Country	Location
73005	2062	Queen Mary's Peak	Tristan da Cunha	2062	Saint Helena	-37.1117, -12.2887

Pico del Teide, AF660
Rob Woodall, March 2007

Bob, Brent and I assembled in Tenerife, intent on climbing the big volcano. In 2007 you had to visit a certain office on a Tuesday afternoon to obtain a permit. We arrived on a Saturday and didn't want to wait until Tuesday. Eschewing the cable car, we hiked up easy snow before swinging right to cross steepish slopes, keeping generally out of sight, and eventually arriving at the summit. It was my first active volcano, with hissing, steaming vents discoloured with yellow sulphur dioxide. We descended the main trail and were caught near the cable car station. The ranger warned of dire consequences but it was unclear whether we would get fined. He seemed keen on a donation. We scraped together seven Euros, which wasn't a lot even in those days.

Pico do Fogo, AF660
Alastair Govan, January 2019

The Cabo Verde islands lie around 700 kilometres off the coast of west Africa and have an African feel, despite being governed by Portugal until 1975. Many islands are semi-desert but those which are high enough to catch the Atlantic cloud are fairly green. The island of Fogo ('fire') is by far the highest. Its main peak, Pico do Fogo, is a dormant volcano that last erupted in 2014, partially burying the village which occupied its huge central caldera.

The caldera, at around 1600 metres, was easily reached by a good road, and from there it was a steep hike up slabby rocks and scree to the rim of a smaller, younger, crater. A short scramble, with some chains to help, took us to the summit. The quickest way down was to walk or run down the slopes of deep volcanic ash. Without gaiters, my boots rapidly filled with sharp granules of ash, requiring four stops to empty out, but this was still easier than descending the gravelly slabs.

AF67 Indian Ocean Islands

The islands in AF670 and AF674 are not shown above. Socotra is in the Arabian Sea east of Somalia.

AF670 North Indian Ocean Islands

Id	Height	Name	Island	Drop	Country	Location
73509	1519	Māshanig / مشانق	Socotra	1519	Yemen	12.5767, 54.0144

AF671 Mozambique Channel

Id	Height	Name	Island	Drop	Country	Location
73504	2361	Mont Karthala / Al Qirṭālah	Grande Comore	2361	Comoros	-11.7592, 43.3675
73508	1595	Mont Ntringui	Anjouan	1595	Comoros	-12.2150, 44.4243

AF672 Madagascar

Id	Height	Name	Drop	Country	Location
73502	2876	Maromokotro	2876	Madagascar	-14.0225, 48.9675
73505	2658	Pic Boby / Pic Imarivolanitra	1874	Madagascar	-22.1950, 46.8850
73507	2643	Tsiafajavona	1658	Madagascar	-19.3492, 47.2433
73510	1475	Ambre-Bobaomby	1374	Madagascar	-12.5963, 49.1522
73511	1972	Pic d'Andohahela	1257	Madagascar	-24.6158, 46.7050
73513	2060	Pic d'Ivohibe	1166	Madagascar	-22.5083, 46.9567
73516	2132	Marojejy	1027	Madagascar	-14.4492, 49.7325

AF673 Mascarene Islands

Id	Height	Name	Island	Drop	Country	Location
73501	3070	Piton des Neiges	Réunion	3070	France	-21.0993, 55.4800
73517	2621	Piton de la Fournaise	Réunion	1027	France	-21.2431, 55.7074

AF674 South Indian Ocean Islands

Id	Height	Name	Island	Drop	Country	Location
73503	2745	Big Ben – Mawson Peak	Heard Island	2745	Australia	-53.1042, 73.5175
73506	1850	Mont Ross – Grand Ross	Kerguelen	1850	France	-49.5942, 69.4942
73515	1237	Mont Henri Rallier du Baty	Kerguelen	1057	France	-49.6092, 68.8651
73512	1242	Mascarin Peak	Marion Island	1242	South Africa	-46.9038, 37.7095
73514	1090	Mont Marion-Dufresne	Ile de l'Est	1090	France	-46.4182, 52.2466

——— Oceania ———

OC70 New Guinea

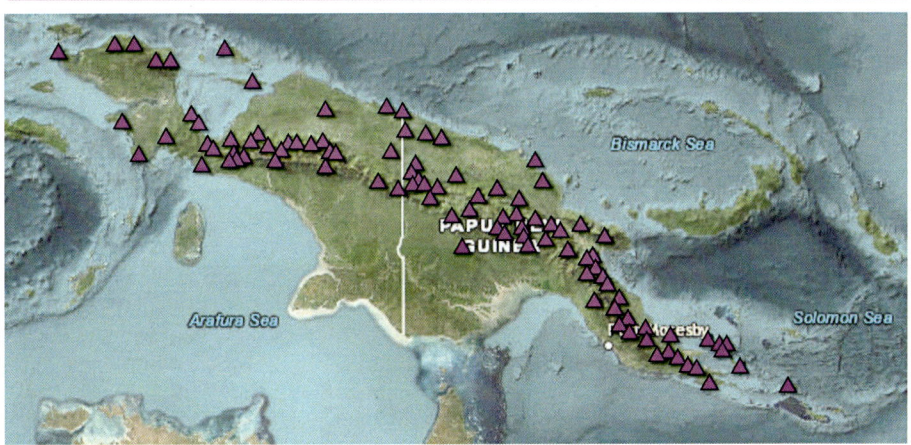

OC700 Western New Guinea Peninsula

Id	Height	Name	Drop	Country	Location
80005	2955	Pegunungan Arfak – Gunung Mebo	2776	Indonesia	-1.1563, 133.9796
80013	2187	Pegunungan Wondiwoi	1994	Indonesia	-2.7333, 134.5842
80016	2500	Bon Irau	1900	Indonesia	-0.6617, 132.8892
80027	1680	Kumawa	1636	Indonesia	-3.9152, 133.0108
80037	1490	Pegunungan Fak Fak	1434	Indonesia	-2.9634, 132.5517
80041	1566	Pegunungan Jamur *	1386	Indonesia	-3.5892, 135.0675
80051	1663	Gunung Fudi / Bukit Gnowo	1326	Indonesia	-3.3617, 133.8642
80062	2461	Tohkier / Kwoka	1217	Indonesia	-0.6542, 132.3134
80078	2726	Niefeb / Oranfebi	1106	Indonesia	-1.1259, 133.5433
80092	1100	Osua Jauer	1018	Indonesia	-2.9725, 134.8025
80067	1184	Gunung Batanta, Pulau Batanta	1184	Indonesia	-0.8576, 130.6240

OC701 Northern New Guinea Coast Ranges

Id	Height	Name	Drop	Country	Location
80002	4150	Finisterre Range – Boising	3709	Papua New Guinea	-5.9537, 146.37523
80012	2230	Pegunungan Gauttier	2007	Indonesia	-2.5708, 138.6742
80017	2034	Cyclops – Gunung Dafonsoro	1893	Indonesia	-2.5067, 140.5255
80025	4121	Mount Sarawaget	1710	Papua New Guinea	-6.3108, 147.0899
80026	1960	Mount Menawa	1648	Papua New Guinea	-3.2939, 141.7232
80030	1675	Adelbert Range – Mount Mengam	1555	Papua New Guinea	-4.7028, 145.2313
80042	1769	Pegunungan Q	1384	Indonesia	-3.8021, 140.6519
80073	1657	Mount Sulen	1145	Papua New Guinea	-3.4080, 142.1868
80074	1660	Mount Bapi *	1144	Papua New Guinea	-3.2006, 141.1301
80085	1193	Mount Bougainville	1039	Papua New Guinea	-2.6544, 141.0329

80022	1807	Manam Volcano, Manam Island	1807	Papua New Guinea	-4.0792, 145.0383
80033	1496	Gunung Sambrawai *, Pulau Yapen	1496	Indonesia	-1.7709, 136.4283
80090	1034	Bonsupiori, Pulau Biak	1034	Indonesia	-0.8068, 135.6056

Boising, OC701
Petter Bjørstad, June 2014

Sometime in 2010 I looked at the list of the 50 most prominent mountains of the world and noticed that all but one had been climbed. The one, called 'Finisterre Range Highpoint', remained mysterious. Therefore, in June 2012, my son Pål and I travelled to Papua New Guinea with the intention of climbing it. I had spent many hours trying to get in indirect contact with the local chief of the Tep-Tep tribe. He had promised to guide us to the highest summit, but he meant the highest summit in Tep-Tep territory, while our peak was located in Nankina land. We returned to Norway with lots of experience and a better understanding of why nobody had ever visited this peak.

It took two more years of research to establish contact with the Nankina tribe and prepare a new expedition. After arriving on the island we travelled by dinghy, then by foot to Gwarawon, the main Nankina village. There we learned that the name of the mountain was Boising and that another village, Kwombwu, was even closer. We walked to Kwombwu, being the first outsiders ever to visit. After discussing our intention with the local people, we eventually succeeded in making the ascent, a project that they fully engaged in. A trail through dense jungle was needed. We had between ten and twenty men help clear a path with their machetes. After camping high on a ridge the peak could finally be attempted. Pål led up ridges with grass to locate a short summit ridge. We built a small cairn before returning to camp. Upon our return to Kwombwu two days later, the village launched a 24-hour 'sing-sing' to celebrate and mark the change from believing that one should never approach this peak to accepting that this ascent could be positive for their future.

The two expeditions required five weeks in the Papua New Guinea jungle and several hundreds of hours spent on prior research and preparations.

Boising, OC701, Mount Wilhelm and Mount Giluwe, OC703
Rob Woodall, August 2015

In August 2015 there was a British expedition to Boising. It had only one previous ascent, by Petter Bjørstad's party a year before. Our attempt failed. The people of the upper reaches wanted more money than we had brought. There was no cash machine, so we were all left empty handed. We were Scott and party to Petter's Amundsen, but we didn't freeze to death, or get eaten.

I had a few days to spare and decided to try for Kanangio, an island peak just off the north coast of New Guinea. I had no information but our hotel staff managed to devise a plan. I would get the bus to Kubugam, a fellow passenger would keep me on track and I would stay with someone local. This all worked nicely. My genial host was the local chief constable. In the afternoon we attended a sports day (darts, basketball and bamboo drums), but no alcohol was allowed. We had arranged for an early boat to the island the next morning, but it didn't arrive. I wasn't sure I would have had enough time to reach the summit even if it had arrived on time.

After these two failures we climbed Mount Wilhelm, the highest point in Papua New Guinea and hence a well-established destination. We reached the top of Mount Giluwe too, which was not difficult to arrange. On the way down the guides captured a cuscus (a type of possum). I think someone paid a ransom and the poor creature was released.

Boising, OC701 (Petter Bjørstad)

Single Cone, OC731 (Rob Woodall)

On Haleakala, OC760 (Petter Bjørstad)

OC702 Maoke Range

Id	Height	Name	Drop	Country	Location
80001	4884	Puncak Jaya – Carstensz Pyramid	4884	Indonesia	-4.0789, 137.1595
80007	4758	Puncak Mandala – Aplim Apom	2760	Indonesia	-4.7087, 140.2894
80011	3750	Pegunungan Weyland – Kobowre	2215	Indonesia	-3.8708, 135.8708
80024	3640	Undundi-Wandandi	1732	Indonesia	-3.5067, 136.4227
80029	3949	Angemuk	1565	Indonesia	-3.5250, 138.5917
80032	3340	Deiyai	1523	Indonesia	-3.9692, 136.1951
80043	3785	Jumbul Ambera	1383	Indonesia	-3.8675, 139.0033
80044	3955	Gunung Antares	1381	Indonesia	-4.8961, 140.9040
80046	3773	Z Chain	1354	Indonesia	-3.6333, 136.9234
80050	4061	Pegunungan Hens – Ngga Nggulumbulu	1327	Indonesia	-3.7584, 137.3109
80055	2884	Gunung Babiloa *	1272	Indonesia	-3.3017, 136.6059
80056	4750	Puncak Trikora	1268	Indonesia	-4.2618, 138.6817
80061	3285	Y Chain	1227	Indonesia	-3.5585, 137.5601
80064	1322	Bukit Buru	1207	Indonesia	-4.2258, 134.9308
80069	3047	Mamaipiri	1181	Indonesia	-4.0558, 135.9593
80070	3856	Gunung Wairima *	1165	Indonesia	-3.5864, 138.2595
80076	3801	Dugudok	1133	Indonesia	-3.5424, 137.8283
80077	3251	Yaramaniapuka	1112	Indonesia	-4.0991, 135.7408
80079	3151	Jimliek	1106	Indonesia	-3.8027, 138.8259
80091	1587	Pegunungan Charles Louis	1019	Indonesia	-3.7508, 135.2450
80094	1332	Pegunungan Legare	1010	Indonesia	-3.4608, 135.7842

OC703 New Guinea Central Highlands

Id	Height	Name	Drop	Country	Location
80003	4509	Mount Wilhelm / Ende-ewa Kombuglo	2971	Papua New Guinea	-5.7796, 145.0292
80009	4368	Mount Giluwe	2504	Papua New Guinea	-6.0431, 143.8862
80010	4104	Mount Kabangama / Minj Milen Ku	2300	Papua New Guinea	-6.0606, 144.6155
80015	3557	Mount Piora	1920	Papua New Guinea	-6.7253, 145.9876
80019	3616	Mount Karoma	1861	Papua New Guinea	-5.7230, 142.4945
80020	2474	Mount Bosavi	1859	Papua New Guinea	-6.6133, 142.8262
80023	3647	Mount Michael	1760	Papua New Guinea	-6.4053, 145.3156
80035	1544	Mount Samsai / Mount Hunstein	1442	Papua New Guinea	-4.5105, 142.6546
80036	2606	Three Pinnacles	1435	Papua New Guinea	-4.8014, 141.3121
80038	2797	Schrader Range	1426	Papua New Guinea	-5.2183, 144.5190
80040	2002	Blue Mountain / Mount Blue	1390	Papua New Guinea	-4.4431, 141.2854
80045	1817	Water Cap	1357	Papua New Guinea	-4.1612, 141.4239
80052	3065	Fiamolu Mountain / Mawi	1317	Papua New Guinea	-4.8772, 142.0665
80054	3465	Mount Ialibu	1283	Papua New Guinea	-6.2342, 144.0770
80058	3546	Mount Otto	1255	Papua New Guinea	-5.9755, 145.4821
80059	3583	Mount Wamtakin	1245	Papua New Guinea	-5.1908, 141.8698
80060	2810	Mount Stolle / Mekil	1238	Papua New Guinea	-4.7925, 141.6643
80065	2569	Mount Karimui	1202	Papua New Guinea	-6.5920, 144.7879

80068	1977	Mount Kasa / Four Corners / Vierkant	1183	Papua New Guinea	-4.6728, 141.4857
80071	3127	Mount Kamanotina *	1152	Papua New Guinea	-6.1566, 145.7544
80072	3708	Yakopi Nalenk / Burgers Mountain	1147	Papua New Guinea	-5.1511, 143.3079
80075	3852	Mount Kumbivera	1137	Papua New Guinea	-5.5082, 143.0482
80080	3809	Mount Hagen	1082	Papua New Guinea	-5.7603, 144.0407
80084	2667	Mount Suaru	1064	Papua New Guinea	-6.3014, 144.6621
80086	2945	Mount Jaka	1037	Papua New Guinea	-5.6672, 144.4629
80096	2144	Maramuni Mountain *	1008	Papua New Guinea	-4.9239, 143.8685

OC704 Owen Stanley Range

Id	Height	Name	Drop	Country	Location
80004	3676	Mount Suckling / Manurep	2932	Papua New Guinea	-9.6661, 149.0082
80006	4036	Mount Victoria	2773	Papua New Guinea	-8.8925, 147.5333
80018	2883	Mount Simpson	1893	Papua New Guinea	-10.0350, 149.5687
80021	1891	Mount Victory / Keraroa	1851	Papua New Guinea	-9.2002, 149.0718
80031	2274	Sibium Mountains	1545	Papua New Guinea	-9.3258, 148.3583
80034	2752	Mount Shungol	1492	Papua New Guinea	-6.8640, 146.7157
80039	1836	Mount Parkes	1419	Papua New Guinea	-8.7109, 147.7705
80047	3449	Mount Kenevi	1347	Papua New Guinea	-9.1197, 147.8452
80048	3278	Mount Amung	1347	Papua New Guinea	-7.4259, 146.5510
80049	2996	Mount Dayman	1340	Papua New Guinea	-9.8361, 149.2896
80053	2397	Mount Kumalu *	1316	Papua New Guinea	-6.9530, 146.5485
80057	1346	Mount Gugu Sari	1259	Papua New Guinea	-10.5681, 150.2271
80066	2877	Mount Missim / Mount Denny	1193	Papua New Guinea	-7.2169, 146.8098
80081	2715	Uranua Mountains	1079	Papua New Guinea	-7.7223, 147.1711
80082	3277	Mount Yule / Zarimai	1075	Papua New Guinea	-8.2080, 146.7838
80083	1770	Ajaura Hills	1066	Papua New Guinea	-9.7469, 148.6679
80088	1850	Mount Atlee-Hunt	1036	Papua New Guinea	-8.1186, 147.5046
80093	3990	Mount Albert Edward – East Dome	1017	Papua New Guinea	-8.4125, 147.4033
80095	2793	Jonangge Mountain	1009	Papua New Guinea	-7.5106, 147.0271
80097	1834	Mount Thompson	1007	Papua New Guinea	-10.1464, 149.8368
80098	1938	Hydrographers Range	1005	Papua New Guinea	-8.9750, 148.3368
80008	2536	Mount Vineuo, Goodenough Island	2536	Papua New Guinea	-9.3325, 150.2050
80014	1947	Mount Kilkerran, Fergusson Island	1947	Papua New Guinea	-9.4617, 150.7683
80028	1711	Mount Kaibole, Fergusson Island	1631	Papua New Guinea	-9.4292, 150.5458
80087	1390	Edagwaba Range, Fergusson Island	1036	Papua New Guinea	-9.6183, 150.6475
80063	1210	Prevost Range, Normanby Island	1210	Papua New Guinea	-10.1033, 151.1850
80089	1036	Mount Koia Tau, Misima Island	1036	Papua New Guinea	-10.6583, 152.6300

Mount Hagen, OC703
Rob Woodall, August 2015

Mount Hagen, the Ribu which gives its name to the airport, was a straightforward day hike from Magic Mountain Lodge, where I was staying. It had five summit candidates, and to the bemusement of my local guide I visited all of them (one involved a tricky scramble). My final day was spent enjoying some of the spectacular bird life. Papua New Guinea is a fascinating destination, but climbing many of its 84 Ribus is likely to be difficult.

OC71 Lesser Australian Ranges

OC712 Central Australia Ranges

Id	Height	Name	Drop	Country	Location
80502	1531	Mount Zeil / Urlatherrke	1325	Australia	-23.4008, 132.3958

OC713 South Australia Ranges

Id	Height	Name	Drop	Country	Location
80504	1171	Saint Mary Peak / Ngarri Mudlanha	1029	Australia	-31.5036, 138.5520

OC714 Tasmania

Id	Height	Name	Drop	Country	Location
80501	1617	Mount Ossa	1617	Australia	-41.8708, 146.0333
80503	1573	Ben Lomond – Legges Tor	1302	Australia	-41.5325, 147.6583
80505	1327	Mount Picton	1023	Australia	-43.1575, 146.6067

Mount Ossa, OC714

Rob Woodall, January 2015

Australia is a vast but ancient and eroded land with only fourteen Ribus, two of which are Ultras. On the way back from New Zealand four of us climbed Mount Ossa in Tasmania. The weather there is notoriously wet. The peak is close to the inexplicably popular five-day Overland Track, but it can also be reached from the east, with a hut stay en route. The trail included long stretches of boardwalk to protect the fragile habit and the sanity of hikers. We arrived at the hut soaked and made the short hike the next morning, struggling up to the summit block in wind and rain, before returning to the hut and escaping the next morning. Tasmania has other Ribus. It's not known whether it has other weather.

OC72 Great Dividing Range

Peaks in this region are shown on the same map as OC71.

OC720 Cape York Ranges

Id	Height	Name	Drop	Country	Location
81002	1611	Bartle Frere / Choorechillum	1319	Australia	-17.3992, 145.8183
81003	1582	Bellenden Ker – Centre Peak	1236	Australia	-17.2592, 145.8592
81005	1218	Mount Elliot	1171	Australia	-19.4883, 146.9675
81007	1374	Thornton Peak / Wundu	1119	Australia	-16.1642, 145.3742
81009	1018	Bell Peak North	1004	Australia	-17.0858, 145.8800
81006	1121	Mount Bowen, Hinchinbrook Island	1121	Australia	-18.3567, 146.2667

OC722 North New South Wales Great Dividing Range

Id	Height	Name	Drop	Country	Location
81008	1586	Brumlow Top	1105	Australia	-32.0025, 151.4475

Brumlow Top, OC722
James Stone

This is a shy swelling on the plateau of the Barrington Tops National Park in New South Wales. It is hidden in the midst of the lush Gondwana rainforest. Whilst a track passes quite close to the summit, it is still a battle through the clawing vegetation to find the actual top, marked by a partially moss-covered cairn. Barrington Tops comprise an ancient, eroded shield volcano and Brumlow Top is likely the highest volcano on the Australian landmass. The nearby Mount Polblue, another short hike through vegetation, was once thought to be the highest in the area, and has a triangulation pillar, but it is now understood to be several metres lower. Brumlow Top also has competition from Round Hill, nearly 200 kilometres further north, which is about the same height and has an air navigation facility, so access to its highest point is uncertain.

OC723 South New South Wales Great Dividing Range

Id	Height	Name	Drop	Country	Location
81001	2228	Mount Kosciuszko / Kunama Namadgi	2228	Australia	-36.4558, 148.2633

OC724 Victorian Alps

Id	Height	Name	Drop	Country	Location
81004	1984	Mount Bogong / Warkwoolowler	1232	Australia	-36.7325, 147.3067

Mount Bogong, OC724
James Stone, January 2018

This is the highest point in the state of Victoria, cut off from the rest of the Great Dividing Range by the valley of the Big River. It comprises a large and exposed plateau with its lower reaches skirted by a forest of Alpine ash. Traditionally the Bogong region was a gathering place for indigenous groups who would meet to trade, undertake ceremonies and eat the protein-rich Bogong moth. There are many routes to the plateau but most climbs are probably undertaken via the Staircase Spur on the north-west of the mountain.

OC73 New Zealand

OC730 New Zealand North Island

Id	Height	Name	Drop	Country	Location
81502	2797	Mount Ruapehu	2797	New Zealand	-39.2896, 175.5626
81504	2518	Mount Taranaki / Mount Egmont	2311	New Zealand	-39.2961, 174.0639
81516	1571	Pukeamoamo / Mitre	1341	New Zealand	-40.7982, 175.4576
81533	1752	Hikurangi	1183	New Zealand	-37.9190, 178.0607

OC731 New Zealand South Island – Lesser South Island Ranges

Id	Height	Name	Drop	Country	Location
81505	2723	Mount Tutoko	2191	New Zealand	-44.5942, 168.0125
81506	2885	Tapuae-o-Uenuku	2022	New Zealand	-41.9958, 173.6628
81507	2319	Single Cone	1956	New Zealand	-45.0716, 168.8078
81508	2608	Manakau	1788	New Zealand	-42.2250, 173.6175
81509	2333	Mount Taylor	1636	New Zealand	-43.5077, 171.3189
81512	1875	Mount Owen	1415	New Zealand	-41.5520, 172.5412

Id	Height	Name	Drop	Country	Location
81513	2102	Moffat Peak	1404	New Zealand	-45.0191, 168.1285
81517	1354	Kā Mauka-Tokoweka	1334	New Zealand	-45.3467, 166.9617
81518	2340	Mount Franklin	1331	New Zealand	-42.0516, 172.6877
81519	2022	Jane Peak	1322	New Zealand	-45.3279, 168.3234
81520	2061	Tooth Peak	1321	New Zealand	-44.9783, 168.3183
81521	1804	Hunter Mountains	1320	New Zealand	-45.6628, 167.4071
81522	2185	Mount Hutt	1292	New Zealand	-43.4717, 171.5258
81523	1749	Ivess Peak	1269	New Zealand	-42.2059, 172.1210
81524	1525	Mount Uriah	1225	New Zealand	-42.0182, 171.6433
81528	1921	Grampian Mountains – Black Rocks	1212	New Zealand	-44.3250, 170.5292
81532	1203	Mount Stokes	1183	New Zealand	-41.0904, 174.1020
81534	1650	Brunel Peaks	1176	New Zealand	-45.7508, 167.7875
81537	2343	Mount Bonpland	1167	New Zealand	-44.8277, 168.2797
81539	1829	Mount Harper / Mahaanui	1150	New Zealand	-43.6582, 171.0519
81540	2098	Mount Saint Bathans	1150	New Zealand	-44.7166, 169.7492
81542	1704	Caroline Peak	1140	New Zealand	-45.9440, 167.1950
81543	1478	Mid Dome	1139	New Zealand	-45.5849, 168.5373
81547	2096	Ailsa Mountains	1107	New Zealand	-44.8878, 168.1834
81548	1791	Maungakura / Red Hill	1098	New Zealand	-41.6267, 173.0575
81549	1577	Bayonet Peaks	1097	New Zealand	-45.1625, 168.6858
81550	1764	Mount Ward East	1093	New Zealand	-45.6108, 167.1908
81551	1963	Mount Pisa	1084	New Zealand	-44.8725, 169.1908
81553	1606	Mount Mantell	1080	New Zealand	-41.9792, 172.2833
81555	2474	Mount Christina	1076	New Zealand	-44.7930, 168.0481
81561	2122	Pariroa / Castle Mount	1053	New Zealand	-44.8483, 167.7800
81563	1892	Mount Lyall	1051	New Zealand	-45.2752, 167.5364
81565	1314	Expedition Peak	1043	New Zealand	-44.9910, 167.3463
81566	1760	Mount Richmond	1040	New Zealand	-41.4742, 173.3958
81567	2293	Somnus	1038	New Zealand	-44.6644, 168.2212
81572	1859	Mount Irene	1029	New Zealand	-45.1779, 167.3594
81574	1043	Treble Mountain	1023	New Zealand	-46.0025, 166.6992
81575	2182	Raglan Range	1022	New Zealand	-41.9866, 173.0344
81577	2173	Dillon Cone	1016	New Zealand	-42.2719, 173.2241
81531	1196	Mount Grono, Secretary Island	1196	New Zealand	-45.2653, 166.9520
81557	1069	Mount Clerke, Resolution Island	1069	New Zealand	-45.6879, 166.6865

OC732 New Zealand South Island – Southern Alps

Id	Height	Name	Drop	Country	Location
81501	3724	Mount Cook / Aoraki	3724	New Zealand	-43.5950, 170.1421
81503	3033	Mount Aspiring / Tititea	2471	New Zealand	-44.3842, 168.7275
81510	1648	Skippers Range	1598	New Zealand	-44.4342, 168.1700
81511	1925	Mount Victor	1432	New Zealand	-44.0325, 169.1833
81514	1894	Benmore Peak	1396	New Zealand	-44.4167, 170.0942

81515	2830	Mount Earnslaw / Pikirakatahi	1359	New Zealand	-44.6225, 168.4108
81525	2145	Mount Franklin	1225	New Zealand	-42.8700, 171.6594
81526	1356	Mount Bruce Murray	1223	New Zealand	-42.7170, 171.3357
81527	1900	Mount Longfellow	1220	New Zealand	-42.6925, 172.2908
81529	2640	Mount Hooker	1201	New Zealand	-43.8308, 169.6733
81530	2643	Mount Dechen	1198	New Zealand	-43.7975, 169.7558
81535	2408	Mount Murchison	1169	New Zealand	-43.0041, 171.3769
81536	1748	Ben Lomond	1168	New Zealand	-45.0070, 168.6156
81538	2875	Mount D'Archiac	1153	New Zealand	-43.4650, 170.5817
81541	1998	Castle Hill Peak	1148	New Zealand	-43.2579, 171.7698
81544	2536	Mount Pollux	1127	New Zealand	-44.2325, 168.8733
81545	2620	Mount Edward	1122	New Zealand	-44.4667, 168.5850
81546	1633	Mount Oakden	1111	New Zealand	-43.2447, 171.4163
81552	1860	Mount Binser	1083	New Zealand	-43.0268, 171.8606
81554	1204	Mount Te Kinga	1079	New Zealand	-42.6604, 171.5001
81556	1835	Mons Sex Millia	1075	New Zealand	-42.5350, 172.4500
81558	1373	Mount Turiwhate	1067	New Zealand	-42.7628, 171.2906
81559	3151	Mount Sefton	1063	New Zealand	-43.6825, 170.0420
81560	1455	Glen Dene Ridge	1055	New Zealand	-44.5468, 169.1677
81562	1680	Purple Hill	1052	New Zealand	-43.1087, 171.8126
81564	2275	Mount Rolleston	1048	New Zealand	-42.9112, 171.5125
81568	1497	The Pyramid	1038	New Zealand	-42.4656, 171.9176
81569	2024	Mount Turnbull	1035	New Zealand	-42.8522, 172.0544
81570	1873	Mount Crichton North	1033	New Zealand	-45.0202, 168.4840
81571	1845	Gray Hill	1032	New Zealand	-42.9540, 171.9639
81573	1909	Mount Nerger	1024	New Zealand	-43.9983, 169.1358
81576	1695	Mount Ida	1016	New Zealand	-43.2166, 171.5322
81578	2194	Mount Enys	1014	New Zealand	-43.2333, 171.6350
81579	1385	Mount Harata	1014	New Zealand	-42.3754, 171.9058
81580	2175	McKerrow Range	1009	New Zealand	-44.3100, 169.2792
81581	2525	Centaur Peaks	1001	New Zealand	-44.6354, 168.5749

Skippers Range, OC732
Rob Woodall, January 2015

It is never a good sign when your chosen summit does not have a name. The Skippers Range Highpoint had no known ascents and we had no plans to climb it until we discovered that New Zealand helicopter flights were quite affordable. Even better, a tourist couple had booked a flight to Milford Sound, so we could be tourists then be dropped off at the peak. Not at the summit of course – we identified a spot just above the forest. The pilot explained how to leave the chopper as he would be unable to safely leave the controls. We first visited Lochnagar (an actual lake, not a mountain as in Scotland). Milford Sound was spectacular. The peak was a pleasant 600-metre ascent in four hours. In the pub that night another pilot told us that he took hunters to the area regularly.

OC75 Melanesia

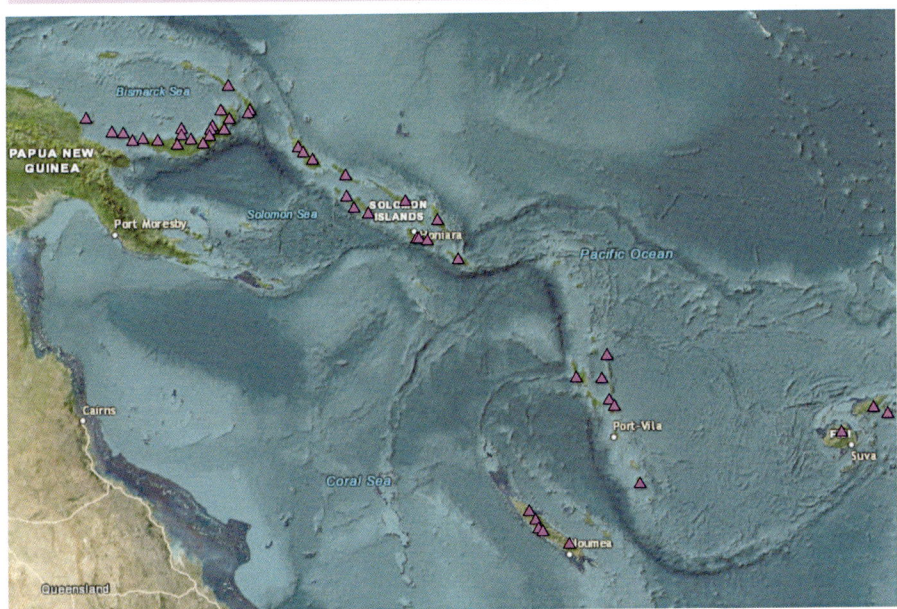

OC750 Bismarck Archipelago

Id	Height	Name	Island	Drop	Country	Location
82502	2340	Mount Taron / Mount Agil	New Ireland	2340	Papua New Guinea	-4.4008, 152.9383
82516	1502	Lengtien Mountains / Lelet Plateau	New Ireland	1437	Papua New Guinea	-3.3717, 152.0108
82529	1920	Verron Range	New Ireland	1202	Papua New Guinea	-4.5317, 152.8567
82504	2334	Ulawun	New Britain	2334	Papua New Guinea	-5.0508, 151.3308
82505	2316	Nakanai Mountains	New Britain	2072	Papua New Guinea	-5.1867, 151.8350
82509	2063	Mount Sinewit	New Britain	1716	Papua New Guinea	-4.7458, 152.0533
82510	1824	Mount Talawe	New Britain	1699	Papua New Guinea	-5.5375, 148.3925
82512	1951	Whiteman Range	New Britain	1645	Papua New Guinea	-5.8125, 149.8383
82517	2248	Mount Bamus	New Britain	1424	Papua New Guinea	-5.1983, 151.2400
82526	1750	Karas Range	New Britain	1234	Papua New Guinea	-4.3875, 151.7142
82527	2185	Hargy Mountain *	New Britain	1221	Papua New Guinea	-5.4517, 151.2308
82531	1305	Mululus	New Britain	1147	Papua New Guinea	-5.5583, 150.4075
82532	1360	Mount Andewa	New Britain	1142	Papua New Guinea	-5.6100, 148.9992
82533	1155	Mount Wangore / Mount Bola	New Britain	1138	Papua New Guinea	-5.1417, 150.0375
82537	1105	Mount Welcker	New Britain	1075	Papua New Guinea	-5.4167, 150.0267
82540	1920	Mount Welu *	New Britain	1045	Papua New Guinea	-5.7317, 150.9400
82507	1839	Mount Uluman / Mount Kunugui	Karkar	1839	Papua New Guinea	-4.6775, 145.9775
82511	1658	Mount Bel	Umboi	1658	Papua New Guinea	-5.6150, 147.9658
82519	1378	Tolokiwa Volcano	Tolokiwa	1378	Papua New Guinea	-5.3142, 147.5900
82524	1280	Mount Reaumur / Dowi	Long Island	1280	Papua New Guinea	-5.2567, 147.0900

OC751 Solomon Islands

Id	Height	Name	Island	Drop	Country	Location
82501	2715	Mount Balbi	Bougainville	2715	Papua New Guinea	-5.9050, 154.9950
82514	2251	Mount Takuan	Bougainville	1517	Papua New Guinea	-6.4433, 155.6092
82544	1893	Mount Bagana	Bougainville	1010	Papua New Guinea	-6.1375, 155.1958
82503	2335	Mount Popomanaseu	Guadalcanal	2335	Solomon Islands	-9.7033, 160.0608
82522	1920	Mount Kaichui	Guadalcanal	1313	Solomon Islands	-9.7842, 160.5075
82543	1932	Mount Latinarau	Guadalcanal	1012	Solomon Islands	-9.7117, 160.1583
82508	1768	Mount Veve	Kolombangara	1768	Solomon Islands	-7.9517, 157.0767
82523	1303	Mount Kalourat	Malaita	1303	Solomon Islands	-8.9717, 160.9217
82528	1219	Mount Sasari	Santa Isabel	1219	Solomon Islands	-8.1750, 159.5542
82535	1080	Mount Vangunu	Vangunu Island	1080	Solomon Islands	-8.6875, 157.9975
82538	1063	Rendova Peak	Rendova Island	1063	Solomon Islands	-8.4692, 157.3533
82539	1050	Makira	Makira	1050	Solomon Islands	-10.5900, 161.8175
82546	1006	Mount Maetambe	Choiseul / Lauru	1006	Solomon Islands	-7.0850, 157.0067

OC752 Vanuatu

Id	Height	Name	Island	Drop	Country	Location
82506	1879	Tabwémasana	Espiritu Santo	1879	Vanuatu	-15.3625, 166.7542
82515	1496	Manaro	Aoba	1496	Vanuatu	-15.4045, 167.8396
82518	1413	Lopevi Volcano	Lopevi	1413	Vanuatu	-16.5092, 168.3433
82525	1270	Maroum	Ambrym	1270	Vanuatu	-16.2467, 168.1192
82534	1084	Mount Tukosmera	Tanna	1084	Vanuatu	-19.5767, 169.3875
82542	1016	Mount Teu	Mere Lava	1016	Vanuatu	-14.4642, 168.0392

OC753 New Caledonia

Id	Height	Name	Drop	Country	Location
82513	1629	Mont Panié / Taaluny	1629	New Caledonia	-20.5886, 164.7702
82520	1618	Humboldt	1325	New Caledonia	-21.8800, 166.4226
82530	1501	Mé Maoya / Mémwâwia	1156	New Caledonia	-21.3678, 165.3354
82536	1381	Hîgo / Tchingou	1076	New Caledonia	-20.9016, 165.0059
82545	1330	Boulinda	1006	New Caledonia	-21.2318, 165.1471

OC754 Fiji

Id	Height	Name	Island	Drop	Country	Location
82521	1324	Tomanivi / Mount Victoria	Viti Levu	1324	Fiji	-17.6150, 178.0183
82547	1241	Uluigalau	Taveuni	1241	Fiji	-16.9000, 179.9867
82541	1032	Nasorolevu	Vanua Levu	1032	Fiji	-16.6267, 179.3975

OC76 Polynesia

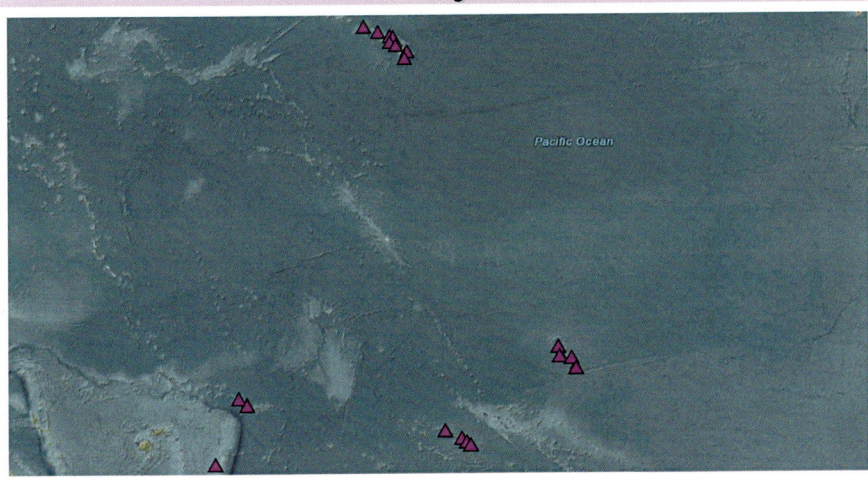

OC760 Hawaii

Id	Height	Name	Island	Drop	Country	Location
83001	4230	Mauna Kea – Pu'u Wekiu	Hawaii	4230	USA	19.8207, -155.4680
83004	4190	Mauna Loa	Hawaii	2180	USA	19.4755, -155.6057
83002	3055	Haleakala / Pu'u Ulaula	Maui	3055	USA	20.7097, -156.2533
83006	1764	Pu'ukukui	Maui	1729	USA	20.8904, -156.5863
83007	1600	Kawaikini	Kauai	1600	USA	22.0587, -159.4974
83008	1515	Kamakou	Molokai	1515	USA	21.1067, -156.8683
83011	1231	Ka'ala	Oahu	1231	USA	21.5081, -158.1429
83017	1030	Lānaʻihale	Lanai	1030	USA	20.8123, -156.8732

OC761 Central Polynesia

Id	Height	Name	Island	Drop	Country	Location
83012	1229	Puoko	Nuku Hiva	1229	French Polynesia	-8.8612, -140.1739

OC762 Samoa

Id	Height	Name	Island	Drop	Country	Location
83005	1858	Mauga Silisili	Savai'i	1858	Samoa	-13.6183, -172.4867
83015	1160	Mount Le Pu'e	Upolu	1160	Samoa	-13.9386, -171.7312

OC763 Southern Polynesia

Id	Height	Name	Island	Drop	Country	Location
83003	2241	Mont Orohena	Tahiti	2241	French Polynesia	-17.6214, -149.4768
83009	1332	Mont Roniu	Tahiti	1319	French Polynesia	-17.8249, -149.2130
83010	1269	Temetiu	Hiva Oa	1269	French Polynesia	-9.8085, -139.0717
83013	1207	Mont Tohiea	Moorea	1207	French Polynesia	-17.5506, -149.8223
83014	1203	Oave	Ua Pou	1203	French Polynesia	-9.3918, -140.0740
83016	1125	Touaouoho	Fatu Iva	1125	French Polynesia	-10.5001, -138.6396
83018	1018	Tefatua / Mont Toomaru	Raiatea	1018	French Polynesia	-16.8350, -151.4535
83019	1015	Kao	Kao	1015	Tonga	-19.6683, -175.0158

Relative mountains of the ocean

Back in 1980, David Byrne of Talking Heads noted that 'there is water at the bottom of the ocean'. This statement is indeed accurate but for some reason Byrne made no note of all the mountains down at the ocean floor. Known as seamounts, these submersed mountains are defined as isolated rises in elevation of 1000 metres or more from the surrounding sea floor which do not reach the surface of the sea. Aquatic Ribus, if you will, all of which are rarely seen by human eyes. Seamounts have a negative elevation as even the tallest must remain submerged below sea level to qualify.

Estimates of how many seamounts exist vary widely. According to Dean Goodall in *Introduction to Seamounts*, at least 9951 have been mapped, but the National Oceanic and Atmospheric Administration suggests the actual number may be over 20000. A new one with a height of around 1500 metres was discovered in 2023 by researchers mapping the sea bed off Guatemala for Schmidt Ocean Institute, a private foundation set up in 2009 to advance research, knowledge and sharing of information about the oceans. One of the foremost seamount researchers is Lucy Woodall, but she appears not to be related to the leading terrestrial Ribu bagger Rob Woodall (he who would all mountains climb).

A standard protocol for reaching the summit of seamounts has yet to be established. Some people might be content to reach a summit by diving from the ocean surface, but the more dedicated seamount baggers would aim to begin their ascents from the ocean floor.

There are also at least 283 guyots, which are flat-topped seamounts – also known as tablemounts – created by wave action near the surface of the ocean. These guyots can have summit plateaus exceeding ten kilometres in diameter, so finding the location of the summit could be extremely challenging.

There are many more underwater Ribus than terrestrial Ribus yet they are largely out of reach for non-amphibious peak baggers. Given that less than 10% of the deep sea floor has been well-mapped, there is substantial research work yet to do on them, though private companies have been collecting their own bathymetric data, which tends to be held outside of the public domain. Some seamounts are active volcanoes and the Pacific Ocean is home to more of them than any other ocean. Seamounts appear to be used by whales as navigational aids and are often sites of high biodiversity.

Some mountains straddle both submarine and terrestrial zones and therefore cannot be defined as seamounts. These include Mauna Kea on Hawaii, which extends 5251 metres from the sea floor to the surface of the ocean and continues rising for another 4230 metres above sea level. All of the peaks in this book are based on 'wet prominence', whereby all permanent water, snow and ice are regarded as features of the surface of Earth. This is the standard version of topographic prominence. Contrast this with the concept of 'dry prominence' which assumes that the Earth's surface is a solid bottom such as the ocean floor. Changes in sea level would not have any impact on figures based on dry prominence as they would remain the same whether or not the oceans existed.

With a total of 9481 metres of relative height from the bottom of the ocean, Mauna Kea is the second most prominent mountain on the planet according to the dry prominence model, after Mount Everest, which has a dry prominence of 19760 metres due to the Challenger Deep at the southern end of the Mariana Trench near Guam, which is the lowest known point of the sea bed at minus 10911 metres.

It makes sense for the Ribus project to use sea level as zero for mountain height measurements and to disregard what we cannot see, so the wet prominence model is much more intuitive than the dry prominence model. As the wet prominence of Mauna Kea is 4230 metres, it comfortably qualifies as one of the fifty most prominent Ribus.

Antarctica

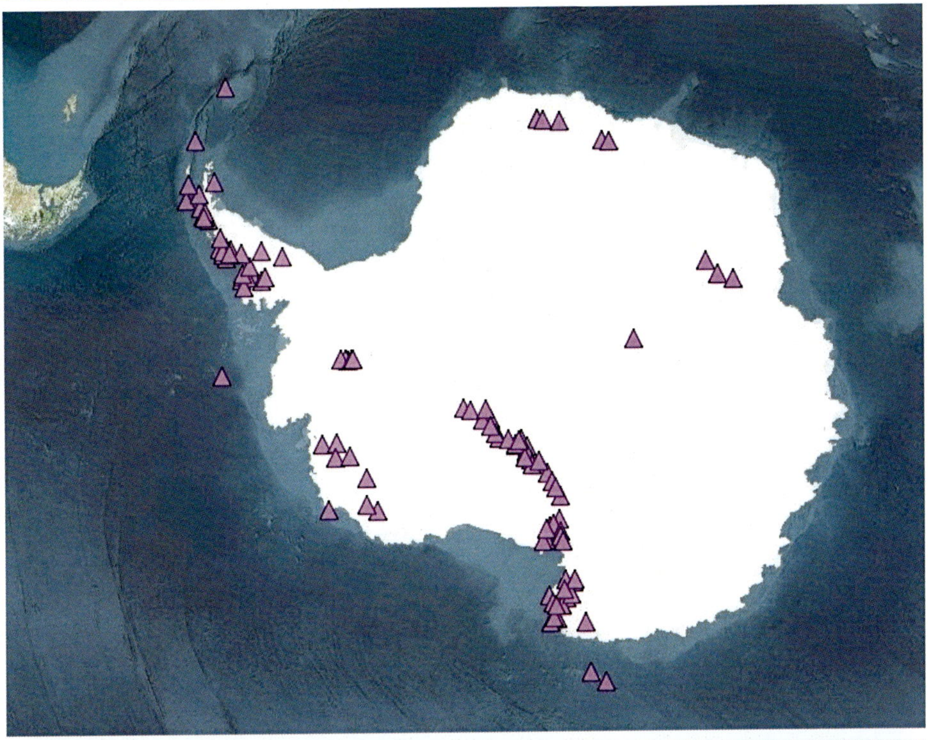

Mount Sidley, AN803 (James Stone)

AN80 West Antarctica Ranges

AN800 Antarctic Peninsula

Id	Height	Name	Island	Drop	Location
90008	3239	Mount Hope	Antarctica	2193	-69.7983, -64.4558
90013	2250	Mount Rendu	Antarctica	1980	-67.4500, -67.0592
90025	1946	Bartholin Peak	Antarctica	1479	-67.2955, -66.6850
90026	2415	Mount Matin	Antarctica	1427	-65.1558, -63.6067
90032	2046	Mount Lagally	Antarctica	1291	-67.1442, -67.0833
90033	3184	Mount Jackson	Antarctica	1283	-71.3608, -63.4275
90037	1585	Rudozem Heights – Glavinitsa Peak	Antarctica	1246	-67.6433, -66.6982
90038	2120	Gravier Peaks	Antarctica	1227	-67.2117, -67.3025
90045	1675	Mount Edgell	Antarctica	1088	-69.4392, -68.2683
90046	1980	Mount Bain	Antarctica	1062	-66.5525, -65.4400
90048	2040	Hadley Upland	Antarctica	1021	-68.5167, -66.4258

Antarctic Peninsula Islands

Id	Height	Name	Island	Drop	Location
0003	3075	Alexander Island Peak *	Alexander Island	3075	-69.1919, -70.7058
90010	2985	Mount Stephenson	Alexander Island	2158	-69.8233, -69.7092
90021	2095	Colbert Mountains	Alexander Island	1589	-70.6492, -70.1283
90023	2580	Elgar Uplands	Alexander Island	1548	-69.5475, -70.6433
90041	2360	Mount Calais	Alexander Island	1146	-69.1800, -70.2367
90047	1990	Dimitrova Peak	Alexander Island	1061	-69.2358, -71.4108
90050	2050	LeMay Range	Alexander Island	1013	-70.7567, -69.2500
90004	2825	Mount Français	Anvers Island	2825	-64.6238, -63.4380
90049	1520	Mount William	Anvers Island	1017	-64.7844, -63.6667
90005	2560	Mount Gaudry	Adelaide Island	2560	-67.5433, -68.6092
90022	2250	Mount Bouvier	Adelaide Island	1551	-67.2175, -68.1733
90006	2520	Mount Parry	Brabant Island	2520	-64.2594, -62.4061
90011	2040	Mount Foster	Smith Island	2040	-62.9950, -62.5516
90016	1772	Mount Irving	Clarence Island	1772	-61.2758, -54.1300
90017	1700	Mount Friesland	Livingston Island	1700	-62.6708, -60.1864
90018	1645	Mount Verne	Pourquoi Pas Island	1645	-67.7475, -67.4758
90051	1585	Mount Arronax	Pourquoi Pas Island	1000	-67.6575, -67.3733
90020	1617	Mount Haddington	James Ross Island	1617	-64.2141, -57.6211
90024	1500	Enigma Peak	Rothschild Island	1500	-69.5508, -72.7075
90027	1415	Mount Bridgman	Liard Island	1415	-66.8200, -67.3950
90028	1415	Luigi Peak / Savoia Peak	Wiencke Island	1415	-64.8532, -63.4264
90034	1280	Blaiklock Island Peak *	Blaiklock Island	1280	-67.5592, -67.0525
90035	1265	Mount Nivea	Coronation Island	1265	-60.5840, -45.4750
90039	1160	Hansen Island Peak *	Hansen Island	1160	-67.1092, -67.6092
90040	1160	Mount Britannia	Rongé Island	1160	-64.7138, -62.6926
90042	1125	Tower Hill	Trinity Island	1125	-63.7108, -60.7183

AN801 West Antarctic Ice Cap

Id	Height	Name	Drop	Island	Location
90019	1640	Lars Christensentoppen	1640	Peter I Island	-68.8292, -90.6308

AN802 Ellsworth Mountains

Id	Height	Name	Drop	Island	Location
90001	4892	Mount Vinson	4892	Antarctica	-78.5255, -85.6171
90029	4157	Mount Anderson	1411	Antarctica	-78.1483, -86.1856
90031	3817	Mount Goldthwait	1323	Antarctica	-78.0142, -85.9806
90036	2776	Mount Ulmer	1264	Antarctica	-77.6114, -86.0503
90043	4852	Mount Tyree	1125	Antarctica	-78.4086, -85.8669

AN803 Coastal West Antarctica

Id	Height	Name	Drop	Island	Location
90002	3162	Mount Siple	3162	Siple Island	-73.4392, -126.7272
90007	4275	Mount Sidley	2503	Antarctica	-77.0397, -126.1014
90009	3520	Mount Tahake	2175	Antarctica	-76.2817, -112.1258
90012	3595	Richmond Peak	2014	Antarctica	-75.7975, -115.8136
90014	2634	Mount Murphy	1865	Antarctica	-75.3453, -110.7375
90015	3652	Mount Frakes	1807	Antarctica	-76.7992, -117.6592
90030	3478	Mount Berlin	1333	Antarctica	-76.0558, -135.8242
90044	2978	Mount Andrus	1114	Antarctica	-75.8217, -132.3067

Mount Sidley, AN803

James Stone, January 2017

This is the highest volcano in Antarctica and one of the Volcanic Seven Summits. It lies in a 80-kilometre volcanic chain comprising the Executive Committee range. It rises some 2000 metres from the surrounding ice sheet. It is remarkably remote and access is only feasible through a logistics provider such as Antarctic Logistics and Expeditions or a national scientific expedition.

Mount Sidley is a complex, polygenetic stratovolcano which was discovered in 1934 when it was overflown by a US mission. It was first climbed in 1990 and for a time was thought to be the highest mountain in Antarctica.

The volcano's main features are a five-kilometre wide crater blasted out of the side of the mountain together with rime-covered rocks that are scattered around its upper reaches, often referred to as 'mushrooms'. The mountain is now visited regularly by climbers looking to climb all the Volcanic Seven Summits.

AN81 Transantarctic Mountains

AN810 Victoria Land

Id	Height	Name	Drop	Island	Location
90502	4163	Mount Minto	2641	Antarctica	-71.7858, 168.7533
90507	3501	Mount Murchison	2005	Antarctica	-73.4208, 166.3008
90509	3654	Mount Supernal	1826	Antarctica	-73.0592, 165.6992
90512	2732	Mount Melbourne	1755	Antarctica	-74.3500, 164.6900
90515	2026	Mount Brewster	1603	Antarctica	-72.9550, 169.3783
90522	3750	Mount Hewson	1430	Antarctica	-73.9667, 162.6367
90524	3300	Mount Payne	1382	Antarctica	-72.8175, 167.8617
90525	2085	Hargreaves Peak	1378	Antarctica	-71.6183, 170.5558
90527	2581	Mount Ford	1264	Antarctica	-70.9542, 162.8700
90528	3245	Mount Hancox	1263	Antarctica	-72.6267, 166.9917
90531	3719	Mount Sabine	1245	Antarctica	-71.9175, 169.5533
90535	2474	Navigator Nunatak	1204	Antarctica	-73.2658, 164.2600
90542	2903	Mount Lepanto	1115	Antarctica	-72.7375, 168.4417
90553	2820	Mount Monteagle	1003	Antarctica	-73.7208, 165.4667
90508	2000	Hawkes Heights	2000	Coulman Island	-73.5475, 169.6950

AN811 Prince Albert – Mcmurdo

Id	Height	Name	Drop	Island	Location
90501	3794	Mount Erebus	3765	Ross Island	-77.5258, 167.1675
90510	3300	Mount Terror	1804	Ross Island	-77.5108, 168.5717
90505	4025	Mount Lister	2191	Antarctica	-78.0608, 162.6850
90514	3525	Mount McClintock	1611	Antarctica	-80.2233, 157.5158
90516	2609	Mount Discovery	1586	Antarctica	-78.3717, 165.0183
90521	2765	Mount Harmsworth	1466	Antarctica	-78.6817, 160.9275
90532	2723	Mount Morning	1233	Antarctica	-78.5008, 163.5292
90536	2060	Mount Coates	1197	Antarctica	-77.7917, 162.1633
90541	1829	Mount Theseus	1127	Antarctica	-77.4583, 162.2742
90545	1540	Mount Brigham	1096	Antarctica	-77.1175, 162.2933
90547	3070	Timber Peak	1083	Antarctica	-74.1717, 162.3817
90551	1035	Mount Aurora	1009	Antarctica	-78.2325, 166.3675

Mount Erebus, AN811

Ross Island has four volcanoes, of which two are Ribus. It has been described as the sixth highest island on Earth and also the southernmost island reachable by sea. However, as the persistent ice sheet connects it to the Antarctic mainland, it is not considered to be a topographically genuine island for the list of Ribus. The highest point, Mount Erebus, was the location of the Air New Zealand Flight 901 disaster in 1979 when a sightseeing flight crashed into the volcano. One of those on board was mountaineer Peter Mulgrew, who had replaced his friend Sir Edmund Hilary as the commentator on the ill-fated flight.

AN812 Queen Alexandra Range

Id	Height	Name	Drop	Island	Location
90503	4528	Mount Kirkpatrick	2611	Antarctica	-84.3283, 166.4500
90504	4160	Mount Miller	2297	Antarctica	-83.3433, 165.7958
90506	4351	Mount Markham	2134	Antarctica	-82.8442, 161.3275
90513	4480	Mount Elizabeth	1733	Antarctica	-83.8933, 168.4033
90523	4303	Mount Bell	1404	Antarctica	-84.0658, 167.4808
90530	3239	Hunt Mountain	1252	Antarctica	-82.0883, 159.2825
90537	3207	Mount Albert Markham	1158	Antarctica	-81.3908, 158.2417
90540	3313	Mount Reid	1134	Antarctica	-83.0417, 166.0267
90543	2819	Mount Fox	1109	Antarctica	-83.6400, 169.2233
90544	3010	Mount Field	1103	Antarctica	-80.8850, 158.0267
90552	3620	Mount Lecointe	1006	Antarctica	-83.1425, 161.1858

AN813 Queen Maud Mountains

Id	Height	Name	Drop	Island	Location
90511	4250	Mount Kaplan	1801	Antarctica	-84.5542, 175.3450
90517	4125	Prince Olav Range	1542	Antarctica	-85.0683, -171.2158
90518	3938	Nilsen Plateau	1538	Antarctica	-86.2675, -158.0625
90519	4084	Flat Top	1528	Antarctica	-84.6875, 172.0000
90526	4069	Mount Fridtjof Nansen	1310	Antarctica	-85.3467, -167.5392
90529	3965	Mount Odishaw	1260	Antarctica	-84.6944, 174.9081
90533	2525	Mount Zanuck	1220	Antarctica	-85.9542, -151.1200
90534	3560	Teller Peak	1216	Antarctica	-85.9517, -135.4717
90538	3310	Johansen Peak	1155	Antarctica	-86.7100, -148.1500
90539	2927	Mount Ellsworth	1138	Antarctica	-85.7567, -160.9942
90546	3380	Mount Westminster	1094	Antarctica	-84.9983, 169.5400
90548	3450	Mount Rosenwald	1035	Antarctica	-85.0633, -179.0158
90549	2781	Mount Borcik	1020	Antarctica	-86.1908, -153.5217
90550	3648	Mount Usher	1017	Antarctica	-84.9442, 172.1450

AN814 Horlick Mountains

Id	Height	Name	Drop	Island	Location
90520	3941	Faure Peak	1514	Antarctica	-85.7092, -128.5775

Johansen Peak, AN813

This is the southernmost Ribu. It is in La Gorce Mountains and is named after Hjalmar Johansen, a member of Roald Amundsen's party in 1911. There are no recorded ascents and probably no unrecorded ones either.

AN82 East Antarctica Ranges

AN820 Queen Maud Land Coast

Id	Height	Name	Drop	Island	Location
91006	3020	Gessnertind	1167	Antarctica	-71.7608, 6.9092
91007	2781	Vikinghoegda	1110	Antarctica	-72.0800, 23.1258
91008	2945	Habermehltoppen	1060	Antarctica	-71.8167, 6.9083
91009	2410	Nipehovden	1050	Antarctica	-71.9192, 24.6558
91010	2931	Ulvetanna	1045	Antarctica	-71.8592, 8.3292
91011	2750	Tambovskajatoppen	1033	Antarctica	-71.6800, 12.3458

AN821 Wilkes Land Coast

Id	Height	Name	Drop	Island	Location
91001	2170	Brown Peak	2170	Sturge Island	-67.3717, 164.7483
91003	1274	Clemence Massif	1274	Clemence Massif	-72.1411, 68.7414
91004	1190	Young Island Peak *	1190	Young Island	-66.3592, 162.3550

AN822 East Antarctic Ice Cap

Id	Height	Name	Drop	Island	Location
91002	4087	Dome Argus	1338	Antarctica	-80.4758, 76.8414
91005	3220	Mount Menzies	1177	Antarctica	-73.4606, 61.8883
91012	1720	Mount Stinear	1008	Antarctica	-73.0786, 66.3186

Dome Argus, AN822

Inaccessibility is relative, but the southern pole of inaccessibility is especially inaccessible, being the point on the Antarctic continent furthest from the Southern Ocean. It is much more difficult to reach than the South Pole, not least because there is some disagreement about where exactly it is. A small number of expeditions have made it to the approximate area, including the Russians, who set up a research station crowned with a bust of Lenin. The southern pole of inaccessibility is one of the three important points in the interior of the continent, along with the South Pole and the local Ribu, Dome Argus.

As the highest ice dome on the Antarctic Plateau, Dome Argus hides a multitude of secrets. It constitutes a single Ribu at present, yet hundreds of metres below the ice is an entire range of mountains called the Gamburtsev Subglacial Mountains. They are thought to be rather like the European Alps and to extend for over 1200 kilometres. It is probable that at some stage in the distant future this range will be uncovered and a large collection of new Ribus will emerge from their obscurity, to be named by any advanced lifeforms that may exist at that time. This range was discovered in 1958 by the 3rd Soviet Antarctic Mission and named after Soviet geophysicist Grigoriy Gamburtsev.

Much further east from Dome Argus is the Denman Glacier, which covers a deep canyon with bedrock over 3500 metres below sea level. Denman Canyon is the deepest natural location on land (or at least not covered by liquid water) anywhere on Earth. It is also a potential negative Ribu depending on whether the layers of solid ice blocking the entire descent to its base are considered to be grounds for disqualification. The Bentley Subglacial Trench in West Antarctica is another contender at minus 2555 metres.

The relative importance of prominence

Most people understand the idea of separate mountains and mountain ranges but are not necessarily interested in a more detailed and precise analysis. However, anyone drawn to the idea of climbing hills in a specific list is likely at some point to question the criteria used and to wonder why some peaks they have seen or climbed are not included. The use of topographic prominence provides a simple, precise and unambiguous principle.

Advantages of prominence

In 2005 a book on prominence was published, entitled 'The Finest Peaks: Prominence and other Mountain Measures', by Adam Helman. This was the first book published on this topic and has been of great value to anyone researching the topic in detail. Helman described two models to help illustrate why the concept of prominence works so well for producing lists of peaks.

The first one is the 'traveling climber' model. A hiker stands at the top of a mountain (Peak A) and gazes over at another, higher one (Peak B) on the other side of the valley. He or she decides to hike from one peak to the other, naturally trying not to lose more height than necessary, usually by following the highest connecting ridge between the two peaks and making the re-ascent in the most efficient way. The lowest point on that highest connecting ridge between the two peaks is the key col. If Peak B is higher than Peak A, the prominence of Peak A will be its elevation minus the height of the key col. For example, if Peak A is the south summit of Everest and Peak B is Everest, then the climber on the south summit will need to drop down only eleven metres on the ridge to the col at 8738 metres before re-ascending 111 metres up to the top of Everest. Ignoring the obvious challenges associated with high-altitude climbing, this meagre drop of eleven metres helps demonstrate why the south summit is not regarded as an independent peak.

The second model is the 'receding flood model'. This can be illustrated by Gunung Merapi and Gunung Merbabu on the island of Java in Indonesia and featured on the front cover. Imagine that sea level rose sufficiently to submerge the lower peak, Gunung Merapi, at 2930 metres. Gunung Merbabu is 3145 metres high and would appear as a small island 215 metres high above the water's surface. As this flood recedes (or the sea level begins to drop slowly) Gunung Merapi appears as a small island too, slowly growing in height (and prominence) as the water level falls. At this stage, the height of Gunung Merapi is equal to its prominence (assuming the water level is regarded as zero). As the water level continues to recede, eventually the original key col, at 1574 metres, is no longer submerged and is revealed as a land bridge that connects Gunung Merapi to the higher Gunung Merbabu.

At this point, Gunung Merbabu becomes the highest peak of the newly-shared island. However, Gunung Merapi is still distinct from Gunung Merbabu, having 1356 metres of topographic prominence. Even if sea level was permanently up at the key col, any hiker wishing to climb Gunung Merapi would still have to make an ascent of at least 1356 metres, assuming there were no roads leading higher toward the summit. If we zoomed out from these two peaks whilst the flood was receding to observe the island of Java as a whole, we would see other high peaks emerging from the waters, not least Gunung Semeru, which at 3676 metres is the highest on the island of Java and therefore has a key col at sea level and a prominence equal to its elevation.

This model reveals that mountains can be identified as objectively independent using prominence criteria. One can also think of prominence as the difference between the summit elevation and the lowest contour ring that encircles this peak but no higher peak.

As you descend from a summit, eventually you will either reach sea level or a contour that encircles the peak in question plus a higher peak. This higher peak can be regarded as a parent peak, and the topographic network of any landmass can be discovered, somewhat like a family tree. This system provides a mathematical hierarchy of peaks. However, although a parent peak would always be higher and on the other side of the key col from its child, there are at least three different ways of defining parentage. It could be the nearest higher neighbour, the nearest more prominent neighbour, or the island parent itself, which is the highest point of the landmass. In some cases, the parent peak will have all three of those characteristics simultaneously.

Disadvantages of prominence

The most significant criticism of using prominence to create lists of hills can be demonstrated with examples of twin peaks, where one peak qualifies as a Ribu but the other does not. Adam Helman refers to this issue as the 'winner takes all' problem.

For example, there may be two peaks of very similar height about ten kilometres from each other on an immense plateau in a country that has not been well surveyed. Different data sources disagree as to which peak is the higher. Only one of these peaks is a Ribu. It is the highest peak of the range and region as a whole. The other one has a prominence of just 80 metres. Whichever is the higher is the queen of the range and the lower is a mere subsidiary peak. Should they be resurveyed and the results found to be the other way around, then the status of the two peaks would switch. In cases like this, most climbers will wish to visit both candidates if possible, firstly to be on the safe side regardless of future survey results and secondly to enjoy what could be two different and enjoyable hikes. Would the survey results mean that one peak was no longer worth climbing and that the higher of the two was suddenly better? Obviously not, but such cases illustrate that using prominence to calculate the status of a mountain requires a winner that takes everything and a loser, possibly by only a few centimetres, that may well be forgotten.

Another potential criticism of prominence is that the key cols are sometimes so distant from significant mountain peaks that they do not relate to human experience but rather to mathematics. Less prominent peaks tend to have a nearby key col that may form part of a hike to the summit and part of the same experience. Others, such as Denali, are completely different in this regard. Denali is the highest and most prominent peak in North America, therefore from its summit there is no peak higher until South America. However, the use of mathematics rather than human experience can be embraced rather than criticised as it can enhance our limited understanding of the land we walk on.

Traditionally, the key col for Denali has been located in an otherwise indistinct village field near Rivas in Nicaragua, about 7700 kilometres away. To travel there by vehicle would require a journey of over 10000 kilometres, taking at least five days of non-stop driving. On foot it might take a year or more for a long-distance walker. It would therefore be quite some experience to include a visit to Denali's key col as part of the broader goal of reaching the summit. It is interesting to note that a field in Nicaragua is the lowest point of the highest natural ridge connecting the continents of North America and South America, but the key col for Denali has complications. There is an artificial lower col even further away at the Culebra Cut on the Panama Canal, which cuts through the continental divide. This col is 26 metres above sea level and has been accepted as the key col for the list of Ribus. The Nicaraguan village field was the col until the Panama Canal was completed, but the reality today is that the Culebra Cut is lower and is a long-standing feature of the landscape that is not likely to change in the near future.

This means that the key col for Denali is about 24 metres lower than on some peak lists whose custodians apply different rules about the impact of human activity on key cols. A similar development has affected the prominence of Kilimanjaro in Africa. When the Suez Canal was completed it cut the land bridge between Africa and Asia and effectively turned Africa into an island. There are no locks on the Suez Canal so it is at the same level as the sea at either end. This means that Kilimanjaro now has prominence equal to its elevation.

Prominence in Britain

In Britain the history of lists of hills usually starts with Hugh Munro, creator of the famous list of peaks in Scotland over 3000 feet high, originally published in 1891 and now known as the Munros. Inclusion in this list was determined by height and subjective judgement, as Munro never specified the prominence required for a peak to be listed, but its importance as a concept was implicit in his subdivision of the list into tops and separate mountains. In the 1920s, John Corbett compiled a list of peaks between 2500 and 3000 high with a prominence of 500 feet. This was the first peak list to specify prominence criteria, albeit in addition to elevation, but it was not published until 1953, several years after Corbett's death.

Feet and metres almost converge on round numbers at certain points – 1500 metres is not far off 5000 feet and 600 metres is not far off 2000 feet. In 1984, Terry Marsh produced a book called 'The Summits of Snowdonia: A Guide to the 600-Metre Mountains of Snowdonia'. A second book covering all Welsh peaks over 600 metres high followed the following year. These seem to have been the first British summit lists to include metric criteria, though this was sometimes combined with subjective elements.

In 1989, Scotsman Eric Yeaman published his 'Handbook of the Scottish Hills'. This too was metric and inclusion on this list required a prominence of 100 metres or more. Isolated peaks which were a minimum of five kilometres on foot from a higher peak were also included. No separate minimum height was required and so relative height (prominence) was prioritised over absolute height (elevation). Yeaman's book appears to have been the first published list to include a criterion for drop but none for absolute height. His list later led to the Humps, a list of around 2980 British hills with 100 metres of prominence.

Whereas Yeaman's list covered only part of Great Britain and remained largely unknown outside small circles of enthusiasts, Alan Dawson's 'The Relative Hills of Britain', published in 1992, introduced the concept of a Marilyn, a hill with a prominence of 150 metres or more, in England, Scotland, Wales and the Isle of Man. This was based on meticulous research of British Ordnance Survey maps. Although the 1542 Marilyns were listed in order of elevation, and their prominence figures were not given, this publication had a wider impact and arguably cemented the importance of prominence as the primary criterion for inclusion in a peak list.

In the same book, Dawson included a list of hills of England and Wales over 2000 feet high with a prominence of 30 metres. These criteria were extended to Scotland in 2004. In 2010 the lists became fully metric and all of Britain was covered in a single list of hills over 600 metres high with 30 metres prominence, the Simms ('Six-hundred Metre Mountains').

Prominence globally

In 1930, the German and Swiss mountaineer Günter Dyhrenfurth used the concept of prominence to begin compiling lists of peaks over 7000 metres high, after having been part of the first ascent of Jongsang Peak (7462m). In the USA, a group known as the Colorado

Fourteener Completers were using the concept of prominence by the 1960s to identify separate peaks with a minimum elevation of 14000 feet. Imperial measurements were usual then but most more recent lists – especially those created in Europe – have either been metricated or been metric from the outset.

It was Earth scientist Steve Fry who came up with the term Ultra (for 'ultra major mountain'), in the USA during the 1980s, for mountains with a prominence of 5000 feet (1524 metres) or more. Fry used the word 'prominence' but listed the peaks in order of elevation. With the steady move in recent decades from imperial to metric measurements, the concept of an Ultra was amended to include all peaks with a prominence of 1500 metres.

In 2004, Jonathan de Ferranti, Eberhard Jurgalski and David Metzler compiled a list of the fifty most prominent peaks worldwide, which they called Earth's 'Fifty Finest'. This seems to have been the start of a period of prominence research by international teams using the internet as a means to research and collaborate.

In 2005, Adam Helman's book was published. It included an article on prominence algorithms written by his friend Edward Earl, a software engineer. This article described Earl's WinProm project, an application for calculating prominence based on United States geological survey data converted into a digital elevation map. Without WinProm, manually locating each key col for mountains across the world would have been an extremely challenging and laborious task, prone to human error and requiring an enormous number of topographic maps. With WinProm the process was effectively semi-automated, but researchers still had to use the program rigorously and then analyse and verify every output manually. This is covered in more detail in the next chapter.

Reflections on prominence

Many guides and porters have the job of climbing one single mountain several times a month for years or even decades, usually with a new group of people. They can climb the same mountain numerous times and it will be different on every occasion. Depending on the weather and conditions on the day, they might find that on one occasion they have a leisurely picnic at the top in warm sunshine and a few weeks later find that they are dealing with a life-threatening situation on the same spot. Other people are able to find motivation and satisfaction in climbing lots of different mountains rather than the same one many times, using prominence or elevation as their guiding principles.

Regardless of whether a summit is new or familiar, most climbers know that on some days they may think of little but what they are going to eat that evening, while on other outings they might reach a decision on a crucial event in their life, have a moment of transcendental inspiration, or come up with a new idea or concept, as happened on Gunung Lawu, when the idea for the Ribus first emerged. For some reason, nobody thought to create a list using the 1000-metre prominence criterion until 2009, when Andy M Dean and I created a regional list of Ribus covering the Indonesian archipelago.

Once the list was created, I was inclined to spend every weekend on night trains, rickety buses, motorbikes and domestic flights trying to climb new Ribus. I would often arrive at Gambir train station in central Jakarta at around 5am on a Monday morning, direct from the hike, then head straight in to work at school and try to get a new write-up done for the Gunung Bagging website from my desk in between lessons. I had no idea at the time that all this would eventually lead to a book, but I am sure that this would not have happened without the desire to climb and appreciate mountains. That desire was at least as strong as the desire to classify and tabulate the peaks, and to attempt to apply a clear topographic structure to the complex and often chaotic landscape of the planet.

The research process

At some point in time, artificial intelligence may be able to compile a list like the Ribus in a matter of minutes. For the time being, it takes several people several years to put it all together. After our small, international group of keen hikers and prominence enthusiasts agreed to begin the Ribu research project via the Baggers without Borders online forum, we had to start amassing suitable sources of data. To create a list of mountains based on elevation or prominence requires as many sources as possible, particularly for those parts of the world where no official published elevation data exists and there are no reports of the peaks having been climbed. Several data sources have been used in the project.

Topographic maps

Traditional maps printed on paper are available at varying scales for many regions of the world. Some are military map series covering the entire globe in sections. These include the Army Map Service series produced by the US Department of Defense. Others are produced by government-funded agencies such as the Ordnance Survey in Britain and the Philippines' National Mapping and Resource Information Authority. There are some useful freely-available digital topographic maps for certain regions, such as Central America, or for the entire world from a single source, such as the Russian Topo Maps (currently illegal in Russia). Different topographic maps use different contour ring intervals and provide different levels of certainty. Numerous peaks and cols do not have spot heights and so contour rings are used to estimate their heights. A col that has an elevation of somewhere between 4000 feet and 4100 feet on a topographic map means that the correct figure could be anywhere within a range of 30 metres. Such cases need further data from other sources such as digital elevation models (DEMs).

Digital topographic map layers

Google Maps terrain layer, ArcGIS, OpenStreetMap and OpenTopoMap are all sources that have been worth consulting. Some of them may be from the same origin and some may have voids or major errors in certain areas, but the contour lines can assist in most cases when comparing figures with those shown on traditional topographic maps. Many of these sources also include summit spot heights and names, but with varying degrees of accuracy.

Peakbagger website

Some map layers that are not easy to find elsewhere are visible as a layer on the map on individual peak pages on the Peakbagger.com website.

8000ers website

The highest mountains of the world attract a lot of attention. Eberhard Jurgalski has researched all peaks over 6650 metres high and made his work available to others via the 8000ers.com website. This data source was very useful in the Ribus project in certain regions, not only for elevation figures but also for mountain names.

Digital elevation models

The project team has consulted DEM data where available, including from the Space Shuttle Radar Topography Mission (SRTM), Copernicus GLO-30 from the European Space Agency (ESA), Advanced Land Observing Satellite (ALOS), Terra Advanced Spaceborne Thermal Emission and Reflection Radiometer (ASTER), Reference Elevation Model of Antarctica (REMA) and Polar Geospatial Center (PGC).

The use of DEMs has been essential given the scale of the project, but inevitably these models are prone to error. In densely-forested areas, or urban areas, DEMs can give figures that represent the tops of trees or buildings rather than the ground. In most cases the DEMs tend to slightly under-estimate summit heights, because measurements are taken every few metres. If readings are taken every 30 metres they may miss a peak altogether and give two separate lower readings from either side of it, so steep-sided peaks are often not accurately-represented by DEMs. On average, figures from SRTM data seemed to be about fifteen metres lower than the published elevation from other sources. A rule of 'SRTM plus 15m' was not a bad one at the beginning of the project, but DEM data is becoming more accurate and this trend is expected to continue.

Some recent work has been done to correct elevation readings prone to errors caused by forest canopies and buildings. FABDEM (Forest And Buildings removed Copernicus DEM) was released in 2021 and is a global elevation map that uses artificial intelligence to remove building and tree height biases from the Copernicus GLO-30 model. However, the average height of trees varies enormously depending on terrain and elevation. For example, stripping away a standard fifteen metres from a summit area where the vegetation is only three or four metres high is not going to lead to accurate results, but this technology is likely to improve in the future.

Since the mid-1990s, Jonathan de Ferranti in Scotland has become an authority on numerous worldwide digital elevation models. He has assessed and combined various DEM sources and local topographic maps to form the most error-free central dataset covering the entire planet. He also worked to generate and refine the list of Ultras, along with Aaron Maizlish, manager of the Peaklist.org website. Jonathan's own website, Viewfinder Panoramas, offers numerous computer-generated panoramic drawings.

Between 2005 and 2010, Andrew Kirmse worked on the Google Earth project, with one focus being to create a terrain database from numerous sources. As this work coincided with a growing interest in prominence, based on his hiking and peak bagging experiences, he decided to contact Edward Earl about the WinProm software. In 2014 they began to collaborate on an updated form of WinProm, to be used for a global analysis. Work was still ongoing when Edward Earl died on a hiking trip in 2015. Andrew Kirmse continued to work on the project, using Jonathan de Ferranti's global dataset. In 2017, Kirmse released a dataset covering the entire planet and all summits down to a prominence of 100 feet (30.5 metres).

Kirmse also calculated an isolation figure for all peaks globally, where isolation was defined as the distance from a given point to the nearest point with a higher elevation. This raised some interesting results in contrast with a list based purely on prominence, as smaller peaks on remote islands have considerable isolation figures. Kirmse re-ran his prominence analysis in 2022 using data from a new source, the Copernicus GLO-30 DEM, and published the results in early 2023.

In one of several tragic cases linked to mountain list compilers and authors of writings on topographic prominence, but not directly related to the act of climbing mountains, Steve Fry, initiator of the Ultras name and concept, was murdered in 2019. Correlation is not causation and the cases are not linked, but Steve Fry, Adam Helman and Edward Earl and all prematurely no longer with us.

Lidar

Lidar is a survey technology that uses the reflection of light from the ground as a method of calculating the elevation of numerous points over a large area of terrain. Lidar data is available in some areas and is usually accurate to within half a metre, though its accuracy is also affected by trees, buildings and other constructions. Governments are increasingly using Lidar for topographic surveying, as modern Lidar data capture very high point densities. Lidar is now capable of generating bare earth models with an accuracy of a few centimetres in some cases, depending on terrain.

Amateur surveyors

There are several surveying teams, usually comprising dedicated hikers, with sufficient equipment and knowledge to conduct topographic surveys and release high-quality results. For example, in Britain over 3000 summits have been surveyed using equipment and software that make use of the Global Navigation Satellite System (GNSS). In the USA, Eric and Matthew Gilbertson have been resurveying the highest peaks in Washington state and publishing the results on their Country Highpoints website, as Eric has explained:

I'm working on many peakbagging lists like the world country highpoints and the Washington hundred highest, and it is very important to me that I climb the correct peaks on these lists. I would hate to put in all the effort for an international expedition only to climb the incorrect country highpoint. Sometimes I discover that peaks have not been surveyed carefully enough to know which is actually the highest in a certain country, or whether a peak is high enough or prominent enough to be on the Washington state hundred highest. So I've gone and surveyed peaks myself.

I'm a mechanical engineer by training, and I have access to surveying equipment from the Civil Engineering department at Seattle University, where I teach. My main ground survey tools are a 20-arcsecond mechanical theodolite, a differential GPS unit (capable of two centimetres of absolute vertical accuracy), and several 10-arcminute surveyor sight levels. Before conducting ground surveys I also use Lidar data if available and satellite-based measurements.

My ground surveys have established new country highpoints in Saudi Arabia (Jabal Ferwa), Togo (Mount Atilakoutse), Gambia (Sare Firasu Hill), Guinea Bissau (Dongol Ronde), and Uzbekistan (Alpomish). I have also discovered that the highest point of Kyrgyzstan (Pik Pobeda) does not have a single true summit, as three key locations along a 700m-long ridge are close enough in elevation that yearly snow conditions determine the highest point in any given year.

In the USA a typical survey I've conducted is to determine which of He Devil or She Devil peak in Idaho is higher and thus the Ultra-prominent peak. I brought my theodolite and sight levels to each peak to take angular inclination/declination measurements looking at the other peak. I also took a two-hour differential GPS measurement on each summit with my Spectra Promark 220 with Ashtech antenna. I processed the dGPS results using OPUS, an online tool provided by the US Government. I found that She Devil is 7.9 centimetres taller than He Devil, and is thus the Ultra-prominent peak.

Online trips reports and GPS data

Many hikers enjoy documenting their outings and these reports can include invaluable information, especially for parts of the world where few other sources exist. Some websites have offered GPS data for thousands of mountain hikes. A single height reading is not reliable on its own, as hand-held GPS devices can be affected by vegetation and weather conditions and are usually only accurate to within around ten metres. However, several independent readings with similar summit elevation figures can help researchers to reach a reasonably accurate figure.

The central Ribus database

The existing list of over 1500 Ultras provided a great starting point, and my own research had produced figures for the peaks in Indonesia, Malaysia and Timor-Leste, but this data needed reassessing and we were still left with well over 5500 peaks to research.

By 2019, the research team needed a central place to store and amend data. Computer graphics researcher and keen hiker Oscar Argudo put together a Web-based app using the Python programming language that has allowed numerous editors to edit the dataset simultaneously. Oscar used Andrew Kirmse's 2017 database as a starting point and another database of geographical names to locate possible names for the peaks in Kirmse's dataset, all of which were nameless to begin with.

The web-app allowed team members to compare information on digital map layers using all the above sources. After completing a certain region, the latest dataset could be exported in XLS, KML and GPX formats. Summit and col locations could be manipulated where required, and colour-coded to illustrate confidence in the data. In the many cases of twin peaks, where the lower one had been wrongly identified in the dataset as higher, the cols were exchanged manually. Extreme concentration and fine judgements were often required.

As the project moved forward, some editors with more free time available took on much larger responsibilities and others found themselves overwhelmed with the sheer scale of the task. One or two were quite justifiably too busy climbing mountains (as the world emerged from Covid-19 lockdown) to be able to slave into the early hours of the morning comparing different maps, checking different spellings of a mountain name, and trying to edge the project closer to completion.

Just as the project seemed to be reaching the finish line, Andrew Kirmse released a database update in 2023. This was unexpected but actually good timing, and the team ran some analyses to check for peaks that had different data on the new dataset as compared to the original one from 2017. With a few changes to the structure of the database, and the implementation of a modified version of the PEMRACS system as the basis for geographical divisions into regions, we were nearing some sort of conclusion. But, just as the list of Ultras or P1500s was not the end of the story when they were announced to the world, this list of Ribus or P1000s is not the end either.

Beyond Ribus

The next logical step after Ultras and Ribus could be P500s. However, there has been more interest from hikers in peaks with 600 metres of prominence, known as Majors or P600s. The 600-metre figure in hill lists has its origins in imperial measurements, being a close approximation of 2000 feet (609.6 metres), a figure for summit elevations often used in Britain to distinguish a mountain from a hill.

As the prominence threshold for inclusion in a list is reduced, the number of entries increases exponentially. There are thought to be well over 30000 peaks with over 600 metres of prominence, more than enough to constitute a project spanning several lifetimes. Perhaps it will be the use of artificial intelligence that enables researchers to create a worldwide list of P600 peaks.

Accuracy of digital elevation models for the Pyrenees

by Oscar Argudo

The starting point of the Ribus project was the first automated analysis of prominences on global elevation data made by Andrew Kirmse in 2017. He used a version of the Shuttle Radar Topography Mission (SRTM) elevation dataset, with a spacing of three arc seconds (about 90 metres), improved by Jonathan de Ferranti with higher resolution sources and topographic maps. The result of Kirmse's analysis was a dataset of all the peaks in the world with more than 100 feet (30.5 metres) of prominence. In late 2022, Kirmse redid the analysis using a 30-metre resolution global dataset, the Copernicus GLO-30, adding about 50% more peaks with 30 metres of prominence (P30s). Therefore, one natural question arose: how complete and accurate were these datasets?

In 2017, Toni Braza and I had been working for a couple of years on listing all the P30 summits of Catalonia and the P100 summits of the Pyrenees. We used an automatic analysis on elevation datasets of five-metre resolution from IGN (Institut Géographique National), followed by manual checking of peak and col elevations using topographic maps with one-metre precision or better. Since the Pyrenees were a well-mapped area, and one I was familiar with, I decided to compare map-checked values with results obtained by Kirmse and the output of running his code on the IGN grids. The following table summarises the number of peaks retrieved using the automatic analysis in each of the datasets and the numbers after our manual check, which we regarded as more accurate, assuming that there were no errors in the spot heights of the topographic maps and that we did not make any errors during manual verification.

	SRTM (90m)	GLO-30 (30m)	IGN (5m)	Map-checked
P >=100m	1938	2252	2412	2459
P >=200m	624	672	706	720
P >=300m	283	294	308	310
P >=500m	91	90	99	102
P >=600m	57	58	60	60
P >=1000m	9	9	11	12

The first trend to notice is that the more detailed the elevation model, the more peaks are retrieved from the analysis, although there are always fewer than in reality. This is to be expected. The sampling (spacing) of the elevation grid can easily miss the highest point of a peak or the lowest point in a col. Thus, elevation grids tend to under-estimate peak elevations and over-estimate cols, which results in lower prominences and fewer peaks.

To illustrate the effects of different elevation grid resolutions, the first images overleaf show a photograph of an area of the Maladeta massif (where Pico de Aneto and other high peaks of the Pyrenees are located) along with datasets of different resolutions. The 5m grid data from IGN contain a lot of the details we can perceive in the photograph. A 30m grid (in this case from SRTM instead of Copernicus GLO-30) has lost most of the terrain texture and some peaks have been smoothed, but overall most of the features perceivable in the picture still seem to be present. This is not the case with the 90-metre grid, where an over-smoothed terrain model has already lost some identifiable peaks. There seems to be just one Ribu missing from IGN totals: Pic de Soularac (2368m, P1007). The software analysis identifies it as having a prominence of 996.4m. Most of the difference is explained by the peak elevation being lower in the IGN grid: 2360m. This peak is also missing from GLO-30 and SRTM analyses, with reported prominences of 987m and 951m respectively.

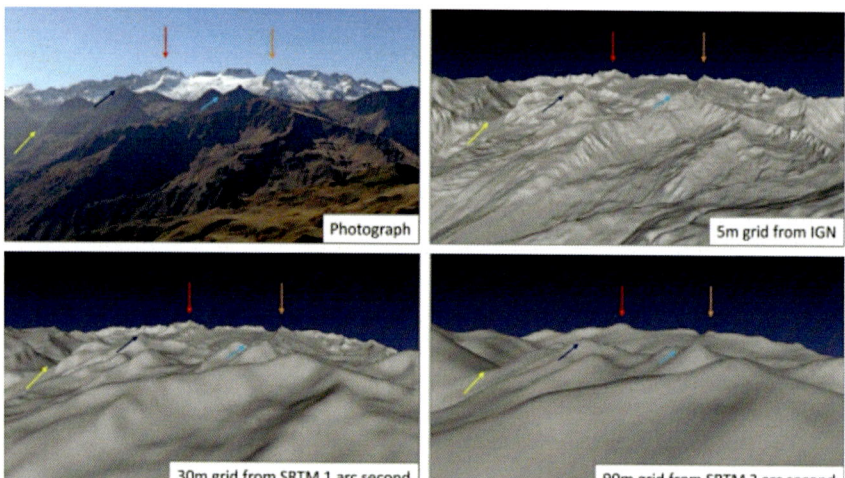
Visual comparison between different elevation datasets around Maladeta massif

Pic de Soularac (left) and Pic Carlit (right)

Cap de la Gallina Pelada (left) and Vignemale (right)

Pic du Midi d'Ossau (left) and Collarada (right)

Pic Carlit (2921m, P1001) is missing as a Ribu in both SRTM and GLO-30 models, with reported prominence 963m and 990m. In this case, while there is consensus among sources that peak elevation should be 2921m, the map-checked prominence varies on topographic maps due to differing elevations of its key col. Col de Puymorens is reported as 1915m in OpenStreetMap, as 1917 in France IGN, and 1919 in Spain IGN. This highlights the importance of checking various sources, and to keep track of a marginal Ribus list in the event that improved data modifies their status.

The last Ribu missing in SRTM and GLO-30 datasets changes in each case. GLO-30 lists Cap de la Gallina Pelada (2321m, P1007) but misses Vignemale (3298m, P1026), with a computed prominence of 972m. SRTM, on the other hand, does the opposite: it includes Vignemale but misses Cap de la Gallina Pelada, assigning a prominence of 983m.

A lower computed prominence from digital elevations is the most common cause of missing peaks for a given threshold, as all the cases above illustrate. Most of these cases can be spotted by manually checking not only the peaks above the cut-off prominence, but also those a few metres below. How much below? It depends on the source and the desired cut-off, keeping in mind that as we lower the prominence threshold the number of peaks included increases exponentially. From the P600 summits of the Pyrenees (about 60 peaks), we found that SRTM had an average prominence error of 24 metres, whereas IGN had an average prominence error of four metres. Of course, there is no way to be 100% certain that we have not missed any peak that appeared to have a much lower prominence than it has in reality.

In some rare occasions, a reported peak from the analysis should not be included in the list at all. It could be the case of identifying an incorrect high point location (wrong peak), an incorrect col location (reporting one col instead of another), or the correct peak and col not being present at all in the elevation dataset. For example, all automated analyses reported Collarada (2883m, P800) as a Ribu, instead of Pic du Midi d'Ossau (2884m, P1089). The reason is that all three elevation grids had a much lower altitude for Pic du Midi d'Ossau, probably because of its steepness. Consequently, their respective key cols were also swapped. Pic du Midi d'Ossau is not only a Ribu but also one of the most beautiful mountains in the Pyrenees. However, just one metre of difference could demote it to P800, in favour of Collarada. Without prior knowledge of it being higher it would have been easy to miss this case due to the peaks being about fifteen kilometres apart.

Luckily, cases like this one are rare. Most of the small differences in elevation that could swap the prominence of two peaks occur between neighbouring high points. For the P600 peaks of the Pyrenees, we found the mean distance between reported peak and actual peak to be 81 metres in the SRTM dataset, whereas in IGN it was nearer 5-10 metres. Thus, most of the time a higher elevation location will be apparent close enough on a map. For the Ribus project we have taken care to incorporate as many data sources as possible and compare them to existing lists. Identified cases of peaks with similar elevations that could be swapped in their prominence have been labelled as possible twin Ribus.

In summary, peak listing has been greatly facilitated in recent years thanks to the analysis software developed initially by Edward Earl and continued by Andrew Kirmse, as well as better and more complete datasets, like those compiled by Jonathan de Ferranti. However, there is still a huge manual effort in checking reported prominence values against maps. We are aware that there is no such thing as a definitive peak list. There could be some corrections as better data and measurements become available and the land itself changes. This publication represents the current list to the best of our knowledge and after several years of effort.

Restless Earth

There are currently 1566 Ultras and 5584 non-Ultra Ribus. It is almost certain that there are not exactly 7150 Ribus. By the time of publication this list of them is likely to be out of date. Inevitably, more Ribus will be discovered in future and possibly a few will no longer qualify or will have their summit location moved significantly. There are many reasons why the Ribus dataset will never be a static entity.

Melting ice

Many summits are covered in snow or ice and many key cols are covered by glaciers. These are all melting at different rates but in many cases sufficiently quickly to mean that new height readings need to be taken every few months rather than every few years. The melting may decrease prominence in some cases and increase it in others. Dome Argus is the highest ice feature of Antarctica and is thought to be the coldest naturally occurring place on Earth. Underneath many hundreds of metres of ice lies a sub-glacial mountain range thought to be similar in size to the European Alps, with sharp mountain peaks and valleys. For now they are ghost peaks, encased within hundreds of metres of ice and hidden from view.

Volcanic activity

When a volcano erupts violently it can change the shape of a mountain summit. In 2010 Gunung Merapi in Indonesia erupted and blasted the lava dome and highest parts of the crater wall to pieces, reducing the elevation from 2968m to about 2930m. If Gunung Merapi keeps behaving in this manner it may end up blowing itself out of the list of Ribus.

Almost 1000 kilometres east of Gunung Merapi is Gunung Tambora, on the island of Sumbawa. As the island summit at 2722 metres high, Gunung Tambora is easily a Ribu, but its highest point is on the edge of an immense crater six kilometres in diameter and at least 800 metres deep, not far off having enough anti-prominence to qualify as a negative Ribu. Something truly cataclysmic happened here in 1815. The height of Gunung Tambora before this eruption is thought to have been around 4300 metres. This relatively recent volcanic event wiped about 1500 metres off the top and moved its summit location by several kilometres. An event of such magnitude will surely happen again.

Also in Indonesia is Anak Krakatau (child of Krakatoa), in the Sunda Strait between Java and Sumatra. After a huge 1883 eruption, about which several books have been written, the volcano appeared to have entered a much quieter phase, yet the 'child' emerged from the surface of the ocean in 1927. By the early part of the 21st century, Anak Krakatau was growing by several metres per year and was estimated to have been around 350 metres high in 2018, just before a devastating lateral collapse of the south-western flank of the cone caused a tsunami. I had been invited to Anyer for the fateful weekend by a Norwegian friend who later had to run from the tsunami. Luckily I declined the invitation in favour of a trip to Java's south coast, as I had been to the Krakatau islands group for a camping trip just four weeks earlier to observe the eruptions. After that event, the volcano's maximum height was just 157 metres and a brand new lake had formed on the island. Digital and physical topographic maps of this volatile location are always some way behind the reality, sometimes by years, during which great changes have occurred. Anak Krakatau has since been growing again. If it continues to grow several metres per year it will qualify as a Ribu by about 2300, but even if it does it is not likely to stay in the list for very long. It is possible that a future eruption will be so massive that it is again reduced to below sea level, before re-emerging as Cucu Krakatau – 'grandchild of Krakatoa'.

Human activity

The construction of a Chinese airport has already damaged one mountain so severely that it no longer qualifies as a Ribu (see page 225). There will probably be similar cases in future as construction, destruction and population growth continue. Key cols can also be affected when new infrastructure is built. A small group of diggers could easily turn a Sub-Ribu into a Ribu over the course of an afternoon, though the digger operators or infrastructure corporations would not have that as their primary motivation. Whether such artificial cols are accepted is ultimately dependent on the perspective of the creator or custodian of the relevant peak list. Should an artificial col take on a natural appearance over time, with vegetation growing as on any other col, then it is hard to argue against its acceptance.

Data development

For many regions of the world the data available is far from ideal. In many cases, deciding on the most probable height of a mountain or col is a matter of judgement. If one source suggests a figure of 2430m and another suggests 2440m, do we opt for one or the other or use the average? The answer depends on the quality of data sources. Some have missing areas, sections of low resolution or can be affected by human error. Good editors look at all the sources available, assess the data quality then make a judgement on the outcome based on the data. This is not an easy task. Better sources of data in future are likely to lead to changes in the list. Over a period of five years we discovered several peaks that qualify as Ultras but were not originally included due to the data sources available when the list was compiled. There were also some that were demoted from Ultra to Ribu status.

The Titiwangsa range of mountains in the Malay peninsula have several peaks between 2171m and 2183m high. Until recently, Gunung Yong Belar was regarded as the highest (based on SRTM data analysis) and was therefore listed as an Ultra. It was later found that local topographic maps, supported by relatively recent surveys, showed Gunung Korbu to be two metres higher, at 2183m. This meant that Gunung Yong Belar should not have been classed as an Ultra and was not even a Ribu, having only 615 metres of prominence. Just two metres, imperceptible to the human eye, made all the difference for inclusion on the list. The two peaks are over eight kilometres apart and can not be climbed in the same outing, unless the outing takes about five days, negotiating an obstacle course of dense jungle, thick mud and slippery logs.

Some pairs of peaks can be climbed within an hour of each other if close enough. The most interesting cases are those which require different approaches or are so far apart that they might be in different countries. Not many Ribus pose that problem, but there are certainly some where the summit could be relocated to a nearby peak found to be a metre or two higher. Unlike the cases of melting glaciers and volcanic destruction, the physical world has not changed after a new survey or model, but our understanding of it has.

Sea level change

The baseline of zero metres is very important. A change of one metre would cause a peak 1000 metres high to become only 999 metres. The implications for the list of Ribus in the longer term are significant, especially for islands where the highest point only just makes it into the list by a metre or two. The great author JG Ballard remarked that reality is 'a stage set that could be dismantled at any moment'. It is both unfortunate and fascinating that elements of the environment which people assume to be most enduring, such as the outline of a mountain, are anything but enduring when we zoom out from the timespan of a single human life and consider our local terrain over the course of millennia.

The Seven Summits

The highest points of the seven continents of the world are known as the Seven Summits. Reaching the top of them all is a huge mountaineering challenge that has spawned several related lists. The following table represents the usual version of the Seven Summits.

Id	Height	Name	Continent	Drop	Country	Location
64001	8849	Mount Everest / Chomolungma	Asia	8849	China, Nepal	27.9879, 86.9248
41001	6963	Cerro Aconcagua	South America	6963	Argentina	-32.6533, -70.0108
30001	6190	Denali / Mount McKinley	North America	6164	USA	63.0691, -151.0062
72001	5895	Kilimanjaro	Africa	5895	Tanzania	-3.0764, 37.3540
90001	4892	Mount Vinson	Antarctica	4892	None	-78.5255, -85.6171
80001	4884	Puncak Jaya – Carstensz Pyramid	Oceania	4884	Indonesia	-4.0789, 137.1595
54001	5642	Elbrus / Mingi Taw	Europe	4741	Russia	43.3525, 42.4375

The table below includes alternative entries. Europe EC means Europe excluding the Caucasus Mountains, Australia TNZ refers to Australia, Tasmania and New Zealand, Australia M refers to the Australian mainland and Tasmania, while Australia OT refers to the country and its overseas territories. Mawson Peak is rarely considered as it is on Heard Island, an overseas territory of Australia that is not part of the Australian continent and is difficult to reach and land on. All eleven entries in both tables qualify as Ribus.

Id	Height	Name	Continent	Drop	Country	Location
51501	4806	Mont Blanc / Monte Bianco	Europe EC	4693	France, Italy	45.8325, 6.8650
81501	3724	Mount Cook / Aoraki	Australia TNZ	3724	New Zealand	-43.5950, 170.1421
73503	2745	Big Ben – Mawson Peak	Australia OT	2745	Australia	-53.1042, 73.5175
81001	2228	Mount Kosciuszko	Australia M	2228	Australia	-36.4558, 148.2633

There is little disagreement about the inclusion of Everest, Aconcagua, Denali, Kilimanjaro and Mount Vinson, but the entries for Europe and Oceania are less obvious. The boundary between Europe and Asia is not universally agreed upon. Some geographers argue that the Kuma-Manych Depression in south-western Russia separates the two continents. If Elbrus is regarded as Asian then its place in Europe is taken by Mont Blanc. The uncertainty over the entry for Oceania is due to the lack of a clear definition. The term Australasia usually includes New Guinea as well as Australia, Tasmania and New Zealand, but a modified version excludes New Guinea because half of it is in Indonesia, which is regarded as an Asian country. Oceania includes all of these plus Melanesia, Micronesia and Polynesia.

The immense challenge of climbing to the top of all Seven Summits was first achieved in 1985 by American Dick Bass. He regarded mainland Australia as a continent and therefore chose Mount Kosciuszko as one of his seven. Shortly afterwards, Reinhold Messner suggested the replacement of Kosciuszko by the much harder Carstensz Pyramid on Puncak Jaya in Indonesian Papua, the highest peak in Australasia and Oceania. This has since become the most popular version of the Seven Summits list, though many people also climb Mount Kosciuszko as it is the simplest of all and can be reached in a few hours.

The inclusion of Puncak Jaya depends on the island of New Guinea being regarded as part of a continental landmass. If the continent is Oceania or Australasia then it counts, but if the landmass is Australia then the entry must be the highest peak on the Australian mainland. If we disregard New Guinea as part of Australasia then Mount Cook in New Zealand should be included, as it is the highest peak of Australia and New Zealand.

The concept of individual continents is to some extent a cultural one. Before the construction of the Suez Canal in 1858 and the Panama Canal in 1914, there were just two major landmasses (the Americas and Eurasia-Africa) plus two very large islands (Australia and Antarctica). With the Suez Canal, Africa technically became an island as the key col for Kilimanjaro became zero (sea level) rather than about ten metres. The Panama Canal divided the Americas in two, so the key col for Denali moved from a Nicaraguan village to between canal locks at the Culebra Cut, which is about 24 metres lower. Asia and Europe still share the huge landmass known as Eurasia, so it is inevitable that dividing it in two will be awkward.

Plate tectonics offer an alternative solution to the definition of continents, with Eurasia becoming one, and both Elbrus and Mont Blanc off the list due to Everest being the entry for Eurasia. Puncak Jaya would be included as the highest part of the Indo-Australian plate, while 4230-metre Mauna Kea in Hawaii would be introduced as the seventh summit, being the highest peak on the Pacific plate. There are plenty of other, minor, plates but none of them correspond to continents.

As the concept of the Seven Summits has become increasingly well known, some mountaineers have considered what the second-highest peaks would be on each continent. They concluded that they would be even harder to climb than the highest Seven Summits.

Id	Height	Name	Continent	Drop	Country	Location
30002	5956	Mount Logan	North America	5250	Canada	60.5671, -140.4056
62501	8611	K2 / Chogori	Asia	4015	China, Pakistan	35.8816, 76.5127
72003	5199	Mount Kenya – Batian	Africa	3825	Kenya	-0.1523, 37.3089
40503	6893	Ojos del Salado	South America	3680	Argentina, Chile	-27.1092, -68.5408
80007	4758	Puncak Mandala	Oceania	2760	Indonesia	-4.7087, 140.2894
54006	5205	Dykhtau	Europe	2002	Russia	43.0517, 43.1325
90043	4852	Mount Tyree	Antarctica	1125	None	-78.4086, -85.8669
51507	4634	Monte Rosa	Europe EC	2165	Switzerland	45.9368, 7.8667
81004	1984	Mount Bogong	Australia M	1232	Australia	-36.7325, 147.3067

Another way of creating a list of the Seven Second Summits would be based on prominence alone. That would create the following list, assuming that Elbrus and Puncak Jaya are included in the primary list of Seven Summits.

Id	Height	Name	Continent	Drop	Country	Location
40001	5731	Pico Cristóbal Colón	South America	5539	Colombia	10.8390, -73.6867
30002	5956	Mount Logan	North America	5250	Canada	60.5671, -140.4056
51501	4806	Mont Blanc / Monte Bianco	Europe EC	4693	France, Italy	45.8325, 6.8650
61501	5610	Kūh-e Damāvand	Asia	4667	Iran	35.9550, 52.1100
83001	4230	Mauna Kea – Puu Wekiu	Oceania	4230	USA	19.8207, -155.4680
71501	4543	Ras Dashen	Africa	3989	Ethiopia	13.2367, 38.3725
90501	3794	Mount Erebus	Antarctica	3765	None	-77.5258, 167.1675
81501	3724	Mount Cook / Aoraki	Australia TNZ	3724	New Zealand	-43.5950, 170.1421

Had Mont Blanc been included in the primary list rather than Elbrus, then Etna on Sicily would take the spot for Europe. If New Zealand were excluded from Australasia, but New Guinea were not, then Boising in Papua New Guinea would make an appearance.

The peaks on the Seven Second Summits list were first climbed by Christian Stangl in 2013. Later the same year he became the first person to reach the Seven Third Summits, though there is even more uncertainty about which peaks should be included owing lack of clarity about definitions of separate continents and separate mountains.

Elbrus, with the higher west peak on the left (James Stone)

K2, the second highest mountain on Earth (Oscar Argudo)

The Volcanic Seven Summits

Inclusion on this list is determined by volcanic activity, whether current, historical or ancient. This is more complex than it sounds, for 'volcanic summits' refers to volcanic mountains rather than minor eminences. Volcanic cones are excluded if they form part of volcanic fields with relatively little prominence. This notably excludes Ka-er-daxi at 5808 metres in the Kunlun volcanic field in Tibet, with a prominence of around only 300 metres. There are also a cluster of obscure mountains east of Ka-er-daxi which may turn out to be volcanic, but all are small volcanic landforms rather than volcanic mountains and all have less than 600 metres of prominence. The highest is Yinshi, at over 5870 metres, and the most prominent is Xiaolan (5798 metres high).

The Volcanic Seven Summits concept was first widely publicised by Amar Andalkar in 1999. Just two of the continental Seven Summits are included – Kilimanjaro and Elbrus. The first mountaineer to climb them all appears to have been Mario Trimeri in 2011. Once again, definitions of Europe and Australasia have led to multiple options, though the version in which Australasia includes Papua New Guinea as part of Oceania is the most widely accepted, as shown in the first table below.

Id	Height	Name	Continent	Drop	Country	Location
72001	5895	Kilimanjaro	Africa	5895	Tanzania	-3.0764, 37.3540
33501	5636	Pico de Orizaba	North America	4922	Mexico	19.0303, -97.2698
54001	5642	Elbrus / Mingi Taw	Europe	4741	Russia	43.3525, 42.4375
61501	5610	Kūh-e Damāvand	Asia	4667	Iran	35.9550, 52.1100
40503	6893	Ojos del Salado	South America	3680	Argentina, Chile	-27.1092, -68.5408
80009	4368	Mount Giluwe	Oceania	2504	Papua New Guinea	-6.0431, 143.8862
90007	4275	Mount Sidley	Antarctica	2503	None	-77.0397, -126.1014

If Elbrus is regarded as Asian rather than European then Etna becomes the entry for Europe while Elbrus becomes the entry for Asia, as it is around 32 metres higher than Kūh-e Damāvand in Iran. If New Guinea is excluded from Australasia then Mount Ruapehu in New Zealand becomes part of the list. If the concept of the Australian continent is narrowed down to the Australian mainland then lowly Brumlow Top becomes part of the list. It is an easy hike with a short ascent from the nearest road, but there is no view from the top and no indication that this was once a volcano. Alternative candidates:

Id	Height	Name	Continent	Drop	Country	Location
52001	3323	Etna / Mongibello	Europe EC	3323	Italy	37.7505, 14.9948
81502	2797	Mount Ruapehu	Australasia TNZ	2797	New Zealand	-39.2896, 175.5626
73503	2745	Big Ben – Mawson Peak	Australia OT	2745	Australia	-53.1042, 73.5175
81008	1586	Brumlow Top	Australia M	1105	Australia	-32.0025, 151.4475

The highest Australian volcano is the recently-active Mawson Peak on Heard Island in the southern Indian Ocean, but this is not part of the Australasian continent. The Australian mainland now has no active volcanoes, but significant volcanic activity once occurred on what is now the east coast. Just as there are issues with defining the continents, there are also issues with defining a volcano. Volcanic cones are excluded, but if an ancient volcanic mountain does not appear to have any typically volcanic features such as fumaroles, lava or a crater, has not erupted in millions of years and would not be identified as being volcanic by anyone other than researchers, then is it still a volcano at all?

All the Volcanic Seven Summits are Ribus. However, all are dormant volcanoes and some no longer resemble volcanoes (Etna, Ruapehu, and Mawson Peak are active but are not regarded as official entries). Mount Sidley has not erupted for millions of years. Elbrus has not erupted since around 50AD. Kūh-e Damāvand has not erupted for 7000 years, though there are active fumaroles on the mountain. Ojos del Salado last erupted over 1000 years ago, though there may have been some small eruptions during the 1950s. Pico de Orizaba erupted in 1846, which compared to the others is very recent. Mount Giluwe has not erupted for hundreds of thousands of years. Kilimanjaro is not regarded as extinct and does have fumaroles on its slopes, but there are no recorded historical eruptions.

If recent volcanic activity within the last 100 years is required then the list would look quite different. This time-span marks the approximate limit of human memory and lifespan. Many volcanoes lie dormant for centuries before recommencing activity, so a single lifetime is too short to notice the characteristics of such volcanoes. Adopting the 100-year rule would give the following table, based on elevation rather than prominence:

Id	Height	Name	Continent	Drop	Country	Location
65501	4753	Vulkan Klyuchevskaya Sopka	Asia	4653	Russia	56.0558, 160.6417
71001	4045	Mount Cameroon – Fako	Africa	3919	Cameroon	4.2180, 9.1735
90501	3794	Mount Erebus	Antarctica	3765	None	-77.5258, 167.1675
52001	3323	Etna / Mongibello	Europe	3323	Italy	37.7505, 14.9948
33502	5413	Volcán Popocatépetl	North America	3033	Mexico	19.0227, -98.6279
83004	4190	Mauna Loa, Hawaii	Oceania	2180	USA	19.4755, -155.6057
40531	6145	Volcán San Pedro	South America	2024	Chile	-21.8877, -68.3914
81502	2797	Mount Ruapehu	Australasia TNZ	2797	New Zealand	-39.2896, 175.5626
73503	2745	Big Ben – Mawson Peak	Australia OT	2745	Australia	-53.1042, 73.5175

If the rules favoured prominence over elevation, then the only changes would be in South America where Cotopaxi is lower but more prominent than Volcán San Pedro, and in Oceania where Ulawun is lower but more prominent than Mauna Loa.

The Hawaiian islands present a problem for compilers of lists of mountains based on continents, and the Arctic island of Jan Mayen further calls into question the continental divisions, as it has the planet's northernmost active volcano, Beerenberg (2277 metres). Jan Mayen is part of the western Eurasian plate, yet tens of millions of years ago it formed part of the eastern edge of the Greenland plate. Knowing where to draw the line with tectonic plates is difficult. There is also an Arabian plate which is home to an extinct volcano.

That there are seven continents on Earth is widely accepted, but defining some of them can be quite complicated. There are several legitimate outcomes based on varying criteria according to political, administrative, conventional, cultural and even tectonic boundaries. My own opinion is that the entry for the continent which includes the Australian mainland should be based on the definition of Oceania that includes Australia, New Zealand, New Guinea, Melanesia, Micronesia and Polynesia, and that all entries for a worldwide list of mountains representing their continent should have a minimum topographic prominence of 1000 metres and therefore qualify as Ribus. As to whether the Caucasus Mountains are part of Europe or Asia, perhaps there is no clear answer to this other than by reducing the number of continents and invoking the concept of Eurasia.

Summit cairn on Brumlow Top, an ancient Australian volcano (James Stone)

Jim Irwin on the Moon, with Mount Hadley beyond (David Scott)

Relative mountains of the Moon

The list of Ribus in this publication does not include data relating to other celestial bodies, but there is extensive information available about the relative mountains of the Moon.

There is no surface water or sea level on the Moon. That means there is no difference between wet prominence and dry prominence, but we need a baseline for measurement. The NASA standard for establishing a 'zero' in place of sea level is based on a nominal mean radius. Since the Clementine mission in 1994, the figure used is 1737.4 kilometres from the centre of the Moon, though 1730km was used by the Defense Mapping Agency in the 1970s and 1737.988km by the Army Mapping Service in the 1960s. Another method would be to locate the deepest crater and make zero metres the lowest point of that.

The Clementine mission was launched with a key aim of making scientific observations of the Moon, but its data has been superseded by that from NASA's Lunar Reconnaissance Orbiter (LRO) between 2009 and 2013. The best modelling data comes from the Lunar Orbiter Laser Altimeter (LOLA) on board the LRO. The LOLA collected over 6.5 million measurements, and the resultant DEM data allegedly has an accuracy of about one metre. As in most or all digital elevation models, some voids exist and have been filled by interpolation.

There are also topographic maps produced by NASA in the 1970s with a scale of 1:250000. Together these maps form the Lunar Topographic Orthophotomap series and include many named mountains and craters, some of which have since been changed.

The Moon has no active volcanoes or tectonic plates. The vast majority of its mountains have been created by asteroid impacts in the distant past, so it appears that the Moon may have a larger number of negative Ribus – craters with a depth of 1000 metres or more – than Ribus with positive prominence. Adam Helman has called this 'negative prominence' whereas Andrew Kirmse referred to 'anti-prominence' and has identified several such features on Earth, though none have an anti-prominence of over 1000 metres.

The highest peak on the Moon is believed to be the Selenean summit along the north-eastern rim of Engel'gardt crater. This is 10786 metres above the mean radius. The slope to the summit has an average angle of only three degrees, discounting numerous impact craters, so it would be a long, steady slog to the highest point rather than a steep climb. However, the low gravity would help speed up progress.

Perhaps the most beautiful photograph of a mountain on the Moon was taken in 1971 by Commander David Scott during the Apollo 15 mission, the fourth to land on the Moon. It shows the lunar module pilot Jim Irwin standing next to the lunar roving vehicle. In the background is the high summit plateau of Mount Hadley, supposedly the second-highest peak on the Moon with around 4000 metres of relative height. It is not clear how far Mount Hadley was from the camera, but NASA sources estimated the distance as eighteen kilometres. The mountain was named after the English mathematician John Hadley.

Before the Apollo 11 crew landed on the Moon they had to undergo a huge amount of training at various locations. One of these places was Hawaii, where in 1965 Buzz Aldrin and other NASA astronauts hiked to the top of Mauna Loa to study its lunar-like surface.

There are advantages and disadvantages to mountaineering on the moon. There is no rain, wind or mist, there are no angry landowners or shooting parties and there are stunning views back to Earth. The ability to leap over any tricky technical sections of terrain is helpful but likely to consume more oxygen than a steady plod. Transportation costs are even greater than on Earth, local accommodation options are severely lacking, and it is inconvenient to arrange a return visit if you find that the list has been changed while you were away, so that a peak you bounded up has been superseded. There are no country pubs, few other hikers to greet, a dismal lack of wildlife, and an altogether eerie calm.

Top 50 Ribus by prominence

Id	Height	Name	Drop	Country	Location
64001	8849	Mount Everest / Chomolungma	8849	China, Nepal	27.9879, 86.9248
41001	6963	Cerro Aconcagua	6963	Argentina	-32.6533, -70.0108
30001	6190	Denali / Mount McKinley	6164	USA	63.0691, -151.0062
72001	5895	Kilimanjaro – Kibo – Uhuru	5895	Tanzania	-3.0764, 37.3540
40001	5731	Pico Cristóbal Colón	5539	Colombia	10.8390, -73.6867
30002	5956	Mount Logan	5250	Canada	60.5671, -140.4056
33501	5636	Pico de Orizaba / Citlaltépetl	4922	Mexico	19.0303, -97.2698
90001	4892	Mount Vinson	4892	Antarctica	-78.5255, -85.6171
80001	4884	Puncak Jaya – Carstensz Pyramid	4884	Indonesia	-4.0789, 137.1595
54001	5642	Elbrus / Mingi Taw	4741	Russia	43.3525, 42.4375
51501	4806	Mont Blanc / Monte Bianco	4693	France, Italy	45.8325, 6.8650
61501	5610	Kūh-e Damāvand	4667	Iran	35.9550, 52.1100
65501	4753	Vulkan Klyuchevskaya Sopka	4653	Russia	56.0558, 160.6417
64002	8125	Nanga Parbat / Diamer	4614	Pakistan	35.2385, 74.5893
83001	4230	Mauna Kea – Pu'u Wekiu, Hawaii	4230	USA	19.8207, -155.4680
63001	7439	Jengish Chokusu / Pik Pobeda	4137	China, Kyrgyzstan	42.0363, 80.1208
63002	5445	Bogeda Feng	4122	China	43.8000, 88.3350
40501	6267	Volcán Chimborazo	4120	Ecuador	-1.4678, -78.8170
69001	4095	Gunung Kinabalu – Low's Peak	4095	Malaysia	6.07508, 16.5583
64003	7782	Namjag Barwa	4093	China	29.6317, 95.0550
31001	4392	Mount Rainier / Tahoma	4037	USA	46.8529, -121.7604
62501	8611	K2 / Chogori	4015	China, Pakistan	35.8816, 76.5127
71501	4543	Ras Dashen	3989	Ethiopia	13.2367, 38.3725
34001	4220	Volcán Tajumulco	3980	Guatemala	15.0430, -91.9037
30003	4671	Mount Fairweather	3976	Canada, USA	58.9064, -137.5265
40502	4988	Pico Bolívar	3964	Venezuela	8.5408, -71.0483
67001	3952	Yù Shān / 玉山	3952	Taiwan	23.4700, 120.9573
72002	5109	Mount Stanley / Ngaliema	3924	DR Congo, Uganda	0.3856, 29.8729
64004	8586	Kānchenjunga	3923	India, Nepal	27.7025, 88.1475
71001	4045	Mount Cameroon – Fako	3919	Cameroon	4.2180, 9.1735
62502	7708	Tirich Mīr	3918	Pakistan	36.2551, 71.8428
72003	5199	Mount Kenya – Batian	3825	Kenya	-0.1523, 37.3089
69002	3805	Gunung Kerinci, Sumatera	3805	Indonesia	-1.6966, 101.2642
68001	3776	Fuji-san / 富士山, Honshu	3776	Japan	35.3608, 138.7275
34002	3819	Cerro Chirripó	3767	Costa Rica	9.4843, -83.4889
90501	3794	Mount Erebus, Ross Island	3765	Antarctica	-77.5258, 167.1675
70001	4167	Djebel Toubkal	3758	Morocco	31.0600, -7.9150
69003	3726	Gunung Rinjani, Lombok	3726	Indonesia	-8.4117, 116.4581
81501	3724	Mount Cook / Aoraki	3724	New Zealand	-43.5950, 170.1421
73001	3718	Pico del Teide, Tenerife	3718	Spain	28.2728, -16.6423

80002	4150	Finisterre Range – Boising	3709	Papua New Guinea	-5.9537, 146.3753
41002	4058	Cerro San Valentín	3695	Chile	-46.5958, -73.3450
30601	3694	Gunnbjørn Fjeld	3694	Greenland	68.9195, -29.8985
40503	6893	Ojos del Salado	3680	Argentina, Chile	-27.1092, -68.5408
69004	3676	Gunung Semeru, Jawa	3676	Indonesia	-8.1079, 112.9227
63301	7556	Minya Konka / Gongga Shan	3646	China	29.5958, 101.8792
40504	5398	Alto Ritacuba	3629	Colombia	6.4846, -72.2965
60001	5137	Büyük Ağrı Dağı / Greater Ararat	3610	Türkiye	39.7021, 44.2984
62503	7649	Kongur Shan	3580	China	38.5933, 75.3125
30004	4996	Mount Blackburn	3534	USA	61.7317, -143.4375

The 4000ers

There are 22 mountains worldwide with a prominence of 4000 metres or more. These 4000ers are spread across all continents, with peaks in North America, South America, Europe, Asia, Africa, Oceania and Antarctica. Aside from Everest, the only other 4000ers with an elevation over 8000 metres are Nanga Parbat (8125m) and K2 (8611m). Three of the 4000ers are on islands rather than continental landmasses: Puncak Jaya in New Guinea, Mauna Kea in Hawaii and Gunung Kinabalu in Borneo. It is unclear if anyone has climbed all 22 of the 4000ers.

It appears that the top 50 most prominent mountains have all been climbed but that nobody has climbed all of them. The 68th most prominent peak, Sauyr Zhotasy in China (3840m with a prominence of 3252 metres) is probably the most prominent peak in the world which had not been climbed by 2024.

Mont Blanc, the 11th most prominent mountain in the world (Oscar Argudo)

Top 50 Ribus by elevation

Id	Height	Name	Drop	Country	Location
64001	8849	Mount Everest / Chomolungma	8849	China, Nepal	27.9879, 86.9248
62501	8611	K2 / Chogori	4015	China, Pakistan	35.8816, 76.5127
64004	8586	Kānchenjunga	3923	India, Nepal	27.7025, 88.1475
64015	8485	Makalu	2393	China, Nepal	27.8895, 87.0886
64017	8188	Cho Oyu	2349	China, Nepal	28.0942, 86.6608
64005	8167	Dhaulagiri I	3358	Nepal	28.6973, 83.4933
64007	8163	Manaslu	3103	Nepal	28.5500, 84.5600
64002	8125	Nanga Parbat / Diamer	4614	Pakistan	35.2385, 74.5893
64009	8095	Annapurna I	2987	Nepal	28.5958, 83.8202
62526	8080	Gasherbrum I / Hidden Peak / K5	2155	China, Pakistan	35.7248, 76.6960
62559	8051	Broad Peak / K3	1701	China, Pakistan	35.8134, 76.5652
62580	8034	Gasherbrum II / K4	1531	China, Pakistan	35.7578, 76.6532
64010	8027	Shisha Pangma / Gosainthan	2909	China	28.3550, 85.7786
64013	7937	Annapūrna II	2437	Nepal	28.5350, 84.1217
64055	7893	Himalchuli	1643	Nepal	28.4367, 84.6392
62514	7885	Disteghil Sar	2512	Pakistan	36.3258, 75.1883
64265	7871	Ngadi Chuli / Peak 29	1021	Nepal	28.5033, 84.5667
62552	7852	Kunyang Chhish	1751	Pakistan	36.2050, 75.2067
62517	7821	Masherbrum / K1	2416	Pakistan	35.6417, 76.3058
64006	7816	Nanda Devi	3139	India	30.3759, 79.9706
62505	7795	Batura Sar	3120	Pakistan	36.5103, 74.5232
62509	7788	Rakaposhi	2800	Pakistan	36.1425, 74.4900
64003	7782	Namcha Barwa	4093	China	29.6317, 95.0550
62567	7760	Kanjut Sar I	1630	Pakistan	36.2058, 75.4167
64011	7756	Kāmet	2820	India	30.9195, 79.5929
64016	7751	Dhaulagiri II	2390	Nepal	28.7633, 83.3883
62528	7742	Saltoro Kangri	2147	Pakistan, India	35.3993, 76.8486
64255	7711	Jannu / Kumbhakarna	1036	Nepal	27.6817, 88.0442
62502	7708	Tirich Mīr	3918	Pakistan	36.2551, 71.8428
64012	7694	Naimonanyi / Gurla Mandhata	2787	China	30.4383, 81.2950
62521	7672	Saser Kangri	2310	India	34.8668, 77.7533
62568	7668	Chogolisa I / Bride Peak	1613	Pakistan	35.6133, 76.5747
62844	7650	Trivor	1010	Pakistan	36.2882, 75.0845
62503	7649	Kongur Shan / 公格尔峰	3580	China	38.5933, 75.3125
62689	7611	Shispare Sar / Pasu	1216	Pakistan	36.4408, 74.6808
64008	7570	Gangkhar Puensum	2997	Bhutan, China	28.0474, 90.4550
63301	7556	Minya Konka / Gongga Shan	3646	China	29.5958, 101.8792
62750	7545	Skyang Kangri / Staircase	1125	China, Pakistan	35.9240, 76.5647
64053	7538	Kula Kangri	1659	China	28.2267, 90.6167
62625	7530	Yukshin Gardan Sar	1365	Pakistan	36.2501, 75.3736
62608	7518	Saser Kangri II	1413	India	34.8044, 77.8058

62550	7516	Mamostong Kangri	1791	India	35.1417, 77.5775
62511	7509	Muztagh Ata	2697	China	38.2758, 75.1167
62504	7495	Pik Imeni Ismail Samani	3403	Tajikistan	38.9433, 72.0158
62533	7492	Noshaq	2017	Afghanistan, Pakistan	36.4325, 71.8292
62560	7464	Teram Kangri I	1694	China, India	35.5798, 77.0789
64121	7462	Jongsang Ri	1327	China, India, Nepal	27.8818, 88.1349
62524	7457	Malubiting	2248	Pakistan	36.0033, 74.8758
63001	7439	Jengish Chokusu / Pik Pobeda	4137	China, Kyrgyzstan	42.0363, 80.1208
62535	7428	K12	1970	Pakistan, India	35.2958, 77.0225

The 8000ers

The highest thirteen Ribus are all over 8000 metres high. They are all located in the Himalayan or Karakoram ranges. Understandably, they have attracted considerable attention by mountaineers and there is a specific list of peaks called the 8000ers.

Interestingly, there are not thirteen 8000ers but fourteen. This is because Lhotse – at 8516m the fourth-highest mountain in the world – has a prominence of only 610 metres. It may be one of the highest peaks but it is a long way short of being a Ribu. It is overshadowed by Everest which is only three kilometres away to the north. Like any other mountain, Lhotse's prominence is derived from its elevation minus the height of the key col, which is the South Col between it and Everest at 7906m. Whether or not Lhotse is a separate mountain depends entirely on how you define what a separate mountain is, but it is certainly not a Ribu. All of the other 8000ers are not just Ribus but Ultras, with the second-least prominent 8000er being Gasherbrum II (8034m), which has a prominence of 1531 metres, which is two and a half times the prominence of Lhotse.

The 8000ers had all been successfully climbed by 1964, when a Chinese team reached the top of Shisha Pangma. The first person to claim to have reached the top of all of them was the Italian climber Reinhold Messner in 1986. However, in recent years some earlier expeditions have been scrutinised using new technology to more precisely locate the summit locations. In 2023, researcher Eberhard Jurgalski claimed that Messner was five metres below the true summit of Annapurna when he climbed it in 1985. This could have been due to the poor visibility on the day, but more probably because the precise summit location was not accurately known back then, with eight possible summits along the three-kilometre long summit ridge. A good counter-argument to Jurgalski is that minor summit features in snow do change over time.

The highest unclimbed Ribu is currently Gangkhar Puensum (7570m) which lies on the border between Bhutan and Tibet and is off-limits due to local religious beliefs. Indeed, all mountaineering has been banned in Bhutan since 2003.

There are several peaks over 8000 metres high that are not included in the accepted list of 8000ers, though the exact height and prominence of them is uncertain. The most prominent is believed to be Broad Peak Central, about 8011m high with prominence of around 190 metres. Two other peaks thought to have over 100 metres prominence are Yalung Kang (Kanchenjunga West Peak) at 8505m with around 135m prominence, and Kanchenjunga South Peak, 8476m with around 116m prominence. Subsidiary peaks of Lhotse and Annapurna are thought to have over 50m prominence. Although these figures are small compared to the 1000 metres required for Ribu status, climbing an extra 50 or 100 metres takes a huge amount of effort at elevations over 8000 metres.

Top 50 islands

Id	Height	Name	Island	Drop	Country / Terr.	Location
80001	4884	Puncak Jaya – Carstensz Pyramid	New Guinea	4884	Indonesia	-4.0789, 137.1595
83001	4230	Mauna Kea – Pu'u Wekiu	Hawaii	4230	USA	19.8207, -155.4680
69001	4095	Gunung Kinabalu – Low's Peak	Borneo	4095	Malaysia	6.0751, 116.5583
67001	3952	Yù Shān / 玉山	Taiwan	3952	Taiwan	23.4700, 120.9573
69002	3805	Gunung Kerinci	Sumatera	3805	Indonesia	-1.6966, 101.2642
68001	3776	Fuji-san / 富士山	Honshu	3776	Japan	35.3600, 138.7275
69003	3726	Gunung Rinjani	Lombok	3726	Indonesia	-8.4117, 116.4581
81501	3724	Mount Cook / Aoraki	South Island	3724	New Zealand	-43.5950, 170.1421
73001	3718	Pico del Teide	Tenerife	3718	Spain	28.2728, -16.6423
30601	3694	Gunnbjørn Fjeld	Greenland	3694	Greenland	68.9195, -29.8985
69004	3676	Gunung Semeru	Jawa	3676	Indonesia	-8.1079, 112.9227
69005	3440	Latimojong – Bulu Rantemario	Sulawesi	3440	Indonesia	-3.3851, 120.0243
52001	3323	Etna / Mongibello	Sicilia	3323	Italy	37.7505, 14.9948
90002	3162	Mount Siple	Siple	3162	Antarctica	-73.4392, -126.7272
34501	3098	Pico Duarte	Hispaniola	3098	Dominican Rep	19.0232, -70.9980
90003	3075	Alexander Island Peak *	Alexander	3075	Antarctica	-69.1919, -70.7058
73501	3070	Piton des Neiges	Réunion	3070	France	-21.0993, 55.4800
83002	3055	Haleakala / Puu Ulaula	Maui (Hawaii)	3055	USA	20.7097, -156.2533
69009	3031	Gunung Agung	Bali	3031	Indonesia	-8.3407, 115.5036
69010	3030	Gunung Binaiya – Puncak Siale	Seram	3030	Indonesia	-3.1733, 129.4556
71002	3011	Pico Basilé / de Santa Isabel	Bioko	3011	Eq Guinea	3.5883, 8.7616
69011	2963	Ramelau – Foho Tatamailau	Timor	2963	Timor-Leste	-8.9065, 125.4935
69501	2954	Mount Apo / Apo Sandawa	Mindanao	2954	Philippines	6.9873, 125.2710
42501	2934	Mount Paget	South Georgia	2934	UK Overseas Ter	-54.4498, -36.5253
69502	2926	Mount Pulag	Luzon	2926	Philippines	16.5975, 120.8992
73502	2876	Maromokotro	Madagascar	2876	Madagascar	-14.0225, 48.9675
30009	2869	Shishaldin Volcano	Unimak Island	2869	USA	54.7555, -163.9705
73002	2829	Pico do Fogo / Pico de Cano	Fogo	2829	Cabo Verde	14.9504, -24.3424
90004	2825	Mount Français	Anvers Island	2825	Antarctica	-64.6238, '-63.4380
81502	2797	Mount Ruapehu	North Island	2797	New Zealand	-39.2896, 175.5626
73503	2745	Big Ben – Mawson Peak	Heard Island	2745	Australia	-53.1042, 73.5175
69017	2722	Gunung Tambora	Sumbawa	2722	Indonesia	-8.2466, 117.9588
82501	2715	Mount Balbi	Bougainville	2715	Papua NG	-5.9050, 154.9950
52002	2706	Monte Cinto	Corse	2706	France	42.3800, 8.9458
69018	2700	Gunung Kapalatmada	Buru	2700	Indonesia	-3.3007, 126.2199
40002	2595	Monte Shipton	Isla Grande	2595	Chile	-54.6628, -69.5921
30602	2594	Barbeau Peak – First Peak East	Ellesmere	2594	Canada	81.9150, -75.0101
69503	2582	Mount Halcon	Mindoro	2582	Philippines	13.2625, 120.9950
90005	2560	Mount Gaudry	Adelaide	2560	Antarctica	-67.5433, -68.6092
80008	2536	Mount Vineuo	Goodenough	2536	Papua NG	-9.3325, 150.2050
64501	2524	Pidurutalagala	Sri Lanka	2524	Sri Lanka	7.0010, 80.7754
90006	2520	Mount Parry	Brabant Island	2520	Antarctica	-64.2594, -62.4061
69505	2465	Mount Kanlaon	Negros	2465	Philippines	10.4100, 123.1300

53002	2456	Psilorítis – Tímios Stavrós	Kríti	2456	Greece	35.2267, 24.7708
73003	2423	Roque de los Muchachos	La Palma	2423	Spain	28.7542, -17.8848
69024	2367	Poco Ngandonalu	Flores	2367	Indonesia	-8.6517, 120.4480
73504	2361	Mont Karthala	Grande Comore	2361	Comoros	-11.7592, 43.3675
73004	2350	Montanha do Pico	Pico (Açores)	2350	Portugal	38.4687, -28.3993
82502	2340	Mount Taron / Mount Agil	New Ireland	2340	Papua NG	-4.4008, 152.9383
68002	2339	Vulkan Alaid	Ostrov Atlasova	2339	Russia	50.8608, 155.5650

Pico del Teide, Tenerife, the ninth most prominent island summit (Alan Dawson)

Gunung Semeru behind smoking Gunung Bromo and Gunung Batok, from Tengger Caldera (Andy M Dean)

Sub-Ribus

Sub-Ribus are mountains with a prominence of over 990 metres but less than 1000 metres, so they miss Ribu status by under ten metres. Currently, 226 Sub-Ribus have been identified.

Id	Height	Name	Drop	Country	Location
63784	6566	Bobogawu	999	China	30.6108, 86.4325
63785	6252	Goyon Kangri I	999	China	30.5842, 95.0517
64290	5905	Yejiang Shan *	999	China	28.4853, 87.2753
63786	5790	Dongna Shan *	999	China	31.9650, 94.2513
64291	5696	Chhote Lek	999	Nepal	29.9317, 81.6967
64289	4420	Kumey Parvat *	999	India	28.0792, 93.1158
30476	2921	Herron Mountain *	999	USA	63.0567, -151.4758
31470	2543	Castle Peak	999	USA	48.9822, -120.8623
31825	2383	Lamarque Peak	999	Canada	58.2886, -127.5622
31457	2380	Mount Skukum	999	Canada	60.1949, -135.4870
30477	2256	Junjik Mountain *	999	USA	68.3867, -147.2100
32201	2154	Deception Cone	999	Canada	56.8517, -124.7628
68730	2054	Loi Se	999	Myanmar	22.3375, 98.4600
51685	1963	Hoher Nock	999	Austria	47.7828, 14.3236
33621	1960	Cerro La Aguja	999	Mexico	18.5371, -102.2925
41375	1941	Cerro Lago *	999	Chile	-51.4150, -73.4450
70533	1803	Jabal Sabidana / جبل سيدن	999	Sudan	18.0715, 36.8460
33622	1580	Cerro Aguja Grande	999	Mexico	26.9447, -108.4611
81582	1429	Lake Kakapo Peak *, South Island	999	New Zealand	-45.9430, 167.0524
65733	1302	Gora Yana *	999	Russia	69.9533, 134.3408
69221	1265	Bukit Pelamau, Borneo	999	Malaysia	3.939201, 4.8492
80100	1180	Wagura	999	Indonesia	-2.7883, 133.8667
31456	1095	Frederick Sound Peak	999	Canada	51.0216, -126.7507
63789	5325	Da Mu Ji / 达木吉	998	China	32.1533, 96.7042
40871	3773	Rabadilla de Vaca / Cuco	998	Ecuador	-4.2492, -79.1075
30937	2940	Sortebræ Bjerg	998	Greenland	69.0092, -27.6733
31826	2864	Highland Peak	998	USA	37.8939, -114.5789
30479	2781	Chitistone Peak *	998	USA	61.5958, -142.1342
67219	2241	Da Haituo Shan / 大海坨山	998	China	40.5750, 115.8186
31458	2197	Quijano Peak	998	Canada	59.6481, -134.9167
30478	2182	Lansing Mountain *	998	Canada	63.8425, -131.8055
68731	2130	Nauzuarzo Tlāng	998	India	23.8383, 93.2542
42031	2070	Pedra Bonita	998	Brazil	-22.7567, -45.8425
68732	1543	Phnom Thom / ភ្នំធំ	998	Cambodia	11.8425, 103.8483
68733	1512	Barak Parvat *	998	India	24.6667, 93.3608
50123	1506	Snøhetta	998	Norway	68.6895, 18.3277
81011	1378	Mount Carbine Tableland	998	Australia	-16.4208, 145.2717
30938	1280	Gabbrofjeld	998	Greenland	68.2017, -31.6417
81010	1259	Mount William	998	Australia	-21.0166, 148.5986
67540	1252	Siran	998	Russia	53.2475, 136.9692

50063	1211	Kambsmyrarhnjúkur	998	Iceland	65.9433, -17.7758	
64525	1187	Malayagiri	998	India	21.3683, 85.2700	
64292	6556	Tsho Karpo Kang	997	Nepal	29.3683, 82.7783	
62859	6500	Skirish Sar	997	Pakistan	36.3003, 75.3742	
40872	5788	Nevado León Muerto	997	Chile	-26.1000, -68.5333	
40873	5167	Cerro Toro	997	Bolivia	-18.9633, -66.4367	
41376	3795	Cordón de Mayan	997	Argentina	-36.2767, -70.0915	
32202	3201	Foster Peak	997	Canada	51.0656, -116.1641	
67220	2550	Wanjiaping Shan *	997	China	31.7458, 109.6242	
51687	2483	L'Étale	997	France	45.8497, 6.4473	
53108	2273	Golem Rid / Bik Doruk	997	North Macedonia	41.4542, 20.6458	
30480	2195	Mount Williams	997	USA	60.7225, -144.9008	
69222	2070	Gunung Siel, Buru	997	Indonesia	-3.3317, 126.4783	
62858	1993	Gora Takhku	997	Uzbekistan	40.3960, 65.9522	
30481	1910	Wade Lakes Mountain *	997	Canada	60.1117, -137.2443	
69223	1200	Bukit Raya, Borneo	997	Indonesia	-1.5333, 111.0817	
53109	997	Óros Kouvára – Profítis Ilías, Ándros	997	Greece	37.8515, 24.8604	
30939	997	Nalungiussaq, Nutaarmiut	997	Greenland	72.7183, -55.4758	
62860	6651	Tahu Rutum	996	Pakistan	36.1183, 75.4975	
63792	6340	Kuoduo Shan *	996	China	30.5075, 83.0675	
63790	5958	Xiaruoduo	996	China	28.3850, 100.4175	
40874	5655	Chila	996	Peru	-15.4061, -72.1669	
64293	5522	Chawa Laji Shan *	996	China	29.0967, 88.2858	
63791	4365	Tangdui Shan *	996	China	28.5458, 98.4267	
41378	4140	Cerro Cenicero	996	Chile	-31.3689, -70.7878	
61633	3410	Kūh-e Mazār	996	Iran	30.8095, 56.7746	
90554	3335	Mount Hirschel	996	Antarctica	-72.1983, 169.5258	
31828	3109	Capitan Mountains	996	USA	33.6013, -105.3437	
51688	2656	Großer Krottenkopf	996	Austria	47.3117, 10.3558	
31827	2449	Penfold Peak	996	Canada	52.8314, -120.5700	
61113	2270	Kūh-e Davān	996	Iran	29.7342, 51.6633	
30483	2169	Takhin Peak *	996	USA	59.2156, -136.1067	
41377	2081	Volcán Yanteles	996	Chile	-43.5033, -72.8142	
81583	1958	Mount Alexander, South Island	996	New Zealand	-42.7242, 171.6067	
30482	1572	Axis Peak	996	USA	60.4517, -149.6133	
67221	1490	Qiānniú Gǎng / 牵牛岗	996	China	30.0285, 119.0021	
61634	1376	Shin Strgai / Sheikh Badin	996	Pakistan	32.2950, 70.8066	
31459	1106	Ursula Peak	996	Canada	53.4894, -128.8120	
63793	6356	Qiaqing Shan *	995	China	30.5106, 94.6378	
62862	6250	Khrebet Ilyksu	995	Pakistan	36.6075, 75.5869	
62861	6065	Pik Beleuli	995	Tajikistan	39.1725, 72.7650	
63794	5370	Gajixiaoza Shan *	995	China	30.9467, 97.6300	
40876	3942	Cerro Negro	995	Peru	-17.3983, -70.2833	
40875	3165	Cerro Palpito	995	Colombia	5.9896, -73.8159	

32203	3077	Smoky Dome	995	USA	43.4931, -114.9363
66569	2631	Sevrey Uul	995	Mongolia	43.6017, 102.0458
70023	2561	Lqars n'Tsguiniyn / Isk n'Aït m'Raw	995	Morocco	32.0508, -4.7150
51033	2228	Urbión	995	Spain	42.0114, -2.8785
65045	2201	Gora Reka Chet *	995	Russia	53.5758, 94.7650
31829	2170	Simpson Peak	995	Canada	59.7236, -131.4481
41380	2110	Cerro Resbalin *	995	Chile	-46.3175, -72.5200
65735	2089	Gora Ukelayat *	995	Russia	62.0200, 170.8383
73518	2075	Pic Mananatana *	995	Madagascar	-21.7058, 46.9092
31830	1994	Nina Peak *	995	Canada	55.8767, -124.7947
30484	1985	Tiekel South *	995	USA	61.2944, -145.3479
41379	1801	Cerro Montura O El Foyel	995	Argentina	-41.6392, -71.5525
69224	1785	Gunung Sidole / Bulu Sinio, Sulawesi	995	Indonesia	-0.5434, 119.9592
67541	1615	Gora Alin' / Гора Алинь	995	Russia	50.6652, 138.7415
80101	1540	Pegunungan Maskur *, New Guinea	995	Indonesia	-3.0633, 134.1992
65737	1513	Gora Nayakhan *	995	Russia	62.3692, 158.6308
65736	1319	Momon *	995	Russia	55.6583, 136.6183
67222	1175	Dàmào Shān / 大帽山	995	China	24.1184, 115.1070
65734	1136	Gora Arman' / Гора Армань	995	Russia	59.8082, 149.9527
42032	1098	Pedra da Jamanta	995	Brazil	-23.3100, -44.6058
81584	1055	Mount Cullen, South Island	995	New Zealand	-41.3375, 173.8317
69225	995	Gunung Manukoko, Atauro	995	Timor-Leste	-8.2700, 125.5758
31460	995	Mount Woronkofski, Woronkofski	995	USA	56.3900, -132.4887
64294	6011	Pangbok *	994	India	33.9900, 76.4979
62863	5825	Keke Tuleke Shan *	994	Afghanistan, China	37.1883, 74.4750
40878	5553	Suri	994	Peru	-17.0683, -69.9919
63795	5550	Baishitougou Shan *	994	China	39.1183, 95.4983
40877	5043	Cerro Rosado	994	Argentina	-23.9775, -65.9400
31832	3099	International Mountain	994	Canada	50.9683, -117.0942
41382	2734	Cerro Pino Solo	994	Argentina, Chile	-38.5181, -70.8644
30486	2561	Raven Throat Peak	994	Canada	62.9556, -127.0111
71568	2475	Äsebot Terara	994	Ethiopia	9.2717, 40.5742
63796	2454	Hkaiyat Bum	994	Myanmar	26.1861, 97.2108
30487	2414	Cloud Peak	994	USA	68.4031, -148.4622
31831	2245	Cry Lake Mountain *	994	Canada	58.6764, -128.9270
31461	2120	Flemer Peak	994	Canada	59.7466, -136.3742
65738	2110	Gora Gromovaya	994	Russia	61.2397, 144.6822
31833	2033	Shilsky Peak *	994	Canada	60.1697, -130.5722
72558	1841	Serra Inago	994	Mozambique	-15.0625, 37.3416
90555	1700	Mount Kowalczyk	994	Antarctica	-77.9333, 163.7883
30485	1684	Kiwi Peak *	994	Canada	65.1933, -134.4628
67223	1384	Méihuā Dǐng / 梅花顶	994	China	24.4882, 113.4124
42033	1265	Pedra da Santa Maria	994	Brazil	-21.0117, -41.2408
34079	1248	Cerro Corre Viento	994	Honduras	15.8331, -86.1830

30941	1185	Taconite Mountain *, Ellesmere	994	Canada	82.8367, -77.4597
41381	1145	Monte Spoerer	994	Chile	-53.4103, -71.9000
30940	1110	Qaarusuup Qulaa	994	Greenland	65.7158, -52.7975
50124	1078	Gora Sedova, Novaya Zemlya Severny	994	Russia	74.0757, 56.2649
40086	1055	Cerro Sobenes *, Isla Nalcayec	994	Chile	-46.1737, -73.7392
50125	1041	Skittentinden	994	Norway	69.6756, 18.4424
63797	6098	Janghgaida Rinag	993	China	33.4767, 87.6467
63798	6020	Wei Xueshan	993	China	36.1367, 90.0725
64295	5258	Harshin Jot	993	India	32.3038, 77.3308
40879	4215	Cerro Pacococha *	993	Peru	-13.5519, -73.3094
68737	3465	Lomu Parvat *	993	India	26.0128, 95.1447
31834	3350	Mount Grafton	993	USA	38.6923, -114.7425
90052	3248	Mount Allen	993	Antarctica	-78.6950, -85.0211
66570	3185	Hemu Shan *	993	China	48.6492, 87.4456
68736	2830	Tao Phoung Chan	993	Vietnam	22.6108, 103.6858
62046	2650	Jabal Bayá, 'Än	993	Saudi Arabia	20.7792, 40.7983
61635	2479	Dra Khel	993	Pakistan	27.9606, 66.7505
71031	2335	Mont Mbam	993	Cameroon	5.9517, 10.7168
60110	2259	Çîyayê Lînki	993	Iraq	37.0892, 43.7317
68735	2245	Lasan Parvat *	993	India	25.0750, 93.7575
32204	2003	Blanchard Peak *	993	Canada	57.2247, -125.0250
68734	1996	Yaoqu Shan *	993	China	21.7017, 101.4900
68079	1756	Sobo-san, Kyushu / 祖母山	993	Japan	32.8281, 131.3470
50126	1590	Storfonn	993	Norway	61.6722, 6.6029
67224	1140	Taibai Ding / 太白顶	993	China	32.3778, 113.2764
69567	1140	Mount Sacripante, Leyte	993	Philippines	10.5350, 124.8300
50127	993	Sandhornet, Sandhornøya	993	Norway	67.1113, 14.0679
64296	6162	Cuochuanmi Shan *	992	China	28.0678, 87.1631
63799	5915	Mami Gongba Shan *	992	China	32.0653, 83.7606
63123	5450	Ayidingkule Shan *	992	China	41.9016, 79.8441
63800	4920	Arpalikkania	992	China	36.8567, 84.1658
40880	4609	Pico Mifés	992	Venezuela	8.7593, -70.8064
61115	3425	Kuh-e Zerreh	992	Iran	32.0051, 50.7372
31836	3033	Cantata Mountain	992	Canada	51.5869, -117.8278
32205	2976	Willard Peak	992	USA	41.3829, -111.9746
31835	2826	Fays Peak	992	Canada	50.5812, -117.2994
51690	2341	Thaneller	992	Austria	47.4264, 10.7247
72559	2274	Himalaya	992	Mozambique	-19.3892, 32.7923
31462	2267	Mount Crerar	992	Canada	50.0803, -123.6447
30942	2190	Rodebjerg	992	Greenland	66.3567, -36.4450
61114	2160	Lavye	992	Iran	32.9728, 48.6761
65739	2152	Gora Mandyčan *	992	Russia	61.8017, 150.4217
51689	2007	Rax – Heukuppe	992	Austria	47.6892, 15.6892
30488	2002	Zenazie Mountain	992	Canada	59.7731, -132.9578

30490	1660	Mount Williwaw	992	USA	61.1036, -149.5139
67542	1578	Maebong-san / 매봉산	992	North Korea	38.9867, 127.1475
68738	1550	Kaladan Parvat *	992	India	22.6283, 92.9167
30489	1490	Mount Hardscrabble *	992	USA	58.6703, -154.9792
34521	1400	Morne Trois Pitons	992	Dominica	15.3714, -61.3278
69568	1338	Mount Lunitan, Luzon	992	Philippines	15.1622, 120.1733
69226	1336	Olet Takan, Sumbawa	992	Indonesia	-8.8367, 117.4900
1239	992	Sgurr Alasdair, Skye	992	United Kingdom	57.2067, -6.2238
62864	6751	Kunchang Kangri	991	India	34.6183, 78.0775
63801	5962	Quanshuigou Shan *	991	China	36.5300, 84.0942
63124	4385	Ewirgol Shan *	991	China	43.1192, 87.3342
40881	4325	Cerro de Santurbán	991	Colombia	7.3775, -72.8447
66571	3720	Gora Bardam-Ula	991	Mongolia	48.3288, 89.8188
63802	3428	Bumrawng Bum	991	Myanmar	26.9997, 97.2133
61116	3284	Kūh-e Sīāh Chūvā	991	Iran	33.3875, 49.9500
33623	3250	Cerro Yucucui	991	Mexico	17.4756, -97.7227
67226	2933	Laojiung Shan	991	China	31.5342, 110.4717
31837	2880	Snowcrest Mountain	991	Canada	49.5519, -116.5172
80102	2654	Morton Peaks, New Guinea	991	Papua New Guinea	-7.3508, 146.0060
32206	2478	Bloodroot Peak *	991	Canada	53.8769, -119.4053
65743	2353	Gora Hastah *	991	Russia	66.3361, 141.4593
31465	2138	Reclusion Peak	991	Canada	52.9722, -127.6347
66051	2094	Gora Bambujka *	991	Russia	55.6892, 115.1508
65742	2057	Gora Čadjah *	991	Russia	56.0074, 129.2850
68739	2045	Salween Bum *	991	Myanmar	22.1119, 98.6071
30491	2035	Mile Benchmark	991	USA	60.9572, -143.7450
65740	2015	Vysokaya Gora / Высо́кая Гора́	991	Russia	60.7075, 139.2033
53110	1644	Chionístra / Χιονίστρα	991	Greece	39.5153, 20.5189
69227	1235	Bukit Mererong, Borneo	991	Malaysia	3.1717, 113.9400
31463	1098	Elephant Head Mountain	991	Canada	53.2085, -128.8813
31464	1061	Mount Parry	991	Canada	52.8810, -128.7590
69569	1026	Mount Arayat, Luzon	991	Philippines	15.2053, 120.7425
64297	6321	Brammah Parvat	990	India	30.2752, 80.6482
62865	5645	Shaitantosh	990	Tajikistan	38.0342, 72.9050
32207	3662	Medicine Bow Peak	990	USA	41.3604, -106.3175
71569	2940	Giangero	990	Ethiopia	7.8083, 37.4833
61636	2890	Kuh-e Aj'e-Pa'in	990	Iran	30.8356, 54.8458
32208	2863	Rocky Mountain	990	USA	47.8124, -112.8005
31839	2548	Dos Cabezas Peaks	990	USA	32.2223, -109.6121
63803	2530	Lóngchán Yán / 龙缠岩	990	China	32.4733, 104.3492
33624	2430	Sierra Almagre	990	Mexico	27.6280, -103.9049
61637	2171	Marithal	990	Pakistan	27.2097, 67.1589
30492	2136	Tele Mountain *	990	Canada	62.5128, -131.8509
69228	1964	Gunung Pugung, Sumatera	990	Indonesia	-4.9758, 103.8600
67543	1955	Gora Yako / Гора Яко	990	Russia	48.6804, 138.2478

31838	1923	Ord Mountain	990	USA	34.6749, -116.8152
30494	1894	Nushralutak Peak *	990	USA	67.6861, -156.5227
31466	1829	Kimsquit Ridge	990	Canada	53.0706, -127.1911
41563	1580	Serra Padauari *	990	Brazil	1.4142, -64.1258
61117	1573	Asiabe-Tudiru	990	Iran	27.3111, 54.8158
30493	1396	Nahanni Butte	990	Canada	61.0857, -123.3818
32516	1250	Four Peaks – South Peak	990	Canada	59.4672, -63.9633
42034	1025	Pico da Pedra Branca	990	Brazil	-22.9319, -43.4732
80099	990	Gunung Samlor, Pulau Waigeo	990	Indonesia	-0.0417, 130.8517

Hoher Nock, 1963m Sub-Ribu in Austria (Rob Woodall)

Sgurr Alasdair (right), 992m Sub-Ribu on Skye in Scotland (Alan Dawson)

Index of countries and territories

This table of countries and territories includes the numbers of Ultras, Ribus and Sub-Ribus found within each. Numerous peaks are found on international borders and have been counted as being in more than one country. Canada has the most Ribus with 932, followed by China (893) and the USA (643). Other countries with more than 100 Ribus are Russia (467), Chile (381), Greenland (244), Argentina (235), Indonesia (235), Iran (212), India (187), Pakistan (174), Mexico (148) and Türkiye (104). In Europe the countries with most Ribus are Italy (98), Norway (92), Greece (59) and France (48).

The same order of top three countries applies to Sub-Ribus, with Canada having 33, China 31, and the USA 23. However, China has more Ultras (189) than Canada (139). There are 145 countries or territories with at least one Ribu, with 121 having at least one Ultra. Lots of countries have no Ribus at all, including Andorra, Bangladesh, Belarus, Belgium, Botswana, Brunei, Burkina Faso, Estonia, Finland, Gambia, Ghana, Guinea-Bissau, Hungary, Israel, Jordan, Latvia, Liberia, Lithuania, Luxembourg, Mali, Mauritania, Moldova, the Netherlands, Paraguay, Qatar, Senegal, Singapore, South Sudan, Uruguay and Zambia.

Country or Territory	Pages	Ultras	Ribus	Sub-Ribus
Afghanistan	163-164, 170-174, 176-177	15	94	1
Albania	141-143	6	20	
Algeria	262-264	3	12	
Angola	276	2	8	
Antarctica	295-300	45	116	3
Argentina	86, 95-109, 115-116	60	235	4
Armenia	150	2	5	
Australia	247, 254, 280, 286-287	2	14	2
Austria	131-132, 134-135	13	57	4
Azerbaijan	150, 161	2	7	
Bhutan	204-205	6	18	
Bolivia	94-98	15	84	1
Bosnia and Herzegovina	141-142		6	
Brazil	112-114	9	52	5
Bulgaria	145-146	4	9	
Cambodia	245	2	2	1
Cameroon	266	2	16	1
Canada	9, 13-24, 31-52, 59-64, 67-69	139	932	33
Cabo Verde	279	2	4	
Chad	263-264	2	6	
Chile	84-86, 92, 94-109	78	381	8
China	169, 173-205, 221-232, 240-243	189	893	31
Colombia	84, 88-90	21	54	2
Comoros	280	2	2	
Costa Rica	77	3	9	
Côte d'Ivoire	266		1	
Croatia	141-142		3	
Cuba	79	1	3	
Cyprus	155	1	1	
Czechia	140		1	

Country or Territory	Pages	Ultras	Ribus	Sub-Ribus
Democratic Republic of the Congo	271	5	11	
Djibouti	269	1	3	
Dominica	80		1	1
Dominican Republic	80	3	5	
Ecuador	86, 90	15	30	1
Egypt	155, 264	2	10	
El Salvador	76-77	4	9	
Equatorial Guinea	266	2	2	
Eritrea	268-269	2	7	
Ethiopia	267-269	19	53	2
Fiji	292		3	
France	80, 123, 125-129, 138-139, 280	10	48	1
French Polynesia	293	1	8	
French Southern and Antarctic Lands	280	1	3	
Georgia	149-150	3	20	
Germany	131-132, 140	1	11	
Greece	142-146	18	59	2
Greenland	21, 24-30	50	244	5
Guatemala	75-76	6	15	
Guinea	266		3	
Guyana	111		1	
Haiti	80	2	4	
Heard Island and McDonald Islands	280	1	1	
Honduras	76-77	8	23	1
Iceland	118	1	8	1
India	175-177, 187, 191-192, 197-200, 203-207, 239	51	187	11
Indonesia	246-257, 281-282, 284	86	235	8
Iran	153-154, 157-164	54	212	7
Iraq	154-157	2	11	1
Ireland	122		1	
Italy	128, 132, 134-135, 138-139	22	98	
Jamaica	80	1	1	
Japan	233-237	21	54	1
Kazakhstan	179-180, 182, 221-222	6	23	
Kenya	268-269, 272-274	6	25	
Kosovo	141-143		4	
Kyrgyzstan	169-170, 179-181	12	67	
Lao	240-245	5	47	
Lebanon	155	2	3	
Lesotho	277	1	2	
Libya	264		1	
Madagascar	280	3	7	1
Malawi	276	1	5	

Country or Territory	Pages	Ultras	Ribus	Sub-Ribus
Malaysia	241-242, 246-249	10	36	2
Mexico	43, 58, 71-76	27	148	4
Mongolia	210, 218, 220-222	18	42	2
Montenegro	141-142		5	
Montserrat	80		1	
Morocco	261-262	5	14	1
Mozambique	276	1	12	2
Myanmar	190-193, 239-242	16	79	4
Namibia	276	1	5	
Nepal	200-203	25	78	2
New Caledonia	292	1	5	
New Zealand	288-290	10	81	3
Nicaragua	76-77	2	9	
Niger	263		3	
Nigeria	266		8	
North Korea	232	1	11	1
North Macedonia	142-143, 146	4	7	1
Norway	118-121	6	92	4
Oman	167	4	10	
Pakistan	163-164, 171-177, 197-198	47	174	6
Panama	77, 84	2	9	
Papua New Guinea	281-285, 291-292	30	84	1
Peru	84, 90-95	22	96	4
Philippines	258-260	29	66	3
Poland	140		2	
Portugal	124, 279	2	7	
Puerto Rico	80		1	
Romania	140	4	8	
Russia	118, 121, 140, 147-150, 209-222, 231-234	68	437	16
Rwanda	271	2	3	
Saint Helena	279	1	1	
Saint Kitts and Nevis	80		1	
Saint Vincent and the Grenadines	80		1	
Samoa	293	1	2	
Sao Tome and Principe	266	1	1	
Saudi Arabia	155, 166	2	23	1
Serbia	141-142, 145		5	
Sierra Leone	266	1	2	
Slovakia	140	1	3	
Slovenia	134-135, 142	2	7	
Solomon Islands	292	2	10	
Somalia	269	1	1	
Somaliland	269		2	

Country or Territory	Pages	Ultras	Ribus	Sub-Ribus
South Africa	277, 280	2	25	
South Georgia and South Sandwich Islands	115-116	2	6	
South Korea	232	2	8	
South Sudan	268, 272	2	6	
Spain	124-127, 279	7	33	1
Sri Lanka	207	1	4	
Sudan	264, 268, 272	3	13	1
Suriname	112		1	
Sweden	119-121	2	15	
Switzerland	128-132	8	36	
Syria	155	1	4	
Taiwan	230	2	9	
Tajikistan	169-170, 173-175, 179	20	77	2
Tanzania	271-274	11	31	
Thailand	240-242, 245	4	34	
Timor-Leste	256	2	6	1
Tonga	293		1	
Türkiye	151-155	24	104	
Turkmenistan	168-169	2	2	
Uganda	271-272	5	10	
Ukraine	140	1	2	
United Kingdom	80, 116, 122		3	1
United States of America	8-15, 32-45, 51-58, 64-69, 293	129	643	23
Uzbekistan	169, 180	1	7	1
Vanuatu	292	1	6	
Venezuela	84, 88, 111-112	17	62	1
Vietnam	226-227, 243-245	10	58	1
Yemen	166-167, 280	4	16	
Zimbabwe	276	1	2	

Totals for Australia, France, the United Kingdom and the USA do not include peaks in their overseas territories, but islands that are an integral part of a country, such as Guadeloupe (France) and Tenerife (Spain), are included in their country totals. French Southern and Antarctic Lands include the islands of Kerguelen and Ile de l'Est (page 280).

Island peaks

Being the largest island on Earth it is perhaps not surprising that Greenland also has the most Ribus (185). Other islands with ten or more Ribus are New Guinea (88), New Zealand's South Island (74), Borneo (61), Baffin Island (53), Sumatera (38), Vancouver Island (33), Sulawesi (32), Ellesmere Island (30), Honshu (29), Jawa (28), Luzon (24), Mindanao (20), New Britain (13), Hokkaido (12), Isla Grande de Tierra del Fuego (11) and Isla Wellington (10).

Ribu density

by Alan Dawson

The largest countries tend to have the most Ribus, but some smaller countries have lots of Ribus for their size. Ribu density is a measure of the Ribus per million square kilometres. For example, the area of the UK is around 244380 square km. It has three Ribus, so its Ribu density is 12.28 (3*1000000/244380). The table below shows the Ribu density of the 25 countries with over 65 Ribus, plus twelve countries that have at least eighteen Ribus and Ribu density over 100. The Area figure is shown in million square kilometres.

Country	Area	Ribus	Ribu Density	
Switzerland	0.04	36	871.9	▲▲▲▲▲▲▲▲▲▲▲▲▲▲▲▲▲▲▲▲▲▲
Albania	0.03	20	695.7	▲▲▲▲▲▲▲▲▲▲▲▲▲▲▲▲▲▴
Austria	0.08	57	679.6	▲▲▲▲▲▲▲▲▲▲▲▲▲▲▲▲▲
Tajikistan	0.14	77	538.1	▲▲▲▲▲▲▲▲▲▲▲▲▲▴
Nepal	0.15	78	530.0	▲▲▲▲▲▲▲▲▲▲▲▲▲
Chile	0.76	381	503.9	▲▲▲▲▲▲▲▲▲▲▲▲▴
Bhutan	0.04	18	468.8	▲▲▲▲▲▲▲▲▲▲▲▴
Greece	0.13	49	447.0	▲▲▲▲▲▲▲▲▲▲▲
Kyrgystan	0.20	67	335.1	▲▲▲▲▲▲▲▲▴
Italy	0.30	98	324.4	▲▲▲▲▲▲▲▲
New Zealand	0.27	81	299.5	▲▲▲▲▲▲▲▴
Georgia	0.07	20	286.9	▲▲▲▲▲▲▲
Norway	0.39	92	238.2	▲▲▲▲▲▲
Phillipines	0.30	66	220.0	▲▲▲▲▲▴
Honduras	0.11	23	204.5	▲▲▲▲▲
Pakistan	0.88	174	197.2	▲▲▲▲▲
Papua New Guinea	0.46	84	181.5	▲▲▲▲▴
Vietnam	0.33	58	175.1	▲▲▲▲▴
Afghanistan	0.65	94	144.2	▲▲▲▴
Japan	0.38	54	142.9	▲▲▲▴
Türkiye	0.78	104	132.7	▲▲▲▴
Iran	1.65	212	128.6	▲▲▲
Indonesia	1.90	325	123.4	▲▲▲
Myanmar	0.68	79	116.8	▲▲▲
Lao	0.24	47	114.0	▲▲▲
Greenland	2.17	244	112.7	▲▲▲
Malaysia	0.33	36	109.1	▲▲▴
Ecuador	0.28	30	105.8	▲▲▴
Canada	9.99	932	93.3	▲▲▴
China	9.71	893	92.0	▲▲▴
Argentina	2.78	235	84.5	▲▲
Bolivia	1.10	84	76.5	▲▲
Mexico	1.96	148	75.3	▲▲
Peru	1.29	96	74.7	▲▲
USA	9.37	643	68.6	▲▴
India	3.29	187	56.9	▲▴
Russia	17.10	467	27.3	▴

One ▲ represents Ribu density of about 40. In many countries the mountains are packed together in relatively small areas – in Greenland the Ribus are all around the coast, while Russia, Canada, China and USA have high mountain ranges and vast areas with no Ribus.

The greatest Ribu density is to be found on islands. Some islands comprise one mountain and little else, such as several of the Aleutian Islands and some of the islands of Greenland.

As with countries, the largest islands tend to have more Ribus, but there are some smaller islands with eight or more Ribus and high Ribu density. Heard Island, between Australia and Antarctica, has one Ribu and is only 368 square km, giving Ribu density of 2717.4. South Georgia has three Ribus, with density 768.6, while Tahiti has two, with density 1870.9. Tahiti is part of French Polynesia, which has eight Ribus on seven different islands and an overall Ribu density of 1919.8.

The table below includes the fifteen largest islands in the world plus all islands with eight or more Ribus, but not Australia or Antarctica which are regarded as continental landmasses. Baffin Island, Victoria Island, Ellesmere Island and Vancouver Island are all part of Canada. Sumatera, Jawa and Flores are part of Indonesia, Timor is split between Timor-Leste and Indonesia. Luzon and Mindanao are part of the Philippines, while New Britain is part of Papua New Guinea. Isla Wellington is part of Chile, as is most of Isla Grande de Tierra del Fuego, but 38% of it belongs to Argentina, with one marginal Ribu.

Island	Area	Ribus	Ribu Density	
Greenland	2.130	185	86.8	▲▲
New Guinea	0.785	88	112.0	▲▲▲
Borneo	0.748	61	81.5	▲▲
Madagascar	0.587	7	11.9	▲
Baffin Island	0.507	53	104.4	▲▲▲
Sumatera	0.443	38	85.8	▲▲
Honshu	0.228	29	127.2	▲▲▲
Victoria Island	0.217	0	0	
Great Britain	0.209	3	14.3	▲
Ellesmere Island	0.196	30	152.9	▲▲▲▲
Sulawesi	0.181	32	177.1	▲▲▲▲▲
South Island, NZ	0.146	74	507.4	▲▲▲▲▲▲▲▲▲▲▲▲▲
Jawa	0.139	28	201.7	▲▲▲▲▲
North Island, NZ	0.116	4	35.8	▲
Luzon	0.110	24	218.3	▲▲▲▲▲▲
Iceland	0.102	8	78.6	▲▲
Mindanao	0.097	20	205.1	▲▲▲▲▲
Hokkaido	0.078	12	153.9	▲▲▲▲
IG de Tierra del Fuego	0.048	11	229.2	▲▲▲▲▲▲
New Britain	0.035	13	369.9	▲▲▲▲▲▲▲▲▲
Taiwan	0.034	9	260.8	▲▲▲▲▲▲▲
Vancouver Island	0.031	33	1054.8	▲▲▲▲▲▲▲▲▲▲▲▲▲▲▲▲▲▲▲▲▲▲▲▲▲
Timor	0.028	8	284.2	▲▲▲▲▲▲▲
Flores	0.014	9	635.9	▲▲▲▲▲▲▲▲▲▲▲▲▲▲▲
Isla Wellington	0.005	10	1800.0	▲▲▲

Author and contributors

Daniel Patrick Quinn is a project manager, lecturer, writer, researcher and composer who currently lives on the outskirts of Wick, Caithness, Scotland. He started his hill bagging career with the Wainwrights as a teenager and soon progressed on to Marilyns and Hewitts before moving to Indonesia to teach English, study gamelan music and explore prominent volcanoes. He has lived in Knodishall, Morecambe, Bolton-le-Sands, London, Edinburgh, East Lothian, Port Carlisle, Jakarta, Hong Kong, Kendal and Stornoway. He is artistic director for the acclaimed music group One More Grain and has lectured on various subjects at the University of the Highlands and Islands.

Oscar Argudo is a computer graphics researcher and lecturer at Universitat Politecnica de Catalunya in Barcelona, Spain. In his leisure time he enjoys being out in nature, chasing summits or exploring natural arches. His passion for mountain climbing started during a trip to Japan when he climbed Mount Fuji. Looking for automated methods to identify peaks from digital elevation models, he learned about prominence and compiled lists of peaks for Catalonia and the Pyrenees. Naturally, he eagerly joined the World Ribus project when he heard about it. Currently residing in Vic, near Barcelona and near the Pyrenees, Oscar previously spent over three years in Lyon, an opportunity to explore numerous locations in the French Alps.

Petter Bjørstad *is* a professor at the University of Bergen, Norway. He started climbing prominent mountains (at age 50) after climbing all the Colorado Fourteeners when living in Boulder, Colorado. He finished climbing the 100 most prominent mountains in Europe in 2014 and the 85 Ribus in mainland Norway in 2021. He is an active (volunteer) mountain guide in the Bergen Mountaineering Club. He has led successful expeditions to Papua New Guinea, Greenland, Alaska and Yukon, among others. He has always enjoyed the planning and subsequent climbing of peaks with little or no prior information.

Sean Caulfield was born in Wexford, Ireland. After graduating from university he worked for several years in the eastern USA, Western Australia and London. In between work projects Sean spent much of his twenties pursuing a love of travel with backpacking trips around Asia and Latin America, climbing some prominent mountains along the way. He moved to Canada in 2017 and now lives in Vancouver. Sean's hobbies include snowboarding, rock climbing and mountain biking, which he incorporates into his passion for climbing peaks in Canada and internationally.

Alan Dawson is the compiler of several lists of British hills, including Marilyns, Grahams, Simms and High Hills. He moved from Liverpool to Glasgow in 1989 and since 2019 has been based in a small village in the Scottish Highlands. He is the author of *The Relative Hills of Britain* (Cicerone Press, 1992), *The 1033 High Hills of Britain* (Pedantic Press, 2021) and *Tales from the Grahams*, with Ann Bowker (Pedantic Press, 2022). After retiring from his work as a digital librarian and researcher, he bought some Leica GNSS surveying equipment and software. Since 2012 he has surveyed over 2500 summits and 2000 cols and has made the results freely available via the Pedantic Press website at pedantic.org.uk.

Andy M Dean is an environmental consultant with a background in geography, remote sensing and geographic information systems. Growing up in Stoke-on-Trent in England, Andy was hiking in the Peak District, Lake District, and North Wales from an early age. After completing a Ph.D in 2003, Andy moved to Vancouver, Canada. Andy's love of summit bagging developed when he moved to Bogor in Indonesia in 2008. He used his technical skills to complete the first Ribu prominence analysis for Indonesia with Daniel Patrick Quinn, and climbed more than 30 Ribus. Leaving Indonesia in 2012, Andy has lived in Calgary, Alberta, and Vientiane in Lao. Vancouver is again his base, with marathon running his current passion.

Jonathan de Ferranti is a topographic researcher who has completed what NASA's Space Shuttle Radar Topography Mission left undone in the mountains, deserts and polar regions. His findings are available via his Viewfinder website at viewfinderpanoramas.org. He has lived near Newburgh, Fife since 1986. By 2024 he had climbed all bar two of the Marilyns in Britain.

Eric Gilbertson is a surveyor and teaching professor in mechanical engineering at Seattle University, USA. He has been peak-bagging since 2009 and has reached the highest point of all fifty states of the USA, with twin brother Matthew. In 2019 he became the fifth person to climb the highest point of all provinces and territories of Canada. His main goal is to climb to the highest point in every country in the world. He has climbed over 140, including 7439m Pik Pobeda in Kyrgyzstan, 8614m K2 in Pakistan and 8586m Kangchenjunga in India. When at home, Eric likes making first winter ascents of peaks in the Cascade Mountains and trips involving different modes of travel such as snow-mobile, zodiac boat, skiing and ice climbing.

Alastair Govan is a retired petroleum engineer living in Aberdeen in Scotland. His first notable hill was one of the Scottish Munros in 1978, aged 19, and he completed this list and several other British lists over the next few decades. Overseas peak bagging didn't really start until 2007, focused initially on European country high-points then on Ultras and other summits. He likes to visit new places and experience the local culture as well as taking in a few peaks.

Anne Gray is an amateur photographer based in Scotland with a passion for wildlife and wild places, particularly the polar regions, polar bears, cheetahs, tigers and whales.

David Jamieson is a professional ecologist based in Scotland who spends much of his recreational time visiting attractive landscapes and climbing any mountains that happen to be there. After climbing all the Scottish Munros he ventured onto smaller UK hills and higher and more prominent summits across continental Europe, Africa, South America and New Zealand. Since retiring from work he has had even more time to pursue his peak-bagging passion with wife Deana, two active sons and any friends who can be persuaded to join him on the slopes.

Jude Newton-Stock is a spatial analyst based in Melbourne, Australia. Despite his fear of heights he was drawn to mountains as a young child and began peak-bagging in his late teens. He appreciates all mountains, large and small, and enjoys the cultures, people and biomes encountered on the way. Jude is also passionate about music and preserving the environment.

Martin Richardson is a keen peak bagger based in Yorkshire in England. He has climbed 210 Ribus, mostly in Europe, and over 8000 of the hills in Britain with at least 30 metres drop.

James Stone is a British/Australian ex-lawyer based in Yorkshire in England. Until becoming semi-retired he concentrated on British hill lists such as the Munros but later widened his interests to peaks worldwide and was one of the first few people to have climbed the Volcanic Seven Summits. He also occasionally manages to struggle up 6000-metre peaks in the Andes and has also climbed prominent peaks in Mexico, Central America, Spain and New Zealand.

Mark Trengrove is a keen peak-bagger, most active in Britain, with forays to Ireland, Europe, and occasionally beyond. His greatest love is for the uplands of Wales, Scotland and Greece. He publishes hill and mountain lists for numerous countries on the Europeaklist website and also acts as moderator for the Baggers without Borders forum (BwB) and webmaster for its website.

Deividas Valaitis is an avid mountain hiker and photographer with a passion for scaling high peaks and navigating challenging terrains. He has climbed over 700 mountains with a prominence of more than 600 metres. In recent years, he has expanded his focus to include Ribus and Ultras. His adventures are featured on his website, p600.org.

Rob Woodall is a civil engineer based in Peterborough in eastern England, working for Anglian Water, which covers the least hilly part of the UK. He has been ticking off various British hill lists since the 1980s and was one of the first two people to climb all 2979 British hills with 100 metres of prominence. His overseas focus has been P600 peaks, but especially Ultras and Ribus. Rob also bags islands, trig points and benchmarks, and has visited all the British trig pillars.

Nikolaus Żuliński lives and works as a bookseller in his hometown of Wien (Vienna), Austria. In 2009 he came across the Gunung Bagging list of the Ribus of Indonesia and Malaysia and began applying this concept to mountains in Europe. Since then he has been trying to climb about ten Ribus per year, thus keeping the chance alive to climb all 567 Ribus of Europe before his 80th birthday. Having some competence in several European languages, he tries to contribute to the World Ribus Project by improving the quality of its corpus of toponyms.

Glossary

8000er – A mountain that is at least 8000 metres above sea level. There are fourteen of them, all in the Himalaya and Karakoram mountain ranges in Asia.

Copernicus GLO-30 – A digital elevation model produced by the Copernicus Programme, a fleet of Earth observation satellites managed by the European Union and European Space Agency to carry out environmental monitoring and other applications.

Corbett – A mountain in Scotland between 2500 and 3000 feet high (762-914 metres) that has a topographic prominence of at least 500 feet (152.4 metres).

DEM – Digital Elevation Model. A digital representation of terrain elevation data, where each cell in a grid contains a value representing the height of a point on the Earth's surface. DEM data is collected using remote sensing techniques such as Lidar and radar.

FABDEM – Forest And Buildings removed Copernicus DEM. This is a global elevation model that removes building and tree height biases from the Copernicus GLO-30 DEM.

GNSS – Global Navigation Satellite System. A broad term that encompasses various satellite networks including GPS, Russia's GLONASS, Europe's Galileo, China's BeiDou, and India's NavIC. Some GNSS receivers can use signals from multiple satellite constellations to improve accuracy of location and elevation data.

GPS – Global Positioning System. A system that relies on a network of satellites orbiting Earth which transmit signals that can be picked up by GPS receivers, such as those found in smart phones, car navigation systems and hand-held GPS devices. By calculating the time it takes for signals from multiple satellites to reach the receiver, GPS devices can calculate the receiver's exact position, providing accurate location information.

IGN – Institut national de l'information géographique et forestière (National Institute of Geographic and Forest Information). It is the national mapping agency of France.

Lidar – Laser Imaging, Detection and Ranging. A method for determining distance by targeting an object with a laser and measuring the time for the reflected light to return to the receiver. Using Lidar in aerial surveys enables surface heights to be measured.

Marilyn – A British hill of any height with a prominence of at least 150 metres. The term is sometimes applied to hills in Ireland and other countries that meet the same criterion.

NASA - National Aeronautics and Space Administration.

P100 – A summit with a prominence of at least 100 metres, also referred to as a Hump.

P150 – A summit with a prominence of at least 150 metres, also referred to as a Marilyn.

P600 – A peak with a prominence of at least 600 metres, sometimes referred to as a Major.

P1000 – A peak with a prominence of at least 1000 metres, also referred to as a Ribu.

P1500 – A peak with a prominence of at least 1500 metres, also referred to as an Ultra.

PEMRACS – Peakbagger Mountain Range Classification System. A broad hierarchical system that divides the entire land surface of the Earth into mountain ranges and sub-ranges.

Ribu – A peak with a prominence of at least 1000 metres. The term is drawn from the Indonesian and Malay word for 'thousand'.

SRTM – Shuttle Radar Topography Mission. A project by NASA and the German Aerospace Center to obtain global, high-resolution digital elevation models of the Earth's surface using radar data collected during the Space Shuttle Endeavour mission in 2000.

Ultra – A peak with a prominence of at least 1500 metres.

Acknowledgements

Many thanks to:

Andrew Kirmse for the invaluable datasets that were a brilliant starting point for the Ribus project, and which originated from Edward Earl's pioneering WinProm program for calculating topographic prominence.

Eberhard Jurgalski for his work on the 8000ers and the 8000ers.com website.

Adam Schneider for the GPS Visualizer website and images.

Greg Slayden for the Peakbagger.com website and his long-standing and unwavering commitment to managing and developing an immense database of peaks across the world.

Scott Surgent for information on some peaks of the USA.

Java Lava hiking group in Jakarta for organising many great weekend trips including one on which the Gunung Bagging co-founders originally met and conceived of the original regional list of Ribus. Special thanks to Nick Hughes for support during the early days of the Ribus project.

The numerous regional editors for the Ribus project not already listed in the contributors section, with regions of expertise shown in brackets: Keith Bennett (Argentina and Chile), Mihai Giurgiulescu (Armenia, Azerbaijan, Bulgaria, Georgia, Iran and Romania), Min He (China), Steven Song (Canada), Andrew Tomkins (Algeria, Morocco and Sudan), Alvaro Vivanca (Chile), and Leibo Zhu (China).

Saint Mary Peak (OC71), an isolated Ribu in South Australia (Petter Bjørstad). The peak most distant from any other Ribu is Queen Mary's Peak in Tristan da Cunha, Saint Helena

References

Publications

Brown, H, Johnstone, S, and Bennet, D, *The Corbetts and Other Scottish Hills*
Scottish Mountaineering Trust, 1990

Dawson, Alan, *The Relative Hills of Britain*
Cicerone Press, 1992 (revised edition pending)

Goodall, Dean, *Introduction to Seamounts*
Amazon, 2015

Helman, Adam, *The Finest Peaks: Prominence and Other Mountain Measures*
Trafford Publishing, 2005

Wallace, Alfred Russel, *The Malay Archipelago*
Macmillan, 1869

Websites

8000ers	8000ers.com
Andrew Kirmse	andrewkirmse.com
Baggers without Borders	groups.google.com/g/baggingwithoutborders
Clach Liath	clachliath.com
Country Highpoints	countryhighpoints.com
Europeaklist	sites.google.com/site/europeaklist
Every Mountain in the World	everymountaingintheworld.com
GeoNames	geonames.org
GPS Visualizer	gpsvisualizer.com
Gunung Bagging	gunungbagging.com
Peakbagger	peakbagger.com
Peaklist	peaklist.org
Pedantic Press	pedantic.org.uk
P600	p600.org
Viewfinder Panoramas	viewfinderpanoramas.org
World Ribus	worldribus.org

Contact details

Please send any comments or enquiries about this book to ribus@pedantic.org.uk
For enquiries about other Pedantic Press publications, contact press@pedantic.org.uk

Also published by Pedantic Press...

**The 1033 High Hills of Britain,
by Alan Dawson, 2021**
PPB003

'A fantastic book! The stories, articles and photos complement the factual data perfectly'
'a very interesting read and a source of inspiration'
'beautifully crafted, a mine of information'

**Tales from the Grahams:
231 medium-sized hills of Scotland,
by Alan Dawson and Ann Bowker, 2022**
PPB004

' captures the nature of the Grahams much better than other books'
'I am exceedingly impressed with both volumes'

**Ten Tables of Grahams
by Alan Dawson, 2022**
PPT004

Illustrated booklet offering all the data in the official list of Grahams

**The Revised Relative Hills of Britain:
The Marilyns, by Alan Dawson, 2025**
PPB006

Definitive book on the Marilyns, the long-awaited follow-up to The Relative Hills of Britain

E-books by Daniel Patrick Quinn...

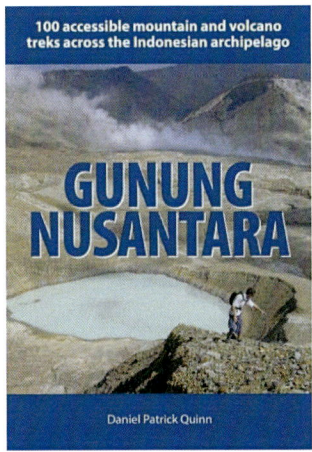

Gunung Nusantara
by Daniel Patrick Quinn, 2021

English-language introduction to 100 accessible mountain treks across the Indonesian archipelago

Exploring Malaysia's Mountains
by Daniel Patrick Quinn, 2024

Guide to fifty mountain treks across Malaysia, including Sarawak, Sabah, Peninsular Malaysia

Albums by Daniel Patrick Quinn...

Ridin' the Stang,
2005

Acting the Rubber Pig
Redux, 2014

I, Sun
2016

Albums by Daniel Patrick Quinn with One More Grain...

Beans on Toast with
Pythagoras, 2022

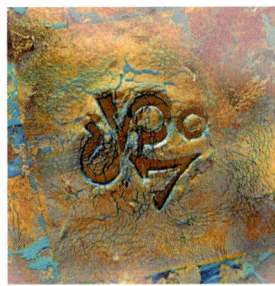

One More Grain,
2023

Modern Music,
2023

Printed by Inky Little Fingers, England